Retrospect and Prospect
in the Psychological
Study of Families

Retrospect and Prospect in the Psychological Study of Families

Edited by

James P. McHale
Wendy S. Grolnick
Clark University

2002

LAWRENCE ERLBAUM ASSOCIATES, PUBLISHERS
Mahwah, New Jersey   London

Lawrence Erlbaum Associates, Inc., Publishers
10 Industrial Avenue
Mahwah, New Jersey 07430

Cover design by Kathryn Houghtaling Lacey

Library of Congress Cataloging-in-Publication Data

Retrospect and prospect in the psychological study of families / edited by James P.
McHale, Wendy S. Grolnick.
    p. cm.
  Includes indexes.
  ISBN 0-8058-3797-3 (alk. paper)
   1. Family—Research. 2. Family—Psychological aspects. I. McHale, James P. II.
Grolnick, Wendy S.

HQ10 .R46 2002
306.85'07'2—dc21

2001042310

Books published by Lawrence Erlbaum Associates are printed on acid-free paper,
and their bindings are chosen for strength and durability.

Printed in the United States of America
10 9 8 7 6 5 4 3 2 1

To my dear wife Trang, who gives light and meaning to the road ahead and to the Tharneys, McHales, Caseys, and Southworths—the families at my center and foundation

J. P. M.

To Jay, Allison, and Rebecca, who teach me more each day about the wonder of being part of a family

W. S. G.

Contents

Preface   ix
Foreword   xv
    Philip A. Cowan

PART I: RETROSPECT AND PROSPECT IN THE PSYCHOLOGICAL   1
STUDY OF PARENTING

1.   Mothering: Retrospect and Prospect   5
       Wendy S. Grolnick and Suzanne T. Gurland

2.   Fathers and Families   35
       Louise B. Silverstein

3.   Parenting in the New Millennium: Prospects, Promises,   65
       and Pitfalls
       Ross D. Parke

PART II: RETROSPECT AND PROSPECT IN THE PSYCHOLOGICAL   95
STUDY OF MARITAL AND FAMILY GROUP DYNAMICS

4.   Retrospect and Prospect in the Psychological Study   99
       of Marital and Couple Relationships
       Kelly M. Flanagan, Mari L. Clements, Sarah W. Whitton,
       Michael J. Portney, David W. Randall, and Howard J. Markman

5.   Retrospect and Prospect in the Psychological Study   127
       of Coparenting and Family Group Process
       James P. McHale, Allison Lauretti, Jean Talbot, and Christina
       Pouquette

6.   The Road Ahead for Research on Marital and Family   167
       Dynamics
       Martha J. Cox and Kristina S. M. Harter

PART III: RETROSPECT AND PROSPECT IN THE   189
PSYCHOLOGICAL STUDY OF FAMILIES AS SYSTEMS

7.   Retrospect and Prospect in the Psychological Study   193
     of Sibling Relationships
     Douglas M. Teti

8.   Retrospect and Prospect in the Psychological   225
     Study of Families as Systems
     Kurt Kreppner

9.   Looking Toward the Horizon: Present and Future   259
     in the Study of Family Systems
     Patricia Minuchin

PART IV: TAKING STOCK   279

10. Family Research and the Law: Can Family Research   283
     Help Solomon? Contributions and Challenges
     Sandra T. Azar

11. Family Influences on Behavior and Development: 321
     Challenges for the Future
     Michael Rutter

Author index   353
Subject index   373

Preface

As the 21st century begins, psychologists who have dedicated their research careers to generating a meaningful body of knowledge that can be called on to promote the welfare of children and families find themselves facing new challenges from many fronts. Within the United States, an unswerving movement toward a society that promises to be ever more pluralistic and to boast a wide array of family arrangements demands that our field move beyond its traditional view of family life—a view that many critics within academia have criticized as being historically and culturally myopic. At the same time, many grass roots movements within the United States cry out for a return to "traditional family values." Shunning evidence suggesting the viability of numerous functional family forms (given adequate societal supports), many religious and political leaders throughout the United States argue that we are ignoring the one, surefire solution to society's woes: returning men to leadership roles in the family and rewarding families that form and maintain stable, heterosexual marital unions. Views of what is wrong with society are plentiful. In some corners, mothers continue to be blamed for all our children's ills. More and more, however, fathers have become the new "culprits," held culpable for being absentee figures in their children's lives. Charismatic public figures urge a return to no-nonsense parenting, empowering some struggling young mothers and fathers but simultaneously and unwittingly sanctioning other parents who already lean toward abusive methods to reframe their harsh and overzealous ministrations to children as "responsible parenting." There have even been voices maintaining that in the end, families do not actually matter at all because it is children's peer relationships that ultimately steer them down paths toward good or ill. And amidst the often rancorous debates, millions of children still suffer abuse, struggle to cope effectively after family dissolution, endure a revolving door of multiple foster placements, or live on the streets with no home at all.

Both laypersons and public figures look to psychologists for help with their questions about children's woes, and psychologists in turn look first to the family interior to search for answers. This propensity to scrutinize family dynamics is perhaps a hallmark of how psychologists have sought to understand and help children for nearly 100 years. Fortunately, a relatively recent and heartening trend in our field has been to expand the focus of study beyond parent-child dyads, and beyond family systems influences, to factors impinging on the family from the sociocultural surround. At the turn of the new millennium, however, the bedrock of what psychologists know about families owes principally to research efforts driven by questions about what helps and what hurts within the complicated interiors of modern—though, alas, most often two-parent nuclear—families. The efforts of psychology's family researchers have been inspired by a hope that the information their studies yield will ultimately be of practical use to those who legislate and to those who make judicial decisions that affect the lives of children and families. But does the pool of knowledge owing to the research efforts of family psychologists actually reach the eyes and ears of those who need to know what we know? And, perhaps more to the point, what is it exactly that we think we know?

In April 1999, a number of the field's most active family researchers convened at Clark University in Worcester, Massachusetts, to honor the father of family therapy, the late Clark psychologist John Elderkin Bell, and to ponder several of these issues. The group took on as its primary mission working to clarify what it is that psychology has learned about families over the past 50 years, since Bell's pioneering efforts in working therapeutically with whole family groups when children had been referred to him for treatment. With two exceptions, the working group that gathered at Clark was composed of scientists trained as psychologists, an arrangement that presented both advantages and disadvantages. On the one hand, the composition of the group allowed for an extraordinarily rich exchange of ideas about the contributions of psychologists, along with a critical evaluation of the knowledge base that composes our field. For 2 days, group members pondered the claims made in one another's papers, critiqued one another's interpretations, and sought to attain some synthesis in a closing, day-long round table discussion. Hence, the chapters in this volume have each benefited from the critical eyes of several knowledgeable family psychologists. As for the disadvantages, the family research base with which psychologists are most familiar—unlike the knowledge base in the fields of anthropology and sociology—is one launched by investigations of families in clinical distress and augmented largely by studies of White, middle-class, heterosexual couples raising children in nuclear families. Members of the working group recognized this nucleocentric bias, of course, and most took pains to integrate their perspectives on families with scholarship emanating from fields outside of psychology. In so doing, however, the contributors remained clear that what they hoped to accomplish in their collaborative effort was a summation of what *psychology* has contributed to family studies, with the principal focus on the psychological and emotional interiors of modern families.

To adequately represent the field, a volume of encyclopedic proportions would be required. Such an exhaustive cataloging is not what this volume offers. This said, however, it does strive to provide an accurate and reasonably comprehensive overview of main lines of thought, ongoing conceptual and methodological quandaries, and lines of influential research that characterized our field in the year 2000. In the chapters that follow, each author or series of authors provides a brief and necessarily selective, but representative, overview of both the past ("retrospect") and the road ahead ("prospect") in outlining major contributions of family research by psychologists. All authors were asked to challenge themselves with the same question as they prepared their contributions: Within the broad topic area that you are addressing, what is it that we really think we know about what matters within families?

Happily, conference participants agreed that we have some reasonable answers to this question. Much of what the contributors outline—indeed, much of what family psychologists have learned over the last half century—should be of interest not only to our colleagues in anthropology and sociology who study families themselves, but also to child and family advocates of all persuasions and to those concerned with charting responsible public policy. But as the authors outline, most of the answers we are in a position to provide at present are nonetheless delimited, qualified, or not yet firmly established. Still, as the field flourishes and replication studies beget further replication studies, and as we and our colleagues take full hold of the dawning awareness that a number of our basic assumptions about "optimal" family functioning are both historically and culturally specific, there lies on the horizon the promise of major new advances in the days and years ahead. As we examine where research in family psychology has been and where we need to go now, our efforts must carefully and respectfully chart not only the dilemmas but also the strengths and promise of the myriad arrangements that will characterize families in the 21st century. At the same time, we must resist the temptation to close the books on two-parent, nuclear families. We still have much to learn about the psychosocial interiors of all types of families, including nuclear families. We recognize that the brief retrospective glimpses provided throughout this book cannot begin to do justice to the collective efforts of those psychologists who have dedicated their careers to family research, but we hope that the ideas they have inspired—many of which have fueled the "prospect" segments of the volume—help chart an agenda that will be of use to the field in the years ahead.

ACKNOWLEDGMENTS

As is true of most volumes of this nature, this effort owes its debt to a great number of instigators and supporters who have touched the lives of its editors and contributors. As will be chronicled at various places throughout the volume, this book and our field owe perhaps their greatest tribute to former Clark University professor and clinician John Elderkin Bell. Bell's revolutionary move in assembling families together as a group to reckon with the distress being expressed by a child changed the face of our field forever. We are also grateful to Bell's son, Colin, who taught us a great deal about his father in the days and weeks leading up to the Clark University Family Conference held in April 1999 that launched this book. We also wish to acknowledge an intellectual debt to Mary D. S.

Ainsworth, whose unparalleled capacities as a theorist and researcher set a standard for our field that will endure as long, and reach as far, as family research will ever take us.

More locally, we want to offer our thanks to the Hiatt family for their kind endowment to Clark University to support endeavors such as this one. We are grateful to the Francis L. Hiatt School of Psychology's Executive Committee for its belief in the timeliness of this effort and its generous support of the conference itself. The volume's various contributors—both in their collegial but searching challenges to one another during the conference itself, and in their thoughtful and scholarly pursuit of provocative chapters afterward—helped make this effort and invigorating and rewarding one for us. Judi Amsel at Lawrence Erlbaum Associates supported our idea for the volume, and was a good friend and advocate during the early stages of its development. Sondra Guideman, also at LEA, was a great help in bringing the book to fruition. We also want to thank Joyce Lee and Deborah Burbank, who editorial and administrative assistance helped shepherd the book along, and Pat Pulda, whose wit and perspective helped buoy us a various times throughout the project.

Last, we wish to offer some personal words of thanks to those who stood patiently by us during the evolution and refinement of the volume. In particular, our partners Trang McHale and Jay Kimmel were sources of support and encouragement. Other friends and colleagues, including Bud Ruby, Ken Rywant, Loren Bush, Penny Vinden, and Mike and Jeni Southworth, provided priceless relief and respite that helped keep the effort moving forward. To all those whose contributions helped make this book a reality, we thank you.

Brief Editor Biographies

James P. McHale is Associate Professor of Psychology and Director of Clinical Training at Clark University. He received his B.S. in psychology from the University of South Florida, his Masters in developmental psychology from Tulane University, and his PhD in clinical psychology from the University of California, Berkeley. His research, which has been supported by the National Institute of Mental Health and the National Institute of Child Health and Development, has examined the nature of interadult parenting support, coordination, and distress in families of young children, and the effect of different coparental dynamics on children's socioemotional development. He is editor, with Philip Cowan, of Understanding How Family-Level Dynamics Affect Children's Development, published by Jossey Bass in 1996.

Wendy S. Grolnick is Associate Professor of Psychology at Clark University. She received her B.A. in psychology from Cornell University, and her Masters and PhD in clinical psychology from the University of Rochester. She has published extensively in the area of the development of children's motivation and self-regulation. Her research, which has been supported by NIMH, the William T. Grant Foundation, and the Spencer Foundation, has focused on the effects of home and school environments on children's motivation, and on factors affecting the environments that parents and teachers create for their children. She is currently working on a new book to be published by Lawrence Erlbaum Associates on antecedents and consequences of parental control.

James P. McHale
Wendy S. Grolnick

Foreword

Philip A. Cowan
University of California, Berkeley

The initial stimulus for this exciting and original volume was a conference organized at Clark University to honor John Elderkin Bell, the father of family therapy. It is hard to conceive now, 50 years after Bell's seminal contributions in the 1950s, what a shift in world view he stimulated by seeing whole families in his clinical practice, even when the person referred was a young child. It was an almost shocking departure from the practice of treating children in individual therapy, with mothers seen as "collateral" to the treatment process, and fathers rarely seen at all.

If the first half of the 20th century was the time of grand theories of individual development (Freud, Jung, Watson, Gesell, Piaget, Skinner), the second half can now be seen as an attempt to understand the development and psychopathology of the individual in context, with the family as a primary biological, social, and psychological influence on development across the life span. Although Sociology and Anthropology have longer histories in focusing on the family, the move to study families in Psychology and Psychiatry came first from family therapists in the 1950s with Bell and Ackerman on the East Coast, and Bateson, Jackson, Satir, and Haley on the West Coast. These theorist-clinicians, and others that followed (especially Bowen, Beavers, Epstein, Framo, McGoldrick, the Minuchins, Walsh, Wynne, and Whitaker) set a challenge for researchers that has not entirely been met. Instead of an individually focused view in which psychopathology and adaptation were located in the patient, they argued for the importance of understanding the system in which the patient lived. From this deceptively straightforward premise a new paradigm took hold.

Family systems theories share six major assumptions:

1. The whole is greater than (different from) the sum of its parts;
2. The system is composed of interconnected subsystems (parent-child, marital, sibling);
3. Because subsystems are interconnected, a change in any individual relationship affects all the other individuals and relationships in the family;

4. Causality is multidirectional rather than linear (e.g., parents affect children and children affect parents);
5. Systems have self-balancing and self-regulating properties; and therefore,
6. Interventions in systems help us to understand how they operate.

The unmet challenge of these views, addressed by many of the authors in this volume, is to create research paradigms and methods adequate to assess dynamic, multidirectional family systems as they move naturally through transitions across the life span. In addition, we need to systematically evaluate research on intervention and family change.

Slowly, clinical family system theories began to affect research on nonclinical populations. Bronfenbrenner's "ecological approach" for example, was a new systemic blueprint for studying children in the 1970s. Only gradually, however, did the focus of developmental research actually expand from children alone, or mothers and children, to fathers, the quality of the relationship between the parents, sibling relationships, and the legacies of adaptive and maladaptive family patterns transmitted across the life span and across generations. More recently, the contextual approach to development has expanded again to include systems outside the family—peers, work, neighborhoods, and the subcultures and cultures that shape social institutions and the meaning systems by which we make sense of an ever-changing world.

And so, in the five decades since Bell's initial contributions, we have moved from focusing on the developmental trajectories of individual children and adults to trying to understand the pivotal role played by family systems. The family, or more accurately, families, are at the very center of the study of psychological development. At their best, families function as safe havens in a heartless world, protecting men, women, and children from the vicissitudes of increasingly complicated contemporary cultures. At their worst, families manufacture harm through unregulated conflict or the chill of emotional indifference among family members.

James McHale and Wendy Grolnick have produced an outstanding edited text that is not simply a compendium of isolated chapters commissioned from independent authors. Each chapter benefits not only from the editors' supervision, but also from the opportunities for interchange provided at the conference that generated the separate reports. The reader gets a sense of the authors talking with each other and commenting on each other's ideas.

The book comes at a particularly important historical time. The authors make a good case for the fact that, although a great deal has been accomplished in family research, there are important tasks left undone. In the world outside of academic research, it is a time in which a heated discourse on families has entered daily discussions of law and policy in many industrialized nations. In the United

States and Great Britain, for example, both conservatives and liberals acknowledge the importance of fostering family values, but they have not agreed on what values should be encouraged for what kind of families. Should heterosexual marriage continue to have a privileged position in comparison to cohabitation and same-sex unions? Is divorce harmful to children in the long term, and, if so, should laws make divorce harder to obtain? What does parenting and marital research have to say about child custody? Does welfare reform benefit children by encouraging parents to work to increase the family standard of living, or does it harm children by taking parents out of the home during critical developmental periods? Although the authors in this book make clear that current research does not provide unequivocal answers to questions about laws and policies regarding families, their discussions of recent findings about marriage and parenting will certainly contribute to a more differentiated discussion of these central societal issues.

The Scope of This Book

At the end of each decade, and especially at the end of the millennium, it has become fashionable to publish large handbooks, often spread across multiple volumes, in order to summarize a field of study. This book manages to summarize the state of knowledge in family systems research with an economy of space and style, giving multiple approaches their due economically and without excessive polemic:

Multiple Methods and Measures

The history of family studies began with reports on family life primarily by women. Observational methods came into prominence in the 1970s and 1980s, at first with a disdain for self-reports that risked casting the baby out with the bathwater. But now, as in this book, many researchers and theorists pay attention to both the inner and outer view of family life, demonstrating that these perspectives reveal different but complementary realities.

Multiple Theories

The chapters deal with a number of theories of stability and change in family life. Biological, psychological, and social forces affecting change are described in many chapters. Theories that focus on internal events (e.g., attachment), external events (e.g., social learning theory) and interactions between internal and external events are all taken seriously.

Building up the study of the family system: Multiple levels of analysis. As implied in the "psyche" part of Psychology, the field began with a focus on individuals. Even with the emphasis on family systems, until very recently family research was a study of mothers, fathers, and children and their relationships taken two by two. Retrospect and prospect in the psychological study of families begins with a section describing research on parent-child relationships, followed by a summary of two decades of research on the importance of parents' marital quality as it affects the life of adults in the family and also as it affects the children. Sibling relationships, long neglected in family studies, have their own chapter at the beginning of a third section. Then, the book ventures into the "new look" in family research based on the assumption that there is unique explanatory power to be gained by looking at the properties of the family system as a whole. Ironically, we are back where clinical family systems theory began, but now with a set of methods and measures that are more in synchrony with the systemic view of family life.

Multiple Social Contexts. Acknowledging that the study of families has so far focused disproportionately on European-American two-parent families, the authors do a valiant job of summarizing existing research on how cultural differences affect family life and how future research must take these differences into account in interpreting what is adaptive and maladaptive about different family processes and structures. We cannot ignore the certainty that optimal family functioning can be defined only for a particular context at a particular historical time.

Application, Intervention, and Social Policy. Not just in a closing chapter, but throughout the volume, the authors pay attention to the "so what?" questions that parents, politicians, journalists, and the general public often raise when they hear about research published in scientific journals. Although it is not easy to match research-based probabilistic statements about risks and benefits to the need for policy makers to establish universal rules, there is an ongoing consideration in this book of the links between the two fields.

Major Themes

A number of major themes are threaded throughout the chapters. The first, inherent in the structure of the book, is the assumption that it is necessary to study individuals embedded within families as systems that are embedded within larger social systems. Second is an emphasis on the study of both normative and nonnormative transitions as a way of highlighting both the resilience and maladaptation that stems from inevitable changes along the life span. Third is a story of the diversity of family arrangements and family processes that lead to adaptation; there is no single blueprint for optimal family life. The fourth theme is both obvious and surprising. One would think that the study of families would inherently be developmental in outlook. For decades, however, in their emphasis on properties of the system as a whole, family system theorists ignored the fact that systemic relations among a 24-year-old father, a 22-year-old mother, and a 2-year-old child, might be different from the same family at 34, 32, and 12, and again at 74, 72, and 52. The authors in this book document some of the past findings concerning family development, make a welcome move past the early childrearing years to explore adolescence and adulthood, and urge more study of developmental lifespan aspects of family systems in the future.

As I read the chapters, one theme that was not prominently featured by the authors seemed to jump out from the pages. Differences between families that are effective and supportive to the development and happiness of the individual members, and families that are ineffective or discouraging of development and well-being, often center around the expression and control of strong emotion. For example, one of the two central dimensions of parenting style is warmth (the other is structure). In another example, one of the key variables in couple relationships that affects children's development is whether the parents can prevent negative affect from escalating out of control and provide children examples of how the inevitable conflicts of family life can be resolved. As families transmit meanings from the culture to the child, they become actively involved in the regulation of family communication, and many of the moves toward regulation are triggered by sudden shifts from positive to negative emotional tone and meaning in the communication process.

In the final chapter, Rutter makes a central point that I would like to applaud and underline. The authors in this book make an exceedingly good case for the progress made by family research since the 1950s, and for the fascinating potential of new findings in the decades ahead. Rutter reminds us that while many authors make causal claims about the connections between family process or structure and children's outcomes, we need to be both careful and humble about these claims because they are based on studies that use single- assessment correlational designs. Addressing this point, intervention studies cited by the authors become especially important. Although intervention designs do not have the power to establish causal connections in a definitive fashion, they provide much stronger support for claims about the direction of effects than do correlations. The intervention results reported in this book provide strong support for the premise that families not only matter, they also have important effects on the developmental pathways of all the individuals and relationships within them. The issue here is not to abandon correlational studies, but rather to improve both correlation and intervention research designs. In order to be credible in their contributions to public policy debates, researchers must be careful not to let their ideology outstrip their findings. The authors in this book do an excellent job of generating interest in what is currently known without inflating their claims and thereby misleading the public.

I invite readers to plunge into this volume for a special treat. Here are contributions from a strong group of active researchers and theorists, ranging from relatively new investigators to established masters of the field, laying out a carefully drawn map of where family research has been (the "retrospect" part of the title) and where prospectors should go as they open up new territory in the study of family processes and outcomes. This book serves an essential guide for what is proving to be an eventful and exciting journey.

I

RETROSPECT AND PROSPECT IN THE PSYCHOLOGICAL STUDY OF PARENTING

The first part of this volume is devoted to research on parenting. Without question, most of psychology's theories about family influences on development have viewed parent–child relations as the origin of both adaptive and maladaptive functioning. And until recently, with few exceptions, most empirical studies of parent–child relations in family psychology have been studies of mothers. Fittingly, then, in chapter 1 of this volume, Wendy Grolnick and Suzanne Gurland provide a critical discussion of mothering research, followed by a thoughtful overview of the voluminous and sometimes controversial literature on parenting. In chapter 2, Louise Silverstein reviews the much briefer history of research studies on fathers by psychologists, clarifying myths and arguing forcefully that we as a field should do all we can to hold future family researchers responsible for attending to fathers as well as mothers in their investigations. Ross Parke closes this first part of the volume by looking ahead to the future of parenting research in our field.

In their chapter on mothering, Grolnick and Gurland begin with a historical look at the way mothers have been depicted in the literature. They argue that the history of theorizing about mothering has been one of "mother blaming," an exclusive focus on mothers as responsible for children's negative behavior. They also suggest that, at the same time mothers have been the recipients of excessive blame, their roles in their children's lives have been ignored as they are seen as the backdrop against which other caretakers are considered. Following this thesis, the chapter turns to a review of literature on parenting. In reviewing the literature, the authors highlight two parenting dimensions that most researchers agree benefit children: warmth-involvement and control. Both empirical and theoretical support for the importance of these dimensions is garnered. Grolnick and Gurland pay special attention to control and argue that confusion over this dimension has resulted from the failure of researchers to differentiate parents being "in control" from parents being "controlling." The authors further argue that parenting dimensions that facilitate compliance may be different from those that facilitate internalization, and parenting researchers would do well to be clear about which of these outcomes is their focus. In the final part of the chapter, the authors explore current conditions of mothering including employment and solo parenting. Their review of the literature supports the idea that economics play a large part in the ways these issues affect mothering. The chapter concludes with a list of future directions for research, including a developmental view of parenting dimensions, a focus on transitions, and an understanding the determinants of parenting.

Silverstein's chapter on fathers begins with a historical exploration of myths about fathers (e.g., children do not become attached to fathers, fathers are uninvolved in their children's lives, marriage is essential to father involvement) and how they might have come about. Reliance on a reified evolutionary psychology, namely biological imperatives, and oversimplified politically biased views are identified as two such determinants. Following this is a review of empirical works on the positive and negative consequences of father involvement and changes over time in father involvement. Silverstein identifies responsivity and emotional availability as key characteristics of fathers that facilitate development, mirroring some of the conclusions of Grolnick and Gurland's chapter on mothers. In the next part of the chapter Silverstein explores fathering in different subcultures. She stresses the diversity within and across subcultures and refutes the stereotypes of African American men as disengaged and uninvolved with their children. Using her own research, she argues for the use of qualitative research, which can help us understand how men construct their fathering roles and what barriers prevent their involvement in their children's lives. The final part of the chapter is a larger scale look at the institutions and policies (e.g., child custody, child support, workplace climate) that limit fathers' involvement in their children's lives and how these can be countered. She argues that no less than a challenge to dominant paradigms and assumptions will be necessary to change the current state of affairs.

In his chapter, Parke explores the directions in which parenting researchers must proceed in the next decade. First, he argues that parenting research must move beyond simplistic notions of parent and child effects to complex understanding of bidirectional and cyclic processes. Next, he suggests that researchers adopt a true developmental perspective. Such a perspective necessitates recognition that, not only do children develop, but so do parents as individuals, parents as a couple, and the family as a unit. Taking a developmental perspective also requires attention to transitions in family lives, both normative and nonnormative, and the effects of these transitions on trajectories of individuals, couples, and families. In the next part of the chapter, Parke explores the role of gender in family roles, asking questions such as what are the unique and overlapping contributions of mothers versus fathers? New work on children in gay and lesbian families showing positive child outcomes and gender identities similar to those in traditional families challenges us to rethink the roles of men and women in families and to ask whether it is exposure to mothers and fathers or to different interactive styles that is most important. Our views of parenting are also challenged by research on new reproductive technologies. Parke reminds us that understanding what is universal and specific about parenting requires us to take into account historical contexts and to conduct research across different cultures. The difficulties in taking such routes, such as cross-cultural equivalence of measures, and ideas for conquering them are explored.

1

Mothering:
Retrospect and Prospect

Wendy S. Grolnick
Suzanne T. Gurland
Clark University

In this volume of works on the family, it seems apt to begin with a chapter on mothers. In the history of research on the family, for better or worse, the mother was the first and primary target of focus. To be sure, mothers are multifaceted and play multiple roles—they are women, partners, breadwinners, and caretakers, among other things, and much feminist writing has been devoted to how mothers manage their multiple roles and identities (e.g., Reddy, Roth, & Sheldon, 1994). In this chapter we keep within the spirit of the volume and focus on mothers as parents, highlighting how mothers parent their children. In doing so, we attempt to address questions such as: What do we know about "effective" mothering? What is the state of mothering today?

RETROSPECT IN THE STUDY OF MOTHERING

In thinking about the history of research on mothering, we were struck by the paradox of two historical trends. The first was the ubiquitous emphasis on mothers in the clinical and early developmental literatures. It was all about mothers. Mothers were the cause of all of children's problems.

The second trend, paradoxically, was the virtual absence of mothers from the parenting literature because parenting had become synonymous with mothering. Much of the "parenting" research from the 1930s to the

1970s actually involved only mothers. In this literature, however, mothers were "invisible" because they were the standard backdrop against which other caretakers were measured. Scarr (1998) pointed out that the history of child care is one in which special notice was granted only to caregivers other than the child's mother.

We start with the early work focusing exclusively on mothers as the source of children's problems. Although mother blaming began earlier than the birth of psychoanalysis, Freud's theory of neurosis, emphasizing the mother's frustration of her children's instincts, began a systematic blaming of the mother. The associated work of Spitz (1950) and Bowlby (1944, 1951) in early institutions continued the focus on mothers, this time stressing the importance of her physical presence. During and after World Wars I and II, many children were orphaned. These children were placed in orphanages that met the children's physical, nutritional, and medical needs, but, of course, they did not include a mother. In addition, to quell the epidemic of tuberculosis, authorities took effected children from their parents and placed them in isolation sanitariums. Though the institutions were well intentioned, the children raised there showed severe psychological dysfunction and an inordinate number became physically ill and died. Bowlby (1944) reported that these terrible consequences were the result of their mothers' absence and coined the "maternal deprivation" hypothesis. In his article, "Maternal Care and Mental Health," Bowlby (1951) extended this work to all forms of mother–child separation. Later accounts of institutional effects, of course, pointed out that children were not only without mothers, but also without any social stimulation or love (Rutter, 1972). Yet, at the time, mothers' absence alone was viewed as the cause of the negative outcomes experienced by these children. In other work conducted around the same time, theorists argued that schizophrenic individuals had been adversely affected during their early childhoods by damaging relationships with their mothers. Fromm-Reichmann (1949) theorized about "schizophrenogenic mothers" whose parenting characteristics were thought to induce later schizophrenia in their children. During the 1940s and 1950s mother blaming was a clear and dominant trend.

Later empirical work continued the focus on mothers using biological models. Early models of mother–child attachment, for example, focused on the importance of early bonds between mothers and their children. Klaus and Kennell (1976) used the animal model of imprinting as a basis for a theory of mother–child bonding. In this theory, the mother forms a bond to her child during a limited time after the child's birth. Presumably, this is a biological process related to the hormonal state of the mother. The experience in the first hours after birth, and whether this bond is formed, were said to have long-lasting effects on the child. For example, Klaus and Kennell compared mothers given early and extended contact with their newborns during the first few days with those who received "routine" hospital care. These authors reported that mothers in the extended-contact group soothed their infants more, and displayed more eye contact and fondling of the infant than mothers in the routine-care group, and that differences between the groups persisted up to one year. Later studies using appropriate controls, however, found no differences between groups receiving extended care versus routine care (Svejda, Campos, & Emde, 1980).

The early studies focusing on the exclusive and direct role of mothers in determining outcomes for children were not without positive consequences. Spitz (1950) and Bowlby's (1951) work on institutions was pivotal in institutional reform. The bonding literature resulted in new hospital procedures in which mothers are typically given opportunities for extensive contact with their infants, and childbirth is viewed as a normal, healthy human experience (Goldberg, 1983). However, the early work also led to a distorted view of the sanctity of mothers' presence and to guilt about her absence. Mothers who miss opportunities to be with their children at birth (e.g., parents of premature infants) may feel their ability to care for their infants will be impaired. Mothers who are employed may get the message that they are damaging their children. Fathers get the message that they are peripheral (cf. Silverstein, chap. 2, this volume).

Although we think of mother blaming as a thing of the past, Caplan and Hall-McCorquodale (1985) argued that it persists, albeit in more subtle ways, in the clinical literature. In their quantitative study of mother blaming in nine major clinical journals, Caplan and Hall-McCorquodale found that mothers were held responsible for 72 child disorders whereas fathers were held responsible for none. Their compelling illustrations include case studies in which fathers were described using neutral or positive characteristics (e.g., age and occupation) whereas mothers were described using negative characteristics (e.g., poor emotional functioning). One case study mentioned a father's abuse and alcoholism briefly, yet blamed the child's problems on the mother's overprotection.

Why does mother blaming persist? It cannot be accounted for by issues such as greater recruitment of mothers into studies or actual relations between risk of psychopathology for children of disturbed mothers versus disturbed fathers, which tend to be equal (Phares & Compas, 1992). Furthermore, it is not that mothers are held accountable for all of children's behavior, as there is some evidence that mothers and fathers are held equally responsible for children's positive behavior (Phares, 1993). A more contextual explanation is required. Ruddick (1980) suggested mother blaming is a result of the power differential between men and women: "Almost everywhere the practices of mothering take place in societies in which women of all classes are less able than men of their class to determine the conditions in which their children grow. Throughout history, most women have moth-

ered in conditions of military and social violence, as well as economic deprivation, governed by men whose policies they could neither shape nor
control" (p. 355). Such circumstances silence mothers and make them easy
scapegoats when their children misbehave or develop various forms of
psychopathology.

Mother blaming, then, has been a dominant and pervasive trend that, despite spawning a few positive institutional reforms along the way, has primarily placed undue culpability on mothers for children's negative outcomes. What is more, the trend has persisted in less explicit ways in
contemporary research, undeterred by empirical data pointing to the inadequacy of "maternal deprivation" or other mother-blaming theories in explaining child outcomes. For researchers aiming to remedy this state of affairs, however, there is the danger of yet another extremist position: the
"invisible mother" problem alluded to earlier.

In attempting to shift the focus away from mothers as exclusively responsible for their children's psychological distress or well-being, researchers are tempted to treat mothers and fathers as interchangeable and to ob-
scure the unique circumstances in which mothers parent. On the other
hand, to take a non-mother-blaming view is to recognize the similarities between mothers and fathers. Both, after all, are parents attempting to meet
their children's needs, and we should therefore expect continuity across
the mothering and fathering styles that are best for children. Radin (1981),
for example, suggested that it is fathers' warmth, and not their masculinity,
that predicts children's levels of competence, achievement, and sex-role
identity. Thus, our aim is to view mothering in a way that is consistent with
the goals of all parenting generally, but that avoids placing undue blame or
responsibility on mothers, and that recognizes the importance and uniqueness of the circumstances surrounding mothers' contributions to their children's development.

Indeed, several advances have helped the research community move toward this more balanced view of mothers and mothering. With regard to
psychopathology, for example, researchers now acknowledge the role of biology in affective, schizophrenic, and anxiety disorders, among others. This
recognition of the multidetermined nature of psychopathology helps to ren-
der the pure mother-blaming stance obsolete. Similarly, mothering is now
recognized as a bidirectional process in which the mother is not the only
determinant of the child's outcomes or of the quality of the parent–child relationship. Bell's (1968) pioneering work on the effects of children on their
parents alerted us that parents parent at least partly in response to the
characteristics of their children. A case in point is the key role of temperament in determining parenting. In our own work, for example, parents who
saw their adolescents as more difficult tended to be more controlling and
less involved with them (Grolnick, Weiss, McKenzie, & Wrightman, 1996)

than those who saw their children as easier to handle. Rutter and Quinton (1984), in their longitudinal study of family illness, showed that children with adverse temperamental features were more likely than other children to be targets of maternal hostility, criticism, and irritability. In addition to this recognition of children's own contributions, other key influences on children have also been identified and studied: notably the father, the peer group, and the neighborhood. All of these advances encourage a balanced view in which our focus is broadened away from an exclusive mother-blaming stance, but we also do not lose sight of mothers' unique contribution as they face challenges and take on particular roles with their children.

In this chapter on mothering, we aim to achieve such a balanced view. We begin by reviewing what we know about the effects of different types of parenting on children, stressing the consensus and controversy in the field. We then discuss modern circumstances surrounding mothering. In particular, we focus on maternal employment, once the rarity but now the norm, and on mothers parenting solo, also a growing trend. Throughout, we remain true to the notion of consistency across caregivers in what is best for children by reviewing findings from the parenting literature that apply equally to mothers and fathers. We also, however, maintain a focus on mothers in context, appreciating that mothers play an important and unique role in their children's lives and that all mothers mother under complex circumstances that can enrich, constrain, or otherwise impinge on their ability to provide emotional resources to their children. Finally, we offer suggestions for future research that may shed new light on mothering.

REVIEW OF LITERATURE

Before beginning our review of the literature, we point out that recent critiques, such as that by Harris (1995), have questioned whether parents, never mind mothers versus fathers, matter at all. A major tenet of this critique has been the argument that nearly all studies finding that parents influence their children's development have employed correlational designs that cannot allow researchers to determine cause and effect (Collins, Maccoby, Steinberg, Hetherington, & Bornstein, 2000). Although it is not possible to randomly assign children to parents and thereby conduct definitive studies, many contemporary studies do use complex statistical procedures, employ longitudinal designs to control for child effects, examine jointly characteristics of children and parents as they affect child outcomes, and examine multiple influences simultaneously (e.g., parents and peers; Collins et al.). The consensus from such work has been that parents do indeed influence their children.

Thousands of studies have been conducted on mothering and parenting, ranging in focus from mother–infant interaction to maternal psychopathology to maternal education and employment status. It is impossible to comprehensively review these thousands of studies, so we have chosen to focus on two important themes. First, we address *dimensions of parenting* and attempt to show that, viewed from the proper perspective, the literature yields a more consistent picture than it might appear at first blush. Second, we review findings that support consistent *relations between parenting style and child outcomes*, with an emphasis on "good" parenting as dependent on what we take to be the appropriate telos of children's development.

Recall that our treatment of these two themes draws on the parenting literature, so that for the most part we are focusing on findings that are equally applicable to mothers and fathers. We intend for this focus to stress the notion that mothers are neither no more nor no less accountable for the satisfaction of children's needs than are other caregivers. In subsequent sections, however, we highlight the features of the parenting context that we believe apply uniquely to mothers.

Consensus Regarding Parenting Dimensions

There is no doubt that the parenting literature is replete with a sometimes confusing array of terms to describe various parenting styles and parenting dimensions. Some researchers, for example, have used terms such as responsive parenting, sensitive parenting, democratic versus autocratic, controlling versus autonomy supportive, and restrictive versus nonrestrictive. If we want to determine what makes for good parenting, we have to wade through these terms, in many cases looking beyond the words themselves to particular researchers' usages and meanings, and evaluate the way particular parenting dimensions are measured. Our task is further complicated by the not-infrequent differential use of the same terms. Baumrind's (1967) notion of control, for example, refers to demands for maturity, whereas Barber's (1996) control refers to psychological pressures on children.

The mire of terminology can make it appear that no two researchers are yielding consistent findings. However, when parenting questionnaires, made up of multiple self-report parenting items or ratings of parents drawn from observations, have been factor analyzed over the last 35 years, they have consistently yielded two dimensions.

The first dimension, variously referred to as maternal warmth, acceptance, responsivity, involvement, or child centeredness, captures maternal provision of emotional and material resources to children. In our work, we have referred to this dimension as involvement. Schaefer's (1959) factor analysis revealed a warmth–hostility dimension based on ratings of high affection, positive reinforcement, and sensitivity to the child's needs and desires on one end, and ratings of rejection and hostility on other end. Baldwin (1955) and Becker (1964) found evidence of a dimension that ranged from warmth to coolness. Pulkkinen (1982) distinguished parent-centered versus child-centered parenting, and Parker, Tupling, and Brown (1979), using the Parent Bonding Instrument, identified caring and empathic versus rejecting or indifferent parenting. Baumrind's (1967) typological scheme identified authoritative parents as warm and accepting and authoritarian parents as cold and aloof. Evidence for the underlying similarity of these differently named constructs comes from shared correlates, found consistently across studies. Warmth has been found to be associated with higher self-esteem in classic studies by Coopersmith (1967). Involvement has been linked to self-esteem (Loeb, Horst, & Horton, 1980) as well as to higher levels of achievement and motivation and lower levels of delinquency and aggression (Hatfield, Ferguson, & Alpert, 1967). We present this simply for now, but argue later that the effects of warmth and involvement depend on other dimensions. At this point, however, we can conclude that warm, responsive, and involved caretaking produces positive effects (see Fig. 1.1).

There is a second dimension that emerges in factor analyses of parenting instruments. This dimension has been far more perplexing than involvement. What unites the second dimension emerging across different factor analyses is its relationship to control of one kind or another. Descriptions such as controlling versus permissive, firm control versus lax control, psychological control versus psychological autonomy, restrictive versus permissive, and controlling versus autonomy supportive have been used to identify this dimension (see Fig. 1.2).

But what is control and how does it relate to parenting? Here is where the confusion begins. Do we mean being "in control"—acting as an authority and presenting children with tasks to be mastered (i.e., control versus chaos)? Or do we mean controlling the children, in the sense of pushing

Parenting Dimension 1

- Warmth vs.Hostility (Schaefer, 1959)

- Warmth vs.Coolness (Becker, 1964)

- Child-Centeredness (Pulkinnen, 1982)

- Caring and Empathic vs.Rejecting and Indifferent (Parker, 1979)

- Involvement (Grolnick & Slowiaczek, 1994)

- Acceptance vs.Rejection (Rohner, 1986)

FIG. 1.1. Parenting dimension 1.

Parenting Dimension 2

- Democratic vs. Autocratic (Baldwin, 1948)
- Firm Control vs. Lax Control (Baumrind, 1965)
- Psychological Control vs. Psychological Autonomy (Schaefer, 1959)
- Controlling vs. Autonomy Supportive (Deci & Ryan, 1985)
- Restrictive vs. Permissive (Becker, 1964)

FIG. 1.2. Parenting dimension 2.

them to act in specified ways without soliciting the children's input (control versus support for autonomy)? These are different definitions. In practice, what has happened is that researchers have entered different items into their factor analyses and come out with different dimensions. Those who have pit being in control against allowing children to control their lives (e.g., unilateral child decision making versus joint decision making) have come up with dimensions ranging from permissive to restrictive, or indulgent to authoritative. For example, entering items such as "I like to know where my child is at all times" versus "It doesn't matter when my child comes home, he will eventually" yields a dimension from restrictive to permissive. In this paradigm, maternal practices such as monitoring, acting as an authority figure, and maintaining rules and guidelines are viewed in opposition to not engaging in these maternal practices and, instead, allowing children's urges to prevail without intervention. By contrast, pitting items such as "I am always telling my son how to behave" against "I like my son to choose his own way of doing things" (items from the Child Report of Parent Behavior Inventory; Schaefer, 1965) yields a dimension from control to support for autonomy. This dimension taps the extent to which parents impose their own will on children versus provide children with opportunities to make decisions and then support children in those decisions.

If, as in the first dimension, we take control to mean being in control—that is, being an authority, making age-appropriate demands, setting limits—we find clear consensus that children do better when parents act as authorities. Children need rules, guidelines, and limits for optimal development. Baumrind (1967), for example, showed that children of permissive parents lacked self-control and self-reliance and were described as immature. If, as in the second dimension, we take control to mean controlling children—that is, placing paramount value on compliance, pressuring children toward specified outcomes, and discouraging verbal give-and-take and discussion, as opposed to supporting children's initiations, providing reasons, and respecting children's viewpoints—we find a clear, yet opposite, consensus that control has negative consequences for children. Authoritarian homes, for example, high in rules and regulations and stressing obedience and conformity produce children who lack initiative, spontaneity, and social competence with peers. Girls in such families have been described as dependent; boys, aggressive (Baumrind, 1967).

Despite the consensus among researchers using equivalent definitions, confusion in the literature persists. An example is Lewis' (1981) critique of Baumrind's work. Lewis began with the idea that there is a conflict between Baumrind's finding that firm control is positive for children's adjustment, and attribution theory, which stressed that functionally superfluous control undermines children's taking on behaviors in the absence of adult surveillance. But, as Baumrind (1983) argued in her reply to Lewis, firm control is not equivalent to functionally superfluous control. Rather, firm control is parents' making age-appropriate demands on children, for example, to do chores, to help themselves, and to follow through on what is asked of them.

Here is where the two definitions of control meet. The age-appropriate demands made by parents who are "in control" can vary greatly in their style of delivery. If the demands communicate an inflexible set standard for compliance, the parents are both "in control" and "controlling." In Lewis's words, they are exercising functionally superfluous control. On the other hand, the same demands, made with a different style of delivery, can communicate an openness to discussion and a valuing and respect of children's input. In this latter case, the parents are "in control" but not "controlling." Rather, they are supportive of their children's autonomy. Thus, the apparent contradiction noted by Lewis is resolved when we recognize that these different definitions of control can coexist, and that one of them (controlling children versus supporting their autonomy) can be used to characterize the style of the other (being in control versus being permissive).

When we look closely at researchers' findings and how they have measured parenting constructs, we find that parenting can be usefully and consistently organized along two primary dimensions: a warmth and involvement dimension and a control dimension separable into two meanings of control. The evidence provided in support of these dimensions, however, is derived largely from factor analyses, and we may wish to ask whether they hold up, not only from this empirical perspective, but also from a theoretical standpoint. One such perspective is to consider parenting from the perspective of our evolutionary origins. Parenting is an evolved system, and evolution has shaped humans to parent in particular ways in response to environmental cues. We argue that the major dimensions of warmth and involvement and control uncovered by researchers are not random or coincidental, but rather they have evolved through natural selection because they conferred a reproductive advantage to the species over evolutionary time.

Most psychologists are familiar with the evolutionary logic of attachment theory. Because in the environment of evolutionary adaptedness there were dangers, predators, and other threats, juveniles who kept their parents in close proximity survived in greater numbers than their peers who wandered from their parents and encountered fatal dangers. Thus, natural selection conferred a reproductive advantage on children and parents who maintained close proximity, and we, as modern-day humans, are the heirs of this evolved system (Bowlby, 1969). This is the familiar attachment system. The infant uses the parent as a base from which to explore, derives comfort from her in times of stress, and regulates proximity to her using felt security as a barometer (Sroufe & Waters, 1977).

Less familiar is the work on the evolutionary basis of the affective system. MacDonald (1992) posited a human affectional system, distinct from the attachment system that centers on fear. He argued that this affectional system developed to assure parental provision of resources and investment of time and energy into childrearing. Trivers (1974) coined the term *parental investment* to refer to parents' tendencies to invest resources of any kind in their offspring. MacDonald suggested that this tendency is based in a positive reinforcement system in which parents feel intense love and caring for their offspring, which makes them want to help and to make sacrifices. A parallel system in children results in their feeling intense love for parents and a desire to be with them. Clearly, it has been adaptive for parents to invest in children because human young have a long period of dependency (necessary to accommodate the growth of their large brains) that requires substantial investment from parents if the young are to survive. If this account has merit, we would have sound basis for findings that warm, involved parenting has positive outcomes. In other words, warmth-involvement as a dimension of parenting makes theoretical sense from an evolutionary standpoint, beyond making empirical sense as a reliable result of factor analyses.

Can a similar argument be made regarding the parental dimension of control? Any such argument would be more speculative, because less work has been directed toward an evolutionary theory of control. However, there are theoretical reasons to believe that control, like warmth and involvement, has evolved as a parenting dimension through natural selection. Although programmed to invest in their children, humans are a flexible species; how they do so is likely to be determined by the environment. Cues in their environments help parents to know how much to invest. A cue of resource scarcity, for example, would prompt parents to delay reproduction.

Among some animals, competition and adversity in the environment are associated with fewer and more widely spaced offspring and prolonged parental care.

So-called *K-selected* species, such as humans, which evolved in stable environments, are sensitive to the levels of competition and adversity in the environment. If the environment is highly stable, there is competition among offspring and parents typically invest in fewer offspring to help make them as competitive as possible. They may do so by investing in children's performance and other outcomes. Similarly, if the environment is highly aversive, parents also increase their investment in children's outcomes.

High levels of psychological investment in children's outcomes may result in controlling parenting. And if parents perceive environmental cues as competitive, they may invest in ways that lead to controlling involvement even when living in a stable environment. Are parents likely to pick up such competitive cues in modern Western culture? We believe the answer is yes. Schools and other institutions (e.g., sports leagues) are centered around competition, grades, and other social comparisons. They may provide cues of threat (albeit subjective and "man-made" threat). For many families, objective threat and adversity in the environment are a fact of life.

These ideas are consistent with research from political psychology. In times of threat, individuals become more authoritarian whereas in times of ease they becomes less so (e.g., Sales, 1973). In our lab we have been conducting studies to determine whether parents who anticipate competition and threat in the future world that their children will inhabit are more controlling than parents who expect the world to be more cooperative and less harsh. In one study (Grolnick & Gurland, 1999), we found that parents who were more concerned about the future tended to value obedience in their children more than those who were less concerned. Furthermore, parents who were more concerned tended to be more controlling with their children. This study provided preliminary support for our theory that parents adjust their levels of control to cues of adversity.

Does this mean that controlling parenting was associated with positive growth and development at some point in our evolutionary history? Not necessarily. Just because a characteristic is in our repertoire does not mean it was (or still is) adaptive for children's growth. It may have been adaptive when literal survival (i.e., be controlled or be eaten or mauled by a lion) was on the line. Although controlling responses to such threats to survival may have been adaptive in the environment of evolutionary adaptedness, they may never have facilitated development. There is also evidence, as we review later, that controlling responses are negative across contexts today. Regardless of whether this modern twist on our evolutionary heritage is supported by the data, the recognition that evolution would have selected for variation in levels of control suggests that control, like warmth and involvement, is both a theoretically and an empirically sound dimension along which to organize our understanding of parenting.

Thus far, we have claimed that there is more consensus in the parenting literature than might be suspected, once the problems of differing terminology have been addressed, and that the two dimensions that emerge—warmth and involvement and control (in both of its usages)—have both theoretical and empirical support for being included in discussions about parenting. But what are the boundaries of this consensus? Are there populations for whom these findings do not hold? The work of Baldwin, Baldwin, and Cole (1990), in which restrictive parenting was positive for children from higher risk families, is often cited as an example that controlling parenting, contrary to our claimed consensus, is good in high-risk families. Yet, restrictiveness in the Baldwin et al. study referred to having rules rather than enforcing them in a controlling manner. In fact, they found that although restrictiveness was positive only for high-risk families, democracy was positively correlated with competence in both groups. Furthermore, both the successful high- and low-risk families displayed a low value for obedience and a high value for responsibility. The results of the Baldwin et al. study supported the importance of being in control, rather than being controlling, in an area where danger and high levels of crime prevailed. Further, results of various studies converge on the negative effects of authoritarian parenting across socioeconomic status (SES) and racial groups (e.g., Dornbusch, Ritter, Leiderman, Roberts, & Fraleigh, 1987). (Recall that authoritarian families are high in rules and regulations, but also strongly value compliance and obedience.) Chen's work in China (e.g., Chen, Dong, & Zhou, 1997) showed that authoritative parenting is positively associated with competence and adjustment. (Recall that authoritative families, distinct from authoritarian families, are high in rules and regulations, but value children's input and self-reliance and responsibility over compliance and obedience). Chirkov and Ryan (1999) also showed that Russian high school students who saw their parents as more autonomy supportive showed better mental health outcomes than those who saw their parents as more controlling. Thus, the consensus remains robust across many socioeconomic, racial, and geographic boundaries.

In our work (e.g., Grolnick & Ryan, 1989; Grolnick, Ryan, & Deci, 1997), we have studied parenting and parental control from within the framework of self-determination theory (Deci & Ryan, 1985). Self-determination theory identifies three innate needs—the need for autonomy, the need for competence, and the need for relatedness—and posits three environmental dimensions based on these needs: autonomy support to control, structure, and involvement that map, respectively, onto the three innate needs. Autonomy support refers to the degree to which the environment provides choice, encourages self-initiation, and minimizes the use of controls. Controlling communications, whether overt, such as in physical punishment, or covert, such as in controlling praise, pressure children toward specified outcomes. Structure refers to information about the relations between behaviors and outcomes. Conveying information about socially sanctioned behaviors and naturally occurring consequences to various behaviors are examples of structure. Such structure, however, can be provided in either an autonomy-supportive manner or a controlling manner. Language that pressures children or close surveillance that ensures compliance make the structure controlling. By contrast, simply conveying information in a reasoned and empathic way allows the structure to provide guidance while supporting children's autonomy. Involvement refers to the dedication of resources to the child. Involved parents put time and energy into their parenting, and they sacrifice when possible.

Grolnick and Ryan (1989) interviewed 114 parents of third- through sixth-grade children about how they motivate their children to engage in school and home-related activities such as doing homework, going to bed on time, and doing chores. Independent raters scored the hour-long interviews and generated summary scores for autonomy support, involvement, and structure. Autonomy support related to teacher ratings of children's competence and adjustment, and to children's grades and achievement scores. Parental involvement was positively related to teacher-rated competence and adjustment, and to school grades and achievement. Parental provision of structure was positively related to children's understanding of how to control their successes and failures in school and in general.

There is consensus on the positive effects of each of the three dimensions, but few studies have focused on the interplay among different parenting dimensions and attempted to separate involvement, for example, from control. We report on two studies from our laboratory that examined the interplay of involvement and control.

The first study is part of our longitudinal work on parent involvement (Grolnick, 1993). A diverse sample of 209 parents, their children, and children's teachers participated. We assessed parent involvement (school, cognitive, and personal) using parent, teacher, and child ratings. We also assessed children's experiences of that involvement from positive to negative (e.g., "I feel good when my mother talks to my teacher" and "I don't like to talk about what happens at school with my mother"). What made children feel negatively about their parents' involvement was its controlling nature; children who saw their parents as autonomy supportive tended to be positive about their parents' involvement, whereas children who saw their parents as controlling tended to be negative about their parents' involvement. The relative importance of each of the two dimensions (level of involvement and quality of involvement) depended on what outcomes were examined. For grades, level of involvement was key. Parents who were more involved had children who were doing better in school. For motivation, however, the quality of involvement was key. Regardless of the level of involvement, autonomy support was associated with more autonomous motivation. There was one interaction between level and quality of involvement for perceived competence. For children in the high-involvement group, quality did not matter. For children in the low-involvement group, perceived competence was higher if quality was positive.

A second study, conducted with Weiss, focused on adolescents in 7th through 11th grades (Weiss & Grolnick, 1991). Adolescents reported on parent involvement and autonomy support. They also reported on their own internalizing and externalizing symptomatology on the Achenbach Youth Self-Report. They divided parents into groups of the most involved (top 15%), moderately involved (middle 70%), and the least involved (bottom 15%). Results showed the high-involvement group and the high-autonomy support group both reported the fewest internalizing symptoms and the fewest externalizing symptoms (see Figs. 1.3 and 1.4). Significant interactions also occurred for both types of symptoms, indicating the combination of high-involvement and low-autonomy support yielded a high level of symptoms (in some cases higher than for the low-involvement groups).

The findings from these two studies contextualized our earlier, tentative claim that there is consensus on the positive effects of parental warmth and involvement. When parents are involved in an autonomy-supportive manner, that involvement is associated with desirable child outcomes. When they are involved in a controlling way, however, the involvement can have deleterious effects on child outcomes.

Parental Involvement by Autonomy Support

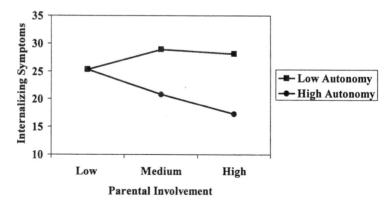

FIG. 1.3. Parental involvement by autonomy support (internalizing symptoms).

Parental Involvement by Autonomy Support

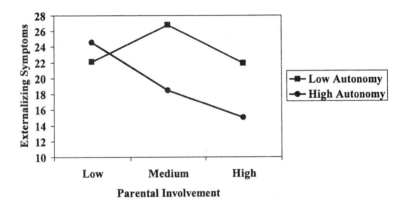

FIG. 1.4. Parental involvement by autonomy support (externalizing symptoms).

The interplay between structure and control has also been examined. (Baumrind actually never did the comparisons of parents high in firm control and differing only in their responsiveness.) Pomerantz and Ruble (1998) examined the interplay between exercising control (what we refer to as structure) and whether that structure is conveyed in a controlling or an autonomy-granting way. Controlling behaviors were those that were likely to (a) make children feel they were controlled by external forces (e.g., receiving a reward for doing well in school), (b) conveyed that performance was key (e.g., mother picks the topic for a report versus allowing the child to do so), or (c) conveyed incompetence (e.g., mother helps the child before the child asked for assistance). Autonomy-granting structure (a) made children feel their behavior emanated from them (e.g., mother attributes child's good performance to ability or enjoyment of task), (b) conveyed that mastery was key (e.g., encourage child to pick his or her own topic), or (c) communicated confidence in the child (e.g., stand by while encouraging the child to solve the problem by himself or herself). Pomerantz and Ruble looked at the effects of structure with autonomy granting, structure alone, autonomy granting alone (no help), and no response to the child's work. Results suggested that when mothers used controlling structure more, children blamed themselves more for their failures. Autonomy granting structure was associated with more intrinsic motivation. Autonomy alone had no effect. As with involvement and control, structure and control also yield specific outcomes depending on the interplay of the two dimensions.

What can we conclude from this review of research on parenting dimensions? First, although factor analyses of parenting questionnaires have consistently yielded two factors, the second factor has been largely determined by the items and methods of measurement used by different researchers, and it may actually represent a confound of two dimensions. Indeed, the studies reviewed indicate there are at least three dimensions to parenting, which must be investigated individually. Second, parenting dimensions can be traced back theoretically to the evolutionary origins of caregiving and protection of children. Third, the interplay of the parenting dimensions is key, in that the evidence supports specificity of outcomes for various combinations of dimensions. Finally, we must ask, using theoretically based formulations, what may be universal about parenting dimensions and outcomes. Although studies do not suggest that controlling parenting is positive in any culture, individuals in different cultures may interpret their surroundings differently; what may be controlling to one group may not be so for another. For example, Rohner and Pettengill (1985) found that, in contrast to U.S. samples where control and acceptance are negatively correlated, in Korean families, children's reports of their parents' control and acceptance are positively correlated. Such a finding suggests that children in different cultures may interpret the same behaviors on the part of parents differently. Furthermore, associations between parenting and outcomes may depend on the way different outcomes are valued in different cultures. For example, Chen et al. (1997) found that authoritativeness in parents was associated with shyness in children in China. However, contrary to the case in the United States, shyness is a highly valued trait in China. Thus, although work converges on the positive effects of autonomy-supportive parenting on child outcomes, these outcomes may differ in different cultures. These complexities of relations between parenting and child outcomes must be attended to if we are to fully understand effective parenting across cultural groups.

What Is "Good" Parenting Depends on What We Desire for Children: Compliance Versus Internalization

If the goal of socialization is simply to produce obedient, compliant children, the goal can be easily attained through the constant and controlling imposition and enforcement of rules. If, however, the goal of socialization is not just for children to comply, but to engage in behaviors volitionally and to accept and endorse the behaviors or develop a value for them, parents must facilitate children's internalization of the regulation of their own behavior. We believe in the latter goal of socialization. In our work, we have conceptualized internalization not as an all-or-none process but as a continuum.

Internalization refers to the processes by which individuals acquire beliefs, attitudes, or behavioral regulations from external sources and progressively transform the external regulations into personal attributes, values, or regulatory styles. Internalization is conceived of as a natural process, part of children's innate propensities to master their internal and external worlds (Grolnick, Ryan, & Deci, 1997). Further, internalization proceeds optimally if (a) controls in the environment are not too strong—controls undermine children's activity, keeping regulation tied to external contingencies; (b) children have a developmentally appropriate understanding of the regulations they are to internalize; and (c) relational support is available, in the form of caring, nurturing adults with whom children can identify.

Even children who regulate their own behavior do so for different reasons, and these reasons can provide a window into the degree to which the regulation of a particular behavior has been internalized. Ryan and Connell (1989) have outlined a continuum to capture the different degrees to which behaviors or values are internalized (see Fig. 1.5). Initially, children regulate behavior through external contingencies (e.g., I do my schoolwork because I'd get in trouble if I don't). A greater degree of internalization is seen in introjected regulation; in this case, externally imposed regulations have been "taken in" by the child but maintained in essentially their original form. At this level of internalization, children self-regulate through internally imposed pressure and self-critical affects such as guilt and shame (e.g., I do my homework because I'd feel guilty if I didn't). A third form, more internalized yet, is regulation through identification. In this case, the child identifies with the value of the behavior and sees it as important for his or her goals (e.g., I do my homework because it helps my learning). Finally, in integrated regulation, there is a fuller internalization where the regulation is assimilated into other existing values and belief systems.

In our work, we have argued that autonomy-supportive parenting, combined with structure and involvement, facilitates the internalization process, whereas controlling parenting undermines it. Grolnick and Ryan (1989) found that parents with more autonomy-supportive styles had children who reported more autonomous regulation in school. Lamborn, Mounts, Steinberg, and Dornbusch (1991) found that children reared in authoritarian families did well on measures of obedience and conformity but had low perceived ability and low social competence. Thus, if the goal is conformity

Types of Regulation

FIG. 1.5. Types of regulation.

and obedience, authoritarian parenting is the way to achieve it. But if the goal is autonomous self-regulation and its attendant benefits, such as areas of self-regulation, moral development, and conscience, the data converge in favor of autonomy-supportive parenting and demonstrate the deleterious effects of controlling parenting on the process of internalization. We provide evidence for these conclusions in two domains.

Moral Development. Prosocial and moral behaviors can be motivated by different processes. Two dimensions are particularly salient: egoistic to altruistic and exogenous to endogenous. Eisenberg-Berg and Hand (1979) have shown that, with age, reasons for prosocial action tend to change from being more hedonistic and approval oriented to more internalized or empathically oriented. Children at lower levels of moral development focus on external pressures, avoidance of punishment, attainment of rewards, or preservation of their own interests. Such foci indicate that the value of prosocial action has not yet been internalized. Supporting the undermining effects of control on moral development, Hoffman (1970) showed that power-assertive parenting was associated with low moral development. Powers (1982) examined parents' behavior during family discussions of moral dilemmas. Her findings showed that it was not the degree of cognitive stimulation in the parents' discussions that predicted high levels of moral development in the children, but rather how supportive versus interfering the parents were in these discussions. Parents who were more supportive and less likely to interfere had children who were higher in moral development. Walker and Taylor (1991) examined parents' moral stage, children's moral stage, and the way families discussed moral dilemmas. The stage of the parent was not as highly related to the stage of the child as was the way the family discussed dilemmas. The parents whose children increased most in moral reasoning over a 2-year period were those who elicited the children's opinions, asked clarifying questions, and checked the children's understanding. In contrast, styles in which children were challenged and confronted and styles in which parents simply provided their opinions (which were described as akin to lecturing) were associated with lesser increases in moral reasoning over the 2 years.

Conscience. Conscience has been defined as the development, maintenance, and application of generalizable internal standards of conduct for one's behavior. Kochanska conducted a series of studies looking at the origins of conscience in toddlers. Kochanska and Aksan (1995) distinguished between *situational compliance*, in which there was cooperation without any feeling of moral obligation, and *committed compliance*, which had a more internalized, self-regulated quality in which spontaneous self-correction of behavior, enthusiasm, and persistence were evident, even when the parent ceased to intervene. Such committed compliance was more likely when parent–child relationships were characterized by high mutual, positive affect. Mutually responsive orientations were also associated with parents' reports of children's internalization (Kochanska, 1997), as was discipline that was gentle rather than power assertive.

These studies demonstrate that greater internalization of behavior regulation is encouraged through autonomy support. Some studies, however, missed the point that there are degrees of internalization and instead viewed overt behavior as an index of a dichotomously conceived internalization. The outcomes of such studies typically focused on whether the child engages in (or refrains from performing) some particular behavior (e.g., not cheating when the child thinks he or she is not being watched; compliance in the absence of monitoring). However, what appears to be the same overt behavior can be regulated differently, and with different consequences for children's experience. Such behaviors can be regulated by introjection, involving anxiety, guilt, and shame, or by identification, involving smooth regulation and minimal internal conflict. Although the behavior may be the same, the consequences for the child (anxiety, worry, defensive coping) of introjected versus identified regulation may be different.

Deci, Eghrari, Patrick, and Leone (1994) conducted a laboratory experiment with college students that addressed how factors that facilitate introjection may differ from those that facilitate identification. Specifically, participants were asked to engage in a highly boring task in one of eight conditions formed by the factorial crossing of the presence versus absence of three facilitating behaviors: providing a meaningful rationale for doing the task, providing an acknowledgement of the participants' feelings of finding the task boring, and emphasizing choice. The dependent variables were (a) the amount of time participants voluntarily spent on the task in a later session when they were alone and had not been asked to do it, and (b) participants' reports of feeling free, enjoying the task, and finding it important. Results indicated that participants in conditions with more facilitating behaviors spent more subsequent free time on the task and reported more positive feelings than those in conditions with fewer facilitating behaviors. Thus, supporting individual self-determination by explaining the reasons for a requested behavior, validating individuals' feelings about it, and minimizing controls increase the likelihood a regulation will be internalized.

Even more interesting for the purposes of our discussion was the fact that data from the participants in the supportive conditions in the Deci et al. (1994) study revealed a strong, positive correlation between the amount of free time the students spent on the tasks and their self-reports of freedom, enjoyment, and importance, thus suggesting integration of the regulation. By contrast, data from subjects in the nonsupportive conditions revealed a negative correlation between free-time behavior and the same self-reports, indicating these individuals engaged in the behavior because they thought they should rather than because they liked it or believed it was important. These nonsupportive-condition individuals were therefore subject to the conflict and tension associated with introjected forms of regulation, whereas their supportive-condition counterparts experienced the freedom and enjoyment of identified regulation. Once again, if the goal were merely to get the individuals to engage in the task, any type of regulation would do. But the autonomy afforded by the supportive conditions is necessary for the larger goals beyond task compliance.

Another example of a controlling parenting behavior that can lead to incomplete internalization and negative experiential consequences is the use of love withdrawal as a disciplinary technique. Research has shown that this technique leads to high compliance but unsophisticated moral reasoning. We suggest that the use of love withdrawal, because of its controlling nature, tends to promote introjected rather than identified or integrated forms of internalization. Thus, a child from a home in which parents rely on this technique may act in parent-valued ways, but the behavior is likely to have negative affective consequences such as low self-esteem (Cooper-smith, 1967).

The main points from the previously described studies are that parenting strategies and styles that facilitate obedience and compliance may be different from those that facilitate internalization, and that the same behavior can be demonstrated by children for different reasons and with different consequences for their moral development, conscience, and well-being. This difference in degrees of internalization allows researchers to conclude that rewards, contingency programs, and token economies have positive effects, but that these interventions also undermine children's self-regulation. What parents are encouraged to do depends on what they want for or from their children: If parents want their daughter to clean her room right now, they should promise her a candy bar, but if they want their daughter to recognize the value of keeping her room clean and to do so willingly without being reminded, the candy bar will not work. Overall, this work illustrates that focusing exclusively on behavioral outcomes, rather than including the child's experience, may miss important aspects of the socialization process.

The preceding review emphasizes two key themes that have emerged from the parenting literature: that there is a reasonable degree of consensus regarding the parenting dimensions of warmth and control, and that different parenting styles are associated with different child outcomes. These themes apply to mothers, fathers, and other caregivers and therefore do not require us to differentiate, for example, mothering dimensions from fathering dimensions. Rather, children have particular psychological needs, and the dimensions that are critical to the satisfaction of those needs are consistent across caregivers. Discussing such dimensions has the added benefit of removing blame from mothers, as fathers and other caregivers are equally implicated in determining the outcomes relevant to children's development.

MOTHERING AND CURRENT CIRCUMSTANCES

The findings discussed in the previous sections suggest that we, as a field, are actually in relatively good position with respect to our understanding of parenting dimensions and their relations to children's outcomes. Identifying the parenting styles that are best for children, however, says little about the day-to-day practicality of modern mothers' actually providing such parenting for their children. Current circumstances, such as high rates of maternal employment outside the home and the changing nature of family constellations away from once-typical, two-parent, nuclear families toward solo-parent families may shape the way mothers parent their children. These two exemplars of contemporary circumstances illustrate the point that mothering, as all parenting, is not a static part of the personality but a dynamic process affected by the context in which it occurs. Like our earlier discussion that emphasized shared responsibility across caregivers, this section on mothers in context also helps reduce mother blaming by recognizing that mothers do not parent in a vacuum, but rather are subject to modern circumstances that can influence their parenting.

Maternal Employment

The number of women in the labor force has dramatically increased in many modern societies. In 1970, 30% of married women with children under the age of six were employed in the United States; this number rose to 45% in 1980 and 57% in 1987. Current estimates are that three fourths of school-aged children's mothers work, as do more than half of the mothers of infants under age one (Behrman, 1996).

The effect of maternal employment on children has been a point of intense controversy. Findings have ranged from the negative (e.g., reports of increases in avoidance during the strange situation in the 1980s and early 1990s; Belsky & Braungart, 1991; Vaughn, Gove, & Egeland, 1980) to the neutral (e.g., Harvey's, 1999, study of the National Longitudinal Survey of Youth (NLSY) showing virtually no adverse effects of maternal employment) to the conditional (Desai, Michael, & Chase-Lansdale's, 1990, finding that negative effects were apparent only among high-income boys).

The complexity of these findings is due at least in part to the fact that quantity and quality of time spent with parents and time in childcare are not equivalent. In the United States, the National Institute on Child Health and Human Development Early ChildCare Research Network has focused on the effects of the quality of day care and concluded that child outcomes are good when quality is high. The conclusion that working mothers spend less time with their children has also been qualified by the recognition that, although working mothers may spend less time in traditional child care activities, they may actually spend more time in shared housework and leisure time activities (Bryant & Zick, 1996). Our task here is not to review the myriad studies on employment, but to point out that the parenting literature cannot ignore the fact that mothers are working and most children are parented by working parents. Developing a more comprehensive understanding of the way work and parenting intersect is a crucial task for parenting researchers in the coming years.

One area on which there is already a fair amount of consensus is the effects of work stress. Studies show that stress at work spills over into the marital interaction (Bolger, DeLongis, Kessler, & Wethington, 1989; Crouter, Perry-Jenkins, Huston, & Crawford, 1989) and that fathers are more behaviorally and emotionally withdrawn when they have had a more demanding day at work (Repetti, 1994). How about mothers? Repetti and Wood (1997) asked this question in a study with mothers and their 3- to 6-year-old children. They looked at mothers' perceived workload and the quality of social interactions with coworkers and supervisors over a 5-day period. They then had parents and observers report on the quality of mother–child interaction those evenings. Results suggested that the higher the perceived workload on a particular day, the more withdrawal mothers reported and the less behaviorally and emotionally involved and the less caring and loving observers reported them to be with their children. Thus, although work status may or may not affect parenting, work stress clearly does.

Mothers Parenting Solo

The number of families headed by single women has increased dramatically over the last 3 decades. In 1960, less than 7% of all children in the United States lived in a female-headed household. By 1985, the proportion had increased to more than 21%. If this trend continues, soon one half of American children may live in a female-headed household for at least some of their years before age 18. There is evidence that single parenthood makes it difficult for mothers to provide autonomy-supportive, structured, and involved environments for children.

Hetherington, Cox, and Cox (1982) found that disrupted family status is associated with less social control and less supervision of children. Simons and Johnson (1996) later reported that, according to observer ratings, child report, and mother report, divorced mothers engage in a wide range of more "dysfunctional" parenting practices, including the use of harsh discipline, coercion, low monitoring, criticism, and lack of follow-through on punishment, when compared with married mothers. In our studies, mothers from single-parent homes were less involved at their children's schools than were mothers from two-parent homes (Grolnick, Benjet, Kurowski, & Apostoleris, 1997).

The less-than-optimal parenting practices observed more frequently in single-parent families have negative consequences for children. Statistics show, for example, that children from disrupted or never-married families are less likely to complete high school and more likely to have low earnings than those from intact families (McLanahan, Astone, & Marks, 1991). Children whose parents lack the warmth, monitoring, and reasonable discipline associated with effective parenting are at greater risk for conduct problems and psychological distress (Maccoby, 1992; Maccoby & Martin, 1983).

How are we to explain the differences in parenting practices among single versus married mothers? There are at least three explanations for such disruptions:

1. Direct effects of a second parent. There is some evidence that the presence of a second parent reinforces the parenting authority of the first (Dornbusch et al., 1985; Thomson, McLanahan, & Curtin, 1992), and that, in the absence of a second parent, authority is weakened and intergenerational boundaries clouded (Knok, 1988). Further, children in mother-only families receive less maternal time than children in two-parent families.

2. Gender Socialization. Other researchers suggest parenting practices differ because of gender role socialization. They contend that discipline is a traditionally male role and that women may not have been socialized to enforce disciplinary procedures. Indeed, there is evidence that single fathers exercise greater parental control than do single mothers (Santrock, Warshak, & Elliott, 1982). However, if married women were socialized in much the same way as single women, why should divorced mothers be less effective disciplinarians than their married counterparts?

3. Stress and Depression. An alternative explanation, for which there is strong research support, suggests that differences in family structure produce their effects on parenting practices through maternal stress and emotional well-being (e.g., Brody & Forehand, 1988; Hetherington et al., 1982; Simons, Beaman, Conger, & Chao, 1993). Stress is highly associated with the poverty and economic pressures single parents experience. In 1983, 50% of all mother-only families were poor, compared with 12% of married families. Not only do single mothers have higher poverty rates, but their poverty is more persistent and more severe than that of married mothers (Duncan & Hoffman, 1985). Single mothers are likely to experience income insecurity and the associated economic stresses and pressures. After a divorce, mothers, on average, retain 67% of their predivorce incomes. Fathers, by contrast, retain 90% of their incomes (McLanahan et al., 1991). Simons and Johnson

(1996) found that, among divorced mothers, economic pressure has a direct negative effect on the quality of parenting, as well as an indirect effect through depression. Women in poverty are more likely to use power-assertive techniques in disciplinary encounters and to be less supportive and affectional (McLloyd & Wilson, 1991). Likely because of the worry and frustration associated with economic pressures, these mothers may be too preoccupied to engage fully in the parental practices witnessed among their married peers. Furthermore, research suggests that a caring spouse increases encouragement, advice, and assistance during times of emotional distress, decreasing the probability that stress will "spill over" into the parenting role (Simons & Johnson, 1996). Note, however, that the key finding concerns the presence of a caring partner; it is well known that the presence of a spouse who creates distress compromises effective parenting by mothers.

Thus, single-parent status, largely in connection with the stress of economic pressure, creates conditions that can impede mothers' provision of involved, structured, and autonomy-supportive parenting. Consequently, single-parent status can be seen as a risk factor for diminished outcomes for children. The message to policymakers should be clear. The challenge is to create supportive structures to help relieve the depressive symptoms and stress attendant to economic distress, and to make adaptive parenting possible.

DIRECTIONS FOR RESEARCH

Parenting researchers must take several directions in the years ahead to fully understand the roles of mothers in their children's lives. These directions are as follows:

1. Researchers must determine the salience and centrality of parenting dimensions across development and context. Is it possible that at different developmental periods different parenting dimensions (e.g., involvement or structure) might be more key? In one study on language development we found that at the early stages of language learning (18 months), amount of maternal language stimulation (involvement) was a key predictor of language competence. At 24 months, maternal autonomy support was predictive but amount of speech was not (Sewell & Grolnick, 1993). Attention to the developmental components of parenting dimensions is clearly a direction for future work.

2. Researchers must specify the role of parenting dimensions at critical periods. For example, Barth and Parke's (1993) work showed that children of parents who were more controlling had more difficulty transitioning into

school. Grolnick, Kurowski, Dunlap, and Hevey (2000) and Lord, Eccles, and McCarthy (1994) demonstrated that parental resources of involvement and autonomy support help children make successful transitions to junior high. These studies suggest attention to transitions is a key issue for parenting researchers (see also Kreppner, chap. 8, this volume).

3. Researchers must revisit the question Belsky and Braungart (1991) posited in 1984 about the determinants of parenting. In particular, it is important to take an updated look at the personal, contextual, and institutional factors that affect parenting. For example, one institutional reason parents in high-risk areas are less involved in their children's school lives is that teachers in high-risk areas are less likely to involve such parents than are teachers in low-risk areas (Grolnick et al., 1997). What may be interpreted as personal lacunae may actually be institutionally based. However, to identify such possibilities, researchers must look beyond the family to the contexts in which families live.

4. Researchers must develop greater clarity on how and why single parenthood and employment affect parenting. Along with this focus, they need to spend energy on the development of policies and practices that reduce the negative effects of stress on mothers (cf. Silverstein, chap. 2, this volume, for a similar point about fathers).

5. Researchers must specify the cues parents are picking up from the environment, identify how these cues affect parenting practices, and establish under what circumstances they result in positive versus negative outcomes. As we have argued, evolutionary psychology stands to provide a useful framework for understanding how parenting can go awry.

To address these issues, a nonblaming stance, but one that acknowledges the unique roles of mothers, is needed. Research based on such a stance is most likely to meet the challenges in the study of motherhood in the years ahead.

REFERENCES

Baldwin, A. L. (1955). *Behavior and development in childhood*. New York: Dryden Press.
Baldwin, A. L., Baldwin, C., & Cole, R. E. (1990). Stress-resistant families and stress-resistant children. In J. Rolf, A. S. Masten, D. Cicchette, K. H. Nuechterien, & S. Weintraub (Eds.), *Risk and protective factors in the development of psychopathology* (pp. 257–280). New York: Cambridge University Press.
Barber, B. (1996). Parental psychological control: Revisiting a neglected construct. *Child Development, 67,* 3296–3319.
Barth, J. M., & Parke, R. D. (1993). Parent–child relationship influences on children's transition to school. *Merrill Palmer Quarterly, 39,* 173–195.
Baumrind, D. (1967). Child care practices anteceding three patterns of preschool behavior. *Genetic Psychology Monographs, 75,* 43–88.

Baumrind, D. (1983). Rejoinder to Lewis's reinterpretation of parental firm control effects: Are authoritative families really harmonious? *Psychological Bulletin, 94*, 132–142.

Becker, W. C. (1964). Consequences of different kinds of parental discipline. In M. L. Hoffman & L. W. Hoffman (Eds.), *Review of child development research* (Vol. 1, pp. 169–208). New York: Russel Sage Foundation.

Behrman, R. E. (Ed.). (1996). Financing child care. *The Future of Children, 6*(2).

Bell, R. Q. (1968). A reinterpretation of the direction of effects in studies of socialization. *Psychological Review, 75*, 81–95.

Belsky, J., & Braungart, J. M. (1991). Are insecure-avoidant infants with extensive day-care experience less stressed by and more independent in the strange situation? *Child Development, 62*, 567–571.

Bolger, N., DeLongis, A., Kessler, R. C., & Wethington, E. (1989). The contagion of stress across multiple roles. *Journal of Marriage and the Family, 51*, 175–183.

Bowlby, J. (1946). *Forty-four juvenile thieves, their characters and homelife.* London: Bailliere, Tindall, & Cox.

Bowlby, J. (1951). Maternal care and mental health. *Bulletin of the World Health Organization, 3*, 355–533.

Bowlby, J. (1969). *Attachment and loss. Vol. 1: Attachment.* New York: Basic.

Brody, G. H., & Forehand, R. (1988). Multiple determinants of parenting: Research findings and implications for the divorce process. In E. M. Hetherington & J. D. Arasteh (Eds.), *Impact of divorce, single parenting, and stepparenting on children* (pp. 117–133). Hillsdale, NJ: Lawrence Erlbaum Associates.

Bryant, W. K., & Zick, C. D. (1996). An examination of parent–child shared time. *Journal of Marriage and the Family, 58*, 227–237.

Caplan, P. J., & Hall-McCorquodale, I. (1985). The scapegoating of mothers: A call for change. *American Journal of Orthopsychiatry, 55*, 610–613.

Chen, X., Dong, Q., & Zhou, H. (1997). Authoritative and authoritarian parenting practices and social and school performance in Chinese children. *International Journal of Behavioral Development, 21*, 855–873.

Chirkov, V. I., & Ryan, R. M. (1999). *Control versus autonomy support in Russia and the U.S.: Effects of well-being and academic motivation.* Unpublished manuscript.

Collins, W. A., Maccoby, E. E., Steinberg, L., Hetherington, E. M., & Bornstein, M. H. (2000). Contemporary research on parenting: The case for nature and nurture. *American Psychologist, 55*, 218–232.

Coopersmith, S. (1967). *The antecedents of self-esteem.* San Francisco: Freeman.

Crouter, A. C., Perry-Jenkins, M., Huston, T. L., & Crawford, D. W. (1989). The influence of work-induced psychological states on behavior at home. *Basic and Applied Social Psychology, 10*, 273–292.

Deci, E. L., Eghrari, H., Patrick, B. C., & Leone, D. R. (1994). Facilitating internalization: The self-determination theory perspective. *Journal of Personality, 62*, 119–142.

Deci, E. L., & Ryan, R. M. (1985). *Intrinsic motivation and self-determination in human behavior.* New York: Plenum.

Desai, S., Michael, R. T., & Chase-Lansdale, P. L. (1990). Maternal employment during infancy: An analysis of "Children of the National Longitudinal Survey of Youth (NLSY)." In J. V. Lerner & N. L. Galambos (Eds.), *Employed mothers and their children: Reference books on family issues* (Vol. 17, pp. 37–61). New York: Garland Publishing.

Dornbusch, S. M., Carlsmith, J. M., Bushwall, S. J., Ritter, P. L., Leiderman, H., Hastorf, A. H., & Gross, R. T. (1985). Single parents, extended households, and the control of adolescents. *Child Development, 56*, 326–341.

Dornbusch, S. M., Ritter, P. L., Leiderman, P. H., Roberts, D. F., & Fraleigh, M. J. (1987). The relation of parenting style to adolescent school performance. *Child Development, 58*, 1244–1257.

Duncan, G. J., & Hoffman, S. D. (1985). Economic consequences of marital instability. In M. David & T. Smeeding (Eds.), *Horizontal equity, uncertainty, and economic well-being* (pp. 427–467). Chicago: University of Chicago Press.

Eisenberg-Berg, N., & Hand, M. (1979). The relationship of preschoolers' reasoning about prosocial moral conflicts to prosocial behavior. *Child Development, 50,* 356–363.

Fromm-Reichmann, F. (1949). Notes on the development of treatment of schizophrenics by psychoanalytic psychotherapy. *Psychiatry, 11,* 263–273.

Goldberg, S. (1983). Parent–infant bonding: Another look. *Child Development, 54,* 1355–1382.

Grolnick, W. S. (1993). *Factors influencing the level and characteristics of parents' involvement in their children's schooling.* Grant funded by the William T. Grant Foundation.

Grolnick, W. S., Benjet, C., Kurowski, C. O., & Apostoleris, N. (1997). Predictors of parent involvement in children's schooling. *Journal of Educational Psychology, 89,* 538–548.

Grolnick, W. S., & Gurland, S. T. (1999). *Threat and parenting.* Unpublished manuscript.

Grolnick, W. S., Kurowski, C. O., Dunlap, K. G., & Hevey, C. (2000). Parental resources and the transition to junior high. *Journal of Research on Adolescence, 10,* 465–488.

Grolnick, W. S., & Ryan, R. M. (1989). Parent styles associated with children's self-regulation and competence in school. *Journal of Educational Psychology, 81,* 143–154.

Grolnick, W. S., Ryan, R. M., & Deci, E. L. (1997). Internalization within the family: The self-determination theory perspective. In J. E. Grusec & L. Kuczynski (Eds.), *Parenting and children's internalization of values* (pp. 135–161). New York: Wiley.

Grolnick, W. S., Weiss, L., McKenzie, L., & Wrightman, J. (1996). Contextual, cognitive and adolescent factors associated with parenting in adolescence. *Journal of Youth and Adolescence, 25,* 33–54.

Harris, J. R. (1995). Where is the child's environment? A group socialization theory of development. *Psychological Review, 102,* 458–489.

Harvey, E. (1999). Short-term and long-term effects of early parental employment on children of the National Longitudinal Survey of Youth. *Developmental Psychology, 35,* 445–459.

Hatfield, J. S., Ferguson, L. R., & Alpert, R. (1967). Mother–child interaction and the socialization process. *Child Development, 38,* 365–414.

Hetherington, E. M., Cox, M., & Cox, R. (1982). Effects of divorce on parents and children. In M. E. Lamb (Ed.), *Nontraditional families: Parenting and child development* (pp. 233–285). Hillsdale, NJ: Lawrence Erlbaum Associates.

Hoffman, M. L. (1970). Conscience, personality, and socialization techniques. *Human Development, 13,* 90–126.

Klaus, M. H., & Kennell, J. H. (1976). *Maternal–infant bonding.* St. Louis, MO: Mosby.

Knok, S. L. (1988). The family and hierarchy. *Journal of Marriage and the Family, 50,* 957–966.

Kochanska, G. (1997). Mutually responsive orientation between mothers and their young children: Implications for early socialization. *Child Development, 68,* 94–112.

Kochanska, G., & Aksan, N. (1995). Mother–child mutually positive affect, the quality of child compliance to requests and prohibitions, and maternal control as correlates of early internalization. *Child Development, 66,* 236–254.

Lamborn, S. D., Mounts, N. S., Steinberg, L., & Dornbusch, S. M. (1991). Patterns of competence and adjustment among adolescents from authoritative, authoritarian, indulgent, and neglectful families. *Child Development, 62,* 1049–1065.

Lewis, C. C. (1981). The effects of parental firm control: A reinterpretation of findings. *Psychological Bulletin, 90,* 547–563.

Loeb, R. C., Horst, L., & Horton, P. J. (1980). Family interaction patterns associated with self-esteem in pre-adolescent girls and boys. *Merrill-Palmer Quarterly, 26,* 203–217.

Lord, S. E., Eccles, J. S., & McCarthy, K. A. (1994). Surveying the junior high school transition: Family processes and self-perceptions as protective and risk factors. *Journal of Early Adolescence, 14,* 162–199.

Maccoby, E. (1992). The role of parents in the socialization of children: An historical overview. *Developmental Psychology, 28,* 1006–1017.

Maccoby, E. E., & Martin, J. A. (1983). Socialization in the context of the family: Parent–child interaction. In P. Mussen (Ed.), *Handbook of child psychology* (pp. 1–101). New York: Wiley.

MacDonald, K. (1992). Warmth as a developmental construct: An evolutionary analysis. *Child Development, 63,* 753–774.

McLanahan, S. S., Astone, N. M., & Marks, N. F. (1991). The role of mother only families in reproducing poverty. In A. C. Huston (Ed.), *Children in poverty* (pp. 1–78). New York: Cambridge University Press.

McLloyd, V. C., & Wilson, L. (1991). The strain of living poor: Parenting, social support, and child mental health. In A. C. Huston (Ed.), *Children in poverty* (pp. 105–135). New York: Cambridge University Press.

Parker, G., Tupling, H., & Brown, L. B. (1979). A parental bonding instrument. *British Journal of Medical Psychology, 52,* 1–10.

Phares, V. (1993). Perceptions of mothers' and fathers' responsibility for children's behavior. *Sex Roles, 29,* 839–852.

Phares, V., & Compas, B. E. (1992). The role of fathers in child and adolescent psychopathology: Make room for daddy. *Psychological Bulletin, 111,* 387–412.

Pomerantz, E. M., & Ruble, D. N. (1998). The role of maternal control in the development of sex differences in child self-evaluative factors. *Child Development, 69,* 458–478.

Powers, S. I. (1982). *Family environments and adolescent moral development: A study of psychiatrically hospitalized and non-patient adolescents.* Unpublished doctoral dissertation, Harvard University.

Pulkkinen, L. (1982). Self-control and continuity from childhood to adolescence. In P. B. Baltes & O. G. Brim (Eds.), *Life-span development and behavior* (Vol. 4, pp. 63–105). New York: Academic Press.

Radin, N. (1981). The role of the father in cognitive, academic and intellectual development. In M. E. Lamb (Ed.), *The role of the father in child development.* New York: Wiley.

Reddy, M. T., Roth, M., & Sheldon, A. (1994). *Mother journeys: Feminists write about mothering.* Duluth, MN: Spinsters Ink.

Repetti, R. L. (1994). Short-term and long-term processes linking job stressors to father–child interaction. *Social Development, 3,* 1–15.

Repetti, R. L., & Wood, J. (1997). Effects of daily stress at work on mothers' interactions with preschoolers. *Journal of Family Psychology, 11,* 90–108.

Rohner, R. P., & Pettengill, S. M. (1985). Perceived parental acceptance–rejection and parental control among Korean adolescents. *Child Development, 56,* 524–528.

Ruddick, S. (1980). Maternal thinking. *Feminist Studies, 6,* 354–380.

Rutter, M. (1972). *Maternal deprivation reassessed.* Harmondsworth, England: Penguin.

Rutter, M., & Quinton, D. (1984). Parental psychiatric disorder: Effects on children. *Psychological Medicine, 14,* 853–880.

Ryan, R. M., & Connell, J. P. (1989). Perceived locus of causality and internalization: Examining reasons for action in two domains. *Journal of Personality and Social Psychology, 57,* 749–761.

Sales, S. M. (1973). Threat as a factor in authoritarianism: An analysis of archival data. *Journal of Personality and Social Psychology, 28,* 44–57.

Santrock, J. W., Warshak, R., & Elliott, G. L. (1982). Social development and parent–child interaction in father-custody and stepmother families. In M. E. Lamb (Ed.), *Nontraditional families: Parenting and child development* (pp. 289–315). Hillsdale, NJ: Lawrence Erlbaum Associates.

Scarr, S. (1998). American child care today. *American Psychologist, 53,* 95–108.

Schaefer, E. S. (1959). A circumflex model for maternal behavior. *Journal of Abnormal and Social Psychology, 59,* 226–235.

Schaefer, E. S. (1965). Children's reports of parental behavior: An inventory. *Child Development, 36,* 413–424.

Sewell, M. C., & Grolnick, W. S. (1993). *Relations among toddlers' language development, parent control style, and stress.* Unpublished master's thesis, New York University.

Simons, R. L., Beaman, J., Conger, R. D., & Chao, W. (1993). Childhood experience, conceptions of parenting, and attitudes of spouse as determinants of parental behavior. *Journal of Marriage and the Family, 55,* 91–106.

Simons, R. L., & Johnson, C. (1996). Mother's parenting. In R. L. Simons (Ed.), *Understanding differences between divorced and intact families: Stress, interaction, and child outcome. Understanding families* (Vol. 5, pp. 81–93). Thousand Oaks, CA: Sage.

Spitz, R. A. (1950). Possible infantile precursors of psychopathology. *American Journal of Orthopsychiatry, 20,* 240–248.

Sroufe, L. A., & Waters, E. (1977). Attachment as an organizational construct. *Child Development, 48,* 1184–1199.

Svejda, M. J., Campos, J. J., & Emde, R. N. (1980). Mother–infant bonding: Failure to generalize. *Child Development, 61,* 775–779.

Thomson, E., McLanahan, S. S., & Curtin, R. B. (1992). Family structure, gender, and parental socialization. *Journal of Marriage and the Family, 54,* 368–378.

Trivers, R. (1974). Parent–offspring conflict. *American Zoologist, 14,* 249–264.

Vaughn, B., Gove, F., & Egeland, B. (1980). The relationship between out of home care and the quality of infant–mother attachment in an economically disadvantaged population. *Child Development, 51,* 971–975.

Walker, L. J., & Taylor, J. H. (1991). Family interactions and the development of moral reasoning. *Child Development, 62,* 264–283.

Weiss, L. A., & Grolnick, W. S. (1991). *The roles of parent involvement and support for autonomy in adolescent symptomatology.* Paper presented at the Society for Research in Child Development, Seattle, WA.

2

Fathers and Families

Louise B. Silverstein
Yeshiva University

I first became interested in studying fathering from a feminist perspective, as a way to "make the world safe" from psychology's overfocus on mothers. Although this tendency to both idealize and demonize mothers is characteristic of the entire field of psychology, I argue that the origin of this overfocus on mothers is Bowlby's (1951) maternal deprivation syndrome and his expansion of that syndrome into maternal attachment theory.

Maternal attachment theory as articulated by Bowlby and Ainsworth (Bowlby, 1969; Ainsworth, Blehar, Waters, & Walls, 1978) proposed that the mother, because of her unique biological relationship to her child, also has a unique psychological role. According to attachment theory, the early (in the first year) mother–child relationship produces an emotional template that determines the quality of all subsequent emotional relationships. Within this paradigm, fathers and other important figures in the child's life are peripheral. Therefore, mother blaming becomes theoretically inevitable.

It was with intense relief, therefore, that I read Rutter's (1974) monograph, *The Qualities of Mothering: Maternal Deprivation Reassessed.* I thought it would be the "book to end all books" in deconstructing Bowlby's (1951) maternal deprivation syndrome and shifting the focus from mother to the more complex systems of relationships within which child development is embedded. Obviously, despite Rutter's efforts and those of others (e.g., Lewis, 1997), the world is not yet safe from the myth that the most important issue in a child's life is who his or her mother is, and what that mother does or does not do.

In 1992, Phares and Compas reviewed eight clinical psychology journals and found that almost half (48%) used only mothers, whereas only 1% used only fathers. In 1996, Phares and I (Silverstein & Phares, 1996) examined dissertation research and found that although the number of studies that relied only on fathers had increased to 10%, the percentage that relied only on mothers had also increased to 59%. Thus, the bias toward using only mothers in research continues to the next generation of psychologists.

Lewis (1997) pointed out that the full range of potential relationships available to children has not yet been explored or even contemplated in child development research. The current chapter on fathering research is my contribution to decreasing the tendency within psychology to equate parenting with mothering.

RETROSPECTIVE RESEARCH SUMMARY

Popular culture has created the impression that the fathering role has progressed in a linear fashion from an all-powerful, remote patriarch to an egalitarian, involved caregiver. However, historians of fatherhood (Mintz, 1998; Pleck & Pleck, 1997) pointed out that the evolution of fathering has not been linear. Rather, men's roles in families have varied across historical periods, and within any given period by race, ethnicity, class, and geographic region.

For example, during the colonial period, most U.S. fathers were intensely involved with their children. Work and home were not separated, so men spent most of their time at home with their family. However, the degree of power and authority that men experienced within their families varied by class, race, and geographic region. Burton and Snyder (1998) pointed out how White men of privilege enjoyed a position of moral authority and economic power within their families and constructed the lives of slaves and working-class White men. The economic advantages conferred by slavery allowed most plantation owners to establish stable, patriarchal family structures. African slave families, in contrast, relied on the economic contribution and child-care efforts of both men and women; thus, their relationships tended to be more egalitarian.

If we consider more recent history, the past 20 years of psychological research on fathers has been oriented toward refuting the maternal attachment paradigm that defined fathers as peripheral to child development. Any summary of this body of knowledge must begin with the work of Lamb, who has been the most prolific and influential scholar in this area. When Lamb published his first book on fathering in 1976, his goal was to convince social scientists, psychologists in particular, that fathers played a significant role in child development. To a large extent, that goal has been achieved in that there is now widespread acceptance that fathers have an important role to play, beyond that of provider, in the lives of their children.

However, this body of fathering research has been characterized by a relatively narrow methodological focus. The participants have been almost exclusively White, middle-class men. Few studies of ethnic minority men were undertaken before 1990. Studies have interviewed mothers about what fathers do, or have interviewed and observed fathers. Few studies have asked children about their relationships with their fathers. Most of the paradigms have been dyadic, looking at father–child interaction.

An exception to this dyadic focus is Parke, Power, and Gottman's (1979) early systemic hypothesis that fathers, in addition to having a direct effect on a child, also had significant indirect effect through their relationships with the child's mother. As noted by other contributors to the volume, however, only recently has this revolutionary idea of expanding the focus beyond dyads to the context of family systems and subsystems been gaining recognition and acceptance among developmental psychologists.

The Mythology of Fatherhood

Early Myths: The Biological Imperative. Between the mid-1960s and the mid-1980s, a substantial amount of empirical research on the father's role began to emerge. The early work was organized around refuting specific ideological beliefs that were corollaries to maternal attachment theory (see Table 2.1). For example, Schaffer and Emerson (1964) asked whether and when infants formed attachments to their fathers. Similarly, Frodi, Lamb, Leavitt, and Donovan (1978) examined whether fathers were as responsive to infants as were mothers. The interaction between racism and "momism" generated research questions that singled out African American fathers as particularly uninvolved and irresponsible (Wilson, 1987).

These myths were successfully deconstructed in a wide range of studies during the first decade of fathering research. Most of the studies involved White families in the United States and Sweden. However, a small number of

TABLE 2.1
Cultural Mythology About Families

Early myths: The biological imperative
1. Fathers don't matter—the quality of the child's attachment to mothers is unique.
2. Mothers are more "sensitive" to infants because of their biological experiences of pregnancy, parturition, and lactation.
3. Black fathers are generally uninvolved, irresponsible fathers.
Later myths: The myth of masculinity
4. Fathers play with children significantly more than mothers do, especially in terms of rough and tumble play.
5. Fathers are necessary as a sex role model in order for boys to develop a masculine gender identity.
Current myths: The marriage imperative
6. Fathers are essential.

---

studies also reported similar findings for African American families in the United States (H. McAdoo, 1988) and AKA Pygmy families in Africa (Hewlett, 1991). Thanks to this important work, we now know that in two-parent families, children become attached to both parents at about the same time during the first year of life. Moreover, observational studies of children in traditional Euro-American families have indicated no preferences for either parent. However, most children prefer their mothers when stressed, probably because mothers are the primary caretakers in most families (see Lamb, 1997a, for an extensive review of the development of father–infant relationships).

We also know that neither mothers nor fathers are "natural" caregivers. Lamb (1987b), in an observational study of parental behaviors during the newborn period, reported that both parents learn on the job. However, by the end of the first year, mothers are significantly more competent caretakers and appear more sensitive to their infant's cues. This is because the mother has spent significantly more time with the infant than has the father. Therefore, the mother knows her child much better. Given her greater competence, as well as her gender socialization that has emphasized nurturing and child care, most mothers more easily embrace caregiving, whereas fathers more often defer to mothers. These behavioral tendencies further exacerbate the skill differential.

Hunter and Davis (1994) pointed out that research on African American men has generally focused on their victimization by various social problems, rather than on normative life issues. African American men have been characterized as either victims or offenders. Thus, early fathering research focused on poor and teen fathers. These groups were seen either as being deadbeat dads or victims of institutionalized racism.

To counteract these negative stereotypes, Cazenave (1979) studied a group of African American middle-income fathers. He found that the provider role was the most often cited aspect of their family role, and the most salient aspect of their masculine identity. Similarly, J. L. McAdoo (1988), in a series of studies in the 1980s, studied middle-income African American fathers. He found that these fathers were actively involved in the socialization of their children, displaying warm and loving patterns of interaction. In a study comparing 40 African American and 40 White middle-class fathers, he found that approximately 75% of both groups of fathers were warm, loving, and nurturant.

Overall, more recent fathering research has been instrumental in dispelling many negative stereotypes about African American fathers. For example, in a nationally representative sample of new young fathers, Lerman (1993) found that nonresident African American teen fathers were more likely than nonresident White teen fathers to contribute to their children's support. Other studies of African American fathers indicated that African American fathers in dual-shift, working-class families, or in families where the fathers were chronically unemployed (Bowman & Forman, 1998; Pleck, 1997) were more likely to participate in child-care tasks than middle-income White fathers.

In addition to refuting these early myths about the unimportance of fathers and the negative stereotypes about African American fathers, one of the most significant developments in this first decade of fathering research was operationalizing the concept of paternal involvement. In the early years of researching fathers, much of the thinking about fathering behaviors was matricentric; that is, researchers used mothering behaviors as the standard against which to compare fathers' behaviors. Similarly, many studies of fathers interviewed only mothers.

In an effort to improve the methodology, a series of studies in the late 1980s by Lamb, Pleck, and Levine (1986; Lamb, Pleck, Charnov, & Levine, 1987) coined the term "paternal involvement." They defined three levels of involvement: accessibility, the father being present but not necessarily interacting with the child; engagement, the father interacting directly with the child; and responsibility, an executive function such as remembering when the child needs to go to the dentist or arranging for babysitters. This theoretical construct advanced research in several ways: It moved the research focus away from a matricentric model, it provided for a standardized way of observing fathering across studies, and it increased the complexity of thinking about how fathers were involved with their children.

Later Myths: The Myth of Masculinity. As fathering studies continued to proliferate, some early findings have proven to be artifacts of U.S. cultural gender ideology. For example, U.S. fathers have consistently been observed to spend much time playing with their children. Rough-and-tumble play is especially characteristic of fathers' but not mothers' interactions with children (see Lamb, 1997b, for a discussion of fathers and play). This observed difference in parenting behaviors was originally interpreted as a biologically based sex difference (Brazelton, Yogman, Als, & Tronick, 1979; Lamb, 1987b).

As more cross-cultural data have become available, rough-and-tumble play has not proven to be a universal characteristic of all fathers. For example, fathers in Israeli kibbutzim (Sagi, Lamb, Shoham, Dvir, & Lewkowicz, 1985) and Swedish fathers (Frodi, Lamb, Hwang, & Frodi, 1983) have not been observed to play with infants more than mothers. In AKA pygmy culture, an African tribe of hunter-gathers in which mothers and fathers share work and caregiving equally, it is aunts or other adults who engage in rough-and-tumble play (Hewlett, 1991). Similarly, U.S. fathers with nonworking wives played with their infants more than did mothers, but this pattern was reversed in families with working mothers (Pedersen, Cain, Zaslow, & Anderson, 1982). Thus rough-and-tumble play is contextually based and appears to be influenced by variations in patterns of caretaking.

As observational data have been analyzed more carefully, it turns out fathers do not play with children more than do mothers (Lamb, 1997a). Rather, play is a greater proportion of most fathers' total interaction with a child; although mothers play as much as do fathers, they also engage in many other forms of interaction. Thus, the conclusion that fathers spend more time playing with young children is inaccurate.

Another cornerstone of the myth of masculinity is that boys need a male role model to learn how to behave like men. However, Pleck (1995) amassed much research that has shown boys can achieve a masculine gender identity without a male role model. The work of Patterson (1995; Patterson & Chan, 1997) on the developmental outcomes of children raised in lesbian mother families has further substantiated Pleck's findings.

Current Myths: The Marriage Imperative. In the mid-1990s, the pendulum swung full circle. Whereas in 1976, researchers found mothers essential and fathers peripheral, neoconservative social scientists such as Popenoe (1996), Blankenhorn (1995), Pruett (1998), and Biller (Biller & Kimpton, 1997) now claim that fathers have a unique and essential role to play in child development. Just as Bowlby (1951) concluded that the negative developmental outcomes of infants institutionalized during World War II were caused by the single variable of separation from mother, these authors claimed that the roots of many social problems (i.e., child poverty, urban decay, societal violence, teenage pregnancy, poor school performance) can be traced to the absence of fathers. Biller and Kimpton (1997, p. 147) even used the term *paternal deprivation* in a manner parallel to Bowlby's maternal deprivation.

This neoconservative perspective is based on the proposition that the biologically different reproductive functions of men and women automatically construct gender differences in parenting behaviors. Mothering and fathering are seen as distinct social roles that are not interchangeable, and marriage is presented as the social context within which responsible fathering is most likely to occur.

Blankenhorn (1995) and Popenoe (1996) have relied heavily on evolutionary psychology to support this argument. Evolutionary psychologists, in turn, have relied on Trivers' (1972) paternity hypothesis, which states that, all other things being equal, male mammals maximize their evolutionary fitness by impregnating as many females as possible, while investing little in the rearing of offspring. Female mammals, in contrast, invest much physiological energy in pregnancy and lactation and thus are motivated to invest a corresponding amount of time and energy in parenting. The exception to the absence of male parental investment is when the males are assured of the paternity of their offspring.

Many feminist behavioral ecologists, such as Smuts (Smuts & Gubernick, 1992) and Hrdy (1997), have shown Trivers' hypothesis to be inaccurate in predicting male involvement with infants among nonhuman primates (e.g., Smuts & Gubernick, 1992). Low levels of infant care do not characterize all primate males. Male involvement exists on a continuum from active nurturing, to benign neglect, to infanticide.

Rather, Smuts and Gubernick (1992) refuted the paternity hypothesis with what they call the reciprocity hypothesis. They found that the amount of time and energy males invest in nurturing and protecting infants varies depending on the reciprocal benefits males and females have to offer each other within a particular bioecological context. Male care of infants is low when either males or females have few benefits to exchange. The probability of male care of infants increases when females have substantial benefits to offer males (e.g., when females can offer males increased mating opportunities or provide them with political alliances that enhance their status within the dominance hierarchy). Paternity certainty does not universally generate high levels of male involvement with infants. Rather, male care of infants is high when males and females within a given ecological context have mutual benefits to exchange. As bioecological contexts change, so do fathering behaviors, especially among primate males.

Although the paternity hypothesis has been shown to be inaccurate in predicting paternal involvement, it has generated another cornerstone of current fatherhood mythology: that marriage is the best way to insure men will behave responsibly toward their children. This neoconservative argument (Blankenhorn, 1995; Popenoe, 1996) proposes that, because men do not have a biological predisposition to nurture, they must be provided with a social structure in which they can be assured of paternity, that is, the traditional nuclear family.

It is accurate that, in general, married men have more contact with their children and more frequently provide them with economic support than do divorced or never-married fathers (Hetherington & Stanley-Hagan, 1997). However, the reasons for this are not clear. Several factors have been implicated in the nonpayment of child support by unmarried fathers. These include father's age and employment status, level of conflict with the child's mother, and geographical proximity (Hetherington, Bridges, & Insabella, 1998). The relative importance of these factors may vary across ethnic and class groupings.

For example, Stier and Tienda (1993) have shown that for poor inner-city men, economic status is the clearest predictor of payment of child support. Using interviews from more than 800 resident and nonresident fathers living in poor neighborhoods in Chicago, these researchers found that fathers who were currently employed were three times more likely to support their nonresident children than fathers who were not working.

The final component of the neoconservative argument is that, if men can be induced to care for young children, their unique, masculine contribution significantly improves developmental outcomes for children. From the essentialist perspective, Blankenhorn (1995) stated, "fatherhood privileges children.... Conversely, the primary consequences of fatherlessness are rising male violence and declining child well-being" (pp. 25–26).

These claims represent an oversimplification of the data. On average, children from divorced families have been shown to be at greater risk for a range of problems than children from nondivorced families. However, 75% of children from divorced families exhibit no negative effects (see Hetherington et al., 1998, for a review). Furthermore, the negative effect of divorce is considerably reduced when the adjustment of children preceding divorce is controlled. Overall, the research suggests divorce does not irretrievably harm most children.

Hetherington et al. (1998) pointed out that divorce is not a single event, but rather a cycle of negative events: beginning with marital conflict, followed by dissolution of the current family structure, and ending with the formation of separate households. In most families, at least one parent remarries, forming a new, blended stepfamily. Divorce occurs more frequently in second marriages, reinitiating the disruptive cycle of loss and conflict. This cycle entails economic stress, disrupted attachments, and often separation from the family home and neighborhood.

In his deconstruction of Bowlby's (1951) maternal deprivation hypothesis, Rutter (1974) illustrated that the negative developmental outcomes observed in institutionalized infants were caused by the disruption of the child's entire life circumstances, rather than simply separation from mother. Likewise, it seems probable that the link between marital transitions and the risk of negative developmental outcomes is due to the disruption in the entire life circumstances of children, rather than simply to the absence of a father.

In their simplification of the evidence, Blankenhorn (1995) and Popenoe (1996) have also failed to acknowledge the potential costs of father presence in some families. Engle and Breaux (1998) have shown that some fathers' consumption of family resources in terms of gambling, purchasing alcohol, cigarettes, or other nonessential commodities may actually increase a family's stress level.

AREAS OF CURRENT INQUIRY

What Are the Consequences of High Paternal Involvement?

Although the empirical literature does not support the contention that fathers are essential, a large body of research evidence suggests that higher levels of positive paternal involvement are associated with positive outcomes for children (see Pleck, 1997, for a review of the research on paternal involvement). High levels of paternal involvement have both direct and indirect positive consequences for families. As an example of an indirect consequence, affectionate fathering has been associated with positive sibling interaction. Similarly, high paternal involvement has been shown to increase positive maternal interactions.

In terms of direct consequences for children, substantial engagement and accessibility by fathers have been associated with positive outcomes in children of all ages. Among these outcomes are cognitive competence, self-esteem, social skills, and less gender role stereotyping (see Biller & Kimpton, 1997; Hosley & Montemayor, 1997, for reviews). For daughters, a close and warm relationship with dad has been linked to a sense of competence, especially in mathematics. For adolescents, particularly boys, father involvement is associated with lower drug use, lower rates of involvement in criminal activity, and lower likelihood of becoming a teen parent.

Research findings on the effect of high father involvement on mothers and marriage have been mixed. Baruch and Barnett (1986) found that greater father involvement was associated with lower overall life satisfaction for mothers. Snarey (1993) associated positive father involvement with marital satisfaction later in life. Overall, an equal number of studies have associated high paternal involvement with positive and with negative marital satisfaction.

A similarly mixed picture exists in terms of the consequences of high father involvement for fathers. High father involvement has been associated with more work–family stress. In some studies, more involved fathers have reported they do not have enough time for their careers (Pleck, 1997). Snarey (1993), in contrast, found that high engagement was related to greater career success at midlife. Other studies have reported that high involvement leads to greater empathy, an increase in parenting skills, and higher self-perceived competence (e.g., Hawkins, Christiansen, Sargent, & Hill, 1993). It may be that high involvement causes short-term stress but leads to long-term positive outcomes, both in terms of marital adjustment and work productivity. Much more research is needed to understand these complex issues.

Have Married Men Significantly Increased Their Involvement in Childcare and Household Management?

One issue about which there is continuing controversy is the extent to which paternal involvement in child care has increased over the past three decades. Some researchers have argued that paternal involvement has increased significantly (Lamb, 1987b; Pleck, 1985). Others have argued that both maternal and paternal involvement have increased, so that the proportional involvement of fathers has not changed significantly (LaRossa, 1988). Hochschild and Machung (1989) have taken the position that the proportion of responsibility for child care and household management that working mothers continue to assume represents a second full-time job, or "second shift."

It is difficult to identify the amount of involvement of the "average" U.S. father, because levels of involvement vary significantly by social class (Erikson & Gecas, 1991). The most involved fathers are those in dual-shift, working-class families, where the mother's absence because of work requires the father to be more involved. These fathers assume, on average, about one third of the child-care responsibilities. The lowest level of paternal involvement has been observed in upper middle-class families where fathers pay for other-than-mother care. Thus, estimating the average level of paternal involvement may not be meaningful.

It seems accurate to conclude that U.S. fathers have significantly increased their overall levels of involvement, but remain significantly less involved than mothers, particularly in terms of assuming responsibility. After an extensive review of the literature, Pleck (1997) estimated that fathers of young children are engaged with them, on average, slightly less than 2 hours a day on weekdays and about 6.5 hours on Sundays. Estimates of accessibility range from 2.8 to 4.9 hours on weekdays and about 10 hours on Sundays. However, Pleck concluded that a father's average share of responsibility remains substantially lower than a mother's. Research has not yet identified one area in which fathers assume primary parenting responsibility. In addition, mothers tend to assume responsibility for the most unpleasant jobs that neither parent wants to perform.

Several factors have been shown to affect levels of paternal involvement, including the father's motivation, the mothers' employment status, and institutional supports. Workplace policies have had an especially chilling effect on paternal involvement. Pleck (1993) has shown that "family friendly" benefits, such as parental leave, flexible hours, and job sharing, are rarely used by fathers. Fathers report that the culture of the workplace tolerates women's use of these options for decreasing family–work stress, yet it considers men who use these options as unmanly and uncommitted to their jobs. Pleck found that, even when a company offered paternal leave, fathers tended to use a combination of vacation and sick days, rather than openly using their paternal leave.

The relative proportion of paternal versus maternal involvement continues to be an issue of controversy. However, there is a consensus that we have not yet reached equality. The absence of workplace policies that encourage men in their fathering roles seems to be exacerbating this situation.

What Is the Role of Fathers in Psychopathology?

Research on how paternal involvement is related to psychopathology in children is much more sparse than research on normative development. Historically, poor child outcomes have been explored in terms of paternal absence rather than involvement. In addition, there has been an over-reliance on retrospective studies using adult memories of individuals' relationships with their fathers.

Phares (1996) has been a pioneer in research on the father's role in the development of psychopathology in children. Phares found that several causal factors are beginning to be explored. These include the effect of the father's pathology, his behavior toward his children, and the effect of marital conflict on child psychopathology. Overall, two major factors influencing child development have been identified as risk factors: a father's emotional availability and his responsivity to his child's needs (Lee & Gotlib, 1991). The two characteristics of emotional availability and responsivity in both mothers and fathers appear to mediate the effect of disruptive family situations (e.g., parental divorce, parental conflict, and parental psychopathology) on children's adjustment.

One factor limiting knowledge about the father's role in developmental psychopathology has been the failure to include fathers in research and therapy. Overall, the research suggests fathers do not volunteer as readily as mothers, but when efforts are made to recruit fathers, they participate in both therapy and research. Phares (1997) has argued that the bias against the role of fathers in child development has generated a tendency in therapists and researchers to exclude fathers. The absence of fathers in clinical research and therapy has given rise to the myth that fathers are difficult to recruit. However, when institutional practice automatically includes fathers (including nonresident fathers) and offers flexible appointment times, fathers have been shown to participate almost as frequently as mothers.

In summary, there is a consensus that fathers play multiple, complex, direct, and indirect roles in their children's lives. Researchers are beginning to view fathers as part of the complex social system of the family in which each person affects every other person in a reciprocal fashion. Similarly, scholars are beginning to recognize the interconnectedness of family and work stress and satisfaction for fathers as well as mothers.

How Do Fathering Identities Vary Across Subcultures?

Psychologists have theorized on how the father's role influences child development and behavior without benefit of systematic cross-cultural studies. Fathering research within the United States has traditionally obscured differences between men of privilege and working-class men, between gay men and nongay men, and between men of different ethnoraces. Until recently, individuals and families that differed from White, middle-class, heterosexual nuclear families have been viewed principally through the lens of pathology. Thus, the strengths and adaptive strategies of ethnic minority families, especially African American families (see McHale, Lauretti, Talbot,

& Pouquette, this volume), and of gay and lesbian parents have too often been overlooked. Beginning in the early 1990s, research on ethnic minority fathers from an adaptive–resilient framework began to emerge.

Hunter and Davis (1994) challenged the dominant definition of African American men as dysfunctional as a result of their struggle with oppression and disenfranchisement. They pointed out that the discourse around African American women has emphasized strength in relation to adversity, whereas the discourse around African American men has focused on victimization and failure. To counter this discourse pathology, Hunter and Davis developed a conceptualization and methodology that provided African American men with an opportunity to define their own sense of manhood. This research methodology involved three steps: generating ideas, sorting ideas, and constructing a concept map. This procedure attempted to preserve the richness of an ethnographic approach, while producing a quantitative representation of the data.

In one study that involved interviews with 32 men, the men emphasized the concepts of self-definition, family connections, and spirituality as the most important components of manhood. This concept map included some aspects of traditional masculinity in terms of having the freedom to pursue a self-definition and to assume a leadership role in the family. However, other concepts emerged, such as "being emotionally sensitive" and "being sensitive to one's femininity," which were not typical of traditional masculinity ideology. Allowing the men to define themselves illustrated the complexities of their self-definitions and roles.

Roopnarine, together with several colleagues, has studied fathers from a cross-cultural perspective. His study of African American fathers from two-parent, stable families indicated these fathers spent about two thirds as much time as mothers in child-care tasks (Ahmeduzzaman & Roopnarine, 1992). In a later study of dual-earner African American families (Hossain & Roopnarine, 1993), mothers were found to invest significantly more time in direct infant care than were fathers, whether mothers worked part time or full time. However, when compared with White fathers, these fathers were more involved with their infants.

Roopnarine has also studied fathers in the English-speaking Caribbean (Roopnarine, Snell-White, & Riegraf, 1993). He found that family-formation strategies and paternal involvement varied among African Caribbean, Indo-Caribbean, and Amerindian subcultures. Indo-Caribbean families tended to have traditional marriages and relatively high paternal involvement. Amerindian families had relatively low paternal involvement.

Among families of African descent in Jamaica, Roopnarine and Benetti (1996) identified a "marital career" in which most men had children early in life within the context of informal and short-lived partnerships. As they grew older, they usually become more committed to their partners, and established a common-law relationship in which the couple lived together and assumed traditional roles. By about age 50, half of the men he interviewed were legally married. This pattern varied by class and was less common among middle-class couples who tended to have fewer and more stable marriages.

This pattern of partner shifting was accompanied by child shifting, that is, children from prior unions were often given to grandparents for varying periods so they would not be an economic or emotional drain on a new partnership. Child shifting meant that these men were likely to be parenting children from their current partner's prior union, and that some of their own children were likely to be parented by a stepfather. Roopnarine and Benetti speculated that these patterns might be remnants of slavery, when families were so frequently disrupted that partner shifting was inevitable. Immigration patterns further exacerbated the lack of contact between parents and children.

The extent to which child shifting negatively affects the father–child relationship has not been sufficiently explored. However, in contrast to the stereotype of all Caribbean fathers as marginal to their families, Roopnarine and Benetti found that Jamaican fathers assumed much responsibility for infants. Fathers in common-law relationships reported spending about 4 hours a day feeding, playing with, and cleaning their infants. Even in visiting relationships, many fathers reported spending 2 hours a day with their infants. Thus, some nonresident fathers were able to remain involved with their children, despite the multiple and complex relationship systems within which they were embedded.

This study of Caribbean fathers reflected the diversity among Caribbean families. Roopnarine and Benetti did not assume that nonnuclear family structures automatically meant fathers were uninvolved with their children. This study has implications for fathers in the United States, in that it describes a cultural context that supports nonresident father involvement. Identifying the factors that provide social support for nonresident fathers to remain involved with their children has direct relevance for U.S. social policy.

In my qualitative research with Auerbach (Auerbach, Silverstein, & Zizi, 1997; Silverstein, Auerbach, Grieco, & Dunkel, 1999), we have been conducting focus groups of fathers from subcultures within U.S. society. We have interviewed Haitian Christian fathers; Promise Keeper fathers; gay fathers; Modern Orthodox Jewish fathers; four groups of Latino fathers (Puerto Rican, Dominican, Mexican); and both divorced and married middle-class, suburban fathers from dual-career families. All of the participants were volunteers. The focus group format is organized around six opened-ended questions regarding their relationships with their fathers, their fantasies about becoming a father, the ways in which being a father has changed the way they think about themselves, and the effect of fathering on their relationships with their wives and their families of origin.

We chose a qualitative research paradigm because we wanted to focus on the men's subjective experiences of fathering, rather than generate hypotheses from our experiences and theoretical perspectives. This paradigm has proven to be successful in identifying similarities and differences among groups.

The two groups of gay fathers we studied proved to be more different from each other than we had anticipated. One group had children in a heterosexual marriage and then established a gay identity later in life (Benson, 1996). The second group had established a gay identity and lifestyle first and then decided to have children (Quartironi, 1995). Some aspects of the men's experience were similar; for example, both of these groups reported having few social supports for integrating their gay identity and their fathering identity. The straight community was negative about their gay identities, and the gay community was generally unsupportive of their fathering identities. However, there were important differences in the fatherhood identities of these two groups. In general, the group that had been married had more traditional ideas about parenting roles. Most of these men had been traditional fathers in terms of focusing on the provider role and being relatively uninvolved in caretaking. In contrast, the men who had established a gay identity first and a fathering identity later had deconstructed parenting. They had developed their own ideology of degendered parenting. They spoke of being a "Mommy-Daddy," rather than a father, and insisted they did not believe in mothering or fathering, but simply parenting.

The more traditional gay dads felt isolated, as they struggled with when and how to disclose their gay identities to their children. One man was still struggling with whether to get divorced. Many of the fathers in this group had joined gay parenting support groups, but some remained without social supports. The Mommy-Daddy dads, in contrast, were much more politically active. These fathers had joined gay and lesbian parenting groups to provide themselves with both emotional support and avenues for social activism. All of the fathers in this group were active in the school system, challenging institutionalized heterocentrism and homophobia, in an effort to protect their children from prejudice.

Another group of fathers who experienced a lack of social support was the group of nongay, divorced fathers (Weil, 1996). These dads were heterosexual men for whom being a father was a central part of their manhood. However, they had difficulty remaining actively involved fathers after divorce. Like the gay Mommy-Daddy dads, they had formed their own support (a fathers' rights) group to lobby for social action in the form of legal changes to child custody and visitation policies. Like the gay dads, they were also heavily involved with their children's schools in an effort to find more opportunities to interact with their children. However, unlike the gay dads, these men had not yet generated a new ideology that defined their postdivorced fathering role. They were still struggling with the transformation of their role from fathering to "visitation." This lack of a positive ideology was reflected in their anger toward the legal system and toward their wives.

We also studied fathers from several religious fundamentalist groups. These include Haitian Christian fathers, Promise Keepers, and Modern Orthodox Jewish fathers. To our surprise, all of these men were engaged in transforming their fathering role from a more traditional and emotionally distant provider to a more emotionally responsive and involved caregiver. All of these fathers reported their religious ideology was helping them in this transition because it prescribed a warm and loving relationship with their children. They also described a religious community that provided a system of social supports to help them deal with their anxiety about engaging in nontraditional, caregiver behaviors.

There are many limitations to this type of research, for example, using a convenience sample, relying on self-report data and researcher-designed questions, and using a group format. However, by focusing on the subjective experiences of the fathers, this project, like that of Hunter and Davis (1994), has given the men a chance to define themselves.

In addition to allowing the men's voices to be heard, this research paradigm has changed the researchers. Both of us had expected that the men in the fathers' rights group would be more interested in taking revenge against their wives than being emotionally involved with their children. Instead, we found that these men, although definitely angry with their wives, were genuinely heartbroken about their separation from their children and were creatively engaged in working toward more contact with them. Similarly, we had assumed the religious groups would reflect extremely patriarchal constructions of fatherhood. In contrast, although their ideology was patriarchal, their behavior indicated these men were actively involved in reconstructing fatherhood in the direction of a more egalitarian and nurturing role.

How Can We Understand Fathering Within a Multigenerational, Systemic Context?

As we begin to think about fathering from a more complex, systemic perspective, we need research models that can reflect this complexity. One such model is that of the family genogram (see Fig. 2.1). The genogram was developed as a systematic means of depicting the complex, multigenerational patterns of relationships within an extended family (McGoldrick & Gerson, 1985). It provides a visual representation of the reciprocal matrix of relationships within which individuals are embedded.

A FAMILY WITH TWO MOTHERS
AND A DONOR UNCLE

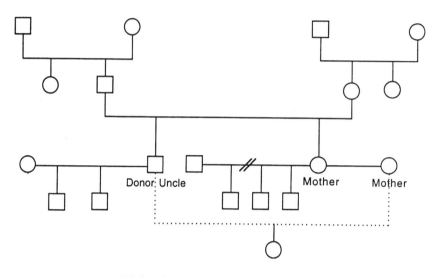

FIG. 2.1. Genogram of a post-modern family.

In the genogram, circles represent women and squares represent men. Circles and squares that are connected with a solid line indicate a marriage or life partnership. A line interrupted by two diagonal lines indicates a divorce. The three-generational family pictured is a lesbian mother family. One of the women is the child's biological mother. The biological father is the brother of the other woman. This means one of the social mothers is also the child's biological aunt. Thus, both mothers have a biological connection to the child. The genogram indicates the aunt-mother had been married previously and has three sons.

Genograms have routinely been used in family therapy. However, they have not been used widely as research tools. The visual nature of the genogram provides an illustration of the additional data that can be gathered when behavior is reconceptualized beyond a dyadic, or even triadic, context.

Another model that has the potential to reflect the complexity of human relationships is the life-course paradigm used by Burton (1990; Burton & Snyder, 1998) and her colleagues. This paradigm moves the subject of inquiry beyond the interior of family life, providing a framework that is historical, contextual, and developmental. It assumes that individuals are affected by social change and are change agents; that social groups within society are interdependent; and that historical events differentially affect individuals depending on class, race, and ethnicity.

Burton and Snyder (1998) have used these concepts of reciprocal continuity, social interdependence, and temporal context to illuminate how White, privileged men have structured the fathering identities of men of color and poor White men. Institutionalized racism has continued to privilege White men of all classes. For example, the exclusion of African American men from most union jobs has benefited working-class White men. Similarly, the unequal sentencing of drug offenses, resulting in large numbers of young African American men in prison has generated a booming prison economy in many White, rural communities. The lack of investment in the education of poor, ethnic minority children structures their ability to participate in the current technological revolution. Because the breadwinner role has continued to be a cornerstone of fatherhood, these limitations on the economic viability of African American men have impeded their ability to provide for their children.

How Can We Help Men Change to Become More Responsible and Involved Fathers?

Given the positive consequences for children and families of high, positive father involvement, one societal priority should be to increase paternal involvement for both resident and nonresident fathers. This goal has proven to be elusive.

Zill and Nord (1996) have tried to tease out the causes and consequences of involvement of noncustodial parents. They analyzed data from the Survey of Income and Program Participation for 1990 and 1991. They found that nonresidential fathers who had voluntarily entered into an agreement to pay child support were significantly more likely to pay than fathers who had court-ordered child support arrangements imposed upon them. Fathers who had voluntarily agreed to pay support also maintained more frequent contact with their children. Similarly, fathers who had a written agreement stipulating frequency and scheduling of visitation had significantly more contact with their children than did fathers who had no such agreement. Their level of contact was the same as fathers who had joint custody. However, an explicit agreement about visitation was not associated with more frequent payment of support in the same way the voluntary agreement about support led to more frequent contact.

What conclusions can we draw from these findings? Do fathers who pay child support see their children more frequently as a way of monitoring their investment? Should social policy mandate mediation as a way of establishing voluntary arrangements for child support? Is an explicit visitation agreement the equivalent of joint custody? Much more research is needed in this area before we can confidently recommend how to help noncustodial fathers remain involved with their children.

Levine and colleagues (Levine, Murphy, & Wilson, 1993; Levine & Pitt, 1995; Levine & Pittinsky, 1997) have focused on how to help men become more involved in various settings, including corporate culture, early childhood centers, schools, and social service agencies. This work is effective because it includes concrete, specific strategies for institutions. For example, Levine and colleagues provide sample questionnaires that a school or a social service agency could give to fathers to assess their interest in being involved. Similarly, Levine provides a checklist for corporate managers to follow to enhance the probability that a father's paternity leave will not disrupt work or be viewed negatively by coworkers.

In my view, one of the most important contributions that Levine's work has made is to identify the resistance to father involvement within the social service community. Levine has pointed out that, because our cultural gender ideology identifies women as primary caregivers, many agencies are staffed primarily with women. Many of these professional women have had negative experiences with men in their own lives. These personal experiences generate a reluctance to reach out to fathers.

When men do become involved, the result is often conflict between mothers and fathers about child management. Because many mental health professionals have not been trained to work effectively with families, they do not know how to manage conflict. Thus, the conflict cannot be transformed into dialogue and negotiation. Father involvement then becomes a failed evolutionary experiment, and the agency reverts to an all-female environment.

Auerbach and I have conceptualized the problem in terms of gender theory. U.S. cultural gender ideology continues to characterize activities such as nurturing infants and caretaking young children as primarily "feminine" tasks. Although more girls are now encouraged to engage in activities that were previously associated with male culture, such as sports, science, and computer studies, boys have not been encouraged to participate in activities that were previously associated with female culture. In general, it is still little girls who are socialized to give care.

Therefore, when we attempt to redefine fathering as nurturing rather than providing, we must realize we are asking men to exhibit behaviors that have been historically considered feminine. We are asking men to enact cross-gender behavior. When we consider how to help men change to become more nurturing and involved fathers, we are really asking: What facilitates cross-gender behavior change?

In our view, two major components help men enact cross-gender behavior: (a) a facilitating ideology that prescribes the new behaviors; and (b) a system of social supports that helps individuals manage the anxiety that inevitably accompanies change, particularly change that violates current cultural norms.

If we are to develop a facilitating ideology, one that encourages men to accept equal responsibility for the care and well-being of infants and young children, we must reconstruct traditional masculinity ideology. Traditional masculinity ideology defines fathering primarily in terms of the provider role. A new fathering ideology is needed that defines a "real man," not only as a good provider, but also as an emotionally involved father.

Most families now require mothers and fathers to share the provider role. In a survey of 1,502 U.S. families, 48% of married women reported they provided half or more of the family income (Families and Work Institute, 1995). However, an equivalent pattern of men more equitably sharing the nurturing role has not yet emerged. What we are suggesting is that, because men and women are now both primary providers, masculinity ideology needs to evolve so the nurturing role is elevated to the same status as the provider role in the socialization of boys and men.

Another aspect of traditional masculinity that must be changed is that a father's commitment to his child is based on his relationship with the child's mother. When the romantic relationship dissolves, the connection between father and child becomes vulnerable to dissolution. However, if gender ideology were to define the father–infant bond as equally sacrosanct as the mother–infant bond, a father's involvement with his child would become independent of his relationship with the mother. A "real man" would stay involved with his children, whether or not he remained committed to the children's mother.

This ideological change is particularly important given three recent demographic trends: the increasing tendency across all ethnic and class groupings for the birth of a couple's first child to precede marriage, the high rate of divorce, and the increasing number of blended families. Without an ideological commitment to strong father–child bonds, these demographic patterns of partner shifting and child shifting are likely to interfere with the continuity of father–child (and in some cases mother–child) relationships.

One component of our current gender ideology that makes this ideological shift so difficult is the assumption that reproductive biology constructs psychological attachment. It seems so natural to believe that carrying a child in one's body would result in a more intense and enduring emotional connection. My belief in the power of the biological imperative led me to recommend exploring the possibility of male pregnancy (Silverstein, 1996). I still believe this phenomenon would help deconstruct the myth of maternal attachment theory. However, this idea has not attracted large numbers of men. Therefore, I am now recommending that social scientists educate themselves about evolutionary theory and cross-species behavior, so that inaccurate claims about the biological basis of male promiscuity and the absence of paternal involvement among male primates can be effectively challenged (see Silverstein & Auerbach, 1999).

If masculinity ideology were revised to embody these two components—redefining fathering as nurturing as well as providing, and conceptualizing the father–infant bond as independent of the father–mother bond—it would become an ideology that facilitated, rather than thwarted, increased paternal involvement and responsibility. These shifts in gender ideology would transform nurturing from a cross-gender to a gender-consistent behavior for men.

Until a new masculinity ideology evolves, men need widespread social supports. Just as the feminist movement of the 1970s provided consciousness-raising groups to help women reject traditional feminine role prescriptions, our research suggests men would profit from similar support groups for men.

For example, the Promise Keeper fathers in our study expressed how comforting it was to meet weekly with other Christian men to discuss their struggles to become more emotionally connected to their wives and children (Silverstein et al., 1999). They reported that it was "good to know that you are not alone," that it was important for "one man to give another man permission to be vulnerable," and that "you have to break down to be a man." These quotes indicate the importance of getting permission *from other men* to violate the cultural prohibitions embedded in traditional masculinity against men expressing their feelings and acknowledging vulnerability.

In addition to support from same-sex peers, men need support from their wives. The finding that high paternal involvement often leads to increased marital conflict (Baruch & Barnett, 1986) has been used to suggest mothers do not want to share power in the sphere of child care. This may be true for some mothers who have little power in other spheres. However, it is equally likely that some amount of conflict is inevitable when any two people begin to share responsibilities that had previously been managed by only one of them. These tasks, however, are especially emotionally loaded because they represent a culturally gendered division of labor. Therefore, we expect anxiety to be high and conflict to ensue. Couples need support as they work together to restructure the traditional division of labor.

The final area of social support that men need is from institutions, particularly the workplace. Key aspects in the climate of the workplace need to be transformed. Recent research has indicated that fathers, as well as mothers, worry about the effect of their work lives on their children. Other studies are beginning to show that men who are actively involved with their children increase their productivity at work (Snarey, 1993). If employers come to believe that men who are more actively involved with their children are more productive at work, policies such as parental leave, job sharing, and flextime may become routine. Similarly, public rituals usually reserved for women, such as baby showers and birth announcements in corporate newsletters, may become part of the fathering culture at work.

How Can We Design Social Policy That Encourages Responsible Fathering Without Discriminating Against Mothers?

The United States is engaged in a social policy debate between neoconservative and progressive ideologies. The social policy recommendations emanating from each ideological position contrast sharply. Neoconservative social scientists claim that wide-ranging social problems—that is, crime, violence, and drug abuse—emanate from broken homes or never-married single-mother families (e.g., Blankenhorn, 1995; Popenoe, 1996). Their solution to these social problems is to return fathers to families. They are recommending rewarding married couples and withholding support (both economic and social) from all other parents who do not live in two-parent married families. They want to make divorce more difficult to obtain, including repealing no-fault divorce legislation. Their message, on balance, is that families can make it on their own, if only they contain two parents. This perspective alleviates the need for public investment in large-scale family support policies.

This point of view has already generated social policy initiatives. A congressional seminar organized in April 1998 by Senator Brownback (R-Kansas) issued several recommendations, including revisions to the tax code that would reward couples who marry and eliminating taxes altogether for married couples with three or more children (Wetzstein, 1998).

Some federal legislation has placed a similar emphasis on the advantages of marriage. For example, the 1996 welfare reform law begins by stating, "Marriage is the foundation of a successful society" (Welfare Reform Act, 1996, p. 110). In 1997, Louisiana passed a Covenant Marriage Act that declares marriage a lifelong relationship and stipulates more stringent requirements for separation and divorce. A housing project in Hartford, Connecticut, now provides economic support to married couples (not to mother-headed families) and special opportunities for job training to men (not to women) who live with their families (LaRossa, 1997).

Progressive social scientists, in contrast, believe that the complex social problems plaguing U.S. society are the result of complex global trends such as the postindustrial technological revolution, the decrease in male employment and corresponding increase in female employment, and anti-welfare state social policies (e.g., Dodson, 1998; Stacey, 1996). This point of view recommends providing all families, but especially poor families, with wide-ranging economic and social supports such as maternity benefits; paid parental leave; and high-quality, subsidized child-care centers. The progressive perspective has generated little legislation. The 1995 Family Leave Act, which allows parents to take unpaid leave to care for newborn infants and elderly parents, is a weak substitute for the kind of paid parental leave families need.

Although the neoconservative agenda claims that strengthening families is its primary concern, the social policy emanating from the neoconservative perspective is unlikely to be helpful to children and families. For example, repealing no-fault divorce is likely to intensify the stress of divorce on children because it will prolong legal battles over who is at fault. Stacey (1998) pointed out that making divorces more difficult to obtain may have the unintended consequence of making people less likely to marry. Similarly, the 1996 Defense of Marriage Act, which describes marriage as exclusively heterosexual, puts the millions of children living with gay and lesbian parents at risk in terms of custody disputes, economic supports, and so on.

A social policy agenda that would be likely to return fathers to families would have to deal with the chronic unemployment and incarceration of inner-city men. This would require a commitment to improving education, in contrast to building prisons. Similarly, increasing paternal involvement in all fathers would require a widespread system of social supports to help balance the competing demands of work and family responsibilities. This type of progressive social policy agenda would require a substantial commitment of public funds.

FUTURE DIRECTIONS

A Commitment to Nonsexist Research

If, as social scientists, we are serious about changing gender ideology, we need to make a commitment to change ourselves. Phares (1992) described the entire body of knowledge within developmental psychology as "a sex-biased dataset." One strategy that every researcher can implement is to refuse to engage in research about mothers unless fathers are also involved. I have taken that stand in terms of sitting on doctoral dissertation committees and collaborating with other faculty members on research projects, and it is not a popular one.

This commitment to including fathers in developmental research would be more effective if it were adopted more widely in the scholarly community. For example, it could become part of the American Psychological Association's (APA) ethical guidelines, as well as editorial policy for APA journals.

A Commitment to Qualitative Research Paradigms

Until recently, psychology has been characterized by an unflagging commitment to quantitative research paradigms. Correlational studies based on data collected for other research purposes continue to be more respectable than qualitative studies organized around lived experiences and life-course strategies. This has been particularly true of research on fathering in that many studies continue to draw conclusions about fathers without actually speaking to them. For example, the neoconservative position on father absence is based on correlational analyses using data from the National Longitudinal Survey of Youth. This is particularly problematic because this study interviewed only mothers.

Even in studies where fathers have been included, much of the data being analyzed had been collected with other research questions in mind. Thus, much of the information needed to draw conclusions about fathering must be inferred. An example of this is the Zill and Nord (1996) study on nonresident fathers. This study relied on the Survey of Income and Program participation, in which important data relating to father involvement had to be inferred. For example, how are fathers who voluntarily entered into a child support agreement different from fathers who could not come to an agreement with their ex-wives? Is there something different about their experiences with their own fathers, their history of caretaking their children, or the level of conflict with their ex-spouses? The answers to these questions are necessary for designing social policy initiatives and could be explored through qualitative interviews.

The most common objection to qualitative research is that it is not generalizable because most studies are based on intensive data analysis of a small number of participants. This insistence on generalizability is interesting given that the quantitative paradigm has produced an androcentric, heterocentric, and hopelessly Eurocentric body of knowledge. Rather than singling out qualitative studies as being unrepresentative, it seems more accurate to assume that any series of studies emanating from a single theoretical framework, whether quantitative or qualitative, has little generalizability. Every study needs to be replicated with additional samples and informed by different theoretical perspectives before the results can be accepted with any degree of certainty.

In my view, qualitative research, because it is hypothesis generating rather than hypothesis testing, is particularly well suited to studying populations about whom little is known. I argue that, because of our bias toward the maternal attachment paradigm, fathers are one such population about whom relatively little is known. Lewis (1997) estimated there are "probably thousands of studies in the literature about the child's relationship with the mother, but to date only seventeen known studies have compared the child's attachment to the father" (p. 140). The lack of information is particularly true for poor, ethnic minority, and gay fathers.

A Commitment to Multiculturalism

Just as we need to make a commitment to nonsexist research, we need to make an authentic commitment to multiculturalism. There are several concrete steps each of us could take in this regard: We could begin by refusing to participate in research or make presentations on panels or symposia where different ethnicities and sexual orientations are not represented. However, a true commitment to multiculturalism requires a commitment to examine one's own gender and racial identity.

In the late 1980s, O'Neil, Egan, Owen, and Murry (1993) developed a workshop called "The Gender Role Journey." This workshop helped men and women explore their gender socialization experiences. They were asked to identify the ways in which they had learned about traditional gender role norms, the developmental events that led them to question those norms, and the kinds of sanctions they had received for violating cultural expectations. Individuals were encouraged to explore their gender stereotypes, particularly concerning misogyny and homophobia. At the end of the workshop, each person could identify where they were on their journey of defining an authentic gender identity, more or less free of cultural prescriptions.

Similarly, Helms (1990) developed an equivalent scale for studying Black and White Racial Identities. This scale helps individuals identify their attitudes toward race, both their own and that of others. The scale is constructed as a developmental journey, although progress is not thought to be linear. Regression to earlier stages is common before constructs are internalized and integrated into one's sense of self.

In terms of White racial identity, an individual in the earliest stage denies feelings about race. Everyone is thought to be "the same." Later stages use stereotypes to understand racial differences or to idealize the other and feel rejecting toward one's own race. In the final stage (if one ever achieves it) one feels comfortable with one's own cultural and racial embeddedness and is aware of similarities and differences between oneself and others. Unconscious racism is acknowledged and attempts are made to dispel one's stereotypes and biases.

This kind of work is challenging for White people because White privilege allows Whites to choose not to attend to being White. How can we hope to do nonracist research and therapy if we are not aware of our own racial identity? If we are authentic in our commitment to understanding difference, we have a responsibility to begin this type of self-exploration.

Another aspect of our journey must be to acknowledge the privilege that accompanies race and class. Burton and Snyder (1998) called our attention to the way White men structure the experiences of poor, African American fathers. Almeida (1998) identified "the third shift," the struggle for women of color to fulfill their own child-care and household responsibilities after working long hours caring for the children of White families. Hardy and Laszloffy (1998) exhorted us to commit ourselves, not just to avoiding racism within ourselves, but to adopting an antiracist social action agenda. Unless we are determined to address the interlocking relations between gender and power and between race and power, we have little chance of creating an inclusive body of knowledge.

CONCLUSIONS: TO THE NEXT GENERATION
OF FATHERING RESEARCHERS

My recommendations to the next generation of fathering researchers relate to the process, rather than to the content, of research endeavors: Avoid dichotomous thinking and develop a tolerance for conflict. This advice is relevant, not only to fathering researchers, but to anyone interested in authentic scientific inquiry.

In 1992 when, as a new faculty member, I announced my interest in studying fathers, I was advised to "forget fathers" and continue my research interest in early day care. Ignoring this advice, I continued to think about how to explore fathering behaviors. I described my idea for a qualitative study of the subjective experiences of fathers to a prominent fathering researcher. "That's very interesting," he said, "but it's not research." This told me a lot about my chances for funding the kind of research in which I was interested.

In June 1999 Auerbach and I published an article pointing out that the empirical research as a whole indicated fathers (and mothers) were important but not essential to healthy child development. The public outcry against the article was so intense that the U.S. House of Representatives debated whether to pass a resolution condemning the article. (Ultimately, the congressmen sponsoring the resolution decided on a less formal "Dear Colleague" letter.)

In my experience, when we challenge dominant paradigms, especially those that are misogynist, racist, and homophobic, many people will not thank us for doing so. Those of us committed to this process must be prepared to experience a significant amount of distress. Often, there is no safe place to stand as we question power relations.

In addition to tolerating conflict, we must be committed to overcoming our cognitive tendency toward either–or thinking. In the last two decades, families in the United States have become more diverse. There is no longer one dominant form of family life. Gay, lesbian, and transexual parents; single mothers by choice; and interracial adoptions are transforming the societal landscape. In contrast to the diversity of these social trends, those of us conducting research and designing social policy are accustomed to thinking about human behavior in dichotomous categories: nature–nurture, male–female, gay–straight, Black–White, normal–pathological.

In addition to our natural cognitive proclivity toward dichotomous thinking, there is tremendous pressure from religious fundamentalists and the political right to define the traditional two-parent, heterosexual family as the optimal context for children and to reject all other family structures as deficit models. In this political atmosphere, it is difficult to maintain a both–and approach to scientific inquiry.

Nevertheless, the complexity of human behavior requires a corresponding complexity in our thinking about research and social policy. We must continue to ask questions that reflect this complexity. For example: How can we design social policy to support fathers, but not at the expense of mothers? How can we acknowledge that fathers (and mothers) are important, at the same time we show that children can flourish in families without fathers (or mothers)? How can we establish a legal standard of child custody and visitation that is flexible enough to protect a child from an abusive parent and allow that parent to maintain a relationship with the child?

As you design your research questions, challenge yourself to take a both–and position. Gather your courage to maintain your equilibrium when the objections to your work emerge. Remember that everything is political, and that the political is always personal.

ACKNOWLEDGMENT

I want to thank Carl Auerbach for his collaboration and support. Although the words are mine, many of the ideas in this chapter have emerged as a result of our work together.

REFERENCES

Ahmeduzzaman, M., & Roopnarine, J. L. (1992). Sociodemographic factors, functioning style, social support, and fathers' involvement with preschoolers in African American intact families. *Journal of Marriage and the Family, 54,* 699–707.

Ainsworth, M. D. S., Blehar, M. C., Waters, E., & Walls, S. (1978). *Patterns of attachment: A psychological study of the strandge situation.* Hillsdale, NJ: Lawrence Erlbaum Associates.

Almeida, R. V. (1998). The dislocation of women's experience in family therapy. *Journal of Feminist Family Therapy, 10,* 1–22.

Auerbach, C., & Silverstein, L. (Symposium Co-chairs). (1997, November). *Is parenting gendered? A postmodern conversation.* National Conference on Family Relations, Arlington, VA.

Auerbach, C., Silverstein, L., & Zizi, M. (1997). The evolving structure of fatherhood: A qualitative study of Haitian American fathers. *Journal of African American Men, 2,* 59–85.

Baruch, G. K., & Barnett, R. C. (1986). Consequences of fathers' participation in family work: Parents' role strain and well-being. *Journal of Personality and Social Psychology, 51,* 983–992.

Benson, A. (1996). *The fathering experiences of gay fathers. A qualitative research study.* Unpublished research project, Ferkauf Graduate School of Psychology, Yeshiva University, Bronx, NY.

Biller, H. B., & Kimpton, J. L. (1997). The father and the school-aged child. In M. E. Lamb (Ed.), *The role of the father in child development* (3rd ed., pp. 143–161). New York: Wiley.

Blankenhorn, D. (1995). *Fatherless America: Confronting our most urgent social problem.* New York: Basic Books.

Bowlby, J. (1951). *Maternal care and mental health.* Geneva, Switzerland: World Health Organization.

Bowlby, J. (1969). *Attachment and loss: Vol. 1. Attachment.* New York: Basic Books.

Bowman, P. J., & Forman, T. A. (1998). Instrumental and expressive family roles among African American fathers. In R. Taylor, J. Jackson, & L. Chalters (Eds.), *Family life in Black America* (pp. 216–261). Newbury Park, CA: Sage.

Brazelton, T. B., Yogman, M. W., Als, H., & Tronick, E. (1979). The infant as a focus for family reciprocity. In M. Lewis & L. A. Rosenblum (Eds.), *The child and its family* (pp. 29–43). New York: Plenum.

Burton, L. M. (1990). Teenage pregnancy as an alternative life-course strategy in multigenerational Black families. *Human Nature, 1,* 123–143.

Burton, L., & Snyder, A R. (1998). The invisible man revisited: Comments on the lifecourse, history, and men's roles in American families. In A. Booth & A. C. Crouter (Eds.), *Men in families. When do they get involved? What difference does it make?* (pp. 31–40). Mahwah, NJ: Lawrence Erlbaum Associates.

Cazenave, N. A. (1979). Middle income Black fathers: An analysis of the provider role. *Family Coordinator, 28,* 583–593.

Covenant Marriage Act, LSA-R.S. §272 *et seq.* (1997).

Dodson, L. (1998). "This river runs deep": Father myths and single mothers in poor America. In C. Daniels (Ed.), *Lost fathers. The politics of fatherlessness in America* (pp. 109–126). New York: St. Martin's Press.

Engle, P. L., & Breaux, C. (1998). Fathers' involvement with children: Perspectives from developing countries. *Social Policy Report. Society for Research in Child Development, 12,* 1–23.

Erikson, R. J., & Gecas, V. (1991). Social class and fatherhood. In F. W. Bozett & S. M. H. Hanson (Eds.), *Fatherhood and families in cultural context. Springer series: Focus on Men* (Vol. 6, pp. 114–137). New York: Springer.

Families and Work Institute (1995). *Women. The new providers.* New York: Whirlpool Foundation Study.

Frodi, A. M., Lamb, M. E., Hwang, C. P., & Frodi, M. (1983). Father–mother–infant interaction in traditional and nontraditional Swedish families: A longitudinal study. *Alternative Lifestyles, 5,* 142–163.

Frodi, A. M., Lamb, M. E., Leavitt, L. A., & Donovan, W. L. (1978). Fathers' and mothers' responses to infant smiles and cries. *Infant Behavior and Development, 1,* 187–198.

Hardy, K. V., & Laszloffy, T. A. (1998). The dynamics of a pro-racist ideology. In M. McGoldrick (Ed.), *Re-visioning family therapy* (pp. 118–128). New York: Guilford.

Hawkins, A. J., Christiansen, S. L., Sargent, K. P., & Hill, E. J. (1993). Rethinking fathers' involvement in child case: A developmental perspective. *Journal of Family Issues, 14,* 531–549.

Helms, J. (Ed.). (1990). *Black and White racial identity.* Westport, CT: Greenwood Press.

Hetherington, E. M., Bridges, M., & Insabella, G. M. (1998). What matters? What does not? Five perspectives on the association between marital transitions and children's adjustment. *American Psychologist, 53,* 167–184.

Hetherington, E. M., & Stanley-Hagan, M. M. (1997). The effects of divorce on fathers and their children. In M. E. Lamb (Ed.), *The role of the father in child development* (3rd ed., pp. 191–211). New York: Wiley.

Hewlett, B. S. (1991). *Intimate fathers.* Ann Arbor, MI: University of Michigan Press.

Hochschild, A., & Machung, A. (1989). *The second shift. Working parents and the revoluion at home.* New York: Viking.

Hosley, C. A., & Montemayor, R. (1997). Fathers and adolescents. In M. E. Lamb (Ed.), *The role of the father in child development* (3rd ed., pp. 162–178). New York: Wiley.

Hossain, Z., & Roopnarine, J. L. (1993). Division of household labor and child care in dual-earner African-American families with infants. *Sex Roles, 29,* 571–583.

Hrdy, S. B. (1997). Raising Darwin's consciousness: Female sexuality and the prehominid origins of patriarchy. *Human Nature, 8,* 1–49.

Hunter, A. G., & Davis, J. E. (1994). Hidden voices of black men: The meaning, structure, and complexity of manhood. *Journal of Black Studies, 25,* 20–40.

Lamb, M. E. (Ed.). (1976). *The role of the father in child development.* New York: Wiley.

Lamb, M. E. (Ed.). (1987a). *The father's role: Cross-cultural perspectives.* Hillsdale, NJ: Lawrence Erlbaum Associates.

Lamb, M. E. (1987b). Introduction: The emergent American father. In M. E. Lamb (Ed.), *The father's role: Cross-cultural perspectives* (pp. 3–25). Hillsdale, NJ: Lawrence Erlbaum Associates.

Lamb, M. E. (1997a). The development of father–infant relationships. In M. E. Lamb, (Ed.), *The role of the father in child development* (3rd ed., pp. 104–120). New York: Wiley.

Lamb, M. E. (Ed.). (1997b). *The role of the father in child development* (3rd ed.). New York: Wiley.

Lamb, M. E., Pleck, J. H., Charnov, E. L., & Levine, J. A. (1987). A biosocial perspective on paternal behavior and involvement. In J. B. Lancster, J. Altmann, A. S. Rossi, & L. R. Sherrod (Eds.), *Parenting across the lifespan: Biosocial perspectives* (pp. 111–142). Hawthorne, NY: Aldine.

Lamb, M. E., Pleck, J. H., & Levine, J. A. (1986). Effects of increased father involvement in two-parent families. In R. A. Lewis & R. E. Salt (Eds.), *Men in families* (pp. 141–158). Newbury Park, CA: Sage.

LaRossa, R. (1988). Fatherhood and social change. *Family Relations, 37,* 451–457.

LaRossa, R. (Chair). (1997, November). *Perspectives for encouraging father involvement.* National Conference on Family Relations, Arlington, VA.

Lee, C. M., & Gotlib, I. H. (1991). Family disruption, parental availability and child adjustment. In R. J. Prinz (Ed.), *Advances in behavioral assessment of children and families* (Vol. 5, pp. 171–199). London: Kingsley.

Lerman, R. I. (1993). A national profile of young unwed fathers. In R. I. Lerman & T. Ooms (Eds.), *Young unwed fathers* (pp. 27–51). Philadelphia: Temple University Press.

Levine, J. A., Murphy, D. T., & Wilson, S. (1993). *Getting men involved. Strategies for early childhood programs.* New York: Scholastic.

Levine, J. A., & Pitt, E. W. (1995). *New expectations. Community strategies for responsible fatherhood.* New York: Families and Work Institute.

Levine, J. A., & Pittinsky, T. L. (1997). *Working fathers. New strategies for balancing work and family.* New York: Addison-Wesley.

Lewis, M. (1997). *Altering fate. Why the past does not predict the future.* New York: Guilford Press.

McAdoo, H. (1988). *Black families.* Newbury Park, CA: Sage.

McAdoo, J. L. (1988). Changing perspectives on the roles of the black father. In P. Bronstein & C. P. Cowan (Eds.), *Fatherhood today: Men's changing role in the family* (pp. 79–92). New York: Wiley.

McGoldrick, M., & Gerson, R. (1985). *Genograms in family assessment.* New York: Norton.

Mintz, S. (1998). From patriarchy to androgyny and other myths: Placing men's family roles in historical perspective. In A. Booth & A. C. Crouter (Eds.), *Men in families. When do they get involved? What difference does it make?* (pp. 3–30). Mahwah, NJ: Lawrence Erlbaum Associates.

O'Neil, J. M., Egan, J., Owen, S. V., & Murray, V. M. (1993). The gender role journey measure: Scale development and psychometric evaluation. *Sex Roles, 28,* 1–19.

Parke, R., Power, T. G., & Gottman, J. (1979). Conceptualizing and quantifying influence patterns in the family triad. In M. E. Lamb, S. J. Suomi, & G. R. Stephenson (Eds.), *Social interaction analysis: Methodological issues* (pp. 231–252). Madison, WI: University of Wisconsin Press.

Patterson, C. J. (1995). Lesbian mothers, gay fathers, and their children. In A. R. D'Augelli & C. F. Patterson (Eds.), *Lesbian, gay, and bisexual identities over the lifespan* (pp. 262–290). New York: Oxford University Press.

Patterson, C. J., & Chan, R. W. (1997). Gay fathers. In M. E. Lamb (Ed.), *The role of the father in child development* (3rd ed., pp. 245–260). New York: Wiley.

Pedersen, F. A., Cain, R., Zaslow, M., & Anderson, B. (1982). Variation in infant experience associated with alternative family roles. In L. Laosa & I. Siegel (Eds.), *Families as learning environments for children* (pp. 203–221). New York: Plenum.

Phares, V. (1992). Where's poppa? The relative lack of attention to the role of fathers in child and adolescent psychopathology. *American Psychologist, 47,* 656–664.

Phares, V. (1996). *Fathers and developmental psychopathology.* New York: Wiley.

Phares, V. (1997). Psychological adjustment, maladjustment, and father–child relationships. In M. E. Lamb (Ed.), *The role of the father in child development* (3rd ed., pp. 261–283). New York: Wiley.

Phares, V., & Compas, B. B. (1992). The role of fathers in child and adolescent psychpathology: Make room for daddy. *Psychological Bulletin, 111,* 387–412.

Pleck, J. H. (1985). *Working wives, working husbands.* Beverly Hills, CA: Sage.

Pleck, J. H. (1993). Are "family supportive" employer policies relevant to men? In J. C. Hood (Ed.), *Men, work, and family* (pp. 217–237). Newbury Park, CA: Sage.

Pleck, J. H. (1995). The gender role strain paradigm: An update. In R. F. Levant & W. S. Pollack (Eds.), *A new psychology of men* (pp. 11–32). New York: Basic Books.

Pleck, J. H. (1997). Paternal involvement: Levels sources, and consequences. In M. E. Lamb (Ed.), *The role of the father in child development* (3rd ed., pp. 66–103). New York: Wiley.

Pleck, E. H., & Pleck, J. H. (1997). Fatherhood ideals in the United States: Historical dimensions. In M. E. Lamb (Ed.), *The role of the father in child development* (3rd ed., pp. 33–48). New York: Wiley.

Popenoe, D. (1996). *Life without father.* New York: Martin Pressler Press.

Pruett, K. D. (1998). How men and children affect each other's development. *Zero to Three, 18,* 3–11.

Quartironi, B. (1995). *The new gay fathers: An exploratory study of their experiences, perceptions, and concerns.* Unpublished research project, Ferkauf Graduate School of Psychology, Yeshiva University, Bronx, NY.

Roopnarine, J. L., & Benetti, S. (1996, May). *Caribbean fathers: Marginalized and distant?* Paper presented at the National Center for Fathers and Fathering, Philadelphia, PA.

Roopnarine, J., Snell-White, P., & Riegraf, N. (1993). *Men's roles in family and society: Dominica, Guyana, and Jamaica.* Kingston, Jamaica: UNICEF and UWI.

Rutter, M. (1974). *The qualities of mothering. Maternal deprivation reassessed.* New York: Aronson.

Sagi, A., Lamb, M. E., Shoham, R., Dvir, R., & Lewkowicz, K. S. (1985). Parent-infant interaction in families on Israeli kibbutzim. *International Journal of Behavioral Development, 8,* 273–284.

Schaffer, H. R., & Emerson, P. E. (1964). The development of social attachments in infancy [Special Issue]. *Monographs of the Society for Research in Child Development, 29*(94).

Silverstein, L. B. (1996). Fathering is a feminist issue. *Pychology of Women Quarterly, 20,* 3–27.

Silverstein, L. B., & Auerbach, C. F. (1999). Deconstructing the essential father. *American Psychologist, 54,* 397–407.

Silverstein, L. B., & Auerbach, C. F., Grieco, L., & Dunkel, F. (1999). Do Promise Keeper fathers dream of feminist sheep? *Sex Roles, 40,* 665–688.

Silverstein, L. B., & Phares, V. (1996). Expanding the mother–child paradigm: An examination of dissertation research 1986–1993. *Psychology of Women Quarterly, 20,* 39–54.

Smuts, B. B., & Gubernick, D. J. (1992). Male–infant relationships in nonhuman primates: Paternal investment or mating effort? In B. S. Hewlett (Ed.), *Father–child relations: Cultural and biosocial contexts* (pp. 1–31). New York: Aldine de Gruyter.

Snarey, J. (1993). *How fathers care for the next generation. A four decade study.* Cambridge, MA: Harvard University Press.

Stacey, J. (1996). *In the name of the family.* Boston: Beacon.

Stacey, J. (1998). Dada-ism in the 1990's: Getting past baby talk about fatherlessness. In C. Daniels (Ed.), *Lost fathers. The politics of fatherlessness in America* (pp. 51–84). New York: St. Martin's Press.

Stier, H., & Tienda, M. (1993). Are men marginal to the family? Insights from Chicago's inner city. In J. C. Hood (Ed.), *Men, work, and family* (pp. 23–33). Newbury Park, CA: Sage.

Trivers, R. L. (1972). Parental investment and sexual selection. In B. Campbell (Ed.), *Sexual selection and the descent of man 1871–1971* (pp. 136–179). Chicago: Aldine.

Weil, F. (1996). Divorced fathers: A qualitative study. Unpublished research project. Ferkauf Graduate School of Psychology, Yeshiva University, Bronx, NY.

Welfare Reform Act, 104 U.S.C. §2110 (1996).

Wetzstein, C. (1998, April 15). Congress urged to provide economic, social incentives to preserve family. *The Washington Times*, p. 10.

Wilson, W. J. (1987). *The truly disadvantaged: The inner city, the underclass, and public policy.* Chicago: University of Chicago Press.

Zill, N., & Nord, C. W. (1996, November). *Causes and consequences of involvement by non-custodial parents in their children's lives: Evidence from a national longitudinal study.* Paper presented at the National Center on Fathers and Families, Philadelphia, PA.

3

Parenting in the New Millennium: Prospects, Promises, and Pitfalls

Ross D. Parke
University of California, Riverside

Where should parenting research move in the next decade? No one has a crystal ball but based on past research and theory, as well as shifts in the roles that parents play in the larger matrix of socialization forces, some predictions and prescriptions can be offered. Understanding advances in various ways. Incremental progress should continue to be embraced, because most of our insights derive from cumulative increases in knowledge base. At the same time, we should be aware of paradigm shifts that will catapult us toward new levels of insight about parenting. These paradigm shifts can take the form of methodological breakthroughs, as well as new ways of conceptualizing the central issues of parenting.

As Grolnick and Gurland (chap. 1, this volume) and Silverstein (chap. 2, this volume) highlight, early theories of parenting were characterized by several features, including a unidirectional pattern of influence, typological approaches, a mother orientation, and nondevelopmental conceptualizations. Fortunately, major advances achieved over the last 30 years in our conceptualization of parenting have challenged many of these assumptions.

In this chapter I visit the role of historical and cultural factors in parenting, a life-course view of parenting, the distinctive roles of mothers and fathers, the independence and interdependence of parenting roles, ways of conceptualizing parenting, methods of assessing parenting, the relative influence of parents in the larger matrix of socialization, and the effect of new reproductive technologies on parenting. Some of these issues are continu-

ing controversies in the field; others represent new challenges for researchers and practitioners as we begin this new millennium.

THEORETICAL ISSUES IN THE STUDY
OF PARENTING

Issues of Generalizability

Historical Generalizability. Is it appropriate to assume that any model
of parenting can be accounted for by the same set of principles in different
historical periods? Probably not! As historians, sociologists, and anthropologists have illustrated, the historical context is a powerful determinant of
parenting ideals as well as practices (Elder, Modell, & Parke, 1994). Psychologists, however, have generally ignored historical influences and instead
have focused largely on historical and universal laws of human behavior. It
is important to underscore the value of a historical approach to parenting
and remind ourselves that historical analyses can serve several functions.
Such an approach affords unique opportunities to assess the generalizability of our explanatory principles in different historical periods. Historical
variations such as war, famine, or economic depression represent important and powerful natural experiments that permit opportunities for theory
and model testing, often under conditions that are much more drastic than
developmental researchers could either ethically or practically engineer or
produce in either the laboratory or the field. Elder's (1974) explorations of
economic depression on family functioning and life-course development of
children in the United States is a classic example of this approach. Recent
work (Conger & Elder, 1994) in which the effect of economic hardship during the 1980s and 1990s provides a unique opportunity to assess the historical boundedness of family—employment relationships. Tracing how historical shifts in family organization in turn alter parenting processes would be
an interesting and profitable enterprise. For example, during wartime the
increased degree of father absence accompanied by a higher percentage of
mothers in the workplace and children in day care provides unique opportunities to document how these shifts affect parenting (Tuttle, 1993). Re-
gional conflicts in the Middle East, Eastern Europe, Africa, and Ireland at
the close of the 20th century remind us that the effect of war and violence
on children and families remains a continuing concern as well as an opportunity to better understand how parenting is altered by war-related stress
(Leavitt & Fox, 1993). Moreover, historically based redefinitions of maternal
and paternal roles provide important opportunities to assess how changing
cognitive constructions of parental roles modify parent—child relationships
(Silverstein, chap. 2, this volume).

Cultural Generalizability. Just as history provides naturally occurring variations, so do cross-cultural contexts provide opportunities for exploring the boundary conditions of our theories. Social scientists have increasingly recognized that culture shapes the nature, timing, and rate of development. This recognition is part of our shift away from endorsement of a positivistic assumption that psychological laws of development are applicable universally. Examining this assumption by replicating findings in other cultural contexts has become a much more common ideal. In a stronger form, family scholars have argued that trying to develop universal theories of parenting is a futile enterprise because culture organizes behavioral patterns in fundamentally unique ways (see Gauvain, 1995; Rogoff, 1990; Whiting, Edwards, Ember, & Erchak, 1988).

Assuming for the moment a new generation of culturally sensitive and informed researchers working from sensible conceptualizations of parenting effects on young children's adjustment, one of the major problems that will face those who engage in cross-cultural research or research on different ethnic groups within a culture is the equivalence of measures across groups. In recognition that the most commonly used measures of family values and functioning have been developed and standardized in White middle-class populations, significant efforts have been made in recent years to develop culturally and linguistically equivalent measures. One recent advance has been to use focus groups consisting of members of the ethnic group of interest to generate items and issues that are culturally relevant (Erkut, Alarcon, Coll, Tropp, & Garcia, 1999). Focus groups are also being used as an integral part of the scale-construction process by making recommendations for wording changes and identifying culturally inappropriate items. A second advance has been to use translation and back translation to ensure that meaning is retained in the translation process. As part of this process, a dual-focus approach (Erkut et al., 1999) has been articulated, in which new concepts and items that arise during the translation process are generated simultaneously in both languages. Recent work by Knight, Virdin, and Roosa (1994) has provided models for establishing scalar equivalence of commonly used questionnaires for assessment of family functioning. Recent theoretical and statistical advances in scaling can be usefully applied to this issue of cross-group equivalency as well. Specifically, Reise and his colleagues (Flannery, Reise & Widaman, 1995; Reise, Widaman, & Pugh, 1993) have used item response theory (IRT) techniques to address the equivalence of scales across groups. The utility of this approach for establishing gender equivalence (Flannery et al., 1995) and cross-cultural equivalence (China versus United States; Reise et al., 1993) suggests this strategy can be used to establish scalar equivalence across different ethnic groups within our own culture as well. The thorny methodological issues in this area are by no means resolved, but the increased awareness of these problems has spurred significant recent advances in this area (Betancourt & Lopez, 1993).

Variations in family organization and structure evident in different societies represent another critical point of departure. Do extended family arrangements require that we completely rethink our prevailing models of parenting, especially when the responsibility is shared across several caregivers? Although progress continues to be made in describing relationships between parents and children in different cultures (Bornstein, 1991; Lamb, 1987; Roopnarine & Carter, 1992) and in different ethnic groups within a country or region (McLoyd, 1989; Parke & Buriel, 1998), this work represents only a beginning. As this work proceeds, it will be important to extend the focus so that parenting is located in its full systemic context, with parallel attention given to marital, sibling, and family systems.

Level of Analyses in Parenting Research:
Beyond a General Style of Parenting

Another emerging theme concerns the level of generality or specificity we should strive for in our attempts to understand parenting processes. The field has gone through phases in which we have alternated between a search for common dimensions used to develop typologies of parenting and a search for more specific aspects of parent–child interaction, which may be more useful in accounting for child outcomes (Patterson, 1993). Baldwin and Baumrind have been among the major proponents of typologies, which have dominated the field for the past 30 years. However, recent studies have raised serious questions about the generalizability of parental styles across either SES or ethnic-cultural groups. Two issues are key: First, are the base rates with which parents use different styles of parenting similar across groups? Second, are the effects of particular parenting styles (e.g., authoritative) on children's adaptation similar across different groups? In contrast to middle-class families, low-SES families are more likely to use authoritarian styles of parenting, in response to the ecological conditions such as increased danger that may characterize the circumstances of poverty (Furstenberg, 1993). Moreover, whereas authoritarian parenting has been linked to negative child outcomes in middle-class Anglo samples, these same strategies are linked with positive outcomes in low-SES families (Baldwin, Baldwin, & Cole, 1990), although interpretation of the evidence remains controversial (Steinberg, 2000). Evidence from cross-ethnic studies (e.g., Chao, 1994) is also relevant, challenging the notion that there is universal advantage to authoritative styles of parenting. It is clear that contextual and cultural considerations need to be given more attention in typological approaches to child rearing.

More direct challenges to the utility of typological approaches have come from Collins and Repinski (in press), Dix (1991), and Kozilius, Gerris, and Fellings (in press), all of whom have argued that the pendulum has now swung back to focus on more specific aspects of parenting. These specific aspects include parent and child expectations and attributions and molecular aspects of parent–child interactions such as contingent responsiveness. All of these authors have made impressive cases for recognizing that parenting behaviors shift as a function of either different dimensions of relationships (Collins & Repinski), different types of transgressions (Kozilius et al.), or different contexts (Dix; see also McHale, Lauretti, Talbot, & Pouquette, chap. 5, this volume). For example, Dix has shown that parental responses to children's transgressions vary with parental mood, the severity of the transgression and the child's response to the misbehavior. Instead of a general style that is evident in all contexts and for all types of misdeeds, parents are likely to calibrate their reactions to suit the specific features of the transgressions.

Although these studies collectively raise serious questions about the validity of parenting theories that do not recognize the specificity of parenting behavior as a function of various factors (e.g., relationships, context), it is likely that parents do, nonetheless, develop a more general style of parenting as well (Grolnick & Gurland, chap. 1, this volume). This focus raises a central question for theories of parenting, namely: How do we move from measuring specific parental reactions to accurately capturing more general styles of responding? This can be viewed as a short-term versus long-term problem, but also a level-of-analysis issue. A major challenge for our field is to reconcile these two ways of viewing parenting, namely as a general style of responding and as a specific set of behaviors, attitudes, and beliefs that are enacted differently in specific contexts, in response to different events, or even in reaction to different children. Both are probably valid but what are the processes by which short-term reactions to specific situations become consolidated into long-term habitual ways of responding (see Patterson, 1993)?

Beyond Parent Effects and Child Effects

Bidirectional and cyclic processes of influence have become more common in recent parenting frameworks. Family scholars are recognizing not just the child's role in the socialization process but also the "bidirectional nature of the parent–child interaction with the parent's explicit understanding and acknowledgment of the child's active contribution or agency as an essential feature of parenting" (Grusec, Goodnow, & Kuczynski, 2000). This perspective is consistent with the view of parenting as a coconstructed process, in which both parent and child play active roles in interpreting the meaning of the other partner's behavior. Although there has been considerable progress made in our appreciation of the parent as a "meaning maker" in the socialization process (Goodnow & Collins, 1991; Miller, 1988), less progress has been made in discovering children's understanding of their role as an active agent and as an interpreter of parental socialization goals and actions. One promising framework that moves us in this direction is the recent work of Kuczynski (Kuczynski & Hildebradt, 1997; Lollis & Kuczynski, 1997). As these authors have argued, we need a theory of parenting that recognizes more explicitly the dual role of child and parent in the emergence and maintenance of parenting beliefs and practices. Just as Bell (1968) reminded us decades ago, children play an active role in shaping their own development; similarly, parenting is a jointly negotiated and constructed process in which children and adults play shifting roles as the child develops (see also Maccoby, 1984).

Beyond a Non-Developmental View of Parenting

It is profitable to place the study of parenting in a life-span developmental perspective. Several tenets of a life span view merit attention. First, the focus on both normative and nonnormative events is of relevance to the study of parenting. Second, this viewpoint emphasizes multiple developmental trajectories. Although the individual development of adults (and children) within a family is important, these can only be understood with reference to the developmental pathway followed by larger units of analysis such as the husband–wife dyad or the parent–child dyad, as well as the family unit itself (McHale & Cowan, 1996; Parke, 1988; Sigel & Parke, 1987). Moreover, it is argued not only that the concept of multiple developmental trajectories recognizes that individuals, dyads, and family units may follow disparate developmental pathways, but also that it is necessary to acknowledge the tension and interplay among these trajectories to fully understand the development of children in the context of their families.

Individual Adult Development. Although developmental psychologists have traditionally focused on the developmental pathways followed by individual children, a handful of studies have investigated changes in individuals across adulthood. As Erikson (1982) reminded us, development is a lifelong process that does not cease in childhood. Adults' reactions to their family roles over time change as a function of the development of the individual partners. Individual adult development can be viewed from two perspectives: developmental status and cultural agenda. First, adults' cognitive, social, emotional, and biological capabilities help determine the level and quality of their understanding of family-centered events, as well as the type of intrapersonal resources and coping strategies available to deal with the vicissitudes of changing family relationships. We have only recently begun to describe and understand the normative changes that occur in functioning across different developmental domains in young and middle adulthood (Schaie & Willis, 1991). Even so, however, it is unlikely that developmental status alone, in terms of cognitive, physical, or socioemotional functioning, will prove a useful predictor of individual contributions to parenting. Instead, a sociocultural agenda needs to be considered as well, one that locates of adults along various educational, occupational, and social-relational dimensions. Individuals may or may not be in harmony with these dimensions as they negotiate transitions. Consider the case of work. The increased rate of maternal employment and the gradual move toward greater wage equity for males and females has transformed the nature of parenting roles (Coltrane, 1996). Findings reveal that women who stay home but desire employment outside the home are more depressed than women who stay home and are satisfied with this homemaker role (Hock & DeMers, 1990). The implications of the former situation for parenting are clearly detrimental (Conger & Elder, 1994). Or consider the case of educational attainment. When one spouse continues to gain advanced educational credentials while the other trails in educational attainment, this dysynchrony in the educational trajectories of the individuals could create strain on the marital relationship and indirectly affect the parent–child relationship. The individual trajectories of men and women may be at odds and prompt greater or lesser strain on the couples' relationship and on their roles as parents.

Individual Development of the Child. As we think about parenting trajectories, children's individual developmental changes must be considered as well. Here again, two perspectives are useful: a developmental status perspective, in which children's cognitive, social, and biological functioning are considered, and a cultural agenda perspective, in which the timing of the child's transitions into various social settings such as elementary school, junior high school, or college is taken into account. Often these two perspectives interact in determining children's reactions to family events. Children who are experiencing puberty at the same time another transition is occurring (e.g., the transition to junior high school) respond differently from children who are responding to a single transition (Simmons & Blyth, 1987). Moreover, recent research suggests that children of different ages respond differently to interadult conflict (Cummings & Davies, 1994).

My proposition is that the study of parenting needs to address how the child's developmental status interacts with the developmental position of his or her parents. For example, the formation of a stepfamily is more problematic when the children are adolescents than either younger or older (Hetherington, Bridges, & Insabella, 1998). Earlier research on divorce has indicated marital breakup is not independent of the child's development. For example, divorce or separation is more likely to occur when the child (or children) have completed high school than at earlier points in the child's development (Emery, 1998; Hetherington et al., 1998; Hetherington, Stanley-Hagan, & Anderson, 1989).

Beyond Individual Trajectories: The Dyad and Family As Developmental Units of Analysis. As authors throughout this volume show, it is critical to take account of the dyads that can compose families. In families with more than one parent, these could include the parenting dyads (e.g., each partner with the child), sibling dyads, and the adult partner dyad. In addition, there is now substantial evidence that these dyadic subsystems are interdependent (Parke & O'Neil, 2000). For example, the quality of the husband–wife relationship has been regularly linked to the quality of parenting (Cummings & Davies, 1994). Sensitively tracing how shifts in the quality of one dyadic subsystem lead to shifts in other dyadic units remains a continuing challenge for parenting researchers (see Kreppner, chap. 8, this volume).

Finally, families as units change across development and respond to change as units. Little is known about the ways different types of family units connect with parenting units. Several theorists (Boss, 1983; Reiss, 1981; Sameroff, 1994) have proposed useful typologies of families as units of analysis. Reiss, for example, has outlined various family paradigms, each guided by a set of enduring assumptions about the social world that are shared by all family members. Differences in paradigms, in turn, are related to the extent to which families seek outside help for their problems and to their views of the social world as ordered or chaotic. Virtually no data are available concerning how parenting is differently linked to variations in family paradigms. This is an area ripe for future research.

Normative and Nonnormative Transitions. A life-course perspective underscores the importance of distinguishing normative and nonnormative transitions. Normative transitions that affect parenting include events such as the parent's reentry into the workplace and the entry of children into day-care or school contexts. In contrast to traditional views that families follow a scripted and stage-like course (e.g., Hill & Rodgers, 1964; Waller, 1938), a life-course view recognizes that the timing of these normative events can dramatically alter the effect of these transitions (Elder, 1984, 1998). The timing of the onset of parenthood can alter the course of marital relationships and the quality of parenting itself (see Bradbury, 1998, for review). Early- and late-timed parenthood has different implications for role distributions between couples. As Daniels and Weingarten (1982) have found, late-timed parents are more likely to share household and child-care responsibilities more equally. Moreover, early- and late-timed parents follow different work trajectories. Late-timed mothers are more likely to follow a pattern of parenting followed by a return to work. The implications of these patterns on parenting relationships over time merit examination. Similarly, the effect of children's normative transitions on parenting merit attention. The transition to elementary school may alter women's work patterns, which, in turn, may alter the nature of parent–child relationships because of the parents' reduced availability necessitated by increased job commitments. The transitions to puberty, junior high school, and college all represent potential emotional and financial stressors that may affect parenting.

A life-course view underscores not only the idiosyncratic patterns of timing of entry into various normative transitions, but also the importance of nonnormative transitions. The effect of nonnormative transitions, such as unemployment on parenting, has a long history. Elder's (1974) classic work on the effect of the Great Depression on family functioning illustrated how nonnormative events can alter the parent–child relationship. Similarly, Conger and Elder's (1994) more recent work on the effect of the Midwest farm crisis on parenting provided further illustration of what unanticipated and nonscripted events can do to the parent–child relationship. In both cases, stress led to increases in parental depression and in harsh and inconsistent parenting. More work is needed to chart how such events play out across time in parent–child relationships, with children at various stages of development.

Several theorists have provided useful dimensional analysis of stressful events along dimensions such as predictability, intensity, duration, and controllability (Moos & Schaefer, 1986; Parke & Beitel, 1988). Many stressful events, such as the birth of a preterm baby, residential mobility, and death of a family member, merit careful consideration. Do these disparate life stressors trigger similar or different parenting effects? A better understanding of how parents cope with different types of stressful events will ultimately provide a richer understanding of the determinants of the developmental course of parenting.

Little attention has been paid to the role of child-centered nonnormative transitions or unexpected life events on parent–child relationships. Drug or alcohol use, school failure, and childhood accidents are all nonnormative events that bear scrutiny for their effect on parenting. In recent years, an increasing number of adult children have been returning home (see Minuchin, chap. 9, this volume). What effect does this unexpected event have on marital and parent–child relationships? This question is of conceptual interest because it reminds us of the potential effect of child events on parenting, and vice versa. Clearly, there are bidirectional effects across generations that can be exaggerated by certain types of child transitions.

Finally, the interplay between normative and nonnormative transitions merits more attention. Do parents react differently when normative and nonnormative events co-occur? For example, the cumulative effect of several sources of stressful change, such as the birth of an infant and the loss of a job, is not well understood. Cumulative stress theories warrant more attention from parenting researchers (Rutter, 1987; Sameroff, 1994).

How does a focus on transitions affect the longitudinal study of parenting? This perspective has major implications for such studies in that it helps investigators select appropriate time points for follow-up evaluations in their design of a longitudinal project. Time alone is unlikely to always be the best basis for selecting retest points in a study. And although age may be of some value for children, adult age per se is less likely to be a particularly helpful guideline. Rather, a focus on normative and nonnormative transitions might be expected to provide a more useful set of guidelines for selecting time points for follow-up (Fine & Kurdek, 1994; Parke, 1994).

Although the focus on transitions as an organizer for longitudinal work is well understood and generally accepted, the related issue concerning how soon after the transition to seek effects is less clear. What are the meaningful break points in substantiating and reporting follow-up effects? In the final analysis, we are going to need a better set of theories about the temporal course of change in parent–child relationships if we are to provide useful guidelines to investigators about the most appropriate time points likely to be sensitive to the earlier event. Real progress awaits better theories that integrate our descriptive data.

RETHINKING THE ROLE OF GENDER
IN PARENTING

In this section I consider several issues concerning the role of gender in parenting. First, I offer my perspective on the question of whether mothers and fathers are redundant or whether they make unique contributions to children's development. Second, I ask whether biological fathers are unique relative to nonbiological fathers. Third, I consider whether fathers play a unique role relative to other members of the household. Finally, I review studies pertinent to whether both fathers and mothers are necessary for "optimal development" or whether two individuals of the same gender can raise children with equally optimal outcome. The debate about the "essential father" was raised by Silverstein and Auerbach (1999) and in thoughtful review again by Silverstein (chap. 2, this volume), but it can easily be extended to debates about the "essential mother" as well.

Are Mothers and Fathers Redundant?

Research with western, Anglo families has taught us that mothers and fathers make both unique and overlapping contributions to children's development (Lamb, 1997; Parke, 1996). In the "big picture," parenting involves certain basic functions, such as protection, nurturance, and instruction. Both parents, regardless of gender, can and usually do contribute to the fulfillment of these functions. At the same time, mothers and fathers in two-parent nuclear families assume distinctive roles. Normatively, fathers and mothers in such families distribute their time with children differently. In spite of the rhetoric about social changes in gender roles, mothers still spend more time in caregiving relative to fathers; in turn, men are more likely to spend a greater proportion of their discretionary time with children in play and recreational activities (Coltrane, 1996; Parke, 1996). One of the major challenges of the next decade will be to carefully monitor these patterns to determine if continual changes in roles of males and females in the workplace lead to increased homogenization of roles in parenting (Parke & Brott, 1999).

Critical to the debate concerning the distinctiveness of mother and father roles is the effect of biological factors as provocateurs to the roles that males and females assume (see Silverstein, chap. 2, this volume). One intriguing set of findings is that male monkeys show the same rough-and-tumble style of play as do human fathers who have been studied (Parke & Suomi, 1981). Augmenting this finding is evidence indicating that male monkeys also tend to respond more positively to bids for rough-and-tumble play than do females (Meany, Stewart, & Beatty, 1985). Maccoby (1988) posited that "perhaps (both monkey and human) males may be more susceptible to being aroused into states of positive excitement and unpredictability than females" (p. 761), speculation that is consistent with gender differences in risk taking and sensation seeking (Zuckerman, 1991). In addition, human males, whether boys or men, tend to behave more boisterously and show more positive emotional expressions and reactions than do females (Charlesworth & Dzur, 1987). Together, these pieces of the puzzle necessitate our remaining open to the possibility that predisposing biological differences between males and females play some role in the play-recreational patterns of mothers and fathers.

Do Fathers Play a Unique Role Relative to Nonbiological Fathers?

Stepparent data reveal less adequate child outcomes for stepfathers than for biological fathers. However, there is enormous variability both in the internal dynamics of stepfamilies and in terms of how well children fare with nonbiological fathers (Hetherington et al., 1998). As Amato (1993) noted, "We get a very different picture dependent upon whether we emphasize central tendency (which leads us to conclude that children in stepfamilies are worse off) or dispersion (which leads us to conclude that substantial overlap exists in the outcomes for children in different family structures)"

(p. 36). Traditionalists consistently focus on the differences in central tendency, whereas nontraditionalists consistently focus on the overlap in distributions. Both lenses are correct, of course, but no simple conclusion is warranted. Even the controversial evidence of Daly and Wilson (1996) that child homicide rates are higher for stepfathers has proven open to challenge. Malkin and Lamb (1994) found that it was biological parents who were more likely than nonbiological parents to severely abuse or kill their children, rather than to cause them major physical injuries. Children appear to be at greater risk for abuse in stepfamilies, but the risks do not necessarily come from the stepparent (Sternberg, 1997).

Do Fathers Play a Unique Role Relative to Other Members of the Household?

Some data indicate that children exhibit fewer problems if a second adult, regardless of whether this adult is a father or father figure, resides in the household, especially if the person is a grandmother (Kellam, Ensminger, & Turner, 1977; Stolba & Amato, 1993). Other, more recent data suggest that children in grandmother-single parent families may not fare so well, in part because of intergenerational conflict between caregivers (Chase-Landsdale & Brooks-Gunn, 1995). Some data suggest that regardless of household composition, fathers play a unique family role such that even after controlling for the number of adults in the household, fathers continue to exhibit a unique effect on children's development (Pedersen, 1980). At this point, it seems safest to conclude that the data are unclear about the uniqueness or distinctiveness of fathers (Silverstein, chap. 2, this volume; Silverstein & Auerbach, 1999).

Gay and Lesbian Couples: What Do We Know About How Children in These Same Sex Households Fare?

Although the evidence is still limited, the recent research on the development of children in gay and lesbian families is another way to assess the uniqueness and necessity of rearing children in homes with both male and female parents. Silverstein has framed this debate in a provocative but helpful way by questioning whether fathers are essential for the successful socialization of children (Silverstein, chap. 2, this volume; Silverstein & Auerbach, 1999). Part of the evidence for her skepticism about the essential father stems from recent work by Patterson and her colleagues indicating that the development of children raised by lesbian and gay parents is well within normal limits (Patterson, 1995; Patterson & Chan, 1997). Recent work by Flaks, Ficher, Masterpasqua, and Joseph (1995) substantiates this picture: Children in heterosexual and lesbian families were not very different in terms of their developmental outcomes. These data are heartening. At the same time, it seems premature to conclude that fathers are replaceable based on this evidence. Studies have relied largely on small samples of highly educated individuals in stable relationships. Furthermore, two other key issues need to be addressed in ongoing work. More needs to be understood about the extent to which role division in lesbian families approximates role division in heterosexual families, and more needs to be understood about the degree to which lesbian couples expose their children to male role models. In the first case, evidence suggests that lesbian couples share household tasks and decision-making responsibilities more equally than do heterosexual couples (Patterson, 1995). At the same time, however, lesbian biological mothers viewed their parental role as more salient than either nonbiological lesbian mothers or heterosexual mothers (Hand, 1991). Moreover, despite the more egalitarian divisions of household labor in lesbian households, there also exists some traditionality in roles, as well. Biological lesbian mothers are more involved in child care than are their partners; nonbiological lesbian mothers spent more time working outside the family (Patterson). This raises the possibility that even in same-gender families, the usual role division concerning child care, which characterizes heterosexual partnerships, may be evident. Whether the nonbiological mothers enact other aspects of more traditional male roles, such as a physical play style, remains to be established. In short, children may be afforded opportunities to experience both maternal and paternal interactive styles in same gender households.

Parents have increasingly been recognized as managers of their children's social environments (Furstenberg, Cook, Eccles, Elder, & Sameroff, 1999; Parke & Bhavnagri, 1989). In this role, they can choose to deliberately expand their children's range of experiences with male figures. At this point, we simply do not have extensive data on how much exposure children raised by lesbian couples have to males outside the family, or whether lesbian mothers intentionally provide this exposure as a means of compensating for the absence of a male figure in the household. Moreover, nothing is known about the duration and frequency necessary to confer any of the potential developmental advantage of exposure to adults of both genders, if indeed such an advantage were one day shown to exist. Perhaps most fundamentally, we lack data on the kind of relationship needed if exposure were to prove helpful.

Although the amount of research on the effects of being reared by two male parents is even more limited than the work on two female parents, the few available data suggest the gender identities of children of gay fathers are similar to those of children of heterosexual fathers (Bailey, Bobrow, Wolfe, & Mikach, 1995). Moreover, as Bozett (1987) reported, the relationships that children develop with their gay fathers are positive. One important challenge faced by children of gay parents, however, is their possible stigmatization by others. An issue that requires concerted attention in this debate is the role of social norms and attitudes toward children growing up in same-gender, child-rearing unions. Beyond the theoretical plausibility of successful adaptation of this type of child-rearing arrangements, our field needs to devote more attention to the level of societal acceptance of these family types as a critical factor that can either facilitate or disrupt the successful adaption children in these families (Patterson & Chan, 1997). Intensive case studies and first-hand accounts of the experience of two men raising children together, such as that found in Green's (1999) book, *The Velveteen Father: An Unexpected Journey to Parenthood*, will also be important.

As is true of lesbian parents, gay parents are more likely than heterosexual couples to share child-rearing duties evenly (McPherson, 1993). More information about the observed and self-reported parenting of gay fathers, such as that provided by Silverstein (chap. 2, this volume), is needed, as well as assessments of the effect of these child-rearing arrangements on the children (Patterson & Chan, 1997). Just as Silverstein and Auerbach (1999) have questioned the essential father, these data on the effects of being reared by gay male parents raise a similar question about the essential mother. As in the case of lesbian couples, an open question concerns the extent to which gay couples provide differential exposure to "maternal" or feminine models and opportunities for interaction with female partners. And, of course, the larger question is whether this exposure, after controlling for parent effects, makes a difference in child outcomes. Recent work on adult mentors confirms conventional wisdom and past research on nonparental adult influence: The effect of nonfamilial mentors on adolescents' social behavior is independent of the effect of parent–child relationships (Greenberger, Chen, & Beam, 1998).

Alternatively, as Silverstein (chap. 2, this volume) suggests, our focus on the gender of the parent may be too narrow a conceptualization of the issue. Instead, it may be helpful to recast the issue to ask whether exposure to males and females is the key, or whether it is exposure to the interactive style typically associated with either mothers or fathers that matters. A study by Ross and Taylor (1989) is relevant. They found that boys prefer the "paternal" play style, whether it is mothers or fathers who engage in the physical and active stimulation. Their work suggests boys may not necessarily prefer their fathers but rather their physical style of play. In another body of work relevant to this issue, fathers and mothers reversed their customary roles (Radin, 1993). In this case, the primary caregiving functions typically fulfilled by women were undertaken by men. Evidence from both the United States (Field, 1978) and Australia (Russell, 1984) suggests that the style of interaction of primary-caregiver fathers is more like primary-caregiver mothers. For example, primary-caregiver fathers smiled more and imitated their babies facial expression and high-pitched vocalizations more than secondary-caregiver fathers (Field). Similarly, Russell found that role-sharing fathers engaged in a less stereotypically masculine style of parenting and instead exhibited a more maternal interactive style (e.g., more indoor recreational activities and less exclusive focus on roughhousing and outdoor games). Finally, Israeli primary-caregiver fathers were more nurturant as reported by both themselves and their children relative to traditional fathers (Sagi, 1982). Together, this evidence indicates that the style of parenting and the gender of the parent who delivers or enacts this style can be viewed as at least partially independent. These types of data will help us eventually address the uniqueness of fathers' and mothers' roles in the family and in their children's development, and they will help provide needed clarity on the important issue of how essential fathers and mothers are for children's development (Silverstein & Auerbach, 1999).

Finally, in keeping with my earlier commentary on historical and cultural change, the increase in families with gay and lesbian parents can be viewed as a series of natural experiments that offer an opportunity to explore the validity of our assumptions about the critical ingredients that define successful parenting. Just as the increase in the use of day care due to the rise in women's employment has permitted valuable tests of certain important tenets of attachment theory (Lamb, 1998), so too should careful studies of same-gender child-rearing arrangements be viewed as unique opportunities for testing our theories about links between gender and parenting.

THE EFFECT OF THE NEW REPRODUCTIVE TECHNOLOGIES ON PARENTING: A CHALLENGE FOR THIS MILLENNIUM

Just as we saw the range of parenting arrangements expand in the 1990s, in this new millennium the routes to parenthood promise to be increasingly diverse. New reproductive technologies are expanding the ways individuals become parents. Recent changes in childbearing include in-vitro fertilization, anonymous and nonanonymous sperm donors, and surrogate mothers (Rodin & Collins, 1991). Djerassi (1999) recently argued that just as "technology's gift to women (and men) during the latter half of the 20th century was contraception, the first 50 years of the new millennium may well be considered the decades of conception" (p. 53).

Various scenarios that may alter our usual ways of conceptualizing families and parenthood are possible. Assisted reproductive technology (ART), including in-vitro fertilization, has produced over 300,000 babies since 1977. Several recent studies have examined the psychological adjustment of children conceived by donor insemination. Although these studies have focused on child outcomes and not on parenting, they nonetheless raise important questions about parent–child relationships in these new technology-assisted families. In Great Britain, Golombok and her colleagues (Golombok, Cook, Bish, & Murray, 1995; Tasker & Golombok, 1997) found no differences in the functioning of children born via donor insemination compared with children in the general population, a finding recently confirmed in the United States by Chan, Raboy, and Patterson (1998). Chan et al. reported that children who had been conceived by artificial insemination were developing normally; moreover, the family interactions and processes that were studied in these families were related to children's outcomes in ways akin to those found in earlier studies of normally conceived children. For example, among two-parent families, regardless of parental gender, "children were rated as better adjusted when their parents reported greater relationship satisfaction, higher levels of love and lower interparental conflict" (Chan et al., p. 453). Neither structural variables nor parental sexual orientation nor the number of parents in the household predicted adjustment. Unfortunately, there was no comparison group of children of nondonor births in this study. As a result, we still have much to learn about the implications for parents or the parent–child relationships of these technology-based conceptions.

Evidence suggests that the sexual orientation of the parents who raise a donor-based child does not make a difference in the child's adjustment. However, we do not know whether important issues such as the disclosure of identity of donors or donor involvement with the family interact with family structural variables (e.g., lesbian or gay versus heterosexual partnerships). Other questions remain as well. Does it make a difference if the identity of the donor is known or unknown? What is the effect of disclosing or not disclosing the nature of the child's conception to the child? What is the effect of disclosing or keeping confidential the identity of the male donor? Does the availability of the male to the child after the birth make a difference in the child's adjustment? Are patterns of parent–child relationships different in couples who have achieved parenthood through in-vitro fertilization after a long period of infertility? Do such parents develop closer relationships with their children? Are they overprotective of their offspring? It would also be important to understand how the partner–partner relationship is altered by this sequence leading to parenthood.

A variant on the new assisted reproductive technology is the increased use of surrogate mothers. This innovation raises questions about the effect of this choice on parent–parent, parent–child, and couple–surrogate mother relationships. Again, issues of disclosure arise as in the case of in-vitro fertilization. Is there any meaningful developmental effect of the child's learning she was born via a surrogate mother? Should the child know the identity of the surrogate mother? What are the implications of contact between the surrogate mother and the child for the child's adjustment? What is the effect of continuing contact between the surrogate mother and the child-rearing family on the parent–parent relationship? Our scientific knowledge about these issues is still limited, though there is an accumulating and thoughtful clinical literature that can serve as a guide for research in this area and as a helpful map for practitioners and policy and legal scholars (see Paulson & Sachs, 1999; Robertson, 1994).

Other developments may have equal or greater implications for future conceptualization of parenting, namely the development of intracytoplasmic sperm injection (ICSI; Palermo, Joris, Devroey, and van Steirteghem, 1992). This procedure allows the fertilization of a human egg by direct injection of a single sperm under the microscope. This is followed by reintroduction of the fertilized egg back into the woman's uterus. Since 1992, more than 10,000 babies have been born as a result of this new conception technology (Djerassi, 1999). Moreover, this procedure raises issues that future scholars of parenting are going to have to consider. Genetically infertile men could become fathers using this new technology. But other uses are more complex. For example, the sperm of deceased men may be used (through ICSI) to produce a child at a later time. A woman may conceive a child at a much older age, which raises important questions about the effect of timing of the onset of parenthood on parent–child relationships. However, because of the increased longevity of women, a woman in her 40s could raise a child at least as long as a 20-year-old in the early 1900s (Djerassi). Our definition of natural and unnatural in regard to the age at which parenting should begin is challenged by these new advances in reproductive technology. Similarly, our definition of parenthood is becoming divorced from biology and instead is a socially constructed category. As Turner (1999) recently commented, "A few decades ago one could have only two biological parents: now a child can have five or six 'parents', sperm donor, egg donor, surrogate mother, and commissioning couple" (p. 14).

As Andrews (1999) argued, one of the most profound technological advances is human cloning. This will permit not merely the production of a new, unique individual, as with other reproductive technologies, but an individual who is a copy of an existing person. Turner (1999) raised the provocative but conceivable scenario, "What will happen when a middle aged father is confronted by an adult 'daughter' who perfectly resembles the young woman he married 20 years before?" (p. 14). Challenges to our conceptions of individuality, identity, and parenting are raised by these new possibilities. To understand the effect of these new technological advances on our social understanding of parenting and kinship relations is one of the major issues we will face in this century.

LOCATING FAMILIES IN A NETWORK
OF SOCIALIZATION INFLUENCES

A major challenge remaining for our field is to determine the unique contribution of families to socialization outcomes and the limits of family effects (Harris, 1995). As Maccoby and Martin (1983) argued in their review of the relations between parental functioning and characteristics of children, "In most cases the relationships that have appeared are not large, if one thinks in terms of the amount of variance accounted for" (p. 82). Their conclusion is still valid, if we assume a narrow view of family influence as the direct effect of parents on their children. However, our increased recognition of the family as a partner with other institutions, such as peers, schools, media, religious institutions, and government policymakers, that influence children's development has significantly expanded our view of the family's role in the socialization process. It suggests the family, directly and indirectly, may have a greater effect on children's outcomes than previously thought. As Parke and his colleagues have argued, families serve not just as direct influences on children but also as indirect influences as managers, mediators, and negotiators on behalf of children in relation to these social institutions (Parke & O'Neil, 2000). Families serve as important gatekeepers and facilitators of opportunities to interact with others outside the family (Furstenberg et al., 1999; Parke, Burks, Carson, Neville, & Boyum, 1994).

The failure to recognize this critical managerial aspect of parenting has led to the oversimplified argument that peers, not parents, are the most important socialization influences in children's development (Harris, 1998). Examined critically, however, this argument fails to recognize not only that children's peer relationships are shaped by the quality of early and ongoing relationships between parents and children, but also that they are influenced by the regulatory guidance through monitoring and supervision that parents provide their children. Peers become important as the child develops, but the early parent–child relationship as well as concurrent parental managerial effectiveness are critical determinants of both the amount and quality of peer influence. Prior work on early and late starter models (Caspi, 1998; Patterson, DeBarshyshe, & Ramsey, 1989) has helped clarify these linkages. Such studies have suggested that early poor relationships in families often lead to potentially antisocial and maladaptive social relationships with teachers and peers and a higher probability of associating with deviant peer groups. In contrast, children who have had a positive set of early family experiences, though just as likely to engage in adolescent experimentation (e.g., drugs, sex), are less likely than early starters to develop habitual antisocial patterns as adolescents.

Unfortunately, our understanding of the ways families influence their children's socialization through their links with other institutions is still poorly understood. Moreover, these agents and institutions (e.g., schools, peers, and so on) play a direct as well as indirect role through the family in the socialization process. Several issues need to be addressed. What are the unique roles that families play in socialization? It seems likely that some kinds of outcomes are specifically due to the family, such as the development of early social attachments, whereas others are influenced largely by other groups such as peers and friends (e.g., tastes in music and fashion). More comprehensive models are needed to chart the relative role of family and other agents at various points in development. Perhaps the most interesting question concerns the ways families coordinate their socialization roles with other agents and institutions. Successful socialization requires a gradual opening up of the family and sharing of responsibility for socialization with other groups. However, we know relatively little about this process of coordination and mutual sharing across socialization agents. It is not helpful to continue to posit linear models of decreasing family influence across development. Instead, we need models that help us understand the changing nature of family influence relative to other groups and the mechanisms that maintain family values and orientation after direct influence has subsided.

Recent work on the intergenerational transmission of working models of relationships (Thompson, 1998) testifies to the prolonged influence of childhood socialization on later adult parenting roles. In fact, this work has anticipated one of the major themes of future research: the effect of childhood socialization patterns on later adult development, not just in parenting, but in other types of adult relationships including marital, friendship, and work relationships. Closely related is the issue of how families and other institutions are linked. Recent work has focused on family–peer linkages (Parke et al., 1994), family–work ties (Crouter, 1994), and family–school relationships (Kellam, 1994), but less attention has been devoted to links between the family and religious institutions, or between the family and legal and social service systems. Moreover, the processes that promote or constrain family involvement with other institutions are not well understood. Finally, the bidirectional nature of the linkage needs more attention so we understand the dynamic and mutual influence of families on other institutions and vice versa. This call for a contextualized view of parenting contrasts with more traditional models that locate the critical factors within the parent (e.g., preferences, beliefs, motivations). Both intraindividual and contextual factors need to be incorporated into our models of parenting.

TOWARD A MULTIMETHOD APPROACH
TO UNDERSTANDING PARENTING

Multiple Methods Are Necessary for Understanding Parenting

Psychologists and other social scientists are using multiple methodological approaches in their studies of parents. Although self-reports of parenting continue to be important sources of information about parental beliefs, attitudes, and expectations, observational methods remain the central approach in the psychologists' methodological armature (Holden, 1997; Parke, 1978). For studies of process, the strategy continues to be the best approach. Observational studies of the interaction patterns of fathers and partners and children, or both, have provided important insights into the nature of the affective and social processes that characterize these relationships. Two examples illustrate. In the first example, Carson and Parke (1996) found that reciprocity of negative affect (anger) was characteristic of the interaction patterns of fathers with sons, who in turn were rejected by their peers. The discovery of the nature of the interactive exchange between fathers and children could not have been achieved with other methods. In the second example, infants, under conditions of uncertainty, often turn to their parents for guidance. This phenomenon, called *social referencing*, has been well documented in the infancy literature (Saarni, 1999). Dickstein and Parke (1988) found that fathers in unhappy marriages are less likely to be the targets of social referencing by their infants than fathers in happy marriages. This study illustrates the effect of marital relationships on the father–infant relationship in the first year of life. Moreover, it is again unlikely that this subtle effect of the marriage on infant behavior would have been uncovered without sensitive observational methods. The establishment of this phenomenon then opens the door to more detailed investigations of how marital distress comes to influence infant behavior, sparking studies of maternal gatekeeping and other multiperson processes (Bietel & Parke, 1998).

Reflecting on Sampling: Issues in Psychological Studies of Parenting

It is important to underscore the value of process-oriented studies of parenting, whether based on observational or self-report methods, because they are often dismissed by other social scientists as small-scale studies, implying the sample sizes typical of these studies are too small to draw meaningful conclusions. Furthermore, it is often claimed that the samples are generally nonrepresentative of the general population. In fact, small-scale studies are often replicated both within and across labs. This replication strategy is important for two reasons. First, it increases confidence in the findings by showing the effects are robust across replications. Many times the replications involve variations in procedure and setting, allowing the robustness of the effect to be more meaningfully established. For example, Boyum and Parke (1995) found a relation between paternal negative affect directed toward children and their poor relationship with peers similar to the one Carson and Parke (1996) reported. However, in contrast to the structured lab play context used in the Carson and Parke study, observations in the Boyum and Parke investigation took place at home during a regular family dinner.

The second reason replications across laboratories are important is that they serve as a partial corrective to the nonrepresentativeness of convenience samples. When investigators in rural conservative Pennsylvania, urban liberal Berkeley, California, and central impoverished Baltimore produce similar findings, greater faith in the generalizability of the findings is warranted (e.g., Belsky & Isabella, 1985; Cowan & Cowan, 1992).

At the same time, there is a movement toward multistage sampling approaches that combine the benefits of gaining a more representative sample and retaining the advantages of observationally based work. Recent examples include the Hetherington, Reiss, and Plomin (1994) study of the effects of nonshared environments in stepfamilies. After employing a representative national sampling strategy, these investigators subsequently videotaped the interactions of mothers, fathers, and their adolescents. Although expensive and time intensive, this multimethod strategy goes a long way to resolving the issues involved. A more modest application of this approach was used by Bietel and Parke (1998) in their study of maternal gatekeeping. A large sample ($N = 300$) of mothers was surveyed concerning their attitudes toward the levels of paternal involvement, and a subsample of this larger group was chosen for observational analyses.

**Qualitative and Quantitative Approaches
Are Both Useful**

As I noted earlier, other methods that are increasingly recognized as useful are focus groups, which can help define the issues of importance for fathers (and mothers) in less studied groups such as individual from other cultures or subcultural groups within the United States. Focus groups are commonly used in other disciplines but have less often used been by psychologists. A focus group is a type of group interview that relies on an emergent process of interaction between group members to produce data and insights not otherwise found without such interaction (Morgan, 1988). Focus groups are excellent forums in which to explore the microlevel of family experiences as well as to examine similarities and differences across different genders, socioeconomic classes, and ethnic groups (for application of this approach to studies of fathers, see Silverstein, chap. 2, this volume; Silverstein & Auerbach, 1999). These groups provide a unique opportunity for parents and children to articulate their concerns, values, and goals in a context that is less constrained than the usual interview format. This technique is of particular value in the early stages of research with understudied populations (see Erkut et al., 1999, for illustrations of the use of focus groups with African American and Hispanic American groups). In a recent study of the effects of economic downturn on Latino families (Gomel, Tinsley, Clark, & Parke, 1998), a focus group strategy was used. This proved useful at the beginning of the process of selecting variables, refining study questions, and assessing the cultural equivalence of instruments. As Rutter (chap. 11, this volume) points out, qualitative and quantitative approaches are not incompatible. Quantitative analytic strategies have recently become available for use with the type of qualitative verbal reports generated by focus groups. Recent computer programs (e.g., Nudist program, or 3.3, the Non-numerical Unstructured Data Indexing, Searching and Theory building) allow researchers to explore patterns in the data, which aid in grounded theory construction, and to simultaneously apply a coding scheme to the transcript text and to convert the coded text into quantitative information. Ethnographic methodologies play an important role in family research as well, particularly in gaining a better understanding of contextual factors that affect parental functioning (see Burton, 1995).

Are Nonexperimental Techniques Sufficient?

Reliance on nonexperimental strategies may be insufficient to study the direction of effects of parents, especially fathers, on children and families (Parke, 1995). Experimental studies have been underused in studies of fathers. By experimentally modifying either a parent's level of involvement or style of interaction, researchers should be able to draw firmer conclusions about the direct causative role parents play in modifying both their children's and their partner's development. These experimental approaches can assume various forms, from parenting classes to more delimited efforts aimed at modifying a particular style of interaction (e.g., reducing punitiveness and increasing positive parenting approaches; see, for example, Lamb, 1997). These experimental studies can be undertaken for several reasons. Although their goal is often to increase levels of parental involvement in the hope of improving the child's life chances, a second central but often neglected advantage of experimental interventions is that they can provide a test of a theoretical position (McBride, 1991; Parke, Power, & Gottman, 1979). We need to remain cognizant that intervention, often viewed as an applied issue, and theory testing, often viewed as a basic research issue, are compatible. In fact, one could argue that the intervention strategies most likely to yield the highest payoff in terms of efficacy are theory based. Experimental interventions can assume various forms and can be guided by the multilevel scheme outlined previously. Individual interventions aimed at modifying parenting attitudes, beliefs, and behaviors represent only one level of analysis. At the dyadic level, interventions targeting the marital couple or a spouse who is high in gatekeeping would provide a test of the importance of dyadic factors in determining father involvement. Other types of experimental interventions could involve targeting neither individuals nor dyads alone, but rather links across contexts. These might include programs that provide opportunities for parents to become involved in the activities of child-centered institutions (e.g., schools) by forming partnerships with fathers and mothers (Epstein, 1989). As Silverstein (chap. 2, this volume) notes, another experimental intervention in need of study and refinement is the degree to which changes in the workplace (flextime, leave, reductions in job stress) affect (or fail to affect) fathering behavior or involvement (Levine & Pittinsky, 1998).

In terms of research design, thanks to the influence of behavior geneticists (Plomin, 1994; Plomin & Rutter, 1998; Rowe, 1994), we have seen an increased focus on nonshared environmental designs, which allow measurement of the differential effect of families on different children within the same family (see also Rutter, chap. 11, this volume). Although some have argued for the decreased use of traditional between family designs, which still form the foundation of most of our knowledge of family effects (Plomin, 1994), others (e.g., Hoffman, 1991) have argued for the continued utility of both types of designs to help uncover, for example, "what environmental conditions might lead to sibling similarity and dissimilarity" (Hoffman, 1991, p. 199). More conceptual work is needed to provide guidelines concerning the value of within- and between-family designs for different variables and issues.

CONCLUSION

As Coles (1999) recently noted, "Time holds its mysteries and the future resists our easy grasp, however anxious we be to assert it conclusively" (p. 27). So it is in the case of parenting. However, as I argue in this chapter, reflections on our past progress in unlocking the secrets of parenting suggests some guides for future research and policy decisions. By embracing a view of parenting that recognizes developmental, ecological, historical, and technological possibilities and constraints, we will continue to make substantial progress in our search for understanding both the processes and possibilities of parenting in this new century. By increasing our understanding of parenting in all of its variations, we will not only be better positioned to provide better support and guidance for parents, but we will in the long run benefit our children as well. Few goals could be more important.

REFERENCES

Amato, P. (1993). Children's adjustment to divorce: Theories, hypotheses and empirical support. *Journal of Marriage and Family, 55*, 23–38.

Andrews, L. B. (1999). *The clone age: Adventures in the new world of reproductive technology.* New York: Holt.

Bailey, J. M., Bobrow, D., Wolfe, M., & Mikach, S. (1995). Sexual orientation of adult sons of gay fathers. *Developmental Psychology, 31*, 124–129.

Baldwin, A. L., Baldwin, C., & Cole, R. E. (1990). Stress-resistant families and stress-resistant children. In J. E. Rolf & A. S. Masten (Eds.), *Risk and protective factors in the development of psychopathology* (pp. 257–280). New York: Cambridge University Press.

Bell, R. Q. (1968). A re-interpretation of the direction of effects in studies of socialization. *Psychological Review, 75*, 81–95.

Belsky, J., & Isabella, R. (1985). Marital and parent–child relationships in family of origin and marital change following birth of a baby: A retrospective analysis. *Child Development, 56*, 342–349.

Betancourt, H., & Lopez, S. R. (1993). The study of culture, ethnicity, and race in American psychology. *American Psychologist, 48*, 629–637.

Bietel, A., & Parke, R. D. (1998). Maternal and paternal attitudes as determinants of father involvement. *Journal of Family Psychology, 12*, 268–288.

Bornstein, M. H. (Ed.). (1991). *Cultural approaches to parenting.* Hillsdale, NJ: Lawrence Erlbaum Associates.

Boss, P. G. (1983). The marital relationship: Boundaries and ambiguities. In H. I. McCubbin & C. R. Figley (Eds.), *Stress and the family* (Vol. 1, pp. 26–40). New York: Brunner/Mazel.

Boyum, L., & Parke, R. D. (1995). Family emotional expressiveness and children's social competence. *Journal of Marriage and the Family, 57*, 593–608.

Bozett, F. W. (1987). Children of gay fathers. In F. W. Bozett (Ed.), *Gay and lesbian parents* (pp. 39–57). New York: Praeger.

Bradbury, T. (Ed.). (1998). *The developmental course of marital dysfunction.* New York: Cambridge University Press.

Burton, L. M. (1995). Intergenerational patterns of providing care in African-American families with teenage childbearers: Emergent patterns in an ethnographic study. In V. L. Bengston & K. W. Schaie (Eds.), *Adult intergenerational relations: Effects of societal change* (pp. 79–125). New York: Springer Publishing.

Carson, J., & Parke, R. D. (1996). Reciprocal negative affect in parent–child interactions and children's peer competency. *Child Development, 67*, 2217–2226.

Caspi, A. (1998). Personality development across the life course. In W. Damon (Ed.), *Handbook of child psychology* (5th ed., Vol. 3, pp. 311–388). New York: Wiley.

Chan, R. W., Raboy, B., & Patterson, C. J. (1998). Psychosocial adjustment among children conceived via donor insemination by lesbian and heterosexual mothers. *Child Development, 69*, 443–457.

Chao, R. K. (1994). Beyond parental control and authoritarian parenting style: Understanding Chinese parenting through the cultural notion of training. *Child Development, 65*, 1111–1119.

Charlesworth, W. R., & Dzur, C. (1987). Gender comparisons of preschoolers' behavior and resource utilization in group problem solving. *Child Development, 58*, 191–200.

Chase-Lansdale, P. L., & Brooks-Gunn, J. (Eds.). (1995). *Escape from poverty: What makes a difference for children?* New York: Cambridge University Press.

Coles, R. (1999, Oct. 10). Make room for daddies: Review of J. Green's The velveteen father. *New York Times Book Review,* p. 27.

Collins, W. A., & Repinski, D. J. (in press). Parents and adolescents as transformers of relationships: Dyadic adaptations to developmental change. In J. Gerris (Ed.), *Dynamics of parenting: International perspectives.* Mahwah, NJ: Lawrence Erlbaum Associates.

Coltrane, S. (1996). *Family man.* New York: Oxford University Press.

Conger, R., & Elder, G. H. (1994). *Families in troubled times: Adapting to change in rural America.* New York: Aldine.

Cowan, C. P., & Cowan, P. A. (1992). *When partners become parents.* New York: Basic Books.

Crouter, A. C. (1994). Processes linking families and work: Implications for behavior and development in both settings. In R. D. Parke & S. Kellam (Eds.), *Exploring family relationships with other social contexts* (pp. 9–28). Hillsdale, NJ: Lawrence Erlbaum Associates.

Cummings, E. M., & Davies, P. (1994). *Children and marital conflict.* New York: Guilford.

Daly, M., & Wilson, M. (1996). Evolutionary psychology and marital conflict: The relevance of stepchildren. In D. M. Buss & N. M. Malamuth (Ed.), *Sex, power, conflict: Evolutionary and feminist perspectives* (pp. 9–28). New York: Oxford University Press.

Daniels, P., & Weingarten, K. (1982). *Sooner or later: The timing of parenthood in adult lives.* New York: Norton.

Dickstein, S., & Parke, R. D. (1988). Social referencing: A glance at fathers and marriage. *Child Development, 59,* 506–511.

Dix, T. (1991). The affective organization of parenting: Adaptive and maladaptive processes. *Psychological Bulletin, 110,* 3–25.

Djerassi, C. (1999). Sex in an age of mechanical reproduction. *Science, 285,* 53–54.

Elder, G. H. (1974). *Children of the great depression.* Chicago: University of Chicago Press.

Elder, G. H. (1984). Families, kin, and the life course: A sociological perspective. In R. D. Parke (Ed.), *Review of child development research: The family* (Vol. 7, pp. 80–136). Chicago: University of Chicago Press.

Elder, G. H. (1998). The life course and human development. In W. Damon (Ed.), *Handbook of child psychology* (Vol. 1, pp. 939–992). New York: Wiley.

Elder, G. H., Modell, J., & Parke, R. D. (Eds.). (1994). *Children in time and place.* New York: Cambridge University Press.

Emery, R. (1998). *Marriage, divorce and children's adjustment* (2nd ed.). Newberry Park, CA: Sage.

Epstein, J. L. (1989). Family structures and student motivations: A developmental perspective. In C. Ames and R. Ames (Eds.), *Research on motivation in education* (Vol. 3, pp. 259–293). New York: Academic Press.

Erikson, E. (1982). *The life cycle completed: A review.* New York: Norton.

Erkut, S., Alarcon, O., Coll, C. G., Tropp, L. R., & Garcia, H. A. V. (1999). The dual-focus approach to creating bilingual measures. *Journal of Cross-Cultural Psychology, 30,* 206–218.

Field, T. M. (1978). Interaction behaviors of primary versus secondary caretaker fathers. *Developmental Psychology, 14,* 183–185.

Fine, M. A., & Kurdek, L. A. (1994). Publishing multiple journal articles from a single data set: Issues and recommendations. *Journal of Family Psychology, 8,* 371–379.

Flaks, D. K., Ficher, I., Masterpasqua, F., & Joseph, G. (1995). Lesbians choosing motherhood: A comparative study of lesbian and heterosexual parents and their children. *Developmental Psychology, 31,* 105–114.

Flannery, W. P., Reise, S. P., & Widaman, K. F. (1995). An item response theory analysis of the general and academic scales of the Self-Description Questionnaire II. *Journal of Research in Personality, 29,* 168–188.

Furstenberg, F. F. (1993). How families manage risk and opportunity in dangerous neighborhoods. In W. J. Wilson (Ed.), *Sociology and the public agenda* (pp. 231–258). Newbury Park, CA: Sage.

Furstenberg, F. F., Cook, T. D., Eccles, J., Elder, G. H., & Sameroff, A. (1999). *Managing to make it.* Chicago: University of Chicago Press.

Gauvain, M. (1995). Thinking in niches: Sociocultural influences on cognitive development. *Human Development, 38,* 25–45.

Golombok, S., Cook, R., Bish, A., & Murray, C. (1995). Families created by the new reproductive technologies: Quality of parenting and social and emotional development of the children. *Child Development, 66,* 285–298.

Gomel, J., Tinsley, B. J., Clark, K., & Parke, R. D. (1998). The effects of economic hardship on family relationships among African-American, Latino, and Euro-American families. *Journal of Family Issues, 19,* 268–288.

Goodnow, J., & Collins, W. A. (1991). *Ideas according to parents.* Hillsdale, NJ: Lawrence Erlbaum Associates.

Green, J. (1999). *The velveteen father: An unexpected journey to parenthood.* New York: Villard Books.

Greenberger, E., Chen, C., & Beam, M. R. (1998). The role of "very important" nonparental adults in adolescent development. *Journal of Youth and Adolescence, 27,* 321–343.

Grusec, J. E., Goodnow, J. J., & Kuczynski, L. (2000). New directions in analyses of parenting contributions to children's acquisitions of values. *Child Development, 71,* 205–211.

Hand, S. I. (1991). *The lesbian parenting couple.* Unpublished doctoral dissertation. Professional School of Psychology, San Francisco.

Harris, J. R. (1995). Where is the child's environment? A group socialization theory of development. *Psychological Review, 102,* 458–489.

Harris, J. R. (1998). *The nurture assumption.* New York: Free Press.

Hetherington, E. M., Bridges, M., & Insabella, G. M. (1998). What matters? What does not? Five perspectives on the association between marital transitions and children's adjustment. *American Psychologist, 53,* 167–184.

Hetherington, E. M., Reiss, D., & Plomin, R. (Eds.). (1994). *Separate social worlds of siblings: The impact of nonshared environment on development.* Hillsdale, NJ: Lawrence Erlbaum Associates.

Hetherington, E. M., Stanley-Hagan, M. S., & Anderson, E. R. (1989). Divorce: A child's perspective. *American Psychologist, 44,* 303–312.

Hill, R., & Rodgers, R. H. (1964). The developmental approach. In H. T. Christensen (Ed.), *Handbook of marriage and the family.* Chicago: Rand McNally.

Hock, E., & DeMers, D. K. (1990). Depression in mothers of infants: The role of maternal employment. *Developmental Psychology, 26,* 285–291.

Hoffman, L. W. (1991). The influence of the family environment on personality: Accounting for sibling differences. *Psychological Bulletin, 110,* 187–203.

Holden, G. W. (1997). *Parents and the dynamics of child rearing.* Boulder, CO: Westview Press.

Kellam, S. G. (1994). The social adaptation of children in classrooms: A measure of family childrearing effectiveness. In R. D. Parke & S. Kellam (Eds.), *Exploring family relationships with other contexts* (pp. 147–168). Hillsdale, NJ: Lawrence Erlbaum Associates.

Kellam, S. G., Ensminger, M. E., & Turner, R. J. (1977). Family structure and the mental health of children: Concurrent and longitudinal community-wide studies. *Archives of General Psychiatry, 34,* 1012–1022.

Knight, G. P., Virdin, L. M., & Roosa, M. (1994). Socialization and family correlates of mental health outcomes among Hispanic and Anglo American children: Consideration of cross-ethnic scalar equivalence. *Child Development, 65,* 212–224.

Kozilius, H., Gerris, J., & Fellings, A. (in press). Exploration of mental scripts of perceptions, cognitions and emotions, explaining parenting behaviors. In J. Gerris (Ed.), *Dynamics of parenting.* Mahwah, NJ: Lawrence Erlbaum Associates.

Kuczynski, L., & Hildebradt, N. (1997). Models of conformity and resistance in socialization theory. In J. E. Grusec & L. Kuczynski (Eds.), *Parenting and the internalization of values: A handbook of contemporary theory* (pp. 227–256). New York: Wiley.

Lamb, M. E. (Ed.). (1987). *The father's role: Cross-cultural perspectives.* Hillsdale, NJ: Lawrence Erlbaum Associates.

Lamb, M. E. (Ed.). (1997). *The role of the father in child development* (3rd ed.). New York: Wiley.

Lamb, M. E. (1998). Non parental child care: Context, quality, correlates and consequences. In W. Damon (Ed.), *Handbook of child psychology* (5th ed., Vol. 4, pp. 73–134). New York: Wiley.

Leavitt, L. A., & Fox, N. A. (Eds.). (1993). *The psychological effects of war and violence on children.* Hillsdale, NJ: Lawrence Erlbaum Associates.

Levine, J., & Pittinsky, T. (1998). *Working fathers: New strategies for balancing work and family.* San Diego, CA: Harvest Books.

Lollis, S., & Kuczynski, L. (1997). Beyond one hand clapping: Seeing bidirectionality in parent–child relations. *Journal of Social and Personal Relationships, 14,* 441–461.

Maccoby, E. E. (1984). Socialization and developmental change. *Child Development, 55,* 317–328.

Maccoby, E. E. (1988). Gender as a social category. *Developmental Psychology, 24,* 755–765.

Maccoby, E. E., & Martin, J. A. (1983). Socialization in the context of the family: Parent–child interaction. In E. M. Hetherington (Ed.), *Handbook of child psychology* (Vol. 4, pp. 1–101). New York: Wiley.

Malkin, C., & Lamb, M. E. (1994). Child maltreatment: A test of sociobiological theory. *Journal of Comparative Family Studies, 25,* 121–133.

McBride, B. A. (1991). Parent education and support programs for fathers: Outcomes on paternal involvement. *Early Child Development and Care, 67,* 73–85.

McHale, J. P., & Cowan, P. A. (Eds.). (1996). *Understanding how family-level dynamics affect children's development: Studies of two-parent families.* San Francisco: Jossey-Bass.

McLoyd, V. C. (1989). Socialization and development in a changing economy: The effects of paternal job and income loss on children. *American Psychologist, 44,* 293–303.

McPherson, D. (1993). Gay parenting couples: Parenting arrangements, arrangement satisfaction, and relationship satisfaction. Unpublished doctoral dissertation, Pacific Graduate School of Psychology, San Francisco, CA.

Meany, M. J., Stewart, J., & Beatty, W. W. (1985). Sex differences in social play: The socialization of sex roles. In J. S. Rosenblatt, C. Bear, C. W. Bushnell, & P. Slater (Eds.), *Advances in the study of behavior* (Vol. 15, 1–58). New York: Academic Press.

Miller, S. A. (1988). Parents' beliefs about their children's cognitive development. *Child Development, 59,* 259–285.

Moos, R. H., & Schaefer, J. A. (1986). Life transitions and crisis: A conceptual overview. In R. H. Moos (Ed.), *Coping with life crises: An integrated approach* (pp. 3–28). New York: Plenum Press.

Morgan, D. L. (1988). *Focus groups as qualitative research.* Newbury Park, CA: Sage.

Palermo, G., Joris, H., Devroey, P., & van Steirteghem, A. C. (1992). Pregnancies after intracytoplasmic injection of single spermatozoon into an oocyte. *Lancet, 340,* 17–18.

Parke, R. D. (1978). Parent–infant interaction: Progress, paradigms, and problems. In G. P. Sackett (Ed.), *Observing behavior* (Vol. 1, pp. 69–95). Baltimore, MD: University Park Press.

Parke, R. D. (1988). Families in life-span perspective: A multi-level developmental approach. In E. M. Hetherington, R. M. Lerner, & M. Perlmutter (Eds.), *Child development in life span perspective* (pp. 159–190). Hillsdale, NJ: Lawrence Erlbaum Associates.

Parke, R. D. (1994). Multiple publications from a single data set: A challenge for researchers and editors. *Journal of Family Psychology, 8,* 384–386.

Parke, R. D. (1995). Fathers and families. In M. H. Bornstein (Ed.), *Handbook of parenting* (Vol. 3, pp. 27–63). Hillsdale, NJ: Lawrence Erlbaum Associates.

Parke, R. D. (1996). *Fatherhood.* Cambridge, MA: Harvard University Press.

Parke, R. D., & Beitel, A. (1988). Disappointment: When things go wrong in the transition to parenthood. *Marriage & Family Review, 12,* 221–265.

Parke, R. D., & Bhavnagri, N. (1989). Parents as managers of children's peer relationships. In D. Belle (Ed.), *Children's social networks and social supports* (pp. 241–259). New York: Wiley.

Parke, R. D., & Brott, A. (1999). *Throwaway dads*. Boston: Houghton-Mifflin.

Parke, R. D., & Buriel, R. (1998). Socialization in the family: Ecological and ethnic perspectives. In W. Damon (Ed.), *Handbook of child psychology* (pp. 463–552). New York: Wiley.

Parke, R. D., Burks, V., Carson, J., Neville, B., & Boyum, L. (1994). Family–peer relationships: A tripartite model. In R. D. Parke & S. Kellam (Eds.), *Advances in family research: Family relationships with other social systems* (Vol. 4, pp. 115–145). Hillsdale, NJ: Lawrence Erlbaum Associates.

Parke, R. D., & O'Neil, R. (2000). The influence of significant others on learning about relationships: From family to friends. In R. Mills & S. Duck (Eds.), *The developmental psychology of personal relationships* (pp. 15–47). London: Wiley.

Parke, R. D., Power, T. G., & Gottman, J. (1979). Conceptualizing and quantifying influence patterns in the family triad. In M. E. Lamb, S. J. Suomi, & G. R. Stephenson (Eds.), *The study of social interaction: Methodological issues* (pp. 231–253). Madison, WI: University of Wisconsin Press.

Parke, R. D., & Suomi, S. J. (1981). Adult male–infant relationships: Human and nonhuman primate evidence. In K. Immelmann, G. Barlow, M. Main, & L. Petrinovich (Eds.), *Behavioral development: The Bielefeld Interdisciplinary Project* (pp. 700–725). New York: Cambridge University Press.

Patterson, C. J. (1995). Gay and lesbian parents. In M. Bornstein (Ed.), *Handbook of parenting* (Vol. 3, pp. 255–274). Mahwah, NJ: Lawrence Erlbaum Associates.

Patterson, C. J., & Chan, R. W. (1997). Gay fathers. In M. E. Lamb (Ed.), *The role of the father in child development* (3rd ed., pp. 245–260). New York: Wiley.

Patterson, G. R. (1993). Orderly change in a stable world: The antisocial trait as chimera. *Journal of Consulting and Clinical Psychology, 61,* 911–919.

Pattterson, G. R., DeBarshyshe, B. D., & Ramsey, E. (1989). A developmental perspective on antisocial behavior. *American Psychologist, 44,* 329–335.

Paulson, R. J., & Sachs, J. (1999). *Rewinding your biological clock: Motherhood late in life: Options, issues, and emotions*. San Francisco, CA: Freeman.

Pedersen, F. A. (Ed.). (1980). *The father–infant relationship: Observational studies in the family setting*. New York: Praeger.

Plomin, R. (1994). Genetic research and identification of environmental influences. *Journal of Child Psychology and Psychiatry, 35,* 817–834.

Plomin, R., & Rutter, M. (1998). Child development, molecular genetics, and what to do with genes once they are found. *Child Development, 69,* 1223–1242.

Radin, N. (1993). Primary caregiving fathers in intact families. In A. E. Gottfried & A. W. Gottfried (Eds.), *Redefining families* (pp. 11–54). New York: Plenum.

Reise, S. P, Widaman, K. F., & Pugh, R. M. (1993). Confirmatory factor analysis and item response theory: Two approaches for exploring measurement invariance. *Psychological Bulletin, 114,* 552–566.

Reiss, D. (1981). *The family's construction of reality*. Cambridge, MA: Harvard University Press.

Robertson, J. A. (1994). *Children of choice: Freedom and the new reproductive technologies*. Princeton, NJ: Princeton University Press.

Rodin, J., & Collins, A. (Eds.). (1991). *Women and new reproductive technologies*. Hillsdale, NJ: Lawrence Erlbaum Associates.

Rogoff, R. (1990). *Apprenticeship in thinking*. New York: Oxford University Press.

Roopnarine, J. L., & Carter, D. B. (Eds.). (1992). *Parent–child socialization in diverse cultures*. Norwood, NJ: Ablex.

Ross, H., & Taylor, H. (1989). Do boys prefer daddy or his physical style of play? *Sex Roles, 20,* 23–33.

Rowe, D. (1994). *The limits of family effects*. New York: Guilford.

Russell, G. (1984). *The changing role of fathers.* St. Lucia, Australia: Queensland University Press.

Rutter, M. (1987). Psychosocial resilience and protective mechanisms. *American Journal of Orthopsychiatry, 57,* 316–331.

Saarni, C. (1999). *The development of emotional competence.* New York: Guilford Press.

Sagi, A. (1982). Antecedents and consequences of various degrees of paternal involvement in childrearing: The Israeli project. In M. E. Lamb (Ed.), *Nontraditional families: Parenting and child development* (pp. 205–232). Hillsdale, NJ: Lawrence Erlbaum Associates.

Sameroff, A. (1994). Developmental systems and family functioning. In R. D. Parke & S. Kellam (Eds.), *Exploring family relationships with other social contexts* (pp. 199–214). Hillsdale, NJ: Lawrence Erlbaum Associates.

Schaie, K. W., & Willis, S. L. (1991). *Adult development and aging.* New York: HarperCollins.

Sigel, I., & Parke, R. D. (1987). Conceptual models of family interaction. *Journal of Applied Developmental Psychology, 8,* 123–137.

Silverstein, L. B., & Auerbach, C. F. (1999). Deconstructing the essential father. *American Psychologist, 54,* 397–407.

Simmons, R., & Blyth, D. (1987). *Moving into adolescence: The impact of pubertal change and school context.* Hawthorne, NY: Aldine.

Steinberg, L. (2000, April 1). *We know some things: Parent–adolescent relations in retrospect and prospect.* Presidential address for Society for Research and Adolescence. Chicago.

Sternberg, K. J. (1997). Fathers, the missing parents in research on family violence. In M. E. Lamb (Ed.), *The role of the father in child development* (pp. 284–308). New York: Wiley.

Stolba, A., & Amato, P. R. (1993). Extended single-parent households and children's behavior. *Sociological Quarterly, 34,* 543–549.

Tasker, F. L., & Golombok, S. (1997). *Growing up in a lesbian family: Effects on child development.* New York: Guilford Press.

Thompson, R. (1998). Early sociopersonality development. In W. Damon (Ed.), *Handbook of child psychology* (Vol. 3, pp. 25–104). New York: Wiley.

Turner, J. R. G. (1999, September 19). Ditto: Review of L. B. Andrews' The clone age: Adventures in the new world of reproductive technology. *New York Times,* p. 14.

Tuttle, W. M. (1993). *Daddy's gone to war.* New York: Oxford University Press.

Waller, W. (1938). *The family: A dynamic interpretation.* New York: Dryden.

Whiting, B. B., Edwards, C. P., Ember, C. R., & Erchak, G. M. (1988). *Children of different worlds: The formation of social behavior.* Cambridge, MA: Harvard University Press.

Zuckerman, M. (1991). Sensation-seeking: The balance between risk and reward. In L. P. Lipsitt & L. Mitnick (Eds.), *Self-regulatory behavior and risk-taking: Causes and consequences* (pp. 143–152). Norwood, NJ: Ablex.

II

RETROSPECT AND PROSPECT IN THE PSYCHOLOGICAL STUDY OF MARITAL AND FAMILY GROUP DYNAMICS

The three chapters in this part review what psychologists have learned about interadult relationships in the family, focusing on the dynamics of marital and coparenting relations but also broadening the conceptualization of such dynamics to include recent scholarship on extended families, intergenerational relations, and other family forms beyond the two-parent nuclear family unit. First, in their chapter on couple and marital relationships, Flanagan and colleagues provide a historical overview of the conceptual models and methodological advances that have shaped research on marital partnerships to this point, and they outline future areas of growth for the field. McHale, Lauretti, Talbot, and Pouquette follow with a chapter distinguishing parent–child and marital relations from coparenting and family group dynamics, emphasizing both historical and cultural determinants of family functioning and the significance of interfamily differences within cultures for the development and adaptation of individuals within those families. Cox and Harter round out the collection of papers with a chapter that crystallizes key points from the prior two chapters and outlines additional themes of interest for marital and family researchers in the years ahead.

In chapter 4, Flanagan and colleagues trace the history of research on marital relationships by psychologists, outlining the movement from self-report methods to observational technology. They explain how early work on couples' interactive styles during conflict discussions reliably distinguished distressed from nondistressed couples, sparking intensive studies of negative reciprocity, coercive behavior, and nonverbal affective displays. From this initial, and productive, focus on dyadic engagement styles the field moved in several productive directions, including the documentation of pursuer–distancer dynamics through the use of sequential analyses; analysis of how individual cognitions, perceptions, and causal attributions contributed to spousal behavior and marital satisfaction; and investigation of ways gender differences in physiological arousal might organize the unfolding of spousal behavior during marital conflict.

At the same time, behavioral marital therapy was evolving to incorporate new insights from the research findings, including a focus on cognitions, with preventive approaches informed by research findings also appearing for the first time. The research-intervention connection has been, and remains, important in the marital field for family psychologists. Despite the extraordinary gains in the field, however, much work remains—in isolating factors that strengthen and sustain happy and long-term marriages, including individual, couple, and extrafamilial sources; in investing more effort in understanding couple relationship issues in later life; and, most crucially, in testing the viability of conceptual models and established wisdom about marital functioning by studying successful and distressed marriages cross-culturally and cross-nationally. Additional effort needs to be invested in finding ways to intervene effectively with the 50% of distressed couples who do not respond well to existing marital therapy efforts and in finding ways to sustain the early gains that frequently dissipate for those who show positive response to intervention. Flanagan et al. conclude by noting that although psychologists have already begun contributing empirically grounded expertise to current national debates about issues such as premarital education, their ultimate effect on social policy decisions remains to be determined.

In chapter 5, McHale et al. illustrate the importance of studying inter-adult parenting coordination and other family-group-level dynamics in studies of children and families, distinguishing coparenting and family group processes from parent–child and marital dynamics. They begin by calling on work from the anthropologist Harrell to illustrate how the adaptive functions of family structure and process cannot be understood without reference to the context of broader societal demands impinging on and organizing the family. This broader lens is especially critical because the conceptual models and empirical knowledge base about families within psychology were both borne of studies of families in clinical distress. Psychology has been slow to catch up with its sister disciplines of sociology and anthropology in recognizing that both the two-parent nuclear structure and our current belief system about childhood, marriage, and the marital-parenting interplay are specific to a historical and cultural frame. McHale et al. examine the adaptive nature of other family arrangements and spotlight the scholarship of Crosbie-Burnett and Lewis in illustrating how the pedi-focal orientation of African American families provides a useful model for conceptualizing interadult coordination and its benefits for children. They then turn to new research on individual differences in family group process among nuclear families, reviewing a series of recent studies documenting the importance of coparental solidarity in promoting young children's adjust-ment. Despite the fact that psychology's interest in family group process originated in the clinical work of family therapists 50 years ago, empirical studies of the full family group are relatively new in the child development literature. Given the diversity of modern family arrangements, researchers interested in studying family group dynamics face challenges in the years ahead.

McHale et al. overview ongoing debates in the field about the search for family dynamics that hold similar import for children's socioemotional de-velopment cross-nationally, and they outline several other questions that will challenge students of family group dynamics in the years ahead. Dis-cussing policy-related concerns, their stance is that we need to be doing much more as a society to curb interparental disparagement, undermining, and antagonism, as such antagonism adversely affects children's sense of stability, predictability, and security. Although more research is needed to ascertain the long-term sequela of other family-level variables, such as af-fective climate and degree of disparity in parenting stances, data suggest that even very young children are attuned to interparental and family-group-level dynamics just as they are to parenting and marital behavior. Fu-ture research should also examine whether coparental dynamics are ame-nable to preventive or early interventions, and whether it might be possible to bypass the arguably more intractable marital dynamic in some families to concentrate on and strengthen faltering coparental functioning. Under-standing the dynamics and effects of interadult coordination in families be-yond the two-parent nuclear unit is also a critical research topic in future studies of the family.

In chapter 6, Cox, and Harter remind us that many of the lessons we have learned about the family owe to the astute observations of the early family therapists. Anticipating several of the themes to be explored in part 3 of this volume, they explore ways general systems theory and communica-tions theory informed studies of nonclinical families through the 1980s. Their brief overview of this work and summary of the preceding two chap-ters lead them to propose several pressing issues in need of competent study by marital and family researchers in the years ahead. Among the ma-jor issues they identify are: examining systemwide changes owing to inter-ventions with the marital dyad; scrutinizing more carefully commonalities and differences in marital–parenting linkages across diverse cultural and socioeconomic groups; understanding more about these linkages within adoptive and blended families, families headed by gay and lesbian couples, and families where partners are cohabiting but not legally married; and working to develop theories about times in the family life cycle during which interventions may be most crucial for families. On this latter issue, Cox's own prior work on family transitions is relevant. In the future study of family group dynamics, Cox and Harter advocate studying how families adapt to environmental challenges, expanding our models to fully incorporate both intergenerational continuities and discontinuities, and dedicating intensified efforts to the role of emotion and emotional communication in the family. They also prod researchers to continue the quest for statistical and analytical procedures that can capture the complexity of circular and shifting family dynamics over time. In closing, they echo McHale et al.'s call for thoughtful studies of diverse family groupings, while reminding us that study of the nuclear family also remains far from complete. They take the stance that responsible policy can only proceed through a thoroughly grounded and nuanced understanding of the full family group—regardless of the composition of that group—given that the family group is the major context for both child development and adult functioning. Such an enterprise, they argue, promises to yield important societal benefits.

4

Retrospect and Prospect in the Psychological Study of Marital and Couple Relationships

Kelly M. Flanagan
Mari L. Clements
Penn State

Sarah W. Whitton
Michael J. Portney
University of Denver

David W. Randall
Penn State

Howard J. Markman
University of Denver

Traditionally, the marital relationship has been the centerpiece around which the family is created and grows. Although not all families consist of a married couple, an examination of family research would be incomplete without examination of the research devoted to this part of the family unit. Marital research has attempted to understand the nature of couples' relationships, to determine why relationships succeed or fail, and to develop ways to help troubled relationships.

The nine parts of this chapter provide an overview of the past, present, and future of research with couples. The first third of the chapter describes the progression of the field from the groundwork established by early sociological research, by observational studies, and by the inclusion of longitudinal data and individual differences. The second third of the chapter addresses promising areas of current research, including investigation of contextual influences on relationship development, relationships of long duration and of older couples, and positive aspects of relationships. Finally, the last third of the chapter focuses on efforts to address marital discord, particularly, intervention, prevention, and social policy.

THEORETICAL AND EMPIRICAL FORERUNNERS TO PSYCHOLOGICAL RESEARCH ON RELATIONSHIPS

Across cultures and throughout history, marriage has existed both as a social institution and as an interpersonal relationship. Some of the earliest empirical studies of marital relationships in the United States focused on broad sociological aspects of marriage, such as identifying sociodemographic correlates of marital satisfaction. This pioneering work was largely grounded in data gathered from self-report inventories. The value of this approach can be seen in the continued use of some of these early measures of relationship adjustment or satisfaction (e.g., Locke & Wallace, 1959; Spanier, 1976).

Although psychologists weighed in with their first published study of marriage more than 60 years ago (Terman, Buttenweiser, Ferguson, Johnson, & Wilson, 1938), sociologists dominated the study of marriage until the early 1970s. The newfound interest in marriage by psychologists reflected both societal trends and scientific advances in theory and methodology. First, after remaining essentially unchanged since 1860, marital dissolution rates rose dramatically in the 1970s (Cherlin, 1992). Second, marital distress emerged as the most frequently reported problem among individuals seeking psychotherapy (Veroff, Kulka, & Douvan, 1981).

The growing interest in marriages by psychologists during the 1970s coincided with theoretical emphases and methodological innovations that allowed for more direct investigation of marriages. The introduction of social exchange and social learning theories signaled a shift from an exclusive focus on individual processes in psychopathology to a broader view that allowed for greater awareness and appreciation of contextual and interpersonal contributions to psychopathology. Individuals' interactions with others became a focus of scientific attention, and the marital relationship represented a critical domain of interpersonal functioning. Finally, increasing dissatisfaction with the extensive reliance on self-report questionnaires helped trigger major improvements in observational methodology, which then catalyzed multidimensional empirical investigations. More specifically, the relatively weak associations that continually emerged between marital satisfaction and sociodemographic variables (Burgess, Locke, & Thomas, 1971), combined with more global concerns about self-reports (Mischel, 1968), were key forces leading psychologists to develop more comprehensive marital assessments.

Empirical findings indicated the value in direct observation of family interactions. For instance, Patterson and Reid (1973) found that trained observers and parents differed in their evaluations of child behavior following intervention, suggesting that self-reports may reflect not only current behaviors but also biases of the reporter based on previous interactions. Additionally, technological innovations, making higher fidelity audiovisual recording equipment more reliable and less expensive, contributed to the rapid development of psychological marital research, which integrated self-reports with direct observations of couples.

THE INFANCY OF PSYCHOLOGICAL MARITAL RESEARCH

A central question underlying marital research was, and continues to be: Why are some marriages happy and others unhappy? Identification of risk and protective factors in marriage was central to the task of developing interventions for distressed couples. This focus on the development of effective treatments separated psychological marital research from its sociological predecessor.

Early psychological studies of marriage focused on identifying patterns of spousal behavior that might predict marital outcomes. Even before the first behavioral marital therapy text (Jacobson & Margolin, 1979) was published, researchers had begun to use behavioral principles to understand and intervene in marital relationships (Stuart, 1969; Weiss, Hops, & Patterson, 1973). Specifically, relationship distress was conceptualized as resulting from the deterioration of mutual reinforcement (Stuart, 1969), asymmetrical reinforcement (Patterson & Reid, 1970), and aversive control strategies (Patterson & Hops, 1972).

To investigate these proposed influences on marital outcomes, researchers developed protocols that involved direct observation of couple interactions. Early research examined couples' communication about two topics: problems in their relationships and events of the day. Each discussion was coded on various dimensions by observational systems such as the Marital Interaction Coding System (MICS; Hops, Wills, Patterson, & Weiss, 1972) and the Couples Interaction Scoring System (CISS; Gottman, Notarius, & Markman, 1976; Notarius, Markman, & Gottman, 1983). These early investigations revealed that distressed couples exhibited more behavioral and affective negativity than did nondistressed couples, particularly during problem discussions (Billings, 1979; Birchler, Weiss, & Vincent, 1975; Gottman, Markman, & Notarius, 1977). Because the behaviors of distressed and nondistressed couples were more discrepant during problem discussions than during daily event discussions, marital research was channeled toward the observation and quantification of relationship conflict. Relationship conflict investigations have revealed several robust differences between distressed and nondistressed couples in behavior and affect.

Behavior: Rates and Reciprocity

Early studies indicated that distressed couples' negativity was exacerbated in problem-solving activities. This heightened negativity was apparent in problem-solving behaviors, general negativity, and negative reciprocity. Compared with nondistressed partners, distressed partners were less likely to compromise (Raush, Barry, Hertel, & Swain, 1974), to agree with their partners (Gottman et al., 1977; Margolin & Wampold, 1981; Revenstorf, Hahl-weg, Schindler, & Vogel, 1984; Revenstorf, Vogel, Wegener, Hahlweg, & Schindler, 1980), to offer problem descriptions (Birchler, Clopton, & Adams, 1984; Margolin & Wampold, 1981), to generate positive solutions (Birchler et al., 1984; Floyd, O'Farrell, & Goldberg, 1987; Hahlweg et al., 1979; Margolin, Burman, & John, 1989; Margolin & Wampold, 1981; Revenstorf et al., 1980), to remain engaged in the discussion (Margolin et al., 1989; Ting-Toomey, 1983), to resolve the problem under discussion (Fichten & Wright, 1983; Margolin & Wampold, 1981; Revenstorf et al., 1984), or to attempt to diffuse arguments (Fichten & Wright, 1983; Raush et al., 1974; Revenstorf et al., 1984). Distressed couples also displayed more coercive acts, including guilt inducement and compensation demands (Raush et al., 1974), and personal attacks, including threats, criticisms, and insults (Fichten & Wright, 1983; Hooley & Hahlweg, 1989; Koren, Carlton, & Shaw, 1980; Raush et al., 1974; Revenstorf et al., 1984), than did nondistressed couples.

In addition to specific problem-solving behaviors, distressed couples showed greater general negativity than did nondistressed couples. Distressed partners were less likely to indicate approval of or caring for their partners (Alberts, 1988; Birchler et al., 1984; Gottman et al., 1977; Hahlweg et al., 1979; Hooley & Hahlweg, 1989; Revenstorf et al., 1980; Vincent, 1972), to use humor or acceptance (Fichten & Wright, 1983; Raush et al., 1974; Revenstorf et al., 1984), to demonstrate empathy (Birchler et al., 1984; Wegener, Revenstorf, Hahlweg, & Schindler, 1979), to appear self-confident (Fichten & Wright, 1983; Margolin & Wampold, 1981), or to touch affectionately or positively during discussions (Margolin & Wampold, 1981; Revenstorf et al., 1984) than were nondistressed partners.

Not only did distressed partners exhibit more overall negativity than did nondistressed partners, but the two groups were also found to differ in terms of behavioral reciprocity. Behavioral reciprocity refers to the contingent nature of partners' interaction behaviors such that one partner's behavior increases the probability of the other partner responding in a similar manner. Early observational studies of marriage indicated that distressed couples exhibited greater reciprocity, both of positive and negative behaviors, than did nondistressed couples (Billings, 1979; Gottman, 1979; Gottman et al., 1977; Margolin & Wampold, 1981; Revenstorf et al., 1980). Gottman et al. (1977) argued that distressed couples were more "locked into" their interactions with one another than were nondistressed couples. In this way, distressed couples had more difficulty de-escalating conflict than did nondistressed couples.

Affect

Because of the difficulty of inferring affect from observable behavior, couples' affect during relationship conflict was less commonly studied in early marital research. The few studies that did investigate affect indicated that distressed couples exhibited fewer empathic smiles, less warm voice tone, less laughter, more raised voices, and more coercive gestures than did nondistressed couples (Gottman et al., 1977; Margolin & Wampold, 1981; Revenstorf et al., 1984). Despite the relative scarcity of these findings, couples' nonverbal behavior appeared to be a more reliable discriminator of marital distress than verbal behavior. For instance, Gottman et al. found that the affective codes of the CISS accounted for more variance in couple satisfaction than did the behavioral codes of the CISS.

BUILDING ON THE GROUNDWORK OF EARLY RESEARCH

The emergence of negative behaviors, reciprocity, and affect as hallmarks of distressed couples' interactions had several important effects on marital intervention and research. First, more sophisticated models, incorporating analysis of sequential chains of behavior and examination of longitudinal data, were developed. Second, the focus on couple behavior broadened to include individual differences in cognition, affect, physiology, and psychopathology. Third, behavioral marital therapy was developed (Jacobson & Margolin, 1979) and refined to include constructs such as cognition (Baucom & Epstein, 1990) and acceptance (Jacobson & Christensen, 1996).

Models of Couple Behavior

With the introduction of longitudinal studies of marriage (e.g., Filsinger & Thoma, 1988; Levenson & Gottman, 1985; Markman, 1979, 1981) and the improvement in sequential analysis of couples' behavior (e.g., Allison & Liker, 1982; Gottman, 1979; Margolin & Wampold, 1981; Notarius, Krokoff, & Markman, 1981; Wampold & Margolin, 1982), it became apparent that couples' outcomes could not be adequately understood by measuring base rates of behavior alone. Longitudinal studies revealed that the physiological and communication correlates of concurrent satisfaction were often not correlated, and sometimes negatively correlated, with long-term satisfaction (Levenson & Gottman, 1983, 1985; Smith, Vivian, & O'Leary, 1990; Weiss & Heyman, 1990). For instance, Markman (1981) found that spouses' rating of their partners' behavior was not related to concurrent satisfaction but was positively correlated with satisfaction up to 5 years later. Additionally, Gottman and Krokoff (1989) found gender differences in the relations between behaviors and long-term satisfaction, such that husbands' negativity was associated with concurrent distress but long-term satisfaction whereas wives' positivity was associated with concurrent satisfaction but long-term distress.

At the same time, increasingly sound methods of sequential analysis allowed researchers to develop more complex models of couple behavior. In addition to substantiating the highly reciprocal manner in which distressed couples interact (Alberts, 1988; Hooley & Hahlweg, 1989; Margolin & Wampold, 1981; Ting-Toomey, 1983), sequential analysis revealed another key pattern of interaction commonly found in distressed marriages. Distressed couples were more likely than nondistressed couples to engage in a pattern of interaction characterized by one spouse (usually the wife) demanding change and the other spouse (usually the husband) withdrawing from the interaction (e.g., Christensen, 1987, 1988; Christensen & Heavey, 1990; Roberts & Krokoff, 1990; Sullaway & Christensen, 1983; Wile, 1981). This demand–withdraw pattern differentiated distressed and nondistressed couples beyond verbal and nonverbal base rates (Roberts & Krokoff, 1990).

Individual Differences

As the quality and quantity of empirical evidence amassed, both researchers and therapists recognized that the intense focus on observable interpersonal behaviors came at the expense of investigating complex intrapersonal factors (Bradbury, 1998). Exclusive focus on couple-level behavior necessarily missed important individual differences. Research in the early 1980s demonstrated the importance of attending to individual spouses' thoughts and emotions (e.g., Berley & Jacobson, 1984; Epstein, 1982; Epstein & Eidelson, 1981; Fincham & O'Leary, 1983; Levenson & Gottman, 1983; Margolin, 1983). Three important areas of individual functioning received significant research attention and later shaped the development of marital research and therapy. These areas were: (a) cognition and attribution, (b) affect and physiology, and (c) psychopathology.

Jacobson and Margolin (1979) recognized the potential importance of cognition and included some cognitive components in behavioral marital therapy (BMT). However, the first clear description of the role of cognition in marital interaction was the sentiment-override hypothesis (Weiss, 1980).

Weiss posited that the actual circumstances of an interaction were less in-fluential than spouses' global positivity or negativity in predicting re-sponses to that interaction. That is, in happy relationships partners were more likely to view each other, and each other's behavior, as more positive regardless of the actual behaviors exhibited. Similarly, distressed spouses were more likely to allow their overall negative bias toward their partners and their relationship to color their perceptions of the actual interactions.

In support of this hypothesis, Floyd and Markman (1983) found that an individual's ratings of their partner's communication were more highly cor-related with the individual's own communication behaviors than with the partner's. Floyd and Markman noted that spouses' cognitions may influence not only their own behaviors, but also their perceptions of their partners' be-haviors. Furthermore, the influence of sentiment override may vary across the life span of the marriage, with premarital, happy husbands and married, distressed wives affected more than other spouses (Floyd, 1988; Notarius, Benson, & Sloane, 1989).

In a related area of study, researchers began to examine distressed and nondistressed spouses' causal attributions for partners' behavior. Spe-cifically, maladaptive or negative attributions such as assigning blame or at-tributing hostile or negative intent to their partners were investigated. Maladaptive attributions for partners' behaviors have been shown to pre-dict more negative and less positive spousal behavior, particularly for wives (Bradbury, Beach, Fincham, & Nelson, 1996; Bradbury & Fincham, 1992; Miller & Bradbury, 1995). In addition, negative attributions have also been shown to be associated with marital distress for both husbands and wives (Fincham & Bradbury, 1993; Karney, Bradbury, Fincham, & Sullivan, 1994; Sayers & Baucom, 1995; Senchak & Leonard, 1993; Townsley, Beach, Fincham, & O'Leary, 1991; Vanzetti, Notarius, & NeeSmith, 1992).

In addition to cognition, affect and its related physiological changes be-came a focus of attention from marital researchers interested in identifying important individual differences. Levenson and Gottman found spouses' self-reports of affect during problem discussions to significantly predict concurrent relationship satisfaction (Gottman & Levenson, 1986; Levenson & Gottman, 1983) and wives' self-reports to predict future relationship satis-faction (Levenson & Gottman, 1985). In the same series of studies, the de-gree of similarity between spouses' levels of physiological arousal during conflict discussions accounted for much of the variance in couples' concur-rent satisfaction. Physiological data were generally not predictive of future satisfaction, except for husbands' heart rate (Levenson & Gottman, 1985). Gottman and Levenson (1986) also argued that men were more susceptible to physiological arousal than were women.

Different forms of psychopathology, most notably depression and alco-holism, were also considered important in understanding marital interactions. In the case of depression, studies of couples in which at least one spouse was depressed reliably revealed links between depression and poorer marital functioning. For instance, couples in which at least one spouse is depressed have been shown to have lower relationship satisfaction (Gotlib & Whiffen, 1989), more negative observed interactions (Hautzinger, Linden, & Hoffman, 1982; Hinchliffe, Hooper, & Roberts, 1978; Hops et al., 1987), more negative perceptions of marital interactions (Kahn, Coyne, & Margolin, 1985; Kowalik & Gotlib, 1987), and more negative reactions to marital interactions (Arkowitz, Holliday, & Hutter, 1982) than have couples in which neither spouse is depressed. Furthermore, depression and marital quality appear to have reciprocal effects such that marital distress predicts depressive symptoms (Beach & O'Leary, 1993), especially for women (Fincham, Beach, Harold, & Osborne, 1997) and depressive symptoms predict marital distress, especially for men (Fincham et al., 1997). Similarly, studies of couples in which one partner was alcoholic revealed that alcohol use was generally associated with greater observed negativity (Jacob & Krahn, 1988; Jacob, Ritchey, Cvitkovic, & Blane, 1981).

Prevention and Intervention

Just as early marital research by psychologists was informed by a primary focus on negative behaviors, affect, and reciprocity, so too did the development of marital therapy reflect this behavioral focus. In recent years, BMT (Jacobson & Margolin, 1979), initially designed to lessen negativity in marital relationships, has been recognized as an empirically supported treatment for marital distress (American Psychological Association Task Force on Psychological Intervention Guidelines, 1995; Baucom, Shoham, Mueser, Daiuto, & Stickle, 1998). In fact, BMT was the only treatment for couples in the APA's initial report of empirically supported treatments.

As marital research began to reflect the dawning awareness that individual factors beyond couples' behavioral interactions influenced outcomes, so too did marital therapy evolve to reflect this understanding. For example, in the late 1980s, growing recognition of the importance of cognitions led clinicians to incorporate cognitive interventions into marital therapy. Baucom and Epstein published the first explicitly cognitive treatment of behavioral marital therapy in 1990.

Continuing research and clinical work shaped behavioral interventions as the field attempted to refine and reshape BMT. Although BMT approaches were effective for many couples, roughly one half of distressed couples were not helped in the long term by such interventions (Jacobson & Addis, 1993). Drawing on the strengths of both BMT and other approaches, Jacobson and Christensen (1996) developed Integrative Couple Therapy (originally called Integrative Behavioral Couple Therapy; Christensen, Jacobson, & Babcock, 1995), which focused on strategies of both change and acceptance.

Similarly recognizing that BMT was limited in its ability to restore couples to predistress levels of functioning (Hahlweg & Markman, 1988), but working from a different perspective, Markman and colleagues developed a promising preventive approach for working with couples (the Prevention and Relationship Enhancement Program [PREP]; Markman, Duncan, Storaasli, & Howes, 1987; Markman, Floyd, Stanley, & Storaasli, 1988; Markman, Renick, Floyd, Stanley, & Clements, 1993; Markman, Stanley, & Blumberg, 1994; Silliman, Stanley, Coffin, Markman, & Jordan, in press). Like the therapy approaches described earlier, this prevention program incorporated empirically supported behavioral techniques with cognitive strategies designed to strengthen relationships before marital distress developed.

Reviews of the existing literature (e.g., Silliman et al., in press) demonstrate that, although there are various programs for premarried and married couples, only PREP is empirically based and has been evaluated in terms of long-term prevention effects. In earlier research, a 15-year prospective study of 135 couples planning marriage was designed to identify the interaction patterns that predict divorce and to evaluate a marital distress and divorce prevention program. Results suggest that couples with dysfunctional premarital interaction patterns are at greater risk for marital distress and divorce (Clements, Stanley, & Markman, 2000; Markman & Hahlweg, 1993). Furthermore, couples who learned constructive arguing skills before marriage (in the PREP program) had lower rates of relationship aggression, breakup, and divorce and higher levels of relationship satisfaction during the early years of marriage (e.g., Markman et al., 1988; Markman et al., 1993). These findings have been replicated and extended in several independent investigations (e.g., Behrens & Halford, 1994; Hahlweg & Markman, in press; Halford, 1998; Thurmaier, Engl, Eckert, & Hahlweg, 1992). Among the most recent and heartening findings to emerge are those of Hahlweg and Markman (in press). Among German couples, divorce rates at the 5-year point of a longitudinal study were 4% for PREP couples compared with 24% for control couples (Hahlweg & Markman, in press).

PROSPECT IN THE PSYCHOLOGICAL STUDY OF MARRIAGE

Although the marital research literature has grown large and diverse, there remains a great deal we still have yet to learn. Moreover, the same diversity of research topics that lends richness to the field has also made it difficult to draw firm comparisons or to generalize across research laboratories. Finally, although researchers have begun to examine both individual and couple factors in understanding marriage, consideration of broader contextual factors such as social networks, ethnicity, and culture is really in its infancy.

Integrating Positive and Negative Behaviors and Tasks

The relatively newer focus on social support in marriage has enriched the understanding of marriage that was obtained by an exclusive focus on relationship conflict (Bradbury, Rogge, & Lawrence, 2001). Research has suggested that the provision of social support is an important element in happy marriages (Cutrona, Hessling, & Suhr, 1997; Cutrona & Suhr, 1992; Pasch & Bradbury, 1998; Pasch, Bradbury, & Davila, 1997).

This line of research, however, has been limited in that few studies that examine social support also examine relationship conflict, making it difficult to determine whether the same processes that predict relationship distress in conflict discussions operate in support discussions. In one of the few studies that examined both relationship conflict and social support, Pasch and Bradbury (1998) found that marital negativity and support behaviors (specifically, wives' negative and positive social support behaviors) both made independent contributions to the prediction of distress status 2 years later. This finding is intriguing and raises the question of whether conflict and support behaviors are part of a larger mechanism of general relationship risk (Bradbury et al., 2001).

Similarly, Jacobson and Christensen (1996) have argued that the focus on problem solving inherent in BMT overlooks important relationship behaviors and strengths that should be harnessed in helping distressed couples. The role of relationship dimensions such as social support, acceptance, and team building is an important new area of marital research and has the potential to greatly inform models of marriage.

Family and Socioeconomic Influences on Marriage

Another promising area for marital research is investigation of the roles of immediate and extended family and social support networks on marriage. Although the effects of marital conflict on children have received much research attention (for reviews, see Cummings & Davies, 1994; Erel & Burman, 1995), the examination of children on marriage has largely been limited to studies of the transition to parenthood, most of which suffer from serious methodological and conceptual flaws (for a review, see Clements & Markman, 1996).

Furthermore, although research has established that children of divorce are at increased risk for their own marital distress and dissolution (Amato,

1999), this effect has been widely attributed to the historical experience of parental marital conflict (for a review, see Hetherington, 1999). Effects of the family of origin beyond childhood, such as the provision of social support to married couples, have been largely unexplored.

Similarly, the effects of SES on marital outcome have been well documented, with less marital stability found among couples earning lower incomes (e.g., Nakosteen & Zimmer, 1997; Tzeng & Mare, 1995). However, it is unclear whether income itself is a causal factor or whether income serves as a marker for other environmental stresses such as inadequate day care for children, poor housing, unsafe neighborhoods, or negligible leisure time.

Cultural Influences on Marriage

An additional important marital research topic is ethnicity and culture in marriage. The psychology of marriage as it currently exists is really a psychology of European American middle-class marriage. Even research samples drawn from ethnically diverse American cities such as Los Angeles, Seattle, and Denver have typically been composed of 75% or more European American participants (e.g., Gottman, Coan, Carrere, & Swanson, 1998; Karney & Bradbury, 1997; Markman et al., 1993). Whether these percentages reflect the demographics of those cities, such sample composition is unsuited for examining the applicability of models developed with majority samples in minority groups.

The few existing studies that have attempted to recruit samples of different ethnic or cultural backgrounds have tended to find more similarities than differences between couples' communication patterns. For instance, Lindahl and Malik (1999) found few effects of ethnicity in the relation between the marital and parenting behaviors of Hispanic American and European American families. Similarly, Hooley and Hahlweg (1989) found communication patterns to be similar across German and English couples.

Currently, there is a multinational, multicultural study of couples together for at least 20 years under way in Canada, Germany, Israel, Netherlands, South Africa, South America, Sweden, and the United States (Kaslow & Hammerschmidt, 1992; Kaslow, Hansson & Lundblad, 1994; Kaslow & Robison, 1996; Roizblatt et al., 1999; Sharlin, 1996). In general, findings have paralleled those obtained with U.S. samples. For instance, satisfied and dissatisfied couples differed on time together, sexual relations, and shared goals in Sweden (Kaslow et al., 1994), on commitment and family of origin happiness in Chile (Roizblatt et al., 1999), and on support and respect in Israel (Sharlin, 1996).

Other studies have also evidenced similarly convergent findings. Relationship satisfaction has been shown to be related to communication and problem-solving openness in Ghana (Miller & Kannae, 1999) and economic status in both Ghana (Miller & Kannae) and Finland (Kinnunen & Pulkkinen, 1998). Additionally, in Chinese families, marital quality and parent–child relationship quality have been shown to be positively related (Shek, 1998).

Although these findings are interesting, there is insufficient evidence to conclude that models of marriage developed with middle-class European American couples are globally generalizable. Future research needs to focus attention on this crucial question.

LONG-TERM RELATIONSHIPS AND RELATIONSHIPS OF OLDER PEOPLE

One of the major demographic trends facing the marital research field is that people are living longer. At present, however, we know little about long-term relationships in general, or the relationships of older partners in particular. By necessity, almost all research in this area has been either cross-sectional or retrospective. Hence, knowledge about long-term relationships remains limited by selection effects and retrospective reporting biases. For example, couples who remained together for a long time have been found to report higher levels of satisfaction than couples who did not remain together. Extrapolating findings from a highly select sample of long-term couples to the general population of married couples risks making attributional errors. There is a parallel that can be drawn with findings from the developmental psychopathology literature. Although all adults with Antisocial Personality Disorder had Conduct Disorder as children, not all children with Conduct Disorder develop Antisocial Personality Disorder as adults (Hinshaw & Anderson, 1996). Similarly, reasoning from the later stages of a marital relationship backward may yield different conclusions than reasoning from earlier stages of the relationship forward.

Additionally, the widespread use of retrospective reports has also introduced bias into this literature. Retrospective studies have typically found that marital satisfaction follows a U-shaped trajectory over time, with satisfaction high premaritally, lower in the childrearing years, and rising after children leave the home (e.g., Mackey & O'Brien, 1999; O'Neill, Fishman, & Kinsella-Shaw, 1987; Spanier & Lewis, 1980). In contrast, true longitudinal designs in which satisfaction was assessed at multiple time points has documented a linear decline (Johnson, Amoloza, & Booth, 1992). The most notable example of this retrospective bias was provided by Vaillant and Vaillant (1993) who in a 40-year study found that marital satisfaction did decline linearly, but when participants later recalled their satisfaction over time, they reported a U-shaped trajectory. That is, their retrospective reports contradicted their longitudinally collected data.

POSITIVE ASPECTS OF MARRIAGE

Reflecting the basic tenet of prevention theory that prevention involves both decreasing risk factors and increasing protective factors (Coie et al., 1993), marital researchers have begun to research positive factors that may contribute to marital satisfaction and stability. Many positive factors, including trust (Holmes & Rempel, 1989; Wieselquist, Rusbult, Foster, & Agnew, 1999), empathic forgiveness (Wastell, 1991), social support (Cutrona, 1996; Pasch & Bradbury, 1998), and prorelationship behavior (Rusbult, Verette, Whitney, Slovik, & Lipkus, 1991; Van Lange et al., 1997; Wieselquist et al., 1999), have been examined. Recent research attention has also been focused on four domains of positive relationship behavior: commitment, sacrifice, teamwork, and joint activities.

Commitment

One of the key constructs receiving renewed attention in recent years is relationship commitment. Commitment has been conceptualized as the dedication to continue the relationship over an extended period (Johnson, 1982), as an explicit pledge by the partners expressing the intended continuity of their partnership (Levinger, 1980), and as the tendency to maintain a relationship while feeling psychologically attached to it (Rusbult, 1980, 1983). Stanley has defined commitment as encompassing two related constructs: personal dedication and constraint commitment (Stanley, 1998; Stanley & Markman, 1992). Personal dedication is one's internal devotion to the relationship and thoughtful motivation to maintain growth. In contrast, constraint commitment refers to elements that cause individuals to remain in relationships, regardless of level of devotion. Constraints include the financial, psychological, and social costs associated with terminating the relationship.

Commitment has been shown to be associated with higher relationship satisfaction and stability (Bui, Peplau, & Hill, 1996; Fenell, 1993; Rusbult, 1980, 1983; Rusbult, Martz, & Agnew, 1998; Stanley, 1998; Stanley & Markman, 1992, 1997). Commitment is also associated with behaviors that maintain and enhance the quality of relationships including devaluing of alternatives to the relationship (Johnson & Rusbult, 1989), responding positively when a partner has acted negatively or destructively (Rusbult et al., 1991), and sacrificing self-interest for the partner or relationship (Van Lange et al., 1997).

Sacrifice

In the context of romantic involvement, the term sacrifice has been used to describe acts in which individuals give up some immediate desire in the interest of bettering their relationship or benefiting their partner (Stanley,

1998; Van Lange et al., 1997). That is, in a situation in which self-interest is at odds with the interest of the relationship, choosing to forego self-interest and act in accordance with the relationship is considered a sacrifice. Willingness to sacrifice for one's relationship has been associated with strong commitment, high relationship satisfaction, healthier couple functioning, and longer lasting relationships (Van Lange et al., 1997; Wieselquist et al., 1999). Furthermore, satisfaction with sacrificing is positively related to relationship quality, dedication, satisfaction, and disclosure (Stanley & Markman, 1992).

Despite these indications that sacrifice is a behavior that strengthens and improves relationships, feminist writers have argued that it does so at the expense of the individual making the sacrifice (Jack, 1991; Jack & Dill, 1992; Lerner, 1985, 1988). To reconcile these two positions, Whitton, Stanley, and Markman (2000) have proposed a comprehensive model of sacrifice in intimate relationships, which highlights the importance of individuals' perceptions surrounding their sacrifices for their relationships in determining the outcomes of sacrifice on the relationship and the individual. That is, behavioral sacrifice can be positive or negative for an individual or a relationship, depending on how the sacrificer perceives it. When a personal interest is given up for a relationship benefit of greater value to the sacrificer, sacrifice has a positive influence on both the relationship and the sacrificer's sense of self. However, when sacrifices are not perceived to be in the interest of a greater relationship good, they may have negative relationship and mental health consequences. Consistent with this model, individuals who perceived acts of foregoing self-interest to be less harmful to the self also reported greater relationship quality (Whitton & Stanley, 1999; Whitton et al., 2000). In addition, for males but not females, increased couple identity was related to perceptions of sacrifice as less harmful to the self. In contrast, perceptions of sacrifice as more harmful to the self were related to increased depressive symptomatology for both genders, explaining variance beyond that accounted for by overall relationship quality. Thus, the more likely individuals were to perceive their sacrifices as harmful to themselves, the more likely they were to exhibit depressive symptoms. These findings provided preliminary support for this comprehensive model of sacrifice in intimate relationships.

Teamwork

Teamwork is another positive mechanism that may be important in maintaining and enhancing relationships (Stanley, 1998), particularly during periods of transition or crisis (Belsky & Kelly, 1994; Cowan & Cowan, 1992; Cowan et al., 1985). Specifically, Belsky and Kelly noted that the ability to put aside individual goals to engage in teamwork was essential for a successful transition to parenthood. The importance of teamwork does not appear to be limited to the time of becoming parents; rather, in a nationwide, randomized telephone survey of married couples, Stanley and Markman (1997) found that approaching challenges as a team was a strong correlate of other positive relationship factors.

Cordova (2000) has clarified and operationalized the construct of teamwork as encompassing four domains: accomplishing tasks in a coordinated way; agreeing on tasks, goals, and priorities; feeling supported by the partner; and having confidence in the partner's contribution to couple-level goals. In a study of first-time parents undergoing the transition to parenthood, Cordova found high initial levels of teamwork were associated with healthier marital and parental functioning. Furthermore, lack of teamwork was the best predictor of depression, especially for wives. Taken together, these findings suggest teamwork is a promising construct that should be further researched and included in models of functioning in romantic relationships. Moreover, because the idea of teamwork is familiar and accessible to couples and clinicians, it may be particularly useful in interventions with distressed couples.

Joint Activity

Participating in shared or joint activities may also serve a protective function in marital relationships (Dindia & Baxter, 1987). The positive influence of joint activity on marriage has a strong theoretical basis. Interdependence theory (Levinger, 1980; Lewin, 1948) posited the importance of partner overlap on various dimensions, including joint activity. More interdependence is theorized to lead to more closeness and commitment between partners. Early research documented a positive relation between joint leisure activity and marital satisfaction (e.g., Blood & Wolfe, 1960). More recently, Stanley and Markman (1997) found that how much fun couples had together was one of the most powerful factors in predicting overall relationship satisfaction and commitment. Similarly, Baldwin, Ellis, and Baldwin (1999) found involvement in leisure activities with the partner predicted marital satisfaction.

Based on such information, prevention and intervention programs have included recommendations for spouses to participate in fun activities together. However, such universal recommendations may have been made prematurely. The effect of joint leisure activity on marital quality has been shown to be moderated by perceived communication (Holman & Jacquart, 1988), social skills and positivity (Flora & Segrin, 1998), the meaning and context of the activity (Orthner & Mancini, 1990; Stockdale, 1989), and spouses' individual and joint expectations regarding the activity (Hartman, Stanley, & Markman, 2000). Research on joint activity in marriage has suffered from the lack of a theoretical framework as well as from the lack of systematic measurement and comparison of multiple domains of joint activity (e.g., leisure, religion). The research of Hartman et al. (2000) was designed to more clearly delineate how, to what extent, and under what circumstances joint activity is beneficial to relationships. In particular, these researchers have been examining the roles of cognitive processes (e.g., the fulfillment of expectations) and social exchange theory in shaping individuals' experience of joint activity in intimate relationships.

INTERVENTION: WHAT WORKS AND FOR WHOM

As previously noted, even the most rigorously validated intervention for marital distress is truly effective for only about half of distressed couples in research studies (Jacobson & Addis, 1993). This may be because couples often wait until they have done significant harm to their relationships before seeking treatment (Notarius & Markman, 1993).

In addition, marital therapy may be subject to the same limitations to successful treatment as individual therapy. As Castonguay, Schut, and Constantino (2001) have noted, pretreatment characteristics of the client are important predictors of individual therapy outcome. Notably, hostility has been shown to interfere with the formation of the working relationship in therapy, and this characteristic may be particularly salient in marital work. That is, individuals whose interpersonal relationships are marked by hostility may experience both distress in marriage and difficulties productively engaging in treatment.

In addition, other aspects unique to marital therapy may be important in predicting treatment outcome. For instance, the formation of working relationships in marital therapy is made more complex both in number and in process. In individual therapy, the working relationship is between the client and the therapist whereas in couple therapy four working relationships must be forged (therapist and wife, therapist and husband, therapist and couple, wife and husband). This process may be especially difficult because of the conflictual nature of the relationship that is the target of therapy. In other words, the therapist is given the task of simultaneously forming relationships with two individuals who are at times diametrically opposed to one another.

These and other issues, such as the appropriateness of the underlying model of the particular therapy for a specific couple, may be at the heart of differential couple response to treatment. Thus, Paul's (1967) ultimate question rephrased as, "What treatment, by whom, is most effective for this couple with that specific problem under which set of circumstances?" continues to define an important area of marital research.

PREVENTION: REACHING OUT TO THE COMMUNITY

One key challenge for the future is to disseminate the psychological research of marriage to service providers who naturally have contact with couples in the community. For example, the Markman group has begun to disseminate the PREP program in an existing service delivery system, religious organizations (ROs). ROs were selected as a prime target for effectively helping couples begin their marriages with lower risks because 75% of first marriages occur in ROs. Furthermore, most ROs are both very committed to delivering premarital services and deeply embedded in the culture of couples who are the targets of such services (Stanley, Markman, St. Peters, & Leber, 1995).

Results indicate the clergy and lay leaders have met standards for minimal competency in the training phase of the study, and most have shown acceptable levels of adherence to the program as it has been implemented in the community. Of even greater importance, both the RO PREP and the traditional PREP show comparable effects: Couples in both groups maintain their positive levels of premarital functioning whereas couples not receiving PREP decline (Stanley et al., in press).

Additional efforts to disseminate prevention and intervention programs have also been developed. In collaboration with the nursing field, a version of PREP modified for couples in the transition to parenthood has been developed (Jordan, Stanley, & Markman, 1999). Coffin, Robredo, Williams, and Howard (2000) have implemented PREP with U.S. Navy couples. Finally, efforts have begun to develop and evaluate a video-based, self-directed version of PREP.

SOCIAL POLICY

In the U.S., approximately 40% to 50% of marriages end in divorce, representing more than 1 million divorces and involving more than 1 million children per year (Cherlin, 1992). Furthermore, evidence suggesting that marital distress leads to or exacerbates mental disorders for both adults and children continues to accumulate (see Halford & Bouma, 1997). The data reflecting the staggering costs of marital failure in our society have not been lost on political leaders, religious leaders, the media, and public policy advocates. Hence, the desire to "do something" has grown substantially (Stanley & Markman, 1998) and has been expressed in two major ways in the United States. First, various private organizations have become active marriage proponents (e.g., Smart Marriages, Smart Families conferences, the Association for Couples in Marriage Enrichment, the Family Impact Seminar policy group, and the Family Life Educator initiative of the National Council of Family Relations).

Second, several state governments have considered or have passed legislation encouraging premarital education for couples (e.g., Arizona, Colorado, Florida, Indiana, Louisiana, Michigan, Oklahoma). There have been several high-level panel discussions and debates on these initiatives, with psychologists adding empirical and conceptual expertise to the national debates (e.g., Bradbury et al., 1997; McManus, Spaht, Stanley, Stanton, & Blankenhorn, 1998; Peterson, 1999; Stanley, 1997; Stanley & Markman, 1998). The eventual effect on marriage of such changes in social policy remains to be seen.

CONCLUSIONS

Our review of current and past research serves two purposes. First, in reviewing the literature, the tremendous progress made in the past 30 years of marital research is obvious. In a logical and systematic manner, marital research has moved from examining sociodemographic correlates of marital satisfaction to examining spousal behaviors, reciprocity, and affect and, most recently, to focusing on more complex models of marital interaction that incorporate individual differences and relationship strengths. Furthermore, shifts in methodology from sole reliance on self-report questionnaires to the inclusion of observational and physiological measures have both driven and been the product of theoretical advances. Prevention and intervention programs have been the beneficiaries of the research efforts. Second, a journey through the past encourages an examination of the future. Several interesting and clinically relevant issues have been left unexplored. Specifically, broader contextual factors such as ethnicity, culture, social networks, and the positive aspects of marital relationships should be examined. If the psychological study of marriages continues to progress as it has in the past 30 years, the next 30 years can be expected to bring a much deeper understanding of marital relationship complexities.

REFERENCES

Alberts, J. K. (1988). An analysis of couples' conversational complaints. *Communication Monographs, 55,* 184–197.

Allison, P. D., & Liker, J. K. (1982). Analyzing sequential categorical data on dyadic interaction: Comment on Gottman. *Psychological Bulletin, 91,* 393–403.

Amato, P. R. (1999). Children of divorced parents as young adults. In E. M. Hetherington (Ed.), *Coping with divorce, single parenting, and remarriage: A risk and resiliency perspective* (pp. 147–163). Mahwah, NJ: Lawrence Erlbaum Associates.

American Psychological Association Task Force on Psychological Intervention Guidelines. (1995). *Template for developing guidelines: Interventions for mental disorders and psychological aspects of physical disorders.* Washington, DC: American Psychological Association.

Arkowitz, H. S., Holliday, S., & Hutter, M. (1982, November). *Depressed women and their husbands: A study of marital interaction and adjustment.* Paper presented at the Annual Meeting of the Association for Advancement of Behavior Therapy, Los Angeles.

Baldwin, J. H., Ellis, G. D., & Baldwin, B. M. (1999). Marital satisfaction: An examination of its relationship to spouse support and congruence of commitment among runners. *Leisure Sciences, 21,* 117–131.

Baucom, D. H., & Epstein, N. (1990). *Cognitive–behavioral marital therapy.* New York: Brunner/Mazel.

Baucom, D. H., Shoham, V., Mueser, K. T., Daiuto, A. D., & Stickle, T. R. (1998). Empirically supported couple and family interventions for marital distress and adult mental health problems. *Journal of Consulting and Clinical Psychology, 66,* 53–88.

Beach, S. R., & O'Leary, K. D. (1993). Marital discord and dysphoria: For whom does the marital relationship predict depressive symptomatology? *Journal of Social & Personal Relationships, 10,* 405–420.

Behrens, B. C., & Halford, W. K. (1994, August). *Advances in the prevention and treatment of marital distress.* Paper presented at the Helping Families Change Conference, Brisbane, Queensland, Australia.

Belsky, J., & Kelly, J. (1994). *The transition to parenthood: How a first child changes a marriage: Why some couples grow closer and others apart.* New York: Delacorte Press.

Berley, R. A., & Jacobson, N. S. (1984). Causal attributions in intimate relationships: Toward a model of cognitive–behavioral marital therapy. In P. Kendall (Ed.), *Advances in cognitive–behavioral research and therapy* (Vol. 3, pp. 1–60). New York: Academic Press.

Billings, A. (1979). Conflict resolution in distressed and nondistressed married couples. *Journal of Consulting & Clinical Psychology, 47,* 368–376.

Birchler, G. R., Clopton, P. L., & Adams, N. L. (1984). Marital conflict resolution: Factors influencing concordance between partners and trained coders. *American Journal of Family Therapy, 12,* 15–28.

Birchler, G. R., Weiss, R. L., & Vincent, J. P. (1975). A multimethod analysis of social reinforcement exchange between maritally distressed and nondistressed spouse and stranger dyads. *Journal of Personality and Social Psychology, 31,* 349–360.

Blood, R. O., Jr., & Wolfe, D. M. (1960). *Husbands and wives: The dynamics of family living.* New York: Free Press.

Bradbury, T. N. (1998). Introduction: The developmental course of marital dysfunction. In T. N. Bradbury (Ed.), *The developmental course of marital dysfunction* (pp. 1–8). New York: Cambridge University Press.

Bradbury, T. N., Beach, S. R. H., Fincham, F. D., & Nelson, G. M. (1996). Attributions and behavior in functional and dysfunctional marriages. *Journal of Consulting & Clinical Psychology, 64,* 569–576.

Bradbury, T. N., & Fincham, F. D. (1992). Attributions and behavior in marital interaction. *Journal of Personality & Social Psychology, 63,* 613–628.

Bradbury, T. N., Markman, H. J., Stanley, S. M., Blaisure, K., Geasler, M., & McManus, M. (1997, May). *Legislating premarital education.* Panel discussion presented at the annual Smart Marriages/Happy Families Conference, Washington, DC.

Bradbury, T. N., Rogge, R., & Lawrence, E. (2001). Reconsidering the role of conflict in marriage. In A. Booth, A. C. Crouter, & M. L. Clements (Eds.), *Couples in conflict* (pp. 59–81). Mahwah, NJ: Lawrence Erlbaum Associates.

Bui, K. T., Peplau, L. A., & Hill, C. T. (1996). Testing the Rusbult model of relationship commitment and stability in a 15-year study of heterosexual couples. *Personality and Social Psychology Bulletin, 22,* 1244–1257.

Burgess, E. W., Locke, H. J., & Thomas, M. M. (1971). *The family: From traditional to companionship.* New York: Van Nostrand Reinhold.

Castonguay, L. G., Schut, A. J., & Constantino, M. J. (2001). Psychotherapy research. In W. E. Craighead & C. B. Nemeroff (Eds.), *The Corsini encyclopedia of psychology and behavioral science* (3rd ed., pp. 1346–1350). New York: Wiley.

Cherlin, A. J. (1992). *Marriage, divorce, remarriage* (Revised and enlarged edition). Cambridge, MA: Harvard University Press.

Christensen, A. (1987). Detection of conflict patterns in couples. In K. Hahlweg & M. J. Goldstein (Eds.), *Understanding major mental disorder: The contribution of family interaction research* (pp. 250–265). New York: Family Process Press.

Christensen, A. (1988). Dysfunctional interaction patterns in couples. In P. Noller & M. A. Fitzpatrick (Eds.), *Perspectives on marital interaction* (pp. 31–52). Clevedon, England: Multilingual Matters.

Christensen, A., & Heavey, C. L. (1990). Gender and social structure in the demand/withdraw pattern of marital conflict. *Journal of Personality and Social Psychology, 59,* 73–81.

Christensen, A., Jacobson, N. S., & Babcock, J. C. (1995). Integrative behavioral couple therapy. In N. S. Jacobson & A. S. Gurman (Eds.), *Clinical handbook of couple therapy* (pp. 31–64). New York: Guilford.

Clements, M., & Markman, H. J. (1996). The transition to parenthood: Is having children hazardous to marriage. In N. Vanzetti & S. Duck (Eds.), *A lifetime of relationships* (pp. 290–310). Pacific Grove, CA: Brooks/Cole.

Clements, M. L., Stanley, S. M., & Markman, H. J. (2000). *Marital distress and divorce: Examining mulitiple outcomes from a discriminant analysis perspective.* Manuscript submitted for publication.

Coffin, W., Robredo, K., Williams, B., & Howard, K. (2000, June). *Marriage and family education in the military.* Workshop presented at the annual Smart Marriages/Happy Families Conference, Denver, CO.

Coie, J. D., Watt, N. F., West, S. G., Hawkins, J. D., Asarnow, J. R., Markman, H. J., Ramey, S. L., Shure, M. B., & Long, B. (1993). The science of prevention: A conceptual framework and some directions for a national research program. *American Psychologist, 48,* 1013–1022.

Cordova, A. D. (2000). *Teamwork and the transition to parenthood.* Unpublished doctoral dissertation, University of Denver.

Cowan, C. P., & Cowan, P. A. (1992). *When partners become parents: The big life change for couples.* New York: Basic Books.

Cowan, C. P., Cowan, P. A., Heming, G., Garrett, E., Coysh, W. S., Curtis-Boles, H., & Boles, A. J. (1985). Transitions to parenthood: His, hers, and theirs. *Journal of Family Issues, 6,* 451–481.

Cummings, E. M., & Davies, P. (1994). *Children and marital conflict: The impact of family dispute and resolution.* New York: Guilford.

Cutrona, C. E. (1996). *Social support in couples.* Thousand Oaks, CA: Sage Publications.

Cutrona, C. E., Hessling, R. M., & Suhr, J. A. (1997). The influence of husband and wife personality on marital social support interactions. *Personal Relationships, 4,* 379–393.

Cutrona, C. E., & Suhr, J. A. (1992). Controllability of stressful events and satisfaction with spouse support behaviors. *Communication Research, 19,* 154–174.

Dindia, K., & Baxter, L. (1987). Strategies for maintaining and repairing marital relationships. *Journal of Social and Personal Relationships, 4,* 143–158.

Epstein, N. (1982). Cognitive therapy with couples. *American Journal of Family Therapy, 10,* 5–16.

Epstein, N., & Eidelson, R. J. (1981). Unrealistic beliefs of clinical couples: Their relationship to expectations, goals and satisfaction. *American Journal of Family Therapy, 9,* 13–22.

Erel, O., & Burman, B. (1995). Interrelatedness of marital relations and parent–child relations: A meta-analytic review. *Psychological Bulletin, 118*, 108–132.

Fenell, D. L. (1993). Characteristics of long-term first marriages. *Journal of Mental Health Counseling, 15*, 446–460.

Fichten, C. S., & Wright, J. (1983). Problem-solving skills in happy and distressed couples: Effects of videotape and verbal feedback. *Journal of Clinical Psychology, 39*, 340–352.

Filsinger, E. E., & Thoma, S. J. (1988). Behavioral antecedents of relationship stability and adjustment: A five-year longitudinal study. *Journal of Marriage and the Family, 50*, 785–795.

Fincham, F. D., Beach, S. R. H., Harold, G. T., & Osborne, L. N. (1997). Marital satisfaction and depression: Different causal relationships for men and women? *Psychological Science, 8*, 351–357.

Fincham, F. D., & Bradbury, T. N. (1993). Marital satisfaction, depression, and attributions: A longitudinal analysis. *Journal of Personality and Social Psychology, 64*, 442–452.

Fincham, F. D., & O'Leary, K. D. (1983). Causal inferences for spouse behavior in maritally distressed and nondistressed couples. *Journal of Social and Clinical Psychology, 1*, 42–57.

Flora, J., & Segrin, C. (1998). Joint leisure time in friend and romantic relationships: The role of activity type, social skills, and positivity. *Journal of Social and Personal Relationships, 15*, 711–718.

Floyd, F. J. (1988). Couples' cognitive/affective reactions to communication behaviors. *Journal of Marriage and the Family, 50*, 523–532.

Floyd, F. J., & Markman, H. J. (1983). Observational biases in spouse observation: Toward a cognitive/behavioral model of marriage. *Journal of Consulting and Clinical Psychology, 51*, 450–457.

Floyd, F. J., O'Farrell, T. J., & Goldberg, M. (1987). Comparison of marital observation measures: The Marital Interaction Coding System and the Communication Skills Test. *Journal of Consulting and Clinical Psychology, 55*, 423–429.

Gotlib, I. H., & Whiffen, V. E. (1989). Depression and marital functioning: An examination of specificity and gender differences. *Journal of Abnormal Psychology, 98*, 23–30.

Gottman, J. M. (1979). *Marital interaction: Experimental investigations.* New York: Academic Press.

Gottman, J. M., Coan, J., Carrere, S., & Swanson, C. (1998). Predicting marital happiness and stability from newlywed interactions. *Journal of Marriage and the Family, 60*, 5–22.

Gottman, J. M., & Krokoff, L. J. (1989). Marital interaction and satisfaction: A longitudinal view. *Journal of Consulting and Clinical Psychology, 57*, 47–52.

Gottman, J. M., & Levenson, R. W. (1986). Assessing the role of emotion in marriage. *Behavioral Assessment, 8*, 31–48.

Gottman, J. M., Markman, H. J., & Notarius, C. I. (1977). The topography of marital conflict: A sequential analysis of verbal and nonverbal behavior. *Journal of Marriage and the Family, 39*, 461–478.

Gottman, J. M., Notarius, C. I., & Markman, H. J. (1976). *Couples Interaction Scoring System.* Unpublished manuscript, University of Illinois, Champaign-Urbana.

Hahlweg, K., Helmes, B., Steffen, G., Schindler, L., Revenstorf, D., & Kunert, H. (1979). Beobachtungssystem fur partnerschaftliche Interaktion. *Diagnostica, 25*, 191–207.

Hahlweg, K., & Markman, H. J. (1988). Effectiveness of behavioral marital therapy: Empirical status of behavioral techniques in preventing and alleviating marital distress. *Journal of Consulting and Clinical Psychology, 56*, 440–447.

Hahlweg, K., & Markman, H. J. (in press). Prevention of marital distress: Results of a German prospective-longitudinal study. *Journal of Family Psychology.*

Halford, W. K. (1998, October). *The science of prevention: The big picture.* Invited keynote speech to the National Marriage and Relationship Education Conference, Adelaide, Australia.

Halford, W. K., & Bouma, R. (1997). Individual psychopathology and marital distress. In W. K. Halford & H. J. Markman (Eds.), *Clinical handbook of marriage and couples interventions* (pp. 291–321). New York: Wiley.

Hartman, S., Stanley, S. M., & Markman, H. J. (2000). *The role of joint activity in promoting marital satisfaction and commitment: Personal and social determinants of an overlooked protective factor.* Unpublished manuscript, University of Denver.

Hautzinger, M., Linden, M., & Hoffman, N. (1982). Distressed couples with and without a distressed partner: An analysis of their verbal interaction. *Journal of Behavior Therapy and Experimental Psychiatry, 13,* 307–314.

Hetherington, E. M. (1999). *Coping with divorce, single parenting, and remarriage: A risk and resiliency perspective.* Mahwah, NJ: Lawrence Erlbaum Associates.

Hinchliffe, M., Hooper, D., & Roberts, F. J. (1978). *The melancholy marriage.* New York: Wiley.

Hinshaw, S. P., & Anderson, C. A. (1996). Conduct and oppositional defiant disorders. In E. J. Mash & R. A. Barkley (Eds.), *Child psychopathology* (pp. 113–149). New York: Guilford.

Holman, T. B., & Jacquart, M. (1988). Leisure-activity patterns and marital satisfaction: A further test. *Journal of Marriage and the Family, 50,* 69–77.

Holmes, J. G., & Rempel, J. K. (1989). Trust in close relationships. In C. Hendrick (Ed.), *Close relationships: Review of personality and social psychology* (Vol. 10, pp. 187–220). Newbury Park, CA: Sage Publications.

Hooley, J. M., & Hahlweg, K. (1989). Marital satisfaction and marital communication in German and English couples. *Behavioral Assessment, 11,* 119–133.

Hops, H., Biglan, A., Sherman, L., Arthur, J., Friedman, L., & Osteen, V. (1987). Home observations of family interactions of depressed women. *Journal of Consulting and Clinical Psychology, 55,* 341–346.

Hops, H., Wills, T. A., Patterson, G. R., & Weiss, R. L. (1972). *Marital interaction coding system.* Eugene, OR: University of Oregon Research Institute.

Jack, D. C. (1991). *Silencing the self: Women and depression.* Cambridge, MA: Harvard University Press.

Jack, D. C., & Dill, D. (1992). The Silencing the Self Scale: Schemas of intimacy associated with depression in women. *Psychology of Women Quarterly, 16,* 97–106.

Jacob, T., & Krahn, G. L. (1988). Marital interactions of alcoholic couples: Comparison with depressed and nondistressed couples. *Journal of Consulting and Clinical Psychology, 56,* 73–79.

Jacob, T., Ritchey, D., Cvitkovic, J. F., & Blane, H. T. (1981). Communication styles of alcoholic and nonalcoholic families when drinking and not drinking. *Journal of Studies on Alcohol, 42,* 466–482.

Jacobson, N. S., & Addis, M. E. (1993). Research on couples and couple therapy: What do we know? *Journal of Consulting and Clinical Psychology, 61,* 85–93.

Jacobson, N. S., & Christensen, A. (1996). *Integrative couple therapy: Promoting acceptance and change.* New York: Norton.

Jacobson, N. S., & Margolin, G. (1979). *Marital therapy: Strategies based on social learning and behavior exchange principles.* New York: Brunner/Mazel.

Johnson, D. J., & Rusbult, C. E. (1989). Resisting temptation: Devaluation of alternative partners as a means of maintaining commitment in close relationships. *Journal of Personality and Social Psychology, 57,* 967–980.

Johnson, D. R., Amoloza, T. O., & Booth, A. (1992). Stability and developmental change in marital quality: A three-wave panel analysis. *Journal of Marriage and the Family, 54,* 582–594.

Johnson, M. P. (1982). The social and cognitive features of the dissolution of commitment to relationships. In S. Duck (Ed.), *Personal relationships: Dissolving personal relationships* (pp. 51–73). New York: Academic Press.

Jordan, P., Stanley, S., & Markman, H. (1999). *Becoming parents: How to strengthen your marriage as your family grows.* San Francisco: Jossey-Bass.

Kahn, J., Coyne, J. C., & Margolin, G. (1985). Depression and marital disagreement: The social construction of despair. *Journal of Social and Personal Relationships, 2,* 447–461.

Karney, B. R., & Bradbury, T. N. (1997). Neuroticism, marital interaction, and the trajectory of marital satisfaction. *Journal of Personality and Social Psychology, 72,* 1075–1092.

Karney, B. R., Bradbury, T. N., Fincham, F. D., & Sullivan, K. T. (1994). The role of negative affectivity in the association between attributions and marital satisfaction. *Journal of Personality & Social Psychology, 66,* 413–424.

Kaslow, F. W., & Hammerschmidt, H. (1992). Long term "good" marriages: The seemingly essential ingredients. In B. J. Brothers (Ed.), *Couples therapy multiple perspectives: In search of common threads* (pp. 15–38). New York: Haworth Press.

Kaslow, F. W., Hansson, K., & Lundblad, A.-M. (1994). Long term marriages in Sweden: And some comparisons with similar couples in the United States. *Contemporary Family Therapy, 16,* 521–537.

Kaslow, F. W., & Robison, J. A. (1996). Long-term satisfying marriages: Perceptions of contributing factors. *American Journal of Family Therapy, 24,* 153–170.

Kinnunen, U., & Pulkkinen, L. (1998). Linking economic stress to marital quality among Finnish marital couples. *Journal of Family Issues, 19,* 705–724.

Koren, P., Carlton, K., & Shaw, D. (1980). Marital conflict: Relations among behaviors, outcomes, and distress. *Journal of Consulting and Clinical Psychology, 48,* 460–468.

Kowalik, D. L., & Gotlib, I. H. (1987). Depression and marital interaction: Concordance between intent and perception of communication. *Journal of Abnormal Psychology, 96,* 127–134.

Lerner, H. G. (1985). *The dance of anger: A woman's guide to changing the patterns of intimate relationships.* New York: Harper & Row.

Lerner, H. G. (1988). *Women in therapy.* Northvale, NJ: Aronson.

Levenson, R. W., & Gottman, J. M. (1983). Marital interaction: Physiological linkage and affective exchange. *Journal of Personality and Social Psychology, 45,* 587–597.

Levenson, R. W., & Gottman, J. M. (1985). Physiological and affective predictors of change in relationship satisfaction. *Journal of Personality and Social Psychology, 49,* 85–94.

Levinger, G. (1980). Toward the analysis of close relationships. *Journal of Experimental Social Psychology, 16,* 510–544.

Lewin, K. (1948). The background of conflict in marriage. In G. W. Lewin (Ed.), *Resolving social conflicts* (pp. 84–102). New York: Harper and Brothers.

Lindahl, K. M., & Malik, N. M. (1999). Observations of marital conflict and power: Relations with parenting in the triad. *Journal of Marriage and the Family, 61,* 320–330.

Locke, H. J., & Wallace, K. M. (1959). Short marital-adjustment and prediction tests: Their reliability and validity. *Marriage and Family Living, 21,* 251–255.

Mackey, R. A., & O'Brien, B. A. (1999). Adaptation in lasting marriages. *Families in Society: The Journal of Contemporary Human Services, 80,* 587–599.

Margolin, G. (1983). An interactional model for the behavioral assessment of marital relationships. *Behavioral Assessment, 5,* 103–127.

Margolin, G., Burman, B., & John, R. S. (1989). Home observations of marital couples reenacting naturalistic conflicts. *Behavioral Assessment, 11,* 101–118.

Margolin, G., & Wampold, B. E. (1981). Sequential analysis of conflict and accord in distressed and nondistressed marital partners. *Journal of Consulting and Clinical Psychology, 47,* 554–567.

Markman, H. J. (1979). Application of a behavioral model of marriage in predicting relationship satisfaction of couples planning marriage. *Journal of Consulting and Clinical Psychology, 47,* 743–749.

Markman, H. J. (1981). The prediction of marital distress: A five year follow-up. *Journal of Consulting and Clinical Psychology, 49,* 760–762.

Markman, H. J., Duncan, S. W., Storaasli, R., & Howes, P. (1987). The predication and prevention of marital distress: A longitudinal analysis. In K. Hahlweg & M. Goldstein (Eds.), *Understanding major mental disorders: The contribution of family interaction research* (pp. 266–289). New York: Family Process.

Markman, H. J., Floyd, F. J., Stanley, S. M., & Storaasli, R. D. (1988). Prevention of marital distress: A longitudinal investigation. *Journal of Consulting and Clinical Psychology, 56,* 210–217.

Markman, H. J., & Hahlweg, K. (1993). The prediction and prevention of marital distress: An international perspective. *Clinical Psychology Review, 13*, 29–43.

Markman, H. J., Renick, M. J., Floyd, F. J., Stanley, S. M., & Clements, M. (1993). Preventing marital distress through communication and conflict management training: A 4- and 5-year follow-up. *Journal of Consulting and Clinical Psychology, 61*, 70–77.

Markman, H. J., Stanley, S. M., & Blumberg, S. L. (1994). *Fighting for your marriage: Positive steps for preventing divorce and preserving a lasting love*. San Francisco: Jossey-Bass.

McManus, M., Spaht, K., Stanley, S., Stanton, G., & Blankenhorn, D. (1998, July). *Can legislation lower the divorce rate?* Panel discussion presented at the annual Smart Marriages/Happy Families Conference, Washington, DC.

Miller, G. E., & Bradbury, T. N. (1995). Refining the association between attributions and behavior in marital interaction. *Journal of Family Psychology, 9*, 196–208.

Miller, N. B., & Kannae, L. A. (1999). Predicting marital quality in Ghana. *Journal of Comparative Family Studies, 30*, 599–615.

Mischel, W. (1968). *Personality and assessment*. New York: Wiley.

Nakosteen, R. A., & Zimmer, M. A. (1997). Men, money, and marriage: Are high earners more prone than low earners to marry? *Social Science Quarterly, 78*, 66–82.

Notarius, C. I., Benson, P. R., & Sloane, D. (1989). Exploring the interface between perception and behavior: An analysis of marital interaction in distressed and nondistressed couples. *Behavioral Assessment, 11*, 39–64.

Notarius, C. I., Krokoff, L. J., & Markman, H. J. (1981). Analysis of observational data. In E. E. Filsinger & R. A. Lewis (Eds.), *Assessing marriage: New behavioral approaches* (pp. 197–218). Beverly Hills, CA: Sage.

Notarius, C. I., & Markman, H. J. (1993). *We can work it out: Making sense of marital conflict*. New York: Putnam.

Notarius, C. I., Markman, H. J., & Gottman, J. (1983). Couples Interaction Scoring System: Clinical implications. In E. Filsinger (Ed.), *Marriage and family assessment: A sourcebook for family therapy* (pp. 117–136). Beverly Hills, CA: Sage.

O'Neill, J. M., Fishman, D. M., & Kinsella-Shaw, M. (1987). Dual-career couples' career transitions and normative dilemmas: A preliminary assessment model. *The Counseling Psychologist, 15*, 50–96.

Orthner, D. K., & Mancini, J. A. (1990). Leisure impacts on family interaction and cohesion. *Journal of Leisure Research, 22*, 125–137.

Pasch, L. A., & Bradbury, T. N. (1998). Social support, conflict, and the development of marital dysfunction. *Journal of Consulting and Clinical Psychology, 66*, 219–230.

Pasch, L. A., Bradbury, T. N., & Davila, J. (1997). Gender, negative affectivity, and observed social support behavior in marital interaction. *Personal Relationships, 4*, 361–378.

Patterson, G. R., & Hops, H. (1972). Coercion, a game for two: Intervention techniques for marital conflict. In R. E. Ulrich and P. Mountjoy (Eds.), *The experimental analysis of social behavior*. New York: Appleton-Century-Crofts.

Patterson, G. R., & Reid, J. B. (1970). Reciprocity and coercion: Two facets of social systems. In C. Neuringer & J. L. Michael (Eds.), *Behavior modification in clinical psychology* (pp. 133–177). New York: Appleton-Century-Crofts.

Patterson, G. R., & Reid, J. B. (1973). Intervention for families of aggressive boys: A replication study. *Behaviour Research & Therapy, 11*, 383–394.

Paul, G. L. (1967). Strategy of outcome research in psychotherapy. *Journal of Consulting Psychology, 31*, 109–118.

Peterson, K. S. (1997, April). Does tying the knot put women in a bind? *The USA Today* [On-line].

Peterson, K. S. (1998, July). Making "I do" harder to undo. *The USA Today* [On-line].

Raush, H. L., Barry, W. A., Hertel, R. K., & Swain, M. A. (1974). *Communication, conflict and marriage*. San Francisco: Jossey-Bass.

Revenstorf, D., Hahlweg, K., Schindler, L., & Vogel, B. (1984). Interaction analysis of marital conflict. In K. Hahlweg & N. S. Jacobson (Eds.), *Marital interaction: Analysis and modification* (pp. 159–181). New York: Guilford Press.

Revenstorf, D., Vogel, B., Wegener, C., Hahlweg, K., & Schindler, L. (1980). Escalation phenomena in interaction sequences: An empirical comparison of distressed and non-distressed couples. *Behavior Analysis and Modification, 2*, 97–116.

Roberts, L. J., & Krokoff, L. J. (1990). A time-series analysis of withdrawal, hostility, and displeasure in satisfied and dissatisfied marriages. *Journal of Marriage and the Family, 52*, 95–105.

Roizblatt, A., Kaslow, F., Rivera, S., Fuchs, T., Conejero, C., & Zacharias, A. (1999). Long lasting marriages in Chile. *Contemporary Family Therapy, 21*, 113–129.

Rusbult, C. E. (1980). Commitment and satisfaction in romantic associations: A test of the investment model. *Journal of Experimental Social Psychology, 16*, 172–186.

Rusbult, C. E. (1983). A longitudinal test of the investment model: The development (and deterioration) of satisfaction and commitment in heterosexual involvements. *Journal of Personality and Social Psychology, 45*, 101–117.

Rusbult, C. E., Martz, J. M., & Agnew, C. R. (1998). The investment model scale: Measuring commitment level, satisfaction level, quality of alternatives, and investment size. *Personal Relationships, 5*, 357–391.

Rusbult, C. E., Verette, J., Whitney, G. A., Slovik, L. F., & Lipkus, I. (1991). Accommodation processes in close relationships: Theory and preliminary empirical evidence. *Journal of Personality and Social Psychology, 60*, 53–78.

Sayers, S. L., & Baucom, D. H. (1995). Multidimensional scaling of spouses' attributions for marital conflicts. *Cognitive Therapy & Research, 19*, 667–693.

Senchak, M., & Leonard, K. E. (1993). The role of spouses' depression and anger in the attribution–marital satisfaction relation. *Cognitive Therapy & Research, 17*, 397–409.

Sharlin, S. A. (1996). Long-term successful marriages in Israel. *Contemporary Family Therapy, 18*, 225–242.

Shek, D. T. L. (1998). Linkage between marital quality and parent–child relationship. *Journal of Family Issues, 19*, 687–704.

Silliman, B., Stanley, S., Coffin, W., Markman, H., & Jordan, P. (in press). Preventive interventions for couples. In H. Liddle, D. Santisteban, R. Levant, & J. Bray (Eds.), *Family psychology intervention science*. Washington, DC: APA Publications.

Smith, D. A., Vivian, D., & O'Leary, K. D. (1990). Longitudinal prediction of marital discord from premarital expressions of affect. *Journal of Consulting and Clinical Psychology, 58*, 790–798.

Spanier, G. B. (1976). Measuring dyadic adjustment: New scales for assessing the quality of marriage and similar dyads. *Journal of Marriage & the Family, 38*, 15–28.

Spanier, G. B., & Lewis, R. A. (1980). Marital quality: A review of the seventies. *Journal of Marriage and the Family, 42*, 825–839.

Stanley, S. M. (1997). What's important in premarital counseling? *Marriage and Family: A Christian Journal, 1*, 51–60.

Stanley, S. M. (1998). *The heart of commitment: Compelling research that reveals the secrets of a lifelong, intimate marriage*. Nashville, TN: Nelson.

Stanley, S. M., & Markman, H. J. (1992). Assessing commitment in personal relationships. *Journal of Marriage and the Family, 54*, 595–608.

Stanley, S. M., & Markman, H. J. (1997). *Marriage in the 90s: A nationwide random phone survey*. Denver, CO: PREP.

Stanley, S. M., & Markman, H. J. (1998). Acting on what we know: The hope of prevention. In T. Ooms (Ed.), *Strategies to strengthen marriage: What we know, what we need to know* (pp. 37–54). Washington, DC: The Family Impact Seminar.

Stanley, S. M., Markman, H. J., Prado, L. M., Olmos-Gallo, P. A., Tonelli, L., St. Peters, M., Leber, B. D., Bobulinski, M., Cordova, A., & Whitton, S. (in press). Short term effects of premarital training in a religious, community-based sample. *Family Process*.

Stanley, S. M., Markman, H. J., St. Peters, M., & Leber, B. D. (1995). Strengthening marriage and preventing divorce: New directions in prevention research. *Family Relations: Journal of Applied Family and Child Studies, 44,* 392–401.

Stockdale, J. E. (1989). Concepts and measures of leisure participation and preference. In E. L. Jackson & T. L. Burton (Eds.), *Understanding leisure and recreation: Mapping the past, charting the future* (pp. 113–150). State College, PA: Venture Publishing.

Stuart, R. B. (1969). Operant-interpersonal treatment for marital discord. *Journal of Consulting and Clinical Psychology, 33,* 675–682.

Sullaway, M., & Christensen, A. (1983). Assessment of dysfunctional interaction patterns in couples. *Journal of Marriage and the Family, 45,* 653–660.

Terman, L. M., Buttenwieser, P., Ferguson, L. W., Johnson, W. B., & Wilson, D. P. (1938). *Psychological factors in marital happiness.* New York: McGraw-Hill.

Thurmaier, F., Engl, J., Eckert, V., & Hahlweg, K. (1992). Praevention von Ehe- und Partnerschaftsstoerungen EPL (Ehevorbereitung—Ein Partnerschaftliches Lernprogramm). *Verhaltenstherapie, 2,* 116–124.

Ting-Toomey, S. (1983). An analysis of verbal communication patterns in high and low marital adjustment groups. *Human Communication Research, 9,* 306–319.

Townsley, R. M., Beach, S. R. H., Fincham, F. D., & O'Leary, K. D. (1991). Cognitive specificity for marital discord and depression: What types of cognition influence discord? *Behavior Therapy, 22,* 519–530.

Tzeng, J. M., & Mare, R. D. (1995). Labor market and socioeconomic effects on marital stability. *Social Science Research, 24,* 329–351.

Vaillant, C. O., & Vaillant, G. E. (1993). Is the U-curve of marital satisfaction an illusion? A 40-year study of marriage. *Journal of Marriage and the Family, 55,* 230–239.

Van Lange, P. A., Rusbult, C. E., Drigotas, S. M., Arriaga, X. B., Witcher, B. S., & Cox, C. L. (1997). Willingness to sacrifice in close relationships. *Journal of Personality and Social Psychology, 72,* 1373–1395.

Vanzetti, N. A., Notarius, C. I., & NeeSmith, D. (1992). Specific and generalized expectancies in marital interaction. *Journal of Family Psychology, 6,* 171–183.

Veroff, J., Kulka, R. A., & Douvan, E. (1981). *Mental health in America: Patterns of help seeking from 1957 to 1976.* New York: Basic Books.

Vincent, J. P. (1972). *The relationship of sex, level of intimacy, and level of marital distress to problem-solving behavior and exchange of social reinforcement.* Unpublished doctoral dissertation, University of Oregon, Eugene.

Wampold, B. E., & Margolin, G. (1982). Nonparametric strategies to test independence of behavioral states in sequential data. *Psychological Bulletin, 92,* 755–765.

Wastell, C. A. (1991). Empathy in marriage. *Australian Journal of Marriage and Family, 12,* 27–38.

Wegener, C., Revenstorf, D., Hahlweg, K., & Schindler, L. (1979). Empirical analysis of communication in distressed and nondistressed couples. *Behavior Analysis and Modification, 3,* 178–188.

Weiss, R. L. (1980). Strategic behavioral marital therapy: Toward a model for assessment and intervention. In J. P. Vincent (Ed.), *Advances in family intervention, assessment and theory* (Vol. 1, pp. 229–271). Greenwich, CT: JAI Press.

Weiss, R. L., & Heyman, R. E. (1990). Observation of marital interaction. In T. N. Bradbury & F. D. Fincham (Eds.), *The psychology of marriage* (pp. 87–117). New York: Guilford Press.

Weiss, R. L., Hops, H., & Patterson, G. R. (1973). A framework for conceptualizing marital conflict: A technology for altering it, some data for evaluating it. In L. D. Handy & E. L. Mash (Eds.), *Behavior change: Methodology concepts and practice* (pp. 309–342). Champaign, IL: Research Press.

Whitton, S. W., & Stanley, S. M. (1999, June). Sacrifice in romantic relationships: The role of perceptions. Poster session presented at the convention of the American Psychological Society, Denver, CO.

Whitton, S. W., Stanley, S. M., & Markman, H. J. (2000). *Sacrifice in romantic relationships*. Unpublished manuscript, University of Denver.

Wieselquist, J., Rusbult, C. E., Foster, C. A., & Agnew, C. R. (1999). Commitment, pro-relationship behavior, and trust in close relationships. *Journal of Personality and Social Psychology, 77,* 942–966.

Wile, D. B. (1981). *Couples therapy: A non-traditional approach.* New York: Wiley.

5

Retrospect and Prospect in the Psychological Study of Coparenting and Family Group Process

James P. McHale
Allison Lauretti
Jean Talbot
Christina Pouquette
Clark University

This chapter examines the meaning and relevance of family group dynamics in studies of child and family development. Readers unfamiliar with recent advances in the conceptualization and measurement of coparenting and family group process may wonder what this chapter has to add on the heels of detailed sections on mothering, fathering, and marital relationships, which is why an overview of multiperson family relationship systems is essential in a volume examining research with families and children. For decades, socialization researchers discussed "family influences on development" without studying the family collective. As we discuss, the ways family members relate with one another in different interpersonal contexts do show consistency in many families. In others, however, inconsistencies are the rule, and children growing up in such families can have disparate social experiences with the same partner in different settings. Moreover, researchers have recently articulated various distinctive family group dynamics, reflecting underlying organizational processes, which surface only when families are engaged together as interacting groups. And, although such family group dynamics do not simply represent a recapitulation of attachment, marital, or other intrafamily relationship processes, they do uniquely predict young children's social and emotional adaptation, even after the well-known effects of parenting and marital processes have been considered.

This chapter provides a broad overview of family group dynamics. First, we draw on the work of the anthropologist Harrell (1997) to describe four basic family system formations. We then consider more specifically family groups in the United States and the roots of American psychologists' current belief system about "optimal" family functioning. Next, we spotlight recent research on coparenting and family group process in the nuclear family group and discuss studies linking these dynamics to important indicators of young children's development and adaptation. We emphasize the need to extend this fledgling knowledge base on how coparental and family group processes affect children's development to include family systems beyond the two-parent nuclear family, and we conclude with some thoughts about clinical practice, public policy, and future coparenting and family group research.

UNDERSTANDING FAMILIES AND FAMILY FUNCTIONS

In psychology, those who study families have often begun their work by developing ideas about how "optimal" family functioning supports the growth, development, and successful societal adjustment of family members. Typically, such work has been largely ahistorical and spawned locally, in the individuals' own "backyards." Only later, if then, has such work blossomed to other places and cultures as researchers have wondered whether that which is optimal in one locale is equally optimal elsewhere. Ultimately, however, defining or characterizing family group patterns, processes, and dynamics devoid of their historical or cultural meaning makes little sense (Parke, chap. 3, this volume; Silverstein, chap. 2, this volume). Humans have always organized their families to adapt to the larger social system in which they have reproduced these families (Harrell, 1997). By understanding changes in the principles driving family-based activities in different societies at different periods in history, the adaptive qualities of the myriad family patterns present today come into sharper relief.

Harrell (1997) contended three major historical transformations have fundamentally affected the family and produced four stages of human history thus far. First, *sedentarization* led the earliest societies, nomadic bands, to gradually transform into rank societies. Later, the *formation of social castes* transformed rank societies into complex societies. And most recently, the *industrial-scientific revolution* led many complex societies to become modern societies. With each transformation, societies became larger, socially and culturally more complex, and evolutionarily favored over the preceding type (in the sense that they possessed an advantage when there was competition between societal types). However, because events of evolution also depend on adaptive advantage in particular environments, the three great transformations did not occur at the same time throughout the world, and societies at all levels of complexity have coexisted for centuries.

Harrell emphasized that social formations are more basic than family systems; to understand changes in the nature of the family it makes no sense to posit an evolutionary sequence, but rather to chart changes in the nature of the activities family members have been called on to perform at each stage of social evolution. Because various structural arrangements can be used to carry out necessary activities in any situation, a variety (though, not an infinite variety) of family systems can be viable at different levels of social complexity. Space limitations do not permit us to review all possible family forms at all stages of societal evolution; instead, we summarize prototypic or, in anthropological terms, "ideal" cases to illustrate basic principles germane to research on the family group.

Harrell saw five sets of activities—procurement and processing (division of subsistence labor); regulation of sexuality; socialization of children; and provision of emotional warmth, support, and comfort—as the basic family functions that cut across all social environments in which families exist. Psychologists, of course, have studied extensively the latter two functions (socialization and emotional support), though all five must be considered to understand family organization. Harrell also identified other functions—representing family members in the public sphere, enabling family members in the public sphere, and managing and transmitting property and offices—as important in certain kinds of societies but not in others (when not necessary, these functions do not impinge on the nature of the family system). The following is a synopsis of how these functions have organized families in the four major societal types outlined by Harrell.

The Family as Indistinguishable From the Larger Social Group: Band Societies

Band, or egalitarian societies, are small, nomadic foraging-hunting-gathering societies with flexible group membership (i.e., moving between groups relatively frequently), where concepts of property and possessions are meaningless. Goods not readily consumed or transported are of no value, and nothing gets passed on from generation to generation. Of particular interest, however, is that band societies do not distinguish public from domestic spheres because division of labor—procuring and processing—take place not at the family level, but at the group level. Likewise, socialization of children is by the band and not simply by the child's biological parents or first-degree relatives, and children are emotionally close to multiple others within the group. Band societies rarely feature inherent gendered patterns, indicating that gender differences may best be studied as adaptations to particular environments embedded in larger social formations (Rosaldo, 1980).

The Family as a Bounded Unit Within an Egalitarian Community: Rank Societies

Over time, expansion by foraging groups forced direct between-group competition and prompted bands to settle in one place to produce and depend on agriculture, gardening, livestock raising, hunting, or fishing. Although large groups and settled land necessitated leadership and hierarchy to facilitate social organization and control, leaders in rank societies were charged principally with insuring that all societal members had access to basic goods necessary for social reproduction. Among the strategies relied on by leaders in societies where land was scarce was allocating resources to kinship groups, giving birth to concepts of family groupings and homesteads and relocating divisions of subsistence labor into the family group itself. Hence came the first clear distinction between family and society; moreover, with families now "owning" land, principles of inheritance and of reckoning descent became concerns in family organization. The family was suddenly a group within which property (and offices) were managed and transmitted, where closer restriction of sexuality benefited a system based on kinship, and where the primary responsibility for children belonged to a family group rather than to the society or band as a whole. Socialization and education also became the province of the child's immediate family members.

Harrell's (1997) analysis illustrates the remarkable diversity of rank societies; in some polygynous groups, where land and subsistence goods were plentiful, large households affording substantial labor power were valued (especially by men) to help build wealth and status, aid in military or political exploits, and strengthen alliances through marriage. The family strategies of women in these same societies, however, were geared toward maintaining a balance between available labor and the family's consumptive needs. These differences in focus led certain rank societies to begin conceiving of the public sphere as a male domain and the private, domestic sphere as a female domain. However, in other rank societies, such as many island nations where land was scarce, family organization was different. On small islands, where the ability of chiefs and councils to determine family access to the scarce available land was crucial, there was little of the prestige competition seen in ecologically open rank societies. Family strategies in such nations were diverse and geared toward finding ways (adoption, property rights for multiple groups) to adjust the balance between people and scarce land resources.

The Family as an Insular Unit in a Nonegalitarian Society: Complex Societies

As was the case in the band to rank transformation, complex societies were borne of shortages in subsistence resources. As population growth curtailed universal access to these resources, high-ranking members of society for the first time began exerting differential control by distinguishing families owning land, livestock, or goods from families who could access goods only by subordinating themselves to owners. In short order, social class inequalities were institutionalized through laws and other control mechanisms of the state, with property-owning families confronting the strain of having to continue producing at a high level to retain their ascribed status. By making resource production so central to public status and access to basic goods, the complex society effectively isolated families one from another, pitting them in competition for status determined by success or failure in managing resources needed for the family's advantage.

This competition and isolation marked the sharpest distinction of domestic from public spheres of any stage of social evolution; all family activities were suddenly vital for survival and concentrated in a single type of family group. The family's management and transmissal of property and offices became critical determinants of well-being in both present and subsequent generations. Sexuality had to be strictly regulated both before and outside marriage, and families took nearly exclusive charge of the socialization of children, especially among the majority group, which had no access to formal, literate education. Here too representation became important, as only certain family members (almost always, men) took part in public-sphere activities of critical importance to the welfare of the full family group. This redefined relationship of family in society bred cloistered family groups focused on safeguarding family interests and preserving family status, and there was not much variation in how such family systems operated throughout the world. Across class lines within societies, however, there were indeed differences in family structures and patterns. The principles of complex families outlined previously held principally for property-holding classes; families with no property were not competing with other families. Moreover, because there was no property earmarked for the next generation, the activities and sexuality of young adults from non-property-holding families did not need to be as strictly monitored. Such families showed far greater tolerance of deviance from family norms than property-owning families. Without interests in a common estate, in fact, family structures and patterns in the lower class remained more like those of rank societies.

The Family as Launching Pad: Modern Societies

As goods production became streamlined following the industrial revolution, there came another dramatic shift. Most families in society began making their livings from selling their labor rather than from the fruits of their property. With this major shift, jobs for the first time were earned and kept through individual skill and initiative, and social status came to be allocated to individuals, rather than to families. With activities performed in and for the family group no longer essential to family survival, and with kin-based succession to offices virtually eliminated, there came inevitable shifts in the power parents held over children (including their control of children's sexuality) and in the nature of relationships between junior and senior generations. Greater diversity in family living arrangements also became possible, a diversity that Harrell considered a defining characteristic of modern societies. Modern families are free to invent their own ideologies and to change locales, a freedom that affords unprecedented opportunities but also threatens families with anonymity and loss of nearby kin support. At the same time, this autonomy has given birth to a new ethos—family intimacy. Citing Burgess, Locke, and Thomas (1945), the sociologist Farrell (1999) contended that the modern "companionship family" is a historically recent phenomenon, made possible primarily because modern families are not overwhelmed by the unrelenting work demands faced by families trying to survive in community-centered, property-based complex societies.

FACTORS GUIDING THE FAMILY PROCESS OF MODERN FAMILIES

Understanding the relationship of the family with the public sphere, and the shifting functions of the family group itself in band, rank, complex, and modern societies, is an important first step in understanding family experience and family patterns. As Farrell (1999) noted, family scholars have often been guilty of missing general trends and patterns among family groups, while generalizing too readily about the family as a monolithic institution without attending to individual and group variation or historical change. Certainly, family psychologists are interested in distinguishing among families on the basis of family group process and dynamics, and we consider such variability among nuclear family groups shortly. At the time of this volume, however, a comprehensive understanding of family diversity (including within-culture diversity) along key dimensions of family group process and dynamics that acknowledge the array of different family groupings cross-nationally remains on the distant horizon. At this point, we reiterate that only by understanding families across time and historical venue can we come to an informed appreciation of current family patterns.

Anthropologists and social historians have argued that despite major shifts in the family's functions over periods of societal change (such as other institutions taking over the family's instrumental procuring and processing tasks), what has not changed—and, in many analyses, what remains an important integrative function of the family group in society—is its central role in providing for the socialization of children and the emotional sustenance of its members. We consider these two functions in greater detail.

Adults' Socialization Goals for Children

Contemporary families in complex and modern societies show major differences in the fundamental socialization goals they emphasize. Control, filial piety, and lifelong dedication to the family unit are emphasized in complex societies, whereas actualization, independence, and autonomy are central in modern societies. These socialization goals mirror the means through which parents aide their children in finding success. In the complex society, the principal means of insuring social survival across generations is maintaining enduring ties to family and property (Harrell, 1997; Hibbett & Itasaka, 1967). In modern societies, children must be entrained to create their own success in a social role. However, although most modern families seek to cultivate their children's autonomy and independence, there remains tremendous variability among these families. First, because ownership and transmissal of property are still central to the economic base of many privileged families, farm families, and small merchant or shop-owning families in the United States and other modern societies, many features of family organization characteristic of families in complex societies remain operative in such families. This said, members of the younger generation in modern societies can decide not to continue on in a family business, an option unheard of in premodern societies. Second, family practices remain fundamentally affected by the family's and its subcultural group's interface with the majority culture. For example, mothers of color in the United States, unlike White middle-class mothers, must be concerned with their children's right to exist and are focused on the importance of survival (Collins, 1999). Greater reliance on authoritarian parenting strategies by African American parents may reflect preparation of children for the harsh exigencies of the world beyond their family (Cowan, Powell, & Cowan, 1997). Hence, although modern families may come together around the goal of inculcating children's independence, autonomy, and eventual reliance on spouses and families of procreation for deriving emotional and material support (Sudarkasa, 1999), the roads parents take toward actualizing these goals vary as a function of their position in society.

Emotional Sustenance of Family Members

Not 200 years ago in the United States, children were needed components in the family workforce, viewed by society as sturdy, useful laborers. Today, however, children are seen as fragile, vulnerable innocents. What changed? In colonial America, as in many contemporary complex societies, children were facts of life, valued for their contribution to family labor and for the future caregiving they would afford dependent parents. According to Farrell (1999), they possessed a "sturdiness and early capacity for responsibility ... that gave them the appearance of little adults roughly by the age of seven" (p. 22). Farrell noted that in 18th-century America, rituals of extended mourning rarely followed children's deaths and that newly born children were often given the same names as previous offspring who had died young (Smith, 1977). Modern children, by contrast, are celebrated for their individuality. Now an option for parents, most (though certainly not all) children in modern societies are not required to help families by procuring, processing, or representing, and their labor no longer enables parents' success in the public sphere. The opposite is true; millions of modern American children are passive recipients of their parents' labor often well into their 20s, with parental labor providing the education and opportunities that can further children's own station in life.

Although these are clearly global statements about modern societies intended only to capture prevailing ethos, the point we are making is that the basic emotional interiors of family groups must be seen as rooted in a particular place, time, and history. Family interiors have been steadily changing as families have reinvented the role and place of children. Moreover, the conceptualization of children as precious and in need of sustained protection is only one such change. The emotional significance of children in modern families has also shifted in a second, different manner, one often overlooked without comparative historical analysis. Over the past 200 years, husband–wife relationships have also transformed, from unions of functional interdependence to unions of emotional attachment. In contrast with many complex societies, where women look to their dependent children rather than to their husbands for emotional support, modern marriages have come to possess both affective and erotic components. Dramatic declines in fertility (adults wanting and having fewer children) and increases in adult life expectancies have contributed to this shift, with married partners now spending substantial periods of adult life living without children at home. In other words, as families reinvented children, so too did they reinvent marriages! Yet most of psychology's contemporary family theories overlook this fact, conceptualizing close and intimate husband–wife unions as the natural order of things. Furthermore, nearly all of these theories posit psychopathology as a probable outcome in families where a weak adult union is accompanied by cross-generational parent–child alliances (Nichols &

Schwartz, 1998). Psychology researchers who study families emphasize tensions sparked by the competing demands of children and marriage. And as many chapters in this volume attest, most of our theories maintain that in the absence of intimate, supportive interadult relationships, the odds of parents' being able to engage in responsive, empathic parenting or in synchronous, coordinated coparenting are not very good.

To summarize, two basic family functions that have survived through various historical transformations are the socialization of children and the emotional sustenance of family members. However, socialization goals and emotional attachments within families have shifted as societies have transformed from complex to modern, and it is important not to lose sight of the fact that psychology's preeminent theories about the family are historically, culturally, ethnically, and economically specific. We recognize that in providing this stripped-down functional analysis, we have short shrifted the remarkable within-culture diversity of family types, particularly among modern societies, that must capture our focused attention in the coming decades, and we have neglected many of the important societal factors, including religious and other indigenous belief systems, that likewise help explain important global variations in family functioning and process. Our modest aim in presenting the view afforded by functional family analysis has been to introduce one useful frame for beginning to contextualize such global family variations.

STUDYING FAMILIES AND FAMILY GROUP PROCESS: WHO EXACTLY CONSTITUTES THE FAMILY GROUP?

It bears repeating that in most of psychology's contemporary family theories, the unit of study has been the nuclear, two-parent family. This is perhaps understandable, given psychology's history, but it is also unfortunate because it has led to a myopic view of families. In commenting on the nuclear family of modern western cultures, Bateson (2000) emphasized that this arrangement deviates from the diverse, multifaceted age and sex groupings that have constituted families in every other society in history, describing the nuclear family "not as the ideal of family life, but as a bare and fragile minimum" (p. 19). Moreover, given the variety of adaptive family strategies now possible in modern societies, increasing numbers of contemporary modern families are no longer assuming this form, either. In this section, before reviewing recent empirical advances in the investigation of whole family dynamics among nuclear family groups, we provide a brief and selective look at nonnuclear family arrangements in the early 21st century and the dilemmas that such arrangements will undoubtedly pose for researchers interested in studying "the" family group process.

Many contemporary families continue to be organized by principles of consanguinity rather than , that is, around blood kin rather than marital ties. As in band cultures and many rank cultures, socialization of children in such family groups does not fall solely to the child's biological parents but rather to an extended family group. For example, in family compounds in Africa, blood kin live together and raise children collectively. Although most adult family members living in this kin network are also involved in conjugal or marital relationships throughout their lives, when marital unions end it is the in-married adult who leaves the compound and the children who remain (Sudarkasa, 1999). Extended kin networks are also found in many Oceanic groups, where children are adopted out to kin after infancy and early childhood, retaining emotional connections to both their natal and adoptive families. Historically, some such adoptions have been dictated by availability of subsistence resources, whereas others have been consciously orchestrated to prevent children from forming excessively strong attachments to the natal family, which would compromise the children's abilities to function independently and effectively as fully contributing societal members (Harrell, 1997).

Extended kin networks have also remained important in the United States, where many African American families whose indigenous family and kin systems were disrupted during the slavery years nonetheless managed to retain an ethic of consanguinial kin relations (Rodgers-Rose, 1980; Staples, 1971). Such relations became even more extensive and systematic in the postslavery years, as racial discrimination in the southern labor market necessitated extended paternal leave taking in search of work and migration to northern cities (Darity & Myers, 1984; Giddings, 1982). An ethic of cooperation and sharing—of money, housing, child care, education, and information—developed between households as an adaptation assuring that whatever meager subsistence resources were available were made accessible to all family members. Within the underclass in the United States today, a similar ethic has remained at work, wherein both blood and fictive kin share resources and the care of children across connected households, many of which could not subsist independently (Stack, 1974). However, Roschelle (1997) has presented data indicating that in many areas these social networks may be becoming less available to parents than they have been in decades past (see also McDonald & Armstrong, 2001).

Although modern African American families in the underclass draw on African family heritage in organizing flexibly and adaptively to sustain the family network, prioritizing children's needs, and providing a broad and deep affectional family base, such arrangements also constrain members of the extended network. Rapp (1999) summarized drawbacks of this family structure, which prevents family members from developing alternative family arrangements, except at extreme emotional cost to all members of the group. For although stable, pair relationships within extended family networks are viewed with respect, family members who move toward nuclear systems outside of the family network (as do couples entering into the middle class) leave behind family who had supported them and take with them important resources relied on by others in the extended group. Still, despite the upheaval such movement causes for all concerned, African Americans with the economic means to do so nonetheless raise their children primarily within conjugally focused and centered family groups (Sudarkasa, 1999). Even when such groups include senior relatives, they diverge from systems in which a senior relative (especially a grandmother) holds a position of authority equal to or greater than one or both spouses in that the seniors are subordinated to the conjugal pair who form the core of that group (Sudarkasa, 1999). The link to class is a strong one indeed; in 1980, 62% of African American households earning more than $20,000 and 72% earning more than $50,000 were headed by married couples (Farley & Allen, 1987).

It is not only underclass children whose households diverge from nuclear, two-parent structures. To the contrary, increases in the nonmarital birthrate and escalating divorce statistics indicate that most American children will spend at least part of their childhood in a single-parent-headed family. Single-parent family structures have dominated an ongoing debate about how the nature of family environments affect children's experience; two competing, and at times seemingly irreconcilable, perspectives have been at the center of this debate (Farrell, 1999; see also Silverstein, chap. 2, this volume). The first, based on the notion that nuclear family structures are the key to cultivating the values that strengthen children, has been a movement to put two-parent families first in policy decisions: constraining single-parent family structures by stigmatizing divorce and nonmarital childbearing, and encouraging new cultural models for fathering. The second perspective accepts single-parent families as a modern reality, promoting policies and programs offering tangible forms of support such as expanded earned-income tax credit and assured child support to provide for children's well-being. This perspective (e.g., McLanahan & Sandefur, 1994) maintains that the well-being of children is optimally supported by healthy, secure, employed parents, regardless of whether the parenting individuals are single or married. Proponents of the first position see programs advocated by proponents of the second position as encouraging and rewarding single-parent family structures, and proponents of the second position counter that the top priority is to support children, regardless of the type of family structure in which they live.

Though we do not have ample space in this chapter to review thoroughly the foundations of these two perspectives, we believe fresh perspectives in this debate are sorely needed. One such perspective is provided by Crosbie-Burnett and Lewis (1999), whose thoughtful analysis of post-divorce families illustrates how the *patrifocal* system of law within the United States—defining the family based on the status of adults (i.e., legal marriage, separation, or divorce)—discourages continued, regular interaction by extended kin with children following divorce. This they contrast with the aforementioned ethic of centering families around children—a *pedifocal* family focus characteristic of many African American families. Because the basic family unit in pedifocal systems includes everyone involved in the nurturance and support of a child, regardless of the individuals' actual household membership (Brooks-Gunn & Furstenberg, 1986; Stack, 1974), the center of family relations shifts away from arrangements between legally related members to arrangements based on the child's needs, assuring continuing responsibility for dependent children across changes in relationships among adults. As Crosbie-Burnett and Lewis (1999) explained, such systems and ideologies stand to be of great benefit to postdivorce Euro-American families, maximizing ongoing cooperation and limiting antagonism between adults and their kin because the goal of relating is based not on an exspousal relationship, but a multiparental one (Ahrons & Rodgers, 1987). Indeed, modern postdivorce families face many of the issues that have challenged African American families since slavery: assuring the welfare of children when one or both biological parents are not present in the home, complex and ambiguous roles and responsibilities, permeable family and household boundaries, and having one's family structure defined by the dominant culture as deviant, outside the norm (Crosbie-Burnett & Lewis, 1999).

Pedifocal definitions of the family endorse all adults who contribute to the child's well-being; acting in the best interest of the child rather than the parents means identifying all individuals from both sides of the family who have been positively involved with the child and establishing mechanisms for their continued involvement after divorce, thereby minimizing the child's losses. And perhaps most important, adopting a pedifocal, postdivorce family orientation requires that both adults agree to respect and strengthen, rather than undermine, future parental or other family figures who become involved in the support and nurturance of children, the essence of the coparental or cocaregiving solidarity we outline next. To the extent that there can be functional linkage among multiple adults for the betterment of children (characteristic of the pedifocal orientation of many African American families), children's adjustment can be strengthened.

In summary, because most research on family group process has documented children's development within two-parent nuclear families, greater innovation and sensitivity will be required in future family group research to capture the lived reality of the multitudes of children who do not live in nuclear family units. With the burgeoning of a new knowledge base on multiperson relationship dynamics within nuclear family groups, we now have a critical mass of focused empirical studies that can provide a beginning point for thinking about the dynamics of multiparent family groups. As we have been emphasizing, however, researchers must keep in mind that the organization and accompanying interpersonal dynamics of many families will diverge in significant ways from the adaptations made by this comparison group of primarily middle-class, heterosexual, White married couples (see Cox & Harter, chap. 6, this volume).

CRYSTALLIZING A KEY FAMILY PROCESS: COPARENTING IN A FAMILY GROUP CONTEXT

Whither the Family Group in Developmental Research?

To group-thinking sociologists, anthropologists, and clinicians trained as family therapists, it may sound odd to hear that studies fully incorporating a family group perspective are a very, very new phenomenon in psychology's child development literature. Indeed, up through the mid-1990s, most studies of child development in the field's leading psychology journals limited their conceptualizations of family interiors to parent–child attachment quality, father involvement, or exposure to marital conflict. Though there were myriad studies of two-parent nuclear families showing that responsive parenting was compromised by marital distress, few studies sought to tie everything together by examining the overall socialization climate that the two coparenting partners together were affording their children. This is not to say that pertinent research on family groups was not being conducted— noteworthy publications that provided fresh and creative insights into whole family processes included Reiss' (1981) *The Family's Construction of Reality* and Walsh's (1982, 1993) edited volumes, *Normal Family Processes.* Reiss' innovative work inspired Hauser's (e.g., Hauser et al., 1984) subsequent investigations of whole family process in families of normal, diabetic, and psychiatrically ill adolescents, and the 1993 edition of Walsh's volume provided cogent updates of comprehensive research programs by Beavers, Olson, Epstein, and others outlining several alternative means for distinguishing among families on the basis of how well they met certain basic functions (e.g., how flexibly and adaptively they responded to challenge and change). Given the positive reception Reiss' and Walsh's volumes received from family researchers 20 years ago, it remains a mystery why socialization researchers took so long to fully embrace the potential ramifications of this work for understanding children's early social environments.

Despite the absence of dialogue between child development researchers and family clinicians that continued until Minuchin's (1985) wake-up call in *Child Development*, one important area that *had* attracted the attention of developmental researchers in the late 1970s was coparenting in postdivorce family environments. In a seminal report, Hetherington, Cox, and Cox (1982) showed that children in postdivorce families fared badly when interparental antagonism that had characterized the predivorce family environment continued or escalated after family dissolution (see also Ahrons, 1981; Wallerstein & Kelly, 1980). In subsequent research studies, the lack of consistency in routine as children moved back and forth between parents in custody arrangements, continuing interparental antagonism, and triangulation of children into interadult conflict repeatedly emerged as major predictors of postdivorce adjustment (Buchanan, Maccoby, & Dornbusch, 1991; Camera & Resnick, 1988; Johnston, Campbell, & Mayes, 1985). It is, in retrospect, surprising how many years it took after the publication of these research findings before researchers began to look systematically at the effects of coparenting support, antagonism, and coordination in families that had not undergone divorce.

Coparenting in Two-Parent Families: Some Basic Considerations

Unlike some of the more elusive constructs studied by family clinicians in years past, the notion of coparenting coordination is one that most researchers, and laypersons, readily grasp. Perhaps this is because most parenting partners entertain at least somewhat divergent notions of how they would ideally like to raise their child. Although there is greater ideological consistency between parenting partners within certain cultures and as a function of parent gender, parenting ideologies within families are likely never to be fully consonant. How adults in families where there is more than one actively involved parenting figure reconcile their divergent views is at the core of the coparental alliance.

The notion that children whose parents work collaboratively should fare better than children whose parents work at cross-purposes is straightforward. Establishing an adequate conceptual framework for understanding coparenting cooperation and collaboration has not been as simple. According to the Cowans' (1992) seminal study of how parents coordinate when their children are infants, one way of conceptualizing modern coparenting relationships is to examine how satisfied the parents, especially the mothers, are with the "who does what" of child care. Normatively, most North American women express disappointment with their partners' contributions, expecting more participation than the partners provide. Men, for their part, typically feel that they do more than their partners recognize. Several U.S. studies over the past decade have illustrated that the bigger the discrepancy between what women expect and what men (in the women's eyes) actually do, the greater is the level of marital dissatisfaction the women express in the early postpartum months (Nicolson, 1990; Terry, McHugh, & Noller, 1991; though see Hackel & Ruble, 1992).

But do marked imbalances in child-care labor translate into contentious or emotionally bereft coparental alliances? Although few studies have posed this question, fathers in many traditional cultures have important developmental influence in their children's lives despite assuming no feeding, diapering, or middle-of-the-night responsibilities. Any between-family variability in the degree of support or antagonism between fathers and mothers in such cultures must owe to factors besides degree of paternal involvement in child care. Likewise, many U.S. fathers who fall down on child-care responsibilities are nonetheless strongly invested in the child's and family's emotional life. Such emotional investment—whether in a traditional coparenting family (where mother does 95% or more of the basic care activities) or in a shared coparenting family (where mothers typically still do between 60% and 70% of the basic care activities)—must be incorporated into conceptualizations of the family's coparental alliance. To illustrate, though fathers often devote discretionary time at home to affectively charged play activities with infants and toddlers (see Silverstein, chap. 2, this volume), we know little about how mothers view their partners' pleasurable relationship with the infant when that same partner contributes next to nothing to the work of parenting. Yet to fully understand the emergent family pattern, it is important to understand both the father's proclivity to participate regularly and meaningfully in social exchanges with the baby and maternal response to paternal involvement. Mothers ambivalent about their partner's connection with the baby may engage in exclusionary gatekeeping activities to limit father–child engagement or communicate their negativity toward the partner to the infant through verbal and nonverbal channels. Conversely, mothers who value their partner's emotional exchanges with the child, even in the face of inadequate paternal participation in the work of child care, are more likely to be members of cooperative and cohesive coparenting alliances (Dienhart & Daly, 1997).

Fathers too are active contributors to the family's coparenting system. For example, men in working-class families typically watch, learn from, and model their partners' parenting styles, affording consistency in the care provided for their babies (Entwisle & Doering, 1981). Conversely, men in upper-middle-class families are more likely to pursue their own intuitions and stylistic preferences in engaging with the baby, leaving open the possibility that babies will experience their parents as more different than alike, at least during one-on-one exchanges with the two parents (Entwisle & Doering, 1981). How the two parents behave in concert, when engaged together with their baby as a coparenting team, may be another story.

Observing Coparenting Dynamics During Family Group Interaction

Work from our laboratory, as well as the laboratories of the Cowans (e.g., Cowan, Cowan, Schulz, & Heming, 1994), Fivaz-Depeursinge and Corboz-Warnery (1999), Belsky (e.g., Belsky, Putnam, & Crnic, 1996), Brody (e.g., Brody, Flor, & Neubaum, 1998), Lindahl and Malik (1999), Katz and Gottman (1996), McConnell and Kerig (1999), and others (cf. Kerig & Lindahl, 2000) has converged in suggesting a core set of relational patterns that can be observed in the multiperson group interactions of families with infants as young as 3 months of age. Among the family group dynamics of interest in recent work has been a pattern signifying antagonistic and adult-centered, or hostile-competitive, coparenting dynamics, a pattern marked by a significant imbalance or parenting discrepancy in levels of parental engagement with the child, and a pattern reflecting cooperation, warmth, cohesion, and child centeredness, or, high family harmony. These patterns have been described in slightly different parlance in different reports from the labs enumerated above, but all concur in identifying distinctions between oppositional, disconnected-disengaged, and cohesive-engaged coparenting patterns.

In one of the first studies to focus on observed coparenting dynamics in families, McHale (1995) found hostile-competitive coparenting, parenting discrepancies, and family harmony to vary as a function of marital process. Hostile-competitive coparenting and marked imbalances in mother-father involvement with the child were more common, and harmonious family engagement less common, in the triadic interactions of families for whom independent marital interviews had uncovered signs of distress. Moreover, when these interviews contained high levels of overt, poorly contained conflict, the family's coparenting interactions were more likely to show hostility and competitiveness, with this link continuing even after global marital distress had been controlled for. A similar link was found between nonegalitarian patterns of relating during the marital interview (with one partner dominating) and greater imbalances in mother-father involvement with the child during triadic interactions. However, this latter linkage did not simply reflect the same person domineering during both the marital and family assessments; in fact, the opposite was usually true: more nonegalitarianism in the marital dynamic with the man dominating was balanced by less mutuality in the family group interaction with the woman dominating. These findings, in combination with earlier and more recent investigations from other laboratories (e.g., Dadds & Powell, 1991; Frosch, Mangelsdorf, & McHale, 2000; Jouriles et al., 1991; Katz & Gottman, 1996; Kitzmann, 2000; Lewis, Cox, & Owen, 1989; Lindahl, Clements, & Markman, 1997) helped crystallize the distinction between marital or husband–wife dynamics and coparenting dynamics. One other finding from this study further underscored this critical distinction. Among families high in marital distress, the nature of the relationship between marital and coparenting distress differed depending on whether the couple's child was a boy or a girl. Boys from maritally distressed families were more likely to encounter hostile-competitive coparenting dynamics during family interactions, whereas girls were more likely to encounter larger discrepancies in coparental involvement (McHale, 1995).

This last finding makes sense if we recognize that men largely believe they have something important and unique to contribute to the socialization of sons. Though they may not initially feel the same way about daughters, fathers' hearts are quickly captured by their baby girls, and our data indicate that men engage as actively with their daughters during family interaction as they do with their sons, when all is right in the marriage. However, when the marriage is not going well, at least according to these data, men are more likely to continue involvement with sons but draw away from involvement with daughters. Perhaps not surprising, sustained father involvement with sons combined with the usual intensive involvement by mothers virtually assures that contentiousness between the marital partners will creep into the coparental and family group process. These gender-related findings have also been documented by Ablow (1997) in an analysis of data from the Cowans' (P. Cowan & Heming, 1997; C. Cowan & Heming, 1997) study of early school-aged children. Hence, these observationally based family group data indicate there may be some differential exposure to child-related conflict for boy children. However, the same data from McHale's (1995) investigation indicate that girls with maritally distressed parents are not spared exposure to parenting riffs; there was just less concomitance between marital distress and overt coparenting conflict among girls as a group in this sample. McHale's data substantiated only one of many potential gendered family patterns. Others, including both same- and cross-gendered family alliances, have been documented in research with older children by Christensen and Margolin (1988) and by Sroufe, Jacobvitz, Mangelsdorf, DeAngelo, and Ward (1985).

Patterns of family group process during infancy similar to those just described have also been documented by Fivaz-Depeursinge and Corboz-Warnery (1999), using a different paradigm and methodology. Studying triadic interactions beginning at 3 months postpartum, these researchers have documented different patterns of engagement, body formation, gaze, and affective expression among families. Several of the patterns they have identified parallel those found in McHale's (1995; McHale, Johnson, & Sinclair, 1999; McHale, Kuersten-Hogan, Lauretti, & Rasmussen, 2000) studies: discrepant levels of engagement in the family process by the two adults; sessions colored by multiple combative, intrusive, and interfering exchanges by the partners; and sessions noteworthy for their synchrony, turn taking, coaction, and positive affect. Similar dynamics had previously been charted in the Lewis et al. (1989) report, where important differences among families along a dimension of *triadic competence* (similarly distinguished by variations in action and affect) had become apparent by the end of the child's first year.

Should we be assigning any significance to these early individual differences in family group-level dynamics? Follow-up studies of families in both the McHale and Fivaz-Depeursinge samples, along with recent longitudinal data reported by Frosch and colleagues, indicate we should. Indicators of distress in the interparental and family group process during infancy harken later social and adjustment difficulties by the time children have entered the preschool years. McHale and Rasmussen (1998) found cross-time links between early family dynamics and later parent and teacher ratings of social adaptation, with strongest cross-time links between hostile-competitive coparenting dynamics during infancy and teacher-rated aggression (especially for boys), and between larger parenting discrepancies and parent-rated anxiety (especially for girls). Fivaz-Depeursinge, Frascarolo, and Corboz-Warnery (1996) traced similar linkages between problematic family alliances assessed during the first year and children's clinical symptomatology at age 4. Frosch et al. (2000) likewise linked interadult hostility during family play during the first year to later difficulties, tracing connections between these early family dynamics and insecure mother–child attachments at age 3.

More central to the crux of this chapter is the finding from McHale and Rasmussen's (1998) longitudinal study (a finding consistent with the cross-time data of Frosch et al., 2000; with Belsky et al.'s 1996 data on families of toddler boys; with Seifer, Sameroff, Dickstein, Hayden, & Schiller's 1996 study of infant and toddler children; with McHale, Lauretti, & Talbot's 1998 study of 2-year-olds; and with McHale, Johnson, & Sinclair's 1999 study of 4-year-olds) that family group indices explain a unique and statistically significant proportion of the variance in child outcome measures, even after taking into account the contributions of more traditional family measures. Coparenting and family group process predicted child outcomes after taking into consideration the effects of individual parental well-being and marital quality in the McHale and Rasmussen (1998) study; dyadic, husband–wife marital conflict in the Frosch et al. (2000) report; dyadic, parent–child relationship quality in the Belsky et al. (1996), McHale, Lauretti, and Kuersten-Hogan (1999), and Seifer et al. (1996) investigations; and dyadic parent–child attachment quality in the McHale et al. (1998) toddler study. These are significant findings that bear repeating: What gets captured in measures of the family group process are system-level processes beyond the traditional marital or parent–child relationship dynamics typically assessed in studies of family contributions to early child development. Moreover, recent work by Howes, Cicchetti, Toth, and Rogosch (2000) has substantiated the significance of system-level processes in maltreating families, as well. Their data documented the relevance of family climate and structure, beyond individual maltreatment acts, in families characterized by neglect and physical and sexual abuse. They underscored, too, that family-level disorganization and incompetency negatively affect numerous family members beyond the children involved.

The conceptual independence of coparenting and family group dynamics is far from absolute. Indeed, coparenting and family process are lawfully related to marital functioning, as several of the studies (e.g., Belsky, Crnic, & Gable, 1995; Katz & Gottman, 1996; Kitzmann, 2000; McHale, 1995) have shown. Moreover, in a study that made use of cluster analyses to identify distinctive family-level patterns along four key dimensions of coparenting and family group process (Fig. 5.1), McHale, Lauretti, and Kuersten-Hogan (1999) showed that two of these patterns—the parent-centered, cohesive family type and the child-centered, cohesive type depicted in Fig. 5.1—are linked to high levels of affinity (warmth and creativity) demonstrated by fathers toward their toddler-aged children during independent, dyadic father–child play sessions (Fig. 5.2). At the same time, however, the degree of overlap in family members' behavior across dyadic and family interaction contexts has been modest in the few studies that have examined such overlap, with many components of the family group process proving difficult to reconcile with patterns of behavior enacted within dyadic, parent–child commerce.

Identifying Core Dynamics by Examining Family Members' Behavior in Multiple Contexts

In a set of related studies conducted in the late 1970s and 1980s, Parke (e.g., Parke & O'Leary, 1976), Belsky (1979), Pederson (e.g., Pederson, Anderson, & Cain, 1980), and others showed that parenting behavior changes as parents move from interacting with their children in parent–child dyads to interacting with their children in a family group context. The most robust finding from these research studies was that the frequency of nearly all parent–child behaviors, or the level of parental involvement with the child by both parents, declines from dyad to triad. Subsequently, Gjerde (1986) demonstrated some systematicity to certain parenting changes across contexts. Studying families with adolescent children, he showed that the quality of father–son interaction declines as fathers and sons move from dyadic to family contexts, whereas the quality of mother–son interaction improves as mothers and sons move from dyadic to family contexts. No similar pattern emerged when the cross-contextual patterns of families with adolescent girls were examined. Something different was going on in the dyadic and group contexts, at least where parent–son relationships were concerned.

Family process rated from whole family interaction

Family Type	Coparental Antagonism	Cohesion & Harmony	Child-Centeredness of Family	Parenting Discrepancy
Child-at-Center	Low	Low	High	Moderate
Competitive Coparents	High	Low	Low	Low
Cohesive-Child-Centered	Low	High	High	Low
Cohesive-Parents-in-Charge	Low	High	Low	Low
Excluding	Low	Low	Moderate	High

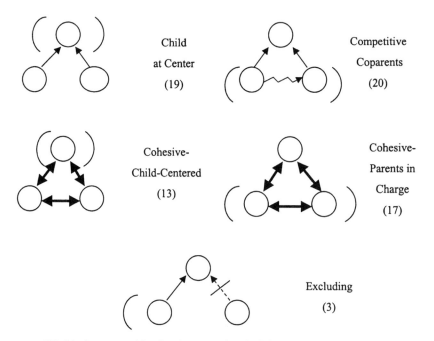

FIG. 5.1. Summary of five family types, identified through cluster analysis of coparenting and family process data, in a sample of two-parent families with 30-month-old children (N = 72).

Though Gjerde's analysis stopped short of telling us whether these shifting patterns earmarked certain families more than others, his findings illustrated that parenting behavior cannot be fully understood devoid of context. We typically think of parenting behavior as a property of the person doing the parenting, but parenting does not always look the same across contexts, even within the same family.

McHale, Kuersten-Hogan, Lauretti, and Rasmussen (2000) illustrated this finding in a study that revealed no association between parenting discrep-

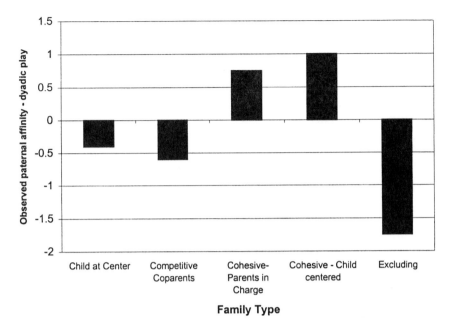

FIG. 5.2. Observational indices of paternal affinity for toddlers (z-scores) as revealed during dyadic father–child play sessions, as a function of family type.

ancy scores formed on the basis of comparing maternal and paternal behavior during family group interactions, and parenting discrepancy scores formed by comparing maternal and paternal behavior during separate, one-on-one interactions with the child. Trying to reconstruct the family group process by combining data from dyadic family subsystems yielded a different picture of what was going on in the family from the picture found when data from family group interaction were examined. Moreover, parents' reports of family functioning were associated with the true family group data, but not with the reconstructed, pseudofamily data (McHale, Kuersten-Hogan, et al., 2000). This makes sense; it seems likely parents base their impressions of family functioning on shared interpersonal commerce occurring within the family group process rather than on events taking place outside of their direct experience.

This said, family events beyond parents' shared coparenting exchanges are relevant in coparental and family functioning. In 1997 McHale introduced the notion of *covert* coparenting processes, communications between parents and children, in the absence of the coparenting partner, that either strengthen and solidify or undermine the child's sense of family integrity. McHale and Rasmussen (1998) found that mothers who acknowledge making more denigrating and disparaging remarks about fathers to their 4-year-old children are more likely to have been party to hostile-competitive coparenting dynamics 3 years earlier, and to have children whose teachers rate them as showing more behavior problems than their peers. For fathers, reports of behavior in promoting family integrity (including more frequent affirming comments about the absent mother and the coparenting group) appear to be most telling. The family interactions of fathers who report engaging in such activities show both greater mutuality in parental involvement and more child centeredness (McHale, Kuersten-Hogan, et al., 2000), and the children of such fathers are rated as showing better social adaptation by parents and teachers (McHale & Rasmussen, 1998). The work of solidifying and maintaining a strong coparenting alliance continues even in the coparenting partners' absence, as Crosbie-Burnett and Lewis' (1999) analysis of pedifocal family systems predicts.

The key point is that the coparental alliance represents a broad, overarching domain that can be fully understood only by examining the behavior of family members in multiple contexts. Lauretti and McHale (1997) provided further evidence for this notion by demonstrating that greater inconsistencies in parenting stances across family contexts are found in families where parents are experiencing marital distress. Their findings indicated that mothers in distressed marriages show a greater decline in responsiveness to their toddler when moving from dyadic to family contexts than do mothers in nondistressed marriages. Fathers in distressed marriages show a decline in engagement with their toddler when moving from dyadic to family settings than do fathers in nondistressed marriages. In short, parenting behavior across family settings is less consistent in the face of marital distress. This may reflect that parents in distressed marriages engage a different relationship standard when parenting alone as opposed to when parenting together. Such inconsistency is particularly disruptive to small children, especially toddlers and preschoolers, for whom predictability helps support the internalization of standards. Here again, we see the importance of including both dyadic and family group data in the same analysis to fully understand the complexity of the family dynamic.

This theme is substantiated by Beitel and Parke (1998), who traced links between both mothers' and fathers' expressed beliefs about parenting and family, and paternal sensitivity with their young infants in dyadic (father and baby alone), triadic (with mother occupied), and triadic (with mother unoccupied) settings. Beitel and Parke found different linkages between parenting beliefs and fathers' behavior with infants depending on whether they were parenting in conjunction with, or outside of, their partners' notice. Examining only dyadic or only triadic family group process would have obscured the different patterns of linkage contingent on family context.

In summary, most of what we currently know about children's experiences with their parents has come from studies of parent–child engagement in parent–child dyads. Yet the data seem clear that the types of social experiences parents afford their children vary as a function of whether they are engaged with and parenting the child alone, or together with their partner. In some families, parenting behaviors and stances are more consistent between parents and across contexts, whereas in other families inconsistency is the rule. Systematic shifts in parenting across contexts tend to earmark families where the adult partners are experiencing marital distress. Moreover, the coparenting interactions of maritally distressed adults are less likely to impress researchers as cohesive (warm-cooperative) and more likely to show signs of hostility-competitiveness, disconnection, or (in rare cases) both. Distress in the coparental alliance predicts, both concurrently and longitudinally, problems in children's social adaptation.

Research evidence supports the contention of family theorists that the family whole can and should be distinguished from the family's component subsystems, while at the same time indicating that it is also possible to trace systematic linkages between family group functioning and certain properties of individuals or dyads in the family. Reiss (1989), along with other family theorists, has emphasized the emergent nature of family group dynamics and drawn important distinctions between the interiorized representations of individual family members and enduring family procedures or practices carried forward by the family as a whole. However, recent data suggest that preschool children's family representations may also covary systematically with family group process.

Do Coparenting and Family Dynamics Shape Children's Social Representations?

The field of attachment research took a quantum leap forward in 1985 when Main, Kaplan, and Cassidy (1985) introduced methods for understanding both parents and children's representational systems with respect to attachment relationships. Following the introduction of the Adult Attachment Interview, Fonagy, Steele, and Steele (1991) showed that mothers' states of mind with respect to attachment during their pregnancy could be linked to the quality of infant–parent attachment 1 year following the infant's birth. More recently, Oppenheim, Emde, and Warren (1997), refining a doll play interview developed to assess children's perceptions of care or harm in caregiver–child relationships, showed that children's working models of attachment could likewise be traced to parent–child attachment quality. In recent years, Dickstein, Fiese, and a consortium of researchers have been exploring both the determinants and sequela of family narratives (Fiese et al., 1999). Here, at the level of representation, researchers have begun teasing apart a distinction similar to the one we have been trying to draw between dyadic and family group process: whether people's conceptions of the family group are conceptually distinct from their states of mind with respect to attachment, attachment being a dyadic and not a family group construct. As one example, von Klitzing, Simoni, Amsler, and Burgin (1999) found that prebirth measures of parents' *triadic capacity*, or propensity to make room for the coparenting partner in their fantasies about the future family process, predict quality of triadic coordination in Fivaz-Depeursinge and Corboz-Warnery's Lausanne Triadic Play after the baby arrives, but not quality of dyadic, parent–child interaction.

Do children also develop conceptions of their family group? Recent evidence suggests they may. For example, McHale, Neugebauer, Asch, and Schwartz (1999) have reported that preschoolers' portrayals of interpersonal aggression while narrating stories about families correlate with their mothers' ratings of family Conflict on Moos' (1974) Family Environment Scale (FES), with depictions of affectionate family exchanges during these stories correlating with maternal FES Cohesion ratings. Preschoolers' depictions of family conflict, aggression, and affection were stable across a 1-month period and were only moderately correlated, and in some cases uncorrelated, with similar measures gleaned from their stories about a day at school. McHale, Neugebauer, et al. argue that children have formed, by preschool age, notions about their family group process that may be distinct from their perceptions of individual parent–child or peer relationship quality.

Children's family representations may help shed light on links between coparenting and family group process, and children's social behavior outside the family. In a study examining linkages between family group process and 4-year-old children's peer behavior on the preschool playground, McHale, Johnson, and Sinclair (1999) found that children whose parents show low coparental support and mutuality during family group interaction exhibit more negative peer behavior on the preschool playground. However, their data also indicated that among boys, this linkage dissipates once the child's perceptions of the family (accessed through doll play and through measures of child discomfort when answering questions about family anger) have been entered into prediction equations, suggesting the perceptions may play a mediating role. In other words, low levels of support and mutuality between coparenting partners (as detected by trained outside observers) only translated into problems with peer relationships for children in the McHale, Johnson, and Sinclair (1999) study if the children perceived something amiss in the family. We think there is a key point embedded within these findings: Data from the study indicated it was not simply overt interparental conflict in the family the preschoolers were tuning into, or not tuning into, but rather the lack of coordination and connection and the level of discrepancy in levels of parental engagement. As Cummings' (e.g., Cummings & Davies, 1994; Cummings, Davies, & Simpson, 1994) work has demonstrated, and as other contributors to this volume note, children must be viewed as active processors of their family's interpersonal dynamics. Our conceptual models must recognize that children's adaptations outside the family are determined, at least in part, by the spin they put on their family circumstances.

CONTINUING QUANDARIES FOR FUTURE RESEARCH ON COPARENTING AND FAMILY GROUP DYNAMICS

When Does Normal Variability in Family Group Dynamics Become Worrisome?

Much of our theorizing about coparenting in two-parent families has been guided by Minuchin's (1974) structural family theory, which emphasizes the importance of an effectively functioning "executive subsystem" for meeting the family's organizational needs. But what are the connections between the family issues discussed by Minuchin, Lidz, Haley, and other family therapists, and the family phenomena we have described in this chapter? One of the earliest submissions from our lab, which ill advisedly referred to parenting discrepancies as "disengagement–enmeshment," drew criticism from a reviewer who demanded to know whether there was any evidence the patterns described in the paper were severe enough to be considered disengagement–enmeshment. We were not able to come up with any, and even today we are deliberating whether patterns such as the ones we have been describing differ in degree, or in kind, from the clinical patterns captured by family therapists in their studies on the dynamics of families referred for treatment. At what point do we make the judgment that competitive coparenting, or discrepant levels of parental involvement, or low levels of family harmony, has become worrisome? Notwithstanding the heuristic value of Bowen's (1966) notion that triangles should be viewed as a central force in all relationships, we are not yet sure that terms such as *triangulation, coalitions*, and other concepts borrowed from family therapy really belong in a literature on family process in nonreferred samples.

At the same time, we need to be sensitive to the possibility that at some critical threshold, what happens between adult caregiving figures does begin to exert some enduring influence over children's developing sense of confidence in themselves and in the predictability of their family relationships. What happens in families where parents cannot agree on standards of conduct, acceptability of emotional expression, or appropriateness of assertive self-expression? Do toddler and preschool children come to learn that certain forms of expression are permissible with one parent but not the other? Or do they fail to make this distinction, expressing themselves similarly across contexts and ending up the constant recipients of punishment from one parent (or, perhaps both) for perceived transgressions, resulting in all the expectable negative effects on self-esteem? Moreover, is coparental solidarity always an optimal state of affairs? Probably not. For example, what becomes of the 3- or 4-year-old child growing up in a closed family system whose parents collude on exacting, harsh, and developmentally inappropriate standards? In such an instance, would not a lack of coparental cooperation (with one parent being more lenient and sensitively attuned) be the best outcome? Looking beyond the adult twosome, would matters be made better or worse for that child by the occasional presence of a sensitive third-party adult (e.g., an involved grandparent, aunt or uncle, or fictive kin)? Would that person's episodic involvement with the child provide enough of an emotional oasis to buffer the child, as is conventional wisdom? Or would the input into a closed system of someone whose methods diverge from the preferences of the coparenting partners disorganize the family such that the child would become the recipient of even harsher treatment? And do families such as these—families with small children who have not yet found their way to the mental health system (but who are providing harsh emotional climates for their children)—find their way into studies of community families in sufficient enough numbers for us to develop a thorough understanding of the individual and family dynamics involved? We have much work to do in refining coparenting constructs and ascertaining their applicability across a broad range of families in varying life circumstances.

What Happens When We Extend Our Focus Beyond Triads?

Although we have used the term family group process liberally in this chapter, most of the empirical bedrock involves studies of the family triad, not broader family groups. Kreppner's (1988) work tracing predictable shifts in family group process following the addition of a second child to the family unit is an important exception. In Kreppner's intensive study of two-parent families, he found that once mothers begin dedicating more of their time to the new child, fathers heighten their involvement with the firstborn relative to previous levels, thereby picking up at least some of the mother's missing attention. What this suggests is that the principles of coparenting may undergo radical revision when more than one child is involved. New interview and observationally based research from our Clark lab contrasting coparenting in one- and two-child families suggests that the norm in nuclear families with two young children is not the same unified, joint family approach as it is in one-child families (McHale, Lauretti, et al., 2000). Rather, most common is a fluid *parallel twosomes strategy*, also identified in Kreppner's sample, wherein each parent engages with one child at a time (though we are also finding a fair degree of variability among two-child families in the extent to which the tetrad comes together as a unit). Variables such as those highlighted by Teti (chap. 7, this volume) including the siblings' genders, core temperamental characteristics, and age difference, play a role in the emergent family dynamic, a dynamic likely to shift as the older sibling matures and additional siblings are added to the family constellation.

Extending conceptual coparenting models beyond family triads and tetrads will be particularly important for families in which a nuclear unit is closely embedded within a larger extended family. In such families, isolating a family triad or tetrad from its broader familial context may lead us to notice signs of miscoordination that would not be evident were the nuclear unit returned to its typical familial context. Coparenting investigations must remain sensitive and attuned to the functional family unit for findings to have any applicability beyond the laboratory.

How Best to Expand Our Empirical Knowledge Base to Include Diverse Family Groupings?

We opened this chapter by examining major societal-level distinctions among different types of family systems, and now we have come full circle. There is an urgent need for comparative studies of family group process in different cultures and subcultures, work that promises to be complex and to once again raise the question: Who is the family group (McHale, Khazan, Rotman, DeCourcey, & McConnell, 2001)? Should we study one or multiple family groups? What sense does it make to seek out common family group dynamics in families where the underlying, organizing principles are so thoroughly different? Is it really possible to understand the family and its principles of organization and process devoid of information about the surrounding community and cultural context (Bronfenbrenner, 1977; Minuchin, chap. 9, this volume)? Many family scholars of color caution against seeking common principles across different groups because such an approach runs a risk of comparing diverse families on dimensions founded within a majority Anglo culture, dimensions that may have different or, in some circumstances, no meaning cross-culturally. What is needed, rather, is new scholarship and indigenous approaches to understanding families across cultures.

Like many family researchers, we are of two minds about this. Our collaborators in China and India anticipated we would find little coparenting conflict in Asian cultures where filial piety, dedication to family, and harmony in the collective are the rule. And indeed, we did find sizeable group differences between Chinese and American mothers' reports of coparental conflict on McHale's (1997) Coparenting Scale (Sarin, Liu, Fan, Rao, & McHale, 1999). Yet at the same time, within a Beijing sample, preschoolers from families where mothers reported comparatively higher coparenting conflict (though still lower than U.S. norms) were more likely than other Chinese preschoolers in the sample to receive elevated behavior problem ratings (which too were milder than those in a U.S. comparison sample; McHale, Rao, & Krasnow, 2000). This finding makes some sense and has parallels in other cultural groups as well. Brody, Flor, and Neubaum (1998), for example, reported that preadolescent African American children show more adaptational difficulties when they come from families higher in coparental conflict, and this is true whether the adults involved are the child's biological mother and father or the child's mother and cocaregiving maternal grandmother (see also Apfel & Seitz, 1999; Chase-Lansdale, Brooks-Gunn, & Zamsky, 1994).

Other data, more removed but nevertheless interesting, come from Gulliver's (1955) account of the Jie, a rank societal group in sub-Saharan Africa relying on cooperation among tribal males to manage different stock in various seasons. Gulliver described how, in this polygynous family system, full brothers were typically closely cooperative but half brothers, who grew up in the same compound as related siblings of cowives, were typically (and, for the group, maladaptationally) antagonistic. Gulliver proposed as one explanation for the contrast between full brothers and half brothers that the half brothers partook, at least vicariously, in the quarreling and rivalry prevalent between cowives. What cannot be determined is whether the contrasts between full brothers and half brothers are as distinctive in societies where cooperation, rather than jealousy and rivalry, between cowives was held up as a societal ideal, as is apparently the case among the Suku (Kopytoff, 1964).

Interparental antagonism strikes us as one family-level process that may be of interest in many different family forms. Are there others? Of all the family processes we have studied in our samples, as well as in Brody's samples of rural Georgia African American families (e.g., Brody & Flor, 1996; Brody, Flor, & Neubaum, 1998; Brody, Stoneman, Smith, & Gibson, 1999) and Lindahl and Malik's (1999) study of Hispanic families in southern Florida, the combination of family warmth and cohesion has emerged as the single most reliable correlate of child adaptation. However, studying this construct cross-culturally, at least using extant self-report measures, can present some dilemmas (see Parke, chap. 3, this volume). An anecdote will illustrate: One item loading highly on the Coparenting Scale's "behavior promoting Family Integrity" factor concerns the frequency with which parents show signs of affection (touches, hugs) toward one another in their child's presence (McHale, 1997). When parents in Bangalore, India ran across this scale item during our focus groups, many wondered why we would ask such a question about conduct improper to reveal to a child. Indeed, behaviors that communicate a sense of family solidarity to children are likely to differ among families of different cultural groups. In exploring anticipated cultural differences, however, researchers would do well to follow the lead of Lau, Lew, Hau, Cheung, and Berndt (1990). Studies of parenting in China have indicated that Chinese parents view training practices (strict discipline, teaching obedience and respect for elders) both as a means of building family solidarity and as a means of demonstrating their love for children. However, Lau et al. discovered that when Chinese adults look back on their own childhoods, they describe their origin families as harmonious only when they remember parental warmth and affection, not when their parents demonstrated firmness without affection.

We have tried to offer some concrete examples of why it will be important for future studies of coparenting and family group process to take full account of broad historical and contextual factors surrounding the family, but even here we have highlighted only certain facets of the social contexts, both formal and informal, in which families are embedded (Bronfenbrenner, 1977). One recent illustration of how interlinking contexts can fundamentally affect coparenting and family group process comes from the work of Crouter, Helms-Erikson, Updegraff, and McHale (1999). These researchers established that coparenting fathers know more about their children's activities, whereabouts, and companions when their wives work longer hours, demonstrating the effect of workplace demands on intrafamilial dynamics. The family's interior is fundamentally affected not only by the larger social context or macrosystem, but also by more local, nested systems such as the parents' workplaces, the family's neighborhood and community supports, and other systems and institutions affecting the child and family's life space (see Minuchin, chap. 9, this volume; Vosler & Robertson, 1998). Attempting to fathom the meaning and adaptability of family group processes without taking account of these external influences neglects the very information that gives these processes meaning.

Admonitions to attend to cultural context are now almost ubiquitous in the published literature. No scientific report, from the undergraduate lab paper to the comprehensive journal review, advances without acknowledgment of cultural constraints. Another needed thrust in future research is the willingness to pose bold and pithy hypotheses about how and why family–child linkages should be expected to differ in different populations, even if such hypotheses prove to be unfounded. Though intrigued by our coparenting findings in Beijing, we understand that rural Chinese family environments are not the same as those in modern Beijing and that we cannot generalize from our Beijing findings to families in Chinese hillsides. Likewise, coparenting coordination in Indian villages or in rural Vietnam, where much of the family's basic caregiving is provided by older children who tend to infants and toddlers for extended periods each day, is unlikely to have the same formative effect on later child development as researchers have been finding in North American or European nuclear families. Indeed, the questions we have been pondering about the significance of coparenting and family group dynamics are probably not even the right questions to be asking to understand families in such societies, and this is where an "emic" approach becomes indispensable.

Moreover, even within the United States, where coparenting research was founded, we have only scratched the surface in developing an understanding of interadult coordination (see McHale et al., 2001, for a review of the current knowledge base on coparenting in diverse family systems). Most coparenting research has involved middle-class, White, heterosexual, married couples, with a smaller but growing body of knowledge available on African American two-parent families and on African American mothers and grandmothers raising children together. However, we continue to know little about coordination (a) between adults raising children together in foster families or between these individuals and birth parents (Erera, 1997; Simms & Bolden, 1991; see also Minuchin, chap. 9, this volume), (b) in two-parent nuclear families where there are also intimately involved grandparenting figures, or (c) in families with lesbian parenting partners who do and do not involve the child's donor father as coparent (Erera & Fredriksen, 1999; Hare & Richards, 1993; Muzio, 1993). Hence, as Azar (chap. 10, this volume) notes, at the moment we can provide little empirically based guidance to courts trying to adjudicate lawsuits where grandparents petition for extensive visitation rights (as in *Troxel v. Granville*, 2000) or where nonbiological family members such as coparenting gay or lesbian partners seek postbreakup visitation rights (as in *V.C. v. M.J.B.*, 1998/2000).

We also know little about the evolution of coparenting relationships among new, unwed parents (Vosler & Robertson, 1998), though at least one current national initiative (Fragile Families and Child Well-Being) promises to provide preliminary data relating to this question by 2005 (Tamis-LeMonda & Cabrera, 1999). And after more than a decade of debate, we still know little about how the coordination or miscoordination of parents and daycare providers influences children's early development (van IJzendoorn, Tavecchio, Stams, Verhoeven, & Reiling, 1998). All of these relationships, among many others, merit timely, competent, and thorough examination (McHale et al., 2001). In our studies of family group process, we must remain conscious that even with the expanded and contextually valid definitions of the functional family unit advocated in this chapter, millions of families still have no cocaregiving figure at all, either within or outside the family household. We will learn a great deal about family function and resilience through careful and respectful study of such family units and the myriad societal contexts within which they function (Sugarman, 1998).

Ultimately, the relevance of coparenting and of the family group process as distinctive features of families' socialization environments must be debated by family scholars within diverse cultures, as well as examined empirically. Based on successive studies of two-parent families with small children in both California and Massachusetts, we are now convinced that the family group process reveals a level of reality distinct from parent–child subsystems. An ongoing thrust in future work must be to develop a thorough understanding of how such group processes come into being and what, if anything, their special significance might be in meeting both the socialization and emotional support functions of the family and the development of its members.

IMPLICATIONS FOR PUBLIC POLICY

One heartening advance in our discipline—reflected in this volume and in our field's leading family research outlet, the *Journal of Family Psychology*—is an increasing awareness among researchers that findings from our studies must inform practice and policy if our work is to have meaning in the lives of families and children. It has been nearly 50 years since family clinicians first began alerting us to the power and complexity of coparenting and family group process, but even within our own discipline there remains confusion and skepticism about whether or how conceptualizing multiperson family group dynamics advances our understanding of child socialization beyond what we already know about parent–child attachment, father involvement, or marital conflict. Perhaps the first step in finally breaking through would be to assure that all graduate students in training read Crosbie-Burnett and Lewis' (1999) essay on lessons to be learned from African American family structure. As Ahrons (1981) noted, coparenting relationships exist even when marriages do not.

But how and in what ways might research-based scholarship on coparenting and family group dynamics enter into the consciousness and shape the deliberations of federal funding agencies, legal systems, and public policy? Consider first the case of divorcing families. In closing their volume *Dividing the Child*, and after considering carefully the debilitating effect of postdivorce coparental antagonism, Maccoby and Mnookin (1992) offered the somber conclusion that mandatory mediation programs during divorce proceedings are likely not to have enduring effects on parents' abilities to create or sustain cooperative postdivorce coparenting relationships. They noted:

> The power of law to achieve cooperative coparenting is severely restrained by an obvious but often overlooked point: some of these families were unable to cooperate *prior* to divorce. Divorcing couples often do not have a history of positive coparenting or even positive relations; thus, it would seem optimistic

to expect the law to create post-divorce relations that were not present pre-divorce. (p. 352)

They went on to note, however, that at present court-annexed mediation typically focuses principally on money, custody, and visitation, with less attention dedicated to helping parents work through long-term coparenting plans. Given Maccoby and Mnookin's findings and those of many others concerning the often disastrous effects of ongoing postdivorce antagonism (Whiteside & Becker, 2000), it seems that finding ways to effectively integrate coparenting interventions into the mediation process would be a national imperative. Yet, despite the introduction in recent years of several programs that show promise (e.g., Emery, Kitzmann, & Waldron, 1999; Johnston & Roseby, 1997; Pruett, 1998), there continue to be many impediments to widespread implementation and evaluation of such programs (Azar, chap. 10, this volume). For example, the legal system is a complicated one for which it can be difficult for research psychologists to gain entry; judicial sanctions, not to mention cooperation between judges and lawyers (who are not always on the same page), are required; and issues pertaining to the protection of human subjects are challenging to negotiate. Funding for controlled clinical research trials is not presently a national priority; divorce has sometimes been perceived as a problem only of the middle class, accompanied by sentiments that people should be left alone to work out family issues on their own. Even so, many courts throughout the United States have been piloting coparenting trials locally (Azar, chap. 10, this volume; Emery, 1999, Hendricks, 1994), with a slowly growing awareness of the value of informed coparenting interventions, at least for divorcing couples (Pruett, Nangle, & Bailey, 2000). Ironically, however, given Maccoby and Mnookin's observations about the organizing influence of predivorce coparenting relationships, similar efforts with nondivorcing couples are rare (Cowan et al., 1997).

Although it is heartening to see our society's growing awareness of the importance of postdivorce coparenting coordination, we must do more. Careful, large-scale studies examining the effectiveness of coparental education (which reaches beyond issues of visitation, drop-off, and pick-up to issues of meaningful coparental coordination; e.g., Bartlett, 2000) when granting divorce needs to become a valued federal funding priority, at the same time as local educational services are made available until the demonstration results come in. Such work must remain sensitive to the complications of high levels of hostility and toxic conflict (Pruett et al., 2000) and of domestic violence, to the threat of ongoing abuse in the postdivorce environment, and to false allegations of abuse voiced in the service of excluding a partner from postdivorce coparenting of children. As Whiteside (1998) has noted, interventions need to be tailored to the unique characteristics and resources of each family.

At the same time as we attend to these compelling emotional issues, we must stop waiting until couples arrive in divorce court. We know from the myriad studies discussed in this chapter and in Azar's summary (chap. 10, this volume) that continuing interadult antagonism is damaging to children. We need to ask why televised public service spots, educational pamphlets provided during well-baby and child visits to parents raising children in both nuclear and extended family systems, and other large-scale advisories regularly addressing this topic are not part of the fabric of society, and take steps to make them so. Any programs and services developed for families also need to be cognizant of how larger system neighborhood and institutional structures impinge on coparenting relations and arrangements, particularly for nonmarital parents and families living in poverty. As Vosler and Robertson (1998) suggested in their review of what we know about nonmarital coparenting, working only at a micro level with families will not remove such family stressors as poor housing, crime, poverty, or lack of quality affordable child care. However, tackling only neighborhood and macro institutional-policy levels may be of little help to multiply-disadvantaged families in which parents wish to coparent a child born nonmaritally. Responsible research efforts must take a multipronged approach to expand our knowledge base about what helps and what does not, with what specific family situations and dynamics and under what types of circumstances.

Beyond interparental antagonism, family psychologists and researchers have made far less progress in demonstrating convincingly the long-term effects of other coparenting and family-level factors such as dissonant, night-and-day parenting stances, or family affective climates. As a result, psychologists are also in less of a position to be prescriptive (as we need to be in curbing active coparental antagonism, animosity, and disparagement). Indeed, researchers must deal with the problem of false positives in their studies in a forthright manner before we can be in a position to offer our best counsel. Such efforts are important and must continue. Indeed, we can envision a time not far from now when findings from our studies will be of use to practitioners deciding whether it is viable to intervene in the family's coparenting system without trying to ameliorate the more intractable marital or conjugal system. When and how such efforts might best be brought to bear in a preventive way should be a consideration in future research initiatives. Few childbirth preparation classes acknowledge the challenges involved in coordinating as coparents, or the importance of strong parental alliances in providing children with the sense of family solidarity that contributes to their felt security (Cummings & Davies, 1996; McHale, 1997).

At this point, we urge practitioners to hear the voices of all family members in portraying their family climate (especially because even the youngest children have a viewpoint, and methods are now available to capture the perspectives of even very young preschoolers), to recognize that coparenting is far more than just the division of child-care labor, to take full account of affective and instrumental contributions made by different adult parenting figures in the child's life, and to evaluate parent–child relationships in both dyadic and family group contexts because the latter frequently reveal facets of the family group process not anticipated from dyadic parenting assessments. This is a vital and exciting new field of research, one that promises to help address several of the field's lingering questions about how family socialization climates shape children's social and emotional development.

REFERENCES

Ablow, J. (1997, April). *Marital conflict across family contexts: Does the presence of children make a difference?* Paper presented at the Society for Research in Child Development, Washington, DC.

Ahrons, C. R. (1981). The continuing coparental relationship between divorced spouses. *American Journal of Orthopsychiatry, 51*, 416–428.

Ahrons, C. R., & Rodgers, R. H. (1987). *Divorced families: A mulitdisciplinary developmental view.* New York: Norton.

Apfel, N., & Seitz, V. (1999, April). *Style of family support predicts teen mothers' subsequent childbearing and parenting success.* Paper presented at the Society for Research in Child Development, Albuquerque, NM.

Bartlett, K. (2000). Improving the law related to post-divorce custody of children. In R. Thompson & P. Amato (Eds.), *The post-divorce family: Research and policy issues* (pp. 71–102). Thousand Oaks, CA: Sage.

Bateson, M. (2000). *Full circles, overlapping lives: Culture and generation in transition.* New York: Random House.

Beitel, A., & Parke, R. (1998). Paternal involvement in infancy: The role of maternal and paternal attitudes. *Journal of Family Psychology, 12*, 268–288.

Belsky, J. (1979). The interrelations of parental and spousal behavior during infancy in traditional nuclear families: An exploratory analysis. *Journal of Marriage and the Family, 41*, 749–755.

Belsky, J., Crnic, K., & Gable, S. (1995). The determinants of coparenting in families with toddler boys: Spousal differences and daily hassles. *Child Development, 66*, 629–642.

Belsky, J., Putnam, S., & Crnic, K. (1996). Coparenting, parenting, and early emotional development. In J. McHale & P. Cowan (Eds.), *Understanding how family-level dynamics affect children's development: Studies of two-parent families* (New Directions for Child Development, No. 74, pp. 45–55). San Francisco: Jossey-Bass.

Bowen, M. (1966). The use of family theory in clinical practice. *Comprehensive Psychiatry, 7*, 345–374.

Brody, G., & Flor, D. (1996). Coparenting, family interactions, and competence among African American youths. In J. McHale & P. Cowan (Eds.), *Understanding how family-level dynamics affect children's development* (pp. 77–91). San Francisco: Jossey-Bass.

Brody, G., Flor, D., & Neubaum, E. (1998). Coparenting process and child competence among rural African-American families. In M. Lewis & C. Feiring (Eds.), *Families, risk and competence* (pp. 227–243). Mahwah, NJ: Lawrence Erlbaum Associates.

Brody, G., Stoneman, Z., Smith, T., & Gibson, N. (1999). Sibling relationships in rural African American families. *Journal of Marriage and the Family, 6*, 1046–1057.

Bronfenbrenner, U. (1977). *The experimental ecology of human development.* Cambridge, MA: Harvard University Press.

Brooks-Gunn, J., & Fustenberg, F. F. (1986). The children of adolescent mothers: Physical, academic, and psychological outcomes. *Developmental Review, 6,* 224–251.

Buchanan, C., Maccoby, E., & Dornbusch, S. (1991). Caught between parents: Adolescents' experience in divorced homes. *Child Development, 65,* 1008–1029.

Burgess, E., Locke, H., & Thomas, M. (1945). *The family: From institution to companionship.* New York: American Books.

Camera, K., & Resnick, G. (1988). Interparental conflict and cooperation: Factors moderating children's post-divorce adjustment. In E. M. Hetherington & J. Arasteh (Eds.), *Impact of divorce, single parenting, and step-parenting on children* (pp. 169–196). Hillsdale, NJ: Lawrence Erlbaum Associates.

Chase-Lansdale, L., Brooks-Gunn, J., & Zamsky, E. (1994). Young African-American multigenerational families in poverty: Quality of mothering and grandmothering. *Child Development, 65,* 373–393.

Christensen, A., & Margolin, G. (1988). Conflict and alliance in distressed and non-distressed families. In R. Hinde & J. Stevenson-Hinde (Eds.), *Relationships within families* (pp. 263–282). Oxford, England: Clarendon Press.

Collins, P. (1999). Shifting the center: Race, class, and feminist theorizing about motherhood. In S. Coontz (Ed.), *American families* (pp. 197–217). New York: Routledge.

Cowan, C. P., & Heming, G. (1997, April). *Preventive interventions for parents of children entering elementary school.* Paper presented at the Society for Research in Child Development, Washington, DC.

Cowan, P., & Cowan, C. P. (1992). *When partners become parents: The big life change for couples.* New York: Basic Books.

Cowan, P., Cowan, C. P., Schulz, M., & Heming, T. (1994). Prebirth to preschool family factors predicting children's adaptation to kindergarten. In R. Parke & S. Kellam (Eds.), *Advances in family research: Vol. 4. Exploring family relationships with other social contexts* (pp. 75–114). Hillsdale, NJ: Lawrence Erlbaum Associates.

Cowan, P., & Heming, G. (1997, April). *Family factors in children's school adaptation: The development of a "mega-model."* Paper presented at the Society for Research in Child Development, Washington, DC.

Cowan, P., Powell, D., & Cowan, C. P. (1997). Parenting interventions: A family systems perspective. In I. Sigel & K. Renninger (Eds.), *Handbook of child psychology* (5th ed., Vol. 4, pp. 3–72). New York: Wiley.

Crosbie-Burnett, M., & Lewis, E. (1999). Use of African-American family structures and functioning to address the challenges of European-American postdivorce families. In S. Coontz (Ed.), *American families* (pp. 455–468). New York: Routledge.

Crouter, A., Helms-Erikson, H., Updegraff, K., & McHale, S. (1999). Conditions underlying parents' knowledge about children's daily lives in middle childhood: Between- and within-family comparisons. *Child Development, 70,* 246–259.

Cummings, E. M., & Davies, P. (1994). *Children and mortal conflict: The impact of family dispute and resolution.* New York: Guilford Press.

Cummings, E. M., & Davies, P. (1996). Emotional security as a regulatory process in normal development and the development of psychopathology. *Development and Psychopathology, 8,* 123–139.

Cummings, E. M., Davies, P., & Simpson, K. (1994). Marital conflict, gender, and children's appraisals and coping efficacy as mediators of child adjustment. *Journal of Family Psychology, 8,* 141–149.

Dadds, M., & Powell, M. (1991). The relationship of interparental conflict and global marital adjustment to aggression, anxiety, and immaturity in aggressive and non-clinic children. *Journal of Abnormal Child Psychology, 19,* 553–567.

Darity, W. A., & Myers, S. L. (1984). Does welfare dependency cause female hardship? The case of the black family. *Journal of Marriage and the Family, 46*, 765–780.

Dienhart, A., & Daly, K. (1997). Men and women co-creating father involvement in a non-generative culture. In A. Hawkins & D. Dollahite (Eds.), *Generative fathering: Beyond deficit perspectives* (pp. 202–225). Thousand Oaks, CA: Sage.

Emery, R. (1999). *Marriage, divorce, and children's adjustment* (2nd ed.). Thousand Oaks, CA: Sage.

Emery, R. E., Kitzman, K. M., & Waldron, M. (1999). Psychological interventions for separated and divorced families. In E. M. Hetherington (Ed.), *Coping with divorce, single parenting, and remarriage: A risk and resilience perspective* (pp. 323–344). Mahwah, NJ: Lawrence Erlbaum Associates.

Entwisle, D., & Doering, S. (1981). *The first birth: A turning point.* Baltimore: Johns Hopkins University Press.

Erera, P. (1997). Step- and foster families: A comparison. *Marriage and Family Review, 26*, 301–315.

Erera, P., & Fredriksen, K. (1999). Lesbian stepfamilies: A unique family structure. *Families in Society, 78*, 263–270.

Farley, R., & Allen, W. R. (1987). *The color line and the quality of life in America.* New York: Russell Sage Foundation.

Farrell, B. (1999). *Family: The making of an idea, an institution, and a controversy in American culture.* Boulder, CO: Westview Press.

Fiese, B., Sameroff, A., Grotevant, H., Wamboldt, F., Dickstein, S., & Fravel, D. (1999). The stories that families tell: Narrative coherence, narrative interaction, and relationship beliefs. *Monographs of the Society for Research in Child Development, 64*(2, Serial 257).

Fivaz-Depeursinge, E., & Corboz-Warnery, A. (1999). *The primary triangle. A developmental systems view of fathers, mothers and infants.* New York: Basic Books.

Fivaz-Depeursinge, E., Frascarolo, F., & Corboz-Warnery, A. (1996). Assessing the triadic alliance between father, mother and infant at play. In J. McHale & P. Cowan (Eds.), *Understanding how family-level dynamics affect children's development: Studies of two-parent families* (New Directions for Child Development, No. 74, pp. 27–44). San Francisco: Jossey-Bass.

Fonagy, P., Steele, H., & Steele, M. (1991). Maternal representations of attachment during pregnancy predict the organization of infant–mother attachment at one year of age. *Child Development, 62*, 891–905.

Frosch, C., Mangelsdorf, S., & McHale, J. L. (2000). Marital behavior and the security of preschooler–parent attachment relationships. *Journal of Family Psychology, 14*, 144–161.

Giddings, P. (1982). *When and where I enter: The impact of black women on race and sex in America.* New York: Morrow.

Gjerde, P. (1986). The interpersonal structure of family interactional settings: Parent–adolescent relations in dyads and triads. *Developmental Psychology, 48*, 711–717.

Gulliver, P. H. (1955). *The family herds: A study of two pastoral tribes in East Africa.* London: Routledge and Kegan Paul.

Hackel, L., & Ruble, D. (1992). Changes in the marital relationship after the first baby is born: Predicting the impact of discrepancy confirmation. *Journal of Personality and Social Psychology, 62*, 944–957.

Hare, J., & Richards, L. (1993). Children raised by lesbian couples: Does context of birth affect father and partner involvement? *Family Relations, 42*, 249–256.

Harrell, S. (1997). *Human families.* Boulder, CO: Westview Press.

Hauser, S., Powers, S., Noam, G., Jacobson, A., Weiss, B., & Follansbee, D. (1984). Family contexts of adolescent ego development. *Child Development, 55*, 195–213.

Hendricks, C. (1994). The trend toward mandatory mediation in custody and visitation disputes of minor children: An overview. *Journal of Family Law, 32*, 491–510.

Hetherington, E. M., Cox, M., & Cox, R. (1982). Effects of divorce on parents and children. In M. Lamb (Ed.), *Nontraditional families* (pp. 238–288). Hillsdale, NJ: Lawrence Erlbaum Associates.

Hibbett, H., & Itasaka, G. (1967). *Modern Japanese: A basic reader* (2nd ed.). Cambridge, MA: Harvard University Press.

Howes, P., Cicchetti, D., Toth, S., & Rogosch, F. (2000). Affective, organizational, and relational characteristics of maltreating families: A systems perspective. *Journal of Family Psychology, 14*, 95–110.

Johnston, J., Campbell, L., & Mayes, S. (1985). Latency children in post-separation and divorce disputes. *Journal of the American Academy of Child Psychiatry, 24*, 563–574.

Johnston, J., & Roseby, V. (1997). *In the name of the child: A developmental approach to understanding and helping children of conflicted and violent divorce.* New York: Free Press.

Jouriles, E., Murphy, C., Farris, A., Smith, D., Richter, J., & Waters, E. (1991). Marital adjustment, parental disagreement about child-rearing, and behavior problems in boys: Increasing the specificity of the marital assessment. *Child Development, 62*, 1424–1433.

Katz, L. F., & Gottman, J. (1996). Spillover effects of marital conflict: In search of parenting and coparenting mechanisms. In J. McHale & P. Cowan (Eds.), *Understanding how family-level dynamics affect children's development: Studies of two parent families* (New Directions for Child Development, No. 74, pp. 57–76). San Francisco: Jossey-Bass.

Kerig, P. K., & Lindahl, K. M. (2001). *Family observational coding systems: Resources for systemic research.* Mahwah, NJ: Lawrence Erlbaum Associates.

Kitzmann, K. (2000). Effects of marital conflict on subsequent triadic family interactions and parenting. *Developmental Psychology, 36*, 3–13.

Kopytoff, I. (1964). Family and lineage among the Suku of the Congo. In R. F. Gray & P. H. Gulliver (Eds.), *The family estate in Africa: Studies in the role of property in family structure and lineage continuity* (pp. 83–116). London: Routledge and Kegan Paul.

Kreppner, K. (1988). Changes in parent–child relationships with the birth of the second child. *Marriage and Family Review, 12*, 157–181.

Lau, S., Lew, W., Hau, K., Cheung, P., & Berndt, T. (1990). Relations among perceived parental control, warmth, indulgence and family harmony of Chinese in mainland China. *Developmental Psychology, 26*, 674–677.

Lauretti, A., & McHale, J. (1997, April). *Shifting patterns of parenting styles between dyadic and family settings: The role of marital quality.* Paper presented at the Society for Research in Child Development, Washington, DC.

Lewis, J., Cox, M., & Owen, M. T. (1989). The transition to parenthood: III. Incorporation of the child into the family. *Family Process, 27*, 411–421.

Lindahl, K., Clements, M., & Markman, H. (1997). Predicting marital and parent functioning in dyads and triads: A longitudinal investigation of marital processes. *Journal of Family Psychology, 11*, 139–151.

Lindahl, K., & Malik, N. (1999). Marital conflict, family process, and boys' externalizing behavior in Hispanic and European-American families. *Journal of Clinical Child Psychology, 28*, 12–24.

Maccoby, E., & Mnookin, R. (1992). *Dividing the child: Social and legal dilemmas of custody.* Cambridge, MA: Harvard University Press.

Main, M., Kaplan, N., & Cassidy, J. (1985). Security in infancy, childhood, and adulthood. A move to the level of representation. *Monographs of the Society for Research in Child Development, 50*(1–2), 66–104.

McConnell, M., & Kerig, P. (1999, April). *Inside the family circle: The relationship between coparenting and child adjustment in two-parent families.* Paper presented at the Society for Research in Child Development, Albuquerque, NM.

McDonald, K., & Armstrong, E. (2001). Deromanticizing black intergenerational support: The questionable expectations of welfare reform. *Journal of Marriage and Family, 63*, 213–223.

McHale, J. (1995). Coparenting and triadic interactions during infancy: The roles of marital distress and child gender. *Developmental Psychology, 31*, 985–996.

McHale, J. (1997). Overt and covert coparenting processes in the family. *Family Process, 36*, 183–210.

McHale, J., Johnson, D., & Sinclair, R. (1999). Family dynamics, preschoolers' family representations, and preschool peer relationships. *Early Education and Development, 10,* 373–401.

McHale, J., Khazan, I., Rotman, T., DeCourcey, W., & McConnell, M. (2001). Coparenting in diverse family systems. In M. Bornstein (Ed.), *Handbook of parenting. Vol. 3: Status and social conditions of parenting.* Mahwah, NJ: Lawrence Erlbaum Associates.

McHale, J., Kuersten-Hogan, R., Lauretti, A., & Rasmussen, J. (2000). Parental reports of coparenting behavior and observed coparenting behavior during the toddler period. *Journal of Family Psychology, 14,* 220–236.

McHale, J., Lauretti, A., DeCourcey, W., Zaslavsky, I., Talbot, J., & Pouquette, C. (2000, July). *Coparenting and triadic dynamics in one- and two-child families.* Paper presented at the International Conference on Infant Studies, Brighton, UK.

McHale, J., Lauretti, A. F., & Kuersten-Hogan, R. (1999, April). *Linking family-level patterns to father–child, mother–child, and marital relationship qualities.* Paper presented at the Biennial Meeting of the Society for Research in Child Development, Albuquerque, NM.

McHale, J., Lauretti, A., & Talbot, J. (1998, April). *Attachment quality, family level dynamics, and toddler adaptation.* Paper presented at the International Conference on Infant Studies, Atlanta, GA.

McHale, J., Neugebauer, A., Asch, A., & Schwartz, A. (1999). Preschoolers' characterizations of multiple family relationship during family doll play. *Journal of Clinical Child Psychology, 28,* 256–268.

McHale, J., Rao, N., & Krasnow, A. (2000). Constructing family climates: Chinese mothers' reports of coparenting behavior and preschool behavior problems. *International Journal of Behavioural Development, 24,* 111–118.

McHale, J., & Rasmussen, J. (1998). Coparental and family group-level dynamics during infancy: Early family predictors of child and family functioning during preschool. *Development and Psychopathology, 10,* 39–58.

McLanahan, S., & Sandefur, G. (1994). *Growing up with a single parent: What hurts, what helps.* Cambridge, MA: Harvard University Press.

Minuchin, P. (1985). Families and individual development: Provocations from the field of family therapy. *Child Development, 56,* 289–302.

Minuchin, S. (1974). *Families and family therapy.* Cambridge: Harvard Press.

Moos, R. (1974). *Combined preliminary manual for the family, work, and group environment scales.* Palo Alto, CA: Consulting Psychology Press.

Muzio, C. (1993). Lesbian co-parenting: On being/being with the invisible (m)other. *Smith College Studies in Social Work, 63,* 215–229.

Nichols, M., & Schwartz, R. (1998). *Family therapy: Concepts and methods* (4th ed.). Needham Heights, MA: Allyn & Bacon.

Nicolson, P. (1990). A brief report of women's expectations of men's behavior in the transition to parenthood: Contradictions and conflicts for counseling psychology practice. *Counseling Psychology Quarterly, 3,* 353–361.

Oppenheim, D., Emde, R., & Warren, S. (1997). Children's narrative representations of mothers: Their development and associations with child and mother adaptation. *Child Development, 68,* 126–138.

Parke, R., & O'Leary, S. (1976). Father-mother-infant interaction in the newborn period: Some findings, some observations, and some unresolved issues. In K. Rieger & J. Meacham (Eds.), *The developing individual in a changing world.* Hawthorne, NY: de Gruyter.

Pederson, F., Anderson, B., & Cain, R. (1980). Parent-infant and husband-wife interactions observed at age 5 months. In F. Pederson (Ed.), *The father-infant relationship: Observational studies in the family setting.* New York: Praeger.

Pruett, M. K. (1998). Divorce in legal context: Outcomes for children. *Connecticut Family Lawyer, 13,* 1–11.

Pruett, M. K., Nangle, B., & Bailey, C. (2000). Divorcing families with young children in the court's family services unit: Profiles and impact of services. *Family and Conciliation Courts Review, 38,* 478–500.

Rapp, R. (1999). Family and class in contemporary America: Notes toward an understanding of ideology. In S. Coontz (Ed.), *American families* (pp. 180–196). New York: Routledge.

Reiss, D. (1981). *The family's construction of reality.* Cambridge, MA: Harvard University Press.

Reiss, D. (1989). The represented and practicing family: Contrasting visions of family continuity. In A. Sameroff & R. Emde (Eds.), *Relationship disturbances in early childhood: A developmental approach* (pp. 191–220). New York: Basic Books.

Rodgers-Rose, L. (1980). *The black woman.* Beverly Hills, CA: Sage.

Rosaldo, M. Z. (1980). The use and abuse of anthropology. *Signs, 5*(3), 389–407.

Roschelle, A. R. (1997). *No more kin: Exploring race, class, and gender in family networks. Understanding families series.* Thousand Oaks, CA: Sage.

Sarin, D., Liu, S., Fan, Y., Rao, N., & McHale, J. (1999, April). *Parenting beliefs, coparenting conduct, and preschool adaptation in India, China, and the United States.* Paper presented at the Eastern Psychological Association, Providence, RI.

Seifer, R., Sameroff, A., Dickstein, S., Hayden, L., & Schiller, M. (1996, April). *Family functioning, infant/toddler outcomes, and parental psychopathology.* Paper presented at the International Conference on Infant Studies, Providence, RI.

Simms, M., & Bolden, B. (1991). The family reunification project: Facilitating regular contact among foster children, biological families, and foster families. *Child Welfare, 70,* 679–690.

Smith, D. (1977). Child-naming patterns and family structure change: Hingham, Mass., 1640–1880. *The Newbury Papers in Family and Community History, 76-5.* Chicago: Newbury Library.

Sroufe, L. A., Jacobvitz, D., Mangelsdorf, S., DeAngelo, E., & Ward, M. (1985). Generational boundary dissolution between mothers and their preschool children: A relationship systems approach. *Child Development, 56,* 317–325.

Stack, C. B. (1974). *All our kin: Strategies for survival in a black community.* New York: Harper & Row.

Staples, R. (Ed.). (1971). *The black family: Essays and studies.* Belmont, CA: Wadsworth.

Sudarkasa, N. (1999). Interpreting the African heritage in Afro-American family organization. In S. Coontz (Ed.), *American families* (pp. 59–73). New York: Routledge.

Sugarman, S. (1998). Single-parent families. In M. Mason, A. Skolnick, & S. Sugarman (Eds.), *All our families: New policies for a new century* (pp. 13–38). New York: Oxford University Press.

Tamis-LeMonda, C., & Cabrera, N. (1999). Perspectives on father involvement: Research and policy. *Social Policy Report, Society for Research in Child Development, 13,* 1–31.

Terry, D., McHugh, T., & Noller, P. (1991). Role dissatisfaction and the decline of marital quality across the transition to parenthood. *Australian Journal of Psychology, 43,* 129–132.

Troxel v. Granville, 530 U.S. 57 (2000). *V.C. v M.J.B.* 163 N.J. 200, 784 A. 2d 539 (1998/2000).

van IJzendoorn, M., Tavecchio, L., Stams, G., Verhoeven, M., & Reiling, E. (1998). Attunement between parents and professional caregivers: A comparison of child-rearing attitudes in different child-care settings. *Journal of Marriage and the Family, 60,* 771–781.

von Klitzing, K., Simoni, H., Amsler, F., & Buergin, D. (1999). The role of the father in early family interactions. *Infant Mental Health Journal, 20,* 222–237.

Vosler, N., & Robertson, J. (1998). Non-marital co-parenting: Knowledge-building for practice. Families in society. *The Journal of Contemporary Human Services, 79,* 149–162.

Wallerstein, J., & Kelly, J. (1980). *Surviving the breakup: How children and parents cope with divorce.* New York: Basic Books.

Walsh, F. (1982). *Normal family processes.* New York: Guilford.

Walsh, F. (1993). *Normal family processes* (2nd ed.). New York: Guilford.

Whiteside, M. (1998). The parental alliance following divorce: An overview. *Journal of Marital and Family Therapy, 24,* 3–24.

Whiteside, M., & Becker, B. (2000). Parental factors and the young child's post-divorce adjustment: A meta-analysis with implications for parenting arrangements. *Journal of Family Psychology, 14,* 5–26.

6

The Road Ahead for Research on Marital and Family Dynamics

Martha J. Cox
Kristina S. M. Harter
University of North Carolina at Chapel Hill

One of the unique cornerstones of family research has been the study of interadult and multiperson relationship systems, and within this domain our field has seen exciting and important progress in recent years. Important insights into the study of marital and family processes are provided by Flanagan and her colleagues (chap. 4, this volume) and by McHale and colleagues (chap. 5, this volume), and important directions for new work on marital and family dynamics are outlined by both sets of authors. In reviewing the progress over the past 30 years of marital research, Flanagan et al. document seminal work in this area, including (a) the identification of negative affect and negative reciprocity as hallmark indicators of marital distress in couple relationships; (b) a progression in the field from a focus on couple behavior to an appreciation for the significance of individual differences in cognition, affect, physiology, and psychopathology; and (c) the emergence of BMT, an empirically supported treatment that has proven helpful in the amelioration of marital distress.

In the chapter on coparenting and family group dynamics, McHale et al. document the relevance of family-group-level dynamics in studies of children and families. They emphasize the importance of appreciating the family at the group level, not just at the individual or dyadic level, to adequately understand the behavior and development of individuals within the family. They also outline from a historical and a cultural perspective how families are organized to adapt to the larger social system in which they are imbedded, and they identify several important directions for future research.

In this chapter we comment on and extend several points raised by Flanagan et al. and McHale et al. and highlight additional gaps in our current understanding of marital and family dynamics. Before doing so, we provide a brief discussion of where the field of family research has been over the last several decades.

WHERE WE HAVE BEEN AND HOW FAR WE HAVE COME

Although the prevention of divorce was one important motivating factor in the growth of research on marital processes, much of the initial interest in marital processes arose from clinical work linking problematic marriages to other disturbances in the family. For years, family therapists have observed clinically that many child problems are associated with other family problems, particularly marital problems (Margolin, 1981). Even in the absence of adequate data to understand this relationship, observations such as these led many therapists to switch their focus of intervention from individuals to the entire family. Framo (1965) and Haley (1967) were among those who made particularly strong and influential statements concerning the importance of the marital relationship in the etiology of disturbances in children. Minuchin (1974) suggested that coalitions formed between parent and child in the absence of a strong marital coalition. The particularly damaging aspect of such coalitions and the accompanying breakdown of generational boundaries seemed to be that the resulting parent–child relationships often were based on the adult's needs rather than the child's needs and thus were not as supportive of the child's developmental tasks. However, these ideas were gleaned more from clinical observation and less from family development investigations.

The lack of family development investigations that would shed light on these clinical observations seemed to arise from a strange division of interest among researchers at the time (Aldous, 1977; Belsky, 1981). Family sociologists had long focused on marriage without regard for the many relationships in the family, notably the parent–child relationship. In contrast, developmental psychologists had attended to the child's development and parent–child relationships. Their focus lacked an appreciation for the effect of the marital relationship or an appreciation that the child developed within a whole family system and was influenced by the functioning of that system at levels beyond the parent–child dyad. In the 1980s, some research began to fill that gap. This research confirmed that marital processes have significant implications for parenting, for the child's experience within the family, and for aspects of the child's development (Belsky, Rovine, & Fish,

1989; Cowan & Cowan, 1985a; 1985b; 1987; Cox, Owen, Lewis, & Henderson, 1989; Lewis, Owen, & Cox, 1988).

In many studies, researchers introduced what proved to be a major innovation opening up new insights into family functioning: assessing the marriage through observation of the couple interacting as well as relying on the partners' self-report. Much of the sociological research on marriage had to that point relied almost exclusively on self-reports of marital happiness or distress. Measurement of individual perceptions of marital satisfaction or distress is important, but it yields different information from direct measurement of marital interactions. In short, researchers began to recognize that individual perceptions of the marriage and systematic observations of marital relationship exchanges represent different levels of analysis.

Several of the longitudinal studies in the 1980s were influenced by systems theories (e.g., Cowan & Cowan, 1985a, 1985b; 1987; Cox et al., 1989; Lewis et al., 1988) and were sensitive to the nature of information gained from a focus on different units of analysis (for recent discussions of systems theories as applied to families, see Cox & Paley, 1997; Sameroff, 1994). Increasingly, these studies began systematically combining observation of couple interaction with individual self-report. In one formative paper, Gottman and Levinson (1984) noted that as early as 1937 Ackerman had suggested that two neurotic individuals could have a happy marriage, that there were emergent properties of dyadic relationships that transcended individual personality characteristics, and that the focus of therapy with couples who were experiencing difficulties should be on interaction patterns. Their analysis underscored how one could see different levels of functioning at different levels of analysis. Ackerman, of course, was followed by several other family clinicians—most notably Bateson and Jackson—whose message (consistent with early systems theories) was essentially that the whole is greater than the sum of parts. In other words, the husband–wife relationship system cannot adequately be understood by isolating its individual members or by taking an average of the two spouses self-reports of marital satisfaction as some researchers had done.

As noted by Flanagan and colleagues (chap. 4, this volume), much of the impetus for the increased focus on observing relationships during the 1980s owed to the wider acceptance of general systems theory and communication theory by family therapists and family researchers, with additional impetus provided by the increased popularity of behavioral theory with its emphasis on observable behaviors and by growing skepticism about self-report data (Miller, Rollins, & Thomas, 1982). Additionally, social exchange theory was being applied to the study of marital relationships (Kelley, 1979), with social developmental psychologists making the same point that examining dyads should be the focus of analysis in studying relationships rather than considering responses of individuals taken separately (Berscheid, 1986; Cairns, 1977).

About this same time, Gottman and his students (among them, Markman) were completing their groundbreaking work on observation of marital processes. Much of this work has been documented by Gottman (1994). In his research studies, Gottman identified key sequences of problem-solving interactions that reliably differentiated (self-reported) distressed from nondistressed couples. This research mapped the terrain for others concerning the marital interactive processes that could be expected to have the most significant implications for parent–child relationships and child development. Markman and his colleagues (e.g., Markman, Floyd, Stanley, & Storaasli, 1988; Stanley, Blumberg, & Markman, 1999) over many years have built on this research on marital processes to develop a set of marital interventions informed by the key findings from the empirical research (i.e., the PREP interventions Markman and Flanagan discuss in chap. 4, this volume). Their interventions focus on the relationship and patterns of interactions between couples associated with later marital dissolution. To date, efficacy of their intervention has been replicated across many studies and in many countries. Yet there is still much ground to cover in these efforts.

FAR BUT NOT FAR ENOUGH

Where Next in the Study of Marriages?

Flanagan et al. (chap. 4, this volume) point to several directions that marital research must take. These include focusing on positive relationship behaviors and strengths that may buoy distressed couples, incorporating broader contextual factors such as ethnicity and socioeconomic influences into marital models, and making more concerted efforts to understand cultural differences in marriages. The authors also document the development of effective prevention and intervention programs and assert that intervention research must continue to address the question of "what works and for whom?" These are important directions for research. However, several other significant directions need to be included in this research agenda.

First, we need a more complete understanding of how marital processes and changes due to marital interventions resonate throughout the whole family system. Flanagan et al. note the importance of considering the benefits of marital interventions for both the marital relationship and the individual adult's mental health. But the effect of marital processes and changes due to marital interventions are likely to be reflected also in parent–child relationships, in the couple's coparenting relationship, and in the child's development. These changes, in turn, are likely to feed back and influence the marriage over time. Moreover, we simply do not know very much yet about the effect of martial processes on other elements of the family system as a function of critical contextual factors such as socioeconomic status, ethnicity, and family composition.

Second, the authors note the importance of better understanding long-term relationships and relationships shared by older adults given that the populations they study are now living longer. At the same time, they find no research that has considered the efficacy of prevention programs such as PREP beyond the first 5 years of marriage. It is important to know whether a single dose of intervention can effectively inoculate couples for the remainder of their married lives, or whether periodic boosters are needed. Given the myriad changes couples experience during their relationship, it seems unlikely that a single dose of prevention would be effective over the life span. Moreover, if boosters are needed, an important question then becomes when such boosters might be most effective. There may be specific times at which additional doses of intervention are required. Such times may be periods of transition for families. Thus, it is necessary to question not only what "works and for whom," but also "when."

Disentangling the Interrelations Among Individual Functioning, Parent–Child Relationships, and Marital Relationships

An abundance of research documents the interdependence between individual functioning, parent–child relationships, and marital relationships. This literature suggests that a change in the family system at one level, such as an intervention at the marriage level, would resonate through the whole system. However, intervention studies normally only look at the effect of marital intervention on the marriage, or possibly on individual functioning, but not on the whole family system.

As several contributors to this volume note, a substantial body of literature has documented associations between marital dissatisfaction or conflict and problematic outcomes for children and adolescents (see Cummings, 1994; Emery, 1982; Grych & Fincham, 1990) as well as disturbances in parent–child relationships (e.g., Cox & Owen, 1993; Easterbrooks & Emde, 1988; Katz & Gottman, 1995). This literature suggests, in fact, that it is through disruption of parenting that marital discord is particularly detrimental for children's development (e.g., Fauber, Forehand, Thomas, & Wierson, 1990; Gottman & Katz, 1989). Given the interdependence of family relationships, it should no longer be surprising when studies indicate that conflict in the marital dyad extends to other parts of the family system (Cox & Paley, 1997; Gano-Phillips & Fincham, 1995). It has been many years since

Minuchin (1974) articulated the importance of families' maintaining a clear, but permeable, boundary between the marital and parent–child subsystems, permitting parents to perform the tasks of socializing their children without sacrificing the mutual support that optimally characterizes the spousal subsystem. In some of the best empirical work on this topic, Cummings (1994) provided data indicating that in families with high levels of parental conflict, this boundary is likely to dissolve, with children attempting to mediate, comfort, or distract their parents during disputes.

Emery, Fincham, and Cummings (1992) have urged professionals not to overlook the direct effect marital conflict can have on children, or the frequently overlooked effect children can have on their parents' marriage. Parents serve as models of adult relationships for their children; in particular, they teach children important lessons about male–female relationships. In so doing, they provide children with examples of how emotions are communicated and how adults attempt to resolve problems (Minuchin, 1988). They may also serve as models for all close relationships, including those involving peers and friends. Thus, when couples have chronic and unresolved conflict, the lessons are likely not to be to the child's benefit. However, exposure to some forms of marital disagreement may actually be of benefit to children, if the disagreements are effectively resolved and if parents model adaptive problem-solving skills (Cummings & Wilson, 1999). The marital relationship helps shape an atmosphere in the family that influences the child's perceptions of the emotional security the family offers.

The effect of the child's perceptions of the patents' marital solidarity may be independent of the effect of the coparenting behavior of the marital pair (McHale et al., chap. 5, this volume). Children who see their parents successfully resolve conflicts and share affection might be expected to feel secure about the future of their family and about their own relationships with their parents. Cummings (1994) has undertaken analyses to test this proposition and has accumulated data suggesting the child's perception of the emotional security afforded by the family appears to be influenced by the amount and type of marital conflict in the home. He suggested that marital conflicts regarding parenting issues may be particularly distressing for children. Children witnessing or experiencing dissonance between adult parenting partners pertaining to the handling of the child may blame themselves for disputes or begin to intervene in these conflicts. This becomes problematic, and the children's intervention in their parents' conflicts places them at increased risk for maladjustment (Cox, Paley, & Harter, in press). As one example, children who intervene in parental conflicts are more likely to become targets for parents' displaced anger than are children who respond by distancing themselves from the conflict (Rosenberg, 1987). Moreover, children's involvement in martial conflict is likely to exacerbate, rather than aide, marital disputes. Neither the immediate nor the cross-time progression of these dynamics is well understood, as this topic has received little attention from marital researchers.

Future research efforts need to keep in mind evidence indicating that children influence their parents' marriages as well as being influenced by them. At the most basic level, a large body of literature documents that the birth of a child is a significant source of stress on the marital relationship (e.g., Belsky & Pensky, 1988, Cowan, Cowan, Herrig, & Miller, 1991; Cox, Paley, Burchinal, & Payne, 1999). There is also growing evidence that various child characteristics, such as child behavior problems or disability status, influence marital dynamics. For example, parents who are able to attribute the cause of marital difficulties to their child's disability can sometimes maintain satisfaction with both the marriage and the coparenting relationship in the midst of distress (Floyd, Gilliom, & Costigan, 1998). Thus, the linkages among marriage, parenting, and child functioning can be complex. Prior findings from studies investigating these linkages provide a mandate to researchers that multiple levels of the family system and the mutual effect of these levels must be incorporated in future investigations of marital and family dynamics (Emery et al., 1992; see also Minuchin, chap. 9, this volume; Parke, chap. 3, this volume).

We must be asking questions such as, "what is the effect of marital interventions such as BMT on the whole family system? Although research on BMT has been largely concerned with the interventions' effectiveness in alleviating marital distress, gains from the intervention might also have other positive ripple effects in the family. Indeed, longitudinal research on marriage and the parenting alliance supports this perspective. In one study, Floyd et al. (1998) found that mothers and fathers with more positive marriages reported relatively higher confidence in their own parenting competence concurrently and showed improvements in feelings of parenting competence over time. Additionally, for the mothers, more positive marriages were associated with a reduction in negative interactions with their children over time compared with mothers in less positive marriages. Nonetheless, marital interventions may need to be broader to deal more effectively with the diverse ways in which couples relate to one another in families (i.e., as marital partners, as coparents) because functioning in different family roles likely feeds back into the marital relationship.

As noted by Flanagan et al. (chap. 4, this volume), there is also a pressing need to study more diverse samples when considering the effects of marital processes on other elements of the family system. Most studies on linkages between marital and parent–child relationships have used samples composed mostly or entirely of Euro-American families or have contained no information on the ethnicity of the sample. Little is known about whether there are different linkages between marriage and parenting across different ethnic groups, or about the import of differences within various ethnic groups (Cox, Paley, & Harter, in press). We also know little about marriage–parenting linkages among families of differing SES. The few studies in this area beyond the typical middle-class samples have focused mostly on lower class or poverty samples. Studies generally have not included a broad range of individuals with regard to SES, despite the evidence that economic stress affects marital and parenting processes (Conger et al., 1992, 1993).

In addition, there is far too little information on links between adult relationships and parent–child relationships in nontraditional families, including adoptive families, blended families, families headed by gay and lesbian parents, and families in which parents are cohabitating but not legally married. Although there may be similarities between traditional and nontraditional families in terms of interparental and parent–child relationships, Cox et al. (in press) noted there may also be unique issues faced by nontraditional families. For example, gay and lesbian couples are likely to experience unique pressures when they live in societies where large segments of the population do not sanction their relationship. For some couples, these unrelenting pressures may have the effect of dividing them as a couple, and hence compromise their parenting. For other gay and lesbian couples, such pressures may have the reverse effect, leading them to pull together in the face of adversity and to form coparenting relationships that are even more cohesive and supportive. As with any group, there are likely various adaptations that nontraditional families must make in their interparental and parent–child relationships. However, the processes that characterize such adaptations have received little attention from investigators.

Transitions as Points of Intervention

In evaluating the efficacy of marital interventions, it would be useful to know if there are times when families or couples benefit most from intervention and are most open to intervention. Looking to the future, if intervention programs are used early in a marriage, with boosters at later points, it will be important for researchers and clinicians to know when these boosters would be optimally implemented. As suggested earlier, transition times in family life may be important times to consider. Transitions are periods when a marriage may be particularly vulnerable because the relationship has to be reorganized to meet new challenges. Identification of couples who are likely to experience increased marital difficulty in the face of transitions is a critical research direction, one that will permit us to focus preventive efforts on the most vulnerable couples. At the same time, understanding the strengths of couples whose relationships are minimally affected by the challenge of transitions may also inform intervention. In this regard, there is no substitute for prospective, longitudinal research studies.

Couples who not only show distress in response to transitions, but who also fail to show recovery over time may be of particular concern. Initial difficulties in a transition may be normative, but the lack of reorganization over time may be a sign of chronic problems that are likely to influence parenting and child development negatively (Cox et al., 1999).

The transition to parenthood may be an important time for prevention efforts to help some couples adjust to major challenges to their relationship. The birth of a child and the need for the couple to reorganize around the care of the infant affect each of the new parents as individuals, as well as the marital relationship. And in circular fashion (Minuchin, chap. 9, this volume) individual and marital adaptations reciprocally affect one another. For example, new parents are at increased risk for depression (Campbell, Cohn, Meyers, Ross, & Flanagan, 1992; Cowan et al., 1991), and maternal depression is highly associated in many studies with marital distress (reviewed by Downey & Coyne, 1990). Cox et al. (1999) found that the extent of adult depressive symptoms as well as the gender of the child and whether the pregnancy was planned or unplanned all predicted patterns of interaction between the couple over the first 2 years after becoming parents. These factors were also important in predicting the way the couple viewed their marriage. The couples who were most at risk for increasing conflict without recovery during the 2 years were those in which husbands and wives experienced depressive symptoms in the context of having had an unplanned daughter. Both having planned the pregnancy and having had a son helped to buffer the marriage of couples where one or both spouses experienced depressive symptoms, in the sense that these couples did not experience the same continuance of negative, conflicted behavior over the 2 years after becoming parents. These data point to two important issues. First, times of challenge or transition may be periods when additional exposure to prevention programs would be important boosters to the original prevention. Second, some couples may need interventions more than others. Having a member who experiences high depressive symptoms seems to be a risk factor, but parental depression combined with unplanned transitions or challenges may heighten the over-time risk still further.

Researchers sometimes fail to appreciate that transition times can also be positive for families, particularly when families process the transitions by calling on assistance from intervention or prevention programs. One important function of the family unit is to sustain family members during times of transition and to instill skills for coping with change in children (Kreppner, chap. 8, this volume). Learning to cope adaptively with change is likely to promote optimal development in children as well as adults across the life span. Thus, instead of narrowly focusing on the negative effects of change on various elements of the family system, future research should also be open to the adaptive ways in which families accommodate to their changing contexts. Such adaptations have the potential to solve some problems while creating others. Parental separation or divorce, for example, can benefit children when the divorce signals an end to children's daily exposure to chronic, hostile marital conflict (Grych & Fincham, 1990). At the same time, however, children with divorced parents also confront many challenges that place them at risk. Buchanan, Maccoby, and Dornbusch (1991), for example, suggested children may feel torn between parents following divorce, which places them at increased risk for depression, anxiety, and deviant behavior (see McHale et al., chap. 5, this volume).

Where Next in the Study of Family Groups?

Despite the compelling nature of the ideas that have come from family systems theories and from family therapists, research has not fully realized the value of these ideas. However, work by McHale et al. (chap. 5, this volume) introduces several promising new research directions and illustrates the importance of moving beyond the husband–wife or parent–child dyad in explorations of family influences on child development. As we noted earlier, family therapists have long recognized the importance of expanding their focus to units beyond the dyad in understanding family processes and disturbances. Both Bateson and Bowen, for example, initially conceptualized schizophrenic behavior as an outgrowth of troubled dyadic interactions (usually between parent and child), but subsequently broadened their perspectives to include triadic interactions and the larger family system (see Hoffman, 1981). They suggested that individual symptoms were indicative of the disturbed organization in the larger family system and that these symptoms maintained the family organization. Recent investigations have provided substantiating evidence in support of these early clinical observations, establishing that families with symptomatic children are often characterized by weak marital alliances and by cross-generational coalitions (Christensen & Margolin, 1988; Gilbert, Christensen, & Margolin, 1984) or by parental coalitions in which "problem" children are scapegoated (Christensen, Phillips, Glasgow, & Johnson, 1983; Vuchinich, Wood, & Vuchinich, 1994). Observing marital partners functioning as coparents (McHale et al., chap. 5, this volume) promises to provide much more informative data regarding the conditions under which conflicted marital interactions may or may not compromise parent–child relationships and child development.

McHale's work and the theoretical framework from which it flows provides strong arguments for the importance of extending the unit of analysis in family research to triadic and whole family interactions. As McHale et al. (chap. 5, this volume) note, however, few studies, using either clinical or normative samples, have taken steps to systematically investigate family units beyond the dyad (Parke, 1988). Most developmental research continues to focus on parent–child dyads, and particularly on the mother–child relationship (Silverstein, chap. 2, this volume). To be sure, circumstances have changed some since Minuchin (1985) challenged the prevailing ideas in developmental psychology about child rearing and its effects based on data drawn from one parent, considered the representative of parenting in the family. Research tells us not only that fathers may offer different experiences for children from mothers (Parke, 1996), but also that interactions between parent and child are affected by the presence of the other parent (Belsky & Volling, 1987; Buhrmester, Camparo, Christensen, Gonzales, & Hinshaw, 1992; Clarke-Stewart, 1978; McHale et al., chap. 5, this volume). Yet although much of parenting occurs in the presence of both parents, relatively few studies have examined the process of coparenting (for exceptions, see Floyd et al., 1998; Floyd & Zmich, 1991; Gable, Belsky, & Crnic, 1995; Maccoby, Depner, & Mnookin, 1990; McHale et al., chap. 5, this volume). The work of McHale and colleagues, and of others pursuing research on coparenting, represents an important direction, and one that future research must continue to follow.

McHale et al. (chap. 5, this volume) raise many other pertinent issues with regard to the study of the family. Further discussion of several of these issues is merited. First, understanding the family in context is critical. This approach includes considering how cultural and intergenerational contexts are associated with family dynamics. Second, the expression and socialization of emotion within families warrants discussion. Finally, the issue of how well our approaches to statistical analyses fit with our concepts of how families function is important to consider.

Understanding Families in Context

As several contributors to this volume note, much of our research on families has been conducted with White, middle-class samples of married couples and their children. However, it is clear that the contexts in which families function vary widely in the United States. Families differ with regard to their economic circumstances, the safety and security of their surrounds, the types of employment opportunities open to their members, and the accompanying socialization goals for their children. Several investigators have underscored the need for a better understanding of the adaptations that poor, minority families make to family structure, organization, and life trajectories in response to environmental challenges (Dilworth-Anderson, Burton, & Johnson, 1993; Harrison, Wilson, Pine, Chan, & Buriel, 1990; Mc-Loyd, 1990a, b; Wilson, 1989). This research demonstrates that what is adaptive in one context may not be adaptive in another, and that making too broad generalizations beyond study samples for policy and clinical practice may be problematic.

Some examples help illustrate. First, as Cox and Paley (1997) noted, work with underrepresented groups frequently challenges many of the traditional notions of family therapists (e.g., Minuchin, 1974), such as what we should consider appropriate boundaries in families. Burton, Allison, and Obeidallah (1995) have suggested that the worlds of adolescents and their parents may overlap to a greater extent in economically disadvantaged minority families than in middle-class families. Some African American fathers and their adolescent sons, for example, are often competing for the same jobs because of high unemployment rates in areas where they live. Stack and Burton (1993) showed in their study of two communities of low-income African American families that grandmothers are often the primary caregivers for grandchildren, while their daughters care for their own grandmothers. Consequently, mothers' relationships with their children were more like sibling relationships than parent–child relationships. In another context, this blurring of generational boundaries may be considered pathological; however, the ability to be more flexible about family roles may be seen as an adaptive strategy for poor, minority families (Harrison et al., 1990).

Second, parents' experiences both in childhood and in current relationships they share with their parents provide a unique context for present-day family functioning. A growing body of research has examined whether the manner in which parents were treated as children or the way they interpret their childhood experiences in adulthood affects the way they treat their children (Putallaz, Costanzo, Grimes, & Sherman, 1998). This work has suggested that cross-generation continuities exist. Although not yet demonstrated empirically, these stabilities across generations may be shown to reflect continuities in parenting practices (Patterson, 1998). As one example, Simons, Whitbeck, Conger, and Chyi-In (1991) found that grandparents who had relied on aggressive parenting practices produced children who as parents were likely to use similar parenting practices. However, discontinuities can also occur across generations, and research needs to consider the conditions under which continuities and discontinuities occur (Kaufman & Zigler, 1989; Rutter, 1998). In one such study, Serbin et al. (1998) found that women with histories of childhood aggression and withdrawal were less likely to transfer symptoms to their children when they had more years of schooling. Thus, parents' level of education may prove to be one mitigating factor in determining whether intergenerational transmission of risk occurs.

Intergenerational continuities and discontinuities may also be evident in coparenting and family-group-level dynamics (McHale, Kuersten, & Lauretti, 1996). The degree to which there is intergenerational continuity in such dynamics depends in large part on patterns of partner selection and the nature of the marital or adult relationships established. However, as noted by

Rutter (1998), this information is difficult to attain given that information should ideally be based on prospective longitudinal data that includes information on both parents. Still, studies that span generations and that include current relationships with the previous generation will help in understanding the pathways by which different family systems are established and maintained.

Emotion in the Family

Increased attention has been devoted to the central role of affect and emotion in family dynamics (Dix, 1991). The emotional relationship between the mother and child and the way in which that relationship shapes the emotional development of the child has been a central part of attachment theory (Cassidy, 1999). However, the rich theoretical formulations of attachment theory have rarely found their way into the marital and family literature. Mostly independent of attachment theory and research, there has been a growing recognition that one of a parent's primary socialization goals for children involves helping them learn to manage their emotions and establish close relationships. Two emerging models dealing with the socialization of emotion have emphasized the significance of parents' responses to children's emotions in shaping the children's social-emotional adaptation. First, Katz, Wilson, and Gottman (1999) have discussed *emotion coaching philosophy* as a characteristic of responsive parenting. They argue that to best promote a child's emotional adaptation, parents must respond empathetically to their child's distress and validate rather than judge the child's emotional reactions. Similarly, Eisenberg, Cumberland, and Spinrad (1998) have proposed that parents who respond in a supportive manner to children's negative emotions teach them ways to effectively manage emotional distress; consequently, they have children who are better able to regulate emotion. In this way, parents normalize children's emotional experience and teach children that a wide range of emotions are acceptable and can be shared in social relationships (Cassidy, 1994). Findings from these research programs indicate that parents' responses to children's emotions have significant bearing on children's social-emotional adaptation (Eisenberg et al., 1998; Katz, 1997; Katz et al., 1999).

Thinking broadly about the role of emotion in interpersonal relationships, attachment research has placed great significance on emotional communication, highlighting the important signaling function of emotion in human relationships. The very young infant, through interaction with the caregiver, is known to move from communication through inborn reflexes that automatically elicit caregiving to communication through explicit, intentional signals that call for regulatory assistance (Sroufe, 1995). There has been almost universal agreement that the role of caregivers in soothing distress is a critical factor in promoting the development of infant self-organization. Caregivers, for example, are known to enhance alertness and to afford self-regulation through their sensitive responsiveness to the child's signals of need for soothing or increased stimulation (Sameroff, 1989; Sroufe, 1995; Tronick, 1989). Most of this work on early communication is dyadic in nature, though the newer work reviewed by McHale et al. (chap. 5, this volume) provides a possible paradigm for conceptualizing emotional influence more broadly.

Parental responsiveness to the child's emotional signals remains important throughout childhood. Collins and Laursen (1992) noted that although parent–child conflict typically increases during adolescence, the negative emotion can serve as an important signal to parents that parenting behaviors need to be modified in response to the changing developmental needs of their children (see also Kreppner, chap. 8, this volume). Holmbeck and Hill (1991) similarly argued that parent–adolescent negative emotion can serve an adaptive function as it can be an impetus to change, adaptation, and development. Likewise, Powers and Welsh (1999) and Graber and Brooks-Gunn (1999) asserted that adolescence is a time when negative emotion in the parent–child relationship occurs normatively as parents and adolescents negotiate the adolescent's growing autonomy and individuation, and that it appears important that families tolerate a moderate degree of negative emotion.

Research on the way emotion is handled in families and not just in dyads, throughout the family life cycle, is an important direction for our field. Such work would enhance our understanding of the social and emotional development of children in their families. However, research on emotion in the family has generally been hindered not only by a lack of consensus over operational definitions of emotion but also by a lack of measures that effectively address emotional experience (Fischer & Tangney, 1995). Progress in developing methodologies that allow family-level investigations of emotion and that accurately assess members' unique emotional experiences would help advance this critical area of research.

Analytic Procedures in Studying the Family

Progress in understanding the development of individuals or relationships in the family is enhanced when investigations take into account circular causal processes reflecting the reciprocal influences of various levels of the family system (Cox & Paley, 1997). Unfortunately, however, not only are our statistical procedures poorly suited to detect circular causality (Rutter, 1987), but also investigators seldom look for circular processes (Emery et al., 1992). Moreover, our typical approach in family research studies is to rely on procedures that consider one variable at a time, despite evidence that the combination of variables is often key. In short, we often neglect a person-oriented approach, choosing instead a variable-oriented approach (Bergman & Magnusson, 1997; Magnusson & Bergman, 1988). McHale's work offers one glimpse at how our future inquiries might pose questions. It suggests that marital conflict may not have the same effect on children when parents continue to coparent well together. At the same time, however, marital conflict is unlikely to be benign, as it may affect a child's sense of emotional security of the family. Hence, marital conflict and poor coparenting may have a different effect from marital conflict with adequate coparenting, which in turn may be different from low marital conflict and good coparenting. Understanding the effects of marital conflict by itself may not be very illuminating. Progress in analytic approaches that keep pace with our theories and models of family systems will be essential if our knowledge in this arena is to progress.

SUMMARY

We have attempted to augment the arguments put forth in the prior two chapters by suggesting several additional research directions that should help guide the next phase of work on marital and family dynamics. Research that tells us more about how relationships in the family influence one another remains an important ongoing thrust (Cox, Brooks-Gunn, & Paley, 1999). These influences are undoubtedly reciprocal, and a charting of different pathways through time will help move our field along and provide important practical information for those who work with families.

Relatedly, we also need a more complete understanding regarding how different kinds of marital interventions resonate through the whole family system at various stages in the family life cycle, and for families in different contexts. The efficacy of marital intervention should not be judged principally on how it affects marital distress and adult functioning, but rather on how the whole family system functions as a result of the intervention. Taking a broader perspective would also allow researchers to consider the various roles adults play in the family (i.e., as marital partners and coparents) and to acknowledge that families may have different goals and values. Because families are composed differently and are affected by different life circumstances, studies using diverse samples must be a priority. In studying interventions, we need to understand not only what interventions work for whom, but also when. The timing of interventions may be particularly critical, and intervention boosters are likely to be needed at key times, such as at family transitions. Marital intervention research needs to consider the times when families or couples may benefit most from intervention and may be most open to intervention.

Interventions work best when they are based on research that illuminates the processes or pathways families follow when they do well over time, and when they fail to do well. As Rutter, (chap. 11, this volume) notes, risk factors tell us little about processes and can often be misleading. Marital conflict, for example, is a known risk factor for child behavior problems. However, research suggests that marital conflict is largely problematic when it is not resolved; when it erodes the ability of adults to be sensitive, warm, and involved with their children; and when it creates a family atmosphere heightening the emotional insecurity of children. Conversely, marital conflicts that are resolved satisfactorily may actually help children gain skill at problem solving in close personal relationships. These are global statements. Research must recognize that these pathways may not generalize to all families and that cultural or other subgroup differences may be important moderators. Again, thoughtful studies of diverse groups are needed. Likely, findings from past studies have been overgeneralized beyond the groups used in the studies. This overgeneralization can be dangerous when such findings lead to ineffective or even damaging interventions. Family research must pay attention to the need for this more specific information about normative and functional family processes in different social contexts.

We need to continue striving for increased sophistication not only in how we conceptualize our models in the family but also in the kinds of methods and analyses we use. Despite the compelling nature of the ideas that have come from family systems theorists and family therapists and the recent conceptual and methodological advances summarized throughout this volume, the value of these ideas has not been fully realized because our progress in methodology and analysis techniques remains slow. Expansion of studies beyond the dyad in families has begun, but still requires innovation in the range of methods appropriate for studying larger units in the family. And as McHale and colleagues note, the definition of what constitutes family for different children in different contexts has been difficult to articulate. We would add that this is also true for the construct of marriage. Adult relationships in families that do not involve marriage are likely as important for the functioning of families as are marital relationships in other families. The types of relationships and family configurations that may be adaptive in one context may not be adaptive in another.

Study of the nuclear family is not yet complete, either. Such studies rarely include a comprehensive understanding of the parents' earlier experiences in their families of origin or of their current relationships with their parents and family members. These intergenerational ties are important, given studies documenting both continuity and discontinuity across generations. Longitudinal studies that span generations, that include assessments of current relationships with the previous generation, and that gauge how the parents understand their earlier experiences in their families while growing up will ultimately be helpful in laying out the trajectories associated with continuities and discontinuities.

We also view the study of emotion in families and the way in which emotion is handled as an important area for future research. Emotions have important communication value, and the way emotions are typically dealt with in family relationships has important implications for the social and emotional development of children, for the long-term relationships between parents and their children, and for children's relationships with others. Refining our definitions of emotion and improving measurement in this area of research remains a major challenge for marital and family researchers.

These directions and those described in the previous two chapters provide a substantial agenda for future research. However, the effort is needed. Understanding more about the full family group as the major context for both child development and for adult functioning promises to yield great benefits that will aide not only in designing intervention and prevention efforts for members of our societies at greatest risk, but also in setting responsible policy to help enhance adaptive functioning and prevent family distress and dysfunction.

ACKNOWLEDGMENTS

Partial support for the preparation of this article was provided by the Department of Education Office of Educational Research and Improvement (Award Number R307A60004) to the National Center for Early Development and Learning and by the National Institute of Child Health and Human Development grant (HD37558) as a part of the NICHD Child and Family Well-Being Network.

REFERENCES

Aldous, J. (1977). Family interaction patterns. *Annual Review of Sociology, 3*, 105–135.

Belsky, J. (1981). Early human experience: A family perspective. *Developmental Psychology, 17*(1), 3–23

Belsky, J., & Pensky, E. (1988). Developmental history, personality, and family relationships: Toward an emergent family system. In R. A. Hinde & J. Stevenson-Hinde (Eds.), *Relationships within families: Mutual influences* (pp. 193–217). Oxford, England: Clarendon.

Belsky, J., Rovine, M., & Fish, M. (1989). The developing family system. In M. Grunnar & E. Thelen (Eds.), *Systems and development* (pp. 119–166). Hillsdale, NJ: Lawrence Erlbaum Associates.

Belsky, J., & Volling, B. (1987). Mothering, fathering and marital interaction in the family triad: Exploring family systems processes. In P. Berman & F. Pederson (Eds.), *Men's transition to parenthood: Longitudinal studies of early family experience* (pp. 37–63). Hillsdale, NJ: Lawrence Erlbaum Associates.

Bergman, L. R., & Magnusson, D. (1997). A person-oriented approach in research on developmental psychopathology. *Development and Psychopathology, 9*(2), 291–319.

Berscheid, E. (1986). Emotional experience in close relationships: Some implications for child development. In W. W. Hartup & Z. Rubin (Eds.), *Relationships and development* (pp. 136–166). Hillsdale, NJ: Lawrence Erlbaum Associates.

Buchanan, C. M., Maccoby, E. E., & Dornbusch, S. M. (1991). Caught between parents: Adolescents' experience in divorced homes. *Child Development, 62,* 1008–1029.

Buhrmester, D., Camparo, L., Christensen, A., Gonzales, L. S., & Hinshaw, S. P. (1992). Mothers and fathers interacting in dyads and triads with normal and hyperactive sons. *Developmental Psychology, 28,* 500–509.

Burton, L. M., Allison, K., & Obeidallah, D. (1995). Social context and adolescence: Perspectives on development among inner-city African-American teens. In L. Crockett & A. Crouter (Eds.), *Pathways through adolescence: Individual development in relation to social context* (pp. 119–138). Hillsdale, NJ: Lawrence Erlbaum Associates.

Cairns, R. B. (1977). Beyond social attachment: The dynamics of interactional development. In T. Alloway, P. Pliner, & L. Krames (Eds.), *Attachment behavior: Advances in the study of communication and affect* (Vol. 3, pp. 1–35). New York: Plenum Press.

Campbell, S. B., Cohn, J. F., Meyers, T. A., Ross, S., & Flanagan, C. (1992). Course and correlates of postpartum depression during the transition to parenthood. *Developmental Psychopathology, 4,* 29–47.

Cassidy, J. (1994). Emotional regulation: Influences of attachment relationships. In N. A. Fox (Ed.), The development of emotional regulation. *Monographs of the Society for Research in Child Development, 59* (2–3, Serial No. 240).

Cassidy, J. (1999). The nature of the child's ties. In J. Cassidy & P. R. Shaver (Eds.), *Handbook of attachment: Theory, research, and clinical applications* (pp. 3–20). New York: Guilford Press.

Christensen, A., & Margolin, G. (1988). Conflict and alliance in distressed and nondistressed families. In R. A. Hinde & J. Stevenson-Hinde (Eds.), *Relationships within families: Mutual influences* (pp. 263–282). Oxford, England: Clarendon.

Christensen, A., Phillips, S., Glasgow, R. E., & Johnson, S. M. (1983). Parental characteristics and interactional dysfunction in families with child behavior problems: A preliminary investigation. *Journal of Abnormal Child Psychology, 11,* 153–166.

Clarke-Stewart, A. (1978). And daddy makes 3: The fathers' impact on mothers and young children. *Child Development, 49,* 489–493.

Collins, W. A., & Laursen, B. (1992). Conflict and relationships during adolescence. In C. U. Shantz & W. W. Hartup (Eds.), *Conflict in child and adolescent development* (pp. 216–241). New York: Cambridge University Press.

Conger, R. D., Conger, K. J., Elder, G. H., Jr., Lorenz, F. O., Simons, R. L., & Whitbeck, L. B. (1992). A family process model of economic hardship and adjustment of early adolescent boys. *Child Development, 63,* 526–541.

Conger, R. D., Conger, K. J., Elder, G. H., Jr., Lorenz, F. O., Simons, R. L., & Whitbeck, L. B. (1993). Family economic stress and adjustment of early adolescent girls. *Developmental Psychology, 29,* 206–219.

Cowan, C. P., & Cowan, P. A. (1985a, April). *Parents' work patterns, marital, and parent–child relationships and early child development.* Paper presented at the meetings of the Society for Research in Child Development, Toronto.

Cowan, C. P., Cowan, P. A., Herring, G., & Miller, N. B. (1991). Becoming a family: Marriage, parenting, and child development. In P. A. Cowan & E. M. Hetherington (Eds.), *Family transitions* (pp. 79–109). Hillsdale, NJ: Lawrence Erlbaum Associates.

Cowan, P. A., & Cowan, C. P. (1985b, April). *Pregnancy, parenthood, and children at three.* Paper presented at the meetings of the Society for Research in Child Development, Toronto, Canada.

Cox, M. J. (1985). Progress and continued challenges in understanding the transition to parenthood. *Journal of Family Issues, 6*(4), 395–408.

Cox, M. J., Brooks-Gunn, J., & Paley, B. (1999). Perspectives on conflict and cohesion in families. In M. Cox & J. Brooks-Gunn (Eds.), *Conflict and cohesion in families: Causes and consequences. The advances in family research series* (pp. 321–344). Mahwah, NJ: Lawrence Erlbaum Associates.

Cox, M. J., & Owen, M. T. (1993). *Marital conflict and conflict negotiations: Effects on infant–mother and infant–father relationships*. Presented at biennial meeting for Society of Research in Child Development, New Orleans, LA.

Cox, M. J., Owen, M. T., Lewis, J. L., & Henderson, V. K. (1989). Marriage, adult adjustment, and early parenting. *Child Development, 60,* 1015–1024.

Cox, M. J., & Paley, B. (1997). Families as systems. *Annual Review of Psychology, 48,* 243–267.

Cox, M. J., Paley, B., Burchinal, M., & Payne, C. C. (1999). Marital perceptions and interactions across the transition to parenthood. *Journal of Marriage and the Family, 61,* 611–625.

Cox, M. J., Paley, B., & Harter, K. S. M. (in press). Interparental conflict parent–child relationships. In J. Grych & F. Fincham (Eds.), *Child development and interparental conflict.* Cambridge, England: Cambridge University Press.

Cummings, E. M. (1994). Marital conflict and children's functioning. *Social Development, 3,* 16–59.

Cummings, E. M., & Wilson, A. (1999). Contexts of marital conflict and children's emotional security: Exploring the distinction between constructive and destructive conflict from the children's perspective. In M. Cox & J. Brooks-Gunn (Eds.), *Conflict and cohesion in families: Causes and consequences* (pp. 105–130). Mahwah, NJ: Lawrence Erlbaum Associates.

Dilworth-Anderson, P., Burton, L. M., & Johnson, L. B. (1993). Reframing theories for understanding race, ethnicity, and families. In P. Boss, W. J. Doherty, R. LaRossa, W. R. Schumm, & S. K. Steinmetz (Eds.), *Sourcebook of family theories and methods: A contextual approach* (pp. 627–646). New York: Plenum.

Dix, T. (1991). The affective organization of parenting: Adaptive and maladaptive processes. *Psychological Bulletin, 110*(1), 3–25.

Downey, G., & Coyne, J. C. (1990). Children of depressed parents: An integrative review. *Psychological Bulletin, 108,* 50–76.

Easterbrooks, M. A., & Emde, R. N. (1988). Marital and parent–child relationships: The role of affect in the family system. In R. A. Hinde, & J. Stevenson-Hinde (Eds.), *Relationships within families: Mutual influences* (pp. 81–103). Oxford, England: Clarendon.

Eisenberg, N., Cumberland, A., & Spinrad, T. L. (1998). The socialization of emotions. In R. F. Baumeister and C. Sedikides (Eds.), *Psychological inquiry: An international journal of peer commentary and review, 9*(4), 241–278.

Emery, R. E. (1982). Interparental conflict and the children of discord and divorce. *Psychological Bulletin, 92,* 310–330.

Emery, R. E., Fincham, F. D., & Cummings, E. M. (1992). Parenting in context: Systematic thinking about parental conflict and its influence on children. *Journal of Consulting and Clinical Psychology, 60,* 909–912.

Fauber, R., Forehand, R., Thomas, A. M., & Wierson, M. (1990). A mediational model of the impact of marital conflict on adolescent adjustment in intact and divorced families: The role of disrupted parenting. *Child Development, 61,* 1112–1123.

Fischer, K. W., & Tangney, J. P. (1995). Self-conscious emotions and the affect revolution: Framework and overview. In J. P. Tangney & K. W. Fischer, (Eds.), *Self-conscious emotions: The psychology of shame, guilt, embarrassment and pride* (pp. 3–22). New York: Guilford.

Floyd, F. J., Gilliom, L. A., & Costigan, C. L. (1998). Marriage and the parenting alliance: Longitudinal prediction of change in parenting perceptions and behaviors. *Child Development, 69,* 1461–1479.

Floyd, F. J., & Zmich, D. E. (1991). Marriage and the parenting partnership: Perceptions and interactions of parents with mentally retarded and typically developing children. *Child Development, 6,* 1434–1448.

Framo, J. L. (1965). Personal reflections of a family therapist. *Journal of Marriage and Family Counseling, 1*, 15–28.

Gable, S., Belsky, J., & Crnic, K. (1995). Coparenting during the child's 2nd year: A descriptive account. *Journal of Marriage and the Family, 57*, 609–616.

Gano-Phillips, S., & Fincham, F. D. (1995). Family conflict, divorce, and children's adjustment. In M. A. Fitzpatrick, & A. L. Vangelisti (Eds.), *Explaining family interactions* (pp. 206–213). Thousand Oaks, CA: Sage.

Gilbert, R., Christensen, A., & Margolin, G. (1984). Patterns of alliance in nondistressed and multiproblem families. *Family Process, 23*, 75–87.

Gottman, J. M. (1994). *What predicts divorce: The relationship between marital processes and marital outcomes.* Hillsdale, NJ: Lawrence Erlbaum Associates.

Gottman, J. M., & Katz, L. F. (1989). Effects of marital discord on young children's peer interaction and health. *Developmental Psychology, 25*, 373–381.

Gottman, J. M., & Levinson, R. W. (1984). Why marriages fail: Affective and physiological patterns in marital interaction. In J. C. Masters & K. Yarkin-Levin (Eds.), *Boundary areas in social and developmental psychology* (pp. 67–106). New York: Academic Press.

Graber, J. A., & Brooks-Gunn, J. (1999). "Sometimes I think that you don't like me": How mothers and daughters negotiate the transition into adolescence. In M. J. Cox & J. Brooks-Gunn (Eds.), *Conflict and cohesion in families: Causes and consequences* (pp. 207–242). Mahwah, NJ: Lawrence Erlbaum Associates.

Grych, J. H., & Fincham, F. D. (1990). Marital conflict and children's adjustment: A cognitive–contextual framework. *Psychological Bulletin, 108*, 267–290.

Haley, J. (1967). Experiment with abnormal families. *Archives of General Psychiatry, 17*, 53–63.

Harrison, A. O., Wilson, M. N., Pine, C. J., Chan, S. Q., & Buriel, R. (1990). Family ecologies of ethnic minority children. *Child Development, 61*, 347–362.

Hoffman, L. (1981). *Foundations of family therapy: A conceptual framework for systems change.* New York: Basic Books.

Holmbeck, G. N., & Hill, J. P. (1991). Conflict in engagement, positive affect, and menarch in families with seventh-grade girls. *Child Development, 62*, 1030–1048.

Katz, L. F. (1997). *Towards an emotional intelligence theory of adolescent depression.* Paper presented at the biennial meeting of the Society for Research and Development, Washington, DC.

Katz, L. F., & Gottman, J. M. (1995). Marital interaction and child outcomes: A longitudinal study of mediating and moderating processes. In D. Cicchetti & S. L. Toth (Eds.), *Rochester Symposium on Developmental Psychopathology: Vol. 6. Emotion, cognition, and representation* (pp. 301–342). Rochester, NY: University of Rochester Press.

Katz, L. F., Wilson, B., & Gottman, J. M. (1999). Meta-emotion philosophy and family adjustment: Making an emotional connection. In M. Cox & J. Brooks-Gunn (Eds.), *Conflict and cohesion in families: Causes and consequences* (pp. 131–166). Mahwah, NJ: Lawrence Erlbaum Associates.

Kaufman, J., & Zigler, E. (1989). The intergenerational transmission of child abuse. In D. Cicchetti & V. Carlson (Eds.), *Child maltreatment: Theory and research on the causes and consequences of child abuse and neglect* (pp. 129–150). Cambridge, MA: Cambridge University Press.

Kelley, H. H. (1979). *Personal relationships: Their structures and processes.* Hillsdale, NJ: Lawrence Erlbaum Associates.

Lewis, J. M., Owen, M. T., & Cox, M. J. (1988). Transition to parenthood III: Incorporation of the child into the family. *Family Process, 27*(4), 411–421.

Maccoby, E. E., Depner, C. E., & Mnookin, R. H. (1990). Coparenting in the second year after divorce. *Journal of Marriage and the Family, 52*, 141–155.

Magnusson, D., & Bergman, L. R. (1988). Individual and variable-based approaches to longitudinal research on early risk factors. In M. Rutter (Ed.), *Studies of psychosocial risk: The power of longitudinal data* (pp. 45–61). Cambridge, MA: Cambridge University Press.

Margolin, G. (1981). The reciprocal relationship between marital and child problems. In J. P. Vincent (Ed.), *Advances in intervention, assessment, and theory* (Vol. 2, pp. 131–182). Greenwich, CT: JAI.

Markman, J. J., Floyd, F., Stanley, S. M., & Storaasli, R. (1988). The prevention of marital distress: A longitudinal investigation. *Journal of Consulting and Clinical Psychology, 56*, 210–127.

McHale, J., Kuersten, R., & Lauretti, A. (1996). New directions in the study of family-level dynamics during infancy and early childhood. In J. McHale & P. Cowan (Eds.), *Understanding how family-level dynamics affect children's development: Studies of two parent families* (New Directions for Child Development, No. 74, pp. 5–26). San Francisco: Jossey-Bass.

McLoyd, V. C. (1990a). The impact of economic hardship on black families and children: Psychological distress, parenting, and socioemotional development. *Child Development, 61*, 311–346.

McLoyd, V. C. (1990b). Minority children: Introduction to the special issue. *Child Development, 61*, 263–266.

Miller, B. C., Rollins, B. C., & Thomas, D. L. (1982). On methods of studying marriage and families. *Journal of Marriage and the Family, 44*, 851–873.

Minuchin, P. (1988). Relationships within the family: A systems perspective on development. In R. A. Hinde & J. Stevenson-Hinde (Eds.), *Relationships within families: Mutual influences* (pp. 7–26). Oxford, England: Clarendon.

Minuchin, P. (1985). Families and individual development: Provocations from the field of family therapy. *Child Development, 56*, 289–302.

Minuchin, S. (1974). *Families and family therapy.* Cambridge, MA: Harvard University Press.

Parke, R. D. (1988). Families in life-span perspective: A multilevel developmental approach. In E. M. Hetherington, R. M. Lerner, & M. Perlmutter (Eds.), *Child development in life-span perspective* (pp. 159–190). Hillsdale, NJ: Lawrence Erlbaum Associates.

Parke, R. D. (1996). *Fatherhood.* Cambridge, MA: Harvard University Press.

Patterson, G. R. (1998). Continuities—A search for causal mechanisms: Comment on the special section. *Developmental Psychology, 34*, 1263–1268.

Powers, S. I., & Welsh, D. P. (1999). Mother–daughter interactions and adolescent girls' depression. In M. J. Cox & J. Brooks-Gunn (Eds.), *Conflict and cohesion in families: Causes and consequences* (pp. 243–282). Mahwah, NJ: Lawrence Erlbaum Associates.

Putallaz, M., Costanzo, P. R., Grimes, C. L., & Sherman, D. M. (1998). Intergenerational continuities and their influences on children's social development. *Social Development, 7*(3), 389–427.

Rosenberg, M. S. (1987). Children of battered women: The effects of witnessing violence on their social-problem solving abilities. *The Behavior Therapist, 4*, 85–89.

Rutter, M. (1987). Continuities and discontinuities from infancy. In J. Osofsky (Ed.), *Handbook of infant development* (2nd ed., pp. 1256–1296). New York: Wiley.

Rutter, M. (1998). Some research considerations on intergenerational continuities and discontinuities: Comment on the special section. *Developmental Psychology, 34*, 1263–1268.

Sameroff, A. J. (1989). Principles of development and psychopathology. In A. J. Sameroff & R. N. Emde (Eds.), *Relationship disturbances in early childhood* (pp. 17–32). New York: Basic Books.

Sameroff, A. J. (1994). Developmental systems and family functioning. In R. D. Parke & S. G. Kellam (Eds.), *Exploring family relationships with others social contexts* (pp. 199–214). Hillsdale, NJ: Lawrence Erlbaum Associates.

Serbin, L. A., Cooperman, J. M., Peters, P. L., Lehoux, P. M., Stack, D. M., & Schwartzman, A. E. (1998). Intergenerational transfer of psychosocial risk in women with childhood histories of aggression, withdrawal, or aggression and withdrawal. *Developmental Psychology, 34*, 1263–1268.

Simons, R. L., Whitbeck, L. B., Conger, R. D., Chyi-In, W. (1991). Intergenerational transmission of harsh parenting. *Developmental Psychology, 27*, 159–171.

Sroufe, L. A. (1995). *Emotional development: The organization of emotional life in the early years.* New York: Cambridge University Press.

Stack, C. B., & Burton, L. (1993). Kinscripts. *Journal of Comparative Family Studies, 24*, 157–170.

Stanley, S. M., Blumberg, S. L., & Markman, H. J. (1999). Helping couples fight for their marriages: The PREP approach. In R. Berger & M. T. Hannah (Eds.), *Prevention approaches in couples therapy* (pp. 279–303). Bristol, England: Brunner/Mazel.

Tronick, E. Z. (1989). Development of the father–infant relationship. In H. Fitzgerald, B. Lester, & M. W. Yogman (Eds.), *Theory and research in behavioral pediatrics* (Vol. 1, pp. 221–229). New York: Plenum.

Vuchinich, S., Wood, B., & Vuchinich, R. (1994). Coalitions and family problem-solving with preadolescents in referred, at-risk, and comparison families. *Family Process, 33*, 409–424.

Wilson, M. N. (1989). Child development in the context of the black extended family. *American Psychology, 44*, 380–385.

III

RETROSPECT AND PROSPECT IN THE PSYCHOLOGICAL STUDY OF FAMILIES AS SYSTEMS

In this part of the book, three authors reflect on how the infusion of systems thinking into the field of developmental psychology has affected theory and research in the years since Minuchin's influential wake-up call in the journal *Child Development* back in 1985. Each of these authors, who have made important contributions to family research over the past decade or so through their active research and innovative thinking, contributes to this effort in different ways.

First, Teti provides an overview of what psychologists have learned about major influences on and subsequent consequences of sibling relationship quality. Focusing on the early years of family formation, Teti shows how studies of sibling relationships have benefited from shedding their myopic focus on sibling rivalry and their exhaustive and largely atheoretical focus on the role of what has been referred to in the literature as "sibling constellation variables." He demonstrates that although studies of such constellation variables as birth order produced some replicable findings, particularly with respect to certain trait variables pertaining to achievement and intelligence, they revealed little about the affective valence of sibling interactions. To fathom differences among families with respect to the functioning of the sibling subsystem, he explains, only approaches that take into account both the adjustment of other family members and the relationships among these members hold promise. Underscoring themes developed elsewhere in this volume, he argues that an understanding of between-family differences will best be served by accounting for how children experience their family circumstances. Teti then goes on to show that the payoff is worth the effort. He reviews studies of siblings as socializing agents, illustrating that although sibling relationships can breed negative behavior when family circumstances go awry, they also buoy the children during times of family adversity and can be a significant factor in the deintensification of one sibling's disruptive behavior problems over time. Such findings, he notes, have important policy implications for decisions made about placement of siblings postdivorce or in foster care. The field will profit now from a greater focus on sibships beyond the early years of family life and through comparative analysis of sibships in Western societies (where virtually all of the prior sibling research by psychologists has been carried out) and non-Western societies (where the essential roles of siblings in the family dynamic diverge in fundamental ways from those of many Western families).

In the chapter that follows, Kreppner endorses the value of a systemic approach, endorsing what he calls a family systems-developmental view in studying families over the life cycle. In this, he contends, researchers need to conceptualize the family network, whatever its composition, as the institution through which meaning and culture are transmitted. Reviewing the ideas of such thinkers as Cassirer and von Uexküll, he builds a case for studying communication in family systems and draws on the ideas of von Bertalanffy and Weiner to emphasize the key notion of regulation of information in the family system. Tracing growing pains in the field (including Kafka's sobering finding that even the elegant double-bind hypothesis could not distinguish families containing a schizophrenic member from so-called normal families), he posits that an important feature of families is their flexibility in communication at major points of developmental change. Presenting data from his own laboratory, and drawing on findings from other labs where relevant, he underscores: (a) the significance of communication and dispute resolution, as well as talk about emotions between parents and between parents and children; and (b) the handling of transitions by families both as groups and (in more detailed analyses) as individuals or dyadic units within the larger group. Not only do normative changes occur in family communication patterns commensurate with children's increasing and changing developmental competencies; individual differences in family-specific modes of handling transitions (especially with respect to flexibility) can also be linked to adolescents' well-being and adjustment. Kreppner closes by offering a set of guidelines he believes should guide any future research efforts on family systems, emphasizing that we keep our eyes on the importance of communication in the family system.

Using the preceding two chapters as background, Minuchin outlines pressing challenges facing systemically oriented family researchers if their work is to be of value to those serving families and children at the turn of the new millenium. Given the diverse circumstances of families in the United States, not to mention the circumstances of families around the world, Minuchin emphasizes that we are unlikely to isolate a tidy set of basic principles that can account for most of what is important to know about children's lives. She points out that increasing numbers of 21st century children are growing up in mixed cultures, with diverse and often contradictory messages coming from both within and outside the family unit. More poignantly, because many children live in the midst of multiple family systems, our models of communication, information flow, and family dynamics must take this reality into account. Arguing that the field is once again ripe for fresh perspectives, Minuchin underscores the importance of taking long views of families without leaving certain epochs (e.g., middle childhood) unattended; focusing on depth dimensions within families; not quitting in the search for statistical models that truly represent complex family interactions in a manner capturing their richness and circularity of influence; creating models simultaneously allowing that periods of relative developmental stability in children (presumably attended by relative stability in child-rearing practices) often co-occur with periods of instability for the family in other realms; and recognizing that because family transition periods themselves have stages, our focus should be on the process of adaptation by children and other family members through these change periods. She illustrates how some of these notions can infuse new life into the study of family systems and subsystems, using the sibling subsystem as a case in point. In particular, she calls for work illustrating how family patterns, attitudes, structures, and experiences give meaning to the developing sibling relationship, suggesting that in this (as in all other work she advocates) thoughtful reliance on case studies should supplement large-scale investigations. In closing, Minuchin highlights two phenomena in modern American society— the growing number of children living in complex structures and the extension of the average life span—demanding intensive study from systems-oriented researchers. She suggests the utility of Bronfenbrenner's concept of mesosystems for future family research, outlines frontiers for the field, suggests means for approaching some of these frontiers, and makes a compelling case for the value of such work to children from different kinds of families. And she reminds us of the imperative that all this work be carried out by culturally sensitive and aware researchers, fully cognizant of cultural and subcultural differences.

Retrospect and Prospect in the Psychological Study of Sibling Relationships

Douglas M. Teti
University of Maryland, Baltimore County

No volume on family relationships would be complete without a look at the role of sibling relationships. The study of sibling relationships is both old and new, as I develop in this chapter. Identifying the antecedents and consequences of sibling relationships presents special challenges for social and personality researchers. Reasons for this are complex and relate to the enormous fluidity and diversity that characterizes sibling behavior. For the most part, systematic examinations of sibling behavior and its contextual determinants and developmental sequelae are relatively recent. This may owe to assumptions implicit in theories of development that assign primacy to parents, and especially mothers, as meaningful socialization agents. Such theories are rooted in western tradition and belief systems, in which siblings are assumed to have little direct effect on child development. Such assumptions may be erroneous. Siblings are influential in their roles as teachers, caregivers, playmates, and support figures throughout the life span.

In psychology, some of the earliest conceptualizations of sibling relationships were those of psychoanalysts (Levy, 1934; Sewall, 1930; Smalley, 1930). These writers viewed sibling behavior primarily in terms of rivalry and competition for parental attention and resources. This unflattering characterization persisted for over 4 decades and did not really change until psychology researchers launched systematic investigations of sibling behavior in the naturalistic confines of their homes during the 1970s. In the meantime, psychologists who studied siblings were preoccupied with documenting whatever relations they could find between children's intellectual abilities, behavioral predispositions, and personality characteristics, and *sibling constellation variables* (e.g., birth order, age spacing, gender composition of sibling dyads). Hundreds of studies adopted this approach (see reviews by Adams, 1972; Cicirelli, 1982; Sutton-Smith & Rosenberg, 1970; Wagner, Schubert, & Schubert, 1979). Although they produced some reliable findings (e.g., that firstborns tended to be more achievement oriented than were laterborns), these studies did little to foster a clear understanding of the kinds of social environments siblings created for one another, nor did they shed light on the manner in which individual differences in the quality of sibling relationships were be shaped by children's relationships with parents.

Pioneering descriptive studies of infant–sibling behavior appeared in the late 1970s by the developmental psychologist Lamb. Lamb's (1978a) laboratory study of 12-month-old infants and their preschool-aged siblings examined differences in young siblings' behavior, assessed whether children or parents were more potent elicitors of interaction, and tested whether sibling behavior was different in the presence of mother versus father. He found that older children offered toys and vocalized more frequently to their infant siblings, whereas infants appeared fascinated by the behavior of the older siblings, imitating them frequently. Children's interaction did not differ as a function of sex of the overseeing parent, although siblings interacted much less frequently with one another than they did with either parent. In a subsequent laboratory follow-up study 6 months later, Lamb (1978b) demonstrated significant stability in sibling interaction across time and increases in the frequency of sibling behavior, especially by the younger sibling.

Although Lamb's work was primarily descriptive, it helped psychologists understand that viewing of sibling behavior only in terms of rivalry and competition misrepresented the multidimensional nature of sibling relationships and did not do justice to the potential power of siblings to influence each other's social and intellectual development. Later studies from Canadian, British, and American psychologists further attested to the variation in sibling behavior and showed that individual differences in such behavior are shaped by both structural and familial influences (Abramovitch, Corter, & Lando, 1979; Dunn, 1983; Dunn & Kendrick, 1982a, 1982b; Furman & Buhrmester, 1985; Teti & Ablard, 1989; Teti, Bond, & Gibbs, 1986; Vandell, Minnett, & Santrock, 1987). Dunn's work in particular was seminal in demonstrating that sibling relationships in the early years can be influenced by the quality of mother–firstborn relationships both before and shortly after the birth of a secondborn.

Dunn (1983) invoked the work of Piaget (1965), Hinde (1979), and others to characterize sibling behavior in terms of two central themes: *reciprocity* and *complementarity*. A reciprocal relationship is one in which each individual creates similar experiences for the other because of commonalities in developmental status and interests. Siblings, particularly those close in age, appear to interact in a manner resembling that seen in same-aged peer relationships, with each child creating similar experiences for the other (e.g., rough-and-tumble play, toy play). By contrast, complementarity characterizes any relationship between two individuals who differ in developmental levels and competencies. Areas of complementarity include teaching and caregiving, which are more often displayed by older siblings, and monitoring, imitation, and play activities, which are more characteristic of younger children. Complementary features of sibling relationships are evident from interviews of the children, who commonly report differences in their sibling relationship along a power-status dimension (Furman & Buhrmester, 1985). Indeed, sibling behavior can take on elements of parent–child relationships in that younger, less experienced children may be taught, nurtured, or "punished" by older, more experienced, "wiser" siblings (Teti, 1992).

Dunn (1983) has argued that the reciprocal features of early sibling interaction are of greater developmental import than the complementary features, particularly in western cultures where older children are called on only occasionally to care for and teach their younger siblings. Still, complementary features of sibling interactions may become important, especially, in later childhood and adolescence, when the cumulative effects of specific complementary interactions may emerge more clearly. Take, for example, the finding that firstborns tend to be overrepresented in positions of high responsibility and authority in adulthood relative to other birth-order positions (Wagner et al., 1979). Perhaps firstborns' tendencies to be teachers, models, and guides for their younger siblings from a young age lead them to seek out such positions because they are reminiscent of family contexts than are known and familiar.

The study of sibling relationships is of value also because they are likely to be the longest lasting of all family relationships. Because siblings often share salient aspects of their environment, but seldom experience these aspects in exactly the same way, they may provide one another with validating information about childhood experiences and new avenues for self-reflection and growth. Indeed, siblings have many opportunities, perhaps more so than do parents, to serve as important sources of support, companionship, antagonism, and socialization throughout the life span. Although the potential of siblings to serve as socialization agents was acknowledged almost 4 decades ago (Irish, 1964), the socializer role of siblings is still poorly understood. It is likely that sibling influences are partly organized by children's relationships with parents and the way parents manage sibling conflict. However, siblings' influence can also be independent of parental input, through observational learning opportunities and providing positive and negative consequences for each other's behavior. There is also evidence that, by late childhood, siblings, especially firstborns versus secondborns, actively try not to be like each other, a process that has been termed *sibling deidentification* (Schacter, 1982; Schacter & Stone, 1987). A child may be motivated unconsciously to carve out a unique and special niche in the family system, an identity that is distinct from that of a sibling, as a means of reducing sibling rivalry and maximizing parental attention and resources. Siblings may thus represent important reference points for each other and may contribute in significant albeit indirect ways to identity formation.

This said, a central argument of this chapter is that the most thorough understanding of sibling influence can only come from an appreciation of how sibling relationships develop within the larger network of family influences. Put more simply, to understanding siblings as socialization agents we need to rely on principles of family systems theory and how these principles apply to families with two or more children. Some of the major systems principles, articulated by Minuchin (1985), include the following: (a) elements within a family system are interdependent and contribute to the functioning of the system as an organized whole; (b) the family system is composed of subsystems (such as individual parent–child subsystems, the marital subsystem, and the sibling subsystem), and the quality of functioning in one subsystem affects quality of functioning in other subsystems; (c) patterns within the family system are not linear but circular, characterized by mutual influences from its individual elements; (d) patterns within the family system tend toward homeostasis and stability; and (e) as an open system, the family can evolve and change in response to changing circumstances.

In the sections that follow, I first offer general descriptions of early sibling behavior by drawing on the systematic behavioral observations of psychologists over the past 2 decades. My focus is on sibling behavior in Western cultures, where most of the work by psychologists has taken place. I then overview commonly studied determinants of sibling relationships, highlighting both the oft-studied sibling constellation variables and the more recent attempts to predict sibling behavior from knowledge about children's temperaments. The family systems perspective of this paper is then revisited with a discussion of family influences on sibling relationships, particularly how sibling behavior can be organized by the quality of the parent–child subsystem and by children's perceptions of differential treatment from parents. I then discuss siblings as socialization agents, a much discussed but as yet poorly understood function of sibling behavior, and how conceptualizations of such a role might differ depending on cultural context. Finally, I conclude with some thoughts about siblings from cross-cultural and social policy perspectives.

CHARACTERIZING THE EARLY SIBLING RELATIONSHIP

General descriptions of interactions between very young siblings are available from research groups in the United States (Lamb, 1978a, 1978b; Teti et al., 1986; Vandell, 1982), Canada (Abramovitch et al., 1979; Abramovitch, Corter, & Pepler, 1980; Abramovitch, Corter, Pepler, & Stanhope, 1986; Pepler, Abramovitch, & Corter, 1981), and Great Britain (Dunn, 1989; Dunn & Kendrick, 1979, 1981, 1982a, 1982b, 1982c). All of these investigations were of two-child families, some were laboratory based (Lamb and Vandell), others were home based (Abramovitch and Dunn), and several consistent findings emerged. To begin, the complementary nature of early sibling interactions was evident in all studies. Older siblings typically led the interactions with their younger siblings, directing a disproportionately larger number of both prosocial and agonistic social behaviors to the infants than the infants did to them. Infants were much more likely to observe what the older siblings were doing, to imitate the older siblings, to take over the toys with which the older children had played, and to submit to the older child's aggression.

What also stood out in this work was the wide range of affect characterizing sibling interactions in the home. Some sibling pairs were predominantly prosocial and nurturant, others hostile and rivalrous. Variability in affect was also a characteristic of many individual sibling dyads, perhaps indicating greater ambivalence. Siblings often directed both nurturant or hostile behavior toward one another, depending on the circumstances. Characterizing early sibling relationships simply as rivalrous or prosocial ignored to the range of affect observed across and within dyads. Nonetheless, several of these studies reported stability in siblings' behavior over time. They also uncovered what appeared to be mutual influences between the siblings' in their behavior. Lamb (1978b), for example, found that the frequency of smiling, vocalizing, looking, laughing, and so on, directed by preschoolers to their infant siblings at 18 months was positively related to the frequency of these same social behaviors shown by infants 6 months earlier.

Dunn's British studies documented the existence of social-cognitive abilities at much earlier ages than prevailing theories of social-cognitive development suggested. This implied the sibling dyad may be an important vehicle for emerging social-cognitive skills, and Dunn and others have subsequently devoted considerable attention to the role of siblings in the development of social understanding (Brown & Dunn, 1992; Dunn & Kendrick, 1982a; Dunn & Munn, 1986; Howe & Ross, 1990; Youngblade & Dunn, 1995). For example, Dunn and Kendrick (1982a, 1982b) reported that firstborn siblings as young as 2- to 3-years-old appeared capable of correctly interpreting the feelings and intentions of their younger siblings. To illustrate: Firstborns commonly remark to their mothers about their infant siblings' emotional states, why the babies are in these states, what they like and dislike, what they can and cannot do, and so on. These findings would not have been predicted by extant theories of social-cognitive development (e.g., Hoffman, 1975), which considered such abilities among 2- to 3-year-olds to be rare.

Two laboratory studies have examined the propensity of preschool-aged children to provide caregiving and nurturance to distressed infant siblings. In a study of 54 mothers and their 30- to 58-month-old children, Stewart (1983) reported that slightly more than half of the children attempted to relieve the distress of their infant siblings when mothers were absent from the playroom. In a subsequent study of similarly aged children and their mothers, Stewart and Marvin (1984) replicated the earlier finding that slightly more than half of the older children provided caregiving, but also reported that the tendency of the older children to do so was related to their perspective-taking abilities. In addition, infants appeared to use older siblings as subsidiary attachment figures (i.e., approaching and maintaining proximity) in the absence of their mothers only when the older siblings behaved as caregivers. When mothers left the siblings alone in the playroom, they were more likely to ask the older child to help take care of the baby when the older child had skills as a perspective taker. Hence, perspective-taking skills appear to be related to the preschoolers' ability to relate and respond to infants' distress. Such a premise was substantiated in a later study by Garner, Jones, and Palmer (1994), who reported that preschool-aged siblings' propensity to direct caregiving to their toddler siblings was associated with preschoolers' ability to identify emotional cues of the main character in a story vignette and with preschoolers' knowledge of caregiving scripts.

Not examined in these studies was the extent to which sibling caregiving was an activity valued by the family. In many non-Western, rural-agrarian societies, older siblings are socialized early to take on some caretaking responsibilities with younger children. Parents are then freed to be more productive at work, contributing to the well-being of the family as a whole (Whiting & Edwards, 1988). Extensive sibling caregiving in North American families is less common, especially among middle-class populations. However, it is more common among North American working-class families (Zukow-Goldring, 1995) and among families who have children with special needs (Lobato, Barbour, Hall, & Miller, 1987; McHale & Pawletko, 1992). Implicit in Stewart and Marvin's (1984) work was the premise that caregiving in older siblings resulted from the emergence of perspective-taking ability in the older child. It is equally plausible, however, to propose a causal arrow that points as much in the reverse direction; that is, perspective taking in older children may develop in response to repeated socialization experiences designed to teach older siblings to recognize when their younger siblings require caregiving, and in response to actual caregiving experiences.

DETERMINANTS OF SIBLING RELATIONSHIPS

Sibling Constellation Variables

Marker variables that define structural features of the sibling relationship within the family are termed *sibling constellation variables*. The most commonly examined constellation variables are birth order, birth spacing, and sex. Constellation variables are germane to any discussion of sibling relationships for the simple reason they are commonly used to refer to, describe, and explain young children's behavior (e.g., "My kids play rough because they're both boys," or "He follows her around because she's the older"). Traditionally, there has been strong interest in the role of sibling constellation variables in the development of personality and intelligence (see reviews by Cicirelli, 1967, 1982; Rosenberg, 1982; Schooler, 1972; Sutton-Smith, 1982; Wagner et al., 1979). Most of the studies of young siblings' behavior and sibling constellation variables have emerged in the last 25 years, and they are briefly reviewed in the following sections.

Birth Order. Given the advanced social and cognitive abilities of older versus younger siblings, older siblings are expected to be more likely to lead and control interactions between siblings and to direct higher levels of both prosocial and agonistic behavior toward their younger siblings than the reverse. Indeed, reports in the United States (Gibbs, Teti, & Bond, 1987; Lamb, 1978a, 1978b; Teti, Gibbs, & Bond, 1989; Vandell, 1982), Great Britain (Dunn & Kendrick, 1979, 1982a, 1982b), and Canada (Abramovitch et al., 1979; Abramovitch et al., 1980; Pepler, 1981) concur that firstborns engage in greater frequencies of both positive and negative social behaviors, and of teaching, and that infant siblings more often follow, imitate, and take over the toys of the older sibling regardless of whether the older siblings are actually interacting with the infants. Similar complementarity in the interactions of preschool- and school-aged siblings has been reported by Brody and colleagues (Brody, Stoneman, MacKinnon, & MacKinnon, 1985; Stoneman, Brody, & MacKinnon, 1984). These researchers found that older siblings took on teacher, managerial, and helper roles more frequently than did younger siblings, and that the younger siblings in turn took on observer, managee, and helpee roles more frequently than did older siblings.

The fact that the more socially and cognitively mature older sibling evidences his or her enhanced social competence during interactions with an infant sibling, and that the infant sibling seems to find this fascinating, is not surprising. Of more theoretical interest, perhaps, is whether young children benefit in some way by repeated interactions with the older, "wiser" sibling. Lamb (1978a, 1978b) speculated that infants may benefit cognitively by observing and imitating the play activities of their older siblings, and Wishart (1986) later supported this hypothesis. Specifically, first-year infants' performance in an object concept task improved after observing a preschool-aged sibling demonstrate the task, relative to a no-demonstration control group. In a later study of older children (5- to 6-year-olds), Hesser and Azmitia (1989) reported that a younger sibling looked at and imitated their older sibling more than a same-aged friend of the older sibling during triadic object play. These results suggest that older siblings may be more likely to influence the behavior of younger siblings than older children outside the family, at least at the ages studied. Koester and Penny (1987) provided further support for this view with their findings that 3-year-old children were more likely to explore an unfamiliar environment in the presence of their older siblings than in the presence of unfamiliar older children. Pepler's (1981) observations of Canadian children also indicate that younger siblings' response to teaching by their older siblings is typically positive, and in an earlier laboratory study of older children, Cicirelli (1972) revealed that younger siblings learned a task more effectively when taught by their older female siblings than by an unrelated peer. In a later study, Cicirelli (1973) further demonstrated that children's performance on a categorization task was facilitated when they were helped by their older siblings relative to when they worked alone.

Thus, the older, more socially and cognitively advanced, wiser sibling is more likely to influence and control the nature of the sibling interaction than is the less mature, younger sibling, although birth order reveals little about the quality of sibling behavior. Younger siblings may benefit from the expanded cognitive and social repertoire of their older siblings, although it is unclear how long term these benefits might be. Such benefits have been addressed within the context of birth spacing effects.

Birth Spacing. Understanding relations between sibling birth spacing and sibling relationships have been more difficult to conceptualize than have birth-order relations. In terms of mutual social influence, closely spaced sibling dyads afford greater similarity between the children in age and developmental status; hence, we might expect children in such dyads to be more accessible to each other, have more common interests and activities, and have more day-to-day opportunities for interaction than would be expected of siblings in widely spaced dyads. What effect spacing might have on sibling relationship quality is less clear. Similarities in interests and needs may lead siblings to compete at high levels for the same toys, for parental attention, and for other material and social resources, stirring greater rivalry in closely spaced dyads than in widely spaced dyads. Indeed, Minnett, Vandell, and Santrock (1983) found that 7-year-olds in closely spaced dyads had more intense and rivalrous relationships than did 7-year-olds in widely spaced dyads. It is also conceivable, however, that in some sibships similarity in interests and activities would facilitate relationship quality and development of a mutually supportive relationship over the long term.

Although siblings in widely spaced dyads are less accessible to each other and experience less intense relationships than do siblings in closely spaced dyads, a wide birth spacing has been considered by some to be intellectually advantageous for both children. The premise behind this is that, as birth spacing increases, so does the effectiveness of the older child as a teacher for the younger child. Cicirelli (1973, 1974), for example, reported that younger children who were taught by siblings who were 4 years older learned a categorization task better than did younger children who were taught by siblings who were 2 years older. However, whether birth spacing relates more broadly to overall intelligence is not clear. Some studies have reported no relation between birth spacing and intelligence (Cicirelli, 1967; Schoonover, 1959). Others have reported that birth-spacing effects on intelligence depend on the sex of sibling (e.g., Koch, 1954, 1955, 1956; Rosenberg & Sutton-Smith, 1969).

A major impetus in the development of interest in birth-spacing effects was the report by Zajonc and Markus (1975; see also Zajonc, 1976; Zajonc, Markus, & Markus, 1979) that large birth spacing mitigates against the detrimental effects of large family size on intellectual performance, especially for laterborn children. Their confluence model was an attempt to explain the negative relations, obtained from aggregate data, between intellectual test scores and family size. In brief, Zajonc and Markus (1975) proposed that the intellectual environment for a given child within a family was diluted with the birth of successive children, under the assumption that intellectual climate can be expressed as an average of the intellectual levels contributed by each member of a family. Assuming that each parent contributes 100 intellectual units to the family (using their example), and each child contributes an increasing number of units as he or she gets older (0 units at birth), the intellectual climate of a given family can be calculated by simply averaging the number of intellectual units contributed by all family members. As family size increases, this average will become reduced as the number of intellectual immature family members increases. For laterborn children, large birth spacings compensate for the negative association between family size and intelligence because such children are born into a family whose intellectual climate benefits from the advanced age and competence of the older children. For firstborns, smaller birth spacings are beneficial in that they provide firstborns with earlier opportunities to function as teachers of the secondborns (to the detriment of the secondborns, however). The importance of sibling teaching to intellectual development was highlighted by the fact that only children's intellectual performances tended to be lower than what the confluence model would have predicted. Zajonc and Markus (1975) provided impressive support for this model on the basis of data aggregated from a population of Dutch individuals born during the famine of 1944, although subsequent attempts to apply the model to sample data have met with little success (Grotevant, Scarr, & Weinberg, 1977; see Scarr & Grajek, 1982, and Steelman, 1985, for reviews).

Against this backdrop, several studies were conducted to examine relations between birth spacing and young siblings' behavior. Except for Minnett et al.'s (1983) study of 7-year-olds, neither the previously described British (Dunn & Kendrick, 1982a, 1982b) nor Canadian (Abramovitch et al., 1979, 1980, 1986; Pepler et al., 1981) longitudinal studies of preschool-aged siblings were able to find relations between qualitative features of sibling interaction and sibling birth spacing. In these studies, close birth spacing was defined as approximately 1 to 3 years, and wide spacing as 3 to 5 years. It is possible that birth-spacing effects on siblings' social interaction do not appear until middle childhood. There is a second possibility, however. When the dependent variables under study are more straightforwardly linked to children's developmental status, relations between birth spacing and sibling behavior are found. Pepler (1981) reported that older siblings in widely spaced dyads engaged in more conceptual teaching than did older siblings in closely spaced dyads. This finding is consistent with Cicirelli's (1973, 1974) report that older siblings of widely spaced dyads were more effective teachers of their younger siblings than were older siblings of closely spaced dyads. In addition, Teti et al. (1986) found that, when infants and their older preschool-aged siblings were together, infants of widely spaced dyads appeared to enjoy a more intellectually and socially stimulating environment than did infants of closely spaced dyads. During 10 minutes of infant–sibling free play, firstborns in widely spaced dyads created significantly more language mastery, concrete reasoning-problem solving, expressive-artistic skill mastery, object play, gross motor, and social game experiences for their infant siblings than did firstborns in closely spaced dyads. In addition, infants and older siblings in widely spaced dyads engaged in significantly less parallel play (play in which each child was involved in their own activity and uninvolved with the other) than did infants and older siblings in closely spaced dyads. However, no relation was found between birth spacing and infants' scores on the Bayley Scales of Infant Development (Bayley, 1969).

Based on these studies, it appears that younger children in widely spaced dyads experience more intellectually stimulating environments created by their older siblings than do younger children in closely spaced dyads. However, empirical work indicates that younger children in widely spaced dyads do not appear to benefit intellectually from these experiences any more than do younger children in closely spaced dyads. It is important to note, however, that these relations have been studied primarily in Western, middle-class samples. Birth-spacing differences in sibling-created intellectual experiences may have little effect in an environment that already provides sufficient intellectual experiences to promote cognitive growth. Such differences may have more influence in lower class environments, especially in which sibling caregiving is more prominent, and in cultures where sibling caregiving is normative. Birth spacing may have its greatest effect when considering the opportunities available for siblings of different ages to engage in meaningful day-to-day interaction. And, like birth order, variations in birth spacing tell us little about the affective valence of sibling interactions.

Sex of Siblings. Interest in sex differences in sibling interactions have been motivated by early findings suggesting that older female siblings are socialized to be more nurturant and prosocial and are more likely to perceive themselves as caretakers than are male older siblings (Koch, 1956; Maccoby & Jacklin, 1974; Sutton-Smith & Rosenberg, 1970). If so, sibships led by an older sister should be more harmonious than should sibships led by an older brother. Other studies have examined the collective effect of both siblings' gender, exploring whether same-sex siblings would be predisposed toward more positive relationships because of more shared interests and activities than would mixed-sex siblings (e.g., Dunn & Kendrick, 1981; Gibbs et al., 1987; Teti & Ablard, 1989). Support for each of these hypotheses has not been straightforward.

The hypothesis that sibships led by older girls should be more harmonious than sibships led by older boys has received some support, although results have not always been consistent. Lamb (1978a) found no sex differences in infant–sibling interaction when the infants were 18 months old. However, when data from 12- and 18-month observation points were combined, older girls were found to be more social than were older boys (Lamb, 1978b). Similar sex differences in the prosocial, nurturant behavior of older siblings were reported by Abramovitch et al. (1979, 1980) when the younger siblings were 20 months old. However, these sex differences were no longer apparent by later observation points (Abramovitch et al., 1986; Pepler et al., 1981). Few sex differences in infant–sibling behavior were found in the Vermont study (Gibbs et al., 1987; Teti et al., 1986) nor in a later laboratory study of sibling interaction, attachment, and caregiving (Teti & Ablard, 1989).

By contrast, more consistent sex differences have been reported in unstructured observations of sibling teaching. In Brody's work, teaching of younger siblings was mostly done by older sisters (Brody et al., 1985; Stoneman et al., 1984). Moreover, regardless of the sex composition of the sibling dyad, female older siblings took on the manager role most frequently (Stoneman et al., 1984). Minnett et al. (1983) reported similar findings with regard to teaching among 7-year-old children and noted that older female siblings praised their younger siblings most often.

Studies examining relations between sibling dyadic sex composition and sibling social behavior have been inconsistent. Dunn and Kendrick (1981) reported that, by infant age 14 months, both older and younger children in same-sex sibling pairs directed more positive behavior toward each other than did children in mixed-sex pairs. Furthermore, children in same-sex dyads showed increases in positive, prosocial behavior between infant ages 8 and 14 months. Conversely, older children in mixed-sex pairs directed more negative, agonistic behavior toward their infant siblings than did their counterparts in same-sex pairs, and both children in mixed-sex pairs increased their negative behaviors toward each other between infant ages 8 and 14 months.

Dunn and Kendrick (1981) explained these findings by invoking a "greater shared interests and activities of same-sexed siblings" hypothesis. However, support for these findings has not been forthcoming from most other research groups. The exception is the Canadian sibling study, in which Pepler et al. (1981) found that negative, agonistic behavior increased in mixed-sex dyads between the secondborns' ages of 20 and 38 months, with a concomitant decline in the amount of imitation of the older children by the younger children. This said, neither this study nor others (e.g., Gibbs et al., 1987) found a relation between sibling behavior and dyadic sex composition. There have even been reports with results opposite those of Dunn and Kendrick. Moreover, Stewart's (1983) laboratory study found that older siblings of mixed-sex dyads provided more caregiving in response to infants' distress than did older siblings of same-sex dyads. This finding was replicated in a subsequent study (Stewart & Marvin, 1984), but only for males. By contrast, Teti and Ablard's (1989) laboratory study of sibling behavior and attachment failed to find any effect of children's sex or dyadic sex composition on older children's caregiving. Finally, in their study of 7-year-olds and their older or younger siblings, Minnett et al. (1983) reported that same-sex sibling dyads showed more negative behaviors than did mixed-sex dyads. No clear picture has emerged from this morass of investigations.

Although older girls may be more nurturant and prosocial when interacting with their siblings than are older boys, it remains unclear what effects, if any, sibling sex and dyadic sex composition have on sibling behavior in early childhood. It does not help that there is no clearly explicated theory that can be used to generate hypotheses about this question. Although Dunn and Kendrick (1981) argued that siblings in same-sex dyads are more prosocial than are siblings in mixed-sex dyads because of a greater level of shared interests and activities, it is equally feasible to argue that shared interests and activities may just as readily foster rivalry and agonistic behavior between two siblings (as reported by Minnett et al., 1983), especially if they lead to competition for the same resources.

Aside from the more clearly established findings that birth order plays a major role in the asymmetry and complementarity of early sibling interaction and that close birth spacings organize more intense sibling relationships than do wide birth spacings, it may be ambitious to expect consistent findings relating sibling interaction to sibling constellation variables, especially when one's interest is in documenting the determinants of sibling relationship quality. Whereas sibling constellation variables may play a role in structural and intellectual aspects of early sibling relationships, such marker variables appear to be of little value in predicting the affective quality of sibling behavior.

Child Temperament

Individual differences in temperamental difficulty have sometimes been invoked to explain variations in sibling relationship quality. The expectation is that the sibling relationships of children with difficult temperaments (e.g., children who are prone to distress, whose threshold of responsiveness to aversive stimulation is low, and who experience difficulty adapting to stress) will be less prosocial and more antagonistic. The few studies that have examined the construct of temperament in this regard have either looked at the older child in the sibling dyad (e.g., Gottlieb & Mendelson, 1990; Thomas, Birch, Chess, & Robbins, 1961) or have evaluated the temperaments of both children, but only in sibling dyads where the children are older (e.g., Brody & Stoneman, 1987). In this work, mothers have been asked to complete questionnaires tapping traditionally defined temperamental dimensions (activity, emotional intensity, mood, persistence). These studies report that children with more difficult temperaments have more difficulty adjusting to siblinghood and enjoy less positive sibling relationships than do children with easier temperaments. It is unclear, however, whether having mothers report on their children's temperaments is a valid means of measuring what is presumably a biologically based construct (Vaughn & Bost, 1999), especially when the children are older. Mothers' reports of temperament, especially for older siblings who are no longer infants, may actually tap a more global and diffuse set of perceived personality variables resulting from the interaction of biologically based child characteristics and parental behavior and disciplinary styles. Indeed, a mother who reports on her older child's temperament may be reporting on her perception of her relationship with her child. How this relates to endogenous temperamental characteristics is unclear. A study of how objective assessments of siblings' temperaments (i.e., lab- or home-based assessments of temperament obtained by a trained observer, such as Bornstein, Gaughran, & Segui, 1991, or Matheny, 1983) shape the development of sibling relationships would be of great value. Such assessments of temperament should be obtained in early infancy, before the cumulative effects of socialization weigh in.

A SYSTEMS VIEW: FAMILY INFLUENCES ON SIBLING RELATIONSHIPS

I now turn attention to the thesis that affective dimensions of young sibling interaction may be more consistently documented by examining sibling relationships within a family systems context. This premise is discussed in the following sections in relation to the move to first-time siblinghood and in terms of putative organizational influences of the parent–child subsystem on sibling relationship quality.

Factors Affecting Children's Adjustment Following the Transition to Siblinghood

Early conceptualizations of sibling relationships as predominantly rivalrous stemmed in part from psychodynamic interpretations of the effect of the birth of a younger sibling (Levy, 1934; Winnicott, 1964). These accounts depicted the event as a major stressor for the older child (see also Moore, 1969). The stress, anxiety, and anger experienced by preschool children in response to a new arrival was viewed as normative, the result of the child's perception that he or she was being displaced by the secondborn in the eyes of the parents. Thus, psychoanalytic theory saw young siblings at a disadvantage from the beginning in that their relationship is marked by feelings of rivalry and resentment in the older child from the moment of the secondborn's birth.

Efforts to provide empirical verification of these claims have met with some success. Transitions to siblinghood can be diverse, though, with some older children showing little outward manifestation of maladjustment. To begin with, virtually all studies that have examined this phenomenon have reported increases in some or all of the following problem areas among many preschool-aged children during the first few weeks following the birth of the second child: dependency and anxiety (e.g., clinginess, whininess, following mother around the house, experiencing sleep disturbances), regression (e.g., demanding a pacifier or bottle at bedtime or developing toileting problems after toilet training had been achieved), withdrawal (becoming quieter or harder to engage in social interaction), and aggressiveness (verbal or physical aggression, or both, directed toward mothers or the new infants, or both; Dunn & Kendrick, 1980; Dunn, Kendrick, & MacNamee, 1981; Field & Reite, 1984; Kendrick & Dunn, 1980; Legg, Sherick, & Wadland, 1974; Nadelman & Begun, 1982; Stewart, Mobley, Van Tuyl, & Salvador, 1987; Taylor & Kogan, 1973; Thomas et al., 1961; Trause et al., 1981; see review by Vandell, 1987). These changes have been linked to concomitant decreases in the amount of maternal attention given to the older children after the birth of the new arrival, and perhaps to the general prenatal-to-postnatal drop offs in prosocial interaction and increases in negative, controlling interactions between mothers and firstborns (Dunn & Kendrick, 1980), particularly when mothers were occupied with their babies (Kendrick & Dunn, 1980). In addition, these changes seem to coincide with increases in the older children's activity levels, heart rates, fantasy play and talk, and general agitation during mothers' hospital stay (Field & Reite, 1984).

Family systems theory (Minuchin, 1985) predicts that the addition of a family member, whether it occurs as a normative event or not, should produce major perturbations in the family system and increased stress for all family members, including older siblings. However, several qualifications are in order. First, much variability characterizes the responses of preschoolers to a baby sibling's birth, and responses can range from strongly negative to more positive and nurturing (Dunn et al., 1981; Legg et al., 1974; Nadelman & Begun, 1982; Thomas et al., 1961). Indeed, Nadelman and Begun noted from maternal reports that older children were highly involved in the care of the newborn, with 71% of the older children assisting in diapering and dressing the baby; 43% helping to bathe the baby; 38% helping to feed the baby; and 68% holding, touching, and hugging the baby. Second, strong negative stress reactions among preschoolers, such as those noted earlier, may in most cases be short-lived. Thomas et al. reported that, among 10 children who manifested stress reactions shortly after the newborns' births, 6 showed mild, brief reactions; 1 showed a more moderate reaction; and 3 children showed more severe, lasting reactions. Thus, the perturbations created by the new arrival tend to dissipate over time as family members adjust to new roles and responsibilities. Third, the nature of reactions to new siblinghood appears to vary with various additional factors. Thomas et al. found the stress reactions to the birth of a newborn to be less severe among older children who already had an older sibling than among firstborn children, suggesting that for the latter group the birth of a baby represents a more salient and threatening environmental change. Thomas et al. also found little distress in response to a newborn's birth among toddlers under 18 months of age relative to older preschool-aged firstborns.

Teti's work on transitions to first-time siblinghood has provided further support for the importance of examining the firstborn's age at the time of the birth and has demonstrated that sibling adjustment is sensitive to individual differences in maternal psychiatric functioning (Teti, Sakin, Kucera, Corns, & Eiden, 1996). In this investigation, firstborn adjustment was assessed pre- and postdelivery using the Waters (1995) Attachment Q-Set, a measure of attachment quality that yields a continuous security of attachment score. A significant drop in firstborn security followed the birth of the sibling, though this drop was moderated by firstborn age. Specifically, the decrease in firstborn security was much less conspicuous for firstborns under 24 months old, relative to firstborns between 2 and 5 years old. These data, together with the earlier findings of Thomas et al. (1961), suggest that very young preschool-aged firstborns find the transition to siblinghood less threatening than do older preschool-aged firstborns. This may relate to social-cognitive differences between younger versus older preschoolers and, in turn, to the ability to experience feelings of displacement in response to a new arrival. Firstborns under 2 years old may lack the social-cognitive sophistication to perceive the new sibling as a rival and a threat to their relationship with their mothers. By contrast, firstborns between 2 and 5 years old possess the requisite social-cognitive abilities to enable the experience of displacement and the ability to identify the secondborn as the locus of their distress (e.g., the reason mothers are spending less time with them).

Teti et al. (1996) also found that substantial decreases in firstborn attachment security, from high levels before the birth of the baby to a drop of at least a standard deviation shortly after the birth (4–8 weeks), were associated with higher levels of maternal psychiatric symptoms before the baby's birth. Thus, decreases in firstborn–mother attachment security is not only predicted by firstborn age, which serves as a rough proxy for social-cognitive sophistication, but also by the quality of maternal functioning as indexed by levels of depression, anxiety, and hostility before the baby's birth. Consistent with Teti et al.'s report of older sibling maladjustment in response to sibling birth are findings from a larger scale study of sibling birth effects on older children's socioemotional and academic functioning during the preschool and early school years. The NLSY reported links between sibling birth and higher, albeit short-lived, levels of behavior problems in older siblings, and lower levels of global self-worth when the older children were 8 years old (Baydar, Hyle, & Brooks-Gunn, 1997). Sibling birth-related differences in self-worth were particularly strong among socioeconomically disadvantaged children. From a systems vantage, sibling birth was also associated with other changes in the family in a separate NLSY investigation. Among these were decreased maternal time spent at her place of employment and concomitant decline in maternal earnings, although these same families also were less likely to undergo marital dissolution than were families who did not experience a new arrival (Baydar, Greek, & Brooks-Gunn, 1997). Both of these studies found sibling birth to be associated with lower levels of verbal attainment (e.g., reading recognition scores) in the preschool and early school-age years of the older sibling.

The collective findings that the introduction of a sibling into an existing family system causes significant perturbations to and subsequent reorganization of that system are consistent with the family systems principles articulated by Minuchin (1985). As Teti et al. (1996) found, however, the nature and extent of responses to a sibling's birth depends on preexisting conditions within the family, including the functional integrity of the family before the birth. Teti et al. demonstrated that mothers who were functioning well before the baby's birth appeared to be more capable of facilitating their firstborns' adjustment to the new baby than did mothers who were functioning poorly.

Linkages Between Parental Behavior and Sibling Relationship Quality

Teti's study and others indicate that the quality of environments parents create for older siblings makes a difference in the quality of adjustment those children make to the birth of their baby brother or sister, as well as in the quality of the sibling relationships that ensue. Thomas et al. (1961) characterized the birth of a sibling as "not an especially disturbing event" among preschoolers whose fathers were active in providing care to the older children before and after the birth. In addition, Dunn et al. (1981) reported greater increases in withdrawal among older preschoolers shortly after the birth of their baby siblings when mothers suffered from fatigue or depression. In a systematic study of the role of parental input in the adjustment of firstborn girls to the birth of a baby sibling, Gottlieb and Mendelson (1990) found that the support reportedly provided to the firstborns by mothers 6 to 10 weeks before the babies' birth interacted with firstborns' level of distress to predict adjustment 5 to 6 weeks after the birth. Specifically, prenatally high-distress firstborns, determined from mothers' reports on rating scales of preschooler behavior, showed reductions in their level of distress if they received high levels of nurturance, approval, and assistance from mothers during the prenatal period. By contrast, prenatally high-distress firstborns, whose mothers reportedly provided little prenatal support, continued to be highly distressed after the babies' birth.

That the mother–firstborn relationship may play a salient role in the quality of early sibling relationships is further evidenced by Dunn and Kendrick's (1982a, 1982b) findings that the affective quality of the first-born–infant relationship was fostered when mothers involved their firstborns in caring for the infants' and in understanding the infants' feelings and intentions. Howe and Ross (1990) reported similar relations between frequencies of mothers' references to firstborns about the babies and older preschoolers' affectively positive interaction and play with their 14-month-old siblings. A logical interpretation of this finding is that firstborns who are included by their mothers in the care of the baby may harbor less feelings of competition and rivalry for their mothers' attention, and thus may be more capable of developing less ambivalent, more prosocial relationships with their baby siblings.

Additional data that appear to tap the quality of the children's relationship with their mothers more straightforwardly also give evidence that sibling relationships may be organized by the parent–child subsystem along affective domains. Brody, Stoneman, and MacKinnon (1986) reported relations between school-aged siblings' prosocial behavior directed to each other and mothers' reported enjoyment of the maternal role. In addition, children were less likely to behave in an antisocial manner toward their siblings when their mothers' used nonpunitive disciplinary techniques. In a study of female siblings in middle childhood, Bryant and Crockenberg (1980) found that children whose mothers showed sensitive attunement to their expressed needs during play were more frequently prosocial and less frequently antisocial during sibling play. Conversely, siblings of insensitive and controlling mothers were more frequently antisocial. Sibling disparagement and discomforting were low when both younger and older siblings had a high proportion of their needs met by their mothers, but equally high when either or both of the children had a low proportion of their needs met. Such a finding is consistent with systemic views of within-family dynamics, which predicts that discrepancies in the way parents treat their children fosters agonistic and competitive relationships between the children (Bank, 1987; Bank & Kahn, 1982).

Three studies (Bosso, 1986; Teti & Ablard, 1989; Volling & Belsky, 1992) have systematically examined the role of attachment security in shaping early sibling relationships. Using Waters and Deane's (1985) attachment Q-sorting technique, Bosso found that more securely attached 18- to 32-month-old older siblings were less negative and more positive toward their infant siblings. These relations were present both in the home and in a university laboratory, and both in and out of mothers' presence. In a subsequent laboratory study, Teti and Ablard likewise assessed preschool-aged siblings' attachment to mothers using the same Q-sorting technique and assessed infants' security of attachment with their mothers using the Strange Situation procedure. When mothers played only with the older child, securely attached infants were less likely to protest and aggress against their mothers or older siblings than were insecurely attached infants. In mothers' absence, more secure older siblings were more likely to direct caregiving toward distressed infant siblings than were less secure older siblings. Of role, when infants ($n = 6$) sought out the older sibling for comfort in mothers' absence, these older siblings were always highly secure. Teti and Ablard identified four sibling security status groups: secure infants with more secure older siblings; secure infants with less secure older siblings; insecure infants with more secure older siblings; and insecure infants with less secure older siblings. Of these four groups, the highest levels of antagonism were observed among insecure infants with less secure older siblings, whereas the lowest levels of antagonism were found among secure infants with more secure older siblings. As Ainsworth, Blehar, Waters, and Wall (1978) have advanced (see review by Teti & Nakagawa, 1990) secure child–mother relationships are fostered when mothers are sensitively responsive to their children's needs, whereas insecure attachments are associated with parental insensitivity and rejection. In a replication and extension of Teti and Ablard (1989), Volling and Belsky (1992) found insecure attachment to mother in infancy predicted sibling conflict in the preschool years. They also reported that prosocial sibling behavior was associated with affectionate fathering.

The results of these studies are consistent with earlier findings on older children (Brody et al., 1986; Bryant & Crockenberg, 1980), which reported positive relations between sibling prosocial behavior and nurturant parent–child relations. From the perspective of attachment theory (Ainsworth et al., 1978; Bowlby, 1969; Bretherton & Munholland, 1998; Sroufe & Fleeson, 1986), children who develop secure relationships with parents are more likely to develop working models of their parents as loving and nurturant and of themselves as worthy of love and support. Furthermore, as Sroufe and Fleeson have speculated, children internalize both the child's and the parent's role in the parent–child relationship, which in turn organizes children's attitudes and behaviors as they enter into new relationships (see also Minuchin, chap. 9, this volume). Thus, although the sibling and parent–child relationships are distinct family subsystems, children's general approach, perception, and behavior toward siblings might be expected to be influenced by the quality of relationship established with a primary attachment figure. Moreover, preschool-aged children's security of attachment to parents might show logical ties to the sensitivity with which parents manage sibling conflict. Although this hypothesis has not yet been tested, parents who intervene in many of the sibling quarrels may be fostering insecure attachments in one or both children by being overly intrusive or by consistently, albeit inadvertently, displaying favoritism for one child over another.

Parenting Two Children at Once: Consequences of Differential Parental Treatment for the Sibling Subsystem

One of the ways parental influence on sibling relations has been studied involves the degree to which siblings are treated similarly versus differently by their parents (Brody, Stoneman, & Burke, 1987; Brody, Stoneman, & Mc-

Coy, 1992; Bryant & Crockenberg, 1980; Kowal & Kramer, 1997; Mchale & Pawletko, 1992; Quittner & Opipari, 1994). Mothers' differential treatment of siblings can appear as early as 2 months of age, with differences in parental treatment linked to affective differences between the children that elicit the mother's differential affective responding (Moore, Cohn, & Campbell, 1997). Research on this issue suggests that parents' differential treatment of siblings tends to have adverse effects. It appears to foster sibling agonism, resentment, and elevated distress in the disfavored child.

At the same time, a critical moderator of the effects of differential treatment of siblings appears to be the way children attribute the causes of differential treatment. As Kowal and Kramer (1997) have demonstrated with 11- to 13-year-olds, 75% of the children who acknowledged the existence of sibling differential treatment did not necessarily perceive it to be unfair. Indeed, differential treatment was tolerated and accepted by the children when it was perceived to be related logically to differences in children's developmental levels, expressed needs, or personal attributes. Children who did not perceive differential treatment as unfair evaluated their sibling relationships more positively than did children who perceived differential treatment as unfair or capricious. These effects are interpretable from an attachment perspective, such that a child who consistently perceives unfair treatment from a parent, and thus has emotional needs that are consistently unmet, is likely to be insecurely attached to that parent and predisposed to experience negative feelings toward both the sibling and the parent. From a broader, systemic perspective, it demonstrates that the putative effect of subsystem characteristics on other subsystems within a family must take into account how those characteristics are being perceived and interpreted by family members. Differential parental attention to or treatment of Child A may not be problematic at all to Child B within the family if: (a) Child B perceives the differences in attention as logical, resulting from differences in developmental status, medical problem, and so on; and (b) Child B already has a reasonably secure relationship with the parent.

In their review of parental effects on the quality of sibling relationships, Furman and Giberson (1995) proposed several paths of influence. These included the quality of parents' relationships with the children; the extent to which parents engage in differential treatment; the manner in which parents respond to sibling conflict; parental attempts to manage their children proactively, so as to facilitate positive sibling behavior and decrease negative sibling behavior; and the quality of the marriage. Ample evidence documents relations between sibling behavior and the first two factors cited by Furman and Giberson, quality of parent–child relationships and differential parental treatment, as the previous discussions attest. Does sibling conflict increase when parents regularly intervene in their children's disputes? Data reviewed by Furman and Giberson suggest so, implying that children are less likely to learn effective conflict management strategies when parents micromanage their children's disagreements. Conversely, parental use of anticipatory management strategies, which can take the form of establishing rules about the acceptability of specific sibling behavior, planning and structuring sibling activities, and making time to anticipate and discuss potential future problems between the children, increases prosocial and decrease agonistic sibling behavior. Finally, marital quality may influence sibling relationships, directly, by providing children with a model for managing relationships, and indirectly, by affecting quality of parenting with the children. Furman and Giberson's account is consistent with the family systems formulations that all elements of a system are interdependent and that the functioning of subsystems within a system affect the functioning of other subsystems (cf. Minuchin, 1985).

SIBLINGS AS SOCIALIZATION AGENTS

Despite early claims about the potential for siblings to serve as socializing agents (Irish, 1964), this sibling role remains poorly understood. Indeed, siblings might be expected to be potent agents of socialization, given the sheer amount of interaction between them during the early years. Intuitively, it seems reasonable to expect that the nature and quality of sibling relationships within their family context might affect patterns of behavior outside that context. For example, a child who intensely rivals a sibling for the affection or attention of a parent may likewise be predisposed to direct rivalrous behavior to peers in the presence of nonparental authority figures. Such influences could only be identified by taking account of family dynamics, as suggested by several family therapy accounts of sibling relations in dysfunctional families (Bank & Kahn, 1982; Brody & Stoneman, 1987; Dunn, 1989). Indeed, several efforts have already documented such similarities in children's behavior with their siblings and with their peers (Berndt & Bulleit, 1985; Vandell, Minnett, Johnson, & Santrock, 1990; Vandell & Wilson, 1987). It is unclear from these studies, however, whether children's relationships with their siblings were influencing their behavior with their peers, or vice versa. In addition, it is unclear if the observed similarities were byproducts of the children's relationship histories with their parents or dispositional characteristics of the children themselves, or both.

The socialization role of siblings has been emphasized to a greater extent in studies of siblings in rural-agrarian cultures (e.g., central Mexican families, the Kwara'ae of the Solomon Islands, the Mandinka of the Republic of Senegal) than in studies of siblings in western, industrialized cultures. This is likely because sibling caregiving is more prominent among the former groups than in the latter (Zukow, 1989a; Zukow-Goldring, 1995). Indeed, there are few studies by psychologists in non-Western groups; most analyses of sibling roles and behavior in nonindustrialized cultures have been anthropological and ethnographic in nature. As the work of Zukow-Goldring (1995) has taught us, older children in rural-agrarian cultures are socialized early to become the part-time caregivers of their younger brothers and sisters, which enables parents to engage more freely and productively in work. Caregiving is not entrusted solely to older children, but is monitored and supervised by adults. Older siblings in these cultures appear to serve as important transmitters of basic cultural knowledge. In addition, sibling caregiving appears to play a central role in the social and intellectual development of both older and younger siblings (Watson-Gegeo & Gegeo, 1989; Weisner, 1989; Whittemore & Beverly, 1989; Zukow, 1989b). What these studies fail to adequately address, unfortunately, is the degree of influence siblings have on each other independent of parental influence. These studies also have not undertaken individual difference analyses by asking whether individual differences in the extent and quality of caregiving within the cultural group differentially affect child socialization outcomes.

In research conducted within the United States, one of the most thorough and systematic analyses of siblings as potential socialization agents has been Patterson's work at the Oregon Social Learning Institute (Patterson, 1984, 1986; Patterson, Dishion, & Bank, 1984). This work was one component of a larger examination of negative coercive exchanges in clinic-referred families with poor child-behavior-management strategies. Patterson found that escalating coercive behavior chains, whose development and maintenance was interpretable from positive and negative reinforcement contingencies, was especially characteristic of sibling dyads in such families. In addition, the siblings of target externalizing children were highly likely to employ coercion and aggression in their exchanges with these children, prompting Patterson to view the sibling relationship as a training ground for the development of externalizing behavior. Younger children learn coercive behavioral patterns through reinforcement and modeling of aversive behavior by a coercive older sibling. These findings suggest that sibling relationships are more likely to be highly antagonistic when at least one sibling consistently exhibits high levels of externalizing symptoms, perhaps especially so when that sibling is older.

In light of these findings, and the tendency for childhood externalizing behavior to remain stable over time (Campbell, 1990; Olweus, 1979) and context (Gelfand, Jenson, & Drew, 1988), it is tempting to presume that sibling relationships among children with clinically diagnosed disruptive behavior problems will inevitably be more conflictual and less supportive and prosocial than will sibling relationships of normal children. Such expectations may be premature, however, in light of the inherent complexity of sibling relationships. As I have outlined, sibling relationships are organized by structural, familial, and constitutional considerations, and these relationship systems may become more independent of family influences as children get older. Although siblings may be instrumental in shaping one another's aggressive behavior, they also may be instrumental in helping along social-cognitive skills and prosocial behavior (Brown & Dunn, 1992; Howe & Ross, 1990), and they may play salient roles in one another's lives by providing emotional and instrumental support (Brody et al., 1985; Buhrmester & Furman, 1987), especially during times of stress (Bank & Kahn, 1982; East & Rook, 1992).

The diversity of sibling relations among children with disruptive behavior problems is illustrated in a recent study of 53 aggressive first and second graders and their siblings (Stormshak, Bellanti, & Bierman, 1996). In this study, only half of the sibling relationships in the sample could be classified as *conflictual* (n = 27, reporting high levels of conflict and low levels of warmth on a sibling relationship questionnaire). The remaining half of the sample was identified either as *involved* (n = 15, reporting moderate levels of conflict and warmth) or *supportive* (n = 11, reporting high levels of warmth and low levels of conflict). This proportional breakdown was corroborated by Teti, Bradley, Hastings, and Zahn-Waxler (2000) in a similar sample of children at risk for disruptive behavior. Moreover, at-risk target children in this study who had a supportive sibling relationship declined in externalizing symptomatology from 5 to 9 years of age, relative to children in conflictual and involved sibling dyads. These findings suggest that children at risk for developing externalizing behavior disorders may learn, via participation in a supportive sibling relationship over time, to behave in more socially appropriate, socially competent ways than children whose sibling relationships are characterized by moderate to high levels of conflict.

Establishing sibling socialization effects independent of parental influence, especially for very young siblings, is a challenging undertaking. Documenting such influences requires systematic, longitudinal examinations of parent–child, child–sibling, and child–peer interaction, and statistical path analyses that attempt to control for the effects of the mother–child relationship before assessing potential causal influences between the sibling and peer systems. Though such analyses remain a frontier for our field, Bryant (1989) has provided one such study of 7- and 10-year-old American children from two-parent families with older siblings spaced 2 to 3 years apart. The 7- and 10-year-old target children in Bryant's study responded to a behavior inventory that inquired about the caretaking they received from their mothers, their fathers, and their older siblings. Socioemotional functioning of the target children was assessed 3 to 4 years later with a separate questionnaire, administered to the target children, that measured empathy, social perspective taking, acceptance of individual differences, attitudes toward competition, attitudes toward individualism, and locus of control. The sibling caretaking practices of the older siblings significantly predicted target children's socioemotional functioning even after statistically controlling for the contributions of mothers and fathers, suggesting that older siblings contributed uniquely to certain aspects of their younger siblings social development. This study can be critiqued for its overreliance on the target children's self-reports, raising concerns about whether some of the contribution of sibling caretaking was the result of monomethod bias. On the other hand, Bryant's findings indicate that, at least in middle childhood, how children see themselves as treated by their siblings has implications for their socioemotional functioning.

It is expected that, as children grow older, sibling relationships will become more independent of the parent–child subsystem and perhaps more susceptible to the growing influences of friendships and peers. The family's organizational influence on siblings should still be apparent, however, to the extent that siblings' predispositions to like each other and to seek out each other for support depend on family influences in the early years. Indeed, it is not unreasonable to suppose that siblings, as a function of the quality of their relationships in the early years, develop perceptions, expectations, or working models of each other that guide their behavior toward each other in predictable ways. In addition, as children grow, the reciprocal features of sibling relationships would be expected to become more predominant, as differences between children in developmental status and competencies diminish.

CONCLUSIONS

This chapter's aims were threefold. First, I hoped to portray the enormous complexity of sibling relationships. Second, I sought to illustrate that sibling rivalry is but one of several dimensions that characterize sibling behavior. Third, I tried to show that whereas sibling constellation variables such as birth order and birth spacing may be helpful in predicting amounts of sibling behavior (as embodied in findings such as at younger ages firstborns direct more behavior to their younger siblings than vice versa and control the interaction), constellation variables are of little value in predicting sibling relationship quality. Understandably, variability in sibling relationships is best approached from the perspective of family systems theory, particularly through an appreciation for the functional integrity of the family and the quality of parent–child relationships. In the Western samples we know the most about, sibling relationships usually thrive when parents have good marriages; exhibit nurturant, supportive, and equitable relationships with their children; afford their children room to resolve their disputes on their own; and work proactively to steer their children into contexts and activities that promote cooperation and reduce friction.

Most studies of sibling relationships by psychologists have been based on middle-class, Western samples. This biases our knowledge base about the nature of sibling relationships. It behooves researchers in our discipline to broaden our perspectives on the roles of siblings by pursuing both descriptive and hypothesis-driven investigations of sibling interaction cross-nationally, particularly in cultures where sibling caregiving is normative. Such work would allow answers to questions both about cultural universals operating within sibling relationships and about meaningful between-culture differences. As just one example, an important distinction between siblings in Western, industrialized cultures and siblings in rural-agrarian settings that feature sibling caregiving is that sibling rivalry in the latter settings is not a characteristic of the relationship. Rather, children learn early in life that they need to work cooperatively with each other and with their parents to fulfill the overarching needs of the family (Watson-Gegeo & Gegeo, 1989; Whittemore & Beverly, 1989). Another potential difference not yet examined empirically is increased salience of siblings who provide consistent caregiving as attachment figures to their younger siblings, a role that should augment their power as agents of socialization. Finally, like studies of siblings in Western, industrialized cultures, investigations of siblings in rural-agrarian settings could seek out individual differences in the quality of family functioning, parent–child relationships, and sibling caregiving to determine whether such differences matter in terms of the quality of children's relationships within the family and in the larger culture (see also McHale et al., chap. 5, this volume). Such investigations would require careful thought about how best to document relationship quality in cultural context. It would be of interest, however to demonstrate that the quality of sibling caregiving in cultures that feature it is sensitive to individual differences in the way parents socialize children into this role, and that this in turn has import for younger children at later points in their development.

As this chapter has illustrated, siblings have the potential to serve as important sources of support and even as potential buffers against the untoward effects of a problematic parent–child relationship (Bank & Kahn, 1982; Dunn & Kendrick, 1982a; Stormshak et al., 1996; Teti et al., 2000). The importance of sibling bonds cannot be overemphasized. Even in Western, industrialized cultures, which deemphasize sibling caregiving, siblings use each other as subsidiary attachment figures and as sources of support in times of stress. The quality of this support likely increases with age as perspective taking grows and as siblings come to appreciate their shared and frequently intertwined histories. Sibling relationships are also typically the longest lasting of all familial relationships; thus, siblings' influence on each other can potentially be felt throughout the life span. Sibling bonds are thus important to promote, protect, and not to be taken for granted. Good parents are likely to understand this intuitively, taking steps to prepare older children for the birth of siblings, involving older siblings in the care of and activities with the new arrival, and minimizing the potential for older children to feel left out or displaced by the infant. Indeed, the quality of older siblings' adaptation to the arrival of a younger sibling may loom large in terms of predicting how the ensuing sibling relationship will develop, as Dunn's work attests (Dunn, 1982a).

Even good parents, however, may lose sight of the importance of sibling bonds when parents are embattled, and, for example, divorce is imminent. When this occurs, the courts must decide on whether siblings should remain together or be split between parents. Split-custody decisions are not typical in American divorce courts (<2%), although they tend to increase when children are older and if they indicate a preference to live separately (Kaplan, Ade-Ridder, & Hennon, 1991). The complexities underlying split-custody decisions are discussed by Azar (chap. 10, this volume). Based on the evidence I have reviewed in this chapter, it seems critical that custody decisions, as well as decisions regarding foster-care placement and adoption of siblings, give top priority to keeping siblings together. The sibling bond functions not only as an emotional support but also as a way of preserving children's sense of family and shared histories. In cases where joint placement is not possible, courts should make provisions to assure frequent sibling visitation unless there exist unusual circumstances that argue against sibling contact (e.g., sibling sexual abuse or violence). As Begun (1995) argued in her discussion of siblings and foster-care placement, when siblings are differentially placed, social workers who are responsible for different children in different foster homes must make special efforts to coordinate efforts to ensure that frequent sibling visitation takes place.

The past 2 decades have witnessed tremendous progress in the study of siblings. Conceptualizations of sibling behavior as primarily rivalrous have been discarded as too narrow, even in the West, and shown to be unrepresentative of the nature of sibling relationships in other cultures. At the same time, much remains to be learned. The specifics of how sibling relationship quality is organized by parent–child subsystems and overall family functioning, cross-cultural perspectives on sibling relationships, the role of the sibling as a transmitter of cultural norms and practices, the role of siblings as socializers of and role models for both adaptive and maladaptive social behavior (such as launching younger siblings on the path to drug use), and the manner in which siblings serve each other as support figures throughout the life span are but a few of the many emerging areas on which the future study of siblings will profitably focus. It is hoped this chapter stimulates additional work toward these ends.

REFERENCES

Abramovitch, R., Corter, C., & Lando, B. (1979). Sibling interaction in the home. *Child Development, 50,* 997–1003.

Abramovitch, R., Corter, C., & Pepler, D. (1980). Observations of mixed-sex sibling dyads. *Child Development, 51,* 1268–1271.

Abramovitch, R., Corter, C., Pepler, D. J., & Stanhope, L. (1986). Sibling and peer interaction: A final follow-up and a comparison. *Child Development, 57,* 217–229.

Adams, B. N. (1972). Birth-order: A critical review. *Sociometry, 35,* 411–439.

Ainsworth, M. D. S., Blehar, M. C., Waters, E., & Wall, S. (1978). *Patterns of attachment: A psychological study of the strange situation.* Hillsdale, NJ: Lawrence Erlbaum Associates.

Bank, S. P. (1987). Favoritism. *Journal of Children in Contemporary Society, 19,* 77–89.

Bank, S. P., & Kahn, M. D. (1982). *The sibling bond.* New York: Basic Books.

Baydar, N., Greek, A., & Brooks-Gunn, J. (1997). A longitudinal study of the effects of the birth of a sibling during the first 6 years of life. *Journal of Marriage and the Family, 59,* 939–956.

Baydar, N., Hyle, P., & Brooks-Gunn, J. (1997). A longitudinal study of the effects of the birth of a sibling during preschool and early grade school years. *Journal of Marriage and the Family, 59,* 957–965.

Bayley, N. (1969). *The Bayley Scales of Infant Development.* San Antonio, TX: The Psychological Corporation.

Begun, A. L. (1995). Sibling relationships and foster care placements for young children. *Early Child Development & Care. Special issue: Social work practice with children, 106,* 237–250.

Berndt, T. J., & Bulleit, T. N. (1985). Effects of sibling relationships on preschoolers' behavior at home and at school. *Developmental Psychology, 21,* 761–767.

Bornstein, M. H., Gaughran, J. M., & Segui, I. (1991). Multimethod assessment of infant temperament: Mother questionnaire and mother and observer reports evaluated and compared at 5 months using the Infant Temperament Measure. *International Journal of Behavioral Development, 14,* 131–151.

Bosso, R. (1986). Attachment quality and sibling relations: Responses of anxiously attached/avoidant and securely attached 18 to 32 month old firstborns toward their secondborn siblings. *Dissertation Abstracts International, 47*(3-B), p. 1293.

Bowlby, J. (1969). *Attachment and loss: Vol. 1. Attachment.* New York: Basic Books.

Bretherton, I., & Munholland, K. A. (1998). Internal working models in attachment relationships: A construct revisited. In J. Cassidy & P. R. Shaver (Eds.), *Handbook of attachment: Theory, research, and clinical applications* (pp. 89–111). New York: Guilford.

Brody, G. H., & Stoneman, Z. (1987). Sibling conflict: Contributions of the siblings themselves, the parent–sibling relationship, and the broader family system. *Journal of Children in Contemporary Society, 19,* 39–53.

Brody, G. H., Stoneman, Z., & Burke, M. (1987). Child temperaments, maternal differential behavior, and sibling relationships. *Developmental Psychology, 23,* 354–362.

Brody, G. H., Stoneman, Z., & MacKinnon, C. (1986). Contributions of maternal childrearing practices and interactional contexts to sibling interactions. *Journal of Applied Developmental Psychology, 7,* 225–236.

Brody, G. H., Stoneman, Z., MacKinnon, C. E., & MacKinnon, R. (1985). Role relationships and behavior between preschool-aged and school-aged sibling pairs. *Developmental Psychology, 21,* 124–129.

Brody, G. H., Stoneman, Z., & McCoy, J. K. (1992). Associations of maternal and paternal direct and differential behavior with sibling relationships. *Child Development, 63,* 82–92.

Brown, J. R., & Dunn, J. (1992). Talk with your mother or your sibling? Developmental changes in early family conversations about feelings. *Child Development, 63,* 336–349.

Bryant, B. K. (1989). The child's perspective of sibling caretaking and its relevance to understanding social-emotional functioning and development. In P. G. Zukow (Ed.), *Sibling relationships across cultures: Theoretical and methodological issues* (pp. 143–164). New York: Springer-Verlag.

Bryant, B. K., & Crockenberg, S. B. (1980). Correlates and dimensions of prosocial behavior: A study of female siblings with their mothers. *Child Development, 51,* 529–544.

Buhrmester, D., & Furman, W. (1987). The development of companionship and intimacy. *Child Development, 58,* 1101–1113.

Campbell, S. B. (1990). *Behavior problems in preschool children: Clinical and developmental issues.* New York: Guilford Press.

Cicirelli, V. G. (1967). Sibling constellation, creativity, IQ, and academic achievement. *Child Development, 38,* 481–490.

Cicirelli, V. G. (1972). The effect of sibling relationship on concept learning of young children taught by child-teachers. *Child Development, 42,* 282–287.

Cicirelli, V. G. (1973). Effects of sibling structure and interaction on children's categorization style. *Developmental Psychology, 9,* 132–139.

Cicirelli, V. G. (1974). Relationship of sibling structuring and interaction on younger sibling's conceptual style. *Journal of Genetic Psychology, 125,* 36–49.

Cicirelli, V. G. (1982). Sibling influence throughout the lifespan. In M. E. Lamb & B. Sutton-Smith (Eds.), *Sibling relationships: Their nature and significance across the life span* (pp. 267–284). Hillsdale, NJ: Lawrence Erlbaum Associates.

Crockenberg, S. (1986). Are temperamental differences in babies associated with predictable differences in care-giving? In J. V. Lerner & R. M. Lerner (Eds.), *Temperament and social interaction in infants and children* (pp. 53–74). San Francisco: Jossey-Bass.

Dunn, J. (1983). Sibling relationships in early childhood. *Child Development, 54,* 787–811.

Dunn, J. (1989). Siblings and the development of social understanding in early childhood. In P. G. Zukow (Ed.), *Sibling interaction across cultures: Theoretical and methodological considerations* (pp. 106–116). New York: Springer-Verlag.

Dunn, J., & Kendrick, C. (1979). Interaction between young siblings in the context of family relations. In M. Lewis & L. Rosenblum (Eds.), *The child and its family* (pp. 143–169). New York: Plenum Press.

Dunn, J., & Kendrick, D. (1980). The arrival of a sibling: Changes in patterns of interaction between mother and firstborn child. *Journal of Child Psychology and Psychiatry, 21,* 119–132.

Dunn, J., & Kendrick, C. (1981). Social behavior of young siblings in the family context: Differences between same-sex and different-sexed dyads. *Child Development, 52,* 1265–1273.

Dunn, J., & Kendrick, C. (1982a). *Siblings: Love, envy, and understanding.* Cambridge, MA: Harvard University Press.

Dunn, J., & Kendrick, C. (1982b). Siblings and their mothers: Developing relationships within the family. In M. E. Lamb & B. Sutton-Smith (Eds.), *Sibling relationships: Their nature and significance across the lifespan* (pp. 39–60). Hillsdale, NJ: Lawrence Erlbaum Associates.

Dunn, J., & Kendrick, C. (1982c). The speech of two- and three-year-olds to infant siblings: "Baby talk" and the context of communication. *Journal of Child Language, 9,* 579–595.

Dunn, J., Kendrick, C., & MacNamee, R. (1981). The reaction of first-born children to the birth of a sibling: Mothers' reports. *Journal of Child Psychology and Psychiatry, 22,* 1–18.

Dunn, J., & Munn, P. (1986). Becoming a family member: Family conflict and the development of social understanding in the second year. *Child Development, 56,* 480–492.

East, P. L., & Rook, K. S. (1992). Compensatory patterns of support among children's peer relationships: A test using school friends, non-school friends, and siblings. *Developmental Psychology, 28,* 163–172.

Field, T., & Reite, M. (1984). Children's responses to separation from mother during the birth of another child. *Child Development, 55,* 1308–1316.

Furman, W., & Buhrmester, D. (1985). Children's perceptions of the qualities of sibling relationships. *Child Development, 56*, 448–461.

Furman, W., & Giberson, R. S. (1995). Identifying the links between parents and their children's sibling relationships. In S. Shulman (Ed.), *Close relationships and socioemotional development: Vol. 7. Human development* (S. Strauss, Series Editor) (pp. 95–107). Norwood, NJ: Ablex.

Garner, P. W., Jones, D. C., & Palmer, D. J. (1994). Social cognitive correlates of preschool children's sibling caregiving behavior. *Developmental Psychology, 30*, 905–911.

Gelfand, D. M., Jenson, W. R., & Drew, C. J. (1988). *Understanding child behavior disorders* (2nd ed.). New York: Holt, Rinehart, & Winston.

Gibbs, E. D., Teti, D. M., & Bond, L. A. (1987). Infant–sibling communication: Relationships to birth-spacing and cognitive and linguistic development. *Infant Behavior and Development, 10*, 307–323.

Gottlieb, L. N., & Mendelson, M. J. (1990). Parental support and firstborn girls' adaptation to the birth of a sibling. *Journal of Applied Developmental Psychology, 11*, 29–48.

Grotevant, H. D., Scarr, S., & Weinberg, R. A. (1977). Constellations with adopted and natural children: A test of the Zajonc and Markus model. *Child Development, 48*, 1699–1703.

Hesser, J., & Azmitia, M. (1989, April). *The influence of siblings and non-siblings on children's observation and imitation.* Paper presented at the biennial meeting of the Society for Research in Child Development. Kansas City, KS.

Hinde, R. A. (1979). *Towards understanding relationships.* London: Academic Press.

Hoffman, M. L. (1975). Developmental synthesis of affect and cognition and its implications for altruistic motivation. *Developmental Psychology, 11*, 607–622.

Howe, N., & Ross, H. S. (1990). Socialization, perspective-taking, and the sibling relationship. *Developmental Psychology, 26*, 160–165.

Irish, D. P. (1964). Sibling interaction: A neglected aspect in family life research. *Social Forces, 42*, 279–288.

Kaplan, L., Ade-Ridder, L., & Hennon, C. B. (1991). Issues of split custody: Siblings separated by divorce. *Journal of Divorce and Remarriage. Special issue: The consequences of divorce: Economic and custodial impact on children and adults, 16*, 253–274.

Kendrick, C., & Dunn, J. (1980). Caring for a second child: Effects on the interaction between mother and firstborn. *Developmental Psychology, 16*, 303–311.

Koch, H. L. (1954). The relation of "primary mental abilities" in five- and six-year-olds to sex of child and characteristics of his sibling. *Child Development, 25*, 209–223.

Koch, H. L. (1955). The relation of certain family constellation characteristics and the attitudes of children toward adults. *Child Development, 26*, 13–40.

Koch, H. L. (1956). Some emotional attitudes of the young child in relation to characteristics of his sibling. *Child Development, 27*, 393–426.

Koester, L. S., & Penny, J. M. (1987, September). *Siblings as facilitators of exploratory play in young children.* Paper presented at the British Psychological Society, Developmental Section Annual Conference. York, England: University of York.

Kowal, A., & Kramer, A. (1997). Children's understanding of differential parental treatment. *Child Development, 68*, 113–126.

Lamb, M. E. (1978a). Interactions between 18-month-olds and their preschool-aged siblings. *Child Development, 49*, 51–59.

Lamb, M. E. (1978b). The development of sibling relationships in infancy: A short-term longitudinal study. *Child Development, 49*, 1189–1196.

Legg, C., Sherick, I., & Wadland, W. (1974). Reaction of preschool children to the birth of a sibling. *Child Psychiatry and Human Development, 5*, 3–39.

Levy, D. M. (1934). Rivalry between children of the same family. *Child Study, 11*, 233–261.

Lobato, D., Barbour, L., Hall, L. J., & Miller, C. T. (1987). Psychosocial characteristics of preschool siblings of handicapped and non-handicapped children. *Journal of Abnormal Child Psychology, 15*, 329–338.

Maccoby, E. E., & Jacklin, C. (1974). *The psychology of sex differences*. Stanford, CA: Stanford University Press.

Matheny, A. P. (1983). A longitudinal twin study of stability of components from Bayley's Infant Behavior Record. *Child Development, 84*, 356–360.

Mchale, S. M., & Pawletko, T. M. (1992). Differential treatment of siblings in two family contexts. *Child Development, 63*, 68–81.

Minnett, A. M., Vandell, D. L., & Santrock, J. W. (1983). The effects of sibling status on sibling interaction: Influence of birth order, age spacing, sex of child, and sex of sibling. *Child Development, 54*, 1064–1072.

Minuchin, P. (1985). Families and individual development: Provocations from the field of family therapy. *Child Development, 56*, 289–302.

Moore, G. A., Cohn, J. F., & Campbell, S. B. (1997). Mothers' affective behavior with infant siblings: Stability and change. *Developmental Psychology, 33*, 856–860.

Moore, T. (1969). Stress in normal childhood. *Human Relations, 22*, 235–250.

Nadelman, L., & Begun, A. (1982). The effect of the newborn on the older sibling: Mothers' questionnaires. In M. E. Lamb & B. Sutton-Smith (Eds.), *Sibling relationships: Their nature and significance across the lifespan* (pp. 13–37). Hillsdale, NJ: Lawrence Erlbaum Associates.

Olweus, D. (1979). Stability of aggressive reaction patterns in males: A review. *Psychological Bulletin, 86*, 852–875.

Patterson, G. R. (1984). Siblings: Fellow travelers in coercive family processes. In R. J. Blanchard (Ed.), *Advances in the study of aggression* (pp. 174–214). New York: Academic Press.

Patterson, G. R. (1986). The contribution of siblings to training for fighting: A microsocial analysis. In D. Olweus, J. Block, & M. Radke-Yarrow (Eds.), *Development of antisocial and prosocial behavior: Research theories and issues* (pp. 235–261). New York: Academic Press.

Patterson, G. R., Dishion, T. J., & Bank, L. (1984). Family interaction: A process model of deviancy training. *Aggressive Behavior, 10*, 253–267.

Pepler, D. J. (1981, April). *Naturalistic observations of teaching and modeling between siblings*. Paper presented at the biennial meeting of the Society for Research in Child Development, Boston.

Pepler, D. J., Abramovitch, R., & Corter, C. (1981). Sibling interaction in the home: A longitudinal study. *Child Development, 52*, 1344–1347.

Piaget, J. (1965). *The moral judgment of the child*. New York: Free Press.

Quittner, A. L., & Opipari, L. C. (1994). Differential treatment of siblings: Interview and diary analyses comparing two family contexts. *Child Development, 65*, 800–814.

Rosenberg, B. G. (1982). Life span personality stability in sibling status. In M. E. Lamb & B. Sutton-Smith (Eds.), *Sibling relationships: Their nature and significance across the lifespan* (pp. 167–224). Hillsdale, NJ: Lawrence Erlbaum Associates.

Rosenberg, B. G., & Sutton-Smith, B. (1969). Sibling age spacing effects upon cognition. *Developmental Psychology, 1*, 661–668.

Scarr, S., & Grajek, S. (1982). Similarities and differences among siblings. In M. E. Lamb & B. Sutton-Smith (Eds.), *Sibling relationships: Their nature and significance across the lifespan* (pp. 357–381). Hillsdale, NJ: Lawrence Erlbaum Associates.

Schacter, F. F. (1982). Sibling deidentification and split-parent identification: A family tetrad. In M. E. Lamb & B. Sutton-Smith (Eds.), *Sibling relationships: Their nature and significance across the lifespan* (pp. 123–151). Hillsdale, NJ: Lawrence Erlbaum Associates.

Schacter, F. F., & Stone, R. K. (1987). Comparing and contrasting siblings: Defining the self. *Journal of Children in Contemporary Society, 19*, 55–75.

Schooler, C. (1972). Birth order effects. *Psychological Bulletin, 78*, 161–175.

Schoonover, S. M. (1959). The relationship of intelligence and achievement to birth order, sex of sibling, and age interval. *Journal of Educational Psychology, 50*, 143–146.

Sewall, M. (1930). Some causes of jealousy in young children. *Smith College Studies in Social Work, 1*, 6–22.

Smalley, R. (1930). The influences of differences in age, sex, and intelligence in determining attitudes of siblings toward each other. *Smith College Studies in Social Work, 1*, 23–40.

Sroufe, L. A., & Fleeson, J. (1986). Attachment and the construction of relationships. In W. Hartup & Z. Rubin (Eds.), *The nature and development of relationships* (pp. 51–71). Hillsdale, NJ: Lawrence Erlbaum Associates.

Steelman, L. C. (1985). A tale of two variables: A review of the intellectual consequences of sibship size and birth order. *Review of Educational Research, 55*, 353–386.

Stewart, R. B. (1983). Sibling attachment relationships: Child–infant interactions in the Strange Situation. *Developmental Psychology, 19*, 192–199.

Stewart, R. B., & Marvin, R. S. (1984). Sibling relations: The role of conceptual perspective-taking in the ontogeny of sibling caregiving. *Child Development, 55*, 1322–1332.

Stewart, R. B., Mobley, L. A., Van Tuyl, S. S., & Salvador, M. A. (1987). The firstborn's adjustment to the birth of a sibling: A longitudinal assessment. *Child Development, 58*, 341–355.

Stoneman, Z., Brody, G. H., & MacKinnon, C. (1984). Naturalistic observations of children's roles and activities while playing with their siblings and friends. *Child Development, 55*, 617–627.

Stormshak, E. A., Bellanti, C. J., & Bierman, K. L. (1996). The quality of sibling relationships and the development of social competence and behavioral control in aggressive children. *Developmental Psychology, 32*, 79–89.

Sutton-Smith, B. (1982). Birth order and sibling status effects. In M. E. Lamb & B. Sutton-Smith (Eds.), *Sibling relationships: Their nature and significance across the lifespan* (pp. 153–165). Hillsdale, NJ: Lawrence Erlbaum Associates.

Sutton-Smith, B., & Rosenberg, B. G. (1970). *The sibling*. New York: Holt, Rinehart, & Winston.

Taylor, M. K., & Kogan, K. L. (1973). Effects of birth of a sibling on mother–child interaction. *Child Psychiatry and Human Development, 4*, 53–58.

Teti, D. M. (1992). Sibling interaction. In V. B. Van Hasselt & M. Hersen (Eds.), *Handbook of social development: A lifespan perspective* (pp. 201–226). New York: Plenum.

Teti, D. M., & Ablard, K. E. (1989). Security of attachment and infant–sibling relationships: A laboratory study. *Child Development, 60*, 1519–1528.

Teti, D. M., Bond, L. A., & Gibbs, E. D. (1986). Sibling-created experiences: Relationships to birth-spacing and infant cognitive development. *Infant Behavior and Development, 9*, 27–42.

Teti, D. M., Bradley, M. E., Hastings, P., & Zahn-Waxler, C. (2000). *Sibling relationships of children at risk for disruptive behavior.* Manuscript submitted for publication.

Teti, D. M., Gibbs, E. D., & Bond, L. A. (1989). Sibling interaction, birth spacing, and intellectual/linguistic development. In P. G. Zukow (Ed.), *Sibling interaction across cultures: Theoretical and methodological issues* (pp. 117–139). New York: Springer-Verlag.

Teti, D. M., & Nakagawa, M. (1990). Assessing attachment in infancy: The Strange Situation and alternate systems. In E. D. Gibbs & D. M. Teti (Eds.), *Interdisciplinary assessment of infants: A guide for early intervention professionals* (pp. 191–214). Baltimore: Brookes.

Teti, D. M., Nakagawa, M., Das, R., & Wirth, O. (1991). Security of attachment between preschoolers and their mothers: Relations among social interaction, parenting stress, and mothers' sorts of the Attachment Q-Set. *Developmental Psychology, 27*, 440–447.

Teti, D. M., Sakin, J., Kucera, E., Corns, K. M., & Eiden, R. D. (1996). And baby makes four: Predictors of attachment security among preschool-aged firstborns during the transition to siblinghood. *Child Development, 67*, 579–596.

Thomas, A., Birch, H. G., Chess, S., & Robbins, A. (1961). Individuality in responses of children to similar environmental situations. *American Journal of Psychiatry, 117*, 798–803.

Trause, M. A., Voos, D., Rudd, C., Klaus, M., Kennell, J., & Boslett, M. (1981). Separation for childbirth: The effect on the sibling. *Child Psychiatry and Human Development, 12*, 32–39.

Vandell, D. L. (1982). *Encounters between infants and their preschool-aged siblings during the first year.* Unpublished manuscript, University of Texas at Dallas.

Vandell, D. L. (1987). Baby sister/baby brother: Reactions to the birth of a sibling and patterns of early sibling relations. *Journal of Children in Contemporary Society, 19*, 13–37.

Vandell, D. L., Minnett, A. M., & Santrock, J. W. (1987). Age differences in sibling relationships during middle childhood. *Journal of Applied Developmental Psychology, 8,* 247–257.

Vandell, D. L., Minnett, A. M., Johnson, B. S., & Santrock, J. W. (1990). *Sibling and friends: Experiences of school-aged children.* Unpublished manuscript, University of Texas at Dallas.

Vandell, D. L., & Wilson, K. S. (1987). Infants' interactions with mother, sibling, and peer: Contrasts and relations between interaction systems. *Child Development, 58,* 176–186.

Vaughn, B. E., & Bost, K. K. (1999). Attachment and temperament: Redundant, independent, or interacting influences on interpersonal adaptation and personality development? In J. Cassidy & P. R. Shaver (Eds.), *Handbook of attachment: Theory, research, and clinical applications* (pp. 198–225). New York: Guilford.

Volling, B. L., & Belsky, J. (1992). The contribution of mother–child and father–child relationships to the quality of sibling interaction: A longitudinal study. *Child Development, 63,* 1209–1222.

Wagner, M. E., Schubert, H. J. P., & Schubert, D. S. P. (1979). Sibship-constellation effects on psychosocial development, creativity, and health. *Advances in Child Development and Behavior, 14,* 57–148.

Waters, E. (1995). The Attachment Q-Set (version 3.0). In E. Waters, B. E., Vaughn, G. Posada, & K. Kondo-Ikemura (Eds.), *Caregiving, culture, and cognitive perspectives on secure base behavior and working models: New growing points of attachment theory and research. Monographs of the Society for Research in Child Development, 60*(2–3, Serial No. 244), 234–246.

Waters, E., & Deane, K. E. (1985). Defining and assessing individual differences in attachment relationships: Q-methodology and the organization of behavior in infancy and early childhood. In I. Bretherton & E. Waters (Eds.), *Growing points of attachment theory and research: Monographs of the Society for Research in Child Development, 50*(1–2, Serial No. 209), 41–65.

Watson-Gegeo, K. A., & Gegeo, D. W. (1989). The role of sibling interaction in child socialization. *Sibling relationships across cultures: Theoretical and methodological issues* (pp. 54–76). New York: Springer-Verlag.

Weisner, T. S. (1989). Comparing sibling relationships across cultures. In P. G. Zukow (Ed.), *Sibling relationships across cultures: Theoretical and methodological issues* (pp. 11–25). New York: Springer-Verlag.

Whiting, B., & Edwards, C. (1988). *Children of different worlds: The formation of social behavior.* Cambridge, MA: Harvard University Press.

Whittemore, R. D., & Beverly, E. (1989). Trust in the Mandinka way: The cultural context of sibling care. In P. G. Zukow (Ed.), *Sibling relationships across cultures: Theoretical and methodological issues* (pp. 26–53). New York: Springer-Verlag.

Winnicott, D. W. (1964). *The child, the family and the outside world.* London: Penguin.

Wishart, J. G. (1986). Siblings as models in early infant learning. *Child Development, 57,* 1232–1240.

Youngblade, L. M., & Dunn, J. (1995). Individual differences in young children's pretent play with mother and sibling: Links to relationships and understanding of other people's feelings and beliefs. *Child Development, 66,* 1472–1492.

Zajonc, R. B. (1976). Family configuration and intelligence. *Science, 192,* 227–236.

Zajonc, R. B., & Markus, G. B. (1975). Birth order and intellectual development. *Psychological Review, 82,* 74–88.

Zajonc, R. B., Markus, H., & Markus, G. B. (1979). The birth order puzzle. *Journal of Personality and Social Psychology, 37,* 1325–1341.

Zukow, P. G. (Ed.). (1989a). *Sibling interaction across cultures: Theoretical and methodological issues.* New York: Springer-Verlag.

Zukow, P. G. (1989b). Siblings as effective socializing agents: Evidence from Central Mexico. In P. G. Zukow (Ed.), *Sibling interaction across cultures: Theoretical and methodological issues* (pp. 79–105). New York: Springer-Verlag.

Zukow-Goldring, P. (1995). Sibling caregiving. In M. H. Bornstein (Ed.), *Handbook of parenting. Vol. 3: Status and social conditions of parenting* (pp. 177–208). Mahwah, NJ: Lawrence Erlbaum Associates.

8

Retrospect and Prospect in the Psychological Study of Families as Systems

Kurt Kreppner

Max Planck Institute for Human Development, Berlin, Germany

In nonacademic circles, the notion that families constitute a primary eco-logical niche affording survival of offspring and socialization of new genera-tions into a common culture is not a controversial one. Within developmen-tal psychology, however, this notion has long been neglected and at times even rejected. Indeed, until human ethologists provided new insights into the significance of primary caretakers and the essential role of care-taker–child relationships during the 1960s and 1970s, the family as a rele-vant developmental context was seldom studied. When family environ-ments were considered by researchers, they were evaluated along such dimensions as number of toys available in the home, housing conditions, quality of neighborhood, and conditions of day care centers.

Though progress was slow, researchers gradually moved beyond stud-ies of the mother–child relationship to consider the roles that fathers play in the child's relational network (Silverstein, chap. 2, this volume). Today, the child–father relationship is viewed by most family psychologists as an important aspect of the natural environment in which children develop. As several contributors to this volume note, however, studying mothering and fathering within families still does not do justice to the richness of the en-tire relationship network that children encounter as they grow up in a fam-ily. To capture the relational experience children encounter in their natural habitats, both the structural aspects of the family's relational network and the emotional climate within which family members exchange information need to be considered. As Cox and Harter (chap. 6, this volume) note, the challenge for researchers is how best to depict the complexity of a network that encompasses multiple relationships in various constellations including dyadic, triadic, and tetradic interaction patterns. What are the ideal tools that would allow us to characterize a family's complex web of relationships, charting the ways family members communicate and establish, maintain, and renegotiate relationships?

In this chapter I try to disentangle disparate aspects of the family as a relevant context for children's development and link individual developmental pathways to the family context. In keeping with the theme of this volume, I discuss relevant ideas from the past, describe recent pertinent research from my own laboratory illustrating essential developmental-systems principles, and offer several guidelines for future research. In the first part of this chapter I summarize several important historical perspectives that spoke to the interplay between development and family, highlighting some influential concepts that gained notoriety with the emergence of systems theory in the beginning of the last century. In doing so, I highlight links between these ideas and more recent orientations in the field of family research. In the second part of this chapter I focus on the key notion of family as a context for development. I present empirical data illustrating the value of considering more than single and static dyadic relationships when assessing environmental influence on individuals. Finally, I present several issues I believe should guide future inquiries examining the family as context for development.

RETROSPECT: PERSPECTIVES ON SYSTEMS, COMMUNICATION, AND CULTURE

Transmission of Meaning and Culture

The family is often defined as an institution enabling the transmission of both genes and culture. In recent years, the first topic has dominated discussions about family transmission whereas the second topic has marshalled considerably less interest. This is a contrast to the zeitgeist of the late 1960s and 1970s, when studies of socialization were a major thrust in studies of development and when the hot topic was careful analysis of interactions between mothers and children. The transmission of culture was also a key element in several compensation programs designed for underprivileged children. In such programs, professionals sought to inculcate cognitive skills in children from poor environments who were believed to be missing out on appropriate levels of stimulation during critical periods of their development. As we entered the new millenium, however, several influential writers had gone so far as to propose that the family as an institution, aside from its role in assuring the transmissal of genes, has little meaningful import for children's cognitive, emotional, and social development (e.g., Harris, 1995; Rowe & Jacobson, 2000). Without question, the unfolding of genetic programs is highly relevant for numerous aspects of developmental processes, but it seems shortsighted to focus principally on genes being transmitted from one generation to the next in the family when meaning and culture are likewise transmitted within this institution. Without the bonds linking generations within the family, the maintenance of motivation to live together and to invest in the next generation becomes tenuous.

Since the time Darwin (1859, 1871) articulated his theory of evolution, biology and infant psychology have made immense progress in substantiating that human beings are a species governed not only by individual experience but also by an endowment reflecting an evolutionary imprint in everyday behavior. The ways meaning and culture are transmitted within the basic intergenerational unit formed by parents and children have frequently been debated by developmentally oriented theorists. The philosopher Cassirer (1944), for example, argued that the transmission of culture constitutes a uniquely human developmental issue. Developmental psychologists such as Baldwin (1894, 1895) and Piaget (1937) have discussed vitalistic perspectives on organism–environment interplay and adaptation. Von Uexküll (1909), assisted by Cassirer and the psychologist Stern (1935), worked on developmental conceptualizations emphasizing the organism's embeddedness in its environment. In these accounts, development was conceived of as being directed into its specific ecological niche. Von Uexküll (1909) articulated a dual approach for elaborating the interplay between organism and environment. He characterized the organism's relatedness to its environment by postulating two networks for information exchange: a network of action by which the individual is forming its environment (*wirknetz*) and a network of perceiving and memorizing information from the environment (*merknetz*). Cassirer (1944) extended von Uexküll's ideas, arguing for a uniquely human adaptation process linking organism to environment that was distinct among the adaptational processes of other species. He underlined the process of *transmission of meaning* during development in the human species. In so doing, he postulated a set of additional, specialized equipment for the human species, a third network besides the networks of action and perception. He called this third network a *symbolic system*, devoted to the symbols present in a child's environment and constituted by language and culture. In Cassirer's words:

> In the human world, we find a new characteristic which appears to be the distinctive mark of human life. The functional circle of man is not only quantitatively enlarged; it has also undergone a qualitative change. Man has, as it

were, discovered a new method of adapting himself to his environment. Between the receptor system and the effector system, which are to be found in
all animal species, we find in man a third link which we may describe as the
symbolic system. This new acquisition transforms the whole of human life. As
compared with the other animals man lives not only in a broader reality; he
lives, so to speak, in a new *dimension* of reality. (p. 24)

This third component represents the essentials necessary to establish a
common meaning system and to communicate on a more abstract and elaborate level independently of immediate needs or emotions. This "new dimension of reality" is both a new tool for understanding and interpreting
one's own experiences and a means for referring to the experiences of others. Thus, the use of symbols can transform cumbersome pieces of perception into elegant strings of meanings. Moreover, the use of symbols affords
the opportunity to partake in the experiences of others beyond one's own
percepts. This enriches the aggregation of individual knowledge and can
lead to a set of categories helpful in interpreting the world.

Each of these aspects is fundamentally important for understanding the
family as a context in which the growing child encounters patterns of communication and schemes of world interpretation opined by other members
of the family. Parents and siblings bring their world views and judgments
about reality into the family's everyday communication, and it is this family
communication that embodies the child's cosmos for the construction of
meaning. Thus, the entire family with its members and their modes of communication can be taken as the relevant ecological niche for the offspring
during infancy, childhood, and even adolescence. Von Uexküll's (1909) articulation of the ecological niche as the context in which the organism adapts
to survive while changing the environmental conditions to meet its own
needs marked the beginnings of a new approach toward understanding the
complex endowment–environment interplay. Cassirer's (1944) articulation
of the symbolic system added the possiblity of an enriched aggregation of
knowledge by referring to information about reality conveyed by abstract
symbols of reality rather than concrete experiences.

The basic idea of the mutual adaptation of organism and ecological
niche—the organism forming its niche as the niche forms the organism—introduced a new way of thinking about adaptation processes, different from
the traditional cause-and-effect logic, to the field of biology. But concepts of
organism–environment interaction or of continuity and change in development still required models that could accommodate the phenomenon of
mutuality, or circular influence. Enter von Bertalanffy (1933, 1956) whose
elaborate systems view in technology and biology, notions of mutual dependency between organism and environment and of adaptation, and description of dynamics and change processes in development filled this void.

Moreover, modern systems theory was propelled further by mathematicians such as Wiener (1948). Wiener is regarded as one of the founding creators of cybernetics and information theory, concepts by which communication was explained in terms of transmission and regulation of information. These ideas were later adapted to model transmission processes inside the family, for purposes as diverse as understanding socialization activities, analyzing family malfunction, or studying changes in interaction and communication patterns during different stages of child development (Duvall & Hill, 1945). The concept of communication as a regulatory tool for socializing the next generation gained more interest as it became enriched by technical information about encoding and decoding procedures as prerequisites for sending and receiving messages. When complex exchanges within a network of interacting members of a family had to be described, these new approaches offered new perspectives to think about the interplay between individual and environment. However, although some psychologists during the 1920s and 1930s had tried to move beyond the narrow mechanical concepts of human functioning that predominated at the time to take a more dynamic look at psychological processes, it was not until the late 1960s that systems concepts were widely applied in describing processes in developmental psychology. Early precursors of nonmechanistic dynamic concepts for the interplay between individual and environment existed in the writings of Lewin, who had argued against structuring the world through a definite order (as had Aristotle) and who had advocated instead classifying according to functions and recurring patterns (as had been proposed earlier by Galilei; see Lewin, 1931). Related examples can be found in the writings of Stern (1935), who proposed a dynamic perspective for describing the interplay between endowment and environment by addressing the *process of convergence* in every individual's developmental pathway. Yet the widespread application of systems concepts and exchange models focusing on specifics of communication in mother–infant relationships did not take hold until the late 1960s, when Bell (1968) championed the principle of bidirectionality in mother–infant interactions.

Development and Change in the Family: Communication and the Regulation of Relationships

Sociologists and psychiatrists began breathing life into the circular model of systems theory when they explored individual pathological behaviors as patterns that regulate and format relationships inside the family and generate structural conditions such as symmetry or asymmetry between family members (Bateson, Jackson, Haley, & Weakland, 1956; Lidz, 1963; Mishler & Waxler, 1968; Wynne, Ryckoff, Day, & Hirsch, 1958). The idea of analyzing families in terms of recurring action–reaction patterns and of considering communication exchanges as negotiations of the status of a family member can be traced to Burgess (1926), a family sociologist who spoke of families as "superpersonalities" and "growing things" (p. 5). He suggested using families' communication patterns to distinguish among types of families, and his emphasis on change in family patterns according to family members' growth pioneered the developmental perspective. This idea was incorporated in a new approach elaborated by Sullivan (1953), who adapted the practice of psychoanalysis for psychotic individuals. Sullivan claimed that schizophrenic men and women could be understood if clinicians could establish a social relationship with these patients. He argued that those suffering from schizophrenia encountered early, disturbed communication patterns in their families, with interruptions in the circle of mutual exchange by which information is typically interpreted as meaningful within a common framework. Sullivan was among the first to notice that after successful therapy, those recovering from schizophrenia often had a recurrence of symptoms upon returning to their families.

Family research flourished during the late 1950s and early 1960s at various institutions such as the Massachusetts Institute of Technology, Yale University, the National Institute of Mental Health in Washington, D.C., and the Mental Research Institute in Palo Alto, California. It was not long before researchers attempted to apply diagnostic concepts featuring specifics of pathological communication formats among family members to normal families. However, early results were sobering. Researchers could not distinguish between so-called normal and pathological families on the basis of their communication patterns! Yet despite the inadequacy of communication analysis and the double-bind concept in distinguishing normal from schizophrenic individuals and their families (Kafka, 1971), the role of communication in the family, the way family members handle information among them, became salient issues in general family research.

Even so, however, most psychologists at that time were hesitant to embrace the new systems approach and its logic of bidirectional effects. It was principally those researchers who dealt with mother–child relationships during infancy who began to look more closely and systematically at exchange rhythms and recurring behavior patterns. A few noteworthy investigations during the 1970s sought to extend analyses of dyadic interactions to larger units such as the triad (Clarke-Stewart, 1978) or the entire family (Belsky, 1981) to study relational effect on developmental pathways. Growing recognition of even very young infants' sensitivity to the quality of relationship, ability to participate in and formulate relationships by various modes of expressive behavior (e.g., Tronick, 1989), and capacity for handling ambiguities in messages coming from interaction partners helped elevate studies focusing on the observation of mother–child communications to a prominent position within developmental psychology.

In many ways, systemic approaches to the person–environment interplay fundamentally changed the traditional perspective on the family as the child's basic environment. First, within a systems approach, the *dynamics* of the system could be characterized by the exchange between family members, rather than the more traditional assessments of physical, environmental features. Among the most important thrusts of this new work were the use of verbal and nonverbal signs to communicate about objects and topics, and about the relationship between communicators. Second, families began being conceptualized as *open systems* adapting to changing needs of their members and of environmental conditions. This was radically different from a static view describing families as institutions that conserve traditional roles, values, and cultural norms. Third, there was an appreciation that the *energy* by which the family as a unit was able to find a state of inner balance or equilibrium (such that all members were motivated to live together and to adapt flexibly to new conditions) was manifest in the quality of communication among these members, rather than in their isolated personality traits.

The application of systems theoretical concepts in developmental research guided biologists and psychologists in their analyses and interpretations of infant activities and reactivities observed in caretaker–infant interactions (Stern, 1974, 1977; Trevarthen & Hubley, 1978). Relational and systemic concepts such as organization, dynamics, and equilibrium afforded new perspectives for understanding mechanisms of well functioning or malfunctioning exchange patterns and their effect on early child development (e.g., Lewis & Freedle, 1973). Within family research, constitution or deconstruction of common meaning in everyday communication became a major topic (Watzlawick, Beavin, & Jackson, 1967). The concept of "pragmatics of human communication" altered our understanding of factors that influence child development, and the regulation of autonomy and dependency in relationships was recognized as a persistent, ongoing process between communication partners.

Furthermore, Watzlawick et al. (1967) illustrated how there are two levels of meaning in every communication between persons: information about the reality that is shared by the communication partners and information about the relationship status or quality of relationship between these partners. Thus, whenever communication is analyzed, both meanings must be considered. The quality of relationship between communication partners affects the ease with which they establish, maintain, or negotiate the status of relationship. Relational characteristics describe factors tapping into the communication partners', and in particular the child's, emotional-cognitive system. Relationship quality also captures children's concrete experiences much more than do formal aspects of family systems. Communication about the meaning of information is facilitated when egalitarian or symmetrical relationships ex-

ist between partners. However, when the relationship is asymmetric or unequal, opportunities for clarifying misunderstandings are reduced.

Within the family, the quality of relationship among members must regularly be negotiated as children's communicative and cognitive skills mature. This important systems-oriented concept characterizing the family as
a fluid communication context has paved the way for a more detailed understanding of family influences on developmental processes in that it allows for an analysis of the degree of flexibility in communication patterns
accompanying major developmental change periods.

The Family and Its Role in the Transmission of Culture

The abilities of human beings to accumulate knowledge and to establish a
canon of common values and norms have inspired researchers to think
about models describing how culture is created, accumulated, transmitted,
and transformed over generations. Such models date back far in our history; one such model was articulated by the philosopher Vico (1744/1966)
during the times of enlightenment. According to Vico's model, culture has
long been transmitted and transformed inside families. Without the institution of family, that is, without a unit that links the old generation with the
next generation, growth of culture is impeded, if not made impossible. In
more recent approaches dealing with the capacity to produce something
like culture, a central topic in comparing developmental processes across
different species has been the acquisition of knowledge, norms, and values
across generations. According to theorists such as Carpenter, Nagell, and
Tomasello (1998), a difference can be found in development over the first 2
years of life when human beings are compared with chimpanzees. Carpenter et al. (1998) drew the following conclusions from the results of their investigations comparing human infants with chimpanzees:

> Certainly, young infants are cultural beings from the beginning in the sense
> that their development takes place within a particular cultural context that in-
> fluences many aspects of their cognitive development. But it is only with the
> emergence of the kinds of social-cognitive abilites that we have investigated
> here that they become able to tune in to other persons and their cognitive
> skills directed to outside entities, that is, in a way that fosters acquisition of the
> conventional use of cultural artefacts such as tools and language—which then
> serve to mediate their subsequent interactions with their environments in
> cognitively meaningful ways. This is the essence of the process of encultur-
> ation. (pp. 131–132)

Infants who grow up in a network of relationships actively participate in relationships as early as 9 months. They begin to exchange meanings with
their communication partners and recognize their intentions. These developmental issues also throw some light on the family as the institution in

which, beyond providing protection of biological functioning, maintenance and transmission of meaning to the next generation is being realized (Bell & Vogel, 1968; Reiss, 1965; Rodgers 1973).

TRANSLATING SYSTEMS PRINCIPLES TO RESEARCH: DEVELOPMENT, RELATIONSHIPS, COMMUNICATION, AND EMOTION REGULATION

Activity of Babies, Infant–Caregiver Relationship, and the Growing Role of the Family in Early Developmental Research

During the 1960s and 1970s, infancy research made important strides in crystallizing key relationship processes between infants and mothers and between infants and fathers. Studies focused on how parents influenced the child's course of development, though there were also some investigations examining how the infant's own activity contributed to the regulation of the relationship with the caregiver (Bell, 1968; Escalona, 1973; Rheingold, 1969). Mutuality even in very early interactions between mothers and children was established by this work. However, a series of important studies also revealed that communication patterns in mother–child dyads did not represent the entire spectrum of infants' early experiences. Different communication patterns between parent and infant could be registered when fathers were observed in interaction with their children during play (Lamb, 1975, 1976; Pedersen, 1975, 1980; for a more detailed analysis of this work on fathers, see Silverstein, chap. 2, this volume). Furthermore, as detailed by McHale, Lauretti, Talbot, and Pouquette (chap. 5, this volume), evidence was also found that parent–child interaction changes in quality and quantity when coparenting partners are present. Gradually, researchers began asking questions not only about single-parent–child dyads but also about the entire family, including the parent–parent or marital relationship (Pedersen, Anderson, & Cain, 1980). In his integrated and interdisciplinary approach, Belsky (1981) suggested that researchers consider applying a holistic strategy in family research. Drawing on systems analogies, he proposed mutual influences among the three relationships in one-child families: the father–child, the mother–child, and the marital relationships.

The Role of Marital Relationships in Child Development During Infancy and Early Childhood

In a longitudinal investigation, Cowan and Cowan (1987, 1988, 1992; Cowan, Cowan, Heming, & Miller, 1991) studied the quality of marital communication patterns and the effect of the marital relationship on children's development. The quality of relationships between partners during pregnancy proved to be the most crucial factor in determining both parents' and children's well-being during the transition period from partners to parents. Couples judged to be higher in marital quality during the pregnancy coped more effectively with the stress associated with the newborn child during the first months after birth. Besides the Cowans' work, many studies have shown that marital functioning remains important for a child's further course of development during infancy and childhood. The development of antisocial behavior in children (Emery, 1982, 1988) and the heightened risk for internalizing problems and a gamut of emotional and cognitive reactions in response to marital conflict (Cummings & Davies, 1994; Gottman & Fainsilber-Katz, 1989) illustrate the influential power of marital relationship quality on children's well-being. Moreover, by focusing on differences in mothers' and fathers' parenting styles, researchers have come to new insights concerning family influences on child development. We are learning it is not so much the difference between parents' models per se, but rather how parents handle these differences (showing mutual support or rejection; see McHale et al., chap. 5, this volume) that affects the child's well-being. In one study, Belsky, Crnic, and Gable (1995) determined that consistent, supportive patterns of coparenting predicted children's coping ability in stressful situations. Another relevant relational aspect that appears to be related to differences in children's development is the manner in which parents and children can talk about emotions (Gottman, Fainsilber-Katz, & Hooven, 1996).

Do direct influences exist between the quality of the marital relationship and the quality of the child's relationship with the parents? A meta-analysis conducted by Erel and Burman (1995) suggested that the answer to this question is yes. Erel and Burman's analysis provided strong support for a spillover hypothesis, that is, the transfer of negativity from one subsystem in the family (parent–parent dyad) to another subsystem (parent–child dyad). However, there was no compelling evidence isolating any particular, concrete, single moderator of this transfer. Although some indicators have pointed to links between children's characteristics and particular negative parental communication styles, such as anger and withdrawal by fathers or high levels of criticism and intrusiveness by mothers (Fainsilber-Katz & Gottman, 1993; Fainsilber-Katz & Kahen, 1993), few studies set out to trace how typical courses of marital communication patterns lead to either harmonic or disharmonic family patterns leading to different child developmental pathways (Gottman, 1994).

In adolescence research, family conversation has been studied by Hauser, Powers, and Noam (1991) and by Grotevant and Cooper (1983, 1985). Elements of conversations in the family such as challenging statements, supporting remarks, and discouraging remarks helped to earmark two formats—enabling and disabling communication patterns—the researchers maintain are highly relevant in the development of the self. Families' idio-syncratic ways of producing meaning may provide valuable information about the social competencies children develop in various contexts (You-niss, 1983, 1989; Youniss & Smollar, 1985). In one recent longitudinal study, Feldman, Fisher, and Seitel (1997) showed that marital satisfaction during the child's adolescence continued to be an important predictor of the young adult's subsequent emotional and physical health 6 years later. It seems clear that the quality of the relationship between parents continues to have an essential effect on developmental pathways even into the ado-lescent years (Davies & Cummings, 1998; Harold & Conger, 1997). One out-growth of this perspective has been an increasing focus on the family mi-crocosm in its many details at specific transition periods during the family life cycle.

As discussed elsewhere in this volume, when couples are heading to-ward divorce, conflict in the marriage spills over and adversely affects the quality of parent–child relationships long before parents ultimately sepa-rate. Numerous studies have shown that children growing up in families en route to divorce, in the context of a deteriorating parent–parent relation-ship, display more behavior problems, maladjustment, poor social skills, and, particularly during adolescence, disengagement from the family than do children from nondivorced families (Block, Block, & Gjerde, 1986; Cherlin et al., 1991; Hetherington, 1979). Moreover, academic achievement and anti-social behavior also appear to be strongly influenced by the process of di-vorce (Zill, 1994). These converging results emphasizing the importance of relationship quality between both parents and children and between moth-ers and fathers illustrate both direct and indirect family effects on chil-dren's developmental pathways.

Dynamics and Transitions in the Family

Dynamics and Family Functioning. Systems theories prompted a new un-derstanding of family functioning during the 1950s and 1960s, focusing on the dynamics among all family members as a central characteristic manifest in family-specific communication patterns. Moreover, a merger between sys-tems-oriented concepts and action-theoretical perspectives provided yet an-other view of family functioning. Researchers such as Kantor and Lehr (1975) focused on the active regulation of closeness and distance among family members by using concepts of space, time, energy, and boundaries to classify families as open, closed, or random systems. In a similar way, Reiss (1981) in-troduced the notion of family "paradigms," specific modes of perception, in-terpretation, and mastery of critical conditions. However, neither Kantor and Lehr's nor Reiss' family models took full account of normative transitions dur-ing children's development in the family. Rather, they dealt with families' different modes of handling nonnormative transitions, or abilities to reorganize their own functioning to survive during a state of uncertainty. Both Kantor and Lehr's and Reiss' approaches characterize families as units embodying an aggregation of rituals and behavior patterns, using common modes to interpret events and specific techniques to maintain relationships inside the family.

As such, the family with its particular mode of exchanging information among members, negotiating members' status, and maintaining meaning and motivation can be conceptualized as a unit characterized by a unique culture that produces representations of reality and styles of communication about these representations.

Normative Transitions. Communication and interaction patterns in the family differ considerably across the life span. For example, the young couple's marital relationship undergoes major changes after the birth of the first child (see Cox & Harter, chap. 6, this volume). Coping with these changes is considered an accomplishment of "family tasks" (Duvall, 1977), analogous to Havighurst's (1948) concept of "developmental tasks." During such critical periods in family life, as when children progress through major developmental periods and demand more autonomy within the family rule system, members negotiate, revalue, reconstruct, and interpret transformations in everyday discussions. Reiss' (1981) model of different types of paradigms influencing modes of reconstruction during times of crises can perhaps be used as a template for analyzing the process of normative transitions.

When children during stable phases of their development do not show major deviations from expected behaviors, open regulation of rules and conflicts about the child's proper conduct normally remain at a minimum. However, during periods of developmental change, new needs and demands have to be integrated into the family's lifestyle and canon of rules. During these transition periods, the threat of sanctions for rules transgressions, followed by transformations in these rule systems themselves, visits every family. Particularly during the transition from childhood to adolescence, the intensity of intergenerational discussions about proper conduct have been emphasized by Hill (1983, 1987) and by Broderick and Smith (1979). Broderick and Smith gave an excellent example of the transition in family rules during early adolescence by elaborating how parents give in, step by step, to their child's demand for more autonomy in keeping his or her room. In the first step, parents adapt their controls to their child's increasing demands for more autonomy, but still retain control. In the second step, they surrender their control attempts. In the final step, they accept their child's manner of maintaining his or her room.

Mismatches between parental control and children's increasing demands can lead to friction in the family's communication culture, that is, the way information is transmitted and interpreted. An analysis of family functioning guided by a relational perspective entails a holistic approach, which addresses not only structural and dynamic aspects of family interaction but also adaptational components such as the degree of flexibility with which extant family relationships and communication patterns can be changed. When guided by a developmental perspective, we come to view the family context as a dynamic environment. As children mature and increase their capabilities to actively transform communication patterns in the family, both parents and children have to renegotiate their relationship status to find a common equilibrium that satisfies each member's idiosyncratic needs. Both Duvall (1977) and McGoldrick and Carter (1982) have elaborated schedules for critical transitions during the family life cycle. Critical periods during normative transitions are those times when well-established interaction and communication patterns lose their effectiveness, and misunderstandings and frustrations mount among all family members. As Cowan (1991) has suggested, it may be useful to classify families with respect to their competence in mastering these transition periods during the life cycle.

Developmental Transitions in the Family: Some Empirical Examples

The Role of Normative Transitions in the Analysis of Family Functioning. In moving from the past to the present, I present a few examples from my work to illustrate the type of analysis I have been advocating. These data represent family changes over two normative family-life transitions. These examples were selected to illustrate changes in communication modes within families across transitions. Parents are faced with a series of time-sensitive tasks in their roles as socialization agents. Initially, they have to capitalize on the appropriate window for conveying rules and norms to their young child. If parents start too early to demand proper conduct, the child may lack the requisite capacity to understand and hence will be unable to obey parental rules. This circumstance might initiate a vicious cycle of mutual misunderstandings and frustrations. However, if parents underestimate the child's developmental status and start too late, an appropriate process of adaptation may be delayed, with a resulting mismatch, accompanied once again by mutual misunderstandings and deviations from expected behavior.

When researchers interested in developmental changes operate exclusively from an individual perspective (focusing, for example, on parents' personality type or parenting styles, or on the child's temperament), they might miss normative changes in parent–child communication modes asso-

ciated with the family developmental process by overlooking a crucial part
of individual development related to the family's competence to master
transitions. By contrast, when researchers are guided by a systems-
developmental perspective (Urban, 1978), their analysis of parents' activities in conveying rules and norms to the child can be conducted in a more
flexible framework. Focusing on continuity and change of communication in
the child's relational context would reveal a new dimension of environmental effects on development: rapidity of increase in explications of rules
when parents believe their child is ready to understand instructions, followed by (after a period of intense transmission of rules and norms) decreases in these activities and leveling off at a new state of equilibrium. Applying such a family-developmental and systems-balancing perspective,
both the design of research and the interpretation of data would be different from investigations concentrating on children and parents as persons.
The following examples illustrate such measurement of parental use of rule
transitions within the family, as guided by a systems-developmental perspective. The data I present are drawn from two longitudinal studies of families observed during critical phases of children's development.

*How to Help Infants Become Functioning Family Members: Charting
Changes in Parents' Socializing Behaviors Between 8 and 16 Months.* The
first study (Kreppner, 1988, 1989, 1991) I discuss observed parent–child interaction and communication during the first 2 years after the birth of a second child. Parents have to reorganize their interaction and communication
modes with this second child in accordance with the child's rapid developmental advancement. However, parents also have to integrate this child into
the already existing canon of interaction and communication modalities that
have been established with the first child. Particularly during the infant's
transition to becoming an actively participating individual in the parent–
child relationship at the stage of "secondary intersubjectivity" (Trevarthen &
Hubley, 1978) at approximately 8 to 9 months, the modality of communication between parent and child is expected to undergo major changes.
    Employing a longitudinal approach, 16 families were observed every
month during the first 24 months after the arrival of the second child. The
first child was about 2 years old at the beginning of the study. During the
study, parents' socialization activities directed toward the second child
(measured using a time-sampling methodology) were charted. Two sets of
activities—control of the situation (as a nonverbal) and transmission of
rules (as a verbal activity)—were plotted and showed a systematic course
over the 2 years (Figs. 8.1 and 8.2). The data revealed that parents change
their communication behavior commensurate with the child's development.
Changes were apparent as the infant achieved secondary intersubjectivity

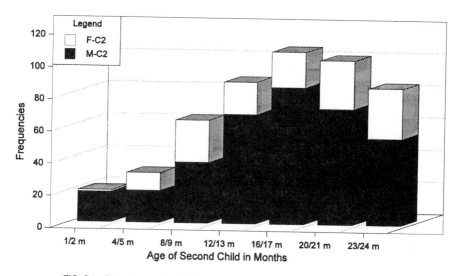

FIG. 8.1. Situation control of mother and father toward the second child.

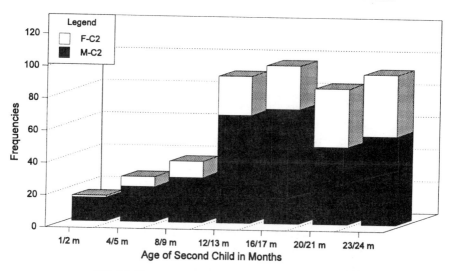

FIG. 8.2. Transmission of rules toward the second child.

at 8 to 9 months and as he or she displayed a growing understanding of language between 12 and 16 months (see Figs. 8.1 and 8.2).

The trajectories of these frequencies over time illustrate an abrupt onset of parents' regulating activities once the infant has reached a new developmental stage of communicative competence. Parents seem to realize the infant's increasing tendency to test parents' emotional reactions to his or her object manipulations, and they react to the child's growing ability to understand single words or instructions. When the child reaches the age of about 16 months, parental regulating activities reach their peak. After this time, both situation control and rule transmission activities slowly decrease toward the end of the second year. The frequency charts reveal major transitions in parental behavior toward the child during this time, when fundamental socioemotional developmental shifts can be observed in the child. Viewed from a differential perspective, these changes could also be construed as capturing family-specific modes in handling transition periods (Kreppner, 1990).

The Transition to Adolescence: Communication Changes Within the Family. In a second longitudinal study (Kreppner, 1995, 1996) focusing on critical phases of family development, continuity and change in parent–child communication were explored during the transition from childhood to adolescence. During this period, another family transition can be observed. In most studies dealing with the child's transition to adolescence, the child's search for a new identity, need to test limits, or process of coping with the different demands of peers and parents have been identified as central issues. From a family systems-developmental view, the child's transition to adolescence offers the opportunity to examine how new patterns of communication between parents and children are established and extant relationships renegotiated. As adolescents are developing a new sense of self and acquiring new skills to affirm their own position against the resistance of the parents, children and parents reorganize their way of living together.

The study from which the following examples are presented was designed to analyze changes in communication patterns between parents and adolescents during the transition period. In addition, modes of different parent–parent communication patterns and their effect on the child's developing sense of self and satisfaction in the family were also examined in a separate investigation (Kreppner & Ullrich, 1998). Links between children's reports of relationship quality and feelings of well-being in the family, combined with analyses of concrete communication behaviors in parent–child exchanges, may guide us to a more thorough understanding of the process by which parents and their children adapt their relationship patterns during major developmental changes.

Sixty-seven children and their parents (47 two-parent and 20 one-parent families) were studied for $3\frac{1}{2}$ years; the children were about 11.6 years old at the beginning, and about 15 years old at the end of the study. To create comparability across families concerning communication behavior in family dyads, observations were conducted by providing structured discussion situations between parents and children and between husbands and wives. Each dyad was asked to discuss several statements printed on stimulus cards such as, "Some in the family do not clean up their room as they should." Each topic on a card was discussed for about 2 minutes. Discussions in these dyadic settings were videorecorded four times: when children were 11.6, 13, 14, and 15 years old. Topics on cards varied over time. The discussions were scored by independent observers from videotape according to categories describing verbal and nonverbal modes of communication (Kreppner & Ullrich, 1996). In addition, adolescents assessed the quality of their relationship with their parents every 6 months, in eight waves of data collection. Altogether, three dimensions were sampled: everyday dependability, emotional ambivalence (dimensions examined by Spiel, Kreppner, & von Eye, 1995), and intensity of discussion in the family (Robin & Weiss, 1980). In addition, all adolescents reported on their feelings of well-being in the family (Skinner, Steinhauer, & Santa Barbara, 1983).

Based on prior research by Hill (1987) some general trends of changes were expected in parent–adolescent communication over time. Foremost among these was an increase in communication formats indicating dissent between the generations in the family. As can be seen from Figs. 8.3 and 8.4, time-specific changes were indeed manifest in communication behaviors between both mother and adolescent and father and adolescent. In both dyads, a similar trend was found: Frequencies for parental communication styles such as "teaching" or "giving attention" decreased during the 3½ years, whereas frequencies for behaviors such as "negotiation" or "exchange of statements" (signifying affirmation of one's own position) increased (see Figs. 8.3 and 8.4).

As for nonverbal communication changes in parent–child dyads, the high degree of closeness shown in relationships with both parents during the first year of our data collection (when the children were about 11.6

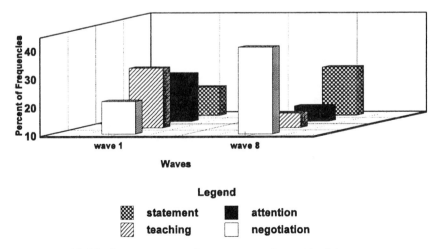

FIG. 8.3. Communication style over time: mothers with adolescents.

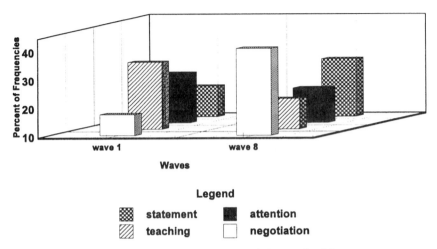

FIG. 8.4. Communication style over time: fathers with adolescents.

years old) decreased considerably by the time the children were 15 years old (Fig. 8.5). There were also changes over time in the nature of mother–father exchanges outside of the child's presence. For example, the exchange of statements between the adults in their discussions peaked when the child was 13 years old (see Fig. 8.6). Furthermore, the degree of tension between the parents during their discussions also peaked at about that same time (see Fig. 8.7).

As these results indicate, a family-oriented approach focusing on phenomena such as continuity and change of communication patterns and favoring the expectation that families have to find a new equilibrium that can

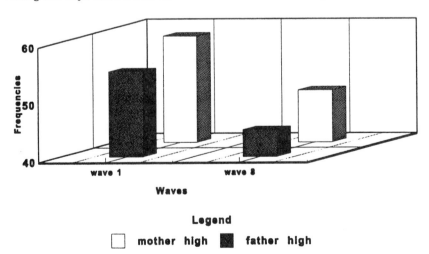

FIG. 8.5. High closeness over time: parents with adolescents.

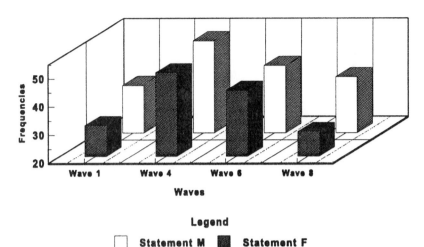

FIG. 8.6. Parental communication over time using statements in mother–father dyad.

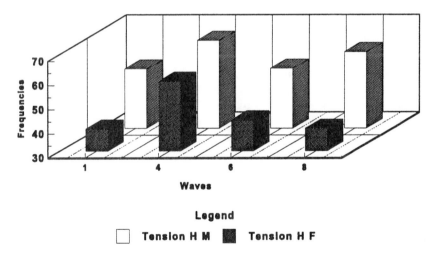

FIG. 8.7. Parental communication over time: tension high in mother–father dyad.

satisfy all members' different needs may carry us to a more thorough understanding of two intimately intertwined processes: family and individual development. If adolescents were considered only as individuals and researchers were concentrating on interactions between parents and their children, changes occurring within the parent–parent dyad would never have been discovered. As several contributors to this volume emphasize, it is only by using a family-systems-oriented approach including all relationships that such changes are investigated and registered. These results lend credence to the value of a family systems-developmental view.

Transition to Adolescence: Differences in Communication Patterns. A related investigation in this second study examined the effects of family communication on adolescent development. In this analysis, adolescents' assessments of the quality of their relationship with their parents were used as a criterion to distinguish among types of families. Three groups of adolescents were distinguished on the basis of having provided consistent responses over time on three of the relationship scales described earlier (see Kreppner, 1996, for details). These three groups described adolescents as showing *secure*, *habitual*, or *ambivalent* relationships with their parents over time. According to a cluster-group scale profile, adolescents in the habitual group showed average dependability, low ambivalence, and low discussion intensity. Adolescents in the ambivalent group expressed a much higher degree of ambivalence with both parents compared with the other two groups, along with average dependability and discussion intensity. Finally, adolescents in the secure group were characterized as showing high dependability with both parents, low ambivalence, and a high amount of discussion intensity. An over-time analyses of adolescents' assessments also revealed, in addition to these three consistent groups, two other groups of adolescents who displayed change patterns during the transition period. One group changed from assessments similar to the habitual group to assessments similar to the secure group. The adolescents in the other group went from assessments similar to the habitual group to assessments similar to the ambivalent group. These two groups were labeled as *consolidating* (from habitual to secure) and *dissolving* (from habitual to ambivalent). Adolescents' continuous assessments of their well-being in their families, a measure not included in the cluster analyses, mirrored different trends in the adolescents' self-rated experiences (see Fig. 8.8).

Differences in communication behaviors across groups were analyzed using log-linear modeling of cross-tabulated frequencies (Fienberg, 1980). Cross-tabulations of frequencies were conducted for every facet of observed communication (for details, see Kreppner & Ullrich, 1996). For each model, parameter estimates of contrasts between levels indicated significant differences.

The most striking changes in family communication were found for groups in which adolescents had rated the quality of the relationship with the parents as being consistently secure or ambivalent. In families of secure adolescents, fathers' use of statements in discussions (exchange of different opinions without a common solution) changed considerably over time. The adolescents, for their part, experienced this mode of exchange as connoting egalitarianism. By contrast, in families of ambivalent adolescents, fathers did not show such time-specific variations in discussing different

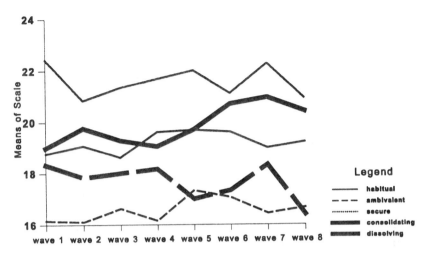

FIG. 8.8. Adolescents' self ratings: well-being in the family.

opinions, and adolescents did not experience the discussion as embedded in an egalitarian relationship (see Figs. 8.9 and 8.10). One interpretation of these findings is that fathers of secure adolescents sensitively lead their children toward a more adult way of discussing controversial issues, whereas fathers of ambivalent adolescents do not show this age-sensitive variation in their behavior.

To follow the two contrasting *change patterns* during the period of transition, parent–adolescent and parent–parent communication patterns of the two groups with dissolving and consolidating adolescents were analyzed in more detail. Findings revealed that in the dyad with their mothers, consoli-

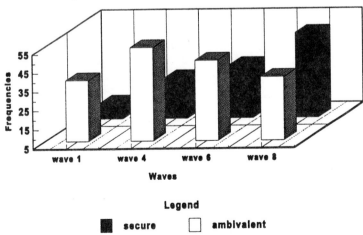

FIG. 8.9. Use of statements over time (constant group): fathers to adolescents.

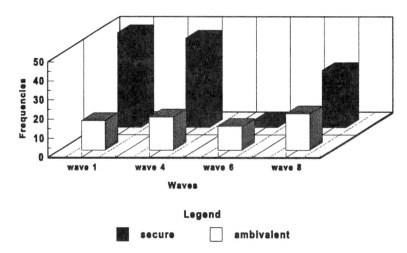

FIG. 8.10. Egalitarian communication (constant group): fathers to adolescents.

dating adolescents exhibited a higher level of integrating behavior, a better ability to regulate distance, and more compromises in their discussions than did dissolving adolescents. Fathers of consolidating adolescents also showed a higher degree of integrating behavior than did fathers of dissolving adolescents (see Fig. 8.11). Moreover, in discussions with their fathers, consolidating adolescents exhibited more "giving way" behavior than did dissolving adolescents (see Fig. 8.12).

Mothers of consolidating adolescents showed more integrating behavior during marital discussions with their husbands outside of the child's pres-

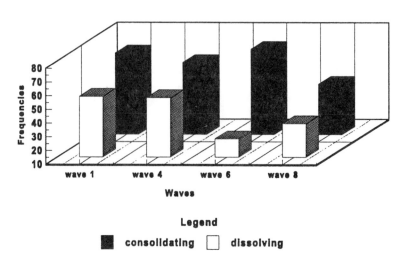

FIG. 8.11. Integrative communication (change group): fathers to adolescents.

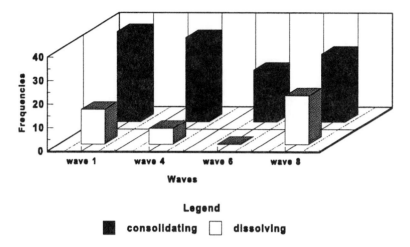

FIG. 8.12. Giving way in discussion (change group): adolescents to fathers.

ence than did mothers of dissolving adolescents (see Fig. 8.13), whereas fathers of consolidating adolescents exhibited more giving way behavior in these discussions with their wives than did fathers of dissolving adolescents (Fig. 8.14). These different communication climates, evident even during parent–parent discussions without the adolescent present, may have served as a communication model for the adolescents when time came to negotiate their demands with the parents.

In sum, parent–child relationships undergo considerable changes during the passage from childhood to adulthood. Families find their way through

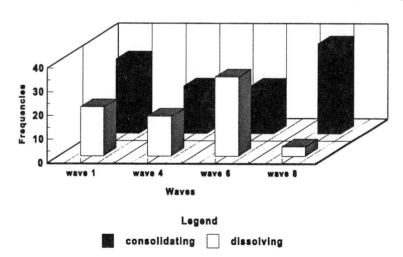

FIG. 8.13. Integrative communication (change group): wives to husbands.

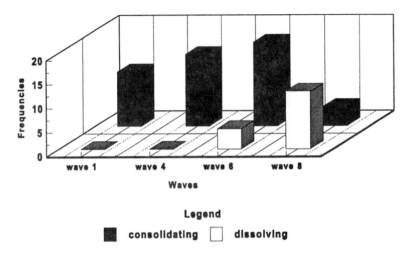

FIG. 8.14. Giving way in discussion (change group): husbands to wives.

this transition period, calling on diverse skills to adapt their communication behavior to their children's growing competences (Kreppner, 2000;
Kreppner & Ullrich, 1998). Families not only adapt their present repertoires
of communication skills when dealing with transition problems, but they
also differ in their flexibility to produce new communication patterns appropriate for meeting their children's changing demands for more autonomy and adult communication.

The different pathways through adolescence outlined here are not static
differences. Rather, they may represent two diverging developmental
trends in family development. Following a time of critical search and ambivalent feelings, adolescents either find a way to reconnect with their families
(as do consolidators), or become convinced that the only path to a new
identity is through leaving the family (as do dissolvers). From a systems
perspective, both modes are adaptive solutions in that they stabilize the extant family system, with or without the child.

PROSPECT: CONCLUSIONS AND A LOOK
TO THE FUTURE

A Perspective on Family Communication Emphasizing
Its Function for the Child's Mastery of Developmental
Transitions

Families are not just well-established groups of individuals with a robust
and never-changing set of intragroup relationships. On the contrary, families are more or less fragile entities that have to continually adapt to

challenges generated both by nonnormative events and by normative individual developmental processes. Families differ considerably in their ability to adapt to the developmental demands of their offspring and in their openness to finding new solutions to new life challenges in a manner that satisfies the different needs of all family members. Families attend to one another's needs and react to developmental changes in various ways. Differences in communication behavior are manifest not only in parent–child dyads, but also in parent–parent dyads. The different modalities through which parent–child communication takes place embody the ways rules, regulations, and values are transmitted inside the family. Moreover, as we have come to understand more about the relatedness between mother–child and father–child communication (e.g., Clarke-Stewart, 1988), the sophistication of our view concerning family effect on child well-being and on the parents' own development has deepened (Silverberg, 1996).

Future longitudinal studies must determine which aspects of verbal and nonverbal communication are most prototypic for the establishment of secure relationships within the family, and which support or impede development. Although warm and guiding parental behaviors and communication styles seem good candidates for facilitating mastery of this transition period, we still do not know enough about the developmental backgrounds and dynamics in family history that produce different qualities of family communication patterns. We have accumulated some knowledge about "transition-competent" families, but we are still far from comprehending the intricate details of communication contexts that directly or indirectly shape the child's secure or ambivalent feelings in the family. The prominent role of fathers in adolescent development, evident in some of the results described here, calls for more theory and more relation-oriented research. Good candidates for more intensive study include time-specific effects of communication exchanges within the family, the role of marital communication in shaping a common communication climate, and the flexibility of exchange modes in all family dyads and triads. The role of critical transition phases in adult development and their effect on the family communication climate in general and on parent–parent communication in particular must be explored further in future research. Upon aggregating this critical background information about communication and interaction practices within families, more concerted efforts are needed to ascertain whether there are any long-term influences of these family differences on differential developmental pathways.

Future perspectives on family research should continue to chip away at the differences in theoretical frameworks inherent in conceptualizations of family functioning and of individual development. Despite advances in recent years, the world of individualistic and psychological thinking about child development and the world of interactionistic and sociological thinking about the institution family remain too far apart to foster easy exchange. Lack of flexibility in creating variables that fit both frameworks, or in transforming variables from one into the other can only promote misunderstandings and distance between the different camps. This said, the progress that has been made is heartening.

A Look to the Future of Family Systems Research

It has been argued that family reseachers should operate with the guiding framework that families are institutions not only for the transmission of genes, but also for the maintenance and transmission of culture. The cultural diversity in family formation and in the organization of parent–child relationships can nonetheless be reassessed under a basic and perhaps even fundamental communication and systems perspective: Relationships between parents and children inside the family have to meet several universal prerequisites to secure the child's survival and to socialize the new member into the respective society. Of course, within this range of conditions, a wide array of possibilities in how these goals are realized is possible. However, although there may be multiple formats for a functioning family life, the need to find a balance, to adapt to the different stages of the child's development, and to convey meaning to the next generation can be regarded as general tasks that must be accomplished by all families in one way or another.

The following is a tentative guideline for future research in family and family development:

1. Family research should strongly focus on the *analysis of relationships,* their quality, history, flexiblity, and resiliency under stress. Nonrelational aspects, such as single members' temperaments, traits, or pathologies should be linked to the various aspects of a family's relationship quality.

2. In family studies, both *verbal and nonverbal exchanges* in a relationship should be analyzed. Exchange about objects, persons, and situations is only one aspect in the communication between two people. The other aspect encompasses the regulation of the relationship between two communicating people, its symmetry or asymmetry, and the range and richness of information that can be exchanged. Although both content and relationship are negotiated in both verbal and nonverbal modes, nonverbal information is crucial for gaining a comprehensive interpretation of meanings conveyed in verbal communication. Meaningful information needs a secure relational base.

3. All relationships in a family have to be regarded when research about families is conducted. By the same token, *all constellations,* such as dyads, triads, tetrads, and so forth, must be considered when relationship patterns

within families are investigated. As studies comparing dyadic and triadic interactions have shown, dynamics between the same persons may vary considerably in different constellations.

4. Family research should always keep as a working hypothesis the assertion that families are institutions in which, among other functions, the *production, maintenance, and transmission of meaning and culture* are central. Thus, future research should focus on the families' differential approaches to meet these functions, particularly on families' successful or unsuccessful modes to produce and transmit meaning across generations.

5. When analyzing communication and interaction within the family we should try to create more variables depicting *relationship characteristics on a molar level*. Microlevel analyses, useful for specific questions and elaborations, often lead to elementaristic and reductionistic interpretations of complex behavior patterns. Research should dedicate more effort to capturing an in-depth dimension when analyzing human communication.[1]

6. As a research strategy, family research could concentrate on specific time windows in family development, that is, periods when *transitions have to be mastered*. During a transition phase, the ways families handle different interests and divergent problem-solving strategies can be observed in full detail. Family-oriented observational investigations could help better characterize the modalities by which families negotiate their extant relationships. Under a developmental perspective, these studies could focus on families' initial attempts to keep well-established balances, on families' changes of strategy after some unsuccessful attempts, and on the family members' final struggle to reach a new state of equilibrium.

7. New methodological approaches are necessary. The follow-up of families through several stages of their lifetime has to take account of the modalities of communication during transition periods. Studies should be able to *segregate relevant from irrelevant* aspects. To achieve this, both larger representative samples and more detailed longitudinal case studies (located in larger samples) are needed.

8. In general, these theory-driven proposals for future research on families should be sensitive to the fact that conducting research with families is always a political issue. Family research is not just another aspect of natural science; it deals with a prominent societal unit that has borne and still bears

---

[1]This is a dimension that Lewin (1927) had labeled as "conditional-genetic"dimension in contrast to the "phenomenal" or surface dimension. By this conditional-genetic dimension he meant the dimension that unveils the conditions that create concrete behavior patterns that are then visible at the surface in different forms. Examples of such molar communication patterns could be varibles such as "capacity to transmit social quality," "model for guidance in a well-organized relationship," "potential for correcting misunderstandings," or "creation of meaning during exchange."

highly controversial political meanings. We must be sensitive to misinterpretations of our results being used to argue for or against specific ideologies. This is amplified when family research has something to say about prospect for the next generation's well-being. In a day of divergent visions, we need to remain aware that research questions that seem appropriate from a scientific perspective will be judged on the basis of societal desirability and political correctness. Ultimately, family as an institution remains a center for cultural identity and a place where old and new imaginations about the building of a future society may collide (see Parke & Buriel, 1998).

A Final Thought

A look forward seems meaningless without a parallel look back. I close by returning to two general perspectives formulated by philosophers discussed earlier in this chapter. Both emphasize the role of communication for the human species and underline the importance of culture. Both see communication and culture as quintessential components for understanding human nature and behavior. And both have criticized approaches in the human sciences as being too mentalistic and reductionistic.

The philosopher Vico made every effort to keep alive a tradition that seemed lost after Descartes and during the times of enlightenment and rationalism. In his book *The New Science*, Vico (1744/1966) argued against the extreme reductionism in Descartes' "cogito" as the only sign of truth for human existence. According to Vico, in introducing his "method of doubt," Descartes neglected all commonsense experiences constituting human nature—among them, historical traditions, jurisprudence, sciences of language, rhetorics, the arts, and political pragmatics. In short, he overlooked all topics in humanities based on human communication. The discursive production and maintenance of meaning, our main focus in family research, thus dates far back in the history of epistemology to an era of philosophical thinking fundamentally different from our current views on logic and reality. What's more, to understand the essentials of human communication, we could look to the period before Descartes, the time of early humanism and renaissance, when law and medical sciences were the prototypes for finding general solutions in the sciences.

The second philosopher whose thoughts remain relevant in the struggle to understand the meaning of human communication is Cassirer. In his famous *An Essay on Man*, Cassirer (1944) couched his humanistic perspective in a more general comment on the nonempirical and reductionistic character of the rational concept of human nature:

> The great thinkers who have defined man as an "animal rationale" were not
> empiricists, nor did they ever intend to give an empirical account of human

nature. By this definition they were expressing rather a fundamental moral imperative. Reason is a very inadequate term with which to comprehend the forms of man's cultural life in all their richness and varieties. (pp. 25–26)

If we accept the premise that families are the institutions in which meaning is produced for the next generation, in which culture is transmitted, and in which the skills for establishing and maintaining relationships and the arts of communication are conveyed, our research on families must address these issues. Happily, such research is already under way. Hauser (1999), for example, has attempted to identify protective factors that could open the door for new family perspectives with relevance for individual development. Moreover, the ongoing longitudinal work in Minneapolis, which follows children from their early attachment relationship in infancy through adolescence and into their establishment of romantic relationships during early adulthood, promises to shed important light on the effect of relationship quality during individual development (Collins, 1998). Moreover, family narratives have gained renewed interest in developmental psychology during recent years. Parents' manner of talking about their histories and families of origin constitute an important feature of the context in which children grow up. Coherence, interaction, and relationship beliefs may all provide inroads toward understanding families' communication contexts (Fiese et al., 1999).

It is inspiring to realize how far we have come since Descartes and his reductionistic cognitive solution for the explanation of human existence. Rich thinking remains alive in family science and is providing a more advanced and open vision of human beings in their interrelatedness with intergenerational and cultural contexts.

REFERENCES

Baldwin, J. M. (1894). Imitation: A chapter in the natural history of consciousness. *Mind, 3*, 26–55.

Baldwin, J. M. (1895). *Mental development in the child and the race.* New York: MacMillan.

Bateson, G., Jackson, D. D., Haley, J., & Weakland, J. (1956). Toward a theory of schizophrenia. *Behavioral Science, 1*, 251–264.

Bell, N. W., & Vogel, E. F. (Eds.). (1968). *A modern introduction to the family.* New York: The Free Press.

Bell, R. Q. (1968). A reinterpretation of the direction of effects in studies of socialization. *Psychological Review, 75*, 81–95.

Belsky, J. (1981). Early human experience: A family perspective. *Development Psychology, 17*, 3–23.

Belsky, J., Crnic, K., & Gable, S. (1995). The determinants of coparenting in families with toddler boys: Spousal differences and daily hassles. *Child Development, 66*, 629–642.

Bertalanffy, L. von. (1933). *Modern theories of development: An introduction to theoretical biology.* London: Oxford University Press.

Bertalanffy, L. von. (1956). General system theory. In L. Bertalanffy & A. Rapoport (Eds.), *General systems. Yearbook of the Society for the Advancement of General Systems Theory* (pp. 1–10). Ann Arbor, MI: Braun-Brumfield, Inc.

Block, J. H., Block, J., & Gjerde, P. F. (1986). The personality of children prior to divorce: A prospective study. *Child Development, 57,* 827–840.

Broderick, C., & Smith, J. (1979). The general systems approach to the family. In W. Burr, R. Hill, F. Nye, & I. Reiss (Eds.), *Contemporary theories about the family* (Vol. 2, pp. 112–129). New York: The Free Press.

Burgess, E. (1926). The family as a unity of interacting personalities. *Family, 7,* 3–9.

Carpenter, M., Nagell, K., & Tomasello, M. (1998). Social cognition, joint attention, and communicative competence from 9 to 15 months of age. *Monographs of the Society for Research in Child Development, 63*(4, Serial No. 255).

Cassirer, E. (1944). *An essay on man. An introduction to a philosophy of human culture.* New Haven, CT: Yale University Press.

Cherlin, A. J., Furstenberg, F. F., Jr., Chase-Lansdale, P. L., Kiernana, K. E., Robins, P. K., Morrison, D. R., & Teitler, J. O. (1991). Longitudinal studies of effects of divorce on children in Great Britain and the United States. *Science, 252,* 1386–1389.

Clarke-Stewart, K. A. (1978). And daddy makes three: The father's impact on mother and young child. *Child Development, 49,* 466–478.

Clarke-Stewart, K. A. (1988). Parents' effects on children's development: A decade of progress? *Journal of Applied Developmental Psychology, 9,* 41–84.

Collins, W. A. (1998, February). *Late adolescent competence in developmental perspective: Issues from a 19-year study.* Session held at the seventh biennial meeting of the Society for Research on Adolescence, San Diego, CA.

Cowan, C. P., & Cowan, P. A. (1987). Men's involvement in parenthood: Identifying the antecedents and understanding the barriers. In P. W. Berman & F. A. Pedersen (Eds.), *Men's transition to parenthood* (pp. 145–174). Hillsdale, NJ: Lawrence Erlbaum Associates.

Cowan, C. P., & Cowan, P. A. (1992). *When partners become parents: The big life change for couples.* New York: Basic Books.

Cowan, C. P., Cowan, P. A., Heming, G., & Miller, N. B. (1991). Becoming a family: Marriage, parenting, and child development. In P. A. Cowan & M. Hetherington (Eds.), *Family transitions* (pp. 79–109). Hillsdale, NJ: Lawrence Erlbaum Associates.

Cowan, P. A. (1991). Individual and family life transitions: A proposal for a new definition. In P. A. Cowan & M. Hetherington (Eds.), *Family transitions* (pp. 3–30). Hillsdale, NJ: Lawrence Erlbaum Associates.

Cowan, P. A., & Cowan, C. P. (1988). Changes in marriage during the transition to parenthood. In G. Y. Michaels & W. A. Goldberg (Eds.), *The transition to parenthood: Current theory and research* (pp. 114–154). Cambridge, UK: Cambridge University Press.

Cummings, E. M., & Davies, P. (1994). *Children and marital conflict: The impact of family dispute and resolution.* New York: Guilford.

Darwin, C. (1859). *On the origin of species.* London: John Murray.

Darwin, C. (1871). *Descent of man.* London: John Murray.

Davies, P. T., & Cummings, E. M. (1998). Exploring children's security as a mediator of the link between marital relations and child adjustment. *Child Development, 69,* 124–139.

Duvall, E. (1977). *Marriage and family development.* New York: Lippincott.

Duvall, E., & Hill, R. (1945). *When you marry.* New York: Association Press.

Emery, R. E. (1982). Interparental conflict and the children of discord and divorce. *Psychological Bulletin, 92,* 310–330.

Emery, R. E. (Ed.). (1988). *Marriage, divorce, and children's adjustment.* Newbury Park, CA: Sage.

Erel, O., & Burman, B. (1995). Interrelatedness of marital and parent–child relations: A meta-analytic review. *Psychological Bulletin, 118,* 108–132.

Escalona, S. K. (1973). Basic modes of social intraction: Their emergence and pattering during the first two years of life. *Merrill Palmer Quarterly, 19*, 205–232.

Fainsilber-Katz, L., & Gottman, J. M. (1993). Patterns of marital conflict predict children's internalizing and externalizing behaviors. *Developmental Psychology, 29*, 940–950.

Fainsilber-Katz, L. F., & Kahen, V. (1993). *Marital interaction patterns and children's externalizing and internalizing behaviors: The search for mechanisms.* Paper presented at the biennial meetings of the Society for Research in Child Development, New Orleans, LA.

Feldman, S. S., Fisher, L., & Seitel, L. (1997). The effect of parents' marital satisfaction on young adults' adaptation: A longitudinal study. *Journal of Research on Adolescence, 7*, 55–80.

Fienberg, S. E. (1980). *The analysis of cross-classified categorical data.* Cambridge, MA: MIT Press.

Fiese, B. H., Sameroff, A. J., Grotevant, H. D., Wamboldt, F. S., Dickstein, S., & Fravel, D. L. (1999). The stories that families tell: Narrative coherence, narrative interaction, and relationship beliefs. *Monographs of the Society for Research in Child Development, 64*(2, Serial No. 257).

Gottman, J. M. (1994). *What predicts divorce?* Hillsdale, NJ: Lawrence Erlbaum Associates.

Gottman, J. M., & Fainsilber-Katz, L. (1989). Effect of marital discord on young children's peer interaction and health. *Developmental Psychology, 25*, 373–381.

Gottman, J. M., Fainsilber-Katz, L., & Hooven, C. (1996). *Meta-emotion: How families communicate emotionally.* Mahwah, NJ: Lawrence Erlbaum Associates.

Grotevant, H. D., & Cooper, C. R. (Volume Eds.). (1983). Adolescent development in the family. *New directions for child development, No. 22.* San Francisco: Jossey-Bass.

Grotevant, H. D., & Cooper, C. R. (1985). Patterns of interaction in family relationships and the development of identity exploration in adolescence. *Child Development, 56*, 415–428.

Harold, G. T., & Conger, R. D. (1997). Marital conflict and adolescent distress: The role of adolescent awareness. *Child Development, 68*, 333–350.

Harris, J. R. (1995). Where is the child's environment? A group socialization theory of development. *Psychological Review, 102*, 458–489.

Hauser, S. T. (1999). Understanding resilient outcomes: Adolescent lives across time and generations. *Journal of Research on Adolescence, 9*, 1–24.

Hauser, S. T., Powers, S. I., & Noam, G. G. (1991). *Adolescents and their families.* New York: The Free Press.

Havighurst, R. J. (1948). *Developmental tasks and education.* New York: McKay.

Hetherington, E. M. (1979). Divorce: A child's perspective. *American Psychologist, 34*, 851–858.

Hill, J. P. (1983). Early adolescence: A research agenda. *Journal of Early Adolescence, 3*, 1–21.

Hill, J. P. (1987). Research on adolescents and their families: Past and prospect. In W. Damon (Ed.), *New directions for child development: Adolescent health and social behavior* (Vol. 37, pp. 13–32). San Francisco: Jossey-Bass.

Kafka, J. S. (1971). Ambiguity for individuation. A critique and reformation of double-bind theory. *Archives of General Psychiatry, 25*, 232–239.

Kantor, D., & Lehr, W. (1975). *Inside the family.* San Francisco: Jossey-Bass.

Kreppner, K. (1988). Changes in parent–child relationships with the birth of the second child. *Marriage and Family Review, 12*, 157–181.

Kreppner, K. (1989). Linking infant development-in-context research to the investigation of lifespan family development. In K. Kreppner & R. M. Lerner (Eds.), *Family systems and life-span development* (pp. 33–64). Hillsdale, NJ: Lawrence Erlbaum Associates.

Kreppner, K. (1990, October). *Differences in parents' cooperation patterns after the arrival of a second child.* Paper presented at the International Conference BABY XXI, Lisbon, Portugal.

Kreppner, K. (1991). Observation and the longitudinal approach in infancy research. In M. Lamb & H. Keller (Eds.), *Infant development: Perspectives from German-speaking countries* (pp. 151–178). Hillsdale, NJ: Lawrence Erlbaum Associates.

Kreppner, K. (1995). Differential experiences within the family during adolescence: Consistencies of relationship assessments and concrete communication behaviors over time. In J. J. Hox, B. F. van der Meulen, J. M. A. M. Janssens, J. J. F. ter Laak, & L. W. C. Tavecchio (Eds.), *Advances in family research* (pp. 103–122). Amsterdam: Thesis.

Kreppner, K. (1996). Kommunikationsverhalten zwischen Eltern und ihren jugendlichen Kindern und der Zusammenhang mit Indikatoren des Selbstwertgefühls [Communication behavior in the family and the development of self-esteem during adolescence]. *Praxis der Kinderpsychologie und Kinderpsychiatrie, 45,* 130–147.

Kreppner, K. (in press). Variations in children's perceived relationship quality and changes in communication behaviors within the family during the child's transition to adolescence: A differential approach. In J. R. M. Gerris (Ed.), *Dynamics of parenting.* Cambridge, MA: Cambridge University Press.

Kreppner, K., & Ullrich, M. (1996). Familien-Codier-System. Beschreibung eines Codiersystems zur Beurteilung von Kommunikationsverhalten in Familiendyaden [Family Coding System. Description of a coding system for the assessment of communication behavior in family dyads]. *Materialien aus der Bildungsforschung, 57;* 39 pages, 2 appendices.

Kreppner, K., & Ullrich, M. (1998). Talk to mom and dad, and listen to what is in between. In M. Hofer, P. Noack, & J. Youniss (Eds.), *Verbal interaction and development in families with adolescents* (pp. 83–108). Greenwich, CT: Ablex.

Lamb, M. E. (1975). Father: Forgotten contributors to child development. *Human Development, 18,* 245–266.

Lamb, M. E. (1976). *The role of the father in child development.* New York: Wiley.

Lewin, K. (1931). Der Übergang von der aristotelischen zur galileischen Denkweise in Biologie und Psychologie [Transition from Aristotelean to Galilean thinking in biology and psychology]. *Erkenntnis, 1,* 421–466.

Lewis, M., & Freedle, R. (1973). Mother–infant dyad: The cradle of meaning. In P. Pliner, L. Krames, & T. Alloway (Eds.), *Communication and affect* (pp. 127–155). New York: Academic Press.

Lidz, T. (Ed.). (1963). *The family and human adaptation.* New York: International University Press.

McGoldrick, M., & Carter, E. A. (1982). The family life cycle. In F. Walsh (Ed.), *Normal family processes* (pp. 167–195). New York: Guilford.

Mishler, E. G., & Waxler, N. E. (Eds.). (1968). *Interaction in families.* New York: Wiley.

Parke, R. D., & Buriel, R. (1998). Socialization in the family: Ethnic and ecological perspectives. In W. Damon & N. Eisenberg (Eds.), *Handbook of child psychology: Vol. 3. Social, emotional, and personality development* (5th ed., pp. 463–552). New York: Wiley.

Pedersen, F. A. (1975). *Mother, father, and infant as an interaction system.* Paper presented at the annual convention of the American Psychological Association. Chicago.

Pedersen, F. A. (Ed.). (1980). *The father–infant relationship.* New York: Praeger.

Pedersen, F. A., Anderson, B. J., & Cain, R. L. (1980). Parent–infant and husband–wife interactions observed at age five months. In F. A. Pedersen (Ed.), *The father–infant relationship* (pp. 71–86). New York: Praeger.

Piaget, J. (1937). *La construction du réel chez l'enfant* [The construction of reality in the infant]. Neuchatel: Delachaux et Niestlé.

Reiss, D. (1981). *The family's construction of reality.* Cambridge, MA: Harvard University Press.

Reiss, I. L. (1965). The universality of the family: A conceptual analysis. *Journal of Marriage and the Family, 27,* 343–353.

Rheingold, H. L. (1969). The social and socializing infant. In D. A. Goslin (Ed.), *Handbook of socialization theory and research* (pp. 779–790). Chicago: Rand McNally.

Robin, A., & Weiss, J. (1980). Criterion related validity of behavioral and self-report measures of problem-solving communication skills in distressed and non-distressed parent–adolescent dyads. *Behavioral Assessment, 2,* 339–352.

Rodgers, R. (1973). *Family interaction and transaction. The developmental approach.* Englewood Cliffs, NJ: Prentice Hall.

Rowe, D. C., & Jacobson, K. C. (2000). Familieneinflüsse: Anlage und Umwelt [Family influences: Nature and nurture]. In K. Schneewind (Hrsg.), *Familienpsychologie im Aufwind* [New impetus for family psychology] (pp. 32–46). Göttingen, Germany: Hogrefe.

Silverberg, S. B. (1996). Parents' well-being at their children's transition to adolescence. In C. D. Ryff & M. M. Seltzer (Eds.), *The parental experience in midlife* (pp. 215–254). Chicago: University of Chicago Press.

Skinner, H. A., Steinhauer, P. D., & Santa Barbara, J. (1983). The family assessment measure. *Canadian Journal of Community Mental Health, 2*, 91–105.

Spiel, C., Kreppner, K., & Von Eye, A. (1995). Die Familien-Beziehungs-Skalen, FBS: Bericht über die Entwicklung eines Screening Instruments zur Erfassung von Beziehung Jugendlicher zu ihren Eltern [Family Relationship Scales, FBS. Report on the development of a screening instrument for the assessment of adolescents' relationship with their parents]. *Diagnostica, 41*, 322–333.

Stern, D. N. (1974). Mother and infant at play: The dyadic interaction involving facial, vocal, and gaze behaviors. In M. Lewis & L. A. Rosenblum (Eds.), *The effect of the infant on its caregiver* (pp. 187–232). New York: Wiley.

Stern, D. N. (1977). *The first relationship. Infant and mother.* London: Open Books.

Stern, W. (1935). *Allgemeine Psychologie auf personalistischer Grundlage.* Den Haag, Netherlands: Martinus Nijhoff.

Sullivan, H. S. (1953). *The interpersonal theory of psychiatry.* New York: Norton.

Trevarthen, C., & Hubley, P. (1978). Secondary intersubjectivity: Confidence, confinding and acts of meaning in the first year. In A. Lock (Ed.), *Action, gesture and symbol* (pp. 183–229). London: Academic Press.

Tronick, E. Z. (1989). Emotions and emotional communication in infants. *American Psychologist, 44*, 112–119.

Urban, H. B. (1978). The concept of development from a systems perspective. In P. B. Baltes (Ed.), *Life-span development and behavior* (pp. 45–83). New York: Academic Press.

Vico, G. (1744/1966). *Die neue Wissenschaft über die gemeinschaftliche Natur der Völker* [The new science. Translated by T. G. Bergin & M. H. Fisch, Ithaca, NY: Cornell University Press, 1948]. Hamburg, Germany: Rowohlt.

von Uexküll, J. J. (1909). *Umwelt und Innenwelt der Tiere* [Environment and inner world of animals]. Berlin, Germany: Springer.

Watzlawick, P., Beavin, J. H., & Jackson, D. D. (1967). *Pragmatics of human communication.* New York: Norton.

Wiener, N. (1948). *Cybernetics.* New York: Wiley.

Wynne, L. C., Ryckoff, I. N., Day, I., & Hirsch, S. I. (1958). Pseudomutuality in the family relations of schizophrenics. *Psychiatry, 21*, 205–220.

Youniss, J. (1983). Social construction of adolescence by adolescents and parents. In H. D. Grotevant & C. R. Cooper (Eds.), *Adolescent development in the family: New directions for child development* (pp. 93–110). San Francisco: Jossey-Bass.

Youniss, J. (1989). Further thoughts on social construction in families. *Journal of Family Psychology, 3*, 61–63.

Youniss, J., & Smollar, J. (1985). *Adolescent relations with mothers, fathers, and friends.* Chicago: University of Chicago Press.

Zill, N. (1994). Understanding why children in stepfamilies have more learning and behavior problems than children in nuclear families. In A. Booth & J. Dunn (Eds.), *Stepfamilies. Who benefits? Who does not?* (pp. 97–106). Hillsdale, NJ: Lawrence Erlbaum Associates.

9

Looking Toward the Horizon: Present and Future in the Study of Family Systems

Patricia Minuchin
Family Studies, Inc.

The past decade or so has brought a relatively new kind of research into the field of development. In the early 1980s, it was possible to cite both the impressive accumulation of knowledge about children's development and the paucity of concepts and research concerning the family as an interactive system. That situation has altered considerably. The emergence in the mid-1980s of the *Journal of Family Psychology*, devoted to the study of the family system, is one important indicator of changing perspectives.

Despite the formidable problems associated with the study of systems, the period has been marked by exploration and expansion. Working from theories that recognize the complexity of interactive patterns, researchers have formulated studies that incorporate multiple methods of data collection, examine the connections among subsystems, and track the evolution of family patterns over time (see, for instance, Cowan, Field, Hansen, Skolnick, & Swanson, 1993; Fiese et al., 1999; Hetherington, Bridges, & Insabella, 1998; Hetheringon, Henderson, & Reiss, 1999; McHale & Cowan, 1996; Mikesell, Lusterman, & McDaniel, 1995; Parke & O'Neil, 1999; Ramey & Juliusson, 1998; Sigel & Brody, 1990).

During this period, systemic developmental research has grown not only more complex but also more differentiated. Perhaps this is a characteristic of most new paradigms. Family therapy, for instance, has moved since its inception from general discussions of systems theory and family functioning to family patterns in specific areas, such as drug and alcohol abuse, chronic illness, divorce and remarriage, family diversity, and the interaction between families and larger systems. In like manner, developmental research has moved toward particular issues and subsystems, searching for more detail and greater depth. Examples and references are necessarily partial, but any list includes the transition to parenthood (e.g., Belsky & Pensky, 1988; Cowan & Cowan, 1992); studies of two-parent families and of triads (e.g., Belsky, Crnic, & Gable, 1995; McHale & Cowan, 1996); childhood illness in a family context (e.g., Cohen, 1999; McHale & Pawletko, 1992; Nixon & Cummings, 1999); development and evolving relationships in divorce and in stepfamilies (e.g.; Banker & Gaertner, 1998; Hetherington et al., 1998; Hetherington et al., 1999); and the recasting of mothering, fathering, and sibling relationships in system terms, as discussed in this volume and elsewhere (e.g., Parke, 1996; Volling & Belsky, 1992).

At the beginning of the new century, the growing body of systemically oriented studies serves as a stimulus for additional research, but the challenge also comes from characteristics of the rapidly changing society around us: postmodern theories concerning the construction of reality; new visions of human possibilities based on neurological research, brain mapping, and increased understanding of genetic structures; and a changing social context that has created various family structures and new ways of defining what is acceptable.

In this part of the volume, retrospect and prospect have been considered both at the most general level of theory and research, concerning total families, and in terms of an influential subsystem, the siblings. With these chapters as baseline, it is possible to highlight important points and raise issues that invite further exploration.

THE FAMILY AS A SYSTEM

As the family is context for the individual, the culture is context for the family. Kreppner has drawn attention to this reality, underscoring what is perhaps the broadest function of the family: the transmission of cultural meanings and expectations to its members, particularly the growing children. That conception includes not only human, symbolic, western, and national cultures, but also ethnic subcultures within which families live, and the value system that is meaningful for a particular family. In this country we are, again, an immigrant society, and we need to be mindful that many children are living within a complex mixture, coping with the contradictions between their inherited family culture and the messages that come from the school, the media, and the peer group.

One of the major issues to be discussed later is the need to know more about children who live in the midst of multiple family systems; who are removed from their families and placed in foster care, or who are related to parents who have moved apart and established new families. These children are important to consider when looking at families as the transmitters of cultural values. They stand at the nodal point of interacting systems, needing to integrate differing views and expectations. Although this is a description of the human condition at all stages of the life cycle, it is particularly demanding for children who may need to process messages that are discrepant and that carry emotional freight. For many months, at the turning of the century, the nation watched while relatives, officials, and politicians fought over the future of a 6-year-old Cuban boy who had been pulled from the waters off the Florida coast. For any observer of the Elian Gonzales fiasco, it was clear the child was the unintended victim, while the battle raged above his head.

In considering the current state of affairs, with respect to studies of the family unit, it seems useful to discuss the general framework for continuing research, review basic points, suggest avenues for further exploration, and note the importance of periods of stability and change.

A Framework for Research: Focus, Freshness, and Methodology

As a statement of the necessary focus for designing systems research, the points presented by Kreppner (chap. 8, this volume) are basic. He highlights the centrality of relationships as the core of understanding families; the relevance of multiple subsystems in determining the overall patterns of the family; the conception of families as evolving over time, through developmental stages and transitional periods; and the focus on communication and interaction during different periods of the life cycle.

It is perhaps not accidental that, in his comments on systemic developmental research, Kreppner moves directly from material on early childhood to studies of adolescence. Family patterns and communication during the middle years, from about ages 6 through 12, are less clearly identified and are less discussed in the literature than are earlier and later periods. Yet, the family is involved in the child's relation to school, the child's growing capacity for independent thinking, decisions about increased responsibility within the family, and the extent to which the child's participation in peer group life is accepted and valued. It may be, for instance, that communication patterns between the parents, and between parents and children, go through changes, as their 8-year-olds become concrete-operational in their thinking, just as these patterns are shown to change in Kreppner's studies of adolescents and their families. There is, however, little research of this nature on families whose children are in the middle years.

The challenge of studying systems beyond the dyad necessarily pushes the field toward new methodology and variables. There are advantages to continuing the work with established dimensions: attachment, socialization, warmth and hostility as formative factors, for instance, and achievement, adaptation, and social competence as criteria. Yet, new variables invite fresh thinking. Several such variables are offered throughout this volume and this chapter, but Kreppner also suggests that it would be useful to formulate studies of the "depth-dimension" variables that shape visible behavior, such as the potential for correcting misunderstandings. Perhaps that potential can be seen as one aspect of conflict resolution in the repertoire of the family. But it is useful not to foreclose, not to appropriate new formulations into the roster of familiar variables before they have been held up to the light and played with. The potential for correcting misunderstandings is a feature of communication that differs from one family to another. Presumably, participation in these patterns provides a template for the developing child concerning behavior in situations that involve disagreements and may move toward conflict. How can this aspect of family communication be operationalized? Does it appear differentially in parent–child, spouse, and sibling communications? What does the child learn, and does this problem-solving orientation carry over into settings outside the family? At how early an age can this reasonably be studied? The example may not be compelling, but the mandate to frame questions and variables in a fresh way seems important.

Some basic features of general systems theory have challenged the field from the beginning to reframe the focus of research and the manner of interpreting data. The concepts of circularity and complementarity, for instance, are central to the systemic explanation of behavior, and they shape the nature of acceptable inferences. They suggest that cause and effect are not linear, that behavior is simultaneously the result of and trigger for other behavior, and that circles are thus more accurate descriptions of human interactions than are straight lines.

The challenge has been difficult for researchers to handle. For some time, the concept of bidirectionality has been incorporated into theories of family interaction, yet much of the research is still couched in terms of the search for cause and effect. There is a continuing effort to determine who has influenced whom, and to what mathematical extent different forces weigh in, using elaborate statistical formulas to hold factors constant and rank their influence.

Because the field has been primarily concerned with children, whose power to influence is generally more limited than that of their parents, the assumption that the forces are unequal makes sense. Yet, that fact must be reconciled with the equal truth that interactions are circular (a more inclusive term than bidirectionality), with all participants functioning as stimulators and responders and with the experiental and observable reality that all the forces in a situation operate at once, refusing to hold still in order to be evaluated sequentially. Sophisticated statistics are still poor representations of interactive behavior, and at times they may be misleading. It may be necessary to separate the questions that can be approached primarily in terms of adult effect on children from the questions that are most productively considered by looking at the circle of interactions. Finding ways to understand and represent complex family interactions remains a frontier for the field.

Periods of Stability and Change

The family life cycle, like that of the individual, is marked by alternating periods of stability and change. There is no predictable pacing or balance, beyond the flow of developmental changes in family members; families may be struck by unexpected disturbances at any time, and some families go through more periods of change than others. The only thing we know for sure is that the life cycle of any family is characterized by both kinds of experience.

Periods of Stability: Established Patterns and Homeostatic Mechanisms. Stability is not a synonym for tranquility. What it means, basically, is that the family has established patterns for relationships and coping. There are rules and routines for handling the events of daily life, involving specific members and hierarchies, and particular ways of expressing affection and dealing with conflict. The patterns are predictable and repeated. Whether they seem functional and desirable to observers, they are acceptable, or at least familiar, to family members.

When there are deviations, the family has its methods, referred to as *homeostatic mechanisms*, for returning the system to a state of equilibrium. In an earlier publication (Minuchin, 1985), homeostasis was described as an "error-activated process by which behavior departing from the expected range of a family's patterns is controlled, via corrective feedback loops, to reestablish familiar equilibrium" (p. 290). If the 12-year-old son brings home unusually poor grades on his school report, for instance, one family might ground him and limit his time watching MTV; another might consult a psychologist about his newly preoccupied and sullen air; another might sit down in a family meeting, during which the parents encourage the 15-year-old sister to be an active participant. In each case, the process is part of the family's attempt at self-regulation, aimed at returning to patterns that are expected and acceptable. For the most part, such mechanisms are adaptive, but they may also perpetuate behavior that is problematic. The homeostatic mechanisms may function so automatically, and so rigidly, that the family is resistant to change, even when circumstances demand flexibility.

Much developmental research assumes families are in a period of relative stability. When a study compares the effects of rigid versus flexible approaches to controlling the behavior of a 3-year-old child, the researchers assume families in the study are in a stable period, socializing their child through patterns that are repeated and that represent their style of child rearing. This is a fair assumption for studies that assess and compare families at a particular stage of the child's life. There is an important caveat, however. The sample may include families who are in transition—who have a new infant or whose household has recently incorporated a grandmother following the death of her spouse. These factors affect the way the family handles the 3-year-old at the moment, and that process may or may not change quality as the family settles down into its new structure.

At this stage of systemic research, it may be appropriate to note that, although the reality of stable and transitional periods in family functioning is generally known, investigators have not usually incorporated this knowledge into their research designs. They have tended to assume the family is in a stable period with established patterns of behavior, unless the sample was selected to study transitions. Assessing the reality of the family, as part of sample selection, would be an important, relatively simple principle in the design of future research.

Periods of Change: Coping With Transitions. When a family faces a new situation, it must inevitably go through a transitional period. During this process, the patterns of family interaction are not stable or predictable, at least for a time. The transition may be essentially developmental, such as the birth of an infant or the departure of the oldest child for college, or it may be an unexpected event, such as the move to a different city or a flood that destroys the family's home. No matter the specifics; the process of disequilibrium and adaptation is essentially the same.

In the flow chart of the transitional process, the sequence moves from the point of change through a period of disarray and confusion, to a search for new and more appropriate patterns that can become stable again, while honoring the realities of the new situation. In studying transitional events, it is important to remember that a period of uncertainty is part of the process and that data collected in the early stages of change may not predict the outcome.

In studying transitions, it may be useful to distinguish between transitions that have an immediate period of "crisis"—an abrupt change, such as the birth of a baby, a death in the family, or the remarriage of a parent—and transitions that have a more evolutionary trajectory, such as the move into adolescence. Kreppner's (chap. 8, this volume) studies of changing patterns over a period of years, as the child moves into adolescence, is an example of systemic evolutionary research. When a family must handle an abrupt change, however, the questions seem different. How do family members handle confusion and tension in the initial period? How do they tolerate ambiguity and mobilize necessary supports? How do they interact with each other, and how are the reactions of the children handled? Do families have different styles for handling the effect of sudden events, and do those styles have different implications for the long run or do various patterns work well enough?

There are models available for thinking about issues and variables in crisis situations. Rolland (1993), for instance, has created a psychosocial typology of life-threatening illness, noting that the challenge to the family depends on whether the onset is acute or gradual, and whether the trajectory is progressive or marked by cycles of improvement and relapse. Minuchin and Minuchin (1994), working with families of cancer patients, have noted that some families mobilize effectively at the point of crisis but have difficulty sustaining their efforts over the long haul, whereas others are shocked and disorganized at first but reorganize over time and are able to provide consistent long-term care. Families in such situations must also balance their protection of the vulnerable member with the acceptance of his or her autonomy, wherever possible, and must adapt that balance to changing realities during the illness. This is a challenge for adults in a family where the ill or disabled member is a growing child. Whether the crisis is centered on the illness of a child or an adult, however, the trauma is the business of the entire family.

With this orientation as a given, recent studies have probed the implications of disability in one child of the family, tracking issues such as the differential treatment of siblings (McHale & Pawletko, 1992) or the extent to which children with disabled siblings are more sensitized to family conflicts and stress than are other children (Nixon & Cummings, 1999). These studies, concerned with stable family patterns, mark an expansion of the field, but there is little available concerning the reorganization of the family when the illness creates a crisis. Studies incorporating the variables and processes that have been noted at a conceptual and clinical level would be a useful contribution, relevant both to the specific understanding of transitions in the face of serious illness and to more general understanding of family reactions to change.

In the developmental literature, there are assessments of children's reactions in situations of family change. Teti (chap. 7, this volume), for instance, reviews the work concerning the birth of a sibling. With rare exceptions, however, there has been little attention to the details of the *process* of adaptation, including the participation of all relevant family members. It may be necessary to gather such material through intensive case studies, combin-

ing observation and interview. Kreppner's earlier work on the reorganization of the family when a second child is born and Dunn's studies documenting how mothers do or do not include their firstborns in caretaking
activities with the infant move in this direction (Dunn & Kendrick, 1982;
Kreppner, Paulsen, & Schuetze, 1982). This kind of work should be extended. Studies of change over time are relevant for both crisis situations
and more evolutionary transitions, but they may call for different research
structures and forms of data collection.

THE SIBLING SUBSYSTEM

Almost any family has several subsystems. Some, such as those involving
the extended family of grandparents, aunts, and uncles, have hardly been
touched by research; others, involving combinations of parents and children, have accumulated a body of subsystem studies, reflecting the long-
term primacy of parent–child relationships in the field. Systemic studies of
sibling interaction are somewhere in between, slowly growing but characterized more by "prospect" than "retrospect."

Not so many decades ago, it would almost have been fair to summarize
the emotional component of sibling relationships as rivalrous and their relative development in intellect and achievement as a probable function of
factors such as birth order. Subsequent studies have provided more elaborate information, but, as Teti (chap. 7, this volume) indicates, the research
focused on discrete constellation variables has not been fruitful. Perhaps
that reflects the limited nature of the questions that have been raised and
the measures that have been employed. Nobody doubts the importance of
sibling gender, family size, or birth spacing and order, but the force of these
factors depends on family patterns: how the children of different genders
are perceived by the parents; how the siblings form a small society, with its
own rules for older and younger, male and female children; how roles and
identities are sorted out among the children; and how allegiances form and
function. We know almost nothing of the implications of such attitudes,
structures, and experiences for the developing child.

The body of systemically oriented sibling research is small. Most studies
involve very young siblings, and, when work is extended to include the family, it deals mostly with mothers. A small number of studies, including Teti's
work, has connected the quality of sibling relationships to the security of attachments to the mother, and to nurturant parent–child relations—a kind of
spillover from one subsystem to another. Questions inevitably arise concerning the attachment to fathers in these families, and, as the children
grow, the network of family alliances and coalitions as these affect sibling
relationships. Alliances and coalitions are versions, or perhaps elabora-

tions, of attachment. They describe the fact that members of a family may form special bonds with other members: a parent and particular child, a child and a grandparent, a child and a favorite uncle, for instance. These alliances are neither good nor bad in themselves, but they are likely to affect sibling relationships in ways that are currently unexplored. In a fledgling area, such as systemic sibling research, it seems advisable to take a bold stance, going beyond what is suggested by attachment, dynamic, or modeling theories to raise the common sense questions that might occur to any thoughtful person. What do siblings carry over from watching the interactions of the adults in their family? How do parents, together, shape differences in the way their children think about themselves? What coparenting issues appear for the first time when the family expands to more than one child: managing differential treatment? fairness? intervention in sibling play, negotiations, or quarrels? How do the issues change over time, or with the advent of a third child? What about siblings in single-parent families? stepfamilies? homeless families? foster families? gay and lesbian families? And so on.

Siblings as Observers of Adult Interaction

From their earliest days, children are watchers of the important adults in their families. In the process, it seems likely they absorb something of the way people relate to each other, even when children are not involved. This probability has not been investigated as a model for sibling interaction. The issue is not one of marital satisfaction, which has been a recognized variable in studying the effect of parent relationships on children, but of documenting specific behavior: how spouses (or other family adults) express affection, help each other, negotiate their decisions, and conduct their arguments.

The question of what siblings take in from observing the interaction of their parents, and how they act this out in their own relationship, is complex. It is possible, for instance, that the oldest child takes in behavior that has to do with authority differently from younger siblings, but that what is internalized is not a simple identification with one role or another for either child. Sroufe and Fleeson (1988) have suggested that children internalize varied aspects of the relationships they have participated in, including attitudes and behavior beyond their own roles, and that this complex internal model is carried forward into new situations. It would be useful to extend this concept through studies of what is observed and integrated of parent interactions by each of the siblings, and what is acted out in their relationship. This would require data both on the consistent patterns of parent interaction, as observed and described by each child, and the recurrent patterns of interaction between the siblings. Research of this kind is apt to be most fruitful with siblings who are no longer toddlers.

Siblings, Parents, and Identity Formation

The involvement of siblings and parents in identity formation warrants discussion. Schachter (1982) provided a useful starting point in her description
and study of what she called *sibling deidentification*, meaning the process by
which siblings actively try to be different from each other. The second
child, she noted, tends to identify with a different parent from the first
child, regardless of whether the parent is of the same sex as the child. With
this concept and finding, she challenged a cornerstone of dynamic theory,
which has posited same-sex parent identification as a normal feature of
child development, and she highlighted the relevance of siblings as a reference point for identity formation.

From a systemic point of view, however, one needs to go farther. Parents
project their expectations onto children, and they tend to see siblings, early
on, as having different personalities and filling different roles. From that
perspective, sibling deidentification is partly a matter of fulfilling prophe-
cies emanating from family adults, rather than a process driven solely by internal dynamics and the sibling relationship. It would probably be most accurate to regard the process as multidetermined and circular. A researcher
might make a start by assembling a family, when there are at least two children of an age to respond verbally, and proceed by asking the family:
What's Annette like? How did she get that way? What about Tom and Jarad?
How are they like each other, and how are they different? How do you think
of yourselves and each other? And so on. Recent work has drawn attention
to family stories created by its members, as these stories relate to family
functioning and child development (Fiese et al., 1999). An extension of this
idea to the realm of individual- and sibling-identity formation would be a
logical and interesting undertaking.

Differential Treatment of the Children

Differential treatment of siblings, as a research area and a question concerning "good parenting," is a complex topic. Siblings come in different
sizes and personalities, with different needs. Sensitive parents may have
general patterns for childrearing but they treat each child differently.
Though children are notoriously vigilant about "fairness," especially during
the middle years, Kowal and Kramer (1997) have suggested they are more
relaxed about the differential treatment of siblings than psychologists have
been. Two thirds of the children in their study, aged 11 to 13, did not perceive differential treatment; of those who did, three quarters thought the
difference was fair and justifiable on the basis of age, personality, and need.

When family structures are complex, as in the case of stepfamilies,
Hetherington et al. (1999) have suggested that the differential treatment of

siblings is most marked when one child is the parent's offspring and the other is a stepchild; however, the effects on adolescent adjustment, in this study, depended on a combination of factors. In general, assumptions about the negative effects of differential treatment are probably most justified when there are notable variations in warmth or hostility, involving evident favoritism or the scapegoating of a particular child.

The recent studies of families with a disabled child are also relevant to this issue. They are a reminder that circumstances may force differential treatment of the family's children, and that the realities are apt to reverberate throughout the system. These studies have reframed the issue, shifting attention from generalized judgments of good or bad to an assessment of family management, sibling relationships, and child development. This is a positive direction for future research, as well as a contribution to policymakers and clinicians concerned with handicapped children. An increased understanding of how families cope with the complexities of daily life in such circumstances, how they balance protection of the handicapped child with the encouragement of his or her autonomy, and how siblings are potential resources for disabled children would be of considerable social value.

The Coparenting of Siblings

When a family has two parents, they are, inevitably, a team, whether or not they pull together. It has been hard, methodologically, to deal with that fact, but there is little opposition to the idea that parents interact in the raising of their child, or that the influence of their behavior is not simply additive. Recent years have seen the emergence of studies on coparenting (e.g., Belsky et al., 1995; McHale & Cowan, 1996), as well as research probing the implications of family interaction in one- and two-parent families.

Ramey and Juliusson (1998), for instance, observed the dinnertime behavior of (White, middle-class) parents and their children (ages 6 to 12) in divorced and two-parent families. They found that the overall amount of social contact between parents and children was comparable in the two situations. Of the several points suggested by this complex study, two are relevant for this discussion. First, when both parents were present, they were equally active, dividing and combining their social contacts with the children; single mothers did double duty, filling in for the absent adult, so that the overall experience for the children was similar, in terms of social interaction. An important corollary of this point is that, if the study had focused only on mother–child behavior, mothers in the intact families would be seen as only half as active as single mothers, and the overall reality would be missed.

The second point concerns the parenting of siblings. Most families in this sample had two or more children, and the general principle that contact with any one child is reduced as the number increases was upheld. However, overall interaction with the group of children was similar. Ramey and Juliusson (1998) took a systems perspective in their discussion of the study, noting that a homeostatic mechanism appears operative in the aftermath of divorce. At least in this sample, increased activity on the part of the mother, when the father was no longer present, returned the family to a familiar state of equilibrium with respect to social interaction at dinnertime.

Research on the coparenting of siblings is sparse. To understand the interaction of parents and children, in a family of more than three people, it is necessary to go beyond each parent's relationship with individual children or with the siblings as a pair or group. The question is how the adults function together. Parents of two or more children need to accept and support their different parenting styles, as they must in relation to any one child, but they must also monitor their favoritism for different children, negotiate their different reactions to sibling quarrels, and so forth.

That parents have different ways of relating to their several children is inevitable and normal. What matters, it appears, is the rigidity of their patterns and the way they handle their differences. Concepts developed in relation to the coparenting of one child, such as the effect of hostile-competitive coparenting (McHale, Kuersten, & Lauretti, 1996), should be extended to sibling situations and elaborated as needed. As of now, there is little specific information, and this is an important area for future research.

LOOKING TO THE FUTURE

Responsible suggestions for the future must take account of social realities. There are at least two phenomena in American society that are the proper concern of family systems theorists, as well as developmental psychologists, and they have not been thoroughly investigated. One involves the growing number of children who live within complex structures. The other involves the extension of the average life span, with implications for the responsibilities of the middle generation. These are the issues of today and tomorrow, and they require attention.

Children in Complex Family Systems

Two groups of children find themselves in the midst of complex family structures: children whose parents have separated, divorced, or remarried; and children from multiproblem poor families and chaotic neighborhoods who have been removed from the families they were born into and are living in foster homes. The two groups overlap only slightly, because they usually come from different parts of the social grid, but they have certain features in common. All these children must relate simultaneously to two sets of people, even if legal and social decisions have placed them in a particular household, and even if, in some cases, the relationship to both sets exists only within the head of the child.

There is a useful model available for framing this kind of situation. More than 2 decades ago, Bronfenbrenner (1979) described the nested systems that compose the child's life space, labeling them microsystem, mesosystem, exosystem, and macrosystem. It is the concept of the mesosystem that is relevant here. Mesosystems refer to settings linked by the fact that the child is a participant in both and the people in both settings are concerned with the child's well-being. Bronfenbrenner was interested in the mesosystem formed by home and school, but the concept applies equally well to the families established around the child as a consequence of divorce, remarriage, or placement in foster care.

We can look to the future, in relation to these mesosystems, considering first divorce and remarriage, then foster placement.

Divorce and Remarriage. There is, by now, a considerable body of research concerning divorce and remarriage. Although various investigators have worked in this area, the progress, as well as the frontiers, can be illustrated by describing the trajectory of Hetherington and her colleagues (e.g., Hetherington & Clingempeel, 1992; Hetherington et al., 1998; Hetherington et al., 1999). Beginning with studies of the effects of divorce on young children, their work has paralleled the evolution experienced by many of these families: The children grow older, the parents marry and establish new families, the children acquire a mix of parental adults, and the stepfamilies contain biological siblings, half siblings, and stepsiblings.

Some generalizations emerge from this work that are useful for clinical interventions, as well as further research. The investigators have noted, for instance, that the quality of family interaction mediates the effects of individual vulnerability, family composition, and stress, and that the principles shaping the adequacy of adolescent functioning are the same in long-term stable stepfamilies as they are in families whose parents have never divorced—satisfying marriages, parent–child relations that are both warm and effectively controlling, and positive sibling interactions. At a more differentiated level, they have found that, in the complex mixture of stepfamily members, the people who have the most difficulty establishing an affectionate relationship are those who have no biological ties, whether siblings or parents and children.

This area of study has moved along vigorously and is producing interesting information. Nobody believes that family breakup is desirable, but the incidence is high and the trend will probably continue. It is important, therefore, to learn as much as possible about minimizing the human costs and maximizing the success of new structures, paying particular, though not exclusive, attention to the experience of the children. Three suggestions for expansion, concerning the extended family, the next generation, and the exploration of new variables, can be briefly noted.

First, it would be useful to construct a map of the child's life space that goes beyond the immediate family. How a child, or any family member, fares, it has been said, is a function of the balance between risks and resources. To fully evaluate the balance, it is necessary to consider central members of the extended family: grandparents, aunts and uncles, and noncustodial parents and members of the new families they may have established.

These family members may be supportive of the child in important ways and at important times; the way they function during periods of transition, in divorce and remarriage, are particularly worth intensive study. The extended system is not always harmonious, however. Conflicts are not uncommon concerning the rights of the extended family to visit and to remain part of the child's life. Sometimes these become legal issues, but problem solving and negotiation, with or without the help of professionals, are more likely to create a cooperative system and to serve the best interests of the child. We need both more extensive investigations and wiser policies.

Second, it would be useful to study the marriages and family systems established by young people who have grown up in these situations. Outcome is usually assessed in individual terms, and we know something about the postdivorce conditions and organization of stepfamilies that shape positive adjustments in children and adolescents. But what happens then? As adults, what kinds of systems do they establish and become part of? The question is not simply whether these young people do or do not divorce, but what they carry over to adult relationships and the tasks of coparenting, keeping in mind that they do not function alone but in interaction with partners who have a history of their own. A study of these new systems would tell us much about resilience, modifiability, and the necessary conditions for creating stable families, despite an erratic history.

Finally, it would be useful to develop new variables, including dimensions suggested by new social phenomena. Consider, for instance, the postdivorce structures created by gay or lesbian parents who leave their original heterosexual marriages to live within a same-sex system. This is a new social reality. It may be useful to maintain an open perspective for studying the child's interaction with the old and new families, creating variables that reflect the complexity of the models for social and sexual roles.

New variables may also be suggested by research findings. The study of stepfamilies described earlier, for instance, suggested that people who do not share the same background are apt to have difficulty in communicating; when they come together in a stepfamily, they do not understand each other's meanings as readily as people with a shared history. Kreppner's (chap. 8, this volume) discussion of culture and meaning seems relevant here, as well as the depth-dimension variable concerning the potential for correcting misunderstandings. Study of the differences among stepfamilies in variables such as these might be useful, both to predict the relative degree of harmony in family functioning and to help increase the capacity for meaningful communication when stepfamilies are in crisis.

Foster Care. Suggestions for the future study of divorce and remarriage can build on retrospect, but the systemic investigation of foster care is almost entirely prospect.

The placement of children in foster care is a major social issue, linked to the reality that the affluent society we are currently celebrating in the United States has, like many of our houses, its corners of shame. Many poor families live in violent neighborhoods, are prone to substance abuse, experience racism, are unable to advance economically, and are disorganized in their daily lives. What is most relevant for this discussion is that children from this population are removed from their homes in large numbers and placed in other families. Sometimes they return home; sometimes they linger in foster placement or are eventually adopted.

We have little systematic information about the experience of the child, the way the quality of interaction in the mesosystem affects the child's well-being, or the foster care policies that would be most constructive for the children and the families. There are dozens of unanswered questions. What do children of different ages make of it all? How do they handle the dilemma of mixed loyalties? the relations to multiple adults who may change over time? the connections and resentments in relation to new and lifelong siblings? What helps them survive? What are the differential effects of hostile, nonexistent, or cooperative relations between adults in the foster and biological families? Are there optimal ways to handle transitional periods?

It is not that we have no leads. A description of the foster care situation, for instance, based on training and consulting in foster care agencies, offers a model that is integrative; appears supportive of families; and takes into account the issues for the children of separation, adaptation, and development (Minuchin, 1995; Minuchin, Colapinto, & Minuchin, 1998). The model is based on the reality that the foster and biological families form a mesosystem, whether recognized or not. In many cases, they can be brought together by the responsible case worker to form a cooperative network on behalf of the child, exchanging information, discussing problems, and collaborating on solutions.

Where this structure has been implemented, it is evident that the two families can often establish a working relationship, and that there are benefits for the child and for members of both families. Given the traditional structures and attitudes of the foster care system, however, it is difficult to implement such a network as a matter of policy. Intensive study, comparing the effects of cooperative family contacts with the effects of families kept separate might be influential in shaping a policy that is psychologically sound. From observing situations in which cooperative relations have been established—and, by analogy, with the positive effects of a good working relationship between parents who are divorced but collaborate on parenting—it is reasonable to predict that this structure may reduce the trauma of separation for the child, shorten the time in foster care (thereby decreasing costs), and increase the possibility that reunification of the original family can proceed successfully.

Such predictions can be tested, and the findings would be important in terms of policy. To approach the many unexplored questions, however, it is probably necessary to study the situation at a more basic level. The method of choice may well be ethnographic. Burton (1997) has pointed out the usefulness of this method as a first step, when meanings, patterns, rules, and behavior have never been systematically examined. This is the state of affairs in relation to foster care. A move into the relevant community to watch, listen, interview, observe in the homes, attend court hearings, read newspapers and case reports, and gather information from the officials and case workers who make the decisions may be a daunting prospect, but it would be invaluable.

It would be remiss to leave this topic without noting that foster care is characterized by recurrent transitions, as children are removed from their families, placed elsewhere, and moved on or returned home. The transitions create an upheaval for everybody, not only for the child but also for members of the biological and foster families who must cope with loss, changes in family composition, and the repeated challenge of reorganization. Further systemic research on foster care must focus on transitional periods, whatever the methodology.

The Middle Adult Generation

People are living longer than they used to in modern America, and the life cycles of individuals and families are more extensive. Social realities suggest that systemic research must be extended upward along the developmental trajectory, continuing to focus on changing family patterns and the adaptation of the individual to new life stages.

The field is well along in studying the interaction between the concerns of young adults (marital relationships, careers, parenting) and the needs of their young children. However, with rare exceptions (see McCaslin, 1993), there has been little effort to consider the difficulties and coping strategies of the "middle generation"—people who are still responsible for their growing children but are becoming concerned for aging parents, even as they continue to cope with work pressures, household matters, finances, and so forth. Because there is little to draw on from the past, a commentary about future systemic research in this area is mostly a matter of raising questions. In doing so, it is useful to revisit themes that have already appeared in the chapter, including periods of stability, family transitions, and sibling relationships.

Periods of Stability. When middle-aged people are designated as the core of systemic studies, the first questions concern family organization. What subsystems are now central, and how can the relationship among subsystems be characterized? In the conduct of daily life, how are decisions made? responsibilities divided? conflict handled and resolved? How are patterns and issues different from those of an earlier stage: for families in general? for each particular family? Because the middle generation often holds positions of responsibility at work, how is the relationship between work and family managed? What determines the comfort and satisfaction of family members at this stage of the family life cycle? With so little known, it is time to build a body of work concerning family organization at stages of life beyond early adulthood.

Transitions. Middle-aged people deal with various transitions involving both their generation (e.g., job changes, moving, divorce, retirement) and the generations below and above theirs. Children move out and perhaps back in, marry or find partners, and produce children. Parents grow older and may become ill, incapacitated, or die. The middle generation often is, or feels, that they are the responsible generation, involved in caretaking, advice, decisions, and financial issues.

When new circumstances arise, whether within or between generations, how are the transitions handled? Who is involved, and how is that decided? How are intervention and autonomy negotiated, if middle-aged people are dealing with their parents or their young adult children? How do different families handle periods of immediate crisis, and how do they reorganize to meet new long-term realities? Models and mechanisms are available to study such situations; an identification of issues important at this stage of the life cycle would mark the beginning of systemic investigations.

Siblings. In middle age, relationships among siblings often become prominent again, and they take new forms. As people grow older and their children move on to build their own lives, the relationship to the "family of orientation" vis a vis the "family of procreation" may shift. Contact with siblings may become more frequent and important, particularly as new issues arise in the original family. How do siblings negotiate their roles in relation to the increasing needs of elderly or ailing parents? How much do they keep contact after the parent generation is gone? What does that depend on? Are the roots in early childhood? What roles do spouses and adult children play in facilitating or blocking contact among older siblings?

Some sibling-oriented questions concern carryover to the next generation. What is the correspondence, for instance, between sibling experience in childhood and the way adults relate to different children and grandchildren in the families they create? How do couples who have grown up with different sibling experiences combine their efforts and negotiate differences in relating to their children, not only when the children are young but also as adolescents and young adults?

Different Subcultures and Ethnic Groups. Though not specifically dealt with earlier in the chapter, a look to the future must include an acknowledgment of diversity. Studies of middle age in the family systems of different subcultures are rare. Burton (1996, 1997) has found that African American adolescents living in high-risk neighborhoods perceive midlife as a time of limited resources and personal despair, rather than a period of security and success, and they are not necessarily confident they will live that long. She has found, also, that among African American women, intergenerational patterns and the timing of transitions are different from those in the broader culture, so that middle-aged women have responsibilities for caretaking that are specific to their subculture. Such studies make an important contribution. For the most part, however, we know little about family systems involving the middle generation in different subcultures, and this area should be marked for further study.

AT THE HORIZON

The first issue of the *American Psychologist* published in the new millennium was dedicated to the further development of a positive psychology; that is, to an emphasis on "happiness, excellence, and optimal functioning" (*American Psychologist*, 2000). This is a message with implications for systemic research. The possibility of maximizing individual potential and pleasure in the coming decades may depend in large measure on what we can learn about the functioning and interaction of complex human systems.

To support such a mission, family-oriented research will need both to map the territory in greater detail and to advance our understanding of how the pieces fit together. In a sense, the task is reminiscent of the conception of organismic development described many years ago by Werner (1948). It is a matter of increasing differentiation—as the work expands into new areas and probes specific subsystems—and of hierarchic integration—

as we come to understand more clearly how the parts are organized, relate to each other, and fit into the whole. The goal is worth the effort.

REFERENCES

American Psychologist. (2000). Special issue on happiness, excellence, and optimal human functioning. *American Psychologist, 55*(1).

Banker, B., & Gaertner, S. (1998). Achieving stepfamily harmony: An intergroup-relations approach. *Journal of Family Psychology, 12,* 310–325.

Belsky, J., Crnic, K., & Gable, S. (1995). The determinants of coparenting in families with toddler boys: Spousal differences and daily hassles. *Child Development, 66,* 629–642.

Belsky, J., & Pensky, E. (1988). Marital change across the transition to parenthood. In R. Palkowitz & M. Sussman (Eds.), *Transitions to parenthood.* New York: Hawthorne.

Bronfenbrenner, U. (1979). *The ecology of human development.* Cambridge, MA: Harvard University Press.

Burton, L. (1996). Age norms, the timing of family role transitions, and intergenerational caregiving among aging African American women. *The Gerontologist, 36*(2), 199–208.

Burton, L. (1997). Ethnography and the meaning of adolescence in high-risk neighborhoods. *Ethos, 25*(2), 208–217.

Cohen, M. S. (1999). Families coping with childhood chronic illness: A research review. *Families, Systems, and Health, 17,* 149–164.

Cowan, C., & Cowan, P. (1992). *When parents become partners.* New York: Basic Books.

Cowan, P., Field, D., Hansen, D., Skolnick, A., & Swanson, G. (1993). *Family, self, and society: Toward a new agenda for family research.* Hillsdale, NJ: Lawrence Erlbaum Associates.

Dunn, J., & Kendrick, C. (1982). *Siblings: Love, envy, and understanding.* Cambridge, MA: Harvard University Press.

Fiese, B., Sameroff, A., Grotevant, H., Wamboldt, F., Dickstein, S., & Fravel, D. (1999). The stories that families tell: Narrative coherence, narrative interaction, and relationship beliefs. *Monographs of the Society for Research in Child Development, 64*(2, Serial No. 257).

Hetherington, E. M., Bridges, M., & Insabella, G. (1998). What matters? What does not? Five perspectives on the association between marital transitions and children's adjustment. *American Psychologist, 53*(2), 167–184.

Hetherington, E. M., & Clingempeel, W. (1992). Coping with marital transitions: A family systems perspective. *Monographs of the Society for Research in Child Development, 57*(2–3, Serial No. 227).

Hetherington, E. M., Henderson, S., & Reiss, D. (1999). Adolescent siblings in stepfamilies: Family functioning and adolescent adjustment. *Monographs of the Society for Research in Child Development, 64*(4, Serial No. 259).

Kowal, A., & Kramer, L. (1997). Children's understanding of parental differential treatment. *Child Development, 68,* 113–126.

Kreppner, K., Paulsen, S., & Schuetze, Y. (1982). Infant and family development: From triads to tetrads. *Human Development, 25*(6), 373–391.

McCaslin, R. (1993). An intergenerational family congruence model. In P. Cowan, D. Field, D. Hansen, A. Skolnick, & G. Swanson (Eds.), *Family, self, and society: Toward a new agenda for family research* (pp. 295–316). Hillsdale, NJ: Lawrence Erlbaum Associates.

McHale, J., & Cowan, P. (Eds.). (1996). *Understanding how family-level dynamics affect children's development: Studies of two-parent families* (New Directions for Child Development No. 74). San Francisco: Jossey-Bass.

McHale, J., Kuersten, R., & Lauretti, A. (1996). New directions in the study of family-level dynamics during infancy and early childhood. In J. McHale & P. Cowan (Eds.), *Understanding how family-level dynamics affect children's development: Studies of two-parent families* (pp. 5–26). San Francisco: Jossey-Bass.

McHale, S., & Pawletko, T. (1992). Differential treatment of siblings in two family contexts. *Child Development, 63,* 68–81.

Mikesell, R., Lusterman, D., & McDaniel, S. (Eds.). (1995). *Integrating family therapy: Handbook of family psychology and systems theory.* Washington, DC: American Psychological Association.

Minuchin, P. (1985). Families and individual development: Provocations from the field of family therapy. *Child Development, 56,* 289–302.

Minuchin, P. (1995). Foster and natural families: Forming a cooperative network. In L. Combrinck-Graham (Ed.), *Children in families at risk* (pp. 251–274). New York: Guilford.

Minuchin, P., Colapinto, J., & Minuchin, S. (1998). *Working with families of the poor.* New York: Guilford.

Minuchin, S., & Minuchin, P. (1994). The family's perspective. In A. Grieco, M. McClure, B. Komiske, & R. Menard (Eds.), *Family partnership in hospital care* (pp. 51–59). New York: Springer.

Nixon, C., & Cummings, E. M. (1999). Sibling disability and children's reactivity to conflicts involving family members. *Journal of Family Psychology, 13,* 274–285.

Parke, R. (1996). *Fatherhood.* Cambridge, MA: Harvard University Press.

Parke, R., & O'Neil, R. (1999). Social relationships across contexts: Family–peer linkages. In W. Collins & B. Laursen (Eds.), *Minnesota symposium on child psychology* (Vol. 30, pp. 211–239). Mahwah, NJ: Lawrence Erlbaum Associates.

Ramey, S., & Juliusson, H. (1998). Family dynamics at dinner: A natural context for revealing basic family processes. In M. Lewis & C. Feiring (Eds.), *Families, risk and competence.* Mahwah, NJ: Lawrence Erlbaum Associates.

Rolland, J. (1993). Mastering family challenges in serious illness and disability. In F. Walsh (Ed.), *Normal family processes* (2nd ed., pp. 444–473). New York: Guilford.

Schachter, F. (1982). Sibling deidentification and split-parent identification: A family tetrad. In M. Lamb & B. Sutton-Smith (Eds.), *Sibling relationships: Their nature and significance across the life span* (pp. 123–151). Hillsdale, NJ: Lawrence Erlbaum Associates.

Sigel, I., & Brody, G. (Eds.). (1990). *Methods of family research: Biographies of research projects* (Volume I: Normal families). Hillsdale, NJ: Lawrence Erlbaum Associates.

Sroufe, L. A., & Fleeson, J. (1988). The coherence of family relationships. In R. Hinde & J. Stevenson-Hinde (Eds.), *Relationships within families: Mutual influences* (pp. 27–47). New York: Oxford University Press.

Volling, B., & Belsky, J. (1992). The contribution of mother–child and father–child relationships to the quality of sibling interaction: A longitudinal study. *Child Development, 63,* 1209–1222.

Werner, H. (1948). *Comparative psychology of mental development.* New York: International Universities Press.

IV

TAKING STOCK

The closing part of this volume comprises two chapters that crystallize what the field of family research needs to be doing and why. Azar's contribution provides a tour through the quandaries and challenges presented to psychologists by the legal system, arguing that these challenges invite new scholarship and focused contributions that would truly make a difference in the lives of some of our societies' most distressed children and families. Rutter then provides a broad-strokes commentary on what psychologists have and have not accomplished, and he offers his perspective on the steps family researchers must be willing to take before their work can provide definitive answers to the powerful questions they have chosen to address.

In her chapter on the legal system in the United States, Azar highlights the relevance of family research in informing decisions made about families' and children's lives by the courts. In the judicial system psychologists testifying as expert witnesses have profited immensely over the past 2 decades from the intensive and productive family research on divorce outcomes. At the same time, work is needed to help understand the divorce outcomes of underrepresented populations, atypical custody arrangements, and the interaction of various contextual factors. By contrast, we are severely hampered by a dearth of incisive data on families and child welfare. Azar's review traces prevailing biases in the U.S. court system, both historically and at the dawn of the 21st century, making the case that in the absence of very specific research findings (what helps, what hurts, under what circumstances, and for what kinds of families), our investigations are of little practical use to decision makers in the court system. Areas in dire need of thoughtful research include circumstances behind and long-term consequences of both severed and preserved attachments in foster care and adoption, clearer definitions of minimally adequate parenting that can provide guidance when situations involving parental fitness and termination of parental rights surface, postdivorce domestic violence, adaptive outcomes of children growing up with gay and lesbian parents, and clarification of modifiable environmental circumstances optimizing outcomes in all of these areas. She emphasizes that our database is currently Anglo-centric and that parenting and family practices and outcomes need to be understood in context. As do others in the volume, she emphasizes the relevance of community standards, while noting that distinctions must be made between validating normative cultural practices diverging from the White, middle-class standard typically invoked by the courts and identifying critical thresholds above which even these normative practices lead to deleterious child outcomes. Not all enactments of cultural practice are normative, even within the culture in which they arise, and our field would profit from a culture-sensitive cataloging of forms of risk. Azar closes by offering a roster of content domains to aid in documenting culture-specific skills and competencies that she believes might help in defining minimally adequate parenting. Systematic data addressing the content domains she enumerates would provide a more thorough grounding for psychologists who may be prevailed on to give testimony that will shape the lives of children in the new millenium.

Rutter's closing commentary ponders what we have truly learned from family research, concluding that we still have a long way to go. He wonders why, if we have learned so much about families, there have not been parallel increases in the mental health of our children. He then challenges family researchers to do their part to assure that the findings they champion are bolstered by rigorous conceptual and methodological undergirdings. He reviews and offers palliatives to various threats to causal inference, among them measurement bias and criterion contamination, the fact that risk environments are not randomly distributed, the pervasive influence of third variable effects, and genetic mediation of supposedly environmental risks. He offers a primer in the key requirements for testing causal hypotheses, calling for high-quality measurement, qualitative and quantitative approaches to research, differentiation of person and environmental effects, and use of quasi-experimental designs, drawing both on findings from his research program and from others' programs. He underscores the reality that most risk processes involve chain effects. In discussing risk and protective processes, he points out that certain features carry risk for certain outcomes while simultaneously being protective against others, and that protective processes often arise from successfully overcoming risk, rather than avoiding it. Rutter then outlines what we do and do not yet know about resilience and goes on to pinpoint some of our most enduring findings concerning main sources of family risk, noting that we must be conscious of both child-specific and familywide effects. He closes with trenchant commentary on several remaining, enduring challenges family researchers must continue to grapple with, including the nature of mediation of environmental effects on the organism, when and how sociocultural contexts matter, whether the childhood years are all important, and whether family influences are indeed the key consideration. The final section of Rutter's chapter presents his take on where we go from here.

10

Family Research and the Law: Can Family Research Help Solomon? Contributions and Challenges

Sandra T. Azar
Clark University and
The Center for Adoption Research

Over the last half century, the legal system in the United States has been called on increasingly to intervene in family life (e.g., divorce, child abuse, domestic violence, elder abuse). In many of these legal interventions, psychologists and other mental health professionals are relied on as expert witnesses with the expectation they will bring scientific expertise to the areas of interest to the courts.[1,2] This expectation has afforded unique opportunities for psychology and related disciplines to contribute usefully to decision making that takes children's needs into consideration. It has, however, also presented major challenges as unique family-based assessment questions are asked of our scientific database. Until recently, the mental health field has focused on making judgments regarding the competencies of individuals (e.g., competency to stand trial), using models of personality and individual development and associated standardized measures. Although legal decision making with individuals has been fraught with difficulties (e.g., violence prediction; Grisso & Appelbaum, 1992), the newer assessment questions in

---

[1] It has been argued that the number of times mental health professionals are involved is not great, but that it is increasing, and, when the case is in conflict, evaluations may carry more weight.

[2] An expert witness provides the decision maker (typically a judge in family matters) with facts and opinions beyond the experience of average people (Stromberg et al., 1988). A person is qualified as an expert by virtue of knowledge, skill, experience, training, or education specific to the question under consideration (Bolocofsky, 1989). In family cases, this means training and experience with child or adult assessment and knowledge of the scientific literature around parenting and family issues.

custody work have frequently stymied professionals. Judges have asked difficult questions, such as the following:

- Can an infant who is 2 months old cross the country and visit with a noncustodial parent without damage?
- Can a mentally retarded parent adequately care for a child with special health needs?
- Is this child bonded to a parent such that terminating parental rights will do damage to him?
- Does this group of four siblings need to be adopted together or can we split them up and have them adopted separately without doing damage?
- Which of two parents is the "psychological" parent of a child?

Such questions have tested the limits of our field's models and knowledge base. Furthermore, when questions are asked about a family whose cultural, racial, or social class background is different from the mainstream of American culture, questions have been raised as to whether we have any expertise to share (Azar & Benjet, 1994).

Newer family research has shown more promise in being able to provide some basis for answering these questions, although as will be seen, it also has major limitations. This chapter will overview the interface between this research and the legal system. It first traces the historical roots of psychology's contributions to child custody decision making and highlights where family research has already made contributions. It then examines the gaps between what is known regarding families' capacities to parent children generally and what are more complex questions within the legal system regarding divorce cases. Contributions outside divorce (i.e., in child welfare cases) have been fewer, and the latter portion of this chapter addresses this topic. To keep the task manageable, this discussion focuses on one custody decision in particular: decision making around termination of parental rights.

In termination of parental rights (TPR) cases the discrepancy between the questions asked and our models and measurement technology may be the greatest, particularly when a family comes from an ethnically underrepresented or economically disadvantaged background. The fundamental question in TPR cases is whether parents' capacities have fallen so far below *community standards* as to place a child in significant harm—a question of parental "unfitness." Given that most child protection cases involve neglect, this question often requires a determination of minimally adequate parenting, a question not easily dealt with using current family research. The tensions produced by discrepancies between our expertise in this area and the needs of the legal process present opportunities for expanding our knowledge. In overviewing the issues here, it is hoped that a research agenda for the field might be charted that will contribute to children's well-being in an area where there is most need.

WEIGHING OF CHILDREN'S NEEDS IN CUSTODY
DECISION MAKING: A NEWER PHENOMENON
IN THE LEGAL SYSTEM

In the United States, the boundary between children's "needs" versus their "rights" in the court system has been a topic of considerable debate. There has been a shift over time within the legal system in its perspective on the relationship between the rights of children and those of their parents (Derdeyn, 1976).[3] In very early historical eras, parental rights were paramount and children were, for the most part, viewed as chattel. Parents, for example, could give their children to others to work off parental debts (Kadushin, 1967). Before the 20th century, fathers were automatically awarded custody of their children in divorce cases because the children were considered their legal property (Melton, Petrila, Polythress, & Slobogin, 1997; O'Donohue & Bradley, 1999). This idea that children were property and the fact that women could not legally own property precluded mothers from being awarded custody. (This also reflected an implicit assumption that men and not women were the wage earners; therefore, women could not support children.)

Over the last century, however, some specification of responsibilities to children began to be articulated. Custody cases in divorce began to consider more explicitly whether a parent would provide for a child's physical needs (use of a limited *best interests* criteria). However, even with passage of community property laws (where women were awarded property with divorce), women still rarely were given custody after divorce.

As the rights of women evolved, so did those of children. In the United States, the invoking of the *tender years doctrine* as the rationale for automatically awarding custody of very young children to mothers following divorce (1830) signaled a shift toward seeing needs besides those of basic survival as worthy of consideration. Even so, questions about mothers' morality and sexual activity could override the tender years doctrine and allow fathers to receive custody.[4]

During the 1960s and 1970s, the tender years doctrine was abolished in some states (although there remains a preference to award custody of very young children and infants to mothers). In its place, a best interests standard became popular (Goldstein, Freud, & Solnit, 1973). This standard placed greater weight on custody being awarded to the parent who could provide environmental stability—the "psychological parent" (i.e., the parent with whom the child had the greatest emotional bond)—and who was the least detrimental alternative. Questions about defining who was the psy-

---

[3]It might be argued that there has been a simultaneous shift historically, as well, to giving the concept of "childhood" itself special privilege and protection (Radbill, 1980). This privileged status may vary by cultural group, as might the range of ages over which it occurs.

[4]Chesler (1991) argued that if fathers choose to fight for custody even today, the power differential is such that they are likely to win.

chological parent, however, quickly arose (e.g., the child may have different psychological needs at different developmental stages, and each child's needs may be specific to that child), as well as issues around the contradiction between meeting psychological needs and providing environmental stability (O'Donohue & Bradley, 1999). Some states have turned to a more concrete *primary caretaker standard* (e.g., in West Virginia this refers to the parent who has invested the most in household management, including caretaking of the children—preparing meals, disciplining, taking children for medical care, putting children to bed at night, and waking in the middle of the night if they require care; Melton et al., 1997). This too can be challenged in that the performance of some of these tasks does not necessarily correlate with the intensity of a child's relationship with a parent.

In this same period, the *battered child syndrome* was first identified (Kempe, Silverman, Stecle, Droegmueller, & Silber, 1962). Statutes were drafted giving states the right to protect children from such harm by their parents. These statutes allowed courts to violate the sanctity of family life and make decisions regarding child custody, including removal of a child from the home, further eroding the primacy of parents' rights to make decisions about their children and opening the family to public scrutiny. Over the decades since, similar measures have been taken regarding children's rights in other care settings (e.g., outlawing corporal punishment by schools), and statutes have been modified to include various forms of maltreatment (e.g., exposure to domestic violence). This strengthened the idea that children had rights of their own, separate from their parents.

With these shifts, courts have begun to take a closer look at the quality of care parents provide children in making custody arrangements, as well as to impose punishment more readily for violations of children's rights to proper care (e.g., child abuse laws). This attention to children's needs has also occurred globally. With the passage of the UN Convention on Children's Rights (United Nations General Assembly, 1989) and the debate that has ensued regarding the United States' and other countries' willingness to follow its articles, has come even greater attention to children as having rights separate from their parents, and, consequently, a need for even greater articulation of their parenting needs. Broadening applications of child protection laws, increasing willingness to terminate parental rights (recent passage of the Adoption and Safe Families Act, 1997), and increases in the rights of other interested parties (e.g., grandparents) are evidence of the shift away from parents' rights to greater consideration of children's rights.

In participating in legal processes that have emerged with this shift in focus, psychology has taken on the responsibility of contributing its views on these topics. Decisions such as terminating parental rights now require an assessment of parents' functional capacities to carry out their role (e.g., provide adequate levels of nurturance, food, shelter, and supervision). In doing such evaluations, psychologists and other mental health professionals have had to go beyond their typical assessment roles (e.g., intelligence testing, personality assessment) and evaluate parental competencies. To do so, they have been forced to draw on existing models of children's development and parents' role in it.

This new role in assessing parental competencies tests the limits of our parenting models and forces us to reevaluate them. This examination has raised concerns regarding the adequacy of these models in guiding us toward answers to these crucial forensic questions (Azar, Benjet, Fuhrmann, & Cavallaro, 1995; Budd & Holdsworth, 1996; Grisso, 1986). In particular, we find ourselves faced with the complex question of whether such models are equally valid for culturally diverse populations or for families from lower socioeconomic backgrounds. This debate has coincided with similar challenges within our field more generally regarding the universality of our models of development and family (Kagitcibasi, 1995). Because our field's predominant models are the starting point for many psychologists' judgments, they play a foundational role in expert witness testimony and evaluations. If they are too narrow or flawed, their indiscriminant use in custody cases becomes problematic from a legal, not to mention a moral and ethical, perspective.

PAST CONTRIBUTIONS OF FAMILY RESEARCH AND FUTURE CHALLENGES

Family researchers have done much to add to the scientific body of work drawn on by expert witnesses in cases involving child custody. Their work, however, has primarily addressed issues in divorce and less so in child protection.

In divorce cases, mental health professionals play several roles both in legal processes affecting families and in the aftermath of the decisions made. First, psychologists act as expert witnesses in disputes over custody in individual cases. They testify either about general scientific knowledge regarding families and children, or, more often, they report on evaluations they have completed with a particular family, using their knowledge about families, parents, and children to interpret their findings and inform decisions.[5] Second, they also can act as consultants to parents on making their own decisions regarding custody arrangements (e.g., through direct service or in advice provided through the media and books). Finally, using outcome data from family research on the effects of legal decisions, mental health

---

[5]Melton et al. (1997) argued that mental health professionals have not been asked to testify often, even in divorce cases. Judges report mental health opinion evidence in 10% or less of cases, and only 25% of judges said they had heard such testimony in most contested cases and none reported receiving such evidence in more than three quarters of cases. However, other reports suggest this figure is increasing and when mental health professionals do testify, it carries weight.

professionals have shaped clinical and legal practice. For example, they have contributed through interventions to help families cope with the legal process and its aftermath more effectively (e.g., through alternative dispute resolution programs designed to make custody and other divorce decisions less conflicted; Emery & Wyer, 1987; Koch & Lowery, 1984; Sprenkle & Storm, 1983), through mandatory divorce education programs that teach divorcing parents about the effect of divorce on children and methods for minimizing its effects (Zibbell, 1992), through prevention programs in schools to help children cope better (Anderson, Kinney, & Gerler, 1984; Pedro-Carroll & Cowan, 1985; Stolberg & Garrison, 1985), through visitation centers for parents who are in such high conflict that they cannot safely transfer children back and forth between homes (Johnston, 1994), and through the use of family mental health consultants in extreme high-conflict divorces to arbitrate ongoing difficulties (Garrity & Baris, 1994). Although there is a growing scientific database informing these roles and programs, it is still limited for the types of ideographic concerns that often arise in custody cases (e.g., what pattern of visitation is best for a 4-month-old child?; Melton et al., 1987, 1997).

In divorce, most custody decisions seek to identify the better of two alternative caretakers (which parent is more optimal). Some limited work is available on high-conflict divorces and on cases where differences between parents appear to be larger. For example, some work has focused on differentiating for courts the distinction between the *labels* applied to parents that suggest risk to children, as with psychiatrically ill parents, and the *actual* functional capacities of such parents to avoid automatic and stereotype-based decision making. Less work is available to inform legal custody issues where children face significant risks, as in child protection cases, especially when they involve low-SES and ethnically diverse families. In these cases, the *minimally adequate* parenting capacity of one or more of the caretakers is in question, as is the potential for *significant* risk to the child. Below, contributions of family research in divorce are reviewed, followed by a consideration of the issues that surface in child protection cases and for which currently available family theory and research are less helpful and in need of more empirical work.

DIVORCE

The Negative Consequences of Conflict and Divorce on Children

The knowledge base on the effects of divorce and conflict within the marital relationship is substantial. Two seminal longitudinal studies have made major contributions (Hetherington, Cox, & Cox, 1978; Wallerstein, 1984, 1985;

Wallerstein & Kelly, 1980). Although both have been subject to methodological criticism (e.g., sampling limitations, lack of quantitative data), they have nonetheless illuminated the effect of divorce and substantiated a pattern of significant stress early in the process and ongoing influence later. These and other cross-sectional studies have suggested that the potential for negative outcomes exist in this transition, and that the continued conflict between parents is the most common family-based factor associated with negative child outcomes (Emery, 1982). In such cases, high contact between the parents (presumably through visitation) is associated with worse outcomes. By contrast, in less conflicted divorces, postdivorce adjustment for children (especially boys) is facilitated by frequent contact with noncustodial parents (typically the father).

Other factors cited as mediating the relationship between divorce and child outcomes include the drop in economic condition that divorce produces for women (usually the custodial parent), the effect of the strain of single parenthood, and the loss of one parental figure (Amato, 1994). All of these studies, however, have been correlational; thus, causality cannot be definitively established. Despite their usefulness in informing clinical interventions and providing global background for expert testimony, forensic writers have argued they do not speak strongly to the kinds of questions often asked of expert witnesses (e.g., determination of visitation patterns; Melton et al., 1997).

Prior studies have also largely neglected the consequences of divorce for non-White children (Amato & Keith, 1991). This is important in that the limited evidence available suggests the effect may differ by cultural group. On the basis of differences found in the effect of single parenthood on African American and White samples, Amato and Keith hypothesized that the effect of divorce may be less for low-SES African Americans. They reason that because one of the predictors of strain for families is the economic drop experienced with divorce (Duncan & Hoffman, 1985; Teachman & Paasch, 1994; Weitzman, 1985), and because there is greater economic strain on minorities in our society generally, the economic drop associated with divorce may be less of a change for low-SES families. A recent study, however, found that African American families where divorce occurs are more likely to move to a poorer neighborhood (South, Crowder, & Trent, 1998), suggesting the reverse. This effect was lessened, however, if the parent moved in with her parents. This fits with Amato's (1994) argument that the extended family support network typical of such families may provide a stronger level of support to the divorced, single, African American mother. More work is needed if family research is to be useful in divorce cases involving diverse families. This is an area of both current and future challenge.

Although some findings have appeared on differential effect of divorce by child gender, the findings on child age and interaction with gender and culture are more mixed (Amato, 1994). To provide fine-tuned information to the courts, more work is needed here as well.

Finally, prior studies raise questions as to whether evaluations of pre-divorce caregiving and parental adjustment at the time of divorce tell us much about later outcomes. Predivorce behavior (e.g., father involvement) may not predict postdivorce relationships with children (Hetherington, 1979; Turner, 1984), and because parents are in the midst of the crisis of the divorce, their present adjustment may likewise not be indicative of their more typical functioning or of long-term outcomes. This raises some question regarding the utility of such information.

Despite limitations, the work on the negative effect of conflict in divorce on children has spurred the legal system to develop methods of helping children (see Johnston, 1994, for a review). This has mostly involved methods for decreasing the conflict. Courts in many states now require parents to attend divorce education programs (typically short one-time didactic presentations) to outline potential problems children may encounter and ways to minimize them (Zibbell, 1992).

Some courts have initiated court-ordered treatment in cases where conflict is extreme. Mediation (alternative dispute resolution) strategies have been attempted as a way to settle divorce cases (develop custody and visitation plans). Such alternative routes to dispute resolution are designed to take the negotiation out of the adversarial atmosphere of courtrooms. These alternatives, however, have not been as consistently successful as hoped in decreasing further conflict, as evidenced by continued litigation of the divorcing parties and lack of improvement in parental and child problems (Melton et al., 1997). Thus, they may not have improved circumstances for children, except where conflict is moderate. In extremely conflictual situations, where ongoing contacts between parents during visitation transfers are marked by high hostility, supervised transfers have been ordered by courts. Visitations centers have also emerged that provide safe places for such transfers. We are just beginning to examine the effects of such arrangements on children's adjustment (see domestic violence discussion and Johnston, 1994).

Custody Arrangements

Father Custody

The best available data suggests that 85% to 90% of the children of divorce live with their mothers (Furstenburg & Cherlin, 1991). Based on the preferences in the assumptions currently operating in courts (tender years, psychological parent, best interests), mothers appear to be considered the better choice for custody. Some argue, however, that this is based on stereotyped perspectives.

Several reviews have raised questions about biased views that father custody is less adequate and therefore not in children's best interests. Although the quality of the available literature can be questioned (e.g., reliance on retrospective reports, sample-selection bias—mostly widowed and abandoned fathers studied), most reviews have concurred there are no data supporting the need for gender preference in custody decisions (Melton et al., 1997; Thompson, 1994). The data on father custody and on fathers in intact families suggest men are able to become competent in "maternal" caregiving while maintaining the brand of physical, rough-housing style of relating to children commonly seen among males (Melton et al., 1987; Thompson, 1994). The greater economic security typically enjoyed by fathers also appears to provide some advantage. Although not increasing the amount of father-only custody, this has led to greater consideration of joint custody arrangements.

Father custody in diverse populations has received less attention. Lawson and Thompson (1999) argued that the dichotomous view of fathers as good versus bad or nurturant versus uninvolved prevalent in the parenting and divorce literature is even stronger when minority fathers are involved. They suggest this is in part due to research focused solely on low-SES fathers and to stereotypes present in society regarding African American men (see also Silverstein, chap. 2, this volume). More work is needed on diverse populations to examine the question of father custody for such groups.

Joint Custody

Family research has shown that both parents are important in lives of children from two-parent families and that fathers and mothers make different, but crucial contributions to children's development. This work and other societal changes have fostered recognition in the legal system of how important it is to maintain relationships with both parents, and this has led to an increase in joint custody arrangements. In such arrangements, both parents retain legal rights and responsibilities to children, but the child may live with one parent (joint legal custody) or move back and forth between parental homes in a more equal arrangement (joint physical custody). Findings from research on joint legal custody suggest it has symbolic value but does not appear to change practices within families, whereas joint physical custody appears to result in more father contact, involvement, and payment of child support (Amato, 1994).

Although initial findings suggested either better adjustment or no difference among children in joint physical custody situations, there may be biases as to who requests such arrangements (i.e., better educated and less hostile parents; Amato, 1994). Also, if joint physical custody is undertaken merely to resolve custody disputes, it may not reduce ongoing conflict between parents and may thus lead to higher risk for children. The residential instability produced by joint custody arrangements may also be stressful for some children. A major contribution from family research would be to clarify the influences of parent, child, family interaction, and contextual factors (e.g., economics) in the success or failure of such arrangements. More refined notions of coparenting capacities (see McHale, Lauretti, Talbot, & Pouquette, chap. 5, this volume) may be of great use in custody determinations.

The Importance of Other Bonds— Attachments Beyond Those to Parents

There has been an increasing interest in legal situations regarding the preservation of contact with extended family and other supports. This has paralleled work in family research on the importance of relationships beyond those between parents and children. In some cases, this has resulted in case law that has pitted the rights of parents against those of other interested parties whose contact with the child may be in children's best interest. Although these topics are being discussed under the heading of divorce, they can also emerge in child protection cases as well (e.g., Should sibling groups be separated and adopted separately if this would be in the best interests of one or more of the children? What should be the legal standing accorded individuals with no biological relationship to the child, but with whom the child may have forged a meaningful psychological bond such as foster parents?). The two most noteworthy areas are the roles of siblings and grandparents in children's lives. Family research has only recently begun to address these two areas and more work is needed. Likewise, other forms of relationships where attachments can be placed in jeopardy and result in legal disputes are in need of study. These include *separations* of partners in gay and lesbian families, where a nonbiologically related partner seeks contact with a child, and the rights of foster parents. Although the latter is not a divorce per se, it has many structural parallels with divorce and thus is discussed in this part of the chapter.

Sibling Relationships. Siblings serve as a support network for and contributor to the development of children (Dunn, 1983; Teti, chap. 7, this volume). The question of whether damage will be done to children by separating siblings occasionally surfaces in divorce cases and often comes up quite often in decision making regarding the ultimate custody of children when parental rights are terminated.

Consideration to splitting up siblings in divorce cases can occur: (a) to avoid visitation conflicts between parents; (b) to sex match children with parents; (c) when children are divided into warring camps with reconciliation unlikely; (d) when siblings have been living apart already for an extended period; (e) when one child has a harmful influence on the other; (f) when one child, but not all the children, would have been exposed to danger living with a particular parent; (g) when disciplinary, physical, or emotional problems exist that one parent is better able to handle; (h) when no bond has yet been formed between siblings due to age differences; (i) when the adult who played a primary role (i.e., the psychological parent) in the child's life was different for each child; and (j) when a parent is partial to one or more children and rejects the others. Some of these, in combination with practical considerations (e.g., an adoptive home may not be possible for a special needs child but can be for the sibling; it would not be appropriate to make the healthier child stay in foster care for an indeterminate period), are the same conditions for splitting siblings in child protection situations. Although the best interests criteria should be used in making such decisions in divorce cases, in practice, decisions are made in a more haphazard manner. (This may be true in child protection cases as well.) In addition, although courts may not make such determinations initially when adjudicating a divorce, they may evolve formally or informally over time. Kaplan, Hennon, and Ade-Ridder (1993) provide a thoughtful overview of the potential costs of splitting siblings in custody disputes from a life-span systemic perspective. These costs include children being used as pawns in parents' battles, ambiguity in family boundaries, intergenerational coalitions forming that negatively affect children's ability to use siblings for support and coping (siblings are a source of homeostasis), role strain on children with conflicting demands being made on them, and practical consequences (e.g., financial support problems). They argue that these risks are great. Yet, despite these concerns, empirical work to guide decision making remains limited, and intensive research is needed in this area.

Grandparents' Rights. As with siblings, family research has begun to focus on the importance of intergenerational connections both to children's outcomes and to adult development (Azar, in press; Tinsley & Parke, 1984). Most states now uphold the right of grandparents to visitation with children once a divorce has occurred and when it is in children's best interests (Melton et al., 1997), although legally no special status is given to grandparents from among people who have developed a special relationship with children (Thompson, Tinsley, Scalora, & Parke, 1989). The triggering conditions for legal cases usually involve death, divorce, or parental incapacities, where contact with grandparents might provide children with some advantages. The legal question is typically the preservation of such contact over the objections of parents (i.e., balancing benefits to be derived by children over the costs of intergenerational conflict; Thompson et al., 1989). There are little data on which to evaluate such decisions.

Some writers have argued that the use of the legal system to resolve such visitation questions may even produce new forms of intergenerational conflict. For example, it may result in the imposition of legal parameters on family-resolution strategies and produce unusual imbalances of power (e.g., parents are typically less financially capable of fighting long court battles than are grandparents, which may force more unwanted and coercive resolutions). The long-term effect of legally imposed visitation on children and families has received little study. The outcomes of high conflict on children might be similar to those found in divorce.

Other Attachments. Children frequently have attachments with other adults in their lives beyond those who are their legal guardians. Until recently, these relationships were not given standing in courts. However, family theory argues that such attachments may be pivotal to children's adaptation; hence, severing these bonds may have negative ramifications. Two in particular are worthy of discussion: children in families headed by gay and lesbian parents where a breakup has occurred and children who have lived for extended periods with foster parents.

Recent legal cases have involved visitation and custody for gay and lesbian couples. Such couples are raising either children who are from a previous heterosexual relationship of one of the partners or children that one partner conceived through artificial means. The parent whose tie to the child is not biological may want continued contact after the breakup of a relationship or, in the latter case, even custody. In the past, he or she might have had no legal recourse to attain contact if the custodial parent objected. There are few data to support decision making on the effect of such relationship breakups on children and the effect of custody arrangements.

Although there is an emerging literature on the effect of being raised by such parents that may be helpful, ways to understand the effect of the loss of such attachments have not been studied. Ahrons (1999) has proposed that gay and lesbian families have kinship networks similar to those of African American families, operating outside the legal marital system. For these families, divorce is less likely to interfere with familial ties (see Ahrons for a discussion of this topic). She has also argued that because familial roles are more ambiguous in such families, children may be better prepared to accept the ambiguity inherent when families change their structure. Gender differences in reaction to loss and investment in keeping connected with one's ex-partner have also been identified as potential sources of differing reactions to relationship breakup, with lesbian couples able to negotiate this transition more easily than gay couples (Ahrons). Clearly, discussion in this area is very speculative and more research is needed.

Foster parenting is another area where custody issues have begun to emerge. More than 500,000 children are placed in foster care each year.

Many of these children are African American or of mixed racial background, have encountered significant maltreatment, and have mental health and physical health problems. Although many return to their families quickly after some intervention, some stay in foster care for an extended time before being returned to their biological parents or placed for adoption. Although there has been some concern that many children encounter multiple placements, others live with a single family. Children's bonds to such foster parents can become strong given the circumstances of their placement and the length of time they sometimes live in such homes. The nature of this attachment and the potential for problems should these bonds be severed by court processes (reunification with biological parents) has not received much attention. Again, this area is ripe for family research (see Minuchin, chap. 9, this volume).

Permanent placement of such children outside of their biological home should reunification not be possible has received some attention. Although studies have examined outcomes in adopted children, only a few have examined interactions in such families (Rosenthal, 1993), and fewer still have examined mixed-race adoptions. There is an emerging literature on adoption disruption, which can occur in 10% to 15% of cases (i.e., adoptions that do not finalize because of adoptive parents' difficulties with the child; Festinger, 1990). As yet, the factors most studied are case history (number of previous placements) and child characteristics (e.g., mental health, abuse history), with less known about the features of families that afford lower risk of disruption. Because courts make adoption decisions, being able to identify risky adoption situations may be crucial. This is another area where family research might make a contribution.

Courts are also creating a myriad of adoptive arrangements. For example, there has been some recent experimenting with open adoptions in child welfare situations. These are typically situations where foster parents become adoptive parents and children may continue to have some limited contact with their biological parents. (Open adoptions have also occurred in more traditional adoptions; Demick, 1993.) Some limited research is available on the outcomes of such arrangements (Berry, 1993), but more in-depth work with larger samples is needed, especially where adoptive parents are related. The nature of long-standing family relationships may have effect. Open adoptions that cross racial lines are also worthy of study (Silverman, 1993).

The "At-Risk" Parent and Divorce

As suggested earlier, some parental conditions can become issues in custody decisions both in divorce and in the child welfare system. Substance abuse, psychiatric illness, and mental retardation are all parental factors that have historically been seen as automatic risks for children and as grounds for legally questioning custody. These groups have higher than average involvement with child protective service agencies and greater risk of losing custody of their children. For example, it has been estimated that as many as 80% of mentally retarded parents will have their parental rights terminated once they enter the child protective service system (Feldman, 1998; Seagull & Scheurer, 1986). Substance abuse has also been found to be associated with higher levels of TPR (Famularo, Stone, Barnum, & Wharton, 1986).

Societal biases may affect judgments regarding the risk these groups pose to children. For example, within community samples, emotional disorders are viewed as the most detrimental to parenting when compared with several disabling conditions (e.g., criminality; MacDonald & Hall, 1969). Similar biases exist in the law. For example, Hayman (1990), discussing mentally retarded parents, noted that "from the perspective of the law, the mentally retarded parent is an oxymoron-in-waiting" (p. 1202). Decision makers may have difficulty transcending their own cognitive biases about these groups (Azar et al., 1995; Budd & Greenspan, 1984).

In contrast to the absolute judgments members of society may make about risk, a growing body of longitudinal family research has been providing data indicating more contingent risk statements are most appropriate. Informed by such data, courts now require not only that the presence of debilitating mental conditions be documented, but also that their functional relationship to parenting problems and child risk be established.

For each of the groups described above, family research evidence has shown variations in risk level and has suggested factors that courts need to weigh in each case. Links among diagnosis, parenting disturbances, and negative child outcomes appear to be more complex than originally thought (McCombs, Thomas, & Forehand, 1991; Tymchuk, 1992; West & Prinz, 1988). For example, among populations of mentally retarded parents in the United States are those who do provide satisfactory basic care (e.g., keeping children clean, adequately fed, clothed; Mickelson, 1947; Tymchuk, 1992). Indeed, with the exception of very low IQ scores (30–49), the absolute level of intelligence may not be systematically related to the adequacy of the care provided. Also, problems have not been found to cut across all areas of parenting (e.g., level of punitiveness, decision-making skills in child-rearing; Tymchuk, 1992). Within low IQ groups, it appears specific skill deficits, such as in problem solving, and contextual stress may distinguish those who show problems from those who do not (Azar, 1995). Heterogeneity of child outcomes have also been found (Martin, Ramey, & Ramey, 1990), further suggesting individual differences.

With substance abuse and other psychiatric disorders, levels of disturbances in parent–child interaction patterns depend on whether the disorder is in active phase (Jacob, 1992; Rodning, Beckwith, & Howard, 1991; Seilhamer, Jacob, & Dunn, 1993). Contextual issues associated with the disorder (e.g., strain) may be the greatest culprit in negative outcomes (Hammen et al., 1987). Drug abuse can be associated with increased marital discord, disconnection from social supports, increased violence exposure, and incarcerations or other separations (Wasserman & Leventhal, 1994). Each of these factors may need to be assessed. Type of disorder and context may also interact. For example, marital discord has been linked to problems in children with depressed mothers, but not in children of schizophrenic parents (Emery, Weintraub, & Neale, 1982).

It is also unclear whether heightened child problems are due to these ill parents' capacity to be a "good enough" parent or to genetic or other biological factors that may have exerted their influence before children's birth (Gottesman & Shields, 1972; see also Rutter, chap. 11, this volume). Furthermore, child factors may temper risk. For example, depressed mothers who enjoyed interactions with their children or received positive responses from them have been found to be more effective in sustaining positive interactions (Cox, Puckering, Pound, & Mills, 1987), suggesting that children's behavioral style or temperament must be considered. Fisher, Kokes, Cole, Perkins, & Wynne (1987), in examining competent offspring of mentally ill mothers, found that competent children more often have a parent (a) with a mood disorder as opposed to a schizophrenic parent; (b) whose disorder was not chronic; (c) whose disorder occurred later in the child's life; and (d) who, if lacking in a warm, active style, was balanced by a father who compensated for this lack in his interaction with the child. In assessing risk, therefore, this complexity needs to be considered.

Mitigating factors, such as parents' willingness and ability to actively participate in the treatment of their disorder (e.g., consistency in taking medication) should also be assessed. If two parents are present, the skills of the nonaffected parent and the nature of extended family and friend support should be assessed as compensatory forces. Low IQ parents with good supports appear to do better (Mickelson, 1947; Seagull & Scheurer, 1986). Also, family emotional climate affects relapse of disorders. For example, heightened criticism, hostility, and intrusiveness are linked to relapse (Brown, Monck, Carstairs, & Wing, 1962).

In summary, where parents have cognitive impairments or psychiatric disorder, or have problems with substance abuse, family research is beginning to articulate contingent statements of risk. Unfortunately, our database varies greatly in how well it provides a basis for making such statements. At this point, it is crucial for expert witnesses to identify exactly which parenting capacities were compromised in the past (e.g., self-regulation, ability to maintain a consistent and helpful social support network, poor modeling of social conventions through criminal activities) and to determine whether these abilities have remained and will continue to remain compromised in the future. Essentially, using family research, expert witnesses must interpret the more fine-grained meaning of risk (e.g., interactive effects, effects over time) and the multitude of other factors that may exacerbate or temper the risk of parental diagnosis. Judgments should be based on empirical data with a statement as to its strength. Overall, family research has shown that answering these functional questions is much harder than the court might presume.

Gay and Lesbian Parents

One group of parents who have been subjected to extraordinary bias regarding their competency are gay and lesbian parents. There are strongly held societal beliefs that "risk" is inherent in their parenting of children, and these ingrained belief sets may increase the likelihood that risk will be raised as an issue in a divorce case. Family researchers have much work to do here, though some relevant evidence has begun to emerge (Falk, 1989). Cross-sectional studies have suggested that the sex role development of children of homosexual single parents does not differ from that of children of heterosexual single parents (Patterson, 1992). This work has focused on lesbian parents, and we know less about fathers (see Silverstein, chap. 2, this volume). Longitudinal studies have yet to be done.

Domestic Violence

Domestic violence has emerged as a major social problem over the last 3 decades. Early research on domestic violence concentrated on treatment and work with female survivors of such violence. Because women often entered domestic violence shelters with their children, a focus on the family as a whole, however, quickly occurred. A family literature has emerged regarding the direct and indirect consequences of exposure to domestic violence to children. At first this work produced important, but global, findings. For example, an overlap between battering and child abuse was found. That is, child abuse is committed at high rates by both batterers (between 47% and 54%) and victims of battering (between 28% and 35%) (Saunders, 1994). Then, more specific data emerged regarding the negative psychological effect of exposure to domestic violence on children. Such exposure alone has been associated with heightened levels of both internalizing and externalizing behavioral problems in children, although variations in outcomes have been observed that depend on child age, gender, appraisal of the conflict, level of involvement in disputes, and co-occurrence of other violence such as child abuse (Fantuzzo, 1999; Margolin, 1998). Little is known about ethnic differences in the effects found.

Based on this work, child protective service agencies and courts have begun to ask questions about children's continued risk of violence exposure after divorce, and domestic violence exposure is now seen as a child protection issue. Longitudinal work with families has started to provide critical information in this area. Recidivism in domestic violence appears high (rates of cessation over 2-year periods have been shown to be only 20%; Quigley & Leonard, 1996, to 40%; Aldarondo & Sugarman, 1996). Predictors of recidivism include severity of marital discord, severity and frequency of marital violence, chronicity or stability of prior violence, and level of psychological aggression the husband exhibits toward the wife. This database provides some guidance for informing courts of the risks involved in continued contact with a violent parent. Because studies involve small samples, interpretations at this point can only be offered cautiously.

CHILD PROTECTION—TERMINATION OF PARENTAL RIGHTS AND FAMILY DIVERSITY

When children have been removed from parental custody because of child protection concerns and the parent has failed to make use of or benefit from provided services (i.e., no evidence of improved parental competency or of decreased potential for violence), the social service agency involved may file in court to TPR). In most states, the parent will no longer have contact with the child if such a ruling occurs, though in some cases parents may be permitted to have limited contact or information (e.g., receiving yearly pictures, or, in recent mediation efforts, being allowed a limited number of visits). An extended family member may also adopt the child and hence regular, ongoing contact may occur. Children may also recontact parents once they reach adulthood. Minority and low-SES parents constitute a high proportion of child maltreatment cases and they are therefore probably overrepresented among TPR cases (American Humane Association, 1985; Lindholm & Willey, 1986). This fact represents unique challenges to expert testimony that will be highlighted as family research's contributions to this topic are discussed.

Termination of parental rights typically involves two questions where family research may be relevant: whether parental *unfitness* exists that has shown itself to be unamenable to intervention and whether TPR is in the best interests of the children (Melton et al., 1997). Certain categories of parental conditions legally allow courts to consider terminating parental rights (e.g., mental deficiency, mental illness; Grisso, 1986), but their presence alone is not enough to constitute legal grounds for TPR. It is incumbent on petitioners to show that the parent's condition significantly affects the child's welfare. Such dispositional questions ultimately require determinations of parental competency (or *fitness* in legal terms) and prediction of risk for violence and maladaptive parenting behavior. Such questions are problematic given our current models, knowledge base, and the availability of valid family and parenting assessment methods (Azar, Lauretti, & Loding, 1998; Budd & Holdsworth, 1996; Grisso, 1986). Moreover, long-term outcomes of children who have been permanently removed from parental custody have not been studied. Thus, answers to questions about whether termination is in the best interest of children currently do not proceed from a strong scientific foundation.

Thresholds for Reporting Maltreatment— The Question of Defining What Is Harmful

In child protection cases, an initial determination of parental fitness and child risk occurs early on—in the reporting process, when an initial determination of significant risk of harm to children gets made and children are removed from the parents' home. It is the continuation of this risk level over a significant period that leads to TPR decisions.

Although we know at gross levels what is harmful to children (e.g., breaking bones), the threshold for determining more subtle forms of harm can sometimes be open to question, especially in neglect (the most common form of maltreatment). The focus of family research has been on optimal parenting, not minimally adequate parenting. The notion that there can be a range of potentially optimal environments can be found throughout developmental theory (e.g., Hartmann's, 1958, "average expectable environments" and Winnicott's, 1958, 1965, "good enough" environment). Only recently, however, has the idea that diverse environments may all lead to adequate child outcomes been discussed in the literature (e.g., in the literature on at-risk children; Cicchetti & Lynch, 1995). Scarr and McCartney (1983), for example, have argued for specification of a range of environments that provide "functionally equivalent" opportunities for adequate development. They have also emphasized the built-in rectifying capacities in children, especially young children, to overcome many environmental challenges. Specific components of such environments have yet to be outlined, and the outer limits of their range have not been specified (Baumrind, 1993). These discussions may ultimately, however, result in more refined models that are useful for the legal process.

Furthermore, family research has begun to recognize ethnic, racial, and class differences in parenting practices (Azar & Benjet, 1994; Azar & Cote, in press). Thresholds for labeling such behavior as abusive or neglectful may vary with the group under consideration. For example, certain acts may be viewed by any culture as abusive or neglectful, whereas others may not. Relying on sibling care of young children (e.g., 8-year-olds caring for siblings), for example, is common in many cultures (Korbin, 1994), but it is viewed as risky in the United States and often labeled as neglect. These differences may color how fit parenting is defined and whether children are seen as at significant risk of harm.

Maltreatment also often coincides with a series of events, any one of which might derail development (e.g., poverty, domestic violence) or act in a compensatory way (e.g., nonperpetrator parent's supportive reactions). Although family systems perspectives consider contextual factors as relevant in understanding family functioning, courts may weigh them differently or not at all in decision making. Definitions of fit parenting may vary with these contextual factors and a universal community standard may not be possible.

Inadequate Models and a Narrow Database of Knowledge

The biggest problem faced by expert witnesses in defining fit parenting is the uneven coverage and limited database on diverse groups in our current models. We are thus constrained in our ability to define crucial domains for the measurement or development of a continuum along which parenting might be placed, and we may be ultimately hampered in our ability to specify predictive models for future harm to children. Furthermore, the ideographic questions that come up in TPR cases demand flexibility on the part of evaluators in positing relevant dimensions to evaluate. Our current theorizing does not typically outline functional links between parental capacities and children's responses. Hence, determining fitness requires understanding a specific parent's capacities and determining how they match both *community standards* and the needs of a *specific* child. This is especially important in that children in TPR cases often have special needs above those of the average child. Family-based researchers are in the best position to develop such process-oriented models, but our research is only beginning to consider the critical issue of parent–child match (Azar & Olsen, in press; Blaher, 1984). In this work, Vygotskyian (1934) and cognitive behavioral approaches may be the most useful models.

Early Models. Complex models of parenting are a relatively new addition to the psychology literature (Azar, 1991).[6] Two categories of models have evolved: developmental models, which articulate the origins of normal development, and clinical models, which are designed to understand the occurrence of maladaptive parenting (i.e., child abuse and neglectful

---

[6]Parke and Buriel (1998) argued that the early models of socialization were "grand" models (based in psychoanalytic or behavioral theorizing) and that such models fell into disfavor and were replaced by mini-models of areas of development.

parenting). Developmental models focus on parents' role in socialization (i.e., the process whereby an individual's standards, motives, attitudes, and behaviors are changed to conform to those seen as desirable and appropriate for his or her present and future role in any society; Parke & Buriel, 1998). Clinical models delineate predictors of extreme aberrant parental behavior (e.g., use of violence) and their consequences to children. These two types of models provide at best a limited understanding of the full range of what is required to parent competently in general and may be limited when it comes to understanding parents from diverse backgrounds (Azar & Benjet, 1994).

Early models have taken two approaches: (a) posing dimensions on which parents vary or (b) positing typologies. Dimensional models typically delineate narrow domains of parental behavior defining optimal parenting (e.g., use of positive affection) or specific risk (e.g., violent parental behavior), but not the full range of ways parenting may fail (e.g., lack of supervision, neglect of medical care). Developmental models also typically focus on predictors of specific but equally narrow child outcomes (e.g., academic achievement). The socialization goals posited are typically what LeVine (1974) called self-actualizing goals (e.g., fostering behavioral capabilities for maximizing cultural specific values—morality, autonomy, achievement), rather than survival goals (e.g., promoting the physical survival and health of children) or economic goals (e.g., promotion of skills that foster economic self-maintenance). These models typically emphasize individually based outcomes, not group-oriented outcomes (e.g., capacities for operating successfully independently instead of goals that bring honor to one's ancestors and that prioritize the meeting of group goals).

In 1964, Becker noted that the two most common dimensions on which parents have been evaluated in the developmental literature are *warmth-hostility* and *control*. He discussed how these are linked to better or poorer child outcomes. Little has changed in the years since in how we think about key parenting dimensions. Parenting typologies, in contrast, have typically outlined categories that involve combinations of narrow-band socialization practices and that predict specific child outcomes (such as self-reliance). These, too, have been oriented more to individual outcomes and to self-actualizing goals. For example, Baumrind (1970) identified three parenting styles (authoritative, authoritarian, and permissive) that vary in levels of control, demandingness, and warmth and positive encouragement. Children of authoritative parents have been shown to have the "best" outcomes in Baumrind's system, with better instrumental competencies.

Although possessing some validity for middle-class, White families in divorce cases, these early dimensional models and typologies are open to debate as frameworks for child welfare custody evaluations. Psychology has constructed its views of family and socialization practices in the image of the Western, middle-class nuclear family. Such forms are not present or the norm in all cultures, and they are not the norm worldwide (see Kagitcibasi, 1990).

For the most part, our predominant models assume that all parents possess the basic physical resources to parent and, thus, that all parenting can take place in the same way. Moreover, they fail to consider how context can influence what is adequate parenting or constrain the expression of certain behaviors (e.g., that the single parent living in a high-crime neighborhood can and should engage in the same set of parenting behaviors as the middle-class mother without a partner who lives in a suburban setting, and that those same parenting practices are "best" for children across all domains of functioning in either setting). These models also assume that all families prioritize the same socialization goals (e.g., all value self-reliance as an outcome). Even a cursory look at other ethnic and social class groups finds these weak assumptions.

When examined closely, the database from which the ingredients for these models were selected is found to be narrow, as are the child outcomes selected for study. This leads to searching questions regarding both representativeness of findings and relevance of constructs identified. For example, two reviews of developmental journals covering 1979 to 1993 found only 3% to 8% of articles had a significant focus on minority samples (Cauce, Ryan, & Grove, 1998; Graham, 1992). Moreover, despite calls for more such research, the situation may have worsened in recent years. If legal criteria demand an understanding of *community standards* for deciding on parenting *failures*, we are not meeting the demand. Our family research base has had little to say about many communities.

Viewing the constructs these models posit and a review of the research based on them reveals the consequences of these faulty assumptions and narrow database. For example, consider the dimensional approach cited above. Cultures differ in their use of affect, as well as in the value they attach to parental control and monitoring. The consequences for children may similarly vary. For example, African American parents are often seen as overly strict and restrictive of their children. Explanations vary for this phenomenon. One notion is that such harsh treatment may reflect a belief by African American parents that the normal range of behavior observed in all children will be less tolerated in their children and hence that their children must outperform other children in a society predisposed to see them as incompetent (Greene, 1990). Viewed from this perspective, higher levels of parental restrictiveness among African American families may be considered adaptive. Indeed, if the clearer rules for social behavior and greater control exhibited in some ethnic groups are perceived by children from these groups as greater involvement and concern, they may provide a sense of security rather than be a source of risk (e.g., Rohner & Pettengill,

1985; Trommsdorff, 1985). Likewise, some cultural groups viewed as engaging in "harsh" punishment and less overt positive affection (e.g., Chinese Americans) are frequently found to cultivate more positive outcomes in areas such as academic achievement (Uba, 1994). The predictive validity of the constructs posited (or the way we define and measure them[7]) may vary with culture.

Similarly, questions have been raised regarding the universality of existing categorical approaches (Chao, 1997). There is some evidence of significant ethnic group differences in parenting styles (Bartz & Levine, 1978). When ethnically diverse or low-SES parents are viewed through the lens of Baumrind's (1970) categories, for example, they typically are not seen favorably. Yet, cultural and physical context may change the predictive validity of typologies (Parke, chap. 3, this volume). For example, under high-environmental-risk conditions, authoritative parenting practices have not always been found to be as beneficial as they are under low-risk conditions, nor have authoritarian practices always been found to be negative in their effect (Baumrind, 1993). Family research is only beginning to explore such interactive effects. How much to weigh such factors has not been determined. Attempts to specify culture- and class-specific dimensions and classifications for different social classes and cultural groups also have been limited (Chao, 1997). Use of our current typologies as the basis for expert testimony needs to be done cautiously until new culturally valid data are available.

Finally, family research findings based on these early models have often emphasized group differences and have not paid attention to similarities found; the literature provides a list of "disturbances" and ignores any strengths identified. This fact may prime expert witnesses similarly to look for or emphasize in evaluations those more deviant factors. Newer work provides evidence for similarities, as well as differences (Bartz & Levine, 1978). Moreover, when confounding factors (such as education level and SES) are considered, different conclusions are reached.

Newer Systemic and Relational Models. Although newer and more elaborated systemic models and relational models have emerged from family research in recent years that promise to rectify some of these issues, many of the same problems are replicated. Newer models have attempted to be broader and to include both family structure and contextual factors (Belsky & Vondra, 1989). Here too, however, alternative family forms (e.g., single parenthood) and contexts (e.g., living with an extended family) are seen as inherently less "ideal" and as a source of risk for children. That is, studies still are not constructed with an eye toward examining strengths of these alternative family forms or contexts. Consideration is not given to the fact that in some cultures the functions of parents are carried out by ex-

---

[7]From a social constructivist perspective, "harshness" is in the eye of the beholder.

tended family members and in such cultures single parenthood may have an influence on children different from the influence of cultures in which two parents carry out all the functions. This suggests that evaluating parent–child dyadic or triadic interactions alone as a way to gauge capacities to meet child needs may be myopic in some groups. Although some family theory has acknowledged the effect of extended family, most research is still dominated by studies of dyads.

Current dyadic models also have problems. Attachment theory is probably one of the most articulated of the relational models (Bowlby, 1982). Attachment researchers have argued that definitions of both optimal (i.e., secure) and inadequate (i.e., anxious-avoidant, anxious-resistant, and disorganized-disoriented) internal working models of attachment and their social consequences are universal across cultures. These views are not without potential bias. As Silverstein (chap. 2, this volume) notes, there is a strong bias toward studying mothers as primary or sole caregivers. This arrangement is not favored in all cultures. Furthermore, when measures of the quality of mother–child attachment, developed with American, White, middle-class samples, have been applied to other cultural and SES groups, they have repeatedly not favored these other groups. Specifically, high proportions of anxious-avoidant attachments are found among European groups and high proportions of anxious-resistant attachments are found among Asian groups.[8] Thus, it is unclear whether definitions of what constitute adequate mother–infant attachment differ by culture, or whether methods for assessing attachment are not universally valid (e.g., Sagi & Lewkowicz, 1987). Context- and culture-specific values may also come into play. Higher levels of "inadequate" attachment among low-SES minority populations could be due to the stress of life in poverty (e.g., Vaughn, Egeland, Sroufe, & Waters, 1979). Asian cultures' emphasis on interdependence (Markus & Kitayama, 1990) and protection of children (Chiu, 1987) may promote transactions that lead to anxious-ambivalent attachments. Experts who invoke such constructs must therefore be aware of their potential bias and limits in our understanding.

Along with models that focus on dyadic relationships, family models have also emphasized social processes within the system as a whole and on contextual factors linked to better family functioning (e.g., social support). Although an improvement over dimensional and typological approaches, some of these family processes may still be value laden. For example, the McMasters model argues for the importance of *directness* of communication (Epstein, Bishop, & Baldwin, 1982). If one takes a culturally relativistic per-

---

[8]Although terms such as European and Asian are used in this chapter, such groups are not homogeneous and cannot be treated as such. These terms are used to highlight differences, and where possible the label is used for the subgroup for which specific data exist. Based on the author's arguments, however, she too may be faulted for using such global labels.

spective, however, the prioritizing of this form of communication may not always make sense. For example, the communication style of Japanese parents toward their infants is described as preparing them to communicate in an indirect and highly implicit manner (Clancy, 1986). Parents may carry this goal into new cultures when they immigrate, continuing to value the importance of reading others' social cues, including indirect gestures and facial expressions, over direct verbal communication (Uba, 1994). A Western outsider observing such family interaction might experience concern over the lack of overt or obvious guidance on the part of the parent. Yet, the parent may be conveying much to their child through looks or gestures overlooked by an untrained observer.

A similar example comes from the language development literature. Although children are seen as developing through their structured interactions with important adults in their lives, not all societies use the same socialization procedures. Although prompting a child as to what to say appears to be a relatively widespread practice, expanding children's utterances, using leading questions, announcing activities and events for them, and using a simplified lexicon and grammar to do so have all been found to vary across cultures (Ochs, 1986). It remains to be seen whether such variation in strategies places children at risk.

Systems theory has also expanded our view to include environmental factors supporting parenting (e.g., social support). Ultimately, this may result in different models of parenting for different social contexts. As yet, however, the relevance for different cultural groups of many of the factors thought to be important by systems theory has received less attention. For example, being an immigrant may limit the nature of one's social network and the environmental resources available (e.g., new immigrants to a culture may find themselves living in poor economic conditions). Socialization practices also may take on different meanings when they are enacted over time within another culture (Pettengill & Rohner, 1985). That is, children may interpret their parents' practices using social comparison and may choose to use their peers in the new culture as the social group they use to delineate norms. This can have a crucial influence on their evaluation of and reactions to parental behavior (Kagitcibasi, 1990).

Environments may also require different types of parenting. In high-risk environments, parental control and skills may need to be of a higher quality *and* qualitatively different from parental control and skills in more benign contexts. Cauce (1995) calls this "precision parenting in an unforgiving environment" (e.g., a parent who lives in an urban high-crime neighborhood may need to possess skill at anticipating risks and weighing one risk against another in more complex ways than a parent who lives in a low-crime, low-risk neighborhood). This also highlights the idea that SES differences may be more relevant than ethnicity when considering risk to children. In fact, ethnic variations in socialization practices have been shown in some studies to disappear when SES is controlled (Kagitcibasi, 1990). Methods for identifying and prioritizing the context- versus person-based factors in evaluating parents' capacities to meet children's needs require further development.

Even some of our more robust contextual factors may affect one subcultural group more than another or may influence different groups in different ways. Take social support, for example. It typically is seen as serving as a buffer against stress (by providing psychological and physical resources) and as reflecting good parental adjustment that may affect children's outcomes (as when parents serve as brokers for children's social contacts and model social behaviors for them). Yet, there may be differences both between and within ethnic groups in the utility of social support as a buffer. One study done with Chinese nationals suggested that support only acted as a buffer for those with an internal locus of control and that, generally, for those with an external locus of control, support had a negative effect (Liang & Bogat, 1994). Similarly, among single mothers, higher social network contact has been associated with lower levels of maternal nurturance (Weinraub & Wolf, 1983). Links between the ability to marshal and maintain a social network and parenting competency are more complex than first thought.

Differences also exist in the relationships from which support may be sought (e.g., family versus nonfamily members). In certain ethnic groups, such as Hispanic populations, greater dependence on family, rather than nonfamily, is the norm (Escovar & Lazarus, 1982; Herrerias, 1988; Keefe, Padilla, & Carlos, 1979). Because abusive parents have been shown to be socially isolated and to demonstrate a preference for contacts with family over those with friends (Salzinger, Kaplan, & Artemyeff, 1983), an evaluator might mistakenly consider the configuration in some ethnic groups a risk factor. These same differences may also affect parents' willingness to use service providers when under stress and, in turn, evaluators' judgments of their ability to marshal resources. Given that compliance with social service providers is weighed heavily in TPR decisions (Famularo, Kinscherff, Bunshaft, Spivak, & Fenton, 1989; Jellinek et al., 1992), cultural differences in use of social services may ultimately affect judgments regarding custody.

Furthermore, in many cultures, the functions of socialization are shared by the extended family network, not just carried out by mothers and fathers. Yet, when courts ask evaluators to assess parental fitness, evaluators do not typically first ask who are the care providers for a child and they do not assess all these individuals as a group. For example, godparents within Hispanic families may mediate parent–child conflict (Falicov & Karrer, 1984). In African American families, there is often an extended kinship network that includes grandmothers, aunts, and cousins who may share mothering of a child and who are referred to as "other mothers" (Greene, 1990). In the eyes of those not versed in the culture's norms and value system, this phenomenon of "multiple mothering" could potentially be seen as pathological (e.g., labeled as an inability to parent alone).

Culture-based social etiquette may even influence the ways social supports are described. For example, for Koreans, it is socially appropriate to be self-effacing regarding family members (Kim, McLeod, & Shantzis, 1992), which may appear as if they are belittling their social supports; this may leave room for misinterpretations (e.g., that a parent is difficult or interpersonally unskilled). More normative data are needed on how different cultural groups describe their relationships.

Finally, challenges faced by minorities within our culture (e.g., discrimination) may produce a set of parental coping strategies that may be misinterpreted (e.g., social isolation) or may produce momentary changes in parenting strategies that occur only under the observation of members of nonminority groups (i.e., they may parent differently when observed by nonminority evaluators; Clark, Anderson, Clark, & Williams, 1999; Greene, 1990). Although family researchers have discussed this to a limited extent, data are only beginning to appear. Such factors may also result in differences in the effect of stressors. Their intensity may be felt differently; thus, they may produce more disregulation for some groups compared with others. This increase in disregulation may be mistakenly labeled by an evaluator as a parent's poorer capacity to handle that stress (i.e., they may make a person attribution as opposed to a contextual attribution). McLoyd (1999), for example, provided evidence that unemployment for an African American in our society may produce more disruption because this group has fewer safety nets (e.g., home ownership may be a less liquid asset because of the neighborhoods where minorities reside).

Social Constructivist View

Recent social constructivist thinking argues for a more radical approach in questioning the constructs in currently available developmental, systemic, and relational models (Azar, 1986; Dix, Ruble, & Zambarano, 1989; Gretarsson & Gelfand, 1988). Such theorists argue for a new look at the transactions within families that encompass an examination of their meaning as seen through the perspective of family members. In some of this work, family members' preconceived role expectations and moment-to-moment interpretations of transactions have been seen as playing a role in the responses they choose. Meanings, in turn, are influenced by the culture in which they are embedded. This opens up the possibility that different factors may be uncovered for understanding parenting capacities that may be equally or more salient than our current factors for different ethnic or SES groups. Ochs (1997) gave the example of prioritizing teaching of rank versus that of providing information as a key socialization goal in some cultures. Within cultures that view the teaching of rank as a priority, a parent who answers a child's questions directly might be viewed as less *fit*. Yet, in our culture, failure to answer children's questions directly may be viewed as being unresponsive. Socialization goals, therefore, require some attention (Kuczynski, 1984). In newer work, there has been a return to these topics under the rubric of studying values, expectations, schema, attributions, and processes of parenting (e.g., problem solving; Azar, 1986, 1989). For instance, it has been argued that parents' reasons for childbearing may differ by culture. In highly developed, posttechnological societies, the "old-age security" provided by children is a less important reason for having another child (Kagitcibasi, 1982). In less developed countries, where formal systems of support for old age are not present, and in the lower classes where these supports are less assured, however, it remains a value. Following from this may be a whole set of differences in parenting practices aimed at producing a child who will provide old-age care (e.g., socialization of deference to others versus autonomy, greater use of sibling caregiving).

Differences in expectations regarding children taking on adult role responsibilities, however, have been linked to parenting risk within the United States. Azar (1986, 1989, 1998) has argued that parental schemas regarding the role of children and how they should relate to parents set the stage for parent–child interaction patterns. If parents' expectations are overly rigid or developmentally inappropriate, parents may misinterpret child behavior and its causes and may ultimately respond in inappropriate ways. A series of studies have demonstrated that parents who engage in maladaptive responses (e.g., child abuse) have more unrealistic expectancies regarding children (Azar, Robinson, Hekimian, & Twentyman, 1984; Azar & Rohrbeck, 1986), and these expectations are correlated with more negative attributions to children, greater use of punishment, and less use of explanation in childrearing situations (Azar, 1998). These expectations include seeing children as having adult perspective-taking capacities and the skills to care for parents' and siblings' needs. Based on these findings, such expectations might be viewed as indicators of risk in a custody evaluation (e.g., as evidence of *role reversal* that would lead to *parentification* of children).

Both African American and Puerto Rican American mothers showed elevated levels of such expectations in a small-scale study by Azar and Houser (1993). African American mothers expected more from young children than did nonminority parents (e.g., capacity to take on care of self and care of others). Low-SES, Puerto Rican mothers also showed a trend for higher expectations of receiving help and affection from children. Thus, a narrative of *role reversal* may be more common in some cultural groups. Findings also indicated, however, that the level at which such expectations become maladaptive must be determined empirically. For example, Azar and

Houser found that within the African American mothers, higher levels of such expectations still differentiated mothers who had been identified for physical child abuse, suggesting there are some levels of what is considered normative for a subcultural group that may still be predictive of negative outcomes for children. The sample in this study was too small to establish which types of expectancies differentiated abusive mothers. However, different content domains where such expectations occur (e.g., self-care versus perspective taking) may not be equally important. Overall, this work suggests that minority parents who verbalize more of such expectations than nonminority parents should not automatically be deemed maladaptive by an evaluator. When such expectancies become maladaptive, which may depend on their frequency or their content needs to be considered more carefully. Research is needed exploring ethnic and social class differences in parental definitions of both their roles and those of their children and tracing how these definitions relate to their behavior and child outcome.

This discussion suggests a great deal of complexity in defining fit parenting and even greater complexity in defining it when a family comes from a diverse group. Ironically, the legal system may be more advanced in its thinking than the current status of family work. For example, custody statutes invoke the concept of *community standards* and legal experts may look to psychologists to inform them as to the relevant reference group for these standards. Addressing this question requires different skills than those used typically by clinicians. Methods for evaluating families and parenting practices are just being developed, and those based on our current models sample too narrow a range of domains and responses (Azar & Benjet, 1994; Grisso, 1986; Heinze & Grisso, 1996). Even if we had valid and reliable measures of the constructs embodied in current models, they may not have the predictive validity required for all groups. Specialized assessment may also be required for some groups. For example, methods for measuring family acculturation are not well developed, nor are methods to weigh the importance of discrepancies among individual members' acculturation.

CONCLUSIONS

Melton and Wilcox (1989), in their review of the changes in family law in the United States, argued that until recently the law had been virtually impervious to the realities of child development and family life and to scientific knowledge in these areas. They argued that judges and lawyers were more concerned with "making moral statements about virtuous family life than in fashioning legal rules to match the social and economic realities of family structure and process" (p. 1214). They noted, however, a recent shift in family law toward legal realism, a jurisprudential philosophy that emphasizes the need to strive for congruence between law and social welfare. Although they welcomed this shift and noted opportunities to generate knowledge to influence policy,[9] they suggested caution in psychology's entering the legal arena and not overstepping its expertise. This chapter echoes their views.

To date, family research has made major contributions to informing expert testimony in custody decision making. Most of our contributions have occurred in divorce. Here, expert witnesses enjoy a substantial database on which to base their judgments. The legal system, in conjunction with psychology, has made strides in creating interventions to buffer the reactions of children and families to the transition of divorce and the legal processes involved. More work remains to be done to clarify the needs of diverse families, the effect of atypical custody and visitation arrangements, and the interactive effects of various contextual factors.

Although some contributions have occurred in child welfare, these have been more modest because of the nature of the questions asked (e.g., determinations of minimally adequate parenting) and of the samples considered (e.g., low-SES and diverse families). Moreover, whereas in divorce family research has played a formative role in identifying the effect of various custody arrangements on children's outcome, it has made only minimal contributions in child welfare. Many questions remain unanswered or answered in only a limited way (e.g., What is the effect of loss of a foster parent on children's outcomes? What is the effect of an open adoption in cases where child maltreatment has occurred? What family-based factors best predict adoption disruption?).

For legal decisions in child welfare, more work is needed in developing culturally sensitive models and in improving the database on which to build these models. With such models, better measurement will become possible and lead to greater utility for legal decision making. This author and others in the field have questioned the idea of universals and argued for the idea of positing of *local* standards (see Azar & Cote, in press). The implementation of local standards necessitates a more culturally sensitive research agenda that may lead to greater openness to diverse pathways to competent parenting (fitness) and the meeting of children's needs. Given our limited data, we cannot abandon current frameworks, but we must use more care in judging their utility for individual families and use a more *functional* approach to judging practices that appear discrepant. Research needs to differentiate factors that are cultural universals from those that need local definitions (Korbin, 1994; Ochs, 1986, 1997). As a framework for doing so, Korbin (1994) has argued for an examination of three kinds of parenting prac-

---

[9]See Rutter (1999) for another excellent discussion of the role of research in the justice system more generally.

tices that may be labeled as a risk to children: (a) cultural practices that are viewed as abusive or neglectful by other cultures, but not by the culture in question; (b) idiosyncratic departures from one's cultural continuum of acceptable behaviors; and (c) societally induced harm to children beyond the control of individual parents and caretakers (e.g., lack of access to high-quality housing and increased risk due to this, such as child lead poisoning; Korbin, 1987). Korbin has argued that not all enactments of cultural practices are normative even within the culture from which they arise. It is the way the practice is enacted that makes it a risk to children within that culture. This fits with our suggestion for local perspectives in evaluating parental fitness. This will require cataloging culture-specific forms of risk that may not currently exist within our lexicon of risky parenting practices.

Existing systemic ideas can provide a base for such theorizing (Belsky & Vondra, 1989; Epstein, Bishop, & Baldwin, 1982), although greater flexibility in the constructs posited are required. For example, there needs to be a greater attentiveness to strengths as well as risks in alternative family structures.

Our research needs to consider more carefully the issue of parent–child match and identify methods to examine it. Vygotskian theory (1934) provides a useful approach in this area. It focuses on an ideographic view of adults' role in children's development. Competent parenting (i.e., parenting that facilitates development) in this view involves responses on the parent's part that are within a child's developmental reach (within what is called the *zone of proximal development*; Rogoff & Wertsch, 1984). The focus is on (a) the specific capacities of the child and (b) the parents' ability to operate in a manner just above where the child is developmentally, moving them to higher levels of functioning. Thus, parents who are insensitive to their children's immaturity and respond in ways that are outside of their range would be deemed less appropriate (e.g., expecting a 4-year-old who does not yet have perspective-taking capacities to comfort them when they are sad and becoming enraged when they do not). Although this model is primarily focused on cognitive development, it can be applied to development in other domains and may provide a useful frame for the evaluation of a parent–child match.

Finally, our models typically delineate the elements of optimal parenting, not the elements required for minimally adequate parenting (the more important question in maltreatment cases). Thus, they do not address the full spectrum of what is required to parent children successfully. For example, criteria for neglect (e.g., lack of supervision), a common element of such cases, are not well developed (Zuravin, 1991). The elements of minimally adequate parenting need to be articulated.

Recently, behavioral and cognitive behavioral family theorists have attempted to address a broader range of factors predictive of child risk and

TABLE 10.1
Sampling of Skill Areas Required to Parent

1. Parenting skills
   Problem-solving abilities
   A repertoire of child-management skills (balance of positive and negative strategies; discipline skills)
   Medical care and physical care skills (e.g., ability to identify needs for medical assistance; capacity to select nutritious foods)
   Safety and emergency response skills
   Capacities for warmth and nurturance (e.g., affective, recognition/expression skills)
   Sensitive and discriminant interactional response capacities
   Capacity to coparent
2. Social cognitive skills
   Perspective taking
   Problem-solving capacities
   Appropriate expectations regarding children's capacities
   Cognitive reflectivity/complexity
   Balancing short- and long-term socialization goals
   Positive attributional style
   Perceptual/observational skills
   Self-efficacy
3. Self-control skills
   Impulse control
   Accurate/adaptive perceptions
   A positive bias
   Self-monitoring skills
   Assertiveness
4. Stress management
   Self-care skills
   Relaxation skills
   Recreational capacities
   Ability to marshal a social support network
   Positive appraisal style
   A breadth of coping capacities (problem-focused coping, emotion focused, avoidant coping)
   Financial planning skills
5. Social skills
   Interpersonal problem-solving skills
   Empathy
   Affective recognition/expression skills
   Assertiveness
   Social initiation skills
   Capacities to respond effectively to a breadth of individuals (e.g., family, friends, employers, social workers, children's teachers)

thus provide assistance in delineating areas for evaluating minimally adequate parenting. Taking a skills approach, Azar and Twentyman (1986), for example, outlined five areas of parental-skill deficits associated with abuse: (a) specific parenting skills (e.g., a wide repertoire of discipline strategies, emergency skills), (b) social cognitive incapacities and disturbances (e.g., unrealistic expectations of children, poor problem solving, negative attributional bias toward children), (c) poor stress coping, (d) anger control problems, and (e) social skills deficits. Table 10.1 provides some examples of skill areas that may fit under each of these headings. This effort delineates a broader set of domains than have been articulated in earlier models of parenting. Recent attempts to apply such approaches to court evaluations are under way (Azar et al., 1998). It is hoped that through a more thorough cataloging of relevant domains, family research will become more inclusive and provide a stronger foundation for expert testimony.

REFERENCES

Adoption and Safe Families Act, 105 US Public Law §89 (1997).

Ahrons, C. (1999). Divorce. An unscheduled family transition. In B. Carter & M. McGoldrick (Eds.), *The expanded family life cycle* (pp. 381–398). Boston: Allyn & Bacon.

Aldarondo, E., & Sugarman, D. B. (1996). Risk marker analysis of the cessation and persistence of wife assault. *Journal of Consulting and Clinical Psychology, 64*, 1010–1019.

Amato, P. R. (1994). Life-span adjustment of children to their parents' divorce. *Children and Divorce, 4*, 143–164.

Amato, P. R., & Keith, B. (1991). Parental divorce and the well-being of children: A meta analysis. *Psychological Bulletin, 100*, 26–46.

American Humane Association. (1985). *National analysis of official child abuse and neglect reports.* Denver, CO: Author.

Anderson, R. F., Kinney, J., & Gerler, E. R., (1984). The effects of divorce groups on children classroom behavior and attitudes toward divorce. *Elementary School Guidance and Counseling, 19*, 70–76.

Azar, S. T. (1986). A framework for understanding child maltreatment: An integration of cognitive behavioral and developmental perspectives. *Canadian Journal of Behavioral Science, 18*, 340–355.

Azar, S. T. (1989). Training parents of abused children. In C. E. Schaefer & J. M. Briesmeister (Eds.), *Handbook of parent training* (pp. 414–444). New York: Wiley.

Azar, S. T. (1991). Models of child abuse. A metatheoretical analysis. *Criminal Justice and Behavior, 18*, 30–46.

Azar, S. T. (1995, April). *Is the intellectually low functioning parent at risk for child maltreatment?* Presented at the biennial meeting of the Society for Research in Child Development, Indianapolis, IN.

Azar, S. T. (1998). A cognitive behavioral approach to understanding and treating parents who physically abuse their children. In D. Wolfe & R. McMahon (Ed.), *Child abuse: New directions in prevention and treatment across the life span* (pp. 78–100). New York: Sage.

Azar, S. T. (in press). Adult development and parenting. In J. Demick (Ed.), *Adult development.* New York: Sage.

Azar, S. T., & Benjet, C. L. (1994). A cognitive perspective on ethnicity, race and termination of parental rights. *Law and Human Behavior, 18,* 249–268.

Azar, S. T., Benjet, C. L., Fuhrmann, G., & Cavallero, L. (1995). Child maltreatment and termination of parental rights: Can behavioral research help Solomon? *Behavior Therapy, 26,* 599–623.

Azar, S. T., & Cote, L. (in press). Sociocultural issues in the evaluation of the needs of children in custody decision-making: What do our current frameworks for evaluating parenting practices have to offer? *International Journal of Law & Psychiatry.*

Azar, S. T., & Houser, A. (1993, November). *Unrealistic expectations, negative attributions, and parenting responses: Further validation of a social cognitive model with African American and Puerto Rican mothers.* Paper presented at the annual meeting of the Association for the Advancement of Behavior Therapy, Atlanta, GA.

Azar, S. T., Lauretti, A., & Loding, B. (1998). The evaluation of parental fitness in termination of parental rights cases: A functional-contextual perspective. *Clinical Child and Family Psychology Review, 1,* 77–99.

Azar, S. T., & Olsen, N. (in press). Legal issues in child abuse and neglect. In W. O'Donohue, D. R. Laws, & C. R. Hollin (Eds.), *Handbook of forensic psychology.* Sarasota, FL: Westview Press.

Azar, S. T., Robinson, D. R., Hekimian, E., & Twentyman, C. T. (1984). Unrealistic expectations and problem solving ability in maltreating and comparison mothers. *Journal of Consulting and Clinical Psychology, 52,* 687–691.

Azar, S. T., & Rohrbeck, C. A. (1986). Child abuse and unrealistic expectations: Further validation of the Parent Opinion Questionnaire. *Journal of Consulting and Clinical Psychology, 54,* 867–868.

Azar, S. T., & Twentyman, C. T. (1986). Cognitive behavioral perspectives on the assessment and treatment of child abuse. *Advances in cognitive-behavioral research and therapy* (Vol. 5, pp. 237–267). New York: Academic Press.

Bartz, K. W., & Levine, E. S. (1978). Childrearing by Black parents: A description and comparison to Anglo and Chicano parents. *Journal of Marriage and the Family, 40,* 709–719.

Baumrind, D. (1970). Socialization and instrumental competence in young children. *Young Children, 26,* 104–119.

Baumrind, D. (1993). The average expectable environment is not good enough: A response to Scarr. *Child Development, 64,* 1299–1317.

Becker, W. C. (1964). Consequences of different kinds of parental discipline. In M. L. Hoffman & L. W. Hoffman (Eds.), *Review of child development* (Vol. 1, pp. 169–207). New York: Sage.

Belsky, J., & Vondra, J. (1989). Lessons from child abuse: The determinants of parenting. In D. Cicchetti & V. Carlson (Eds.), *Child maltreatment* (pp. 153–202). New York: Cambridge University Press.

Berry, M. (1993). Risks and benefits of open adoption. *The Future of Children, 3,* 125–138.

Blaher, J. (1984). A dynamic perspective on the impact of a severely handicapped child on the family. In J. Blaher (Ed.), *Severely handicapped young children and their families* (pp. 3–50). New York: Academic Press.

Bolocofsky, D. N. (1989). Use and abuse of mental health experts in child custody determinations. *Behavioral Sciences & the Law, 7,* 197–213.

Bowlby, J. (1982). *Attachment and loss: Vol. L. Attachment.* New York: Basic.

Brown, G. W., Monck, E. M., Carstairs, G. M., & Wing, J. K. (1962). Influence of family life on course of schizophrenic illness. *British Journal of Preventive and Social Medicine, 16,* 55–68.

Budd, K. S., & Greenspan, S. (1984). Mentally retarded women as parents. In E. Blechman (Ed.), *Behavior modification with women* (pp. 477–506). New York: Guilford.

Budd, K. S., & Holdsworth, M. J. (1996). Issues in clinical assessment of minimal parenting competence. *Journal of Clinical Child Psychology, 25*(1), 2–14.

Cauce, A. M. (1995, June). *Slouching toward cultural competence in research.* Presented at the Family Processes Institute, Ogunquit, ME.

Cauce, A. M., Ryan, K. D., & Grove, K. (1998). Children and adolescents of color, where are you? Participation, selection, recruitment, and retention in developmental research. In V. C. McLoyd & L. Steinberg (Eds.), *Studying minority adolescents: Conceptual, methodological, and theoretical issues* (pp. 147–166). Mahwah, NJ: Lawrence Erlbaum Associates.

Chao, R. (1997, April). *The "meaningfulness" of our most familiar constructs: Research on parenting for ethnically diverse populations.* Paper presented at the biennial meeting of the Society for Research in Child Development, Washington, DC.

Chesler, P. (1991). *Mothers on trial.* New York: Harcourt Brace Jovanovich.

Chiu, L. (1987). Childrearing attitudes of Chinese, Chinese American, and Anglo-American mothers. *International Journal of Psychology, 22,* 409–419.

Cicchetti, D., & Lynch, M. (1995). Failures in the expectable environment and their impact on individual development: The case of child maltreatment. In D. Cicchetti & D. Cohen (Eds.), *Developmental psychopathology: Vol. 2. Risk, disorder, and adaptation* (pp. 32–71). New York: Wiley.

Clancy, P. M. (1986). The acquisition of communicative style in Japanese. In B. B. Schieffelin & E. Ochs (Eds.), *Language and socialization across cultures* (pp. 213–250). Cambridge, MA: Cambridge University Press.

Clark, R., Anderson, N. B., Clark, V. R., & Williams, D. R. (1999). Racisim as a stressor for African Americans. A biopsychosocial model. *American Psychologist, 54,* 805–816.

Cox, A. D., Puckering, C., Pound, A., & Mills, M. (1987). The impact of maternal depression on young children. *Journal of Child Psychology and Psychiatry, 28,* 917–928.

Demick, J. (1993). Adaptation of marital couples to open versus closed adoption: A preliminary investigation. In J. Demick, K. Bursik, & R. DeBiase (Eds.), *Parental development* (pp. 175–201). Hillsdale, NJ: Lawrence Erlbaum Associates.

Derdeyn, A. P. (1976). Child custody contests in historical perspective. *American Journal of Psychiatry, 133,* 1369–1376.

Dix, T., Ruble, D. N., & Zambarano, R. J. (1989). Mothers' implicit theories of discipline: Child effects, parent effects, and the attribution process. *Child Development, 60,* 1373–1391.

Duncan, G. J., & Hoffman, S. D. (1985). Economic consequences of marital instability. In M. David & T. Smeeding (Eds.), *Horizontal equity, uncertainty, and economic well-being* (pp. 427–467). Chicago: University of Chicago Press.

Dunn, J. (1983). Sibling relationships in early childhood. *Child Development, 54,* 787–811.

Emery, R. E. (1982). Interparental conflict and the children of discord and divorce. *Psychological Bulletin, 92,* 310–330.

Emery, R. E., Weintraub, S., & Neale, J. M. (1982). Effects of marital discord on the school behavior of children of schizophrenic, affectively disordered, and normal parents. *Journal of Abnormal Child Psychology, 10,* 215–228.

Emery, R., & Wyer, M. (1987). Child custody mediation and litigation: An experimental evaluation of the experience of parents. *Journal of Consulting and Clinical Psychology, 55,* 179–186.

Epstein, N. B., Bishop, D. S., & Baldwin, L. M. (1982). McMasters model of family functioning. In F. Walsh (Ed.), *Normal family processes* (pp. 115–141). New York: Guilford.

Escovar, P. L., & Lazarus, P. J. (1982). Cross-cultural child-rearing practices: Implications for school psychologists. *School Psychology International, 3,* 143–148.

Falicov, C., & Karrer, B. M. (1984). Therapeutic strategies for Mexican American families. *International Journal of Family Therapy, 6,* 18–30.

Falk, P. J. (1989). Lesbian mothers. Psychosocial assumptions in family law. *American Psychologist, 44,* 941–947.

Famularo, R., Kinscherff, R., Bunshaft, D., Spivak, G., & Fenton, T. (1989). Parental compliance to court-ordered treatment interventions in cases of child maltreatment. *Child Abuse & Neglect, 13,* 507–514.

Famularo, R., Stone, K., Barnum, R., & Wharton, R. (1986). Alcoholism and severe child maltreatment. *American Journal of Orthopsychiatry, 56,* 481–485.

Fantuzzo, J. W. (1999). Prevalence and effects of child exposure to domestic violence. *The Future of Children. Domestic Violence and Children, 9,* 21–32.

Feldman, M. A. (1998). Parents with intellectual disabilities. In J. R. Jutzker (Ed.), *Handbook of child abuse research and treatment* (pp. 401–420). New York: Plenum Press.

Festinger, T. (1990). Adoption disruption: Rates and correlates. In D. Brodzinsky & M. Schechter (Eds.), *The psychology of adoption* (pp. 201–218). New York: Oxford University Press.

Fisher, L., Kokes, R. F., Cole, R. E., Perkins, K., & Wynne, L. C. (1987). Competent children at risk: A study of well-functioning offspring of disturbed parents. In E. J. Anthony & B. J. Cohler (Eds.), *The invulnerable child* (pp. 211–228). New York: Guilford.

Furstenburg, F. F., & Cherlin, A. J. (1991). *Divided families: What happens to children when parents part.* Cambridge, MA: Harvard University Press.

Garrity, C. B., & Baris, M. A. (1994). *Caught in the middle. Protecting the children of high conflict divorce.* New York: Lexington.

Goldstein, J., Freud, A., & Solnit, A. J. (1973). *Beyond the best interests of the child.* New York: Free Press.

Gottesman, I. I., & Shields, J. (1972). *Schizophrenia and genetics. A twin study vantage point.* New York: Academic.

Graham, S. (1992). Most of the subjects were white and middle class. *American Psychologist, 47,* 629–639.

Greene, B. (1990). Sturdy bridges: Role of African-American mothers in the socialization of African-American children. In J. P. Knowles & E. Cole (Eds.), *Woman-defined motherhood* (pp. 205–225). New York: Harrington Park Press.

Gretarsson, S. J., & Gelfand, D. M. (1988). Mothers' attributions regarding their children's social behavior and personality characteristics. *Developmental Psychology, 24,* 264–269.

Grisso, T. (1986). *Evaluating competencies.* New York: Plenum.

Grisso, T., & Appelbaum, P. S. (1992). Is it unethical to offer predictions of future violence? *Law and Human Behavior, 16,* 621–633.

Hammen, C., Adrian, C., Gordon, D., Burge, D., Jaenicke, C., & Hiroto, D. (1987). Children of depressed mothers: Maternal strain and symptom predictors of dysfunction. *Journal of Abnormal Psychology, 96,* 190–198.

Hartmann, H. (1958). *Ego psychology and the problem of adaptation.* New York: International University Press.

Hayman, R. L. (1990). Presumptions of justice: Law, politics, and the mentally retarded parent. *Harvard Law Review, 103,* 1201–1271.

Heinze, M. C., & Grisso, T. (1996). Review of instruments assessing parenting competencies used in child custody evaluations. *Behavioral Science and the Law, 14,* 293–313.

Herrerias, C. (1988). Prevention of child abuse and neglect in the Hispanic community. *Journal of Primary Prevention, 9,* 104–119.

Hetherington, E. M. (1979). Divorce: A child's perspective. *American Psychologist, 34,* 851–856.

Hetherington, E. M., Cox, M., & Cox, R. (1978). The aftermath of divorce. In J. H. Stevens, Jr. & M. Matthews (Eds.), *Mother–child, father–child relationships* (pp. 149–176). Washington, DC: National Association for the Education of Young Children.

Jacob, T. (1992). Family studies of alcoholism. *Journal of Family Studies, 5,* 319–338.

Jellinek, M. S., Murphy, J. M., Poitrast, F., Quinn, D., Bishop, S. J., & Goshko, M. (1992). Serious child mistreatment in Massachusetts: The course of 206 children through the courts. *Child Abuse & Neglect, 16,* 179–185.

Johnston, J. R. (1994). High-conflict divorce. *Children and Divorce, 4,* 165–182.

Kadushin, A. (1967). *Child welfare services.* New York: Macmillan.

Kagitcibasi, C. (1982). Old-age security value of children. Cross-national socioeconomic factors. *Journal of Cross Cultural Psychology, 13,* 29–42.

Kagitcibasi, C. (1990). Family and socialization in cross-cultural perspective: A model of change. In R. A. Dienstbier (Ed.), *Cross-cultural perspectives. Nebraska symposium on motivation* (pp. 135–200). Lincoln: University of Nebraska Press.

Kagitcibasi, C. (1995). Is psychology relevant to global human development issues? Experiences from Turkey. *American Psychologist, 50,* 293–300.

Kaplan, L., Hennon, C. B., & Ade-Ridder, L. (1993). Splitting custody of children between parents: Impact on the sibling system. *Families in Society,* 131–143.

Keefe, S. E., Padilla, A. M., & Carlos, M. L. (1979). The Mexican-American extended family as an emotional support network. *Human Organization, 38,* 144–152.

Kempe, C. H., Silverman, F. N., Stecle, B. F., Droegmueller, W., & Silber, H. K. (1962). The battered child syndrome. *American Journal of the American Medical Association, 181,* 17–24.

Kim, S., McLeod, J. H., & Shantzis, C. (1992). Cultural competence for evaluators working with Asian-Americans. In M. Orlandi (Ed.), *Cultural competence for evaluators: A guide for alcohol and other drug abuse prevention practitioners working with ethnic and racial communities* (pp. 203–260). Washington, DC: U.S. Department of Health and Human Services.

Koch, M. P., & Lowery, C. R. (1984). Evaluation of mediation as an alternative to divorce litigation. *Professional Psychology: Research and Practice, 15,* 109–120.

Korbin, J. E. (1987). Child abuse and neglect: The cross cultural context. In H. Kempe & R. E. Helfer (Eds.), *The battered child* (3rd ed., pp. 21–35). Chicago: University of Chicago Press.

Korbin, J. E. (1994). Sociocultural factors in child maltreatment. In G. B. Melton & F. D. Barry (Eds.), *Protecting children from abuse and neglect* (pp. 182–223). New York: Guilford.

Kuczynski, L. (1984). Socialization goals and mother–child interaction: Strategies for long-term and short-term compliance. *Developmental Psychology, 20,* 1061–1073.

Lawson, E. J., & Thompson, A. (1999). *Black men and divorce.* Thousand Oaks, CA: Sage.

LeVine, R. A. (1974). Parental goals: A cross-cultural view. *Teachers College Record, 76,* 226–239.

Liang, B., & Bogat, G. A. (1994). Culture, control, and coping: New perspectives on social support. *American Journal of Community Psychology, 22,* 123–147.

Lindholm, K. J., & Willey, R. (1986). Ethnic differences in child abuse and sexual abuse. *Hispanic Journal of Behavioral Science, 8,* 111–125.

MacDonald, A. P., & Hall, J. (1969). Perception of disability by the nondisabled. *Journal of Consulting and Clinical Psychology, 33,* 654–660.

Margolin, G. (1998). Effects of domestic violence. In P. K. Trickett & C. J. Shellenbach (Eds.), *Violence against children in the family and the community* (pp. 57–102). Washington, DC: APA.

Markus, H. R., & Kitayama, S. (1990). Culture and the self: Implications for cognition, emotion, and motivation. *Psychological Review, 96,* 224–253.

Martin, S. L., Ramey, C. T., & Ramey, S. (1990). The prevention of intellectual impairment in children of impoverished families: Findings of a randomized trial of educational day care. *American Journal of Public Health, 80,* 844–887.

McCombs, C., Thomas, A., & Forehand, R. (1991). The relationship between paternal depressive mood and early adolescent functioning. *Journal of Family Psychology, 4,* 260–271.

McLoyd, V. (1999, June). *Ethnicity, race, and social class as defining features of families.* Paper presented at the first annual Summer Institute of the Family Research Consortium III, Bretton Woods, NH.

Melton, G. B., Petrila, J., Poythress, N. G., & Slobogin, C. (1987). *Psychological evaluations for the courts: A handbook for mental health professionals.* New York: Guilford.

Melton, G. B., Petrila, J., Poythress, N. G., & Slobogin, C. (1997). *Psychological evaluations for the courts: A handbook for mental health professionals* (2nd ed.). New York: Guilford.

Melton, G. B., & Wilcox, B. L. (1989). Changes in family law and family life. Challenges for psychology. *American Psychologist, 44,* 1213–1216.

Mickelson, P. (1947). The feebleminded parent: A study of 90 family cases. *American Journal of Mental Deficiency, 51,* 644–633.

Ochs, E. (1986). Introduction. In B. B. Schieffelin & E. Ochs (Eds.), *Language socialization across cultures* (pp. 1–160). New York: Cambridge University Press.

Ochs, E. (1997). Linguistic resources for socializing humanity. In J. J. Gumperz & S. C. Levinson (Eds.), *Rethinking linguistic relativity* (pp. 407–437). New York: Cambridge University Press.

O'Donohue, W., & Bradley, A. R. (1999). Conceptual and empirical issues in child custody evaluations. *American Psychological Association, 6*, 310–322.

Parke, R. D., & Buriel, R. (1998). Socialization in the family: Ethnic and ecological perspectives. In W. Damon (Series Ed.) & N. Eisenberg (Vol. Ed.), *Handbook of child psychology: Vol. 3. Social, emotional, and personality development* (5th ed., pp. 463–552). New York: Wiley.

Patterson, C. J. (1992). Children of lesbian and gay parents. *Child Development, 63*, 1025–1042.

Pedro-Carroll, J., & Cowan, E. L. (1985). The children of divorce intervention program: An investigation of the efficacy of a school based intervention program. *Journal of Consulting and Clinical Psychology, 53*, 603–611.

Pettengill, S. M., & Rohner, R. P. (1985). Korean-American adolescents perceptions of parental control, parental acceptance-rejection and parent–adolescent conflict. In I. R. Lagunes & Y. H. Poortinga (Eds.), *From a different perspective* (pp. 241–249). Lisse, Netherlands: Swets & Zeitlinger.

Quigley, R. M., & Leonard, K. E. (1996). Desistance of husband aggression in the early years of marriage. *Violence and Victims, 11*, 355–370.

Radbill, S. X. (1980). Children in a world of violence: A history of child abuse. In C. H. Kempe & R. E. Helfer (Eds.), *The battered child* (pp. 3–20). Chicago: University of Chicago Press.

Rodning, C., Beckwith, L., & Howard, J. (1991). Quality of attachment and home environments in children prenatally exposed to PCP and cocaine. *Development and Psychopathology, 3*, 351–366.

Rogoff, B., & Wertsch, J. V. (1984). *Children's learning in the "zone of proximal development."* San Francisco: Jossey-Bass.

Rohner, R., & Pettengill, S. (1985). Perceived parental acceptance–rejection and parental control among Korean adolescents. *Child Development, 56*, 524–528.

Rosenthal, J. A. (1993). Outcomes of adoption of children with special needs. *The Future of Children, 3*, 77–88.

Rutter, M. (1999). Research and the family justice system: What has been the role of research and what should it be? *Newsletter of the National Council for Family Proceedings, 15*, 2–4.

Sagi, A., & Lewkowicz, K. S. (1987). A cross-cultural evaluation of attachment research. In L. W. C. Tavecchio & M. H. van Ijzendoorn (Eds.), *Advances in psychology series: Vol. 44. Attachment and social networks* (pp. 427–459). New York: Elsevier.

Salzinger, S., Kaplan, S., & Artemyeff, C. (1983). Mother's personal social networks and child maltreatment. *Journal of Abnormal Psychology, 92*, 68–72.

Saunders, D. G. (1994). Child custody decisions in families experiencing woman abuse. *Social Work, 39*, 51–59.

Scarr, S., & McCartney, K. (1983). How people make their own environments: A theory of genotype environmental effects. *Child Development, 54*, 424–435.

Seagull, E. A., & Scheurer, M. D. (1986). Neglected and abused children of mentally retarded parents. *Child Abuse & Neglect, 10*, 493–500.

Seilhamer, R. A., Jacob, T., & Dunn, N. J. (1993). The impact of alcohol consumption on parent–child relationships in families of alcoholics. *Journal of Studies on Alcohol, 54*, 189–198.

Silverman, A. R. (1993). Outcomes in transracial adoption. *The Future of Children, 3*, 104–118.

South, S. J., Crowder, K. D., & Trent, K. (1998). Children's residential mobility and neighborhood following parental divorce and remarriage. *Social Forces, 77*, 667–693.

Sprenkle, D. H., & Storm, C. L. (1983). Divorce therapy outcome research: A substantive and methodological review. *Journal of Marital and Family Therapy, 9*, 239–258.

Stolberg, A. J., & Garrison, K. M. (1985). Evaluating a primary prevention program for children of divorce. *American Journal of Community Psychology, 13*, 111–124.

Stromberg, C. D., Haggarty, D. J., Leivenluft, R. F., McMillian, M. H., Mishkin, B., Rubin, B. L., & Trilling, H. R. (1988). *The psychologist's legal handbook*. Washington, DC: The Council for the National Register of Health Service Providers in Psychology.

Teachman, J. D., & Paasch, K. M. (1994). Financial impact of divorce on children and their families. *The Future of Children: Children and Divorce, 4*, 63–83.

Thompson, R. A. (1994). The role of the father after divorce. *Children and Divorce, 4*, 210–235.

Thompson, R. A., Tinsley, B. R., Scalora, M. J., & Parke, R. (1989). Grandparents' visitation rights. *American Psychologist, 44*, 1217–1222.

Tinsley, B. R., & Parke, R. D. (1984). Grandparents as support and socialization agents. In M. Lewis (Ed.), *Beyond the dyad* (pp. 161–194). New York: Plenum.

Trommsdorff, G. (1985). Some comparative aspects of socialization in Japan and Germany. In I. R. Lagunes & Y. H. Poortinga (Eds.), *From a different perspective*. Lisse, Netherlands: Swets and Zeitlinger.

Turner, J. R. (1984). Divorced fathers who win contested custody of their children: An exploratory study. *American Journal of Orthopsychiatry, 54*, 498–501.

Tymchuk, A. J. (1992). Predicting adequacy of parenting by people with mental retardation. *Child Abuse & Neglect, 16*, 165–178.

Uba, L. (1994). *Asian Americans: Personality patterns, identity, and mental health*. New York: Guilford.

United Nations General Assembly (1989, November). *Adoption of the convention on the rights of the child* (U.N. Doc. A/Res/44/25). New York: Author.

Vaughn, B., Egeland, B., Sroufe, L. A., & Waters, E. (1979). Individual differences in infant–mother attachment at twelve and eighteen months. *Child Development, 50*, 971–975.

Vygotsky, L. S. (1934). *Thought and language*. Cambridge, MA: MIT Press.

Wallerstein, J. S. (1984). Children of divorce: Preliminary report of a ten-year follow-up of young children. *American Journal of Orthopsychiatry, 54*, 444–458.

Wallerstein, J. S. (1985). Children of divorce: Preliminary report of a ten-year follow-up of older children and adolescents. *Journal of the American Academy of Child Psychiatry, 24*, 545–553.

Wallerstein, J. S., & Kelly, J. B. (1980). *Surviving the breakup: How children and parents cope with divorce*. New York: Basic Books.

Wasserman, D. R., & Leventhal, J. M. (1994). Maltreatment of children born to cocaine-dependent women. *American Journal of Diseases of Children, 147*, 1324–1328.

Weinraub, M., & Wolf, B. M. (1983). Effects of stress and social supports on mother–child interactions in single- and two-parent families. *Child Development, 54*, 1297–1311.

Weitzman, L. J. (1985). *The divorce revolution: The unexpected social and economic consequences for women and children in America*. New York: Free Press.

West, M. O., & Prinz, R. J. (1988). Parental alcoholism and child psychopathology. *Annual Progress in Child Psychiatry and Development*, 278–314.

Winicott, D. W. (1958). *Through pediatrics to psycho-analysis: Collected papers*. New York: Basic Books.

Winicott, D. W. (1965). *The maturational processes and the facilitative environment*. New York: International Universities Press.

Wolfe, D. A. (1988). Child abuse and neglect. In E. J. Mash & L. G. Terdal (Eds.), *Behavioral assessment of childhood disorders* (pp. 627–699). New York: Guilford.

Zibbell, R. A. (1992). A short-term, small group education and counseling program for separated and divorced parents in conflict. *Journal of Divorce and Remarriage, 18*, 189–203.

Zuravin, S. J. (1991). Research definitions of child physical abuse and neglect: Current problems. In R. H. Starr & D. A. Wolfe (Eds.), *The effects of child abuse and neglect: Issues and research* (pp. 100–128). New York: Guilford.

11

Family Influences on Behavior and Development: Challenges for the Future

Michael Rutter

Institute of Psychiatry, London

A wealth of research has shown associations between family functioning and children's behavior or development. As a consequence, we have learned much about how families operate and what types of family malfunction seem to carry significant psychological risks for the children. Given this massive increase in the evidence on possible family influences on children's psychological functioning, it might be supposed that it should have been accompanied by a parallel increase in the mental health of our children. It comes as a shock, therefore, that this has not happened. Over the last half century there have been, in all parts of the industrialized world, tremendous improvements in most aspects of physical health. Infantile mortality rates have fallen dramatically, life expectancy has increased greatly, and many of the killing infections of early life have been conquered (e.g., smallpox has been eradicated and neither polio nor tuberculosis is the scourge it used to be). In contrast, systematic research has shown that, over the same period, the rates of psychosocial disorders among young people have increased dramatically (Rutter & Smith, 1995). Drug problems have become much more prevalent, crime rates have soared, suicide rates in young people have gone up at the same time that those in older people have come down, and depressive disorders in younger people have increased. If we know so much about family functioning, why have we not been more successful in improving the mental health of our children? That is a challenge that we must accept. Of course, it would be wrong to overlook the very real gains that have taken place. Even with difficult problems, such as antisocial behavior, methods of prevention and intervention have improved and are associated with benefits, albeit modest ones (Rutter, Giller, & Hagell, 1998). However, we are going to have to do much better in the future.

During recent years, powerful voices have also argued forcefully that, except at the extremes, what happens in the family does not make much difference to how children turn out. Thus, behavior geneticists such as Plomin (1994), Rowe (1994), and Scarr (1992) have argued that many of the associations that have been attributed to environmental effects really represent genetic mediation. Parents pass on genes to their children as well as shaping and selecting the environments of their rearing. These critics accept the reality of the statistical associations reported in the literature but propose that their meaning is different from that usually supposed. Thus, family discord and disruption are associated with risks to the children, but they suggest that is because these reflect genetic susceptibilities rather than environmental influences. Other critics, most notably Harris (1998), have made the same point but have gone on to include two other propositions. First, she noted that much of the research showing associations between parental behavior and child behavior derive from measures based on parental reports. It is suggested, therefore, that there may be some effects within the home but they are situation specific and do not have much implication for children's behavior in other environments. Second, the critics have proposed that, insofar as environmental influences on psychological functioning are important, they mainly derive from the peer group rather than from the family (Harris, 1998). Their reviews have made some valid points that require our attention. Nevertheless, there are many good reasons for concluding that they have overstated their case (Rutter et al., 1998; Rutter, Pickles, Murray, & Eaves, in press; Rutter, Silberg, O'Connor, & Simonoff, 1999a, 1999b).

THREATS TO CAUSAL INFLUENCES

Measurement Bias and Criterion Contamination

Several measurement problems need to be recognized. First, we should be skeptical about conclusions based on studies in which the measure of the family risk variable and the measure of the child outcome variable come from the same informant (usually a parent, but sometimes the young people themselves). In these circumstances there is a strong possibility that the association reflects perceptual biases in the mind of the person making the rating, rather than true causal effects. Even when the independent vari-

able (i.e., the risk factor) and the dependent variable (i.e., the child outcome) derive from different informants, if they both concern behaviors
within the home, there is still the problem of knowing the extent to which
the associations apply to behavior in other circumstances. A further consideration is that research findings have been consistent in showing only
modest intercorrelations among the ratings made by different informants
(Achenbach & Edelbrock, 1978; Horton, Laird, & Zahner, 1999; Simonoff et
al., 1997). This is not just a question of measurement error (although that is
likely to be part of the story) because child, parent, and teacher ratings differ
in their patterns of correlations with other variables. For example, the genetic contributions to child behavior as reported by parents tend to be
higher than those reported by the young people themselves (Eaves et al.,
1997). Researchers have not solved the problem of how to deal with these differences among informants, but there is general agreement on the need for
multiple measures, from multiple informants, preferably repeated over time.
Most reliance needs to be placed on research where that has been the case.

Risk Environments Are Not Randomly Distributed

In many respects, the most serious threat to the validity of causal inferences with respect to environmentally mediated family influences occurs
because risk environments are not randomly distributed (Rutter, Champion, Quinton, Maughan, & Pickles, 1995). The individual differences in environmental risk exposure arise in wide-ranging ways; thus there are important societal effects. Racial discrimination remains an evil, and powerful,
influence in most societies (Brown, 1984; Madood et al., 1997). It is not just
that individuals from ethnic minorities experience personal interactions of
an unpleasant (and sometimes dangerous) nature. In addition, discrimination as it applies in relation to housing, unemployment, and other domains
means that people from ethnic minorities are often likely to experience high
rates of environmental risk exposure. This raises two separate possibilities.
First, it could be that the risk effects derive from acts of discrimination rather
than from the family circumstances with which they are associated. Second,
it is possible that the family circumstances provide the immediate mediating
mechanism for the risk but that the societal factors operate as distal influences earlier in the causal chain. That is, they do not in themselves represent
the causal risk process but they are important because they make it more
likely that the immediate risk mechanisms will arise.

A second way individual differences in environmental risk exposure
arise is through the effects of people's own behavior. This was dramatically
evident many years ago in Robins' (1966) pioneering long-term follow-up of
children who attended a child guidance clinic. She found that the children
who had shown antisocial behavior when young had a greatly increased

rate of risk experiences in adult life as indexed by features such as repeated divorces, rebuffs from friends, social isolation, periods of unemployment, being sacked from jobs, and lack of social support. Longitudinal studies since then have confirmed the associations between deviant behavior in childhood and both acute and chronic life stresses in adult life (Champion, Goodall, & Rutter, 1995). An abundance of evidence reveals that children's behavior influences how other people respond to them (Bell & Chapman, 1986; Rutter, Dunn, et al., 1997) as well as shaping and selecting the social environments they enter. As a consequence, it is essential to use research designs that can differentiate between person effects on the environment and environmental effects on the person. Ordinarily, longitudinal data are essential for that purpose. In practice bidirectional effects are likely to be the usual occurrence, but there can be no causal inference regarding family effects on children unless the design used can test the direction of influence.

Third Variable Effects

A further threat to the validity of causal inferences derives from the pervasive need to consider so-called "third variable" effects. The statistical associations may not derive from any direct reflection of a risk mechanism but rather from the association between the postulated risk variable and with some other factor that truly causes the risk. In other words, it is crucial to differentiate between risk indicators and risk mechanisms. In the past the two have often been confused. For example, for many years the experience of a child being separated from its parents was seen as a major risk for mental health. The finding that this did not apply to happy separations and that the risks associated with parental divorce far exceeded those associated with parental death called the assumption into question (Rutter, 1971). Since then, much research with both children (Fergusson, Horwood, & Lynskey, 1992) and adults (Harris, Brown, & Bifulco, 1986) has shown that the major risk mediation derives from poor parental care or family discord rather than from the separation as such.

Some of the current discussions about whether family conflict is necessarily harmful (Rutter, 1994a; Cummings & Davies, 1994) raise similar questions. One of the problems is that words such as conflict are used to cover a diverse range of circumstances. Disagreements among people are a normal part of human life. It would be absurd to suppose that they are likely to constitute serious risks to mental health. On the other hand, if such disagreements lead to escalating patterns of verbal or physical abuse, of hostile and rejecting remarks, or the scapegoating of individuals in the family, this may well carry risks. We need to go beyond the general concept to ask more specific questions about mechanisms. Does the damage derive from conflict, leading to tense, negative, and discordant interpersonal relationships? Do the main risks derive from a child's personal experience of such bad relationships or are there also risks associated with marital discord, even if the child's relationship with the parents is good? The evidence suggests that, although there may be some risks from marital discord, the greater risks probably derive from the child's experience of adverse parent–child relationships (Jenkins & Smith, 1990; Reiss et al., 1995). In addition, may there also be risks associated with the child witnessing overt physical violence in the home (Moffitt & Caspi, 1998)? Also, may there be risks that derive from the child learning that the way to respond to social problems is to lose control and hurl abuse at other people? No single study is likely to provide a definitive answer on all the key elements in the risk processes, but it is important to appreciate the need to take the step of designing research that can differentiate between indirect risk indicators and direct risk mechanisms.

Genetic Mediation of Supposedly Environmental Risks

The observation many years ago that the correlations between parent and family features and child characteristics were much stronger in biological families than in adoptive families (Jones, 1946) first drew attention to the likelihood that some associations that appeared to involve environmental mediation because the risk variables referred to environments (as would be the case with features such as family discord or parental neglect) actually reflected genetic mediation, at least in part. This is because the environmental risk situations stem from parental behavior that is open to genetic (as well as environmental) influences. Some of the difference in strength of correlations between adoptive and biological families is likely to be a consequence of the narrower range of risk environments in adoptive families (Stoolmiller, 1999), but that is not the whole explanation. A further way in which genes influence environmental risk exposure is through their effects on children's behavior. Thus, adoptee studies have shown that the adopting parents of children born to, but not reared by, antisocial parents are more likely to exhibit negative forms of control than are parents of children who lack that biological risk (Ge et al., 1996; O'Connor, Deater-Deckard, Fulker, Rutter, & Plomin, 1998). The mediation in this case comes about through the genetic effects on the children's disruptive behavior, that in turn influences their interactions with their adoptive parents who are rearing them. The implication of all these findings is that it is necessary to use designs that can differentiate between genetic and environmental mediation even when the risks are statistically associated with variables that describe environments.

Key Methodological Challenges

Family researchers have to accept the reality of the various threats to the validity of their inferences about family influences. Careful attention needs to be paid to the use of research designs that deal with the threats discussed earlier. In addition, however, two other needs must be met. First, it is essential to consider the range of possible alternative explanations for the findings. It is not enough to consider the evidence that supports the investigator's favorite! Rather, designs that pit one postulated mediating mechanism against another need to be used. Second, it is important to use designs that can test whether there is a consistent dose-response relationship under varying conditions—two of the key requirements for testing causal inferences (Rutter, 1994b). Although in some circumstances there may be threshold effects in relation to environmental risks, the causal inference is strengthened by the demonstration that there is a consistent tendency for the risks of an adverse outcome to increase with increases in either the frequency or the severity of the postulated environmental risk factor. This should be evident under varying conditions, a standard expectation in experimental designs that arises from the importance of showing that the risks stem from the postulated risk factor and not from some other associated factor.

KEY REQUIREMENTS FOR TESTING CAUSAL HYPOTHESES

High-Quality Measurement

If there is to be adequate study of family influences of children's behavior, there must be high-quality, sensitive, and discriminating measures of the family environment aspects thought to provide the risks. Although many useful measures are available, they are not as strong as one might wish. They fall under several headings.

The first are questionnaire measures that aim to tap family discord (Busby, Christensen, Crane, & Larson, 1995; Spanier, 1976), family adaptation and cohesion (James & Hunsley, 1995; Maynard & Olson, 1987), family conflict (Straus, Hamby, Boney-McCoy, & Sugarman, 1996), or marital quality and satisfaction (Rust, Bennun, Crowe, & Golombok, 1986). Such scales have reasonable evidence of reliability and validity but they are global in focus, relying on informant perceptions and attitudes and lacking in differentiation of the types of possibly relevant family features and of the extent to which these impinge on the child. The need to focus on the experiences of each child in the family led to the development of scales to access differential parental treatment. The SIDE (Daniels & Plomin, 1985) was the first of these, and the TIRE (Carbonneau et al., in press) represents a more recent development. The findings indicate the value of an approach that focuses on differential treatment, but these scales require further work, if only because of the difficulties in getting parents to recognize that they do respond to their children in different ways.

The second set of measures are standardized interviews. These took a step forward in the 1960s with the development of the Camberwell Family Interview (Brown & Rutter, 1966; Rutter & Brown, 1966). Two features probably constituted the most important advances. First, a distinction was drawn between attitudes and behavior. Both were regarded as important, but researchers appreciated that they required different approaches to measurement. Second, to get around the biases associated with informant perceptions and halo effects, researchers designed the interview to obtain detailed descriptions of behavior as it actually occurred in the family in recent real-life situations. The result was the establishment of reliable and valid measures of qualities as subtle as warmth and hostility. These showed a high level of agreement between the independent accounts given by husbands and wives, and the measures were found to predict later marriage breakdown (Quinton, Rutter, & Liddle, 1984). These measures have stood the test of time and have shown their predictive power in relation to children's behavior (Rutter & Quinton, 1984; Rutter, Maughan, et al., 1997) but they remain limited in the extent to which they cover different aspects of family functioning.

A third type of measure involves quantification of emotional expression. An innovation of the Camberwell family interview was the development of the direct measure of so-called negative "expressed emotion" (Leff & Vaughn, 1985). It was appreciated that it should be possible to obtain a discriminating measure of the parental end of the parent–child relationship by noting the emotions and attitudes expressed in the *way* the child was described when it was left up to the parent to choose to bring out positive or negative aspects. Originally, this was based on accounts of critical and hostile remarks during a lengthy interview, but a shorter version was developed on the basis of similar accounts of negative remarks during a 5-minute period in which the parent was invited to talk generally about the child, without specific probes (Magaña et al., 1986). Two advantages to this measure are that it is focused and that it does not rely on parent perceptions or reporting.

A fourth approach is provided by direct observations of family interaction, either in the home or in the laboratory (Jacob & Tennenbaum, 1988). These observations provide direct measurement of actual behavior without the need for performance ratings or perceptions. They are the only satisfactory way of measuring sequences of behavior. However, they are limited because they are based on very short time samples of behavior in only one

situation. Furthermore, they are extremely demanding in terms of the resources required both for making the observations and for rating them. In
addition, there are several other techniques of value. For example, the
HOME Inventory (Caldwell & Bradley, 1994) uses a combination of parental
reports and direct observations by investigators.

We are far from having a satisfactory range of measures of family functioning. If we are to make the much-needed move from risk indicators to
risk mechanisms, ingenuity and creativity will be required to improve our
measurement techniques. In that connection, there is an inevitable trade-off
between quality of measurement on the one hand and sample size on the
other hand. To provide rigorous tests of causal hypotheses, and to take adequate account of confounding variables, large sample sizes are needed.
This inevitably places constraints on the measurement systems that can be
used. Nevertheless, it is important for investigators to appreciate that false
positive findings are more likely with small samples than with large ones
(Pocock, 1983).

Qualitative and Quantitative Approaches
to Measurement

Family researchers have tended to divide into those who favor qualitative
approaches and those who favor quantitative methods. Any dispassionate
consideration of the situation leads to the conclusion that both are needed.
Nevertheless, it may be helpful to outline the particular contributions to be
made by qualitative approaches (Coverdill, Finlay, & Martin, 1994; Kidder &
Fine, 1987; Seale, 1999). Four stand out as important.

First, quantitative researchers too often rush in with counts, without
having first determined which aspects of family functioning need to be assessed. This is where pilot studies should be used as an essential preliminary to any main study. However, not all pilot studies use qualitative methods optimally. These methods are always important, but they are especially
so when research focuses on children from atypical situations (for whom
preexisting measures may not be most appropriate), or when the interest
lies in aspects of either family functioning or child behavior that have been
little studied, or when the study involves social or cultural groups not included in previous research. Sometimes, misleadingly, qualitative research
is assumed to involve nothing more than a few haphazard unstructured interviews or observations of a few families. Qualitative research has its own
set of methodologies and techniques that involve quantification of qualitative measures.

Qualitative researchers sometimes write as if their methods provided
adequate answers on their own. They do not. It is crucial to pay detailed
and systematic attention to the heterogeneity of all samples, and this requires proper epidemiological methods and, usually, sizeable samples.

Also, the testing of causal hypotheses always requires some form of quanti-fication. It is important that investigators appreciate the need to combine quantitative and qualitative methods, both to determine what should be measured and to find out how it might best be assessed.

The second situation in which qualitative methods are appropriate is when the variable of interest focuses on qualities. This was the case, for ex-ample, with the development of measures of warmth and hostility in the Camberwell Family Interview, although this proceeded to a way of quantify-ing these qualities. The same applied to the concept of attachment insecu-rity (Ainsworth, Blehar, Waters, & Wall, 1978), in which the real advance lay in the appreciation that the most important feature of the attachment rela-tionship was the qualities that provided security rather than elements such as the number of approaches to or withdrawals from the parent. Initially, this was devised as a categorical measure, but, more recently, dimensional versions are being developed (Waters, Vaughan, Posada, & Kondo-Ikemura, 1995). The key feature of this use of qualitative measures is not whether they are categorical or dimensional, but rather their focus on qualities. Moreover, some form of quantification is almost always required.

The third circumstance in which qualitative measures are required is when it is necessary to identify and assess the unexpected. This need is fre-quently present even when the investigator already knows much about some aspects of the situation that needs to be quantified and when meas-ures for such quantification are already available. For example, in both nat-uralistic and experimental studies of diagnostic interviewing of clinically re-ferred samples, one of the most striking findings was the high frequency with which idiosyncratic, but clinically relevant, aspects of family function-ing were identified (Cox, Rutter, & Holbrook, 1981). Similarly, a long-term follow-up of children with developmental disorders of receptive language indicated the high frequency with which they showed subtle, but severe, deficits in social functioning in early adult life (Rutter & Mawhood, 1991; Howlin, Mawhood, & Rutter, 2000). Such deficits did not fit into the prevail-ing systems of psychiatric classification, but they were nevertheless associ-ated with substantial impairments in the individuals' real-life functioning. Again, a follow-up study of children adopted into U.K. families from depriv-ing institutions in Romania showed that quasi-autistic features were often present (Rutter, Andersen-Wood, et al., 1999). If such important features in either family functioning or child behaviors are to be identified and as-sessed, it is crucial to have a method of data collection that allows for a de-tailed description of sequences of behavior and not just yes/no answers to highly focused, closed questions. This has important implications for the style of standardized research interviews.

Fourth, qualitative and quantitative methods often need to be combined when seeking to delineate personal patterns of life trajectories (Singer, Ryff,

Carr, & Magee, 1998). Variable-oriented approaches have a definite place but, for some sorts of questions, person-oriented methods have advantages.

Differentiation of Person Effects and Environmental Effects

Much family research is based on between-group comparisons. Differences between groups are used to infer causal influences within the individual. Farrington (1988) pointed out that it is preferable to investigate within-individual change directly, in relation to specifically conceptualized and measured changed environmental circumstances, rather than to rely on the indirect inferences required for between-group comparisons. Longitudinal data, or the ability to reconstruct measures in a time sequence, are ordinarily required. Nevertheless, longitudinal data are not adequate on their own. To begin with, much apparent change over time merely reflects measurement error (Fergusson et al., 1996). Sometimes the errors may be random, but sometimes they reflect systematic biases deriving from unmeasured aspects of the outcome variable being studied. Appropriate statistical techniques to deal with this issue are essential (Laub, Nagin, & Sampson, 1998; Pickles & Rutter, 1991). Genetic influences may also bring about developmental change. Most obviously, they do so with respect to the onset of the menarche (Pickles et al., 1994). It is not that the genes change as a result of maturation, but rather that the genetic effects influence the programming of developmental changes.

Quasi-Experimental Designs: Experiments of Nature and Natural Experiments

One of the major problems in any correlational study that seeks to test causal hypotheses is that many of the relevant variables are intercorrelated. This limits the ability to take proper account of possible confounding variables; it limits the ability to take adequate account of the nonrandom allocation of risk environments; and it makes it difficult to differentiate between risk mediation stemming from one postulated risk factor and risk mediation stemming from another risk variable. Sometimes animal studies can be used to provide analogues of the human situation. For example, Harlow and Harlow (1969) examined social isolation in Rhesus monkeys, and Hinde and his colleagues studied forms of separation experiences in the same species (Hinde & McGinnis, 1977). Animal studies can be helpful in indicating possible mechanisms and in indicating which ones are implausible, although it is always necessary to check the extent to which one can generalize across species. Accordingly, not only because of the difficulty in finding animal analogues for many postulated family risk factors in humans, but because of the need to study the human situation directly, it is necessary to use quasi-experimental designs in naturalistic situations.

In each case, the key requirement is for the investigator to conceptualize which risks need to be differentiated and to search for sample designs that will enable such risks to be separated or pulled apart. Twin and adoptee designs are used to differentiate between the effects of nature and nurture (Rutter, Bolton, et al., 1990; Rutter, Silberg, et al., 1999a). Twin designs may properly be called an experiment of nature because the biological difference between identical and fraternal twins means the former have all their genes in common whereas the latter share, on average, only half their segregating genes. The adoption design is better described as a natural experiment in that it arises from the human practice of sometimes taking children from their biological parents in infancy and placing them with adoptive parents with whom they have no genetic relationship. Again, this situation allows a separation of nature and nurture. Originally, these two designs (or rather, the many variants of them) were designed to estimate the strength of genetic effects, with the environmental effects inferred from what remained in the variance unaccounted for. However, both twin and adoptee designs can be used to study more directly the effects of measured environments, although there are some important limitations in their use for this purpose (Rutter et al., in press).

There are many other forms of natural experiment. In each case, the key requirement is to think of situations that succeed in pulling apart the relevant variables, to articulate in detail the assumptions on which the designs rest, and to take the necessary steps to test whether those assumptions are met (Rutter et al., in press). A few examples illustrate what is involved.

There has long been an interest in identifying what parents do to foster (or retard) children's language development. Four problems have made this search for family influences difficult. First, children develop language in a wide range of family circumstances and maturational influences play a predominant role, with language developing normally in anything other than abnormal environments. Second, the effects of nature and nurture must be differentiated. Third, the genetic and environmental family risks associated with poor language development overlap with global social disadvantage, making it difficult to separate specific family variables. Fourth, differences in parental behavior that are caused by the children's language problems must be differentiated from parental behaviors that affect the children's language development.

The possibility of a natural experiment arises because of the well-demonstrated finding that, on average, twins lag substantially behind singletons in their language development (Rutter & Redshaw, 1991). The twin–singleton difference in language level may therefore be used as the dependent variable, rather than focusing on individual differences within either twins or singletons. There is no reason to suppose that the genetic influences in twins are different from those in singletons, and twins are no more likely than singletons to come from socially disadvantaged families. Two main types of causal factor are possible (although there are others). First, the language delay might derive from the higher rate of obstetric complications experienced by twins. Second, it could arise from the different patterns of postnatal family interaction associated with twinning. Rutter, Thorpe, and Golding (2000) have studied language delay in twins, using a general population epidemiological sample, with findings pointing to the role of the postnatal environment (using changes between 20 months and 36 months as a way of separating person effects on the environment from environmental effects on the person).

Roy, Rutter, and Pickles (2000) used the very different natural experiment of children being removed from their biological parents in early infancy as a result of parenting breakdown. In these circumstances, some children are placed in long-term residential care in institutions and others are placed in individual families for long-term fostering. The causal question examined here was whether institutional rearing was associated with adverse behavioral effects. The natural experiment relied on the assumption that the two alternative routes involved children who came from comparably adverse family backgrounds; the findings showed they did. Observational measures, as well as questionnaires and interviews, were used to ensure that any differences found were not a consequence of rater biases. The results showed a much higher rate of hyperactivity in the children placed in residential group homes, allowing the inference that this arose as a consequence of their different rearing experiences.

Where adoption results in a radical change in rearing environment for older children, the environmental change may be employed as the natural experiment. Rutter and colleagues used this method with children from depriving Romanian orphanages who were adopted into U.K. families (O'Connor, Rutter, Beckett, et al., 2000; Rutter & the ERA Study Team, 1998; Rutter, O'Connor, et al., 2000). As with other adopting families, these families tended to provide an above average rearing environment. The adoptees from Romania were compared with a nondeprived group of within-U.K. children adopted in the first 6 months of life. Both groups were studied, using a wide range of standardized measures, at 4 and 6 years of age; the measures in both samples were the same. The experimental test of environmental mediation was provided by two means. First, the method relied on the assessment of developmental catch-up during follow-up. Insofar as the children overcame their initial (usually severe) deficits, it may be inferred that the impairments evident at the time they left Romania were a consequence of the adverse rearing conditions experienced in Romanian institutions. The second test was provided by examination of the continuing sequelae in children where this occurred. To make a causal inference, it was necessary to determine whether such deficits were related in a systematic, dose-response fashion to some plausible mediating variable. Results showed that the most important predictive factor was the length of time that the child had experienced psychological privation in Romanian institutions. The degree of malnutrition played some contributory role, but its effects were much weaker than those associated with the duration of privation.

A range of other natural experiments are available and have been used to good effect (Rutter, Pickles, et al., in press). These include changes associated with a harmonious marriage for individuals from a high risk background (Laub et al., 1998; Zoccolillo, Pickles, Quinton, & Rutter, 1992), the changes associated with attending schools of varying qualities (Maughan, 1994; Mortimore, 1995, 1998), the educational gains for mildly retarded children after being adopted into advantaged families (Duyme, Dumaret, & Tomkiewicz, 1999), moves from a high crime to a low crime area (Osborn, 1980), peer group experiences (Rowe, Woulbroun, & Gulley, 1994), migration (McKenzie & Murray, 1999), and time-trend analyses to examine possible factors influencing changes over time in levels of problem behavior (Farrington, Lambert, & West, 1998; Rutter & Smith, 1995). In addition, intervention or treatment designs may be informative. However, the demonstration that such-and-such a treatment is effective does not, in itself, provide any adequate tests of a specific environmental mediating factor. This is because most interventions are multifaceted and the demonstration of treatment benefits does not indicate which environmental change made the most difference. What is required is testing whether changes in the postulated environmental mediating mechanism are related in a systematic way to changes in the outcome behavior of interest. Few treatment studies have been designed to do this, but the design is possible (Dishion, Patterson, & Kavanagh, 1992; Forgatch, 1991; Patterson & Forgatch, 1995) and more use needs to be made of the approach. In the future it should be possible to use molecular genetic findings to provide better leverage on environmental effects, a leverage that will arise because of accurate identification of susceptibility genes that are operating at an individual level (Plomin & Rutter, 1998).

Not as much use has been made of these designs as seems desirable, but they do provide an important potential for a more rigorous testing of family risk mechanisms. However, no one design is wholly satisfactory. Each has its own pattern of strengths and limitations. These patterns vary among the designs, and the message is that the strength lies in using a combination of different samples and different research designs. If these all provide answers pointing in the same direction, there can be considerable confidence in the causal inference. By contrast, if they do not, there needs to be caution in assuming a causal process has been identified.

RISK AND PROTECTIVE PROCESSES

Weak Effects From Single Risk Factors

A general finding from all studies of family risk factors is that single risk factors, if they occur in isolation, have small effects (Fergusson et al., 1996; Kolvin, Miller, Scott, Gatzanis, & Fleeting, 1990; Rutter, 1978). The search for one single family risk variable of overwhelming importance is likely to be futile. The apparent importance of particular family risk variables arises because family risk factors usually occur in combination. Truly single risks are the exception rather than the rule. However, statistical testing for whether a factor has a significant independent effect after taking into account other risk factors is not the same as testing for whether the same factor carries risks when it occurs on its own (Rutter, 1983).

Most Risk Processes Involve Indirect Chain Effects

Attention has been drawn already to the need to differentiate between distal and proximal risk factors. Both poverty and parental loss were used as examples of risk factors that mainly operated in distal fashion by giving rise to other risk processes that operated more approximately. However, it should not be thought that risk factors can be divided in binary fashion into those that are distal and those that are proximal. In many instances, both effects may apply in different connections. Thus, poor parental care is a proximal risk factor in its own right, but it is also a distal risk factor because it may lead to the child's being removed from the home of the biological parents and placed in group residential care. The experience of group care is itself a proximal risk factor, but it is also a distal factor in that it tends to lead to other risk experiences when the child leaves residential care in adolescence (Quinton & Rutter, 1988; Rutter, Quinton, & Hill, 1990). A proper understanding of the ways risk experiences lead to psychopathology requires investigation of the dynamic mechanisms operating over time, in which a series of risk experiences build up to have a cumulative effect that exceeds the effect of any one of the risks in isolation.

Risk and Protective Processes

During recent years, researchers have increasingly appreciated that risks cannot be considered solely in terms of the severity or frequency of adverse risk experiences (Rutter, 1985, 1990). Also, risk and protective factors cannot be regarded as synonymous with hedonically negative and positive experiences. There are several reasons why this parallel cannot be drawn. First, many features carry risk for one sort of outcome but are protective against others. For example, the temperamental characteristic of behavioral inhibition carries a risk for anxiety disorders but it is protective against antisocial behavior (Rutter, Giller, et al., 1998). In internal medicine, hetero-zygote status sickle cell anemia constitutes the best known example. Al-though involved in the risk for sickle cell anemia, it is substantially protec-tive against malaria. In the psychosocial arena, adoption may be viewed as providing some sort of parallel. The experience of being an adopted child probably carries with it some, albeit slight, psychological risks. On the other hand, for children from high-risk biological families, adoption may be substantially protective (Duyme et al., 1999; Maughan, Collishaw, & Pickles, 1998).

Second, it is clear in the somatic arena that protective processes often derive from successfully overcoming risk, rather than from avoiding it. Thus, resistance to infections arises from encountering and successfully overcoming them—either through natural exposure or through immuniza-tion—rather than being brought up in a germ-free environment. It is likely that the same applies with respect to psychosocial risks. Children gain through overcoming challenges and difficulties because such experiences may have a steeling effect. We know relatively little about the features that make a risk experience have a steeling, rather than sensitizing, quality, but it is likely that the key feature is encountering the risk at a time and in a way that leads to successful adaptation. Accordingly, it may be supposed that one important parenting skill probably comprises an ability to judge when children are ready for particular challenges and an ability to help them cope successfully.

RESILIENCE

One of the features of all studies of psychosocial risk factors (within the family and outside it) is that there are huge individual differences in re-sponse. Some children seem to escape most serious ill effects (although that does not necessarily mean they have been totally unaffected or un-scarred) whereas others succumb to lasting psychopathology. During re-cent years there have been increasing attempts to identify the reasons for this individual variation and especially for the factors that promote or fos-ter resilience in the face of serious psychosocial adversity (Rutter, 1999c, 2000a). Substantial methodological problems need to be overcome in study-ing resilience, and we cannot claim to have anything approaching a satisfac-tory knowledge of the relevant protective processes. Nevertheless, certain inferences may be drawn. The findings carry messages for understanding family processes and practicing family therapy.

Thus, resilience does not constitute an individual trait or characteristic. Moreover, children may show resilience in relation to some sorts of stresses and adversities, but not others; similarly, they may exhibit resistance to some sorts of psychopathological sequelae, but yet not others. The concept is important because, if properly dealt with, the findings can provide a better understanding of risk and protective mechanisms, an understanding that should help family therapists devise more effective means of helping individuals living in troubled families. Resilience involves a range of processes that bring together diverse mechanisms operating before, during, and after the encounter with the stress experience or adversity that is being considered, and it is necessary to appreciate how these operate.

Eight features appear to be involved in resilience processes, each of which has an implication for family therapy. First, the overall level of risk is crucial. Damage comes from the accumulation of many risk experiences, with only a small effect from any single experience, however negative. The implication is that reducing the overall level of risks may be helpful, even if considerable risks remain. Second, individual differences in sensitivity to risk are also crucial. These reflect both genetic influences and the effects of prior experiences, including the benefits from overcoming adversity or dealing effectively with challenges in the past. Individual features associated with sensitivity to risk include both temperamental characteristics and cognitive level. Third, the ill effects of psychosocial adversities are influenced by the extent to which the adverse experience directly impinges on the child. The need to consider how each child's position and role in the pattern of family relationships and dynamics differs from that of the other children in the same family has been a central tenet of family therapy from the outset, and empirical research findings provide strong support for the postulate. However, they also underline the need to consider how a child's own behavior shapes other people's responses and hence the interpersonal interactions experienced.

Fourth, a reduction of negative impact constitutes a critical issue in therapy. Parental supervision and monitoring of their children's activities is important in limiting exposure to risks in the peer group and community. Steps to avoid or reduce the scapegoating or targeting of individual children when parents are under stress is also vital. When the atmosphere and experiences at home are bad much of the time, children may choose to distance themselves from the family and it may be helpful for them to do so. The findings from research into resilience emphasize the importance of interventions to reduce the likelihood that vicious cycles of coercive interchange will develop. In addition, however, they serve as a reminder that both risk and protective factors operate in the peer group and community as well as within the family.

Fifth, although there is no one effective coping strategy, it is important to help young people avoid tactics that bring with them risks of a different kind. Thus, reliance on drugs and alcohol may bring its own problems, as may dropping out from education or having a child while still a teenager to escape from a stressful parental family.

Sixth, therapeutic actions need to focus on steps that reduce negative chain reactions that involve the individual's actions outside the family as well as those inside the family. Protection may lie in fostering positive chain reactions, and these need attention in therapeutic planning. Research findings have been important in showing the substantial benefits that may come from turning-point experiences in early adult life that provide a discontinuity with the past and open up new opportunities. Educational provision and a harmonious marriage can both serve this role. Doubtless, such beneficial turning points can arise at any point during life. However, they are more likely when individuals can influence what happens to them. Adolescence is critically important in that connection, with decisions needed on choice of peer group, love relationships, sexuality, use of drugs and alcohol, and persistence in education and work careers.

Seventh, the resilience findings are important in showing the influence of planning and self-efficacy in decision making and in indicating the experiences at home and school that are likely to play a part in determining whether children are able to develop a self-concept that enables them to feel in control of their lives.

Finally, it is important to appreciate what can be done in adult life to counteract the ill effects of earlier adversities in order to make it less likely that psychopathology will persist from childhood to adulthood. On the whole, simply providing positive experiences is of limited benefit, but if there are neutralizing experiences that negate or counteract the ill effects of negative ones, this may be beneficial.

Two other features warrant special mention. First, although the existence of large gender differences in many forms of psychopathology has been known for a long time, the mechanisms involved remain ill understood. In particular, it is not clear how far such differences operate through sex-indexed differential susceptibilities to psychosocial risks (Zaslow, 1988, 1989). It should not be assumed that differential susceptibility operates solely at an individual level. Maccoby (1998) has drawn attention to the marked differences between all-male and all-female peer groups, differences that seem likely to enhance what are initially small differences between boys and girls in individual styles of behavior when considered outside of a social context. Second, growing evidence shows that some genetic factors operate through their leading to increases or decreases in susceptibility to environmental stressors (Rutter, Dunn, et al., 1997). The study of gene-environment interactions poses many problems, not least of which are statistical (Wahlsten, 1990). Nevertheless, if we are to understand the risk and protective processes within the family, this interplay between nature and nurture will have to be better understood.

SOURCES OF MAIN FAMILY RISKS

There is much that we have yet to learn about risk and protective processes within the family. Nevertheless, there has been growth over the last half century or more in the conceptual understanding of how psychosocial risks operate and in the body of empirical research findings on which aspects of family functioning reflect risk mechanisms (Rutter, 1999c). Accordingly, several broad inferences are possible. First, the structure and overall composition of families are of limited importance as proximal risk factors. Thus, for example, being reared by a single parent is a risk indicator for psychopathology. Some slight direct risks may be attributable to being reared by only one parent, but the main risks appear to derive from the fact that being a single parent makes it more likely that all sorts of other risk factors will be present. Similarly, large family size is a risk indicator, albeit not a very strong one, but the main risks probably derive from the consequences large family size may have for patterns of family life in particular social circumstances rather than any direct effect from the number of people living in the home. Although the evidence is more limited, much the same may apply to children being brought up by a lesbian couple rather than a heterosexual one (Golombok & Tasker, 1996). It may be important for children to experience activities and relationships with males as well as females, but being in a lesbian household is not synonymous with a lack of such context. Indeed, in one study (Golombok, Spencer, & Rutter, 1983) children being reared by lesbian couples actually had more contact with adult males than did those being reared by heterosexual women acting as a single parent. The implication from research of these structural aspects of the family all point to the need to examine what the structure does for the functioning of the family as a social group.

Second, the details of which form of discipline and child management are probably of little consequence. It is important that parents exert discipline in a manner that is both responsive to individual children's needs and sensitivities and appropriately definite in terms of expectations. A lot of evidence also suggests that it is important for parents to monitor and supervise their children in an appropriate fashion (Rutter, Giller, et al., 1998). Although it would be going too far to say that the developmental progression for antisocial behavior is fully understood, it does seem that disruptive and aggressive behavior may peak initially in the preschool years, rather than later (Nagin & Tremblay, 1999; Tremblay et al., 1999). Accordingly, although parents may act in ways that foster aggressive or antisocial behavior, probably the main focus needs to be on what parents can do to help children find ways of managing disruptive and aggressive feelings that are part of the normal growing-up process. The concerns in the past over the supposed importance of factors such as when children receive toilet training or when they are weaned have also passed into the sands of time as it became evident that these did not constitute substantial risk factors.

Third, the quality and complexity of conversational interchange in the early experiences probably are important for cognitive, and especially linguistic, development. Thus, this seems to derive from the evidence from cross-fostering studies that offer substantial effects from the qualities of the adoptive home, at least at the social extremes (Capron & Duyme, 1989; Duyme et al., 1999; Schiff & Lewontin, 1986). It is also implicit in the findings from the cognitive development of children adopted from Romanian orphanages (O'Connor, Rutter, Beckett, et al., 2000; Rutter & the ERA Study Team, 1998), although this applies to extreme environments. The twin-singleton comparison provides evidence of influences that are within the normal range. Intervention studies, too, point to the importance of learning experiences within the family (Rutter, 2000b). Although there is no convincing evidence that a high-quality family environment (with respect to conversational interchange and learning experiences) makes much difference as compared with a middle-quality one, both of these seem to have benefits as compared with seriously poor family environments.

Fourth, at least with respect to risks for psychopathology, the quality and continuity of social relationships within the family probably constitute the single most important factor. The risks for antisocial behavior associated with family discord, conflict, hostility, and scapegoating of individual children have been evident in numerous naturalistic longitudinal studies (Rutter & the ERA Study Team, 1998), in genetically sensitive designs (Meyer et al., 2000, Pike, McGuire, Hetherington, Reiss, & Plomin, 1996; Thapar, Harold, & McGuffin, 1998), and there is some evidence from intervention studies that relevant changes in parenting behavior are associated with reductions in children's disruptive and antisocial behavior (Dishion et al., 1992; Forgatch, 1991; Patterson & Forgatch, 1995). The evidence that it is not just the negative effects of discord that are important, but also the lack of continuity in responsive individualized caregiving that matters, derives from the findings of the risks for hyperactive behavior and related features in children reared in an institutional setting (Roy et al., 2000). In addition, loss of a love relationship or a close friendship through rebuff or rejection ranks high among the stressors associated with depression (Brown & Harris, 1978, 1989).

Familywide or Child-Specific Effects?

Behavior geneticists have argued that their findings indicate that, insofar as family circumstances influence children's behavior and development, the effects impinge on individual children to make children in the same family different rather than similar (Plomin & Daniels, 1987; Rowe, 1994; Scarr,

1992). More recent genetic studies that have taken into account measurement error and that have examined the effects of behavior as manifest over time have shown that these claims are overstated (Rutter, Silberg, et al., 1999a). Taken as a whole, the findings suggest there are both familywide and child-specific effects. Nevertheless, it is important to recognize that familywide influences usually impinge differentially on children in the same family. This is partly because parents behave differently toward each child, partly because children vary in the extent to which they get drawn into the family situations that create risk, and partly because experiences do not impinge on a passive organism. Children actively process their experiences, both cognitively and affectively, and the ways they interpret their experiences make a difference to their impact.

EFFECTS OF THE ENVIRONMENT ON THE ORGANISM

In view of the empirical evidence that at least some effects of experiences in early life have consequences that persist through childhood and adolescence, and even into adult life, it is necessary to consider how this persistence over time comes about (Rutter, 1989). Little is known on this topic, and it constitutes a high priority for research in the future. Many possibilities for the mediation of effects need to be considered. For example, there may be effects on neural structure or function. Thus, animal studies suggest that severe stress may lead to neural damage in some circumstances (O'Brien, 1997). This possibility also arises with respect to physical adversities such as malnutrition or obstetric complications. In addition, there may be effects on the neuro-endocrine system. Animal studies have shown this happens in relation to physical stressors (Hennessey & Levine, 1979; Levine, 1962). Finally, the possibility of developmental programming needs to be considered. It is well established that visual input is needed for the organization of the visual cortex, and the same may apply to other sensory systems (Blakemore, 1991). Although many aspects of developmental programming remain controversial, there is evidence of some such process in relation to diet (Barker, 1994) and to the development of immunities (Bock & Whelan, 1991). The possible long-term effects of severe psychological privation on the development of normal social relationships (O'Connor, Rutter, & the ERA Study Team, 2000) may also involve something of this kind, although adequate data to test the hypothesis are not yet available.

Alternatively, the persistence may lie in the alteration of the person's cognitive set, or self-concept, or internal working model. This possibility has received most discussion in relation to the development of attachment relationships (Bretherton, 1990), but similar mechanisms may apply in relation to the vulnerability to depressive disorders in adult life associated with seriously adverse experiences in early childhood (Maughan, Messer, Taylor, Hallings-Pott, & Quinton, 1999) and with the ways in which the experience of abuse may lead to persisting antisocial behavior (Dodge, Bates, & Pettit, 1990; Dodge, Pettit, Bates, & Valente, 1995). Or, the main alteration may be in the person's behavioral habits or styles that first arise as a response to environmental adversity but persist because they have become either self-reinforcing or rewarded in some way by other people. In relation to the association between early psychosocial adversities and persisting antisocial behavior, it is likely that an alteration in patterns of interpersonal interaction is critical. An abundance of evidence shows that antisocial individuals act in ways that provoke negative interpersonal interactions (Rutter, Giller, et al., 1998), and it is likely that vicious cycles of environmental effects on interpersonal interaction, which in turn create stressors for the individual, may promote persistence of antisocial behavior. The different possibility is that the adverse experiences lead to an alteration of the social situation or of the developmental opportunities for the individuals. In this way, persistence lies more in the ways one adverse environment predisposes another, rather than in changes within the individuals. These are not mutually exclusive possibilities, but we must obtain a greater understanding than we have on what are the changes within the organism that predispose to the persistence of ill effects of adverse experiences.

DOES THE SOCIAL AND CULTURAL CONTEXT MATTER?

It is important to consider whether the effects of experiences vary according to social or cultural context (Rutter, 1999b). The evidence suggests that sometimes it does but sometimes it does not, and the need is to determine which applies to particular experiences and contexts. For example, the meaning of illegitimacy has changed radically over time. At the turn of the century, it was the source of major social stigma and usually meant the child was unwanted. By sharp contrast, now many technically illegitimate children are born within a stable family situation in which the parents have chosen not to marry, but in which the child's birth is registered in the names of both parents (Hess, 1995). There is also evidence that the effects of physical punishment may vary by ethnicity (Deater-Deckard & Dodge, 1997), presumably because it has different meanings in different ethnic or cultural groups. It cannot be assumed that experiences have the same meaning in all social contexts or at all times. On the other hand, some psychosocial hazards seem to carry broadly comparable risks in all, or almost all, social circumstances. For example, the adverse effects of serious family discord are fairly ubiquitous across all societies in which their effects have been examined.

Consideration of social context has four main implications. First, it is necessary to differentiate between experiences that truly carry risks because they are directly involved in the risk processes and experiences that are associated with adverse outcomes only because, in the sample studied, they happen to have been associated with other risk features. Second, it is necessary to determine whether the broader social context increases or decreases the risks associated with particular family experiences. Stress research provides examples of such effects (see Rutter, 1981b). Third, we need to appreciate the importance of indirect chain effects by which distal risk factors have effects that depend on their bringing about more proximal risks. The role of poverty in making good parenting more difficult is an example (Rutter, Giller, et al., 1998). Fourth, contextual effects serve as a reminder of the need to appreciate that most causal factors operate in a multifactorial, interactive fashion. Medical models have long appreciated this and have considered the difficulties that follow in moving from findings on risks to prevention policy initiatives (Holland & Stewart, 1997; Wall, 1995). We must put aside the deterministic models associated with psychoanalytic and behaviorist theories, and some other psychological approaches, and catch up with medical thinking on the complexities of causal mechanisms.

ARE THE CHILDHOOD YEARS ALL-IMPORTANT?

There has been much debate over the years on whether early childhood has a predominant influence on people's character (Clarke & Clarke, 1976; Pilling & Pringle, 1978; Rutter, 1981a; Rutter & Rutter, 1993). We have long since moved beyond the oversimplifying dichotomy views about the formative effect of early experiences. They are not determinative because of the strong evidence on the importance of adult experiences in relation to psychopathology of various kinds including antisocial behavior (Laub et al., 1998; Sampson & Laub, 1996) and depressive disorders (Brown & Harris, 1978, 1989). On the other hand, the childhood years are particularly important because early experiences serve to shape and select later experiences (Rutter et al., 1995). At one time the question was whether early experiences had effects that were independent of later experiences. The answer was that usually they did not (Rutter, 1981a). The question was misleading because many of the effects of early experiences rely on indirect chain reactions (Rutter, 1989). Later experiences are not, as a rule, independent of early experiences. The effects derive from continuities and discontinuities in experiences over time. What is needed is a better understanding of how these chain reactions develop and of how both continuities and discontinuities in experiences arise.

IS THE FAMILY THE KEY CONSIDERATION?

Although most psychosocial research has tended to assume that the family constitutes the major influence on children's behavior and development, this assumption has been called into question recently (Harris, 1998; Rowe, 1994; Scarr, 1992). The evidence makes it clear it would be misleading to see the overall family environment as the major influence because of the importance of individual experiences. These may occur either inside or outside the family, but it is the way in which they are experienced by the individual that matters, and the individual's cognitive and affective processing for those experiences may be important.

In addition, the family is not all important because of the evidence on the influence of both the peer group (Rowe et al., 1994) and of experiences at school (Maughan, 1994; Mortimore, 1995, 1998). Family researchers need to be aware of the evidence on these broader environmental influences. The evidence indicates, however, that the family affects children's experiences outside, as well as inside, the home. Thus, families are likely to influence children's choice of peer group and certainly they influence the choice of school. Families, too, are likely to play a role in shaping how children cope with, or adapt to, adverse experiences outside the home. In addition, many of the key experiences are within the family even though they impinge on children in the family in different ways. What is needed is not a polarization between the family and the rest of the environment but rather research that understands how psychosocial influences operate together.

DO FAMILY INFLUENCES REALLY MATTER?

This chapter started by noting some behavior geneticists' dismissal of family influences as being of only marginal importance. As we have seen, although some of their conceptual and methodological criticisms are valid (and need to shape family research strategies), the dismissal is not justified. Empirical research findings based on rigorous strategies designed to test for environmental mediation have shown that features such as family negativity or neglect carry substantial psychopathological risks (Rutter, 2000b).

WHERE DO WE GO FROM HERE?

Research has demonstrated the importance of family influences on children, and studies have provided good pointers on key elements of family functioning. Nevertheless, often the rhetoric of family researchers has exceeded the empirical basis for the claims. More is known than some critics argue, but more doubts and questions exist than some evangelists for the family recognize.

Eight main needs for the future may be identified. First, we must take seriously the need to test causal hypotheses. We have an immense body of evidence on risk indicators but we know much less about risk mechanisms. Accordingly, the first need is to undertake research that will enable us to identify how causal processes operate. Second, if this is going to be done effectively, it will be essential to pit alternative explanations against one another. Too much research in the past has been designed to prove some particular theory. What is required is research that will articulate alternative possibilities and that will use strategies to determine which is the most plausible. Third, we need to have research that can delineate the mechanisms involved in the interplay between persons and environments. Which aspects of people's behavior have the main effects on shaping and selecting experiences and how do those effects play a part in developmental continuities and discontinuities over time?

All research has shown the major differences in the ways people respond to stress and adversity. The fourth need, therefore, is to examine the nature of individual differences in susceptibility and of the risk and protective processes they represent.

Although there is evidence of the influence of the broader social environment, and some evidence on the ways this may influence the impact of experiences within the family, relatively little is known about the strength and nature of social contextual effects and especially of the mechanisms involved. The fifth need is to study these contextual effects and the mechanisms involved.

Too many writings on the family have been concerned with political postures and of theoretical evangelism. We should all be sensitive to the broader societal and political implications of many of the family features that we seek to study, but the sixth need is a dispassionate gathering of the relevant evidence with sensitivity to the issues, and not so much beating of drums.

Sometimes, research is conceptualized solely in terms of testing of hypotheses. As the Nobel laureate biologist Medawar (1982) brought out in his writings about the nature of scientific inquiry, creative ideas and astute observations are just as much an essential part of science as the experimental testing of hypotheses. The seventh need, therefore, is for innovative thinking and astute recognition of key features of family functioning. Finally, we need to question the dogma of the day. Professionals have always made confident statements about this or that aspect of effects of family influences on children, but over the decades the confident statements often reverse what was held to be self-evident in a previous generation. There is a need for constant vigilance to examine the evidence for the inferences based on research, and for careful attention to the samples studied and to the possibility of variations by sociocultural context.

REFERENCES

Achenbach, T. M., & Edelbrock, C. S. (1978). The classification of child psychopathology: A review and analysis of empirical efforts. *Psychological Bulletin, 85,* 1275–1301.

Ainsworth, M. S., Blehar, M. C., Waters, E., & Wall, S. (1978). *Patterns of Attachment.* Hillsdale, NJ: Lawrence Erlbaum Associates.

Barker, D. J. P. (1994). *Mothers, babies, and disease in later life.* London: BMJ.

Bell, R. Q., & Chapman, M. (1986). Child effects in studies using experimental or brief longitudinal approaches to socialization. *Developmental Psychology, 22,* 595–603.

Blakemore, C. (1991). Sensitive and vulnerable periods in the development of the visual system. In G. R. Bock & J. Whelan (Eds.), *The childhood environment and adult disease. Ciba Foundation Symposium 156* (pp. 129–146). Chichester, U.K.: Wiley.

Bock, G. R., & Whelan, J. (Eds.). (1991). *The childhood environment and adult disease. Ciba Foundation Symposium 156.* Chichester, U.K.: Wiley.

Bretherton, I. (1990). Open communication and internal working models: Their role in the development of attachment relationships. In R. A. Thompson (Ed.), *Nebraska symposium on motivation: Vol. 36. Socioemotional development* (pp. 57–113). Lincoln: University of Nebraska Press.

Brown, G. W., & Harris, T. O. (1978). *Social origins of depression: A study of psychiatric disorder in women.* London: Tavistock.

Brown, G. W., & Harris, T. O. (Eds.). (1989). *Life events and illness.* New York: Guilford.

Brown, C. (1984). *Black and white Britain: The Third PSI Survey.* London: Heinemann.

Brown, G. W., & Rutter, M. (1966). The measurement of family activities and relationships: A methodological study. *Human Relations, 19,* 241–263.

Busby, D. M., Christensen, C., Crane, D. R., & Larson, J. H. (1995). A revision of the Dyadic Adjustment Scale for use with distressed and nondistressed couples: Construct hierarchy and multidimensional scales. *Journal of Marital and Family Therapy, 21,* 289–308.

Caldwell, B. M., & Bradley, R. H. (1994). Environmental issues in developmental follow-up research. In S. L. Friedman & H. C. Haywood (Eds.), *Developmental follow-up: Concepts, domains, and methods* (pp. 235–256). San Diego, CA: Academic Press.

Capron, C., & Duyme, M. (1989). Assessment of the effects of socio-economic status on IQ in a full cross-fostering study. *Nature, 340,* 552–554.

Carbonneau, R., Rutter, M., Simonoff, E., Silberg, J. L., Maes, H. H., & Eaves, L. J. (in press). The Twin Inventory of Relationships and Experiences (TIRE): Psychometric properties of a measure of the nonshared and shared environmental experiences of twins and singletons. *International Journal of Methods in Psychiatric Research.*

Champion, L. A., Goodall, G. M., & Rutter, M. (1995). Behavioural problems in childhood and stressors in early adult life: A 20-year follow-up of London school children. *Psychological Medicine, 25,* 231–246.

Clarke, A. M., & Clarke, A. D. B. (Eds.). (1976). *Early experience: Myth and evidence.* London: Open Books.

Coverdill, J. E., Finlay, W., & Martin, J. K. (1994). Labor management in the southern textile industry. *Sociological Methods and Research, 23,* 54–58.

Cox, A., Rutter, M., & Holbrook, D. (1981). Psychiatric interviewing techniques: V. Experimental study: Eliciting factual information. *British Journal of Psychiatry, 139,* 29–37.

Cummings, E. M., & Davies, P. T. (1994). *Child and marital conflict: The impact of family dispute and resolution.* New York: Guilford.

Daniels, D., & Plomin, R. (1985). Differential experience of siblings in the same family. *Developmental Psychology, 21*, 747–760.

Deater-Deckard, K., & Dodge, K. A. (1997). Externalizing behavior problems and discipline revisited: Nonlinear effects and variation by culture, context, and gender. *Psychological Inquiry, 8*, 161–175.

Dishion, T. J., Patterson, G. R., & Kavanagh, K. A. (1992). An experimental test of the coercion model: Linking theory, measurement and intervention. In J. McCord & R. E. Tremblay (Eds.), *Preventing antisocial behaviour: Intervention from birth through adolescence* (pp. 253–282). New York: Guilford.

Dodge, K. A., Bates, J. E., & Pettit, G. S. (1990). Mechanisms in the cycle of violence. *Science, 250*, 1678–1683.

Dodge, K. A., Pettit, G. S., Bates, J. E., & Valente, E. (1995). Social information-processing patterns partially mediate the effect of early physical abuse on later conduct problems. *Journal of Abnormal Psychology, 104*, 632–643.

Duyme, M., Dumaret, A.-C., & Tomkiewicz, S. (1999). How can we boost IQs of "dull children"?: A late adoption study. *Proceedings of the National Academy of Sciences USA, 96*, 8790–8794.

Eaves, L. J., Silberg, J. L., Meyer, J. M., Maes, H. H., Simonoff, E., Pickles, A., Rutter, M., Neale, M. C., Reynolds, C. A., Erickson, M. T., Heath, A. C., Loeber, R., Truett, K. R., & Hewitt, J. K. (1997). Genetics and developmental psychopathology: 2. The main effects of genes and environment on behavioral problems in the Virginia Twin Study of Adolescent Behavioral Development. *Journal of Child Psychology and Psychiatry, 38*, 965–980.

Farrington, D. P. (1988). Studying changes within individuals: The causes of offending. In M. Rutter (Ed.), *Studies of psychosocial risk: The power of longitudinal data* (pp. 158–183). Cambridge, U.K.: Cambridge University Press.

Farrington, D. P., Lambert, S., & West, D. J. (1998). Criminal careers of two generations of family members in the Cambridge Study in Delinquent Development. *Studies in Crime and Crime Prevention, 7*, 1–22.

Fergusson, D. M., Horwood, L. J., Caspi, A., Moffitt, T. E., & Silva, P. A. (1996). The (artefactual) remission of reading disability: Psychometric lessons in the study of stability and change in behavioral development. *Developmental Psychology, 32*, 132–140.

Fergusson, D. M., Horwood, L. J., & Lynskey, M. T. (1992). Family change, parental discord and early offending. *Journal of Child Psychology and Psychiatry, 33*, 1059–1075.

Forgatch, M. S. (1991). The clinical science vortex: A developing theory of antisocial behavior. In D. J. Pepler & K. H. Rubin (Eds.), *The development and treatment of childhood aggression* (pp. 291–315). Hillsdale, NJ: Lawrence Erlbaum Associates.

Ge, X., Conger, R. D., Cadoret, R. J., Neiderhiser, J. M., Yates, W., Troughton, E., & Stewart, M. A. (1996). The developmental interface between nature and nurture: A mutual influence model of child antisocial behavior and parenting. *Developmental Psychology, 32*, 574–589.

Golombok, S., Spencer, A., & Rutter, M. (1983). Children in lesbian and single parent households: Psychosexual and psychiatric appraisal. *Journal of Child Psychology and Psychiatry, 24*, 551–572.

Golombok, S., & Tasker, F. (1996). Do parents influence the sexual orientation of their children? Findings from a longitudinal study of lesbian families. *Developmental Psychology, 32*, 3–11.

Harlow, H. F., & Harlow, M. K. (1969). Effects of various mother–infant relationships in rhesus monkey behaviours. In B. M. Foss (Ed.), *Determinants of infant behaviour* (Vol. 4, pp. 15–36). London: Methuen.

Harris, J. R. (1998). *The nature assumption: Why children turn out the way they do.* New York: The Free Press.

Harris, T., Brown, G. W., & Bifulco, A. (1986). Loss of parent in childhood and adult psychiatric disorder: The role of adequate parental care. *Psychological Medicine, 16*, 641–659.

Hennessey, J. W., & Levine, S. (1979). Stress, arousal, and the pituitary-adrenal system: A psychoendocrine hypothesis. In J. M. Sprague & A. N. Epstein (Eds.), *Progress in psychobiology and physiological psychology* (pp. 133–178). New York: Academic Press.

Hess, L. E. (1995). Changing family patterns in Western Europe: Opportunity and risk factors for adolescent development. In M. Rutter & D. J. Smith (Eds.), *Psychosocial disorders in young people: Time trends and their causes* (pp. 104–193). Chichester, U.K.: Wiley.

Hinde, R. A., & McGinnis, L. (1977). Some factors influencing the effect of temporary mother–infant separation: Some experiments with rhesus monkeys. *Psychological Medicine, 7*, 197–212.

Holland, W. W., & Stewart, S. (1997). *Public health: The vision and the challenge.* London: Nuffield Trust.

Horton, N. J., Laird, N. M., & Zahner, G. E. P. (1999). The use of multiple informant data as a predictor in psychiatric epidemiology. *International Journal of Methods in Psychiatric Research, 8*, 6–18.

Howlin, P., Mawhood, L., & Rutter, M. (2000). Autism and developmental receptive language disorder—A comparative follow-up in early adult life: II. Social, behavioural and psychiatric outcomes. *Journal of Child Psychology and Psychiatry, 41*, 561–578.

Jacob, T., & Tennenbaum, D. L. (1988). Family assessment methods. In M. Rutter, A. H. Tuma, & I. S. Lann (Eds.), *Assessment and diagnosis in child psychopathology* (pp. 196–231). New York: Guilford.

James, S., & Hunsley, J. (1995). The Marital Adaptability and Cohesion Evaluation Scale III: Is the relation with marital adjustment linear or curvilinear? *Journal of Family Psychology, 9*, 458–462.

Jenkins, J. M., & Smith, M. A. (1990). Factors protecting children living in disharmonious homes: Maternal reports. *Journal of the American Academy of Child and Adolescent Psychiatry, 29*, 60–69.

Jones, H. E. (1946). Environmental influences on mental development. In L. Carmichael (Ed.), *Manual of child psychology* (pp. 582–632). New York: Wiley.

Kidder, L. H., & Fine, M. (1987). Qualitative and quantitative methods: When stories converge. In M. M. Mark & R. L. Shotland (Eds.), *Multiple methods in program evaluation. New Directions for Program Evaluation* (No. 35, pp. 57–75). San Francisco: Jossey-Bass.

Kolvin, I., Miller, F. J. W., Scott, D. M., Gatzanis, S. R. M., & Fleeting, M. (1990). *Continuities of deprivation? The Newcastle Thousand-Family Survey.* Aldershot, England: Avebury.

Laub, J. H., Nagin, D. S., & Sampson, R. J. (1998). Trajectories of change in criminal offending: Good marriages and the desistance process. *American Sociological Review, 63*, 225–238.

Leff, J. P., & Vaughn, C. (1985). *Expressed emotion in families: Its significance for mental illness.* New York: Guilford.

Levine, S. (1962). The effects of infantile experience on adult behavior. In A. J. Bachrach (Ed.), *Experimental Foundations of Clinical Psychology* (pp. 139–169). New York: Basic Books.

Maccoby, E. (1998). *The two sexes: Growing up apart, coming together.* Cambridge, MA: Belknap.

Madood, T., Berthoud, R., Lakey, J., Nazroo, V., Smith, P., Virdee, S., & Beishon, S. (1997). *Ethnic minorities in Britain: Diversity and disadvantage.* London: Policy Studies Institute.

Magaña, A. B., Goldstein, M. J., Karno, M., Niklowitz, D. J., Jenkins, J., & Falloon, I. R. H. (1986). A brief method for assessing expressed emotion in relatives of psychiatric patients. *Psychiatric Research, 17*, 203–212.

Maughan, B. (1994). School influences. In M. Rutter & D. F. Hay (Eds.), *Development through life: A handbook for clinicians* (pp. 134–158). Oxford, England: Blackwell Scientific.

Maughan, B., Collishaw, S., & Pickles, A. (1998). School achievement and adult qualifications among adoptees: A longitudinal study. *Journal of Child Psychology and Psychiatry, 39*, 669–685.

Maughan, B., Messer, J., Taylor, A., Hallings-Pott, C., & Quinton, D. (1999, April). *Institutional rearing and intimate relationships in adult life.* Paper presented at the Biennial meeting of the Society for Research in Child Development, Alburquerque, NM.

Maynard, P. E., & Olson, D. H. (1987). Circumplex model of family systems: A treatment tool in family counseling. *Journal of Counseling and Development, 65*, 502–504.

McKenzie, K., & Murray, R. (1999). Risk factors for psychosis in the UK African-Caribbean population. In D. Bhugra & V. Bahl (Eds.), *Ethnicity: An agenda for mental health* (pp. 48–59). London: Gaskell.

Medawar, P. (1982). *Pluto's Republic.* Oxford, England: Oxford University Press.

Meyer, J. M., Rutter, M., Silberg, J. L., Maes, H. H., Simonoff, E., Shillady, L. L., Pickles, A., Hewitt, J. K., & Eaves, L. J. (2000). *Familial aggregation for conduct disorder symptomatology: The role of genes, marital discord, and family adaptability.* Manuscript submitted for publication.

Moffitt, T. E., & Caspi, A. (1998). Implications of violence between intimate partners for child psychologists and psychiatrists. *Journal of Child Psychology and Psychiatry, 39*, 137–144.

Mortimore, P. (1995). The positive effects of schooling. In M. Rutter (Ed.), *Psychosocial disturbance in young people: Challenges for prevention* (pp. 333–363). New York: Cambridge University Press.

Mortimore, P. (1998). *The road to improvement: Reflections on school effectiveness.* Lisse, Netherlands: Swets & Zeitlnger.

Nagin, D., & Tremblay, R. E. (1999). Trajectories of boys' physical aggression, opposition, and hyperactivity on the path to physically violent and nonviolent juvenile delinquency. *Child Development, 70*, 1181–1196.

O'Brien, J. T. (1997). The "glucocorticoid cascade" hypothesis in man. Prolonged stress may cause permanent brain damage. *British Journal of Psychiatry, 170*, 199–201.

O'Connor, T. G., Deater-Deckard, K., Fulker, D., Rutter, M., & Plomin, R. (1998). Genotype-environment correlations in late childhood and early adolescence: Antisocial behavioral problems and coercive parenting. *Developmental Psychology, 34*, 970–981.

O'Connor, T. G., Rutter, M., Beckett, C., Keaveney, L., Kreppner, J., & the English and Romanian Adoptees (E.R.A.) Study Team (2000). The effects of global severe privation on cognitive competence: Extension and longitudinal follow-up. *Child Development, 71*, 376–390.

O'Connor, T. G., Rutter, M., & the English and Romanian Adoptees (E.R.A.) Study Team (2000). Attachment disorder behavior following early severe deprivation: Extension and longitudinal follow-up. *Journal of American Academy of Child and Adolescent Psychiatry, 39*, 703–712.

Osborn, S. G. (1980). Moving home, leaving London and delinquent trends. *British Journal of Criminology, 20*, 54–61.

Patterson, G. R., & Forgatch, M. S. (1995). Predicting future clinical adjustment from treatment outcome and process variables. *Psychological Assessment, 7*, 275–285.

Pickles, A., Neale, M., Simonoff, E., Rutter, M., Hewitt, J., Meyer, J., Crouchley, R., Silberg, J., & Eaves, L. (1994). A simple method for censored age-of-onset data subject to recall bias: Mothers' reports of age of puberty in male twins. *Behavior Genetics, 24*, 457–468.

Pickles, A., & Rutter, M. (1991). Statisical and conceptual models of "turning points" in developmental processes. In D. Magnusson, L. R. Bergman, G. Rudinger, & B. Törestad (Eds.), *Problems and methods in longitudinal research: Stability and change* (pp. 133–165). Cambridge, U.K.: Cambridge University Press.

Pike, A., McGuire, S., Hetherington, E. M., Reiss, D., & Plomin, R. (1996). Family environment and adolescent depression and antisocial behavior: A multivariate genetic analysis. *Developmental Psychology, 32*, 590–603.

Pilling, D., & Pringle, M. K. (1978). *Controversial issues in child development.* London: Elek.

Plomin, R. (1994). *Genetics and experience: The interplay between nature and nurture.* Thousand Oaks: CA: Sage.

Plomin, R., & Daniels, D. (1987). Why are children in the same family so different from each other? *Behavioral and Brain Sciences, 10*, 1–16.

Plomin, R., & Rutter, M. (1998). Child development, molecular genetics, and what to do with genes once they are found. *Child Development, 69*, 1223–1242.

Pocock, S. J. (1983). *Clinical trials: A practical approach.* Chichester, U.K.: Wiley.

Quinton, D., & Rutter, M. (1988). *Parenting breakdown: The making and breaking of intergenerational links.* Aldershot, England: Avebury.

Quinton, D., Rutter, M., & Liddle, C. (1984). Institutional rearing, parenting difficulties and marital support. *Psychological Medicine, 14,* 107–124.

Reiss, D., Hetherington, M., Plomin, R., Howe, G. W., Simmon, S. J., Henderson, S. H., O'Connor, T. J., Bussell, D. A., Anderson, E. R., & Law, T. (1995). Genetic questions for environmental studies: Differential parenting and psychopathology in adolescence. *Archives of General Psychiatry, 52,* 925–936.

Robins, L. (1966). *Deviant children grown up.* Baltimore: Williams & Wilkins.

Rowe, D. C. (1994). *The limits of family influence: Genes, experience and behavior.* New York: Guilford.

Rowe, D. C., Woulbroun, E. J., & Gulley, B. L. (1994). Peers and friends as nonshared environmental influences. In E. M. Hetherington, D. Reiss, & R. Plomin (Eds.), *Separate social worlds of siblings: Impact of nonshared environment on development* (pp. 159–173). Hillsdale, NJ: Lawrence Erlbaum Associates.

Roy, P., Rutter, M., & Pickles, A. (2000). Institutional care: Risk from family background or pattern of rearing? *Journal of Child Psychology and Psychiatry, 41,* 139–149.

Rust, J., Bennun, I. S., Crowe, M., & Golombok, S. (1986). The Golombok Rust Inventory of Marital State (GRIMS). *Sexual and Marital Therapy, 1,* 55–60.

Rutter, M. (1971). Parent–child separation: Psychological effects on the children. *Journal of Child Psychology and Psychiatry, 12,* 233–260.

Rutter, M. (1978). Early sources of security and competence. In J. S. Bruner & A. Garton (Eds.), *Human growth and development* (pp. 33–61). London: Oxford University Press.

Rutter, M. (1981a). *Maternal deprivation reassessed (2nd ed.).* Harmondsworth, England: Penguin.

Rutter, M. (1981b). Stress, coping and development: Some issues and some questions. *Journal of Child Psychology and Psychiatry, 22,* 323–356.

Rutter, M. (1983). Statistical and personal interactions: Facets and perspectives. In D. Magnusson & V. Allen (Eds.), *Human development: An interactional perspective* (pp. 295–319). New York: Academic Press.

Rutter, M. (1985). Resilience in the face of adversity: Protective factors and resistance to psychiatric disorder. *British Journal of Psychiatry, 147,* 598–611.

Rutter, M. (1989). Pathways from childhood to adult life. *Journal of Child Psychology and Psychiatry, 30,* 23–51.

Rutter, M. (1990). Psychosocial resilience and protective mechanisms. In J. Rolf, A. Masten, D. Cicchetti, K. Nuechterlein, & S. Weintraub (Eds.), *Risk and protective factors in the development of psychopathology* (pp. 181–214). New York: Cambridge University Press.

Rutter, M. (1994a). Family discord and conduct disorder: Cause, consequence or correlate? *Journal of Family Psychology, 8,* 170–186.

Rutter, M. (1994b). Beyond longitudinal data: Causes, consequences, changes and continuity. *Journal of Consulting and Clinical Psychology, 62,* 928–940.

Rutter, M. (1999a). Psychosocial adversity and child psychopathology. *British Journal of Psychiatry, 174,* 480–493.

Rutter, M. (1999b). Social context: Meanings, measures and mechanisms. *European Review, 7,* 139–149.

Rutter, M. (1999c). Resilience, concepts and findings: Implications for family therapy. *Journal of Family Therapy, 21,* 159–160.

Rutter, M. (2000a). Resilience reconsidered: Conceptual considerations, empirical findings and policy implications. In J. P. Shonkoff & S. J. Meisels (Eds.), *Handbook of early childhood intervention* (2nd ed., pp. 651–682). New York: Cambridge University Press.

Rutter, M. (2000b). Psychosocial influences: Critiques, findings and research needs. *Development and Psychopathology, 12,* 375–405.

Rutter, M., Andersen-Wood, L., Beckett, C., Bredenkamp, D., Castle, J., Groothues, C., Kreppner, L., Lord, C., O'Connor, T. G., & the ERA Study Team. (1999). Quasi-autistic patterns following severe early global privation. *Journal of Child Psychology and Psychiatry, 40,* 537–549.

Rutter, M., Bolton, P., Harrington, R., Le Couteur, A., Macdonald, H., & Simonoff, E. (1990). Genetic factors in child psychiatric disorders. I. A review of research strategies. *Journal of Child Psychology and Psychiatry, 31,* 3–37.

Rutter, M., & Brown, G. W. (1966). The reliability and validity of measures of family life and relationships in families containing a psychiatric patient. *Social Psychiatry, 1,* 38–53.

Rutter, M., Champion, L., Quinton, D., Maughan, B., & Pickles, A. (1995). Understanding individual differences in environmental risk exposure. In P. Moen, G. H. Elder Jr., & K. Lüscher (Eds.), *Examining lives in context: Perspectives on the ecology of human development* (pp. 61–93). Washington, DC: American Psychological Association.

Rutter, M., Dunn, J., Plomin, R., Simonoff, E., Pickles, A., Maughan, B., Ormel, J., Meyer, J., & Eaves. L. J. (1997). Integrating nature and nurture: Implications of person-environment correlations and interactions for developmental psychopathology. *Development and Psychopathology, 9,* 335–364.

Rutter, M., & the English and Romanian Adoptees (E.R.A.) Study Team (1998). Developmental catch-up, and deficit, following adoption after severe global early privation. *Journal of Child Psychology and Psychiatry, 39,* 465–476.

Rutter, M., Giller, H., & Hagell, A. (1998). *Antisocial behavior by young people.* New York and London: Cambridge University Press.

Rutter, M., Maughan, B., Meyer, J., Pickles, A., Silberg, J., Simonoff, E., & Taylor, E. (1997). Heterogeneity of antisocial behavior: Causes, continuities and consequences. In R. Dienstbier & D. W. Osgood (Eds.), *Nebraska symposium on motivation: Vol. 44. Motivation and delinquency* (pp. 45–118). Lincoln: University of Nebraska Press.

Rutter, M., & Mawhood, L. (1991). The long-term psychosocial sequelae of specific developmental disorders of speech and language. In M. Rutter & P. Casaer (Eds.), *Biological risk factors for psychosocial disorders* (pp. 233–259). Cambridge, U.K.: Cambridge University Press.

Rutter, M., O'Connor, T., Beckett, C., Castle, J., Croft, C., Dunn, J., Groothues, C., & Kreppner, J. (2000). Recovery and deficit following profound early deprivation. In P. Selman (Ed.), *Intercountry adoption: Developments, trends and perspectives* (pp. 107–125). London: British Agencies for Adoption and Fostering.

Rutter, M., Pickles, A., Murray, R., & Eaves, L. (in press). Testing hypotheses on specific environmental causal effects on behavior. *Psychological Bulletin.*

Rutter, M., & Quinton, D. (1984). Parental psychiatric disorder: Effects on children. *Psychological Medicine, 14,* 853–880.

Rutter, M., Quinton, D., & Hill, J. (1990). Adult outcomes of institution-reared children: Males and females compared. In L. Robins & M. Rutter (Eds.), *Straight and devious pathways from childhood to adulthood* (pp. 135–157). New York: Cambridge University Press.

Rutter, M., & Redshaw, J. (1991). Annotation: Growing up as a twin: Twin-singleton differences in psychological development. *Journal of Child Psychology and Psychiatry, 32,* 885–895.

Rutter, M., & Rutter, M. (1993). *Developing minds: Challenge and continuity across the lifespan.* Harmondsworth, England: Penguin.

Rutter, M., Silberg, J., O'Connor, T., & Simonoff, E. (1999a). Genetics and child psychiatry: I. Advances in quantitative and molecular genetics. *Journal of Child Psychology and Psychiatry, 40,* 3–18.

Rutter, M., Silberg, J., O'Connor, T., & Simonoff, E. (1999b). Genetics and child psychiatry: II. Empirical research findings. *Journal of Child Psychology and Psychiatry, 40,* 19–55.

Rutter, M., & Smith, D. J. (Eds.). (1995). *Psychosocial Disorders in Young People: Time Trends and Their Causes.* Chichester, U.K.: Wiley.

Rutter, M., Thorpe, K., & Golding, J. with Greenwood, R. & North, K. (2000). *Twins as a natural experiment to study the causes of language delay.* Report to the Mental Health Foundation, London.

Sampson, R. J., & Laub, J. H. (1996). Socioeconomic achievement in the life course of disadvantaged men: Military service as a turning point, circa 1940–1965. *American Sociological Review, 61*, 347–367.

Scarr, S. (1992). Developmental theories for the 1990s: Development and individual differences. *Child Development, 63*, 1–19.

Schiff, M., & Lewontin, R. (1986). *Education and class: The irrelevance of IQ genetic studies*. Oxford, England: Clarendon.

Seale, C. (1999). *The quality of qualitative research*. London: Sage.

Simonoff, E., Pickles, A., Meyer, J., Silberg, J., Maes, H., Loeber, R., Rutter, M., Hewitt, J., & Eaves, L. (1997). The Virginia Twin Study of Adolescent Behavioral Development: Influences of age, sex, and impairment on rates of disorder. *Archives of General Psychiatry, 54*, 801–808.

Singer, B., Ryff, C. D., Carr, D., & Magee, W. J. (1998). Linking life histories and mental health: A person-centered strategy. *Sociological Methodology, 28*, 1–51.

Spanier, G. B. (1976). Measuring dyadic adjustment: New scales for assessing the quality of marriage and other dyads. *Journal of Marriage and Family, 38*, 15–28.

Stoolmiller, M. (1999). Implications of the restricted range of family environments for estimates of heritability and nonshared environment in behavior-genetic adoption studies. *Psychological Bulletin, 125*, 392–409.

Straus, M. A., Hamby, S. L., Boney-McCoy, S., & Sugarman, D. B. (1996). The revised Conflict Tactics Scale (CTS2): Development and preliminary psychometric data. *Journal of Family Issues, 17*, 283–316.

Thapar, A., Harold, G., & McGuffin, P. (1998). Life events and depressive symptoms in childhood—shared genes or shared adversity? A research note. *Journal of Child Psychology and Psychiatry, 39*, 1153–1158.

Tremblay, R. E., Japel, C., Pérusse, D., McDuff, P., Boivin, M., Zoccolillo, M., & Montplaisir, J. (1999). The search for the age of "onset" of physical aggression: Rousseau and Bandura revisited. *Criminal Behavior & Mental Health, 9*, 8–23.

Wahlsten, D. (1990). Insensitivity of the analysis of variance to heredity-environment interaction. *Behavioral and Brain Sciences, 13*, 109–161.

Wall, S. (1995). Epidemiology for prevention. *International Journal of Epidemiology, 24*, 655–664.

Waters, E., Vaughn, B., Posada, G., & Kondo-Ikemura, K. (1995). Constructs, cultures, and caregiving: New growing points of attachment theory and research. *Monographs for the Society for Research in Child Development, 60* (Nos. 2–3).

Zaslow, M. J. (1988). Sex differences in children's responses to parental divorce: I. Research methodology and postdivorce family forms. *American Journal of Orthopsychiatry, 58*, 355–378.

Zaslow, M. J. (1989). Sex differences in children's responses to parental divorce: II. Samples, variables, ages and sources. *American Journal of Orthopsychiatry, 59*, 118–141.

Zoccolillo, M., Pickles, A., Quinton, D., & Rutter, M. (1992). The outcome of childhood conduct disorder: Implications for defining adult personality disorder and conduct disorder. *Psychological Medicine, 22*, 971–986.

Author Index

A

Ablard, K. E., 194, 203, 204, 210, 211, 223
Ablow, J., 143, 160
Abramovitch, R., 194, 197, 199, 202, 203, 204, 219, 222
Achenbach, T. M., 323, 345
Adams, B. N., 194, 219
Adams, N. L., 102, 117
Addis, M. E., 106, 114, 120
Ade-Ridder, L., 218, 221, 293, 317
Adrian, C., 297, 317
Agnew, C. R., 111, 123, 124, 125
Ahmeduzzaman, M., 46, 60
Ahrons, C., 138, 140, 157, 160, 294, 314
Ainsworth, M. D. S., 35, 60, 211, 219, 329, 345
Aksan, N., 22, 31
Alarcon, O., 67, 86, 89
Alberts, J. K., 102, 104, 116
Aldarondo, E., 299, 314
Aldous, J., 168, 183
Allen, W. R., 137, 163
Allison, K., 178, 184
Allison, P. D., 103, 116
Almeida, R.V., 58, 60
Alpert, R., 11, 31
Amato, P. R., 75, 76, 88, 93, 108, 117, 289, 290, 291, 314
Amoloza, T. O., 110, 120
Amsler, F., 150, 165
Andersen-Wood, L., 329, 350
Anderson, B. J., 253, 256
Anderson, C. A., 110. 120
Anderson, E. R., 72, 90, 325, 349
Anderson, N. B., 308, 316
Anderson, R. F., 288, 314

Andrews, L. B., 81, 88
Apfel, N., 154, 160
Apostoleris, N., 27, 31
Appelbaum, P. S., 283, 317
Arkowitz, H. S., 106, 117
Armitzia, M., 200, 221
Arriaga, X. B., 111, 112, 124
Artemyeff, C., 307, 319
Asarnow, J. R., 111, 118
Asch, A., 150, 164
Astone, N. M., 27, 31
Auerbach, C. F., 47, 53, 54, 60, 63, 74, 76, 78, 79, 86, 93
Azar, S. T., 284, 287, 293, 296, 300, 302, 308, 309, 310, 311, 312, 314, 315

B

Babcock, J. C., 107, 118
Bailey, C., 158, 164
Bailey, J. M., 77, 88
Baldwin, A. L., 10, 16, 29, 68, 88
Baldwin, B. M., 113, 117
Baldwin, C., 16, 29, 68, 88
Baldwin, J. H., 113, 117
Baldwin, J. M., 227, 253
Baldwin, L. M., 305, 311, 316
Bank, L., 214, 222
Bank, S. P., 210, 213, 215, 217, 219
Banker, B., 260, 277
Barber, B., 10, 29
Barbour, L., 198, 221
Baris, M. A., 288, 317
Barker, D. J. P., 340, 345
Barnett, R. C., 43, 54, 60
Barnum, R., 296, 316
Barry, W. A., 102, 122
Barth, J. M., 28, 29

Bartlett, K., 158, 160
Bartz, K. W., 304, 315
Baruch, G. K., 43, 54, 60
Bates, J. E., 341, 346
Bateson, G., 229, 253
Bateson, M., 135, 160
Baucom, D. D., 103, 105, 106, 117, 123
Baumrind, D., 10, 11, 12, 13, 29, 300, 302, 304, 315
Baxter, L., 113, 118
Baydar, N., 208, 219
Bayley, N., 202, 219
Beach, S. R. H, 105, 106, 117, 119, 124
Beam, M. R., 78, 90
Beaman, J., 27, 33
Beatty, W. W., 75, 91
Becker, B., 158, 165
Becker, W. C., 10, 11, 12, 30
Beckett, C., 322, 329, 350
Beckwith, L., 296, 319
Behrens, B. C., 107, 117
Behrman, R. E., 25, 30
Beishon, S., 323, 347
Beitel, A., 73, 91, 148, 160
Bell, N. W., 233, 253
Bell, R. Q., 8, 30, 70, 88, 229, 230, 233, 253, 324, 345
Bellanti, C. J., 215, 217, 223
Belsky, J., 25, 29, 30, 85, 88, 112, 117, 142, 144, 145, 160, 168, 173, 177, 183, 186, 210, 211, 224, 234, 253, 260, 269, 277, 278, 304, 312, 315
Benetti, S., 46, 63
Benjet, C. L., 27, 31, 284, 287, 300, 302, 310, 315
Bennun, I. S., 326, 349
Benson, A., 48, 60
Benson, P. R., 105, 122
Bergman, L. R., 181, 184, 186
Berley, R. A., 104, 117
Berndt, T. J., 155, 163, 213, 219
Berry, M., 295, 315
Bersheid, E., 170, 184
Berthoud, R., 323, 347
Betancourt, H., 68, 88

Beverly, E., 214, 217, 224
Bhavnagri, N., 77, 92
Bierman, K. L., 215, 217, 223
Bietel, A., 84, 85, 88
Bifulco, A., 324, 346
Biller, H. B., 40, 43, 60
Billings, A., 103, 117
Birch, H. G., 207, 208, 209, 223
Birchler, G. R., 102, 117
Bish, A., 80, 90
Bishop, D. S., 305, 311, 316
Bishop, S. J., 317
Blaher, J., 301, 315
Blaisure, K., 116, 117
Blakemore, C., 340, 345
Blane, H. T., 106, 120
Blankenhorn, D., 116, 122
Blankenhorn, D., 40, 41, 42, 55, 60
Blehar, M. C., 35, 60, 211, 219, 329, 345
Block, J. H., 235, 254
Block, J., 235, 254
Blood, R. O., Jr., 113, 117
Blumberg, S. L., 107, 121, 170, 188
Blyth, D., 71, 93
Bobrow, D., 77, 88
Bobulinski, M., 115, 123
Bock, G. R., 340, 345
Bogat, G. A., 307, 317
Boivin, M., 338, 351
Bolden, B., 156, 165
Boles, A. J., 112, 118
Bolger, N., 26, 30
Bolocofsky, D. N., 315
Bolton, P., 331, 350
Bond, L. A., 194, 197, 199, 202, 203, 204, 221, 223
Boney-McCoy, S., 326, 351
Booth, A., 110, 120
Bornstein, M. H., 9, 30, 68, 88, 206, 219
Boslett, M., 207, 223
Boss, P. G., 72, 88
Bosso, R., 210, 219
Bost, K. K., 205, 224
Bouma, R., 115, 119

Bowen, M., 151, 160
Bowlby, J., 7, 14, 30, 35, 40, 42, 60,
  82, 83, 85, 88, 92, 211, 219, 305, 315
Bozett, F. W., 77, 88
Bradbury, T. N., 72, 88, 104, 105, 108,
  109, 111, 116, 117, 119, 120, 122
Bradley, A. R., 285, 286, 319
Bradley, M. E., 215, 217, 223
Bradley, R. H., 328, 345
Braungart, J. M., 25, 29, 30
Breaux, C., 42, 61
Bredenkamp, D., 329, 350
Bretherton, I., 211, 219, 340, 345
Bridges, M., 41, 42, 61, 259, 260,
  271, 277
Broderick, C., 236, 254
Brody, G. H., 27, 30, 142, 154, 160,
  199, 204, 205, 210, 211, 212, 213,
  215, 219, 223, 259, 278
Bronfenbrenner, U., 153, 155, 161,
  271, 277
Brooks-Gunn, J., 76, 88, 138, 154,
  161, 175, 180, 181, 185, 186, 208,
  219
Brott, A., 75, 92
Brown, C., 323, 345
Brown, G. W., 297, 315, 324, 327,
  339, 342, 345, 346, 350
Brown, J. R., 197, 215, 219
Brown, L. B., 11, 31
Bryant, B. K., 210, 211, 212, 215, 220
Bryant, W. K., 26, 30
Buchanan, C. M., 140, 161, 176, 184
Budd, K. S., 296, 287, 315
Buergin, D., 150, 165
Buhrmester, D., 177, 184, 194, 215,
  220, 221
Bui, K. T., 111, 118
Bulleit, T. N., 213, 219
Bunshaft, D., 307, 316
Burchinal, M., 173, 175, 185
Burge, D., 297, 317
Burgess, E. W., 100, 118, 132, 161,
  230, 254
Buriel, R., 68, 92, 177, 178, 186, 252,
  256, 302, 304, 319

Burke, M., 211, 219
Burks, V., 82, 83, 92
Burman, B., 102, 108, 119, 121, 234,
  254
Burton, L. M., 36, 50, 51, 58, 61, 86,
  88, 177, 178, 184, 185, 187, 274,
  276, 277
Busby, D. M., 326, 345
Bushwall, S. J., 27, 30
Bussell, D. A., 325, 349
Buttenwieser, P., 100, 124

C

Cabrera, N., 156, 165
Cadoret, R. J., 325, 346
Cain, R. L., 253, 256
Cairns, R. B., 170, 184
Caldwell, B. M., 328, 345
Camera, K., 140, 161
Camparo, L., 177, 184
Campbell, L., 140, 163
Campbell, S. B., 175, 184, 212, 214,
  220, 222
Campos, J. J., 7, 33
Caplan, P. J., 7, 30
Capron, C., 339, 345
Carbonneau, R., 327, 345
Carlos, M. L., 307, 317
Carlsmith, J. M., 27, 30
Carlton, K., 102, 121
Carpenter, M., 232, 254
Carr, D., 329, 351
Carrere, S., 109, 119
Carson, J., 82, 83, 84, 85, 88, 92
Carstairs, G. M., 297, 315
Carter, D. B., 68, 92
Carter, E. A., 237, 256
Caspi, A., 82, 88, 325, 348, 330, 334,
  346
Cassidy, J., 179, 184
Cassirer, E., 227, 252, 254
Castle, J., 322, 329, 350
Castonguay, L. G., 114, 118
Cauce, A. M., 303, 306, 315, 316
Cavallero, L., 287, 315

Cazenave, N. A., 38, 61
Champion, L. A., 323, 324, 342, 345, 350
Chan, R. W., 40, 62, 76, 78, 80, 88, 92
Chan, S. Q., 177, 178, 186
Chao, R. K., 68, 88, 304, 316
Chao, W., 27, 33
Chapman, M., 324, 345
Charlesworth, W. R., 75, 88
Chase-Lansdale, P. L., 25, 30, 76, 89, 154, 161, 235, 254
Chen, C., 78, 90
Chen, X., 16, 20, 30
Cherlin, A. J., 100, 115, 118, 235, 254, 290, 317
Chesler, P., 316
Chess, S., 207, 208, 209, 223
Cheung, P., 155, 163
Chirkov, V. I., 16, 30
Chiu, L., 305, 316
Christensen, A., 103, 104, 106, 107, 108, 118, 120, 124, 176, 177, 184, 186
Christensen, C., 326, 345
Christiansen, S. L., 43, 61
Chyi-In, W., 178, 187
Cicchetti, D., 144, 163, 300, 316
Cicirelli, V. G., 194, 199, 200, 201, 202, 220
Clancy, P. M., 306, 316
Clark, K., 86, 90
Clark, R., 308, 316
Clark, V. R., 308, 316
Clarke, A. D. B., 342, 345
Clarke, A. M., 342, 345
Clarke-Stewart, A., 177, 184, 230, 249, 254
Clements, M. L., 107, 108, 109, 118, 121, 142, 163
Clingempeel, W., 271, 277
Clopton, P. L., 102, 117
Coan, J., 109, 119
Coffin, W., 107, 115, 118, 123
Cohen, M. S., 260, 277
Cohn, J. F., 175, 184, 212, 222
Coie, J. D., 111, 118

Colapinto, J., 273, 278
Cole, R. E., 16, 29, 68, 87, 88, 89, 297, 317
Coll, C. G., 67, 86, 89
Collins, A., 79, 92
Collins, P., 133, 161
Collins, W. A., 9, 30, 70, 90, 68, 89, 180, 184, 253, 254
Collishaw, S., 335, 347
Coltrane, S., 71, 75, 89
Compas, B. B., 7, 32, 62
Conejero, C., 109, 123
Conger, K. J., 174, 184
Conger, R. D., 27, 33, 66, 71, 73, 89, 174, 178, 184, 187, 235, 255, 346
Connell, J. P., 21, 31
Constantino, M. J., 114, 118
Cook, R., 80, 90
Cook, T. D., 77, 82, 90
Cooper, C. R., 234, 255
Cooperman, J. M., 178, 187
Coopersmith, S., 11, 24, 30
Corboz-Warnery, A., 142, 143, 144, 163
Cordova, A. D., 113, 115, 118, 123
Corns, K. M., 208, 209, 223
Corter, C., 194, 197, 199, 202, 203, 204, 219, 222
Costanzo, P. R., 178, 187
Costigan, C. L., 173, 177, 185
Cote, L., 293, 300, 311, 315
Coverdill, J. E., 328, 345
Cowan, C. P., 85, 89, 112, 118, 133, 158, 140, 142, 158, 161, 169, 173, 175, 184, 233, 254, 260, 277
Cowan, E. L., 288, 319
Cowan, P. A., 70, 85, 89, 91, 112, 118, 133, 140, 142, 158, 161, 169, 173, 175, 184, 233, 237, 254, 259, 260, 265, 269, 270, 277, 278
Cox, A. D., 297, 316, 329, 345
Cox, C. L., 111, 112, 124
Cox, M. J., 26, 27, 31, 140, 142, 144, 162, 163, 169, 171, 172, 173, 175, 181, 185, 186, 288, 317
Cox, R., 26, 27, 31, 140, 162, 288, 317

Coyne, J. C., 106, 120, 175, 185
Coysh, W. S., 112, 118
Crane, D. R., 326, 345
Crawford, D. W., 26, 30
Crnic, K., 142, 144, 145, 160, 177,
    186, 234, 253, 260, 269, 277
Crockenberg, S. B., 210, 211, 212,
    220
Croft, C., 322, 350
Crosbie-Burnett, M., 137, 138, 148,
    157, 161
Crouchley, R., 330, 348
Crouter, A. C., 26, 30, 83, 89, 155,
    161
Crowder, K. D., 319
Crowe, M., 326, 349
Cumberland, A., 179, 185
Cummings, E. M., 71, 72, 89, 108,
    118, 150, 159, 161, 172, 173, 180,
    185, 234, 254, 260, 265, 278, 324,
    346
Curtin, R. B., 27, 33
Curtis-Boles, H., 112, 118
Cutrona, C. E., 108, 111, 118
Cvitkovic, J. F., 106, 120

D

Dadds, M., 142, 161
Daiuto, A. D., 106, 117
Daly, K., 141, 162
Daly, M., 76, 89
Daniels, D., 327, 339, 346, 348
Daniels, P., 72, 89
Darity, W. A., 136, 162
Davies, P., 71, 72, 89, 108, 118, 150,
    159, 161, 234, 254, 324, 346
Davila, J., 108, 122
Davis, J. E., 38, 46, 49, 61
Day, I., 229, 257
Deane, K. E., 208, 210, 224
DeAngelo, E., 143, 165
Deater-Deckard, K., 325, 341, 346,
    348
DeBarshyshe, B. D., 82, 92
Deci, E. L., 12, 16, 21, 23, 29, 30, 31

DeCourcey, W., 152, 164
DeLongis, A., 26, 30
DeMers, D. K., 71, 90
Demick, J., 295, 316
Depner, C. E., 177, 186
Derdeyn, A. P., 285, 316
Desai, S., 25, 30
Devroey, P., 81, 91
Dickstein, S., 84, 89, 144, 149, 163,
    165, 253, 255, 259, 277, 268, 277
Dienhart, A.,141, 162
Dill, D., 112, 120
Dilworth-Anderson, P., 177, 185
Dindia, K., 113, 118
Dishion, T. J., 214, 222, 333, 339, 346
Dix, T., 68, 89, 179, 185, 308, 316
Djerassi, C., 79, 81, 89
Dodge, K. A., 341, 346
Dodson, L., 55, 61
Doering, S., 141, 162
Dong, Q., 16, 20, 30
Donovan, W. L., 37, 61
Dornbusch, S. M., 16, 21, 27, 30, 31,
    140, 161, 176, 184
Douvan, E., 100, 124
Downey, G., 175, 185
Drew, C. J., 214, 221
Drigotas, S. M., 111, 112, 124
Droegmueller, W., 286, 317
Dumaret, A.-C., 333, 335, 339, 346
Duncan, G. J., 27, 31, 289, 316
Duncan, S. W., 107, 121
Dunkel, F., 47, 54, 63
Dunlap, K. G., 29, 31
Dunn, J., 194, 197, 199, 202, 203,
    204, 207, 209, 213, 215, 217, 218,
    219, 220, 221, 224, 266, 277, 292,
    316, 324, 337, 350
Dunn, N. J., 297, 319
Duvall, E., 229, 236, 237, 254
Duyme, M., 333, 335, 339, 345, 346
Dzur, C., 75, 88

E

East, P. L., 215, 220

Easterbrooks, M. A., 171, 185
Eaves, L. J., 322, 323, 324, 327, 337, 339, 339, 345, 346, 348, 350, 351
Eccles, J. S., 29, 31, 77, 82, 90
Eckert, V., 107, 124
Edelbrock, C. S., 323, 345
Edwards, C., 67, 93, 198, 224
Egan, J., 58, 62
Egeland, B., 25, 33, 305, 320
Eghrari, H., 23, 30
Eidelson, R. J., 104, 118
Eiden, R. D., 208, 209, 223
Eisenberg, N., 179, 185
Eisenberg-Berg, N., 22, 31
Elder, G. H., 66, 71, 73, 77, 82, 89, 90, 174, 184
Elliott, G. L., 27, 32
Ellis, G. D., 113, 117
Ember, C. R., 67, 93
Emde, R. N., 7, 33, 149, 164, 171, 185
Emerson, P. E., 37, 63
Emery, R. E., 72, 89, 158, 162, 172, 173, 180, 185, 234, 254 , 288, 289, 297, 316
Engl, J., 107, 124
Engle, P. L., 42, 61
Ensminger, M. E., 76, 90
Entwisle, D., 141, 162
Epstein, J. L., 87, 89
Epstein, N., 103, 104, 117, 118, 305, 311, 316
Erchak, G. M., 67, 93
Erel, O., 108, 119, 234, 254
Erera, P. 156, 162
Erickson, M. T., 323, 346
Erikson, E., 70, 89
Erikson, R. J., 44, 61
Erkut, S., 67, 86, 89
Escalona, S. K., 233, 255
Escovar, P. L., 307, 316

F

Fainsilber-Katz, L., 234, 255
Falicov, C., 307, 316
Falk, P. J., 298, 316

Falloon, I. R. H., 327, 347
Famularo, R., 296, 307, 316
Fan, Y., 153, 165
Fantuzzo, J. W., 298, 317
Farley, R., 137, 163
Farrell, B., 132, 134, 137, 163
Farrington, D. P., 330, 333, 334, 346
Farris, A., 142, 163
Fauber, R., 171, 185
Feldman, M. A., 296, 317
Feldman, S. S., 235, 255
Fellings, A., 68, 90
Fenell, D. L., 111, 119
Fenton, T., 307, 316
Ferguson, L. R., 11, 31
Ferguson, L. W., 100, 124
Fergusson, D. M., 324, 330, 334, 346
Ficher, I., 76, 89
Fichten, C. S., 102, 119
Field, D., 259, 277
Field, T. M., 78, 89, 207, 220
Fienberg, S. E., 244, 255
Fiese, B. H., 149, 163, 253, 255, 259, 277, 268, 277
Filsinger, E. E., 103, 119
Fincham, F. D., 104, 105, 106, 117, 119, 120, 124, 171, 172, 173, 176, 180, 185, 186
Fine, M., 74, 89, 328, 347
Finlay, W., 328, 345
Fischer, K. W., 180, 185
Fish, M., 168, 183
Fisher, L., 235, 255, 297, 317
Fishman, D. M., 110, 122
Fivaz-Depeursinge, E., 142, 143, 144, 163
Flaks, D. K., 76, 89
Flanagan, C., 175, 184
Flannery, W. P., 67, 89
Fleeson, J., 211, 223, 267, 278
Fleeting, M., 334, 347
Flor, D., 142, 154, 160
Flora, J., 113, 119
Floyd, F. J., 102, 105, 107, 109, 119, 121, 170, 173, 177, 185, 187
Follansbee, D., 139, 162

Fonagy, P., 149, 163
Forehand, R., 27, 30, 171, 185, 296, 318
Forgatch, M. S., 333, 339, 346, 348
Foster, C. A., 111, 124, 125
Fox, N. A., 66, 91
Fraleigh, M. J., 16, 30
Framo, J. L., 168, 186
Frascarolo, F., 144, 163
Fravel, D. L., 149, 163, 253, 255, 259, 277, 268, 277
Fredriksen, K., 156, 162
Freud, A., 285, 317
Frodi, A. M., 37, 61
Fromm-Reichmann, F., 6, 31
Frosch, C., 142, 144, 163
Fuchs, T., 109, 123
Fuhrmann, G., 287, 315
Fulker, D., 325, 348
Furman, W., 194, 212, 215, 220, 221
Furstenberg, F. F., 68, 77, 82, 90, 138, 161, 235, 254, 290, 317

G

Gable, S., 145, 160, 177, 186, 234, 253, 260, 269, 277
Gaertner, S., 260, 277
Gano-Phillips, S., 171, 186
Garcia, H. A.V., 67, 86, 89
Garner, P. W., 198, 221
Garrett, E., 112, 118
Garrison, K. M., 288, 319
Garrity, C. B., 288, 317
Gatzanis, S. R. M., 334, 347
Gaughran, J. M., 206, 219
Gauvain, M., 67, 90
Ge, X., 325, 346
Geasler, M., 116, 117
Gecas, V., 44, 61
Gegeo, D. W., 214, 217, 224
Gelfand, D. M., 214, 221, 308, 317
Gerler, E. R., 288, 314
Gerris, J., 68, 90
Gerson, R., 49, 62

Gibbs, E. D., 194, 197, 199, 202, 203, 204, 221, 223
Giberson, R. S., 212, 221
Giddings, P., 136, 163
Gilbert, R., 176, 186
Giller, H., 322, 335, 338, 341, 342, 350
Gilliom, L. A., 173, 177, 185
Gjerde, P. F., 145, 163, 235, 254
Glasgow, R. E., 176, 184
Goldberg, M., 102, 119
Goldberg, S., 7, 31
Golding, J., 332, 350
Goldstein, J., 285, 317
Goldstein, M. J., 327, 347
Golombok, S., 80, 90, 93, 326, 338, 346, 349
Gomel, J., 86, 90
Gonzales, L. S., 177, 184
Goodall, G. M., 324, 345
Goodnow, J. J., 69, 70, 90
Gordon, D., 297, 317
Goshko, M., 317
Gotlib, I. H., 45, 62, 106, 119, 121
Gottesman, I. I., 297, 317
Gottlieb, L. N., 205, 209, 221
Gottman, J. M., 37, 62, 86, 92, 101, 102, 103, 104, 105, 109, 119, 121, 122, 142, 145, 163, 170, 171, 179, 186, 234, 255
Gove, F., 25, 33
Graber, J. A., 180, 186
Graham, S., 303, 317
Grajek, S., 202, 222
Greek, A., 208, 219
Green, J., 78, 90
Greenberger, E., 78, 90
Greene, B., 303, 307, 308, 317
Greenspan, S., 296, 315
Gretarsson, S. J., 308, 317
Grieco, L., 47, 54, 63
Grimes, C. L., 178, 187
Grisso, T., 283, 287, 299, 300, 310, 317
Grolnick, W. S., 8, 15, 16, 17, 18, 21, 27, 28, 29, 31, 33

Groothues, C., 322, 329, 350
Gross, R. T., 27, 30
Grotevant, H. D., 149, 163, 202, 221, 234, 353, 255, 259, 277, 268, 277
Grove, K., 303, 316
Grusec, J. E., 69, 90
Grych, J. H., 171, 176, 186
Gubernick, D. J., 40, 41, 63
Gulley, B. L., 333, 343, 349
Gulliver, P. H., 154, 162
Gurland, S. T., 15, 31

H

Hackel, L., 141, 162
Hagell, A., 322, 335, 338, 341, 342, 350
Hahlweg, K., 102, 103, 104, 107, 109, 119, 120, 121, 123, 124
Haley, J., 168, 186, 229, 253
Halford, W. K., 107, 115, 117, 119
Hall, J., 296, 317
Hall, L. J., 198, 221
Hallings-Pott, C., 341, 347
Hall-McCorquodale, I., 7, 30
Hamby, S. L., 326, 351
Hammen, C., 297, 317
Hammerschmidt, H., 109, 121
Hand, M., 22, 31
Hand, S. I., 77, 90
Hansen, D., 259, 277
Hansson, K., 109, 121
Hardy, K. V., 58, 61
Hare, J., 156, 162
Harlow, H. F., 340, 346
Harlow, M. K., 340, 346
Harold, G. T., 106, 119, 235, 255, 339, 351
Harrell, S., 127, 128, 130, 133, 136, 162
Harrington, R., 331, 350
Harris, J. R., 9, 31, 82, 90, 227, 255, 322, 343, 346
Harris, T. O., 324, 339, 342, 345, 346
Harrison, A. O., 177, 178, 186

Harter, K. S. M., 172, 185
Hartman, S., 114, 120
Hartmann, H., 317
Harvey, E., 25, 31
Hastings, P., 215, 217, 223
Hastorf, A. H., 27, 30
Hatfield, J. S., 11, 31
Hau, K., 155, 163
Hauser, S. T., 139, 162, 234, 255
Hautzinger, M., 106, 120
Havighurst, R. J., 236, 255
Hawkins, A. J., 43, 61
Hawkins, J. D., 111, 118
Hayden, L., 144, 165
Hayman, R. L., 296, 317
Heath, A. C., 323, 346
Heavey, C. L., 29, 31, 104, 118
Heinze, M. C., 310, 317
Hekimian, E., 309, 315
Helmes, B., 102, 119
Helms, J., 58, 61
Helms-Erikson, H., 155, 161
Heming, G., 112, 118, 142, 161, 233, 254
Henderson, S. H., 259, 268, 271, 277, 325, 349
Henderson, V. K., 169, 185
Hendricks, C., 158, 162
Hennessey, J. W., 340, 347
Hennon, C. B., 218, 221, 293, 317
Herrerias, C., 307, 317
Herring, G., 173, 175, 184
Hertel, R. K., 102, 122
Hess, L. E., 341, 347
Hesser, J., 200, 221
Hessling, R. M., 108, 118
Hetherington, E. M., 9, 26, 27, 30, 31, 41, 42, 61, 72, 85, 90, 109, 120, 140, 162, 259, 260, 268, 271, 277, 288, 290, 317, 325, 339, 348, 349
Hewitt, J. K., 323, 327, 330, 339, 345, 346, 348, 351
Hewlett, B. S., 38, 61
Heyman, R. E., 104, 124
Hibbett, H., 133, 163
Hildebradt, N., 70, 91

Hill, C. T., 111, 118
Hill, E. J., 43, 61
Hill, J. P., 180, 186, 236, 241, 255, 327, 334, 350
Hill, R., 72, 90, 229, 254
Hinchcliffe, M., 106, 120
Hinde, R. A., 194, 221, 330, 347
Hinshaw, S. P., 110, 120, 177, 184
Hiroto, D., 297, 317
Hirsch, S. I., 229, 257
Hochschild, A., 43, 61
Hock, E., 71, 90
Hoffman, L. W., 87, 90, 176, 186
Hoffman, M. L., 22, 31, 198, 221
Hoffman, N., 106, 120
Hoffman, S. D., 27, 31, 289, 316
Holbrook, D., 329, 345
Holden, G. W., 84, 90
Holdsworth, M. J., 287, 315
Holland, W. W., 342, 347
Holliday, S., 106, 117
Holmbeck, G. N., 180, 186
Holmes, J. G., 111, 120
Hooley, J. M., 102, 104, 109, 120
Hooper, D., 106, 120
Hooven, C., 234, 255
Hops, H., 101, 106, 120, 122, 124
Horst, L., 11, 31
Horton, N. J., 323, 347
Horton, P. J., 11, 31
Horwood, L. J., 324, 330, 334, 346
Hosley, C. A., 43, 61
Hossain, Z., 46, 61
Houser, A., 309, 315
Howard, J., 296, 319
Howard, K., 115, 118
Howe, G. W., 325, 349
Howe, N., 197, 209, 215, 221
Howes, P., 107, 121, 144, 163
Howlin, P., 329, 347
Hrdy, S. B., 40, 61
Hubley, P., 238, 257
Hunsley, J., 326, 347
Hunter, A. G., 38, 46, 49, 61
Huston, T. L., 26, 30
Hutter, M., 106, 117

Hyle, P., 208, 219

I

Insabella, G. M., 41, 42, 61, 259, 260, 271, 277
Irish, D. P., 195, 213, 221
Isabella, R., 85, 88
Itasaka, G., 133, 163

J

Jack, D. C., 112, 120
Jacklin, C., 203, 222
Jackson, D. D., 229, 253
Jacob, T., 106, 120, 297, 317, 319, 327, 347
Jacobson, A., 139, 162
Jacobson, N. S., 101, 103, 104, 106, 107, 108, 114, 117, 118, 120
Jacobvitz, D., 143, 165
Jaenicke, C., 297, 317
James, S., 326, 347
Japel, C., 338, 351
Jellinek, M. S., 317
Jenkins, J. M., 325, 327, 347
Jenson, W. R., 214, 221
John, R. S., 102, 121
Johnson, B. S., 213, 224
Johnson, C., 26, 28, 33
Johnson, D. J., 111, 120
Johnson, D. R., 110, 120
Johnson, D., 143, 144, 150, 164
Johnson, L. B., 177, 185
Johnson, M. P., 111, 120
Johnson, S. M., 176, 184
Johnson, W. B., 100, 124
Johnston, J. R., 288, 290, 317
Johnston, J., 140, 163
Jones, D. C., 198, 221
Jones, H. E., 325, 347
Jordan, P., 107, 115, 120, 123
Joris, H., 81, 91
Joseph, G., 76, 89
Jouriles, E., 142, 163
Juliusson, H., 259, 269, 270, 278

K

Kadushin, A., 285, 317
Kafka, J. S., 230, 255
Kagitcibasi, C., 287, 306, 307, 308, 317
Kahen, V., 234, 255
Kahn, J., 106, 120
Kahn, M. D., 210, 213, 215, 217, 219
Kannae, L. A., 110, 122
Kantor, D., 235, 255
Kaplan, L., 218, 221, 293, 317
Kaplan, S., 307, 319
Karney, B. R., 105, 109, 120
Karno, M., 327, 347
Karrer, B. M., 307, 316
Kaslow, F. W., 109, 121, 123
Katz, L. F., 142, 145, 163, 171, 179, 186
Kaufman, J., 178, 186
Kavanagh, K. A., 333, 339, 346
Keefe, S. E., 307, 317
Keith, B., 289, 314
Kellam, S. G., 76, 83, 90
Kelley, H. H., 169, 186
Kelly, J. B., 112, 117, 140, 165, 289, 320
Kempe, C. H., 286, 317
Kendrick, C., 194, 197, 199, 202, 203, 204, 207, 209, 213, 217, 218, 220, 221, 266, 277
Kennell, J. H., 6, 31, 207, 223
Kerig, P., 142, 163
Kessler, R. C., 26, 30
Kidder, L. H., 328, 347
Kiernana, K. E., 235, 254
Kim, S., 308, 317
Kimpton, J. L., 40, 43, 60
Kinney, J., 288, 314
Kinnunen, U., 110, 121
Kinscherff, R., 307, 316
Kinsella-Shaw, M., 110, 122
Kitayama, S., 318
Kitzmann, K., 142, 145, 163
Klaus, M. H., 6, 31, 207, 223
Knight, G. P., 67, 90

Knok, S. L. 27, 31
Koch, H. L., 201, 203, 221
Koch, M. P., 288, 317
Kochanska, G., 22, 23, 31
Koester, L. S., 200, 221
Kogan, K. L., 207, 223
Kokes, R. F., 297, 317
Kolvin, I., 334, 347
Kondo-Ikemura, K., 329, 351
Kopytoff, I., 154, 163
Korbin, J. E., 300, 311, 312, 317
Koren, P., 102, 121
Kowal, A., 212, 221, 268, 277
Kowalik, D. L., 106, 121
Kozilius, H., 68, 90
Krahn, G. L., 106, 120
Kramer, A., 212, 221
Kramer, L., 268, 277
Krasnow, A., 154, 164
Kreppner, K., 152, 163, 238, 240, 241, 244, 255, 256, 257, 266, 277, 322, 350
Kreppner, L., 329, 350
Krokoff, L. J., 103, 104, 119, 122, 123
Kucera, E., 208, 209, 223
Kuczynski, L., 69, 70, 91, 90, 308, 317
Kuersten, R., 172, 176, 177, 178, 187, 270, 278
Kuersten-Hogan, R., 143, 144, 145, 146, 147, 148, 164
Kulka, R. A., 100, 124
Kunert, H., 102, 119
Kurdek, L. A., 74, 89
Kurowski, C. O., 27, 29, 31

L

Laird, N. M., 323, 347
Lakey, J., 323, 347
Lamb, M. E., 37, 38, 40, 43, 61, 62, 68, 74, 76, 79, 86, 91, 194, 197, 199, 200, 203, 221, 233, 256
Lambert, S., 333, 346
Lamborn, S. D., 21, 31

Lando, B., 194, 197, 199, 202, 203, 219
LaRossa, R., 43, 55, 62
Larson, J. H., 326, 345
Laszloffy, T. A., 58, 61
Lau, S., 155, 163
Laub, J. H., 330, 333, 342, 347, 351
Lauretti, A. F, 144, 145, 148, 152, 163, 164, 172, 176, 177, 178, 187, 270, 278, 300, 309, 314, 315
Laursen, B., 180, 184
Law, T., 325, 349
Lawrence, E., 108, 117
Lawson, E. J., 317
Lazarus, P. J., 307, 316
Le Couteur, A., 331, 350
Leavitt, L. A., 37, 61, 66, 91
Leber, B. D., 113, 115, 123
Lee, C. M., 45, 62
Leff, J. P., 327, 347
Legg, C., 207, 221
Lehoux, P. M., 178, 187
Lehr, W., 235, 255
Leiderman, H., 27, 30
Leiderman, P. H., 16, 30
Leonard, K. E., 105, 123, 299, 319
Leone, D. R., 23, 30
Lerman, R. I., 38, 62
Lerner, H. G., 112, 121
Levenson, R. W., 103, 104, 105, 119, 121
Leventhal, J. M., 297, 320
Levine, E. S., 304, 315
Levine, J. A., 52, 62, 87, 91
LeVine, R. A., 302, 317
Levine, S., 340, 347
Levinger, G., 111, 113, 121
Levinson, R. W., 169, 186
Levy, D. M., 193, 206, 221
Lew, W., 155, 163
Lewin, K., 113, 121, 229, 251, 256
Lewis, C. C., 13, 31
Lewis, E., 137, 138, 148, 157, 161
Lewis, J. L., 169, 185
Lewis, J. M., 142, 144, 163, 169, 186
Lewis, M., 35, 57, 62

Lewis, R. A., 110, 123
Lewkowicz, K. S., 305, 319
Lewontin, R., 339, 351
Liang, B., 307, 317
Liddle, C., 327, 349
Lidz, T., 229, 256
Liker, J. K., 103, 116
Lindahl, K. M., 109, 121, 142, 154, 163
Linden, M., 106, 120
Lindholm, K. J., 299, 317
Lipkus, I., 111, 123
Liu, S., 153, 165
Lobato, D., 198, 221
Locke, H. J., 100, 118, 121, 132, 161
Loding, B., 300, 309, 314, 315
Loeb, R. C., 11, 31
Loeber, R., 323, 346, 351
Lollis, S., 70, 91
Long, B., 111, 118
Lopez, S. R., 68, 88
Lord, C., 329, 350
Lord, S. E., 29, 31
Lorenz, F. O., 174, 184
Lowery, C. R., 288, 317
Lundblad, A. M., 109, 121
Lusterman, D., 278
Lynch, M., 300, 316
Lynskey, M. T., 324, 346

M

Maccoby, E. E., 9, 27, 30, 31, 70, 75, 82, 91, 140, 157, 161, 163, 176, 177, 184, 186, 203, 222, 337, 347
MacDonald, A. P., 296, 317
Macdonald, H., 331, 350
MacDonald, K., 14, 31
Machung, A., 43, 61
Mackey, R. A., 110, 121
MacKinnon, C. E., 199, 204, 210, 211, 215, 219, 223
MacKinnon, R., 199, 204, 215, 219
MacNamee, R., 207, 209, 220
Madood, T., 323, 323, 347
Maes, H. H., 323, 327, 339, 345, 346, 348, 351

Magana, A. B., 327, 347
Magee, W. J., 329, 351
Magnusson, D., 181, 184, 186
Malik, N. M., 109, 121, 142, 154, 163
Malkin, C., 76, 91
Mancini, J. A., 113, 122
Mangelsdorf, S., 142, 143, 144, 163, 165
Mare, R. D., 109, 124
Margolin, G., 101, 102, 103, 104, 106, 120, 121, 124, 168, 176, 184, 186, 187, 298, 318
Markman, H. J., 101, 102, 103, 104, 105, 107, 108, 109, 111, 112, 113, 114, 115, 116, 117, 118, 119, 120, 121, 122, 123, 124, 125, 142, 163, 170, 188
Markman, J. J., 170, 187
Marks, N. F., 27, 31
Markus, G. B., 201, 202, 224
Markus, H., 201, 224, 318
Martin, J. A., 27, 31, 82, 91
Martin, J. K., 328, 345
Martin, S. L., 296, 318
Martz, J. M., 111, 123
Marvin, R. S., 198, 204, 223
Masterpasqua, F., 76, 89
Matheny, A. P., 106, 222
Maughan, B., 323, 324, 327, 333, 335, 337, 341, 342, 347, 350
Mawhood, L., 329, 347, 350
Mayes, S., 140, 163
Maynard, P. E., 326, 348
McAdoo, H., 38, 62
McAdoo, J. L., 38, 62
McCarthy, K. A., 29, 31
McCartney, K., 300, 319
McCaslin, R., 274, 277
McCombs, C., 296, 318
McConnell, M., 142, 163
McCoy, J. K., 212, 219
McDaniel, S., 278
McDuff, P., 338, 351
McGinnis, L., 330, 347
McGoldrick, M., 49, 62, 237, 256
McGuffin, P., 339, 351

McGuire, S., 339, 348
McHale, J. L., 142, 144, 163
McHale, J. P., 70, 91, 142, 143, 144, 145, 146, 147, 148, 150, 151, 153, 154, 159, 163, 164, 165, 172, 176, 177, 178, 187, 260, 265, 269, 270, 277, 278
McHale, S. M., 155, 161, 198, 212, 217, 222
McHugh, T., 141, 165
McKenzie, K., 333, 348
McKenzie, L., 8, 31
McLanahan, S. S., 27, 31, 33, 137, 163
McLeod, J. H., 308, 317
McLloyd, V. C., 28, 31, 68, 91, 177, 187, 308, 318
McManus, M., 116, 117, 122
McPherson, D., 78, 91
Meany, M. J., 75, 91
Medawar, P., 344, 348
Melton, G. B., 285, 286, 288, 289, 291, 293, 299, 310, 318
Mendelson, M. J., 205, 209, 221
Messer, J., 341, 347
Meyer, J. M., 323, 324, 327, 330, 337, 339, 345, 346, 348, 350, 351
Meyers, T. A., 175, 184
Michael, R. T., 25, 30
Mickelson, P., 296, 297, 318
Mikach, S., 77, 88
Mikesell, R., 278
Miller, B. C., 169, 187
Miller, C. T., 198, 221
Miller, F. J. W., 334, 347
Miller, G. E., 105, 122
Miller, N. B., 110, 122, 173, 175, 184, 233, 254
Miller, S. A., 70, 91
Mills, M., 297, 316
Minnett, A. M., 194, 201, 202, 204, 205, 213, 222, 223, 224
Mintz, S., 36, 62
Minuchin, P., 139, 164, 172, 187, 196, 207, 209, 213, 222, 263, 273, 278
Minuchin, S., 151, 153, 164, 168, 172, 178, 187, 273, 278

Mischel, W., 100, 122
Mishler, E. G., 229, 256
Mnookin, R. H., 157, 163, 177, 186
Mobley, L. A., 207, 223
Modell, J., 66, 89
Moffitt, T. E., 325, 330, 334, 346, 348
Monck, E. M., 297, 315
Montemayor, R., 43, 61
Montplaisir, J., 338, 351
Moore, G. A., 212, 222
Moore, T., 206, 222
Moos, R. H., 73, 91
Morgan, D. L., 85, 91
Morrison, D. R., 235, 254
Mortimore, P., 333, 343, 348
Mounts, N. S., 21, 31
Mueser, K. T., 106, 117
Munholland, K. A., 211, 219
Munn, P., 197, 220
Murphy, C., 142, 163
Murphy, D. T., 52, 62
Murphy, J. M., 317
Murray, C., 80, 90
Murray, R., 322, 333, 348, 350
Murray, V. M., 58, 62
Muzio, C., 156, 164
Myers, S. L., 136, 162

N

Nagell, K., 232, 254
Nagin, D. S., 330, 333, 338, 342, 347, 348
Nakagawa, M., 211, 223
Nakosteen, R. A., 109, 122
Nangle, B., 158, 164
Nazroo, V., 323, 347
Neale, J. M., 289, 297, 316
Neale, M. C., 323, 330, 346, 348
NeeSmith, D., 105, 124
Neiderhiser, J. M., 325, 346
Nelson, G. M., 105, 117
Neubaum, E., 142, 154, 160
Neugebauer, A., 150, 164
Neville, B., 82, 83, 92
Nichols, M., 134, 164

Nicolson, P., 141, 164
Niklowitz, D. J., 327, 347
Nixon, C., 260, 265, 278
Noam, G. G., 139, 162, 234, 255
Noller, P., 141, 165
Nord, C. W., 51, 57, 64
Notarius, C. I., 101, 102, 103, 105, 114, 119, 122, 124

O

O'Brien, B. A., 110, 121
O'Brien, J. T., 340, 348
O'Connor, T. G., 322, 325, 329, 331, 332, 339, 340, 348, 350
O'Connor, T. J., 325, 349
O'Donohue, W., 285, 286, 319
O'Farrell, T. J., 102, 119
O'Leary, K. D., 104, 105, 106, 117, 119, 123, 124
O'Neil, J. M., 58, 62
O'Neil, R., 72, 82, 92, 259, 278
O'Neill, J. M., 110, 122
Obeidallah, D., 178, 184
Ochs, E., 306, 308, 311, 319
Olmos-Gallo, P. A., 115, 123
Olsen, N., 300, 315
Olson, D. H., 326, 348
Olweus, D., 214, 222
Opipari, L. C., 212, 222
Oppenheim, D., 149, 164
Ormel, J., 324, 337, 350
Orthner, D. K., 113, 122
Osborn, S. G., 333, 348
Osborne, L. N., 106, 119
Owen, M. T., 142, 144, 163, 169, 171, 185, 186
Owen, S. V., 58, 62

P

Paasch, K. M., 289, 320
Padilla, A. M., 307, 317
Palermo, G., 81, 91
Paley, B., 172, 173, 175, 181, 185
Palmer, D. J., 198, 221

Parke, R. D., 28, 29, 37, 62, 66, 68, 70, 72, 73, 74, 75, 77, 82, 83, 84, 85, 86, 88, 89, 90, 91, 92, 93, 148, 160, 176, 177, 187, 252, 256, 259, 260, 278, 293, 302, 304, 319, 320
Parker, G., 11, 31
Pasch, L. A., 108, 111, 122
Patrick, B. C., 23, 30
Patterson, C. J., 40, 62, 76, 77, 78, 80, 88, 92, 298, 319
Patterson, G. R., 66, 69, 82, 92, 101, 106, 120, 122, 124, 178, 187, 214, 222, 333, 339, 346, 348
Paul, G. L., 114, 122
Paulsen, S., 266, 277
Paulson, R. J., 81, 92
Pawletko, T. M., 198, 212, 217, 222, 260, 265, 278
Payne, C. C., 173, 175, 185
Pedersen, F. A., 76, 92, 233, 256
Pedro-Carroll, J., 288, 319
Penny, J. M., 200, 221
Pensky, E., 173, 183, 260, 277
Peplau, L. A., 111, 118
Pepler, D. J., 194, 197, 199, 200, 202, 203, 204, 219, 222
Perkins, K., 297, 317
Perry-Jenkins, M., 26, 30
Pérusse, D., 338, 351
Peters, P. L., 178, 187
Peterson, K. S., 116, 122
Petrila, J., 285, 286, 288, 289, 291, 293, 299, 318
Pettengill, S. M., 20, 31, 304, 306, 319
Pettit, G. S., 341, 346
Phares, V., 5, 7, 31, 32, 36, 45, 56, 62, 63
Phillips, S., 176, 184
Piaget, J., 194, 222
Pickles, A., 322, 323, 324, 327, 330, 332, 333, 335, 337, 339, 342, 346, 347, 348, 349, 350, 351
Pike, A., 339, 348
Pilling, D., 343, 348
Pine, C. J., 177, 178, 186

Pitt, E. W., 52, 62
Pittinsky, T. L., 52, 62, 87, 91
Pleck, E. H., 36, 63
Pleck, J. H., 36, 40, 42, 43, 44, 63
Plomin, R., 85, 87, 90, 92, 323, 324, 325, 327, 333, 337, 339, 346, 348, 349, 350
Pocock, S. J., 328, 348
Poitrast, F., 317
Pomerantz, E. M., 19, 31
Popenoe, D., 40, 41, 55, 63
Posada, G., 329, 351
Pound, A., 297, 316
Pouquette, C., 152, 164
Powell, D., 133, 158, 161
Powell, M., 142, 161
Power, T. G., 37, 62, 86, 92
Powers, S. I., 22, 31, 139, 162, 180, 187, 234, 255
Poythress, N. G., 285, 286, 288, 289, 291, 293, 299, 318
Prado, L. M., 115, 123
Pringle, M. K., 343, 348
Prinz, R. J., 296, 320
Pruett, K. D., 40, 63
Pruett, M. K., 158, 164
Puckering, C., 297, 316
Pugh, R. M., 67, 92
Pulkkinen, L., 11, 31, 110, 121
Putallaz, M., 178, 187
Putnam, S., 142, 144, 160

Q

Quartironi, B., 48, 63
Quigley, R. M., 299, 319
Quinn, D., 317
Quinton, D., 9, 31, 32, 323, 327, 333, 334, 341, 342, 347, 349, 350, 351
Quittner, A. L., 212, 222

R

Raboy, B., 80, 88
Radbill, S. X., 319
Radin, N., 8, 31, 32, 78, 92

Ramey, C. T., 296, 318
Ramey, S. L., 111, 118, 259, 269, 270, 278, 296, 318
Ramsey, E., 82, 92
Rao, N., 153, 154, 164, 165
Rapp, R., 136, 165
Rasmussen, J., 143, 144, 146, 147, 148, 164
Raush, H. L., 102, 122
Reddy, M. T., 5, 31, 32
Redshaw, J., 331, 350
Reid, J. B., 101, 122
Reiling, E., 156, 165
Reise, S. P, 67, 89, 92
Reiss, D., 72, 85, 90, 92, 139, 149, 165, 235, 236, 256, 259, 268, 271, 277, 325, 339, 348, 349
Reiss, I. L., 233, 256
Reite, M., 207, 220
Rempel, J. K., 111, 120
Renick, M. J., 107, 109, 121
Repetti, R. L., 26, 31
Repinski, D. J., 68, 89
Resnick, G., 140, 161
Revenstorf, D., 102, 103, 119, 123, 124
Reynolds, C. A., 323, 346
Rheingold, H. L., 233, 256
Richards, L., 156, 162
Richter, J., 142, 163
Riegraf, N., 46, 63
Ritchey, D., 106, 120
Ritter, P. L., 16, 27, 30
Rivera, S., 109, 123
Robbins, A., 207, 208, 209, 223
Roberts, D. F., 16, 30
Roberts, F. J., 106, 120
Roberts, L. J., 104, 123
Robertson, J. A., 81, 92, 155, 156, 159, 165
Robin, A., 241, 256
Robins, L., 323, 349
Robins, P. K., 235, 254
Robinson, D. R., 309, 315
Robison, J. A., 109, 121
Robredo, K., 115, 118

Rodgers, R. H., 72, 90, 138, 160, 233, 256
Rodgers-Rose, L., 136, 165
Rodin, J., 79, 92
Rodning, C., 296, 319
Rogge, R., 108, 117
Rogoff, B., 312, 319
Rogoff, R., 67, 92
Rogosch, F., 144, 163
Rohner, R. P., 20, 31, 304, 306, 319
Rohrbeck, C. A., 309, 315
Roizblatt, A., 109, 123
Rolland, J., 265, 278
Rollins, B. C., 169, 187
Rook, K. S., 215, 220
Roopnarine, J. L., 46, 60, 61, 63, 67, 68, 90, 92
Roosa, M., 67, 90
Rosaldo, M. Z., 130, 165
Roschelle, A. R., 136, 165
Rosenberg, B. G., 194, 199, 201, 203, 222, 223
Rosenberg, M.S., 172, 187
Rosenthal, J. A., 295, 319
Ross, H. S., 78, 92, 197, 209, 215, 221
Ross, S., 175, 184
Roth, M., 5, 31, 32
Rowe, D. C., 87, 92, 322, 333, 339, 343, 349
Roy, P., 332, 339, 349
Ruble, D. N., 19, 31, 141, 162, 308, 316
Rudd, C., 207, 223
Ruddick, S., 7, 31
Rusbult, C. E., 111, 112, 120, 123, 124, 125
Russell, G., 78, 93
Rust, J., 326, 349
Rutter, M., 6, 9, 31, 32, 35, 42, 63, 74, 87, 92, 93, 178, 179, 180, 187, 319, 322, 323, 324, 325, 326, 327, 329, 330, 331, 332, 333, 334, 335, 337, 338, 339, 340, 341, 342, 343, 345, 346, 347, 348, 349, 350, 351
Ryan, K. D., 303, 316
Ryan, R. M., 12, 16, 17, 21, 29, 30, 31

Ryckoff, I. N., 229, 257
Ryff, C. D., 329, 351

S

Sachs, J., 81, 92
Sagi, A., 79, 93, 305, 319
Sakin, J., 208, 209, 223
Sales, S. M., 15, 31
Salvador, M. A., 207, 223
Salzinger, S., 307, 319
Sameroff, A. J., 72, 74, 77, 82, 90, 93,
    144, 149, 163, 165, 169, 187, 253,
    255, 259, 277, 268, 277
Sampson, R. J., 330, 333, 342, 347,
    351
Sandefur, G., 137, 163
Santa Barbara, J., 241, 257
Santrock, J. W., 27, 32, 194, 201, 202,
    204, 205, 213, 222, 223, 224
Sargent, K. P., 43, 61
Sarin, D., 153, 165
Saunders, D. G., 298, 319
Sayers, S. L., 105, 123
Scalora, M. J., 293, 320
Scarr, S., 6, 32, 202, 221, 222, 300,
    319, 322, 339, 343, 351
Schachter, F., 268, 278
Schacter, F. F., 196, 222
Schaefer, E. S., 10, 12, 32
Schaefer, J. A., 73, 91
Schaffer, H. R., 37, 63
Schaie, K. W., 71, 93
Scheurer, M. D., 296, 319
Schiff, M., 339, 351
Schiller, M., 144, 165
Schindler, L., 102, 103, 119, 123, 124
Schooler, C., 199, 222
Schoonover, S. M., 201, 222, 223
Schubert, D. S. P., 194, 195, 199, 224
Schubert, H. J. P., 194, 195, 199, 224
Schuetze, Y., 266, 277
Schulz, M., 141, 161
Schut, A. J., 114, 118
Schwartz, A., 150, 164
Schwartz, R., 134, 164

Schwartzman, A. E., 178, 187
Scott, D. M., 334, 347
Seagull, E. A., 296, 319
Seale, C., 328, 351
Segrin, C., 113, 119
Segui, I., 206, 219
Seifer, R., 144, 165
Seilhamer, R. A., 297, 319
Seitel, L., 235, 255
Seitz, V., 154, 160
Senchak, M., 105, 123
Serbin, L. A., 178, 187
Sewall, M., 193, 222, 223
Sewell, M. C., 28, 33
Shantzis, C., 308, 317
Sharlin, S. A., 109, 123
Shaw, D., 102, 121
Shek, D. T. L., 110, 123
Sheldon, A., 5, 31, 32
Sherick, I., 207, 221
Sherman, D. M., 178, 187
Shields, J., 297, 317
Shillady, L. L., 339, 348
Shoham, V., 106, 117
Shure, M. B., 111, 118
Sigel, I., 70, 93, 259, 278
Silber, H. K., 286, 317
Silberg, J. L., 322, 323, 327, 330, 331,
    339, 340, 345, 346, 348, 350, 351
Silliman, B., 107, 123
Silva, P. A., 330, 334, 346
Silverberg, S. B., 249, 257
Silverman, A. R., 295, 319
Silverman, F. N., 286, 317
Silverstein, L. B., 36, 47, 53, 54, 60,
    63, 74, 76, 78, 79, 86, 93
Simmon, S. J., 325, 349
Simmons, R., 71, 93
Simms, M., 156, 165
Simoni, H., 150, 165
Simonoff, E., 330, 331, 322, 323, 324,
    327, 331, 337, 339, 340, 345, 346,
    348, 350, 351
Simons, R. L., 26, 27, 28, 33, 174,
    178, 184, 187
Sinclair, R., 143, 144, 150, 164

Singer, B., 329, 351
Skinner, H. A., 241, 257
Skolnick, A., 259, 277
Sloane, D., 105, 122
Slobogin, C., 285, 286, 288, 289, 291, 293, 299, 318
Slovik, L. F., 111, 123
Smalley, R., 193, 223
Smith, D. A., 104, 123
Smith, D. J., 321, 333, 350
Smith, D., 134, 142, 163, 165
Smith, J., 236, 254
Smith, M. A., 325, 347
Smith, P., 323, 347
Smollar, J., 235, 257
Smuts, B. B., 40, 41, 63
Snarey, J., 43, 54, 63
Snell-White, P., 46, 63
Snyder, A R., 36, 50, 51, 58, 61
Solnit, A. J., 285, 317
South, S. J., 319
Spaht, K., 116, 122
Spanier, G. B., 100, 110, 123, 326, 351
Spencer, A., 338, 346
Spiel, C., 241, 257
Spinrad, T. L., 179, 185
Spivak, G., 307, 316
Sprenkle, D. H., 288, 319
Sroufe, L. A., 14, 33, 143, 165, 179, 180, 187, 211, 223, 267, 278, 305, 320
St. Peters, M., 113, 115, 123
Stacey, J., 55, 56, 63
Stack, C. B., 136, 138, 165, 178, 187
Stack, D. M., 178, 187
Stams, G., 156, 165
Stanhope, L., 194, 197, 199, 202, 203, 219
Stanley, S. M., 107, 109, 111, 112, 113, 114, 115, 116, 117, 118, 120, 121, 122, 123, 124, 125, 170, 187, 188
Stanley-Hagan, M., 41, 61, 72, 90
Stanton, G., 166, 122
Staples, R., 136, 165
Stecle, B. F., 286, 317

Steele, H., 149, 163
Steele, M., 149, 163
Steelman, L. C., 202, 223
Steffen, G., 102, 119
Steinberg, L., 9, 21, 30, 31, 68, 93
Steinhauer, P. D., 241, 257
Stern, W., 227, 229, 257
Sternberg, K. J., 76, 93
Stewart, J., 75, 91
Stewart, M. A., 325, 346
Stewart, R. B., 198, 204, 207, 223
Stewart, S., 342, 347
Stickle, T. R., 106, 117
Stier, H., 41, 63
Stockdale, J. E., 113, 124
Stolba, A., 76, 93
Stolberg, A. J., 288, 319
Stone, K., 296, 316
Stone, R. K., 196, 222
Stoneman, Z., 199, 204, 205, 210, 211, 212, 213, 215, 219, 223
Stoolmiller, M., 325, 351
Storaasli, R. D, 107, 121, 170, 187
Storm, C. L., 288, 319
Stormshak, E. A., 215, 217, 223
Straus, M. A., 326, 351
Stuart, R. B., 101, 124
Sudarkasa, N., 133, 136, 165
Sugarman, D. B., 299, 314, 326, 351
Sugarman, S., 156, 165
Suhr, J. A., 108, 118
Sullaway, M., 104, 124
Sullivan, H. S., 230, 257
Sullivan, K. T., 105, 120
Suomi, S. J., 75, 92
Sutton-Smith, B., 194, 199, 201, 203, 222, 223
Svejda, M. J., 7, 33
Swain, M. A., 102, 122
Swanson, C., 109, 119
Swanson, G., 259, 277

T

Talbot, J., 152, 164
Tamis-LeMonda. C., 156, 165

Tangney, J. P., 180, 185
Tasker, F. L., 80, 93, 338, 346
Tavecchio, L., 156, 165
Taylor, A., 341, 347
Taylor, E., 327, 350
Taylor, H., 78, 92
Taylor, J. H., 22, 33
Taylor, M. K., 207, 223
Teachman, J. D., 289, 320
Teitler, J. O., 235, 254
Tennenbaum, D. L., 327, 347
Terman, L. M., 100, 124
Terry, D., 141, 165
Teti, D. M., 194, 195, 197, 199, 202,
    203, 204, 208, 209, 210, 211, 215,
    217, 221, 223
Thapar, A., 339, 351
Thoma, S. J., 103, 119
Thomas, A. M., 171, 185
Thomas, A., 207, 208, 209, 223, 296,
    318
Thomas, D. L., 169, 187
Thomas, M. M., 100, 118
Thomas, M., 132, 161
Thompson, A., 317
Thompson, R. A., 293, 320
Thompson, R., 83, 93
Thomson, E., 27, 33
Thorpe, K., 332, 350
Thurmaier, F., 107, 124
Tienda, M., 41, 63
Ting-Toomey, S., 102, 104, 124
Tinsley, B. J., 86, 90
Tinsley, B. R., 293, 320
Tomasello, M., 232, 254
Tomkiewicz, S., 333, 335, 339, 346
Tonelli, L., 115, 123
Toth, S., 144, 163
Townsley, R. M., 105, 124
Trause, M. A., 207, 223
Tremblay, R. E., 338, 348, 351
Trent, K., 319
Trevarthen, C., 238, 257
Trivers, R. L., 14, 33, 40, 63
Trommsdorff, G., 304, 320
Tronick, E. Z., 180, 188

Tropp, L. R., 67, 86, 89
Troughton, E., 325, 346
Truett, K. R., 323, 346
Tupling, H., 11, 31
Turner, J. R. G., 81, 93, 290, 320
Turner, R. J., 76, 90
Tuttle, W. M., 66, 93
Twentyman, C. T., 309, 314, 315
Tymchuk, A. J., 296, 320
Tzeng, J. M., 109, 124

U

Uba, L., 304, 306, 320
Ullrich, M., 240, 241, 244, 256
Updegraff, K., 155, 161
Urban, H. B., 238, 257

V

Vaillant, C. O., 110, 124
Vaillant, G. E., 110, 124
Valente, E., 341, 346
van IJzendoorn, M., 156, 165
Van Lange, P. A., 111, 112, 124
van Steirteghem, A. C., 81, 91
Van Tuyl, S. S., 207, 223
Vandell, D. L., 194, 197, 199, 201,
    202, 204, 205, 213, 222, 223, 224
Vanzetti, N. A., 105, 124
Vaughn, B. E. 25, 33, 205, 224, 305,
    320, 327, 329, 347, 351
Verette, J., 111, 123
Verhoeven, M., 156, 165
Veroff, J., 100, 124
Vico, G., 252, 257
Vincent, J. P., 102, 124
Virdee, S., 323, 347
Virdin, L. M., 67, 90
Vivian, D., 104, 123
Vogel, B., 102, 103, 123
Vogel, E. F., 233, 253
Volling, B. L., 177, 183, 210, 211,
    224, 260, 278
von Eye, A., 241, 257
Von Klitzing, K., 150, 165

Vondra, J., 304, 312, 315
Voos, D., 207, 223
Vosler, N., 155, 156, 159, 165
Vuchinich, R., 176, 188
Vuchinich, S., 176, 188
Vygotsky, L. S., 301, 312, 320

W

Wadland, W., 207, 221
Wagner, M. E., 194, 195, 199, 224
Wahlsten, D., 337, 351
Walker, L. J., 22, 33
Wall, S., 211, 219, 329, 342, 345, 351
Wallace, K. M., 100, 121
Waller, W., 72, 93
Wallerstein, J. S., 140, 165, 289, 320
Walls, S., 35, 60
Walsh, F., 139, 165
Wamboldt, F. S., 149, 163, 253, 255,
    259, 277, 268, 277
Wampold, B. E., 102, 103, 104, 121,
    124
Ward, M., 143, 165
Warren, S., 149, 164
Warshak, R., 27, 32
Wasserman, D. R., 297, 320
Wastell, C. A., 111, 124
Waters, E., 14, 33, 35, 60, 142, 163,
    208, 210, 211, 219, 224, 305, 320, 329,
    345, 351
Watson-Gegeo, K. A., 214, 217, 224
Watt, N. F., 111, 118
Waxler, N. E., 229, 256
Weakland, J., 229, 253
Wegener, C., 102, 103, 123, 124
Weil, F., 48, 64
Weinberg, R. A., 202, 221
Weingarten, K., 72, 89
Weinraub, M., 307, 320
Weintraub, S., 289, 297, 316
Weisner, T. S., 214, 224
Weiss, B., 139, 162
Weiss, J., 241, 256
Weiss, L. A., 8, 18, 31, 33
Weiss, R. L., 101, 104, 106, 120, 124

Weitzman, L.J., 289, 320
Welsh, D. P., 180, 187
Werner, H., 276, 278
Wertsch, J. V., 312, 319
West, D. J., 333, 346
West, M. O., 296, 320
West, S. G., 111, 118
Wethington, E., 26, 30
Wetzstein, C., 55, 64
Wharton, R., 296, 316
Whelan, J., 340, 345
Whiffen, V. E., 106, 119
Whitbeck, L. B., 174, 178, 184, 187
Whiteside, M., 158, 165
Whiting, B. B., 67, 93, 198, 224
Whitney, G. A., 111, 123
Whittemore, R. D., 214, 217, 224
Whitton, S. W., 112, 115, 123, 124,
    125
Widaman, K. F., 67, 89, 92
Wiener, N., 229, 257
Wierson, M., 171, 185
Wieselquist, J., 111, 112, 125
Wilcox, B. L., 310, 318
Wile, D. B., 104, 125
Willey, R., 299, 317
Williams, B., 115, 118
Williams, D. R., 308, 316
Willis, S. L., 71, 93
Wills, T. A., 101, 106, 120
Wilson, A., 172, 185
Wilson, B., 179, 186
Wilson, D. P., 100, 124
Wilson, K. S., 213, 224
Wilson, L., 28, 31
Wilson, M. N., 177, 178, 186, 188
Wilson, M., 76, 89
Wilson, S., 52, 62
Wilson, W. J., 37, 64
Wing, J. K., 297, 315
Winnicott, D. W., 206, 224, 320
Wishart, J. G., 200, 224
Witcher, B. S., 111, 112, 124
Wolf, B. M., 307, 320
Wolfe, D. A., 320
Wolfe, D. M., 113, 117

Wolfe, M., 77, 88
Wood, B., 176, 188
Wood, J., 26, 31
Woulbroun, E. J., 333, 343, 349
Wright, J., 102, 119
Wrightman, J., 8, 31
Wyer, M., 288, 316
Wynne, L. C., 229, 257, 297, 317

Y

Yates, W., 325, 346
Youngblade, L. M., 197, 224
Youniss, J., 235, 257

Z

Zacharias, A., 109, 123
Zahner, G. E. P., 323, 347

Zahn-Waxler, C., 215, 217, 223
Zajonc, R. B., 201, 202, 224
Zambarano, R. J., 308, 316
Zamsky, E., 154, 161
Zaslavsky, I., 152, 164
Zaslow, M. J., 337, 351
Zhou, H., 16, 20, 30
Zibbell, R. A., 288, 290, 320
Zick, C. D., 26, 30
Zigler, E., 178, 186
Zill, N., 51, 57, 64, 235, 257
Zimmer, M. A., 109, 122
Zizi, M., 47, 60
Zmich, D. E., 177, 185
Zoccolillo, M., 333, 338, 351
Zuckerman, M., 75, 93
Zukow, P. G., 213, 214, 224
Zukow-Goldring, P., 213, 214, 224
Zuravin, S. J., 312, 320

Subject Index

A

Adolescence
communication and, 230-234,
240-248
African American males, 38, 39
At-risk children, 323, 324, 334, 335
At-risk parents, 295-298
Attachment research, 14, 35, 149,
179, 180

B

Behavior and family influences,
321-345
child specific effects, 339, 340
childhood years, 342, 343
environment, 330, 340, 341
genetic mediation, 325
high-quality measurement, 326-
328
main family risks, 338, 339
measurement bias, 322, 323
methodological challenges, 326
qualitative vs. quantitative
measurements, 328-330
quasi-experimental designs, 330-
333
resilience, 335-337
risk and protective processes,
334, 335
risk environments, 323, 324
social/cultural contexts, 341, 342
third variable effects, 324, 325
see Family dynamics, Family
process, Family systems

Birth order
see Sibling relationships
Bonding
see Attachment, Mothering,
Parenting research

C

Child
abuse, 286
see family dynamics, Family
systems
Child custody, 285-295
father custody, 290-292
joint custody, 291-292
nonbiological attachments, 294,
295
termination of parental custody,
299-308
Child development
divorce, 140
family groups, 139-143
see Family dynamics, Family
systems, parenting dimensions
Cloning
human, 81, 82
Coparenting, 140-156, 176, 269,
270
adult-centered, 142
attachment research, 149
cross-cultural view of, 152-157
father's role, 141
gender, 140, 141
hostile-competitive coparenting,
142, 143
nonegalitarian patterns, 142
socialization of sons, 143

Culture
transmission of, 226-233

D-E

Depression, 105, 106, 175
Divorce, 140, 271-273, 288, 289, 290
see Marital conflict, Child
custody, Coparenting
Environment, 330, 340, 341

F

Family dynamics, 96, 97, 127-157
band societies, 129, 130, 136
children's conception of family
group, 149, 150
competition, 131
complex societies, 131
contemporary family structure,
135-138
definitions of family, 153
disengagement-enmeshment, 151
diversity, 132, 133
emotional sustenance, 134, 135
extended kin network, 136, 137
industrial-scientific revolution,
128, 129
marital distress, 148
modern societies, 132-134
multicultural studies, 153-155
multiparent family groups, 136-
139
nonmarital birthrate, 137
parallel twosomes strategy, 152,
153
patrifocal system, 138
pedifocal family, 138
public policy, 157-160
rank societies, 130, 136
sedentarization, 128
single-parent family, 137
social formations, 129
socialization goals, 133, 136
stepfamilies, 71, 72
structural family theory, 151

two-child families, 153
underclass children, 136, 137
see Child development, Coparenting, Fathering
Family process, 176-181
analytical approaches to research, 181
dyad, 176, 177
emotion, 179, 180
intergenerational issues, 178
underrepresented groups, 177,
178
see also Coparenting
Family systems, 259-276
depth-demension variables, 262
bidirectionality, 262
change, 264-266
complex family systems, 270, 271
coparenting of siblings, 269, 270
differential treatment of children,
268, 269
divorce and remarriage, 271-273
family interaction, 262, 263
foster care, 273, 274
general systems theory, 262
homeostatic mechanisms, 263,
264
middle adult generation, 274-276
sibling subsystem, 266, 267
siblings and identity formation,
266-268
siblings as observers, 266-268
stable periods, 263, 264, 263, 264
subcultures and ethnic groups,
276
systematic development
research, 259-261
see Psychology and family
systems
Fathering, 36-59, 74-76, 141-143, 148
African American males, 38, 39
biological imperative myth, 37-
39, 75, 76
child shifting, 47
cross-cultural perspective, 46-49
cross-gender behavior, 52

divorced families, 42
ethnic minority fathers, 38, 39, 46
gay fathers, 48
genogram, 49, 50
institutional change, 54
life-course paradigm, 50, 51
marriage imperative, 40, 41, 42
masculinity ideology, 53, 54
masculinity myth, 39, 40, 53
multiculturalism, 57, 58
next research generation, 59, 60
nonsexist research, 56
paternal involvement, 42-44, 51-53
positive/negative consequences of, 42-56
psychopathology, 44, 45
qualitative research paradigms, 56, 57
research, 36-39
social policy, 55, 56
subcultures, 45-49

G

Gay and lesbian parents, 76-81, 156, 298
as caregivers, 294, 295
division of labor, 77, 78
gender identities of children, 77, 78
households of, 74-79
nonbiological child attachments, 294, 295
paternal play style, 78, 79
roles, 77, 78
see also Coparenting
Gender, 76-81, 141, 143
Cross-gender behavior, 52
identity and, 77, 78
nonsexist research, 56
parenting and, 74-79
socialization experiences, 58
Grandparents rights, 152, 156, 178, 179, 293, 294

I

Identity formation
siblings, 266-268
Intergenerational issues, 178
grandparents rights, 152, 156, 178, 179, 293, 294

L

Legal system and family research, 283-314
at-risk parents, 295-298
tender years doctrine, 285, 286
battered child syndrome, 286
child protection, 299-310
children's rights, 284-287, 299-310
context, 303
cultural differences, 152-157, 303, 304
divorce, 288, 289
domestic violence, 298
early models, 301, 302
family researchers, 287-298
father custody, 290, 291
gay and lesbian parents, 298
grandparents' rights, 152, 156, 178, 179, 293, 294
joint custody, 291, 292
maltreatment, 300, 301
newer models, 304-308
parental attachments, 292-295
parental rights, 284-287, 299
parenting models, 300-308
sibling relationships, 292, 293
social constructivism, 308-310
socialization goals, 302
see Coparenting

M

Marital conflict, 171-175, 182
Behavior Modification Therapy (BMT), 173
child perceptions, 172
child's influence, 173

child's reaction, 172
depression, 175
hostile-competitive coparenting,
142-149
marriage-parenting link, 173, 174
nontraditional families, 174
parenthood, 175
transitions, 174-176
Marital processes, 168-183
Marital research, 99-116, 168-183
affect, 103, 105
behavioral principles, 101
boundaries, 172
causal attributions, 105
child problems, 168
cognition, 105
commitment, 111
couple's communication, 101
cultural influences, 109, 110
depression, 105, 106
distressed couples, 101-104
empirical research, 100-104
family system, 170, 171
immediate/extended family, 108
individual differences, 104, 105
intervention, 101, 114, 115
joint activity, 113, 114
longitudinal studies, 104, 169
long-term relationships, 110
marital conflict, 171, 172
marital process, 168-171
negativity, 102
parent-child coalitions, 168-172
positive relationship focus, 170
prevention, 115
problem-solving behavior, 102
reciprocity, 102, 103
research models, 169, 170
sacrifice, 111, 112
sequential analysis, 104
social policy, 115, 116
social support, 108
teamwork, 112, 113
therapy, 106, 107, 114
Masculinity ideology, 53, 54
Masculinity myth, 39, 40, 53

Mothering
biological models, 6, 7, 8
blame, 1, 6-8
early development literature, 5-7
employment, 25, 26
future research, 28, 29
maternal attachment theory, 14,
35
psychoanalysis, 6
sanctity of, 7
single mothering, 26-28
study of, 5-10

P

Parenting dimensions
affective system, 14
attachment theory, 14
compliance, 20-24
conscience, 22, 23
control vs. controlling, 2, 11-24
internalization structure, 20-24
involvement, 10-24
maternal warmth,10-24
moral development, 22
parenting styles, 25-28
self-determination theory, 16-18
self-regulation, 21-23
warmth-hostility, 10, 11
Parenting research, 65-87
beyond generality, 68, 69
bidirectional relationships, 69, 70
cultural generalizability, 67, 68
family paradigms, 72
focus groups, 85, 86
gay and lesbian households, 74-
79
gender, 74-79
historical generalizability, 66
individual adult development,
70, 71
individual development of the
child, 71, 72
life-course view, 72, 73
mothers versus fathers, 74-76
multiple methodologies, 84

nonbiological fathers, 75, 76
nondevelopmental views, 70
nonexperimental techniques, 86, 87
nonnormative transitions, 72-74
normative transitions, 72-74
observational methods, 84
qualitative and quantitative approaches, 85, 86
reproductive technologies, 79-82
sampling, 84, 85
self-reporting methods, 84
social referencing, 84
socialization influences, 82, 83
stressful events, 73
typology approaches, 68, 69
Psychology and Family systems, 225-231
adolescence and communication, 240-248
adolescence research, 234, 235
communication patterns, 230-234
family functioning, 235, 236
future research, 250-253
infant experience, 233
marital relationship, 234, 235
normative transition, 236-238
parents' socializing behaviors, 238-244
systems theory, 229-235
transitions, 248-250
transmission of culture, 226-233
see Adolescence, Family systems, Marital research

R

Reproductive technologies, 79-82
donor identity, 80
human cloning, 81, 82
intracytoplasmic sperm injection, 81

in-vitro fertilization, 79
parent-child relationships, 80
sexual orientation, 80
surrogate mothers, 80, 81

S

Sibling relationships, 193-218
beyond rivalry and competition, 193, 194
birth order, 199, 200
birth spacing, 200-203
caregiving, 198, 199
complementary relationships, 195
differential parental treatment, 211-213
early sibling relationships, 197-199
family systems context, 206-209
firstborn adjustment, 208, 209
infant-sibling behavior study, 152, 153, 194, 198
parental behavior, 209-213
reciprocal relationships, 195
sex of siblings, 203-205
sibling constellation variables, 199
sibling deidentification, 196
social-cognitive skills, 197, 198
socialization agents, 195, 213-216
as support network, 292, 293
temperament of child, 205, 206
transition to siblinghood, 206-209
variability in affect, 197
Surrogate mothers, 80, 81

T

Transitions
family, 248-250
marital, 174-176
siblinghood, 206-209
see Divorce, Marital conflict